JUNO'S *AENEID*

MARTIN CLASSICAL LECTURES

The Martin Classical Lectures are delivered annually at Oberlin College through a foundation established by his many friends in honor of Charles Beebe Martin, for forty-five years a teacher of classical literature and classical art at Oberlin.

John Peradotto, *Man in the Middle Voice: Name and Narration in the* Odyssey

Martha C. Nussbaum, *The Therapy of Desire: Theory and Practice in Hellenistic Ethics*

Josiah Ober, *Political Dissent in Democratic Athens: Intellectual Critics of Popular Rule*

Anne Carson, *Economy of the Unlost: (Reading Simonides of Keos with Paul Celan)*

Helene P. Foley, *Female Acts in Greek Tragedy*

Mark W. Edwards, *Sound, Sense, and Rhythm: Listening to Greek and Latin Poetry*

Michael C. J. Putnam, *Poetic Interplay: Catullus and Horace*

Julia Haig Gaisser, *The Fortunes of Apuleius and the* Golden Ass: *A Study in Transmission and Reception*

Kenneth J. Reckford, *Recognizing Persius*

Leslie Kurke, *Aesopic Conversations: Popular Tradition, Cultural Dialogue, and the Invention of Greek Prose*

Erich S. Gruen, *Rethinking the Other in Antiquity*

Simon Goldhill, *Victorian Culture and Classical Antiquity: Art, Opera, Fiction, and the Proclamation of Modernity*

Victoria Wohl, *Euripides and the Politics of Form*

David Frankfurter, *Christianizing Egypt: Syncretism and Local Worlds in Late Antiquity*

Robin Osborne, *The Transformation of Athens: Painted Pottery and the Creation of Classical Greece*

Joseph Farrell, *Juno's* Aeneid: *A Battle for Heroic Identity*

Juno's *Aeneid*

A BATTLE FOR HEROIC IDENTITY

JOSEPH FARRELL

PRINCETON UNIVERSITY PRESS
PRINCETON & OXFORD

Copyright © 2021 by Princeton University Press

Princeton University Press is committed to the protection of copyright and the intellectual property our authors entrust to us. Copyright promotes the progress and integrity of knowledge. Thank you for supporting free speech and the global exchange of ideas by purchasing an authorized edition of this book. If you wish to reproduce or distribute any part of it in any form, please obtain permission.

Requests for permission to reproduce material from this work should be sent to permissions@press.princeton.edu

Published by Princeton University Press
41 William Street, Princeton, New Jersey 08540
6 Oxford Street, Woodstock, Oxfordshire OX20 1TR

press.princeton.edu

All Rights Reserved

Library of Congress Cataloging-in-Publication Data

Names: Farrell, Joseph, 1955- author.
Title: Juno's Aeneid : a battle for heroic identity / Joseph Farrell.
Other titles: Martin classical lectures.
Description: Princeton ; Oxford : Princeton University Press, 2021. |
    Series: Martin classical lectures | Includes bibliographical references and index.
Identifiers: LCCN 2020044604 (print) | LCCN 2020044605 (ebook) |
    ISBN 9780691211169 (hardback) | ISBN 9780691211176 (ebook)
Subjects: LCSH: Virgil. Aeneis. | Juno (Roman deity)—In literature. |
    Homer—Influence. | Epic poetry, Latin—History and criticism.
Classification: LCC PA6825 .F36 2021 (print) | LCC PA6825 (ebook) |
    DDC 873/.01—dc23
LC record available at https://lccn.loc.gov/2020044604
LC ebook record available at https://lccn.loc.gov/2020044605

British Library Cataloging-in-Publication Data is available

Editorial: Rob Tempio and Matt Rohal
Production Editorial: Sara Lerner
Production: Erin Suydam
Publicity: Alyssa Sanford and Amy Stewart
Copyeditor: Tash Siddiqui

Jacket Credit: Jacket image: Carlo Maratti (1625–1713), *Juno Beseeching Aeolus to Release the Winds against the Trojan Fleet*, ca. 1654–56. Oil on canvas, 24 × 29 3/8 in. (61 × 74.6 cm.). Ackland Art Museum, University of North Carolina at Chapel Hill / Gift of Mrs. Joseph Palmer Knapp, by exchange, 2009.10

This book has been composed in Arno

Printed on acid-free paper. ∞

Printed in the United States of America

10 9 8 7 6 5 4 3 2 1

to the memory of three inspiring teachers
Joseph E. Foley
Nathan Dane, II
Agnes K. Michels

CONTENTS

Acknowledgments   xi
A Note to the Reader   xv

Introduction	1
Why Juno?	1
Form, Content, Context	4
Homer's Aeneid	7
The Systematic Intertext	8
The Dynamic Intertext	15
The Dialogic Intertext	21
The Ethical Aeneid	28
Ancient Perspectives	28
Modern Perspectives	29
Coming Attractions	33
1 Arms and a Man	41
Where to Begin?	41
Enter Juno	48
In Medias Res	52
Displaced Persons	57
Aeolus	59
Neptune	61
Aeneas	66
What Is at Stake?	76
Horace on Iliadic and Odyssean Ethics	77
Horace on Ethical Citizenship	81

Reflections on Juno's *Aeneid* in the Light of Horace's Homer	85
Intertextual Chronology	85
Enigmas of Arrival	90
Intertextual Africa	91
Phorcys' Harbor on the Island of Ithaca	91
Deer Hunting on the Island of Aeaea	95
Disguise and Recognition on the Island of Ithaca	97
Intertextual Dido	107
Unintended Consequences	111
Going Forward	113
2 Third Ways	**114**
None of the Above?	114
Failure Is Always an Option: The Aeneid *and the Epic Cycle*	116
The Narrator's Ambition	116
Juno and Memory	120
The Narrator's Anxiety	123
Aeneas' "Misfortunes"	128
Cyclic Ethics	133
A Second Argo: The Aeneid *and Apollonius*	133
Odyssey and Argosy	135
The *Aeneid* as Argosy	139
Juno's Argonautic Diversion	143
Iliad and *Argonautica*	148
So Many Labors: The Aeneid *as Heracleid*	152
Grappling with Heracles	154
Difference and Essence	159
A Hesiodic Heracles	164
A Heraclean *Aeneid*	166
Weddings, Funerals, and Madness: Dramatic Plots in the Aeneid	167
Setting the Scene	169
The Tragedies of Dido and Aeneas	172
Heraclean Tragedy in the *Aeneid*	176

	Historical Intertexts in Roman Epics	178
	History and Historiography	178
	Homer and Historiography	180
	Myth and History in Livius' *Odyssey*	182
	Myth and History in Naevius' *The Punic War*	186
	Some Conclusions	194
3	Reading Aeneas	196
	A New Kind of Hero?	196
	Aeneas, a Heroic Reader	197
	Books 1–4, Good Kings and Bad	198
	"The Sack of Troy"	199
	"Wanderings"	207
	Aeneas and Dido	217
	Books 5–8, Aeneas' Heroic Education	224
	Sicily	226
	Cumae	232
	Latium	241
	Pallanteum	248
	Books 9–12, Becoming Achilles	253
	A Leadership Vacuum	253
	More Contested Identities	263
	The Reader's Sympathies	272
	Resolutions and Rewards	283
	How to Read the Aeneid	287

Appendix: mene in- *and* mênin   293

Works Cited   299

Index of Passages Cited   331

General Index   345

ACKNOWLEDGMENTS

THIS BOOK has been in the works for some time, during which I have incurred a great many debts which it is a pleasure to acknowledge.

Before anything else, I will always be grateful to my friends and colleagues at Oberlin College for inviting me to give the Charles Beebe Martin lectures in February 2008. That opportunity was the perfect catalyst for a project that had already found its starting point, but did not yet have a definite plan for how to proceed. A short series of closely related lectures proved to be an ideal structure for identifying and working through the major issues. In addition, I was pleasantly surprised to learn that only one previous Martin lecturer, R. S. Conway, had taken the *Aeneid* as his subject, just two years after Paul Shorey launched the series and just a year shy of eight decades before my own.[1] In fact, Conway's subject, "Vergil as a Student of Homer," had a lot in common with mine; but much has changed in the meantime, and even if Vergil can hardly ever be said to be underrepresented in Latin literary studies, this seemed to be one context in which that might be true. The penetrating discussion and good advice I received in response to the lectures was energizing, and it had a very positive impact on the book that has grown out of them. Even more important are the friendships, both new ones made and old ones renewed during my week in Oberlin, which have stayed with me ever since, as I am sure they always will. Here I have to mention especially Ben Lee and Tom Van Nortwick, who were elegant hosts and interlocutors. Kirk Ormand was away on leave during the term of my visit, but he has been enormously helpful, encouraging, and understanding during the book's lengthy gestation period. Now that it is finished, I feel fortunate too that it will be a tangible reminder of that wonderful experience.

During a period of many competing obligations I benefited enormously from several periods of concentrated work without which I might not have been able to finish the book at all. For these I am immensely grateful to a number of institutions. In fall 2013 I was a Resident at the American Academy

---

1. Shorey 1927/1931; Conway 1929/1931.

in Rome, one of the most remarkable living and working environments I have ever found. Much of the credit for that goes to Director Christopher Celenza and Mellon Professor Kimberly Bowes, both of whom through their intellectual leadership, dedicated work ethic, and cheerful humanity set a wonderful example for the entire community. For the progress and the lasting friendships that I made during that time I will never be able to give adequate thanks. In fall 2018 I received a semester of grant support from the Loeb Classical Library Foundation and in spring 2019 I received a Weiler Faculty Fellowship from the University of Pennsylvania School of Arts and Sciences. Together these made possible a full year of leave, which I divided among several wonderful places. For half of the fall term I was hosted by the University of Trent thanks to an exchange agreement with Swarthmore College in which my own department also participates. My thanks to Caterina Mordeglia and Jeremy Lefkowitz, the organizers of this exchange, and to Caterina along with Sandro La Barbera for their friendly hospitality. For the second half of the term I returned to the American Academy as a Visiting Scholar to join a community then being led by Director John Ochsendorf and Mellon Professor Lynne Lancaster, who in every way maintained the high standards of their predecessors while bringing their own distinctive style to the AAR. In the spring term I spent two months in Santa Barbara, California, taking the opportunity to spend more time than usual living near my father-in-law, who is still going strong in his nineties. Although I had no formal affiliation with the University of California at Santa Barbara, members of the Classics Department there, especially Helen Morales and Sara Lindheim, were extremely welcoming, and both the university library and the Goleta Valley Branch library, which was within walking distance of the apartment where my wife and I stayed, proved to be excellent places to work. In March I was Visiting Fellow in the Guangqi International Center for Scholars at Shanghai Normal University, and following that I held a Visiting Fellow Commonorship in Trinity College, Cambridge during Easter Term. I am extremely grateful to Jinyu Liu for the invitation to Shanghai and to her remarkable team of collaborators for their incredibly efficient assistance in arranging a memorable, eye-opening experience, and to Philip Hardie, Richard Hunter, Aaron Kachuck, and Stephen Oakley for their kind assistance and gracious hospitality in Cambridge.

    A number of institutions have given me the opportunity to present various portions of this book as lectures on work in progress. As with the original lectures at Oberlin, these occasions were invaluable to me in testing and refining my arguments. Much of chapter 1 formed the topic of lectures given at Brown University, Haverford College, the Scuola Normale Superiore di Pisa, Trinity College Dublin, Trinity University, Williams College, and the Universities of Florence, London, Oxford, North Carolina (Chapel Hill), Rome ("Tor

Vergata"), and Siena (Arezzo). Part of chapter 2 was the basis of a lecture I gave at Rutgers University and Sapienza University of Rome. Different parts of chapter 3 build on lectures given at Florida State and Penn State. I lectured on related subjects at Baylor University, Swarthmore College, Hunter College, Skidmore College, the University of Colorado (Boulder), the University of California (Los Angeles), and on return visits to Brown, Oxford, and Sapienza. I wish I could thank by name everyone whose enthusiasm or skepticism helped clarify my ideas and my argument, but if I did these acknowledgements would rival the rest of the book in length. That said, I would be remiss if I did not mention, in addition to those named already, Emily Allen-Hornblower, Ronnie Ancona, Alessandro Barchiesi, Ewen Bowie, Sergio Casali, Kerry Christensen, Mario Citroni, Gian Biagio Conte, Erwin Cook, Andrea Cucchiarelli, Edan Dekel, Lowell Edmunds, Jackie Elliott, Jeffrey Fish, Peta Fowler, Christopher Francese, Monica Gale, Leon Golden, Luca Graverini, Tamara Green, Robert Gurval, Stephen Harrison, Stephen Heyworth, Nicolle Hirschfeld, Meredith Hoppin, Matthew Hosty, Thomas Jenkins, Lawrence Kim, Leah Kronenberg, Mario Labate, Giuspeppe La Bua, Maura Lafferty, Elio Lo Cascio, Marc Mastrangelo, Lisa Mignone, Llewelyn Morgan, Glenn Most, Mark Munn, Damien Nelis, Carole Newlands, James O'Hara, Timothy O'Sullivan, Corinne Pache, Timothy Power, Joseph Pucci, Alex Purves, Michael Putnam, Kenneth Reckford, Jay Reed, Victoria Rimell, Deborah Roberts, Alessandro Schiesaro, Alden Smith, Peter Smith, Philip Stadter, Fabio Stok, Oliver Taplin, Stephen Wheeler, and Amanda Wilcox. My colleagues and students at Penn have heard different versions of my arguments in formal and informal settings over the years, and they too have been generous with their feedback, which has had a really decisive effect on the final form of the book. I was exceptionally fortunate in the anonymous readers who were enlisted by Oberlin and the Princeton University Press to vet the manuscript that I submitted in the summer of 2019. Their positive response was obviously instrumental getting the project accepted, and their comments and suggestions were so richly provocative that I added to the book's already long trip down the runway trying to do them justice before resubmitting a final revision. Speaking of the Princeton University Press, everyone there who has contributed to this project—Rob Tempio, Matt Rohal, Sara Lerner, David Campbell, Erin Suydam, Alyssa Sanford, Amy Stewart, and Tash Siddiqui—has done amazing work and has been unfailingly delightful to work with. It goes without saying that none of these friends and colleagues is responsible for the flaws that doubtless remain, and that they deserve nothing but credit for making this a better book than it would have been.

Finally, I am so grateful to my family, who have lived with this project not quite as intimately as I have, but for every bit as long. Three further debts of gratitude are recorded on the dedication page.

A NOTE TO THE READER

I HAVE TRIED to make this book as accessible as possible to all readers of whatever backgrounds. To that end, I decided not to follow certain conventions that are familiar to most classicists, but not to anyone else. Instead, I follow just a few of the most widely used conventions of academic writing, some of which I adapt in ways that I hope are intuitive, but that I explain here just in case.

First of all, I quote Greek and Latin authors only in English whenever possible, which I have found is most of the time. Translations of the texts with which I am primarily concerned, such as the *Aeneid* and its models, are mine unless otherwise stated. I have tried, first, to make these translations illustrate the argument at hand and, second, to make them clear, with no further pretensions. For other Greek and Latin texts I cite what I think is the most easily available translation, with facing Greek or Latin text where possible. Most works of scholarship produced in antiquity have never been translated, so when it is important for the reader to have access to these I translate them if they are short or summarize them if they are long. One such source, Servius' *Commentary on Vergil's Aeneid*, I cite fairly frequently. As specialists will know, there are two ancient versions of this work, but I do not distinguish between them because the difference is never germane to my argument.

When it is necessary to quote the original languages to make an essential point, I do my best to explain that point as simply as possible. I cite Greek mainly in transliteration, the chief exception being when I quote someone who quotes Greek in the original script; in that case I supply a transliteration, as well. I do this because, whenever I find myself reading an argument that quotes a language that I do not know, I find it easier to maintain my concentration if the quotations are transliterated so that I can at least pronounce them, and perhaps understand them to some extent. This may be a personal quirk, but I doubt it is unique to me. I realize that transliteration of Greek may be bothersome to some classicists, but it seems a fairly small hurdle to overcome in comparison to making other readers confront an unfamiliar script.

In references to the subject literature, editions, and translations I use the surname of the principal modern author, editor, or translator and the date of publication as keys to a list of works cited at the back of the book. I sometimes follow the surname with a pair of dates separated by a solidus, as in "Heinze 1915/1993." In this particular case, the first date is the standard edition of Heinze's book and the second is the date of its English translation. I give the first date so that interested readers may more easily keep track of how the interpretations I discuss developed over time, and I give the second in order to identify what I believe will be, for the majority of readers, the most useful or accessible version. With respect to Heinze, the mere fact that the book was translated into English almost ninety years after it was published in German suggests that there is a larger audience for the translation, which happens to be available online, as well. That said, the later date is not always the more convenient or accessible, nor is it always a matter of translation. For instance, "Putnam 1972/1995" is an article first published in *Arethusa*, a journal that is widely available in electronic form, and then republished in a collection of related essays that was not available online as of this writing. Readers who have access to the book will find it the more convenient source for this and several other of Putnam's essays that I cite, but everyone else will find the original, online versions more accessible. That was certainly the case for me with my own copy of the book under quarantine in my campus office, where it remains as I type this sentence almost ten months into the coronavirus pandemic of 2020. During this time, if I wanted to refresh my memory about some particular point, I had to consult whatever online version there might be of this and many other works. Nevertheless, when I cite a particular passage of such a work, I give the pagination that pertains to the later date, whether online or not, for the sake of consistency and simplicity. In the list of works cited, I give full bibliographical information, again separated by a solidus, with inclusive pagination of both versions.

I do not use abbreviations of either ancient or modern works, again in the hope of making the book accessible to all sorts of readers. With the exception of the major Greek and Latin dictionaries, Liddell and Scott's *A Greek–English Lexicon* and the *Oxford Latin Dictionary* edited by P.G.W. Glare, all modern secondary literature, including editions of fragmentary works, are cited by the same system that I use for articles and monographs as described above, and full bibliographical information on those works will be found under the name of the modern author or editor in the list of works cited.

In addition, I generally use English titles for ancient works. A few titles like *Iliad*, *Odyssey*, and *Aeneid* are so familiar that it would be unnecessary and even grotesque to translate them; but a poem like *Nostoi*, which I mention frequently and which is not widely known to modern readers, I call *Homecomings*. That is what *Nostoi* means, after all, so that even if it is slightly less familiar to classicists as a title than *Nostoi* is, it will hardly be unintelligible to them, and it will be much more immediately understandable to everyone else.

Finally, for the text of Vergil, I generally follow Mynors 1969; for Homer, D. B. Monro and T. W. Allen 1912–1920; and, for Apollonius, Race 2008 (which is virtually identical with Vian and Delatte 1974–1996 but is much more easily accessible and is equipped with a translation into English instead of French). Anyone who wants to consult a different edition or translation, whether in print or digital form, of these and most other authors whom I cite will have no trouble doing so.

JUNO'S *AENEID*

Introduction

THE GREAT ITALIAN WRITER and storyteller Italo Calvino once explained: "A classic is a book that has never finished saying what it has to say."[1] If that is true of any book, I believe it is true of Homer's *Iliad* and *Odyssey*, and of Vergil's *Aeneid*. By the same token, conversations among such books are never really finished, either. I am sure most critics and readers have always realized this, even if we sometimes write as if it were possible to sum up such a conversation once and for all. The urge is strong to feel that we have come to terms at last with the stories that matter to us, that we can make sense of the conversations taking place between them, and that we ourselves have something to contribute to the continuing discussions about them. Many of us also feel an urge to make decisions about the issues involved and to persuade others that our decisions are the right ones. Those efforts, no matter how successful, inevitably remain so for only a short time as measured against the lifespans of the works to which they pay tribute. If we are very fortunate, our contributions may add to the general appreciation of those works—not merely in the sense of what everyone knows or agrees to be true about them, but also of what it is possible to say about them, about the depth, magnitude, and seriousness of the conversations that they inspire. If we take issue with the opinions of our predecessors or our contemporaries, that is not in the least to disparage their contributions. It is to celebrate the nature of a true dialogue that aims to increase understanding. For there to be such a thing, we must disagree with one another. If we did not, then all the conversations that mean anything really would come to an end.

Why Juno?

I will have more to say about dialogue, but before I do, I think I should say something about my title. This is not a book about Juno in the *Aeneid*, or not exactly. It is not like Antonie Wlosok's important study of Venus in the *Aeneid*,

---

1. Calvino 1981/1986, 128.

or like John Miller's panoptic survey of Apollo in Augustan poetry, or Julia Dyson Hejduk's about Jupiter.[2] Like most studies of this divinity since Denis Feeney's landmark discussion of gods in epic poetry, it addresses the relationship of Juno in literature to the Juno of history and of cult, but only occasionally and, for the most part, generally.[3] Similarly, it conjures with the allegorical Juno of Michael Murrin and Philip Hardie, but it does not consistently put physical allegory at center stage.[4] Above all, it regards Juno as a character in this poem and in relation to characters in other poems who in some sense share her identity. These aspects are hardly unfamiliar, and I do not claim to reveal very much that is new about Hera or Juno in earlier literature or about relationships among her various avatars. I do believe that my approach to Juno is of some value if only because it is a bit unusual—even though, like most of what I have to say, it is not altogether unprecedented.

The main point is that I explore Juno's familiar role as an oppositional and a transgressive character, and do so to a deliberately exaggerated degree. By "exaggerated" I do not mean that I am overstating this aspect of her role. I mean that I put much more emphasis on it than is usually done because I want to do justice to the poem's own extreme emphasis on Juno's opposition. So extreme is this emphasis that, no matter how vigorously I pursue it, I find that I risk understating its importance. Consider: The first thing that Juno does upon entering the *Aeneid* is to declare her unhappiness with the fact that the Trojan War did not finish off all of the Trojans to the very last one, and she then takes immediate steps to make that happen. She thus reveals herself to be the divine antagonist of this poem's hero. This is a conventional role in epic poetry and one that Juno is extraordinarily well qualified to play. Her previous appearances as Hera in Greek literature, her cultic identity as Tanit in the Punic religion, and her own historical role in supporting the opponents of Roman expansion through the 2nd century BCE, all combine to make Juno not just well qualified, but overqualified for the role of Aeneas' divine antagonist. Her suitability, we might say, is overdetermined. As will happen in cases of overdetermination, an abundance of factors may contribute to one result while not agreeing with one another in important respects.

It is pedantic to point this out, but necessary, because it is no trivial matter that aspects of Juno's role as Aeneas' divine antagonist do not comport with other elements of the poem's design. For instance, and very simply, it has been common since antiquity to consider the first six books of the *Aeneid* as a kind

---

2. Wlosok 1967; Miller 2009; Hejduk 2020.
3. Feeney 1991.
4. Murrin 1980; P. R. Hardie 1986.

of Odyssey. If it is one, then it is ironic that Juno, not Neptune, tries to destroy Aeneas in a storm at sea, as the Homeric Poseidon tries to destroy Odysseus. It is a further irony when Neptune saves the hero from this same storm. One need not make much of these ironies, but on the other hand, if one pays some attention to them, they quickly prove impossible to ignore. Another elementary point is that is that the *Aeneid* is indebted not only to Homer but also to other models. Very prominent among them is the *Argonautica* by Apollonius of Rhodes. This much has been known since antiquity, but demonstration that Apollonian influence is as pervasive as that of Homer, and similar in general character, is a fairly recent achievement, and one with which critics have still not fully come to terms.[5] For instance, Hera, Juno's Greek counterpart, is a more important character in the *Argonautica* than in any other poem that survives from antiquity—with the possible exception of the *Aeneid*. Unlike the Vergilian Juno, however, the Apollonian Hera is not the hero's divine antagonist, but his principal patron. Not only that, but Zeus plays such a minor role in the *Argonautica* that the reader might well regard Hera and not him as the most important deity in that poetic universe.[6] Again, it is possible to treat these antecedents in a way that does not disturb one's sense of Juno's conventional role in the *Aeneid*. That involves treating them in the way that critics used to treat similes in epic poetry, not as overqualified or overdetermined but as overadequate to their specific purpose. One approach to this overadequacy is to say that the reader merely has to identify a "third point of comparison" between the tenor and the vehicle of the simile. One might then enjoy other details from an aesthetic point of view, but in cognitive terms one could disregard them as excess.[7] It is perfectly possible to treat Juno in that same way. Her role in the *Aeneid* is extremely simple: to the point of obsession, she just wants to destroy Aeneas, excluding all other considerations. On the other hand, because this obsessive simplicity arises from a multiplication of overdetermining factors, including those I have just named and many others, Juno's oppositional role takes on a degree of complexity beyond what is found in any of her previous literary, cultic, and historical appearances. This complexity, in my view, is in very large measure what makes the *Aeneid* the poem that it is.

---

5. I refer to Nelis 2001, which I discuss immediately below and in the section of chapter 2 entitled "A Second Argo: the *Aeneid* and Apollonius."

6. Feeney 1991, 62–69, 81–95; Hunter 1993, 78–80, 87–88, 96–100.

7. The ancient critic Servius in his *Commentary on Vergil's Aeneid* 1.497 states the principle that one cannot expect all aspects of the vehicle to be appropriate to the tenor of any simile. The interpretation of "multiple correspondence similes" was put on a new footing by D. A. West 1969. For the particular simile that attracted Servius' comment see chapter 1 note 192.

I should also be clear that although Juno gives me a useful way into these issues, my interest is less in her than in the *Aeneid* itself; it is less in the maker than in the poem that she makes. With this I come to my subtitle, of which there are actually two. For most of the time I was writing this book it had the working title "Juno's *Aeneid*: Narrative, Metapoetics, Dissent."[8] As you know, the subtitle is now "A Battle for Heroic Identity." Both subtitles mean the same thing to me, but the more important question is what they mean to you; so let me next try to help you with that.

Form, Content, Context

My working methods are grounded in literary formalism. I do not insist that this is the best or only way to study literature, and I have learned a lot from those who have actively disparaged formalist criticism. At the same time, I have never been persuaded by most denunciations of formalism as such. The reason is simple. Literature is a form of communication. Writers cannot communicate by telepathy, by direct emotional sympathy, by purely conceptual means. At a minimum, they need things like an alphabet, words, sentences, and some story to tell. These are all formal devices. It is certainly possible to fetishize them as such and to produce quite arid scholarship in the process; but no method in itself can save you from that.

Forms are the means by which writers communicate. Attending to them is a matter of coming to terms not just with the medium of communication but with whatever content may be found within it as well as with the context that surrounds it. It is sometimes hard to tell the difference. Whatever content or context is involved may seem trivial or profound; it may speak to the concerns of our own time or seem totally beside the point. It may speak to you but not to me. With luck, we will both agree—whatever else we may think—that it offers us a way into a discussion that is worth our time.

My choice to focus on "narrative" and "metapoetics" in the original subtitle arose directly from this perspective. Very simply put, the idea behind this book is that the central issues that animate the *Aeneid* are intimately linked to the form of the story that it tells. In Homeric terms, that story is complex. It involves two very different poems that offer different possibilities, specifically in the realm of ethics. In the *Aeneid*, these different possibilities are promoted and contested by forces within the poem that behave as if they were autonomous and could hope to bend the plot in one direction or another, possibly even substituting one plot for another. The different forces stand to some

---

8. Or a variation thereof.

degree outside the plot, but not entirely; they are also functions of it. Specifically, the ones I have in mind are constitutive elements of the epic genre, either indispensable (the epic narrator) or very common (the hero's divine antagonist, whom I have already mentioned). The difference between their respective intentions accounts for the third part of the older subtitle.

In the situation I envision, one of these characters, who is by definition supposed to tell the story, tries to do so but is immediately challenged by another character, Juno, whose role is supposed to be confined within that story; but she does not accept her confinement, expressing her disapproval of the story she believes that narrator has set out to tell. So, transgressive figure that she is, Juno steps across whatever boundary separates characters inside the plot from the narrator who stands outside it. She tries to take control of the poem and make it tell a different story from the one she thinks the narrator wants to tell. Because there is, or it seems there ought to be, some sort of hierarchy by which the narrator is superior to any other character, at least in terms of controlling the plot, I understand Juno to be in dissent with regard to this dispensation. There is more to say about all of this, and I will get to it; but I hope it will be useful for me to have said this much at the beginning, and for the reader to know that the book actually took shape under the triple rubric "narrative, metapoetics, dissent."

How the original subtitle morphed into "a battle for heroic identity" is also easily explained. I have mentioned a relationship between different stories and different ethical possibilities, and it was always clear to me that the formal issues involved are inextricably tied to ethics. This is one of a few areas in which my argument reacts quite specifically to earlier scholarship. Francis Cairns was the first to consider the *Aeneid* in the light of ancient "kingship theory," a branch of ethical philosophy concerned with paradigms of leadership and citizenship, not just in monarchies but in all constitutional forms.[9] This diverse tradition includes a number of works entitled "On Kingship" or something similar, whether they were given that title by their authors or acquired it as a subtitle or second title in virtue of their perceived relevance to the subject.[10] The heroes of the *Iliad* and *Odyssey* loom large in this tradition, and none larger than Achilles and Odysseus themselves.[11] At the turn of the 5th to the 4th century BCE the versatile Odysseus became the preferred paradigm of the "good king" while the intransigent Achilles came to be seen mainly as typifying behaviors to avoid. This preference endured well into the imperial period,

---

9. Cairns 1989, 1–84.
10. Murray 2008, 14–15.
11. Montiglio 2011; see also Richardson 1975 and 1992.

and it is outstandingly exemplified by works emblematic of the Second Sophistic.[12] There is no doubt, however, as Silvia Montiglio has made clear, that it was already the dominant attitude towards Achilles and Odysseus among ethical philosophers during the late Classical and Hellenistic periods of Greek culture, and its impact was felt in Rome well before the *Aeneid* began to be written.[13] In retrospect, the only surprise is that no one thought to interpret the *Aeneid* in light of this tradition before Cairns did so.

A possible explanation is that pejorative representations of Odysseus in Greek tragedy and other "elevated" genres are more familiar to literary scholars than are the philosophical sources of kingship theory.[14] Another is that an essay by the Epicurean philosopher Philodemus of Gadara entitled "On the Good King according to Homer," although it was first published in 1844, was not well understood or even widely read before the mid-1960s.[15] Even then it did not begin to have much impact on students of Latin poetry before the discovery of a treatise by the same author on another ethical subject that is addressed to Vergil and other members of his literary sodality.[16] Cairns, whose book was published the same year as that discovery, was ahead of the curve in grasping that Philodemus' ideas on Homer as a school of ethical heroism must have been familiar to the author of the *Aeneid*.

That said, there is no reason to believe it was through Philodemus alone that Roman intellectuals became acquainted with this branch of ethical philosophy for the first time. "On the Good King" is an elegant tribute to Philodemus' patron, Lucius Calpurnius Piso, probably on the occasion of his assuming some important position in the Roman governmental apparatus, and it would no doubt have made enjoyable and edifying reading for many others. It is very unlikely, however, that it was a revelation to anyone, and very much more likely that it was received as an intriguing effort to reconcile Epicurean ethics with traditional Roman attitudes of service and political engagement, rather than as an introduction to Homeric kingship theory in general.

---

12. Dio Chrysostom, *Discourse* 52, "On Homer" in Crosby 1946, 355–70; "Plutarch," *On the Life and Poetry of Homer* 2.4 ("It is clear from this that in the *Iliad* he is presenting physical prowess, in the *Odyssey* the nobility of the soul"); cf. 2.141–42 in Keaney and Lamberton 1997, 68–69 and 222–25.

13. Rawson 1985, 59, 95, 101; Perutelli 2006, 17–29.

14. Stanford 1954, 102–17.

15. Murray 1965 marked a great turning point; see also the edition of Dorandi 1982 with Murray 1984 and Fowler 1986. A new edition by Jeffrey Fish is awaited; see Fish 2002, 187.

16. Gigante and Capasso 1989; Gigante 2001/2004.

What is clear is that virtually this entire tradition regarded Odysseus as the more admirable and useful of Homer's ethical paradigms.[17] It is therefore not surprising that Cairns interprets the *Aeneid* as promoting an Odyssean model of ethical heroism. Like many others, he starts from the premise that the poem is informed by a strong panegyrical impulse. If such a poem were to propose Achilles as a model of good kingship, it would be swimming against a very strong philosophical tide. As the reader will find, I agree with Cairns and others that the reception of Hellenistic kingship theory looms large on the horizon of expectations that ancient readers will have brought to the *Aeneid*. On the other hand, I do not share the assumption that such factors actually determine what it is possible for the poem to mean; at least, not in any simple way. That is to say, I am more willing than I believe Cairns is to allow that the *Aeneid* might offer an unorthodox or contrarian answer to any given question.

To come back to forms, I am also intrigued by an argument that Cairns offers in support of his argument about kingship—namely, that the Homeric program of the *Aeneid* does not treat the *Iliad* and the *Odyssey* even-handedly, but takes the latter poem as its primary model and the former as a distinctly secondary influence. One easily sees how this serves Cairns' argument that Aeneas is to be understood as a "good king" of the Odyssean type, and not as a negative exemplum, like Achilles. But what is it that justifies treating the poem as primarily an Odyssey, and only secondarily as an Iliad? For Cairns there are two main aspects. I defer one of these for the moment to focus on the primary one, which will serve to introduce a brief survey of relevant critical opinion.[18]

Homer's *Aeneid*

The protagonists of my survey, in addition to Cairns, will be G. N. Knauer, Alessandro Barchiesi, Edan Dekel, and Damien Nelis.[19] I discuss their contributions in chronological order except for that of Nelis, which focuses not on

---

17. Asmis 1991, 39; 1995, 31; Montiglio 2011, passim. Aristotle may be the major exception: see Richardson 1992, 36–40, who also contrasts Aristotle's general approach to Homer with that of critics interested mainly in ethics.

18. In the next section I attempt to account, as briefly as possible, for only the most essential background of my approach to the Homeric *Aeneid*. For the larger context, I refer anyone who may be interested to Farrell 1991, 3–25; 1997; 2005; and 2019.

19. David Quint's contributions, Quint 1993 and 2018, would make him another convincing protagonist, not only as an exemplary exponent of formalist criticism in the service of important ideas—his more recent reading of the *Aenied* being based on the rhetorical figure of

Homer but Apollonius. That said, it is no less important than any of the others for understanding the Homeric *Aeneid*, as we shall see.

The Systematic Intertext

The germ of the idea that the *Aeneid* is more an Odyssey than an Iliad can be traced back to Knauer's 1964 study *Die Aeneis und Homer*, which is still a standard point of reference and seems likely to remain so.[20] This is true even for those who do not agree with any of Knauer's basic assumptions or conclusions. That is because fully one-third of his book, by page count, is comprised of lists documenting practically all of the passages in the *Aeneid* that had been identified as parallel to one or more passages of the *Iliad*, the *Odyssey*, or both, in Knauer's investigation of about seventy-five commentaries and special studies written or published between about 400 and 1962 CE. Of these Knauer collated the twenty-five or so that seemed to him the most informative. These lists are so useful that the book remains a fixture in bibliographies and is widely used, as I say, even by those who profess strong disagreement with almost every other aspect of it. Indeed, I suspect that dissenters are in the majority of those who profit from it in this way.

Let me add that I write these words as someone who was Nico Knauer's departmental colleague from 1984 until his retirement in 1988 and remained his friend until his death in 2018. We did not agree about everything, by any means. I suspect that it was easier for him than it might once have been to befriend a younger colleague who did not share all of his ideas about the *Aeneid*, to name only that, after he moved from Berlin to Philadelphia and had become somewhat acclimated to American academic culture. This was also after his research had largely left classical literature behind to focus on its

---

chiasmus—but also for his pithy observations on the importance of the modern reader's political position and on the recent history of *Aeneid* criticism: see Quint 2018, x–xi and compare the section of this introduction entitled "Modern Perspectives." Because Quint does not fashion himself as an interlocutor in the specific discussion that concerns me here, and also because his own approach to the Homeric problem of the *Aeneid* is altogether so distinctive, it seemed best not to try to describe his position vis-à-vis the others—a project that would be well worth the effort, but would also require a good deal of space—but instead simply to cite his work at opportune moments in the course of my argument.

20. Knauer 1964, 329 remarks that Abrahamson 1963, a posthumous publication that appeared after Knauer had submitted an earlier version of *Die Aeneis und Homer* as his Habilitationsschrift in 1961 (see his foreword), was the only other scholar to that date who had recognized the *Odyssey* as the structural model of the *Aeneid* as a whole.

reception during the early modern period.[21] We did, however, strongly agree about one thing in particular, which is that Vergilian intertextuality (as I call it; I don't believe that Nico ever used that word) is very profitably considered not as an occasional phenomenon, but one with pervasive, systematic, even totalizing tendencies. He is certainly not the first to have had such an idea. The late-antique grammarian and commentator Servius hints at it when he notes that the *Aeneid* consists of Odyssean and Iliadic halves in that order.[22] Elsewhere Servius endorses an even more ancient opinion that describes the poem as "a varied and complex theme; the equivalent, as it were, of both Homeric poems."[23] So the idea of the *Aeneid* as a totalizing imitation of the *Iliad* and *Odyssey* has deep roots. It was always very obvious as well that books 1–6 do not contain the entire *Odyssey* in any literal sense any more than 7–12 contain the whole *Iliad*. Scholars have also long been aware that each half of the poem includes material borrowed from other poems, including the "wrong" Homeric model.[24] A systematic understanding of the entire Homeric program, however, was something new. It was because of Knauer's work that I began to look at Vergil's poetry in this way; and the book you are reading now, even without the additional impetus of Cairns' ideas about kingship theory, might have been much the same, simply as a reaction to Knauer's work and subsequent responses to it.

Knauer approaches his study of this seemingly intractable topic with a disarming simplicity. In an English summary of the book, which he published simultaneously with it, he writes: "If, without requiring the reasons, we assume

---

21. The interest was already evident in Knauer 1964, 31–106, especially 62–106 on the rediscovery of Homer through commentary on the *Aeneid* during the Renaissance (briefly summarized in Knauer 1964a, 61–64). By the time he arrived at Penn he had begun research for the article on Homer for the *Catalogus Translationum et Commentariorum*, a massive undertaking left unfinished, but far advanced at the time of his death. Publication is not imminent, but is anticipated.

22. Servius, *Commentary on Vergil's Aeneid* 1.1; I discuss this passage more fully in the section of chapter 1 entitled "In Medias Res."

23. *argumentum varium ac multiplex et quasi amborum Homeri carminum instar*: I quote David Wilson-Okamura's translation of a passage in Servius' preface to his *Commentary on Vergil's Aeneid*. This preface derives, via the biography of Vergil ascribed to Servius' teacher, Aelius Donatus, from Suetonius Tranquillus, the influential scholar who served as secretary to the emperors Trajan and Hadrian; see Ziolkowski and Putnam 2008, 191.

24. Servius considers *Aeneid* 4 to be an imitation of Apollonius, *Argonautica* 3 and *Aeneid* 5 an imitation of *Iliad* 23. Neither Servius nor anyone else to my knowledge comments on the presence of Odyssean elements in books 7–12 before the 17th-century commentator Juan Luis de la Cerda, whose perspective I discuss in the section of chapter 1 entitled "In Medias Res."

that Vergil really wanted from the very beginning to incorporate both Greek epics in his poem, it is obvious that he had to shorten them drastically."[25] As someone who lived through years of debate as to whether and how one ought to use words like "imitation," "allusion," "reference," and "intertextuality," I am stunned when I reflect on the untroubled directness of this statement. So much have critical perspectives changed that it now seems almost unbelievably naïve; and yet it does take Knauer right into the heart of his problem and lead to immediate results. As his initial focus on the seemingly mechanical, and in a sense trivial problem of shortening seems to suggest, Knauer eventually has to admit that the *Aeneid* does not literally contain the whole *Iliad* and *Odyssey*. The reason, however, is not simply that there was no room. He is very effective in showing how instances of the most common features of archaic epic—formulaic language, typical scenes, and the like—could be combined. There was no need for the *Aeneid* to incorporate multiple episodes of arrival, feasting, or arming for battle: combining many Homeric instances into one or a few would both suffice and, not incidentally, comport well with the classicizing aesthetic of the *Aeneid*.[26] However, the truth is—and Knauer is frank about this—that some elements of the Homeric poems simply "defied transformation."[27] Precisely why they did so is not in fact clear, and the idea that they did so becomes all the more remarkable when one considers that this statement applies to the last nine books of the *Odyssey* (16–24)—which is to say, nearly a quarter of the poem—in their entirety.

In spite of this, there is little doubt that Knauer understands the *Aeneid* as incorporating or transforming virtually or essentially the entire *Iliad* and *Odyssey*. Here is how, after about twelve pages of detailed discussion, he summarizes his findings:

> The plan of Vergil's structural imitations of Homer may now have become at least partly clear: the four great units of action in Homer, the Helen-action and the Patroclus-action in the *Iliad* (not Book 1, the Menis), the Telemacheia and the wanderings of Odysseus in the *Odyssey*, must after a thorough study have seemed to him to be not only comparable but actual parallels between the Homeric epics. Remember only the wrath of the gods

---

25. Knauer 1964a.

26. Shortening and condensation are not the unbending rule, however. Knauer 1964, 227 note 1 records the observation of Ernst Zinn, Knauer's thesis advisor, that *Aeneid* 1–6 contains exactly one invocation of the Muse, at the beginning of the poem (1.8), just like the entire *Odyssey* (1.1), while *Aeneid* 7–12 contains five, the same number as in the *Iliad*. See also the index entry under "Vergils Homerumformung: Längungen homer. Abschnitte" (Knauer 1964, 542).

27. Knauer 1964a, 77.

or the women as cause of war. Such apparent parallelism induced him to unite the two in a single poem, the *Aeneid*—to put it daringly, to treat the same matter a third time.

Then Knauer immediately opens a new paragraph.

The complete structure of the Homeric epics, not simply occasional quotations, was no doubt the basis for Vergil's poem.[28]

If I may rephrase this: Knauer sees the *Aeneid* as a thoroughgoing combination of the entire *Iliad* and *Odyssey*, from a structural point of view, but one that leaves out the events that set in motion the plot of the former (the quarrel between Achilles and Agamemnon in *Iliad* 1) and conclude that of the latter (the punishment of the suitors and the reunion of Odysseus and Penelope in *Odyssey* 16–24). How can both of these statements be true?

There is a great deal that could be said in answer to this question, but I will be brief. First, it is obvious that Knauer did in fact consider the *Aeneid* successful in combining the *Iliad* and the *Odyssey* in their entirety, no matter how much of either it actually left out. Second, and no less remarkably, he believed that the two poems tell essentially the same story, one of heroic deeds undertaken to recover a woman who had been stolen or was under threat of being stolen. Third, there is a certain asymmetry in the Homeric program of the *Aeneid* as Knauer sees it. He insists, and correctly so, that *Aeneid* 1 does not begin with *Odyssey* 1 but with *Odyssey* 5, when the hero is on his way home to Ithaca but is diverted to Scheria, the land of the Phaeacians—just as the *Aeneid* begins with the hero on his way "home" to Italy but diverted to Carthage. The story that Aeneas tells his hosts in books 2–3 about his prior adventures resembles the story that Odysseus tells his own hosts in *Odyssey* 9–12. Some of Odysseus' tales inspire episodes in the *Aeneid* that are not part of Aeneas' own narrative, but are part of the main narrative. For instance, Odysseus' journey to the land of the dead in book 11 (the "Nekyia"), about which he himself tells the Phaeacians, becomes Aeneas' journey to the underworld in book 6, which is told by the epic narrator. The first half of the *Aeneid* is thus not a complete *Odyssey*, but it is convincing as a reworking of the "Phaeacis" (*Odyssey* 5–12). This means that even if the *Aeneid* does not start at the beginning of the *Odyssey*, by the end of its first half it has just about "caught up" with its model. Then, although the poem signals with some fanfare what seem to be Iliadic intentions for its second half, it does not suddenly embark on this project, but instead continues on an Odyssean trajectory for two additional books. Aeneas' arrival in Latium in book 7 and his embassy in book 8 to Pallanteum, a Greek city

---

28. Knauer 1964a, 81.

built on the site of what would be Rome, correspond to Odysseus' arrival on Ithaca and his cautious approach to his own property in *Odyssey* 13–15. With only four books to go, the *Aeneid* is looking like it might be a kind of Odyssey almost from start to finish.[29]

At the same time, however, the catalogue of Italian forces that concludes *Aeneid* 7 corresponds to the catalogue of Greek and Trojan forces that concludes *Iliad* 2.[30] Each catalogue precedes the onset of active combat in its respective poem. Further, in *Aeneid* 8 and 9, the hero is absent while his people are under attack, a situation that corresponds to *Iliad* 3–19, when Achilles stays in his tent while the Greeks are (for the most part) being drubbed by the Trojans. In *Aeneid* 8 and *Iliad* 18 Aeneas and Achilles both receive from their mothers a gift of divine armor, and in books 10 and 20 they both return to battle wearing it and are victorious. Eventually, each slays the greatest hero of the opposing side, Turnus in *Aeneid* 12 and Hector in *Iliad* 22. Knauer thus finds *almost* a complete Iliad within *Aeneid* 7–12, most of it in the last four books. Crucially, however, he also finds that this Iliad is congruent with the second half of the *Odyssey*—that is, with Odysseus' struggle to re-establish himself in Ithaca and overcome Penelope's suitors. On this basis, he infers that in the last books of the *Aeneid* an Iliadic story consisting of Iliadic material *takes the place of* homologous Odyssean elements, but within an Odyssean structure that informs the entire *Aeneid*.

It is obviously possible to take issue with this conception of the Homeric *Aeneid* in whole or in part, but that is in some sense beside the point. What I would like to emphasize is that Knauer presents this conception in quite definite terms, and that he offers it not as his own interpretation of Vergil but as reflecting Vergil's own interpretation of Homer. That is fair enough, of course, but it is worth noting that he regards Vergil's interpretation as quite fixed and definite, not unlike Knauer's own. Looking back on this situation from the perspective of more than fifty years, one can see how it could be done differently. The rigid account that Knauer gives is self-contradictory (a totalizing imitation that leaves out crucial elements of both Homeric poems) in ways that might now seem not merely to undermine his

---

29. See Knauer 1964, 265, 328–29, 343 and Knauer 1964a, 65, 68–73, 76–77.

30. Strictly speaking, the Italian catalogue corresponds to the catalogue of Greek ships, which ends at *Iliad* 2.760 and is followed by the additional 117 lines cataloguing the Trojans and their allies, which conclude book 2. Homer's Trojan catalogue is "transferred" to the catalogue of Aeneas' Etruscan allies in book 10, which also draws on the brief catalogue of Myrmidons at *Iliad* 16.168–97: see Harrison 1991, 106–11, especially 107, on *Aeneid* 10.163–214; Knauer 1964, 297. This is a clear example of how Aeneas' war with Turnus is an intertextual battle for Greek identity, as I discuss in the section of chapter 3 entitled "Becoming Achilles."

conclusions, but rather to open them up to further exploration. One of these might be to imagine the Homeric program of the *Aeneid* not as a fixed structure with a definite meaning, but as something more flexible and provisional. That critical turn has in fact occurred; but before I get to it, let me return for a moment to Cairns.

The early reception of Knauer's work tended to emphasize its rigidity, sometimes approvingly, but not always. Most of those who disapproved did not go on to show how the whole system might be opened up but instead were skeptical of taking such an ambitiously systematic approach in the first place.[31] The bipartite model had survived since antiquity; it obviously wasn't true in every detail, but perhaps that just proved that one should not expect algebraic exactitude from poetry. Some did strongly approve, however.[32] Cairns, who was one of them, took the idea of "The *Aeneid* as Odyssey," the title of chapter 8 of his 1989 book, much, much farther. Although Knauer believed that the *Odyssey* provided the actual scaffolding that supported the entire Homeric *Aeneid*, it was clearly important to him conceptually that the *Aeneid* be, to recall the ancient phrase, "the equivalent, as it were, of both Homeric poems."[33] That is not how Cairns describes it. Building on Knauer's perception of continued Odyssean structural relevance in *Aeneid* 7–12, Cairns argues that the poem is an Odyssey from start to finish and not an organic Iliad, at all. Here is how he puts it:

> The *Odyssey* retains the structural and thematic importance that it had in Books 1–6 well into, and indeed throughout, the "iliadic" Books 7–12, while iliadic or quasi-iliadic episodes surface also in the "odyssean" *Aeneid* 1–6. This makes the *Aeneid*, not a bipartite work divided by subject matter (i.e. voyages or battles), but a unitary *Odyssey* with significant iliadic episodes.[34]

That is really a quite different way of putting it. Nor is that everything. Having conceded the existence of "significant iliadic episodes" throughout *Aeneid*, including books 1–6, Cairns goes on to devote an entire chapter to "The Memorial Games of Anchises" in *Aeneid* 5. Servius begins his commentary on book 5 by stating, "everything the poet mentions here is on display around the tomb of Patroclus [in *Iliad* 23], except there is a chariot race there and a boat race

---

31. See Buchheit 1967 and 1970; Pöschl 1967, 17–19; Wigodsky 1972, 8–12.

32. See, for example, Clarke 1965; C. Hardie 1967; Williams 1967; Wlosok 1973, 130, 139–40.

33. Again I quote David Wilson-Okamura's translation of the preface to Servius' commentary (see note 23 above).

34. Cairns 1989, 178

here."[35] About a century ago Richard Heinze built his masterly analysis of the episode on this assumption. At the same time, Heinze acknowledges, with many others, that Iliadic games are "out of place" in the "Odyssean *Aeneid*."[36] This is an obvious point, which Knauer explains by arguing that the episode was "transferred" from the end of the *Aeneid*, where (he says) it would have been inappropriate, to a location approximating that of some games that take place among the Phaeacians in *Odyssey* 8.[37] There is nothing in this that is the least objectionable or out of line with Knauer's usual methods.[38] Cairns, however, goes much farther by insisting that the Odyssean games are actually the more important model in every respect.[39] One would have thought, after reading the passage of Servius quoted above, that the "Games" of *Aeneid* 5 are a significant Iliadic episode if anything is; but after reading Cairns' chapter on them, one would have been told that they are hardly Iliadic at all.

In case it isn't obvious, I am not really persuaded by this argument. That said, I take Cairns' characterization of the *Odyssey* as dominant in the Homeric program of the *Aeneid* as an important and welcome provocation. I have spoken already of things that are overqualified, overadequate, and overdetermined; now I come to the most important over-compound of all, which is "overreading." One of the things I admire about Cairns is his overreading of both Knauer and the *Aeneid*. Knauer's perspective on the *Aeneid* is rigid, but it contains, if only in spite of itself, the germ of a more dynamic approach. He sees Aeneas as reliving the combined experiences of the angriest, most violent, and most stubborn hero who fought at Troy and also of the wiliest, most

---

35. The two races are the first and, in terms of narration, the longest events in their respective poems. Comparative analysis of the two "Games" episodes, in whole or in part, is a frequent scholarly exercise: see for instance Heinze 1917/1993, 121–41; Otis 1964, 41–62; Willcock 1988. Nelis 2001, 1–21 considers the "Games" of the *Aeneid* in the light of a wider array of models; Lovatt 2005 considers the tradition of epic games episodes from the perspective of Statius, one of Vergil's most important "epic successors" in the phrase coined by P. R. Hardie 1993.

36. Heinze 1917/1993, 121–41.

37. Knauer 1964, 156; 1964a, 65, 72 note 2, 73–74.

38. For a discussion of an important instance, and in my view a programmatic one, see the section of chapter 1 below entitled "Aeolus." Knauer also sees Andromache's mournful greeting of Aeneas in book 3 as "transferred" to the hero's quasi-Odyssean narrative of his "Wanderings" from Andromache's own lamentation for Hector in *Iliad* 22 (Knauer 1964, 276 note 2; 336). Similarly, the heroic funeral given Misenus in *Aeneid* 6 parallels Elpenor's burial in *Odyssey* 11, but it more closely resembles Patroclus' funeral in *Iliad* 23 (Knauer 1964, 136, 220). In general, see Knauer 1964, 330 and 332–45, especially 333–36..

39. Cairns 1989, 215–48.

circumspect, and most versatile. Cairns, instead of seeing the *Aeneid* as drawing more or less equally on two Homeric models, sees one as clearly dominant, and really does not discuss the importance of the other except to downplay or even deny it. Moreover, in contrast to Knauer, he recognizes and even stresses that the two Homeric poems, and especially their heroes, are quite different, specifically in ethical terms, making it clear that he regards Aeneas as an Odyssean "good king." This is, to repeat, not only a quite rigid interpretive structure, but one that moves to shut down any dynamic element that may be have been lying dormant in Knauer's approach. But an important reaction to the rigidity of Knauer's systematic approach, couched explicitly in terms of dynamism, was already in motion.

The Dynamic Intertext

A topic that Cairns treats in a rather gingerly way is the idea that the *Iliad* has often been considered the earlier and the greater of Homer's epic masterpieces. It is an idea that could be found already in ancient commentaries on Homer, as Cairns observes, supporting the observation with a long footnote.[40] Among the modern scholars who discuss this subject Cairns cites Alessandro Barchiesi, whose remarkable monograph *La traccia del modello* appeared five years before Cairns' book on the *Aeneid*. I believe this is Cairns' only citation of *La traccia*, and it is a tribute to his eye for detail and his scholarship; for Barchiesi's main subject is not the Odyssean *Aeneid* at all. Rather, he traces the reception in the most Iliadic portion of the *Aeneid*, and especially, in *Aeneid* 10 and 12, of the Homeric "Patrocleia"—the sequence of the *Iliad* that begins when Achilles' friend Patroclus goes into battle in Achilles' place and is killed by Hector, and ends when Achilles slays Hector in revenge.

Even after more than a quarter-century, and without considering that it was his first book, Barchiesi's project remains amazingly rich and rewarding, full of implications that go well beyond the relationship between these particular texts, and it has been widely influential in at least two ways. To suggest how this is so, perhaps I will be forgiven if I invoke Barchiesi's own famous distinction between Homer as the "genre model" (*modello genere*) and the "example model" (*modello esemplare*) of the *Aeneid*. Under the former aspect, Homer is the master text that showed not only Vergil but all Greek and Latin writers what epic poetry is, as he has continued to show writers and critics ever since. Under the latter aspect, Homer is the author of a particular text or segment of text, or of some treatment of a theme, motif, or idea to which a specific passage

---

40. Cairns 1989, 180 note 15.

of the *Aeneid*, or more than one, may respond. The response can take many forms, whether by repeating the original as precisely as possible, contradicting it, or even omitting it, but most often, on Barchiesi's reading, by modifying or re-imagining it. Such transformations frequently take place under the influence of Homer's reception by readers and critics during the eight centuries or so that separate the *Iliad* and the *Odyssey* from the *Aeneid*. One could say that many of Barchiesi's contemporaries and a generation of younger scholars have looked to his work as a kind of genre model of how to study Latin poetry, especially epic and closely related genres, but certainly not the *Aeneid* alone. Here I am especially interested in Barchiesi's intervention as an example model, and will focus mainly on his specific contribution to the Homeric problem of the *Aeneid*. In that regard, it is worth quoting the opening sentence of his book:

> Twenty years have passed since Knauer published his comprehensive collection of comparisons between the *Aeneid* and Homer: one glimpses in this monumental work the closure—and the definitive balance sheet—of a scholarly activity stretching from ancient inquiries into *furta Vergili* [the poet's "thefts," especially from Homer] right down to the great commentaries of the modern period. But one can also see in this inventory of comparative materials an opening for new research. Space remains, I think, for one who wants to investigate the functions the Homeric model assumes in the composition of the Vergilian text.[41]

It is clear that the young Barchiesi fully grasped Knauer's desire to continue to the fullest extent possible the work of predecessors, even to the inclusion of the competing and indeed contradictory imperatives that any such project must contain. In some sense, much as Knauer conceived of the *Aeneid* as a faithful translation of the Homeric poems, he conceived of his own project as a faithful representation of that relationship assembled from the many individual discernments of it, more or less accurate and much more limited in scope, that he found in earlier commentators. In contrast, Barchiesi declares that Knauer closed the book on that entire tradition. Further, he hints in his sly reference to ancient collections of *furta*, things in the *Aeneid* that were "stolen" from Homer, how much the motivation of those who took part in this tradition changed over time. What some ancient scholars regarded as culpable thefts, many later ones have praised as one of the highest expressions of Vergil's literary genius. In terms of comparison, as we have seen, Knauer's Vergil regarded the *Iliad* and the *Odyssey* as telling, in essence, the same story; similar

41. Barchiesi 1984/2015, xv.

elements in the two poems, he wrote, are "not only comparable," but functionally the same. Again in contrast, when Barchiesi speaks of *Die Aeneis und Homer* as an "inventory of comparative materials," he is probably not responding directly to Knauer's phrase, but he might as well be. His language does not suggest that things that can be compared are necessarily similar but that they are interesting precisely in that they are dissimilar. Finally, Barchiesi's focus on "functions" (plural) suggests a dynamism within the Homeric *Aeneid* that is quite alien to Knauer's conception of a poem that "treat[s] the same matter a third time."

For all of these differences (and there are many more), it is odd to say, but there are certain similarities between the methods of both these scholars. I do not say continuities, because they tend to treat similar issues in different ways. For instance, Knauer follows earlier scholars in supposing that Vergil made use of ancient Homeric exegesis to assist his research.[42] Barchiesi goes much farther than anyone before him in using ancient scholarship to establish the horizon of expectations that Vergil and his readers will have brought to their experience of Homer.[43] Notably, he shows that these expectations are, precisely, *not* identical with those that are based solely on a close acquaintance with the *Iliad* and *Odyssey* themselves: they involve ideas that had grown up around those texts over centuries of reception history. This is one of the ways in which we may regard Homer's meaning itself as not static but dynamic; and in the collisions of meaning that take place between Homer's text and its interpretation by ancient critics, between Greek cultural realities and those of Roman readers, in the intertextual jostling of one Homeric allusion against another within the *Aeneid*, one gets the impression of something very different from Knauer's fixed intertextuality, a pronounced sense that the relationships involved might be and even must be negotiated in different ways.

That said, I would be misrepresenting Barchiesi's work if I suggested that this openness was limitless. A very important part of the way in which he presents interpretive possibilities is that he shows them to the reader, and then often moves on without endorsing them, or else explicitly retreats from doing so. This is perhaps only to be expected in view of the ethical interests of the book. These are not a central concern, but Barchiesi does examine closely the ethical topic of practicing moderation in success (*servare modum*) as a generally recognizable principle that clashes with the behavior of individual Homeric heroes at particular moments and, in the *Aeneid*, with that of Turnus as

42. Knauer 1964, 56 note 2; 69 note 1; 356 note 1.
43. Barchiesi 1984/2015, 1–34.

he slays Aeneas' young protégé, Pallas, and strips the armor from his body as a prize of war. Again I quote:

> Vergil is therefore able to cite in summary form, through the simple opposition between *res secundae* [success] and *servare modum* [practicing moderation], a universally recognized and accepted cultural model: from this an ongoing commentary is cast that allows the reader to ideologize according to his own value system the poem's "Iliadic" content and participate in foreseeing its developments. Thus commented upon, the action takes on a plausible realism. The narrative produces its own *post hoc ergo propter hoc* by construing itself in reading as a necessary concatenation. But this commentary must remain completely incorporated in the narration if it is not to "kill" (as will happen, for example, in Lucan) the free unfolding of epic events by superimposing itself on them. So the Vergilian text cannot help but permit a host of "voices" to coexist within it (voices linking up in various way[s] with the Homeric texts, of which they represent diverse readings and transformations): it accepts the risk of being multivocal and even exploits, for precise communicative ends, the polyphony of its own cultural codes. Perhaps this was the only way to remake Homer without ignoring the distance that inevitably separated it from the complex, civilized world in which the poet lived. Yet this distance is less insurmountable if, once again, we do not consider the Homeric text as a fixed and immutable object but as a layering of historically diverse readings.[44]

This seems as if it could not be more different from Knauer's conception, in which the Homeric text is indeed a fixed and immutable object, even to the extent of denying any important difference between the *Iliad* and *Odyssey* themselves, let alone between those texts as they were understood at different points in their long history of reception. No further comment is required to see how Barchiesi opens up interpretation of the Homeric *Aeneid* to multiple possibilities. And yet, I am not sure in the end precisely how open it remains. A pair of phrases that interest me above are in the description of the Vergilian text: "it *accepts the risk* of being multivocal and even exploits, *for precise communicative ends*, the polyphony of its own cultural codes." What is the nature of this risk, and what are the ends the poem is trying to achieve by taking it? Is the risk simply that of being misunderstood? Multiple voices are often in conflict, as are the welter of voices that modern students of the *Aeneid* have long debated. Ever since Adam Parry first articulated the concept of "two voices," one public and one private, many different readers have attempted to

---

44. Barchiesi 1984/2015, 31.

adumbrate the poem's precise communicative ends with reference to the matter of voices.[45] On the other hand, the risk could be that readers will fail to grasp a multivocality that evokes conflicting responses as a precise communicative end; but that does not seem to be what Barchiesi means. I am not even sure that the multivocality he has in mind resides properly, as it were, within the *Aeneid* itself. Is it rather something that infiltrates the poem along with Homer and the complex history of Homeric interpretation?

We may find at least one answer to this question in Barchiesi's famous paper on "The Lament of Juturna," originally part of the same thesis that became *La traccia*, which was then published separately and is now "reunited with its siblings," the chapters of the original book, in the 2015 translation. The paper addresses a monologue by Turnus' sister, whom Jupiter has raped and "compensated" by granting her divinity and immortality. The monologue speaks to her grief at the impending death of her beloved brother. I quote once more:

> The motif of unhappy immortality, born on the ground of philosophical criticism of Homer, thus inserts itself, thanks to the narrow gap in the epic narrative made possible by the monologic structure that we have examined, in a text that wants to situate itself as a direct continuation of the Homeric tradition: scholars who study (with good reason) the *Aeneid* as an open work, characterized by ideological tensions, in the context of "the crisis of the ancient world," will find this contradiction significant.

And then:

> The undeniable evocation of tragedy that deeply marks Vergil's work establishes, in scenes such as this one, a style that makes an immediate gesture of pathos; but we must note, at the same time, that this expressive register (the aspect of Vergilian style where we can identify and study philologically credible borrowings from tragedy) exhausts and consumes the impulse towards the tragic. From tragedy Vergil carries over a certain violent immediacy that imposes the ego of the characters as a total perspective on the world. But on these originally irreducible personalities the tragic form knows how to enact a principle of synthetic recomposition: the character "learns" from action, changing and being changed by others. All this does not seem possible in the *Aeneid*. . . . Not that the poem lacks potentially tragic material or the required maturity of a dramatic style: its limitation

---

45. Parry 1963; followed by Barchiesi's "'host' of voices" (see note 44 above; actually "una serie di 'voci,'"1984, 51); the "further voices" of Lyne 1987; the skeptical "too many voices" of Traina 1990; and, most recently, the "furthest voices" of Schiesaro 2008, on which see chapter 1, "Enigmas of Arrival," with note 141.

should be located rather in the form of the content, which does not take up the task of recomposing the various worldviews by making them dialectical, but instead brusquely superimposes a dominant perspective—that of Fate.[46]

Here the openness of the *Aeneid*, together with multivocality, looks distinctly illusory and rather like a stratagem. Of course it is more than that, but perhaps some of the risk that Barchiesi has in mind relates to William Empson's throwaway observation, which he attributes to Alexander Pope, that "even the *Aeneid* was a 'political puff'; its dreamy, impersonal, universal melancholy was a calibrated expression of support for Augustus."[47] J. D. Reed in his 2007 book, *Virgil's Gaze: Nation and Poetry in the Aeneid*, cited Empson, but expressed himself with greater nuance when he wrote this:

> Roman origins in the *Aeneid* are an unstable combination of different elements, represented on the narrative level by the contested viewpoints and ambiguity that so often contribute to "Virgilian melancholy." There is certainly enough melancholy in the passages on "ancient cities," but we would do well to remember that the tender feelings of loss that readers often detect in Virgil's account of the cost of Aeneas' mission can be as much an aesthetic channeling of true indignation as they are an acknowledgement of ambivalence about the triumph of Rome.[48]

Ten years later, Reed would complain that different readers reacted to his book as anti-determinist and denying all meaning to Roman identity, on the one hand, but also as upholding the "traditional imperialist" school of interpretation, on the other—with both of these reactions being based on perceptions that Reed is opposed to a notional pessimistic orthodoxy deriving from Parry's "two voices" perspective.[49] Can it be that critics of the *Aeneid*, whether they openly embrace multivocality and polyphony or do not embrace it enough, either way run the same kind of risk as the poem does by permitting so many voices to coexist within it?

---

46. Barchiesi 1978/2015, 111–12.

47. Empson 1935, 1. If Pope actually left this in writing I have not been able to find where. I am grateful to Christine Perkell for first calling my attention to Empson, however, and for a penetrating discussion of this perspective many years ago at a time when I was just beginning to work towards this project, some five years before she published Perkell 1997 as a response to Barchiesi 1978/2015.

48. Reed 2007, 141, quoting Empson. See also Habinek 1998, 164: "Through its central movement of lamentation, [the *Aeneid*] distances the author and reader from their responsibility in the losses generated by imperialism while foreclosing the possibility of resistance on the part of the defeated."

49. Reed 2017.

Barchiesi gives the reader a glimpse of the poem that the *Aeneid* might have been, one engaged in a dialogue with tragedy that is open, and not one-sided or unbalanced; one in which voices of lamentation represent a perspective that the reader need not reject. I have often felt bemused that no one has done as much to convince me of the poem's essentially tragic nature, only to deny the validity of that response. Or, if not to deny its validity, then to encourage a dialogical response, but one that must finally be recognized, not without regret, as an evanescent possibility, a dream version of a poem that ultimately speaks with a single voice. Must that be the last word?

The Dialogic Intertext

Because *La traccia* is devoted to the Iliadic "Patrocleia," one might have inferred that Barchiesi's focus was at odds with Knauer's thinking about the continuing structural relevance of the *Odyssey* in *Aeneid* 7–12; but that would be mistaken. Barchiesi too accepts the idea of an imbalance in favor of the *Odyssey* within the poem's Homeric program. He writes, "The complex texture of relations that bind the *Aeneid* to the two Homeric poems seems analogous to what binds the *Odyssey* to the *Iliad*."[50] This observation, which Barchiesi supports with a page or so of details concerning plot and narration, some of them deriving from ancient scholarship, differs mainly in terms of metaphor from the perspective that Edan Dekel works out in his 2012 book *Virgil's Homeric Lens*. Dekel's central idea is this: "Imitating Homer means first and foremost emulating the Greek poet's own habits. For Virgil, this means first and foremost modeling his intertextual epic on the very first intertextual epic, the *Odyssey*."[51]

In this intriguing conception there are continuities with and departures from the chief insights and contributions of Knauer, Cairns, and Barchiesi. Like Knauer, Dekel regards the second half of the *Odyssey* as congruent in structure and theme with the *Iliad*, but he does not focus, as Knauer does, mainly the mechanical challenge of combining both of the massive Homeric poems. Like Cairns, he sees the *Odyssey* "as a master text for the *Aeneid*," but not merely as the poem's "primary structural or conceptual model."[52] Neither is Dekel concerned to argue that Aeneas is more an Odysseus than a new

---

50. Barchiesi 1984/2015, 71.
51. Dekel 2015, 19.
52. Dekel 2015, 20, where he notes that Cairns also invokes an optical metaphor to argue for "a possible reading of the *Odyssey* as *imitatio cum variatione* [imitation with variation] of the *Iliad* that would have allowed Virgil to look through the *Odyssey* to the *Iliad*" (Cairns 1989, 202).

Achilles, and therefore a "good king."[53] Like Barchiesi, Dekel explores intertextual dynamics and invokes the metaphor of a Homeric "trace" that is, to quote Stephen Hinds' well-known discussion, "also a Homeric 'track' or a 'trail,' which, once encountered in Virgilian territory, has the potential to lead readers in directions determined no less by Homer than by Virgil."[54] As we have seen, the intertextual dynamics that exist between the *Iliad* and *Odyssey* lie mostly outside the limits that Barchiesi set himself, but these dynamics are absolutely central to Dekel's project of reading the *Aeneid* as a reading of the *Iliad* through an Odyssean "lens."

Alluding through one poem to another is a very familiar intertextual procedure to which Richard Thomas has given the felicitous name "window reference."[55] Dekel acknowledges the power of this concept but offers a critique of its limitations.[56] His objections mainly involve what he sees as a tendency to regard the "window," the more proximate model through which one alludes to the more distant one, as hermeneutically inert, more or less. He apparently regards most of those who speak of "window reference" as imagining the ideal window as one that is barely there, or at least as one that does not distort, refract, color, or otherwise alter whatever there may be on the other side. There is something to this, although I think most would acknowledge that even a window with no glass in it frames what one sees and alters it in that way, at least. In any case, it is fair to say that the concept of "window reference" has been understood in new ways since Thomas coined the term, including different ways that the metaphor itself has provoked into existence. Dekel's own optical metaphors of "lenses," "mirrors," and so forth are but the latest instance. (Or so I believe, as of this writing; it is sometimes hard to keep up!)

Dekel also mentions Hinds' influential counter-coinage, "two-tier allusion," which I believe was a product of the debate over basic terminology that I mentioned before (reference, allusion, intertext . . .). That is also what Damien Nelis calls it in his 2001 book, *Vergil's Aeneid and the Argonautica of Apollonius Rhodius*. Dekel mentions Nelis' study in his discussion of "window reference," but he does not devote much attention to it. In a way that is fair enough. Dekel's focus is on Homer and Nelis' is on Apollonius. In fact, though, Nelis' work is essential to understanding the Homeric as well as the Apollonian *Aeneid*, and in ways that speak directly to Dekel's concerns. For instance, when

---

53. Dekel 2015, 108–9 argues on other grounds that Aeneas in book 3 presents himself as improving upon Odyssean leadership. This position contrasts with my own in a number of ways, as will become evident in the section of chapter 3 entitled "Wanderings."
54. Hinds 1998, 101, citing Fowler 1991a, 90.
55. Thomas 1986, 188–89.
56. Dekel 2015, 20–21.

Dekel refers to Hinds' argument "that it is actually impossible to read two texts against one another without privileging one or the other at any given moment of interpretation," he notes,

> While there is a great deal of truth in this formulation, the situation is a bit more complex when we are dealing with three texts. If the *Odyssey* and the *Iliad* are already engaged in an intertextual dialogue, and Virgil composes his *Aeneid* so that it engages that dialogue in yet another dialogue, then we actually have a pair of nested bidirectional relationships. It is possible to read the internal Homeric relationship from the perspective of the *Aeneid*, and the *Aeneid* itself in relation to the Homeric poems.[57]

That is quite correct. And the complexity only increases, I suppose, when four poems are involved. This is the situation that Nelis reckons with. His materials are the *Iliad*, the *Odyssey*, the *Argonautica*, and the *Aeneid*; and "two-tier allusion" or "window reference" is the essential intertextual trope in his conceptual tool kit. Crucially, on Nelis' reading, the Apollonian window is anything but transparent. It is a veritable multicolor, prismatic composition of complex design worthy of Chartres Cathedral; or so Nelis would have it, because the argument of his book is not that the *Aeneid* alludes through a largely inert *Argonautica* to its real, Homeric model, nor that it "corrects" (*à la* Thomas) Apollonius' treatment of Homer in the process.[58] On the contrary, Nelis argues that Apollonius' program largely *determined* that of the *Aeneid*: that the Homeric program of the *Aeneid* amounts to imitating Apollonius imitating Homer.

Nelis expresses himself very clearly about this key point, but I have to confess that I failed to understand it for some time. To describe my difficulty, let me quote James O'Hara's very perceptive, highly appreciative review of Nelis' book. After stressing that Nelis demonstrates persuasively that the Argonautic program extends throughout the *Aeneid*, just as Knauer had argued about the *Aeneid* and Homer, O'Hara writes:

> Many Virgilians will read this book with the disturbing sense that after having gotten used to the dominance of Homer and the choice contributions of Callimachus and Apollonius, we have to change the way we view the poem. The scholar is almost like a sailor or fisherman who has carefully learned the tides, only to look up and see a second moon in the sky (perhaps one that we can only see dimly, through the clouds) exerting its pull on

---

57. Dekel 2015, 23; see Hinds 1998, 102 note 3.

58. In keeping with another allusive technique described by Thomas 1986, 185 as "perhaps the quintessentially Alexandrian type of reference."

the world's waters. This would mean, of course, that everything has changed.[59]

O'Hara's prediction that the book might prove disturbing has been borne out, but in my view the effect of this disturbance has been that very few have actually faced the challenge of calculating the effect of a second moon on those familiar tides. That may be partly because the "two moons" conceit can itself be read in two ways. Perhaps the more obvious way is that the gravitational pull of the second moon is likely to conflict with that of the first, at least some of the time. That way of thinking dominated my initial reaction to Nelis' book. One can see this clearly in something I wrote not long after it appeared, in one of a series of what I have come to think of as interim reports on Vergilian intertexuality.[60] At the time I was used to reckoning with the *Aeneid* in terms that proceeded from Knauer's totalizing perspective on Homer, in which (to pursue the metaphor) the *Iliad* and *Odyssey* are treated as two moons that are never in conflict—or really, as O'Hara's conceit suggests, are together just a single moon. Even if one were to follow Knauer in this, it seemed inevitable that adding Apollonius to the mix as a much more powerful influence than had ever before been suspected would indeed disturb one's sense of order. More than that, it also seemed to me that if this were true of Apollonius, and we simply hadn't realized it, then one had to be prepared, at least in theory, for yet another moon to appear one day, and another and another. In the aforementioned paper I tried to grapple with what such a proliferation of satellites could possibly mean; and it was at this point that I began to surrender any residual allegiance I may have had to the concept of authorial intention in the study of poetic design, and especially in matters of allusion. Frankly, the idea of managing to coordinate separate, but totalizing allusive programs involving two, or really three different poems at once seemed incompatible with the idea that all of the effects that a reader might notice could have been foreseen, even by the most brilliant poet in the world. To admit this was a liberating step, and one result of it is that the reader of the present book, after getting clear of this intro, will notice only one reference to Vergil's intentions (besides this one) in the rest of it, and very few references to Vergil himself, at least in my own "voice." If that had been my only reaction to Nelis' book, I would already have been very much in his debt.

There is, however, an additional, and possibly larger debt, as well. In regard to Nelis' conception of how the Homeric and Apollonian programs work together in the *Aeneid*, I was at first seriously mistaken, assuming that the two

---

59. O'Hara 2004, 376.
60. Farrell 2005; see note 18 above.

moons of O'Hara's image would generally pull in different directions. I did not reckon with the possibility that, if they were aligned, their force would be multiplied. Eventually I understood that the latter possibility agrees much more closely with what Nelis has in mind. His application of "two-tier allusion" to the problem of the Argonautic *Aeneid* is indispensable to his critical method and amounts to a crucial update of Knauer's hermeneutics. One could easily imagine a poet as fashioning any individual passage in such a way as to allude quite clearly to a passage in Apollonius and one in Homer. The passages in both of the Greek poets might have absolutely nothing to do with one another, until the third poet alluded to them simultaneously. That is what I would call "combinatory allusion," which one encounters all the time.[61] It is also the foundation of Knauer's approach to the *Iliad* and the *Odyssey* in the *Aeneid*, although he characteristically prefers to use the word "contamination," which he borrows from the critical vocabulary of Roman comedy. As I have explained, Knauer regards combination or contamination not as an act of debatable interpretation, but as reflecting Vergil's accurate detection of real homologies—intended by Homer!—between the plots of the *Iliad* and *Odyssey*. Such an assumption obviously elides many interpretive possibilities. Still, it was only a short, though crucial step from that assumption to Barchiesi's understanding of the *Odyssey* as occupying a position between the *Iliad* and the *Aeneid*, and then to Dekel's conception of the *Aeneid* as imitating the *Odyssey* imitating the *Iliad*. Both lead towards the notion that the *Odyssey* in some sense guides allusion to, and interpretation of, the *Iliad* in the *Aeneid*. But that is exactly what Nelis says about the *Argonautica*—that Apollonius' imitation of Homer largely determines how the *Aeneid* imitates Homer, as well.

There is an important difference, however, between Nelis and Dekel; possibly Barchiesi, as well, since he adumbrates a general understanding of the relationship between the *Iliad* and *Odyssey* in the Homeric *Aeneid*, though it is not his purpose to analyze the relationship in detail. Dekel does this, and in the process he describes a dialogical relationship between the two Homeric poems that reduces any sense of conceptual hierarchy between them. The impression thereby created is somewhat at odds with the notion of the *Odyssey* as the "lens" though which the *Aeneid* views the *Iliad*. To my mind, this is all to the good. Nelis differs from Dekel, and from Barchiesi, in that he does not

---

61. Thomas 1986, 193 calls this "conflation" or "multiple reference" and considers it "the most complex type of reference." As a friendly amendment to this, I would suggest that complexity is where one finds it, but I would certainly agree that most types of reference are interesting in proportion to their complexity. Knauer might agree with this to an extent, but when he speaks of complexity in allusion he is usually referring to formal and not hermeneutic challenges.

posit any a priori hierarchical relationship between the *Iliad* and *Odyssey*, whether on the basis of narrative chronology, supposed compositional priority, or any other factor. He does not say that the alluding poet must approach one poem through the other. He does say, however—as large numbers of Apollonian critics also do—that the *Argonautica* represents itself as an *Odyssey* in a much more pronounced sense than it fashions itself on the model of the *Iliad*. For this reason, he believes, Apollonius' imitation of the *Odyssey* becomes the basis of almost the entire Homeric program of the *Aeneid*. This position is not quite the same as Cairns'—that the *Aeneid* is really "a unitary *Odyssey* with significant Iliadic episodes"—but it is not incompatible with it. Above all, Nelis believes that the Odyssean character of the *Argonautica* is clearly reflected in the Homeric program of the *Aeneid*. A very significant difference between Nelis and Cairns, however, is that the latter regards "Virgil's ready acceptance of additional influence on his characters, motifs, and emotional tone from Apollonius Rhodius' *Argonautica*" as "external confirmation" of his thesis regarding "the *Aeneid* as *Odyssey*." [62] That is similar to my own initial response to Nelis' work as the revelation of an extensive Apollonian program *added to a conceptually prior* Homeric one. In fact, what Nelis argues, clearly and convincingly, is that the Apollonian program is at least *conceptually parallel* to the Homeric program, and it is difficult not to conclude that it is *conceptually prior* to it. That, it seems to me, is why O'Hara's image is so apt, no matter what may be the direction in which his two moons are pulling. We have been used to thinking of Homer as unique. Nelis shows that Homer is not only not unique, but in at least one important sense he is not even primary.

Among the works that I have been discussing there are some obvious differences as well as some diachronic continuities and discontinuities. All of them, however, have at least one thing in common. Here I quote Dekel: "There is a massive body of literature on local parallels or allusions, and some serious work on the alleged Odyssean or Iliadic 'half,' but there are almost no comprehensive studies of the systematic relationship between the two poets."[63] That is quite true. These studies are the main examples. Again, I do not say this is the only way to approach Vergil's *Aeneid*, or his *Eclogues* or his *Georgics*, for

---

62. Cairns 1989, 179 cites Apollonian influence as "external confirmation" that the *Aeneid* is primarily an Odyssey. The *Argonautica*, he writes, is a "hyper-odyssean epic," and to the extent that the *Aeneid* easily accepts contributions from such a source (one that involves heroic seafaring, that is highly episodic, full of colorful ethnographic elements, and so on), it must be the kind of poem into which such features would readily fit. I will return to this point in the section of chapter 2 entitled "The *Aeneid* as Argosy."

63. Dekel 2012, 14.

that matter, or that it is the best way, or that anyone who neglects it is a miscreant doomed to hermeneutic perdition. I do say that a susceptibility to systematic analysis is highly characteristic of these poems, perhaps to an unusual extent. I would even admit that this may make them a poor model for the study of intertextual effects in other poems.[64] In fact, if I were to amend what I have just written, I might say that the *Eclogues*, the *Georgics*, and the *Aeneid* are unusual in the extent to which they *seem to invite* systematic analysis and to offer the promise of a great reward to anyone who, by virtue of ingenuity or sheer dint of scholarly labor, might be able to encompass the elaborate intertextual vistas that these extraordinary poems *appear* to offer. I also recognize that, to many, this invitation is not enticing at all and that the promised rewards are not in the least tempting, but better avoided as chimerical. These many are not confined to critics who are skeptical of literary formalism *tout court*. After quite a few years of familiarizing myself with the possibilities and the frustrations of such work, I am more convinced than ever that the effort is well worth it, but also more convinced than ever that the skeptic's role is as indispensable as that of the true believer. All of that said, whatever differences I may have with Knauer, Barchiesi, Cairns, Nelis, and Dekel, I share with them a preference for taking a systematic approach.

At the same time, all of the works that I have been discussing share among themselves, to varying extents, the idea that a systematic approach to the Homeric *Aeneid* must be biased, to some degree, towards the *Odyssey*. Of this I admit that I am skeptical, for reasons that will become clear in due course. I am also reluctant to make such an assumption the starting point of my inquiry, rather than accepting it only if that is where my own investigation leads. Further, I am somewhat wary of the various ways in which systematic approaches to the problem tend to become ever more complex, in one way or another. Cairns is something of an exception to this, but he is also in many ways the most forthright and insistent about the dominance of the *Odyssey*. So, in what follows, I will propose a different model that begins, or at least tries to begin, with no bias for or against either of Homer's masterpieces. I will take their differences into account, but will not assign primacy to either of them. I refer to the familiar concept of a two-part Homeric program, and I agree very much with Barchiesi that it is far from irrelevant and should not be discarded. However, like all those whose work I have been discussing, I invoke it only to reiterate that this conception does not tell the whole story. I would go a bit farther to say that precisely because it is far from irrelevant and yet does not tell the whole story, this durable concept paradoxically underlines the contingency of

---

64. See, for instance, Farrell 1997, 222–23 and 228.

all analytical constructs. With that in mind, I have tried to describe fairly the work of five similar but very different accounts of the Homeric *Aeneid*, and I hope I have conveyed my appreciation of what they all have to offer. I also hope it is clear that I think that it would be a mistake to identify any of them with The Truth. Naturally, the same caveat applies to my humble efforts.

The Ethical *Aeneid*

Before I say more about those efforts, there is a bit more to say about ethics. Since Cairns is so explicit about ethical concerns, I return to his idea that the *Aeneid* is primarily an Odyssey and that its hero is an avatar of Odysseus the "good king." On that basis, Cairns concludes that the poem reflects well on the hero's notional descendant, Augustus. This interesting proposal invites the question: if the *Aeneid* were found instead to be primarily an Iliad, would it be necessary to infer that its hero is an avatar of Achilles the "bad king," and that the poem thus reflects poorly on Augustus? I am aware that to pose the question in such bald terms will repel some readers, and I should just say now that if you are one of those, you may just want to stop reading, because I will be posing such questions repeatedly in the coming pages. If you are willing to grant me some leeway, however, I will explain why I do this. It is not my purpose to argue that the *Aeneid* is or is not an Odyssey or an Iliad, or that it combines those poems in some specific proportion, or that it offers a smorgasbord of reflective opportunities for the erudite reader to make of what they will. Instead, I am interested in the heuristic possibilities offered by Cairns' clear-cut approach and am curious to see where they would lead if turned in some other direction. In the case of the Homeric program of the *Aeneid*, there is really only one other principal direction, so I propose to evaluate the alternatives, both of which mean something in terms of ancient and modern ethical assumptions.

Ancient Perspectives

A point very much in favor of Cairns' approach is that ethical criticism was one of the most common modes of discussing and evaluating literature in antiquity. It is overwhelmingly likely that ancient readers were reflexively attuned to the ethics of virtually any story that they read or heard. Certainly they had learned in school to regard Homer as an ethical teacher. It would be rather extraordinary if readers with this background approached a poem like the *Aeneid*, which engages in such a committed way with both the *Iliad* and the *Odyssey*, as if that engagement lacked an ethical dimension or its concern with ethics lacked a Homeric dimension. That much is elementary and obvious, but there will be more to say on the subject very shortly.

Modern Perspectives

A second advantage of focusing on ethics, and specifically on the ancient reception of Homeric ethics, is that it opens a door to discussing possibilities that have been underrepresented in the criticism of epic poetry, and of Roman poetry in general, for some time. This is not the place to attempt a thoroughgoing account of developments in the post–New Critical, post–Harvard School environment of the last three decades or so.[65] It has been and continues to be a period in which an enormous number of new ideas have entered the field as the quantity and variety of texts and subjects that are frequently read and studied by so many classicists has greatly expanded. These developments are obviously altogether positive. At the same time, in my view at least, some of the avenues that it was once possible to explore have surprisingly become much less accessible than was once the case. This is certainly true of the *Aeneid*. New Critical readers with Harvard School leanings once found it possible to find that the poem raises urgent questions about the ethics of power and the means used to procure it. Readers today are more likely to frame their assessment of what the poem might mean by emphasizing that it was written in active engagement with the norms of the epic genre by a poet who enjoyed the friendship and patronage—whatever precisely those words mean—of a person closely associated with the de facto ruler of Rome and its empire. Readers had always been fully aware of these facts, but nevertheless conceived of the poem as speaking to the issues of its moment with reference to broader concerns that transcended that moment. In contrast, many readers now tend to emphasize the limits that immediate political and social realities placed on what any writer could safely say or would even want to say. Comparative studies involving other media play an important role here. In a visual environment saturated with imagery flattering to the Augustan regime, how could mere poetry—particularly poetry that in large part shares an imagistic and conceptual vocabulary with contemporary visual arts—manage to convey a significantly different message?[66] In purely literary terms, as well, generic protocols can be

---

65. The reflections of Giusti 2016, with specific reference to Kennedy 1992, are very pertinent here, as are many of the contributions to Hejduk 2017, of which Reed 2017 (cited above, note 49) is one.

66. In modern times this approach originated with Syme 1939, 459–75 (chapter 30, "The Organization of Opinion"), which was written with direct reference to political propaganda in contemporary authoritarian states. Zanker 1987/1988 represents an updating of this model on the basis of exoteric forms of post-Marxist cultural critique that pervaded the academy in the late 20th century. In my own view, the replacement of "propaganda" with "ideology" in the standard critical lexicon did not really change much. In any case Zanker, like Syme, takes

seen as preventing certain ideas from being expressed or from meaning what they might in some other context. For my own project, these tendencies raise the question of how the *Aeneid* could entertain, even obliquely, the possibility that Augustus' ancestor might be found to be a "bad king" when judged by the standards of philosophical heroism. Cairns does not frame the question in such explicit terms, but the case he presents is consistent with those unstated premises. And yet, to speak directly to those concerns, it is undeniably true that ancient ethical critics of Homer found the *Iliad* to be full of negative exempla. That is to say, the horizon of expectations that surrounded the *Iliad* in particular from the late Classical period onwards both regarded the poem as in some sense the greatest ever written and, in another sense, viewed it as a tragic meditation on human failings. I simply want to ask: Is it not possible that the *Aeneid* was written to challenge the greatest poem ever written on the very same terms? And: Is it possible for the *Aeneid* to engage with the *Odyssey* in ethical terms, and to engage simultaneously with the *Iliad* while *avoiding* analogous ethical issues?

By posing that question I am getting ahead of myself, and I risk forgetting that there is yet another dimension to these ethical questions. When "pessimistic" approaches to the *Aeneid* were still relatively new, one of the most common objections to reading the poem as a critique of its own times and a melancholy meditation on the human condition more generally, asserted that critics who did so were inattentive to the contextual environment that produced the poem and were inappropriately influenced by the times in which they themselves lived.[67] With the proliferation of activity in the field of reception studies during the intervening years, I think I can say that most would now be a bit less likely to make such a charge in such simplistic terms. When was anyone's response to the political or ethical climate of Augustan Rome not conditioned by their own times?

---

virtually no account of how poetry might function differently from architecture or other forms, or of the extent to which the message of any work of art might differ at different points of reception. Elsner 1991 addresses the latter issue from a historical and theoretical perspective that he develops more fully in Elsner 1995 and 2007; see also Hölscher 1987/2004; Rutledge 2012. With regard to the *Aeneid* see Bell 1999; Seider 2013; Schiesaro 2015; Freudenburg 2017. For more general perspectives see Henderson 1998; Fowler 2000, 193–217; Pandey 2018.

67. The interpretation of Putnam 1965, 151–201, that Aeneas wins a "tragic victory" by killing Turnus, which of course was and continues to be hugely influential, provoked a strong reaction that has also been sustained: see von Albrecht 1966, a review of Putnam's book, and 1999, 120, a one-sided review of the controversy to that point. Otis 1976, 27, describes the Aeneas of Putnam and A. J. Boyle as "a product of the Vietnam war and the New Left," but he goes on to admit, "and yet they point, in a curious way, to an actual feature of the *Aeneid*."

It is true, of course, that just as a classic book is one that has never finished telling us what it has to say, it is also one that always seems to be in need of vindication. Often one seeks to vindicate the classics as a vindication of oneself. Such was the case when Victor Pöschl, who contributed more than most to establishing the critical regime that held sway during what is best described as the Cold War years, concluded the introduction to his influential book on the *Aeneid* with these words: "There is more at stake here than just the question of Vergil; it concerns the foundation of Western civilization. We are seeking <u>ties of communication that bind us together</u>. We must, therefore, <u>reestablish a firm place for the *Aeneid* in our cultural consciousness</u> as one of the bibles of the Western world."[68] The words underlined above are underlined in my own copy of Pöschl, which belonged one of my high-school teachers, Thomas Darmody. As I reflect on his reading of the passage, I wonder how it would be received by someone reading it for the first time today. In the light of current debates, I find that different elements of the passage stand out. Those of us who have been "doing Classics" for a long time are so familiar with the concepts of "Western civilization" and "the Western world" that we may take them for granted, even if we automatically align Pöschl's exhortation with the perspective of figures like Theodor Haecker and T. S. Eliot.[69] We have a context for it, and that may blind us to its full significance, just as a lack of perspective may blind first-time readers in a different way.

Pöschl's reasons for writing his book were immediately political in a way that goes beyond the significance of the words quoted above. In fact, only in English translation did Pöschl's original German words gain their full significance. It is now well known that, during the Second World War, Pöschl was a Nazi party member and an officer in the infamous *Schutzstaffel*, better known simply as the SS. Little documentary evidence of his record has survived, certainly nothing to suggest that he was directly involved in the most heinous crimes of that organization.[70] What is clear is that his plea to "re-establish" the *Aeneid* in its proper place—a place that it always seems and perhaps always had seemed to be in danger of losing—is a plea for a return to the "normal" conditions that obtained before the war.[71] What is left unsaid is that only with the translation of his words by Gerda Seligson, a professor of Classics at the University of Michigan who had been Pöschl's fellow student before she was

---

68. Pöschl 1950/1962, 12.

69. Haecker 1931/1934; Eliot 1945; see Ziolkowski 1993; Martindale 1997/2019; Kennedy 1995 and 1997/2019; Thomas 2001, 260–77.

70. Tatum 2013, 25–26; Wlosok 2001, 371.

71. Thomas 2001, 256.

forced to emigrate under the Nazi persecution of the Jews, did Pöschl realize a portion of that restoration.[72] In one sense, then, the "Western civilization" that Pöschl aimed to restore by writing on the *Aeneid* was Europe as he imagined it before the *Nazizeit*. In another, Pöschl was not concerned only with Hesperia, Christendom, and other ancient notions of that kind. To be sure, these concepts are relevant; but virtually every reference to "the West" that was made during the post-war years referred in the first instance to one part of a bipolar world dominated by two competing superpowers. When Pöschl wrote, the dividing line between their spheres of influence, of course, ran right through Germany. Pöschl's desire that Seligson translate his book can thus be read not just as an act of atonement for his service to the Third Reich but also as a future-oriented affirmation of what is still sometimes called the "Western Alliance"—which has been severely tested over the last four years—as against what used to be called the "Eastern Bloc." This all is, or should be, well known; but it is worth remembering as a hedge against any urge to dismiss other acts of modern literary and cultural criticism on the grounds that they are politically motivated, or can be so construed, whether they acknowledge it or not; also against failing to understand that our own critical positions must be politically and culturally determined, probably in ways that are simply not as apparent to us as they will be to those who follow.

I personally feel much too close to the current moment to attempt any serious critique of the way in which recent political history has affected readings of the *Aeneid* and of the Greek and Latin classics over my working lifetime. What I can say is that I have felt quite out of sympathy with what now seem to be the dominant political and cultural trajectories followed by my own country during that time, and also slightly at odds with certain critical trends in my field, in ways suggested by previous remarks. I can further say that my questions about the ways in which my own work does respond, or ought to respond, to all of these developments, especially those in the political and cultural realm, seem much more urgent as I write these words. I do so at the very latest stage in the writing of this book, as I suppose is true of all introductions. Thus it is a time when the aforementioned trajectory of American politics, and its effect on global politics, has reached what I hope will be considered its nadir, if things do not continue to get worse. The acts of the now outgoing administration have exposed weaknesses in the United States constitution and in American political life that have been hiding in plain sight for well over two centuries. The most urgent issue is race and the consequences of building what has become the world's largest economy on a foundation of racial enslavement, but this is

---

72. Tatum 2013, 27–29.

closely tied to other issues of military, economic, and cultural imperialism. For those of us who work in universities, the very existence of those institutions and their continuing role in perpetuating forms of elitism based as much on racial privilege as on intellectual ability, if not in fact primarily on the former, demands an uncomfortable accounting. For classicists, even if we have now grown used to being members of a relatively small and in some sense marginal profession, it is still necessary to reckon with the fact that our subject has at times all too easily been enlisted in support of causes that I hope most of us would repudiate now and would have repudiated then. Finally, like it or not, by the harsh laws of custom and synecdoche we are a convenient signifier of elitism and privilege, whatever our individual personal backgrounds or current circumstances may be.

In view of all that, I would like to think that there are few who would today echo Pöschl by invoking the *Aeneid* as a "bible" and a rallying point for "Western civilization." Of course, I know that there are many who would. In any case, explicit political comment, with either an ancient or a modern focus, will not be a dominant factor in the pages that follow. I have written what I have written simply to explain that, as much as I love the *Aeneid*, I do not believe that I would think it worth devoting so much of my life to it if I did not think it could be read as a work that is critical of its own times and one that challenges readers in our times to do better and be better. If it is a foregone conclusion that in spite of the ethical debates that swirled around Homer himself, it was impossible for the *Aeneid* to engage with both Homeric poems in a way that would make those issues available at a crucial political and cultural moment, then what was the actual point? It may be the case that I am wrong and the *Aeneid* really is, in Bloomian terms, just the "weak misreading" of Homer that many readers have thought it to be.[73] But that is not the way I see it.

Coming Attractions

In what follows, I will investigate the ethical argument of the *Aeneid* as a post-Homeric poem in the largest sense. In chapter 1 I focus on book 1, starting with the opening lines in which the narrator announces his theme. The critical reception of these lines is marked by two common reactions. First, a great many critics have asked whether the proem of the *Aeneid* more closely resembles that of the *Iliad* or that of the *Odyssey*. The fact that they find it necessary to ask this question is noteworthy in itself. Equally important is that there is no

---

73. Bloom 1973; Bloom was not much of a Vergilian, but I have to admit that he had some interesting things to say about Juno: see Bloom 1987, 35–38.

critical consensus. Critics tend to make a definite choice between these alternatives and then defend their decision in equally definite terms. I infer, provisionally at least, from this bipolar critical reception that the narrator introduces his Homeric program with inscrutable intentions. The next person to speak is Juno, however, and she is not inscrutable at all. Both the narrator's introduction of her speech and the speech itself reveal that Juno operates within a wholly Iliadic worldview. By "Iliadic," I mean not that Juno's perspective is entirely confined to the *Iliad* itself. Rather, I mean that she regards the *Iliad* as the centerpiece of a much longer narrative, the main and indeed the only theme of which is her hatred of the Trojans and her quest to destroy them all. This narrative I refer to as the "Long Iliad." It is an ever-expanding Iliad, one that has the Homeric *Iliad* at its core but that extends both backwards and forwards in time to include Juno's seemingly limitless and obsessive hatred and anger. It includes poems such as the pre-Iliadic *Cypria*, which contains one of the origin stories of her grudge against the Trojans, and the post-Iliadic *Aethiopis*, *Sack of Troy*, *Little Iliad*, and *Homecomings* (or *Nostoi* in Greek)—virtually the entire Epic Cycle.[74] When Juno sees Aeneas sailing from Sicily on the last leg of his sea voyage from Troy, she fears that he is about to escape from her "Long Iliad" of persecution and obtain a "homecoming" in Italy. Indeed, knowing something of what Fate has in store for Aeneas, she may have reason to suspect that, unless she acts, his story of difficult and protracted "homecoming" will end with the hero's successful arrival at a long-sought destination and his confirmation as the rightful husband of one woman in particular. This would be a highly Odyssean outcome, even a proto-Odyssean one (since Odysseus is still being detained by Calypso and has not yet reached Ithaca or even Scheria at the time when Juno speaks). That is the last thing Juno wants. She thus intervenes to prevent the *Aeneid* from becoming a successful Odyssey *avant la lettre* and to make it just one more, highly abbreviated, utterly calamitous episode in her "Long Iliad" of Trojan misery instead.

The unusual character of Juno's first speech and her subsequent intervention suggests that she is not content to play a conventional role in the epic as the hero's divine antagonist or some other type of blocking figure. Instead, as others have noted, she behaves as if she were not a creature controlled by the narrator and wholly contained by whatever plot he wishes to pursue. She acts almost as if she stood outside the plot and were in possession of resources

---

74. On the "Long Iliad" and the Epic Cycle, see section of chapter 2 entitled "Failure is Always an Option: The *Aeneid* and the Epic Cycle." *The Sack of Troy* is often called by its Greek title, *Iliou persis*, or the latinized Greek *Iliupersis*. Similarly, *The Little Iliad* is often called by its Latin title, *Ilias parva*, and *Homecomings* by its Greek title, *Nostoi*.

sufficient not just to alter its course but to change its very character. On this basis, I suggest that the *Aeneid* can profitably be considered not as a combination of the *Iliad* and the *Odyssey* into a single poem, but rather as a battle to determine which of Homer's masterpieces it will become. The protagonists in this struggle are the narrator, of course, and Juno, who challenges him repeatedly for control of the plot, in ways similar to what I have just explained. Aeneas has much less ability to take part in this narrative battle, but its outcome is obviously important to him, as well. The poem, after all, is called the *Aeneid*. Whatever else may be true, just as Juno is his divine antagonist, he is the poem's hero. The question is: Will he turn out to be the hero of another Odyssey or another Iliad? From my point of view, the outcome of this battle is most important in an ethical sense: Will he turn out to be another Odysseus, the paradigmatic "good king" of ethical philosophy? Or will he be another Achilles?

The rest of chapter 1, and indeed of the entire book, is a working out of the various assumptions that underwrite this perspective on the poem and of the various critical insights that arise from it. The most important of these I have already mentioned, and that is the ethical dimension, but I approach this via analysis of the Homeric intertext. According to Knauer, it is a straightforward matter: once Aeneas survives the storm, he finds himself in Carthage, where he is entertained at a lavish banquet by Queen Dido. This is what happens to Odysseus, who also survives a storm sent by an angry divinity and finds himself on the island of Scheria where he is entertained at a lavish banquet by King Alcinous. But the intertext sends confusing signals. If one takes all of them seriously, Aeneas' arrival in Africa looks like Odysseus' various arrivals in several quite different places. When Venus arrives to advise him what to do, she engages in an elaborate, not very successful charade that repeats an important encounter between herself and Aeneas' father, Anchises, that takes place outside the *Odyssey* entirely. In virtually all of these cases, it is made clear how different Aeneas is from Odysseus, not because he regularly surpasses the Greek hero but because he utterly lacks those qualities that were thought to make Odysseus a "good king." At the same time, it becomes obvious that Aeneas is still obsessed with Troy and especially with Achilles, whom he considers responsible for his city's destruction, even though the city did not fall until after Achilles was dead. In this opening book Aeneas can be seen as living through a somewhat confused series of proto-Odyssean experiences, but he brings to them an Iliadic mindset that leaves him unprepared to meet the challenges that confront him.

This situation persists for many books, and I consider the implications of it from different angles in the remaining two chapters. Before I summarize that argument, I am sure that an objection will have occurred to most of my readers. Yes, extensive and detailed engagement with the *Iliad* and the *Odyssey* is a basic component of the intertextual *Aeneid*; but it is hardly the only one. I have already mentioned that Venus' meeting with her son imports material that comes from neither the *Odyssey* nor the *Iliad*. That is the least of it. The question that arises is whether the whole idea of a contest between the *Iliad* and the *Odyssey*, however metaphorical, is too narrowly conceived. Granted that the Homeric poems are of enormous importance to the plot, verbal texture, and ethical universe of the *Aeneid*, they are hardly the only sources of such influence. The scope of literary and cultural history relevant to a reasonable estimate of the poem's intellectual and aesthetic range is immense. Nor is that all. The reputation of the *Aeneid* is not founded on its simplicity. In comparison to Homer, both the poem and its hero have sometimes been admired as well as faulted for indirection, indecision, and diffidence. How can the world that it depicts be divided into any pair of sharply defined opposites, even if they are as rich as those offered by Homer's twin masterpieces and their incomparable heroes?

A brief perusal of any commentary on the *Aeneid* will reveal how many different sources, models, and literary parallels of all kinds are cited there to illustrate innumerable affinities that cover almost the entire range of earlier Greek and Latin literature. To speak only of a few canonical genres: Earlier epics in addition to those of Homer—I have already mentioned a few—are of course very frequently cited. Other narrative forms, such as elegy, a near relative of epic that is in many ways so different from it, often appear, as well. This is especially true of narrative elegy, a genre that contains many literary–critical reflections on its similarities to and differences from epic. The idea that the *Aeneid* is in some sense a tragedy is an extremely familiar, extremely powerful force in the critical discourse. History and historiography, too, are clearly essential to the plot of the poem, and the relationship between myth and history is ever before the reader's mind. I have suggested, again following others, that philosophy is responsible for framing some of the central ethical questions that the poem confronts. In the presence of so many different perspectives, how can a choice between any two of them define the universe of possibilities between which the poem, and its reader, must choose?

There is a simple answer to this. The point is that Homer, by ancient critical convention, contains all knowledge and is the source of all wisdom. In literary terms, he is also the source of all genres. There is a lot that could be said on that topic, and much of it has already been suggested by previous studies.[75] I do not attempt to add to this line of inquiry; rather, I assume that any effort to

---

75. On Homer compared to Ocean as the source of all things, see F. Williams 1978, 88–89 and 98–99. On Vergil's comparability to Homer in this sense see P. R. Hardie 1986, 22–25; on

imitate the *Iliad* and *Odyssey* in their entirety must necessarily confront this aspect of Homeric reception. In terms of literary history, then, I take it as axiomatic that the *Aeneid* rivals Homer as the *source* of all genres by, in principle, *incorporating* them all. From this point of view, if there seems to be tragedy in the *Aeneid*, this merely reflects the "fact" that Homer himself is the greatest of tragic poets and his work is the source of the tragic genre. Just as with epic, this status extends to the roles of both genre model and example model, to use Barchiesi's terms again. This means that if the *Aeneid* fashions itself, whether in whole or in part, on a Greek or Roman tragic script, it places itself in a reciprocal relation to tragedy with respect to Homer, not as the source of all tragedy but (again, in principle) the culminating re-integration of tragedy into a totalizing epic structure that rivals Homer. Similarly, if the *Aeneid* can be considered in any way a work of history or historiography, that is because Homer is also the first historian. Most important, if Aeneas shows affinities from time to time with various heroes of epic, tragedy, historiography, and other genres—be it Jason, Heracles, Ajax, Neoptolemus, Fabius, Scipio, Antony, or Caesar—it is because, *ex hypothesi*, Homer's two starkly different, equally great paradigms of heroic excellence encompass all other possibilities between them. Again, I state these principles not as conclusions but as starting points. Instead of arguing for them, I invite the reader to imagine making the opposite case that the Homeric program of the *Aeneid* is actually much more limited than this, and that it must exclude such ambitions. It would quickly become obvious either that the intertextual *Aeneid* is really quite banal, or that everything we know about it suggests—similarly to something that I wrote about Juno above—that we are much more likely to underestimate its ambition than overshoot the mark in trying to do it justice.

Therefore, in chapter 2 I outline the importance of other paradigms—"third ways," as I call them—to the binary contest being waged between Iliadic and Odyssean forces to determine the character of the poem and its hero. As I noted above, many will feel that it is not just a question of whether Aeneas is an Achilles or an Odysseus, or even a combination of the two. According to some critics, he shows his true colors in book 4, where he is exposed as another Jason, who is the equal of neither Achilles nor Odysseus. According to others, he comes into his own late in the game when he is revealed to be another Heracles, who surpasses all of those heroes. And so on. There are many other paradigms that might suggest that a choice between Achilles and Odysseus is simply too limited and too limiting. I therefore discuss a selection of

---

"generic polyphony" and "generic inclusivity" see P. R. Hardie 1998, 57 and Harrison 2007, 207–8, respectively.

what seem to me the most salient possibilities, guided by specific signals within the text of the *Aeneid*, by generic proximity, and by persistent themes within the subject literature. These include the possibility that the narrator of the *Aeneid*—whether he aims to tell the story of another Iliad, another Odyssey, or both—by attempting to rival Homer might fulfill none of these ambitions and simply fail, producing a story typical of Homer's first imitators, the poets of the aforementioned Epic Cycle. In terms of the narrator's project, the ancient critical record makes it very clear what this would mean. The Epic Cycle was proverbial for poor plot construction, unimaginative imitation of Homer, and general second-rateness. In terms of ethics as well as aesthetics, there are clear Cyclic ways of failing to measure up to either Achilles or Odysseus, and I briefly explore just what these might mean for Aeneas. In spite of all this, however, the point of the exercise is to show that becoming neither another Iliad nor another Odyssey, but a failed Cyclic epic instead, would not prevent the *Aeneid* from becoming a highly inferior Iliad or Odyssey, nor would it determine which of those alternatives would (so to speak) win out. Cyclic failure encompasses both possibilities and does not choose between them.

I have said something about Jason and also about Heracles. Both heroes appear in Apollonius and also in Callimachus' *Aetia*, and both these poems are very influential on the *Aeneid*. The ubiquitous Heracles also appears in Hesiod's *Shield of Heracles* and in tragedies by Sophocles and Euripides. All of these, too, have left their impact on the *Aeneid*. In the vast literary record of his exploits, Heracles gravitates towards one or the other pattern of Homeric heroism in his individual appearances without ever really managing to incorporate the best qualities of both at once. Being so diverse, he should in theory multiply the possibilities for Aeneas: being a hero who in any given episode of his career might exemplify almost anything, Heracles can hardly be thought to determine which Homeric hero Aeneas must become. In the *Aeneid*, however, Hercules (the Roman Heracles) is not in fact represented very diversely at all. The poem offers a particular perspective on the hero, and to the extent that Aeneas does emulate Hercules, as Evander for instance invites him to do, he must ignore one set of possibilities and choose quite another.

This is characteristic of all "third ways," whether they are defined as different epic themes or by different narrative genres, including history and historiography.[76] The Homeric antinomy of force versus intelligence—*biê* and *mêtis*

---

76. One important body of material that I do not discuss is Theban mythology, which is prominent in epic and, especially, in tragedy. There is no doubt that this tradition has had a measurable impact on the *Aeneid*: see Weber 2002, Panoussi 2009, Mac Góráin 2013. The area remains dynamic, however, and as yet awaits a thoroughgoing study. For that reason it seemed the better part of valor to leave it open for the present.

or *vis* and *sapientia*—along with its more troubling instantiation as anger versus duplicity—*mênis/ira* and *dolos/dolus*—is a powerful presence in all forms of ethical narrative. As such, it tends to draw all sorts of ethical discussion into its orbit. If this happens in the case of narratives that do not directly concern Homer, such as histories of the Second Punic War, then how much more powerful will its effect be in a poem that actively invites comparison with both of Homer's masterpieces? Beyond this, what is most important to note can be stated simply. While these and no doubt other "third ways" clearly have their effect on the *Aeneid*, and while in the end they do not replace or detract from the Homeric antinomy, but actually reinforce its importance, they call attention to it, precisely, as an antinomy or a dilemma. They do not in themselves solve the problem by making decisions easier for the reader. Instead, they just show how ineluctable the choice really is. And, to repeat, it is a very consequential choice. If the poem is found to be another Odyssey, and its hero a Roman Odysseus, then we may follow Cairns by inferring that Aeneas is being presented as a paragon of ethical heroism in accordance with ancient kingship theory. If instead it is another Iliad, and its hero a new Achilles, then it would be difficult to maintain, against this same tradition, that he is being presented as an exemplary hero worthy of imitation, rather than one to be pondered as a cautionary figure from whose experience the reader might identify behaviors to avoid. That is a specific possibility that neither Cairns nor anyone who has accepted his analysis has acknowledged, but it is the logical concomitant of an approach that takes kingship theory seriously as a context for reading the *Aeneid*.

What, then, is the reader to decide? And, perhaps more important, how? In chapter 3 I approach these questions by tracing the experience of Aeneas through the poem. I begin with the earliest moments in the narrative, which occur in the story he himself tells Dido in books 2 and 3, and continue with his experiences in books 1 and 4, and then all the way to the end of the poem. My aim in doing this is to get some purchase on the hero's own ambitions. To what does he aspire? What does he want to become? It is clear that his "sense of duty," his *pietas*, is an abiding trait, whether he always lives up to it fully or sometimes stumbles. In this, he is merely like any other epic hero, who is always immanently defined by his signature quality, whatever he happens to be doing, and who, over the course of his story, comes all the more impressively to exemplify it. This tells us nothing, however, about any Achillean or Odyssean values that Aeneas may display; and, as I have pointed out, the *Aeneid* gives us a hero who is not only defined by his own immanent quality, but is constantly being measured against Achilles and Odysseus, as well. He is also a hero who has had experience of both Achilles and Odysseus themselves. For this reason, I take the measure of Aeneas' own attitudes and aspirations by considering how he reflects on his experience of both Homeric heroes and how he responds when he finds himself in situations—which the reader will recognize as Iliadic or Odyssean—that call for an Achillean or an Odyssean response. In metaphorical terms, I am in effect assessing Aeneas' memory of his experiences as if he were a reader of Homer. This comparison already tells us something, because Aeneas' "reading of Homer" is very asymmetrical. He is actually a participant in the *Iliad*, but is not even mentioned in the *Odyssey*—much of which, to repeat, has not even happened by the time the *Aeneid* concludes. This gives him a slanted perspective on the Homeric past, one that also appears in his obsessive memorialization of Troy and of the war in which Troy was conquered. At the same time, he has opportunities to remember Odysseus, as well. What is more, even if Iliadic and Odyssean experiences and preferences are not perfectly balanced in Aeneas' "reading of Homer," I will show that elements of both Homeric poems, including appearances of Achilles in the *Odyssey* and of Odysseus in the *Iliad*, are relevant in various ways to the reader's assessment of Aeneas.[77] Finally, to gain some insight into the way that Aeneas makes choices on the basis of his "reading," I consider a series of famous ecphrases from the perspective of how Aeneas reads works of art and of what he does in response to this reading, asking whether the poem offers Aeneas' reactions as a script for readers to follow in making their own choices.

Here I conclude my preview of this book, withholding any spoilers concerning summary judgments on my part. Those, I believe, are unimportant in comparison with decisions that my readers will make. To repeat, it is not my main objective to convince readers that this or that decision is the right one. What I hope is to bring some new perspective into the discussion of what is, after all, an extremely old question, and to recommend some ways of understanding and applying it. In the end, to invoke one last image, I have come to think of the *Aeneid* as more of a Rorschach test than a manifesto, something that reveals readers to themselves instead of urging on them any particular point of view.

And with that, let us turn to the pleasures of the text . . .

---

77. Sharp observations on some of these appearances are to be found in Dekel 2015, 51–62.

1

Arms and a Man

Where to Begin?

The *Aeneid* opens with a brief formal proem announcing its theme and summarizing its plot. Readers have long regarded the poem's first, thematic words, "arms and a man" (*arma virumque*), as emblematic of its Iliadic and Odyssean "halves." Juan Luis de la Cerda, the last and greatest of Vergil's Renaissance commentators, put the case very clearly when he wrote, "the entire *Aeneid* is contained in these two words, 'arms' and 'man,' with an even division between the books. It deals with the man, that is, with Aeneas, in the first six and with arms in the latter six."[1] This view of the poem goes back at least to Servius, who notes more explicitly that the poem's narrator announces his subjects in a different order from that of his narration, "for he tells first of Aeneas' wanderings and afterwards about war."[2] Here Servius anticipates a question that readers might ask and tries to gloss over the problem by referring to a standard rhetorical device—in this case a figure of speech called *hysteroproteron*—basically, "reverse order."[3] Explanations of this sort are not very satisfying, but many of them call attention to issues that were the subject of learned debate in earlier antiquity.[4]

---

1. Cerda 1612/1642, vol. 1, 2. On Cerda and other early modern commentators cited in this book, see Casali and Stok 2019.

2. Servius, *Commentary on Vergil's Aeneid* 1.1 and 264. On Servius and ancient commentary see the revision of Fowler 1997/2019 by Casali and Stok.

3. Cicero notes that this figure is characteristic of Homer (*Letters to Atticus* 1.16.1; see Bassett 1920; Whitman 1958, 97). Does the "inverted" structure of the Homeric *Aeneid* reflect this perception?

4. The point is well made by Ross 1987, 29–30. Servius' commentary is based on that of his teacher, Aelius Donatus, who is known to have made very free use, without attribution, of his predecessors' work: see Naumann 1981; Stok 2010.

So it is in this case. Servius' near contemporary, Macrobius, sheds further light on this issue by relating it to the program of Homeric imitation that students are still taught to recognize in Vergil's masterpiece.

> As for the *Aeneid* itself, didn't it borrow from Homer, taking first the wanderings from the *Odyssey* and then the battles from the *Iliad*? Yes, because the order of events necessarily changed the order of the narrative: whereas in Homer the war was fought at Troy first, with Ulysses become a wanderer on his return from Troy, in Vergil Aeneas' voyage preceded the wars that were subsequently fought in Italy.[5]

The question is discussed in such simple terms that it may strike the modern reader as inconsequential. But one should not be too hasty to draw this conclusion. If we return to Servius' comment on "arms" in line 1 we find this: "Many explain in various ways why Vergil begins with 'arms,' but their opinions are obviously meaningless, since it is clear that he made his beginning elsewhere, as was demonstrated in the foregoing biography of the poet."[6] This biography, which served as a preface to Servius' *Aeneid* commentary, is almost entirely the work of Suetonius, the prolific scholar and imperial official who compiled it several centuries earlier, around 100 CE. In it, Suetonius quotes a four-line summary of Vergil's career, the so-called "pre-proemium," which he says Vergil himself composed to stand immediately before line 1 of the poem. It was supposedly one of just two passages that the editors or literary executors appointed by Augustus actually excised before releasing the *Aeneid* to the public. Few if any now believe this story, and even though Servius did, his own testimony admits that many before him did not and regarded "arms" as the poem's first word. Servius' note also indicates that the choice of this word was a topic of learned discussion within about a century of the poet's death.[7]

It is also possible—I would say, likely—that this part of Servius' comment derives from some predecessor who had his eye on a Homeric commentary,

---

5. Macrobius, *Saturnalia* 5.2.6 in Kaster 2011, vol. 2, 228–29 (slightly modified).

6. Servius, *Commentary on Vergil's Aeneid* 1.1.

7. On the likely date of the pre-proemium see Farrell 2004; on its probable literary context, see Stok 2010; Peirano 2013. On the titular quality of the phrase *arma virumque* in antiquity see Ziolkowski and Putnam 2008, 22–23, with 188–99 for text and translation of the Suetonian *Life of Vergil* (the *Vita Suetoni Donatiana*) and with 202–5 for the corresponding passage of Servius' preface (the *vita Servii*). On the phrase *arma virumque* as a "heroic Leitmotif" see Bloch 1970. For further reflections of the title of the *Aeneid* see Mac Góráin 2018. Cerda 1612/1642, vol. 1, 2 believing the "pre-proemium" to be authentic, conjectures that Vergil's posthumous editors removed it so that the opening of the poem would resemble that of the *Iliad*.

specifically one on the *Iliad*.[8] No such work has come down to us intact, but in the marginal notes, or scholia, that survive in some medieval manuscripts of Homer, we find the following comment: "They discuss why he began with 'anger,' such an ill-omened word. For these two reasons: first, so that by means of this emotion he might cleanse the relevant part of the soul, and so that he might make his listeners more receptive in respect of grandeur."[9] These parallel comments are interesting, not in spite of, but because of the fact that Servius does not share the Homeric scholiast's concern with words of ill omen, catharsis, or the sublime. Remember, Servius himself does not even think that "arms" is the first word of the poem; the ostensible point of his comment is to refute those who do, while no one ever doubted that the *Iliad* begins with "anger." Nevertheless, the similar form of these two comments raises the possibility that they share a common origin. The Homeric scholiast's ultimate source was a commentary on the *Iliad* in monographic form.[10] Servius probably did not use Homeric commentaries directly, but he definitely used earlier *Aeneid* commentaries, and some of these drew on Homeric commentaries by Greek scholars. I therefore infer that in the first issue he raises Servius quotes what one of his predecessors wrote, and that this predecessor was quoting the same *Iliad* commentary that would later be excerpted in the marginal notes of our medieval Homer manuscripts. In its original form, the note that Servius adapts, instead of explaining away the question of why "arms" is the poem's first word, may have dealt with the problem in a more interesting way, like the Homeric commentary on which it is based. Another inference to be drawn from this similarity between the two exegetical traditions is that some ancient Vergilian critic, interpreting the first word of the *Aeneid* as a reference to the poem's Iliadic program, decided to open his commentary on the poem in the same way that one of his Homeric predecessors had opened a commentary on the *Iliad*—and not the *Odyssey*.[11]

There are quite a few borrowings of this kind in Servius and other ancient Vergil commentaries. Many of them are extremely tralatician—notes on geography and mythology, for instance, travel freely among all kinds of ancient exegetical works.[12] It is also clear that Vergil himself made use of such

---

8. For this point and what follows, see Farrell 2008, 119–20.

9. Scholia A on *Iliad* 1.1. On the Homeric scholia in general see Dickey 2007, 18–23.

10. On the history of Homeric commentary in antiquity and its importance to Vergil and his readers, see Hexter 2010.

11. For a parallel late-antique reflection on the opening of the *Aeneid* as Iliadic see McGill 2006. The first word of the *Odyssey* also attracted commentary, on which see Farrell 2021, but the form of that commentary left no discernable trace in ancient scholarship on the *Aeneid*.

12. Mühmelt 1965.

scholarship in his imitation of Homer and other Greek authors.[13] But some comments, including this one, seem to indicate a desire on the commentator's part to emulate Homer's critics in the same way that Vergil emulated Homer. An *Aeneid* commentary that began by asking why "arms" was the poem's first word looks like the work of someone who regarded the *Aeneid* as rivaling the *Iliad* in particular. There would be nothing surprising in this. Propertius, the first Roman writer who specifically mentioned the *Aeneid*, famously called it "something greater than the *Iliad*."[14]

The idea that this correspondence between *arma* and *mênin* signals a more general one between the *Aeneid* and the *Iliad* informs the modern reception of the poem, as we shall presently see. This perspective, however, can be properly understood only with reference to the alternative. It was the Renaissance scholar Fulvio Orsini—also known, and perhaps better known, as Ursinus—who first pointed out that the *Aeneid* proem as a whole resembles that of the *Odyssey*.[15]

> **I sing** arms and a **man, who** first from the coasts **of Troy**
> came to Italy, exiled by fate, and to Lavinian
> shores, **much driven astray**, **he**, on land and **on the sea**,
> by the gods' violence, on account of savage Juno's unforgetting anger,
> after **many sufferings** in war, as well, until he *founded* a city. (*Aeneid* 1.1–7)

> **Sing me**, Muse, the versatile **man, who** was **much driven astray**,
> after he *sacked* the holy citadel **of Troy**,
> and learned **many** people's cities and mind,
> and **endured many sufferings, he, on the sea**, within his heart,
> striving to save his life and the homecoming of his companions.
> (*Odyssey* 1.1–5)

The similarities are obvious. Note in particular that the Latin word for "man" (*virum*) translates the Greek *andra* as literally as possible. In contrast "arms" (*arma*) connotes warfare, but does not actually mean "anger" (*mênin*). In both

---

13. Schlunk 1974; Barchiesi 1984/2015; Schmit-Neuerburg 1999; Casali 2004; Hexter 2010; Farrell 2016.

14. Propertius, *Elegies* 2.34.66, *nescio quid maius nascitur Iliade*. That is not to say that the opinion was universally held. Horace, *Odes* 1.3 bids farewell to Vergil as he embarks upon a sea voyage, which I take as signifying the composition of an Odyssean epic—an inference which not everyone would make, however.

15. Ursinus 1567, 195, lines 16–20. In his introductory note (195, lines 5–14), Ursinus also makes the point that the title *Aeneid*, which is based on the name of the principal hero, is modeled on that of the *Odyssey* and other epics about Heracles or Theseus. I discuss epic treatments of such heroes, especially Heracles, in the section of chapter 2 entitled "Grappling with Heracles."

cases "man" is modified by a limiting relative clause of description alluding to the heroes' difficult journeys from Troy; the words "much" or "many" appear in anaphora; the demonstrative pronoun "he" is used resumptively (according to Greek usage in the fourth line of the *Odyssey* and at the expense of normal latinity in line 3 of the *Aeneid*). Stress is laid upon the heroes' sufferings on the sea. One hero sacks a city, the other founds one; and so on. At the level of diction and sentence structure as well as theme, the opening seven lines of the *Aeneid* do in fact very closely resemble the first five lines—the first complete sentence—of the *Odyssey*.[16]

Ursinus' view of the matter held sway for a long time. In fact, the English commentator John Conington, writing about three centuries after Ursinus, echoes him while adding a surprising point: "'Arma virumque;' this is an imitation of the opening of the Odyssey, ἄνδρα μοι ἔννεπε κ.τ.λ. [andra moi ennepe etc.] ... The words are not a hendiadys, but give the character of the subject and then the subject itself."[17] That is to say, remarkably, in Conington's mind (and in sharp contrast to most ideas about epic poetry) the first word of the poem hardly counts: the reader should construe "arms" as a kind of modifier rather than as a specifically Iliadic element, and should understand that the *Aeneid* begins unambiguously as another Odyssey, announcing its theme with full emphasis on "man." Conington thus anticipates a more recent trend towards interpreting the *Aeneid* primarily in Odyssean terms.[18] However, most readers who consult his commentary today do not find the matter treated so decisively. After Conington's death in 1869, his work was revised and expanded under the supervision of Henry Nettleship, who scrupulously indicated, whenever he added an opinion of his own, that he was speaking only for himself.[19] Amusingly, though, Nettleship decided to present his own, very different idea about the proem just two sentences *before* Conington's, noting that "the first seven lines of the poem will be found to correspond strikingly in rhythm with the first seven lines of the Iliad."[20] (In both poems, the first

---

16. Different commentators place more or less emphasis on these individual elements; compare for instance Conway 1935 and Austin 1971, 29–30 on *Aeneid* 1.3.

17. See Conington 1863, 31 on *Aeneid* 1.1; the same note appears in all subsequent additions.

18. As I discuss in the Introduction.

19. A relatively full publication history, evidently compiled by F. Haverfield, appears in the 5th edition of volume 1 (1898) facing the dedication page; see Conington and Nettleship 1883–1898/1963, vol. 1, iv. In his preface to the 4th edition of volume 2 (1884) Nettleship writes "All notes added by myself are marked by my initials. [H. N.]": see Conington and Nettleship 1883–1898/1963, vol. 2, v.

20. Conington and Nettleship 1963, vol. 2, 3. To be clear, Nettleship's immediate purpose is to support Conington's doubts concerning the authenticity of the "pre-proemium," not to get

complete sentence fills the first seven lines.) Elsewhere Nettleship notes, "the rhythm and general structure of the first seven lines of the Aeneid . . . are taken from the first seven lines of the Iliad," and, "the first two and the last of the seven lines in each case are precisely similar in point of meter."[21] This is only slightly overstated: the pattern of long and short syllables in the three specified lines differs in only two metrical elements while agreeing in thirty-four; they agree further in the placement of major pauses within each line and to a large extent in the length of words found in corresponding positions.[22] If we look beyond meter, we find that the first or second word in line 3 of both poems is *multum* in Latin, *pollas* in Greek, each of which means "much" in the singular and "many" in the plural ("to Lavinian/shores, **much** driven astray," *Aeneid* 1.2–3; "**many** strong souls to Hades did it send, *Iliad* 1.3). If we are prepared to allow for any further rearrangement of words, we find that the first word of the *Iliad*, and with it the theme of "anger," although not broached in the first line of the *Aeneid*, does appear prominently at the very end of line 4, the central line of the initial, seven-line sentence ("on account of savage Juno's unforgetting **anger**," an important phrase, as we shall soon see).[23] A phrase from the *Odyssey* proem, "and endured many sufferings, he, **on the sea**" (1.4), becomes in the *Aeneid* "after many sufferings **in war**, as well" (1.5); thus Odyssean suffering "on the sea" is replaced by Iliadic suffering "in war."[24] In short, Nettleship is quite correct in stating that the correspondences between the proems of the *Iliad* and the *Aeneid* are numerous and detailed.[25]

---

in the first word. But while the two men were friends, the relationship was not free from professional complexities: see Rogerson 2007, 94–106; Harrison 2007.

21. Conington and Nettleship 1963, vol. 3, 519 (an appendix by Nettleship to the 3rd edition of volume 3, 1883).

22. The prosody of *arma virumque cano* is exactly equivalent to that of *mênin aeide thea*, the first words of the *Iliad*; "they constitute a metrical sequence (trochee + amphibrach + iamb) that hexameter poets in general were careful to avoid" (Weber 1987, 261; see also Katz 2018, 56 note 16). McGill 2006 discusses evidence that the equivalence of the two opening phrases was a commonplace of late-antique education.

23. Macrobius, *Saturnalia* 5.2.7 in Kaster 2011, vol. 2, 228–29 compares the Juno's anger in the *Aeneid* to that of Apollo in the *Iliad* as the cause that sets each epic into motion; see Lausberg 1983, 211. Buchheit 1963, 17 on the other hand refers the motif of "anger" in the *Aeneid* to the anger of Poseidon at *Odyssey* 1.20. Austin 1971, 30 regards *iram*, "anger," in *Aeneid* 1.4 as a combined reference to the anger of the Iliadic hero Achilles and the Odyssean god Poseidon.

24. I owe this observation to Kenneth Reckford, a great teacher and friend.

25. On Iliadic elements at the beginning of the *Aeneid* see also Weidner 1869, 69 on *Aeneid* 1.12–33; Fuchs 1947, 191 note 114. Lausberg 1983, 211 sees both of the first two words of the *Aeneid* as alluding to *andra*, the first word of the *Odyssey*, *arma* sonically and *virum* lexically. See also

Within the "single" commentary that bears their names, then, Conington and Nettleship tell the reader of the *Aeneid* different things about the Homeric character of the poem's opening lines. Those who consult the commentary may react variously when confronted with such divergent, but equally authoritative interpretations. Some may choose a side; others may assume that both sides are in some sense right, without feeling a need to say just how; still others may dismiss the problem as unimportant; and there are many other ways of getting on with it, not all of them rigorously logical. Some of the greatest experts even advance two mutually contradictory views. Cerda, for instance, after opining that "arms" and "man" refer to the different themes of the two halves of the poem, later shifts his ground, noting that there is plenty of (Iliadic) warfare in book 2, for instance, and a good deal of (Odyssean) diplomacy in the poem's second half.[26] That is like saying that the balanced, bipartite structure that he had emphasized earlier isn't really there, or that one shouldn't be too fussy about it. By the same token, the user of Conington–Nettleship might easily decide that the *Aeneid* proem alludes to both Homeric poems equally, or else mainly to one or the other; and any difference of opinion or indifference to the balance of Iliadic and Odyssean elements in the proem might extend to the role of Homer in the *Aeneid* as a whole.

Within the spectrum of possible responses to such problems, I would like to focus on two, and on the assumptions that underlie them. The first, more common response, involves two assumptions that seem to be opposites, but in fact are not. These are (1) that the question of whether the *Aeneid* is more of an Iliad or more of an Odyssey is important, that the answer to it exists, that something in the text points to it, and that the matter can be settled, or (2) that the question isn't important after all. These seem like opposite assumptions, but they amount to the same thing, because they involve making a decision that will in large part dictate one's response to the poem as a whole. The second position, which is the one I advocate, requires us not to make these assumptions and to infer from all the reasonable and well-supported arguments on all sides that no single answer can be definitive. Instead, the point must be not to answer the question, or to decide that it is unimportant, but just to ask it.[27] If we do so, and remain attentive to the different opinions that have been expressed since antiquity about the opening lines of the *Aeneid*, the number of questions that we have to consider will quickly multiply. Does the apparently

---

209, where she argues that *irae*, "anger" at the end of *Aeneid* 1.8 alludes lexically to *mênis*, the first word of the *Iliad*, but with reference to divine instead of heroic anger.

26. Cerda 1612/1642, vol. 1, 3 on *arma virumque*.

27. The classic statement of this principle is S. E. Fish 1967/1980, 147–73.

inverted and asymmetrical treatment of "arms" and "man" actually tell the reader anything about the poem that follows? Are we in fact put on notice to expect an Odyssey and an Iliad in equal measure and in that order? Are we being told something else? Or are we simply being advised that we should pay attention and ask questions, but not expect any obvious answers?

The narrator, in short, is not exceptionally clear in telling the reader what kind of poem to expect. It would be difficult to conclude from the opening lines that only one of the Homeric poems will be a relevant intertext; but if both are relevant, it emerges from the critical record that how the *Aeneid* relates to each of them, and how they relate to one another, is hard to say. If the *Iliad* and *Odyssey* are both models for the *Aeneid*, in what sense is this true? Are they compatible models? Complementary ones? Or are they competitive with, even antithetical to one another? Is one prior to the other, in whatever sense (logically, chronologically, aesthetically, thematically, ethically, morally)? If so, which one is that? One kind of reader will feel compelled to decide. But rather than excluding any of these possibilities a priori, it may make more sense, at least for the moment, to keep all of them in play.

Enter Juno

The proem continues with a longer summary of the mythical and historical context that gives the story significance (lines 12–33). Then the action begins. The Trojans have scarcely lost sight of land and begun what ought to be the last stage of their wanderings.[28] Since they are leaving Sicily, we might well infer that their immediate destination is Italy.[29] It is too early, however, to be sure what is happening; in particular, it is almost impossible to orient oneself within the embryonic narrative according to specifically Homeric coordinates.

Aeneas is sailing, however, which is something of which the *Odyssey* contains quite a lot and the *Iliad* almost none at all.[30] We will eventually learn that Aeneas' fitful journey from Troy to Italy corresponds to Odysseus' difficult

---

28. I note in passing the irony involved in Juno's delaying Aeneas' arrival in Italy. Had Aeneas proceeded directly from Sicily to Italy, he might have immediately begun to wage his Iliadic war with Turnus and so missed entirely the distraction of his Carthaginian "Phaeacis." See the section of this chapter entitled "Unintended Consequences."

29. This would presumably be the inference of anyone familiar with the Aeneas legend before Vergil. For this reason, it is just one of the many deceptive elements found in the poem's opening lines.

30. Other than a few raiding parties and their aftermath, including the return of Chryseis in book 1, the *Iliad* hardly speaks of seafaring, to the extent that Achilles' plan to sail home to Phthia (9.356–63) amounts to a threatened abandonment of Iliadic values.

voyage from Troy to Ithaca. More specifically, we will find that Aeneas' Carthaginian adventure corresponds to Odysseus' sojourn among the Phaeacians. That is to say, along with G. N. Knauer, that the *Aeneid* begins with a sequence of major episodes that conforms to the plot of *Odyssey* 5–13.[31] At the same time, we will find throughout this poem that an apparently dominant surface meaning rests upon, but does not quite conceal, a riot of conflicting possibilities roiling in the depths below, some of which occasionally burst through the surface and present themselves for all to see.

So it is here. No sooner have the Trojans embarked upon what may be their Odyssean voyage than Juno appears and delivers the first of her memorable soliloquies. And of the many amazing things that Juno says in this celebrated speech, one of the most amazing is contained in her very first words. To appreciate the effect, it is necessary to look at the Latin first:

mene‿incepto desistere victam
nec posse‿Italia Teucrorum avertere regem?

Shall I withdraw in defeat from what I've **begun**,
unable to keep the king of the Trojans from Italy? (*Aeneid* 1.37–38)

As many readers now acknowledge, Juno's first two words, *mene incepto*, or rather her first two syllables, *mene‿in-*, clearly echo *mênin*, the first word of the *Iliad*.[32] Inevitably, some readers, realizing this fact (or having it pointed out to them), wonder whether it could have any real significance at all.[33] For others, in view of the two words involved—"me" and "beginning"—it is not difficult to discern how they might guide one's interpretation of Juno's opening lines. Literally, Juno asks: "Shall I withdraw in defeat from what I've begun?" But Roman authors often use quite ordinary words with two specific meanings at the same time, an overt primary one and a conventional secondary one that is a literary term.[34] In the *Aeneid*, it is above all the word *finis* (end, destination,

---

31. Knauer actually regards the Odyssean structure of the *Aeneid* as much more extensive than that, as I discuss in the section of the Introduction entitled "The Systematic Intertext."

32. Levitan 1993, 14–15. I have been told that the echo was noticed earlier by a number of scholars, but Levitan was the first to venture into print and to suggest what it might mean.

33. I write this mainly on the basis of discussions, often spirited. Only Conte 2017, 55, I believe, has performed the useful service of stating his objections in writing, making essentially the same points (regarding elision v. synaloepha, prosody, and so on) that I have occasionally heard from others. I explain why I do not find these objections convincing in the appendix that follows chapter 3.

34. The most celebrated example is undoubtedly the one involving anatomical and metrical "feet"; see Ellis 1889, 126; Verrall 1913, 249–67; Kroll 1959, 67; Havelock 1967, 156–57; Quinn 1973,

goal, purpose, fulfillment) that invites this sort of interpretation: it appears prominently in the opening lines of two episodes, virtually framing the epic, in which Jupiter discusses with Venus and Juno the plot of the poem and the fate of the Roman people.[35] By the same token, a word like *incipere*, "to begin"—used at the beginning of a poem and at the beginning of that poem's initial speech, might also possess considerable metapoetic force.[36] Hence the realization that Juno can be understood as saying: "Shall I withdraw in defeat *from the beginning of this poem?*"

There are many reasons why it makes sense to understand Juno in this way. As I have just noted, Aeneas appears to be approaching his fated destination in Italy. Juno evidently thinks that, once he arrives there, her best chance to destroy him will have been lost, so that the most she can accomplish will be to continue to make things difficult by delaying the hero's final victory as long as possible. She spells this out in the second of her great soliloquies in book 7, an obvious companion piece to the one that we are considering now.[37] It therefore makes sense for Juno to regard Aeneas' untroubled passage to Italy at the beginning of book 1 as an event that might force her to withdraw from the poem as soon as it is under way.

But **mene‿incepto** must tell us more than this. If the phrase refers to the beginning of the *Aeneid* as the beginning from which Juno fears she must withdraw, it also refers to the beginning of the *Iliad*, the poem that actually does start with *mênin*. It thus looks suspiciously like a critical intervention, and hardly a disinterested one. As we have just seen, the opening line of the *Aeneid* announces a double theme of "arms" and "man," but does so in a way that invites differing interpretations. The first word, "arms," indicates a thematic field, "warfare," of which the *Iliad* was, for ancient Greek and Roman readers, the

---

139; Hinds 1985, 19 and 1987, 16–17; Barchiesi 1994, 135–37; Clauss 1995, 243–44; Heyworth 2001, 133; Morgan 1999 and 2001; Ferris 2009; Henkel 2014.

35. 1.223 *et iam finis erat*, "and now it was the end"; 12.793 *quae iam finis erit?* "what end will there now be?" with Tarrant 2012, 290.

36. In any case, a certain metapoetic emphasis is hardly uncharacteristic of other Vergilian beginnings (*Georgics* 1.5 *hinc canere incipiam*, "I will now begin to sing"; *adnue coeptis* 1.40, "show favor to the project that I've begun"; see the appendix) or those of other poets writing under Vergil's influence (Ovid, *Metamorphoses* 1.2 *coeptis* with Barchiesi 2005, 138; Valerius Flaccus, *Argonautica* 1.1 *prima ... freta pervia*, "the first seas navigated [by the Argonauts]" with Feeney 1991, 314–15 and Zissos 2008, 72–74).

37. Ursinus 1567, 346 realized that the narrator's introduction to Juno's soliloquy in book 7 (286–92) is modeled on that to Poseidon in *Odyssey* 5 (282–85); Heyne 1830–41, vol. 3, 41 cites the same Homeric passage and draws attention to the similarity between Juno's two soliloquies; see also Cerda 1612/1642, vol. 2, 51 on 7.286; Norden 1915, 6; Pöschl 1950/1962, 24–33.

definitive epic treatment. It thus invites the inference that the *Aeneid* will be a poem of war, another Iliad of sorts.[38] But the second word, "man," literally translates the first word of the *Odyssey*, matching it exactly in lexical and semantic terms. Does this precision correct any mistaken impressions that may have been given previously, making it clear that the poem will really be another Odyssey? If so, in what sense? Or is it to be both an Iliad and an Odyssey? But in that case, why state the twin themes in this way—and especially in this order—when the poem begins with seafaring and ends with war? Is the *Aeneid* to be a kind of Iliad, but really more of an Odyssey? An Iliadic Odyssey, or vice versa? Finally, whatever answer one chooses, what do such phrases actually mean?

Juno's intervention looks like one that she intends to settle the matter. Because she begins with the first word of the *Iliad*, some readers have inferred that she acts not just as a character, but as a kind of narrator, too. "Scarcely has Virgil got going on the story," writes Don Fowler, "when he is interrupted by Juno, complaining at the idea that she has to give up on *her* tale."[39] The fact that Juno begins her speech in mid-line contributes both to the sense that her exordium has been delayed from its "proper" position at the beginning of the line, where any narrative ought to begin, and to the sense that she is interrupting some other narrative that has already begun. Thus Fowler's phrase "*her* tale" is provocative but justified. Moreover, if Juno is a narrator, she speaks as one who specializes in Iliads. Her outburst suggests that she has been following the story up to this point and has heard the poem's theme announced as "arms," but then amplified or corrected so as to introduce a poem about a man, a man coming from Troy, one driven astray, who had suffered a lot on the sea . . . Anyone reading this might be forgiven for inferring that the new poem would turn out to be an Odyssey. In that sense, Juno's first utterance has to be understood with reference to uncertainty about the poem's opening, as a rejoinder to that uncertainty, and even as a protest against the shape that the *Aeneid* is apparently preparing to take. It expresses her desire, even her insistence, that the new poem be no Odyssey at all, but another Iliad instead.

The proposition that Juno functions as a narrator of any kind carries with it a number of important corollaries. For a mere character to behave as if she had a say in what kind of poem she gets to inhabit is, by definition, transgressive. Characters are meant to live within the world of the story, not to usurp a position outside it from which they might manipulate the plot, or reject the

---

38. Warfare is considered the epic theme par excellence in Vergil's *Eclogue 6* (*proelia*, "battles" 3; *bella*, "wars" 7). See Feeney 1999, on the deferral of battle narrative to the end of the *Aeneid* (especially 328 note 1 on this deferral as parallel to Achilles' belated entrance into the battle narrative of the *Iliad*).

39. Fowler 1997, 259.

plot in which they find themselves and exchange it for a different one. Juno, however, is not just any character. Transgression and usurpation are hallmarks of her behavior in every sphere. We are about to consider how she trespasses into Neptune's domain when she tries to destroy Aeneas' fleet. We will also be reminded of more egregious attempts of a similar kind made earlier in her epic career. Because Juno is defined by a propensity towards opposition, her movement from usurping the traditional role of some other character, such as Neptune, to resisting the ineluctable unfolding of Fate, and going even so far as to assert herself as an opponent not only of some other character, but of a poem's narrator, really involves just a few rather small steps.[40] All of that said, it is extremely consequential. Juno's attempt to seize the narrator's role before the *Aeneid* can get well underway requires further consideration of its specific and general effects. Juno the narrator: What kind of story does she tell? And: How well does she tell it?

In Medias Res

Having interrupted the incipient narrative on a stridently Iliadic note, Juno attempts to take control by plunging the reader *in medias res*—which is to say, into the middle of the *Iliad* itself. In order to destroy Aeneas, she bribes Aeolus, the king of the winds, to release his unruly subjects from their cave and let them create a terrible storm at sea.[41] In offering Aeolus this bribe, Juno reprises one of her most famous roles from one of the central books of the *Iliad*, in which, as Hera, she offers a precisely similar bribe to Hypnos, the Greek god of Sleep:[42]

> **To him then Juno,** in supplication, **made this address**:
> "**Aeolus**—for the father of gods and king of men
> has assigned you to calm the waves and raise them with wind—
> a race hateful to me is sailing the Tyrrhenian sea,
> taking Ilium to Italy, and their conquered gods;
> strike force into the winds, overpower and sink their ships,
> or drive apart and scatter their bodies on the waves.
> I have twice seven **nymphs of outstanding beauty**,

---

40. Feeney 1991, 140–37, 149–51; Fowler 1997, 259–62.

41. Aeolus was in antiquity and still is familiar to readers as a character of some importance in the *Odyssey*, but one who does not appear at all in the *Iliad*. I take up the implications of these facts below in the section of this chapter entitled "Aeolus."

42. The correspondence is first noted at Macrobius, *Saturnalia* 5.4.3 in Kaster 2011, vol. 2, 548–49; for discussion see Lausberg 1983, 204–5.

one of whom, the most beautiful, **Deiopea**,
I will join to you in proper marriage and call her yours,
so that, for such services, she may spend all her years with you
and make you the father of lovely offspring."
And Aeolus in answer . . . (*Aeneid* 1.64–76)

To him then Hera the ox-eyed mistress **made this address**:
"**Sleep**, why have these thoughts in your heart?
Do you think Zeus of the great voice will aid the Trojans,
as he grew angry for the sake of Heracles, his own son?
But come, **I will give you one of the youthful Graces
to marry and to be called your wife**,
Pasithea, for whom you long all your days."
So she spoke, **and Sleep** was glad, and spoke **in answer**. (*Iliad* 14.263–70)

According to Knauer, especially evident and elaborate parallels like this one often function as *Leitzitate* or "guide citations," a useful term for close verbal imitations deployed as signposts within episodes of the *Aeneid* modeled closely on episodes of the *Iliad* or *Odyssey*.[43] In this case, the reader is given what looks like a clear signal, and is thus encouraged to infer that the poem begins right in the middle of an episode located right in the middle of the *Iliad*. Moreover, the episode in which Hera bribes Hypnos is not just any episode, and Juno's choice to repeat it in bribing Aeolus is anything but random. The Iliadic episode, still known by the name that ancient critics gave it, "The Deception of Zeus," is famous as Hera's grandest and most transgressive act of self-assertion.[44] In it, she uses sex to distract Zeus from a battle raging upon the plain of Ilium, in which the Greeks, thanks to him, are having the worst of it. Being perhaps the greatest partisan of the Greeks, and detesting the Trojans, Hera cannot endure this and so decides to seduce her husband, enlisting Hypnos to lull him into a deep post-coital coma. While Zeus slumbers, Hera and

---

43. Knauer 1964, 145–47 and 1964a, 66. Knauer 1964, 220 explains that he does not consider Juno's repetition of Hera's bribe to be a *Leitzitat* because he sees the "divine apparatus" as conforming to an Iliadic logic independent of the predominantly Odyssean narrative structure of books 1–6; see however Buchheit 1963, 68 note 261; Lausberg 1983, 204–5. My own view is that every verbal parallel is potentially a *Leitzitat*.

44. The phrase "Deception of Zeus" (*Dios apatē*) is first found in the 12th-century commentary of Eustathius (van der Valk 1971–1987, 368.13, 565.2, 598.4); earlier writers refer to the episode either without a "title" (Plato, *Republic* 3, 390b–c) or with what may be a different one (scholia bT on *Iliad* 14.176; Heraclitus, *Homeric Problems* 39 in Russell and Konstan 2005, 68–73; Plutarch, *Moralia* 19, "Advice to Bride and Groom" 38 in Babbit 1928, 329).

the other gods who favor the Greeks reverse the tide of battle; but before long, Zeus awakens, causes the Trojans to regain the upper hand, and warns Hera what will happen if she ever tries anything like that again. The ironies in Juno's reprise of this scene are rich and beautiful. In the *Iliad*, Hera's stratagem allows Poseidon (at the divine level) to rally a Greek counter-attack, and when Zeus awakens and confronts her, she swears that Poseidon did it all on his own.[45] The fact that Juno resorts to a similar ploy in order to trespass on the realm of Neptune, the Roman Poseidon—and also the nearest thing in the world to Jupiter, the Roman Zeus—is thus a delectable source of readerly pleasure.[46]

Juno's repetition of Hera's marquee performance answers, at least provisionally, our first question about the kind of story she means to tell. If we can judge by her first words and by the bribe that she offers Aeolus, she is determined, in spite of anyone's plan to the contrary, that it be another Iliad. Our second question was about how well she manages it. To this one could say, not very well at all. Her bid for narrative control is no more successful this time than it was before. Juno fails to destroy the Trojans now by bribing Aeolus, just as Hera failed to destroy the Trojans then by bribing Hypnos. Moreover, she does not divert the *Aeneid* into an Iliadic course: as Knauer argues, not just the storm itself but also its immediate aftermath and the subsequent trajectory of the narrative for several books, at least, closely track the adventures of Odysseus. What had seemed an obviously Iliadic *Leitzitat* or guide citation apparently proves misleading.[47]

On the other hand, one could also say that Juno tells her story too well, that she re-enacts Hera's Iliadic stratagem too faithfully, precisely because she repeats the *failure* of her earlier, unsuccessful performance, as well as the performance itself. Fowler takes such things to mean that in the universe of the *Aeneid*, Iliadic repetition stands for "the eternal return of human suffering rather than any hope of an end."[48] So it seems, if we can extend this observation beyond the human condition to that of the gods.[49] And indeed we can; for even

---

45. *Iliad* 14.135–52, 354–401; 15.4–46.

46. Schmit-Neuerburg 1999, 246–53, with reference to ancient criticism of Homer's "Deception of Zeus," sees the reworking of it in *Aeneid* 1 and in the summoning of Allecto in book 7 as opposing the will of Jupiter without making him seem as gullible as his Greek counterpart.

47. Lausberg 1983, 217–18 notes that the "deception" scene is followed by the pronouncement of a significant prophecy by Zeus/Jupiter in both *Iliad* 15 and *Aeneid* 1. This suggests at least that an Iliadic plot structure, even if it does not satisfy Juno's expectations, is far from irrelevant to the plot of the *Aeneid*. Further to this point see the section entitled "Disguise and Recognition on the Island of Ithaca" below in this chapter, especially note 166.

48. Fowler 1997, 262.

49. See Barchiesi 1978/2015.

if gods and goddesses are not supposed to suffer, at the beginning of the *Aeneid* it is Juno who suffers above all, and who in her suffering visits additional suffering on others. It is, as Fowler observes, in her obsessive recidivism to failed Iliadic behaviors that she does so most glaringly.

If Juno's behavior in this prominent episode seems self-defeating, it is that and more; but it is hard to blame her. If one asks why Juno behaves this way, the answer is simple: she is a creature of an Iliadic world. And in light of the new poem's Homeric program, this has two distinct but complementary meanings.

In the first place, Juno, like Achilles, is single-minded in her "anger," her *ira*, her *mênis*. In case any reader had come to the new poem unaware of this fact, the subject is mentioned repeatedly in the opening lines, even before Juno bursts onto the scene.[50] We have noted that the narrator attributes Aeneas' suffering to "savage Juno's unforgetting anger" (line 4). Soon after that he asks, "can heavenly souls can harbor such great anger?" (11). After that he says "even now the savage pains that are the causes of Juno's anger / have not yet left her soul" (25–26). When Juno speaks, her first syllables (*mene_in-* 37), which in Latin barely form an articulate utterance, in Greek say "anger" with great clarity. Finally, when she acts, she causes Aeolus, king of the winds who "soothes their spirits and governs their anger" (57), to release their pent-up anger upon Aeneas.[51] Juno's anger is axiomatic; but it is also fully justified by myth and history. This is especially true if she knows what any reader of the *Odyssey* knows. The *Odyssey* is a tale of homecoming (*nostos*). In fact, it is almost the only *successful* homecoming among the many disastrous homecomings of the Greek victors after the fall of Troy.[52] It is about many other things, as well—travel, adventure, identity, eschatology—but, ultimately, it is about a man who, finding himself far from home, faces numerous challenges of mythic proportions and, through his own endurance, flexibility, and resourcefulness, prevails at last and reaches his goal. In contrast, the *Iliad* is a

---

50. For a provocative meditation on the development of this theme see Freudenburg 2019.

51. Note that the passages cited in this paragraph (7, 25–26, 57) repeatedly associate "spirits" (*animi*) of various kinds with "anger." In his comment on the last of these, Servius glosses *animos* as *ventos*, "winds," as an element of Greek wordplay with *anemos*, "wind," virtually identifying the winds with anger (see O'Hara 1996/2016, 54, 95, and especially 116, with further references). This comports with Juno's own anger and with her allegorical role as "Queen of the Air": see Murrin 1980, 3–25; P. R. Hardie 1986, 229.

52. The mostly disastrous homecomings of the various Greek heroes, other than Odysseus, were recounted in *Homecomings* (*Nostoi*), the last poem of the Epic Cycle in terms of narrative chronology apart from the *Telegony*, a sequel to the *Odyssey*. On the relationship of *Homecomings* to the *Odyssey*, see West 2013, 245, 247–50, with further references.

crucial chapter in the story of Troy's destruction. Therefore, ask yourself: if you were Juno, would you want the new poem to continue this tale of destruction or to end with the long-suffering hero's achievement of a hard-won success?

Juno obviously wants no Odyssean "homecoming" for Aeneas; but she may have concerns that are even more urgent. Above all, Juno evidently believes that this new story must be an Iliad because only an Iliad would give her an opportunity to shape the story as a central participant. This inference is supported by her actual intervention: confronted with the threat of Trojan success, Juno instantly recalls the juicy role that she played, as Hera, in the *Iliad*—the many and memorable episodes in which she opposed the Trojans, her considerable involvement in the narrative—quite apart from the fact that the poem ends with the funeral of her enemy's greatest champion. No surprise then, that in the *Aeneid*, at her earliest opportunity, she re-enacts her most memorable Iliadic star turn, "The Deception of Zeus." Conversely, if one were to run through the episodes of the *Odyssey*, it would be difficult to identify even a single cameo appearance that it would be worth Juno's trouble to reprise.

I mean this quite literally. It happens that the name of Hera, Juno's Greek counterpart, is mentioned only five times in the entire *Odyssey*, not counting a couple of formulaic repetitions. By contrast, she is named one hundred and nineteen times in the *Iliad*.[53] This is a simple and graphic illustration of what all Homer's readers know to be true, that Hera is among the most impressive characters of the *Iliad*, while in the *Odyssey* her role is negligible. For Juno, then, just as weighty as any other factor may be the simple matter of her jealousy and self-regard, characteristics amply rehearsed by the epic narrator in his summary of the goddess's motives for hating the Trojans (*Aeneid* 1.12–28, 36). One could even say, quite apart from hurt feelings, that the opening of the *Aeneid* confronts Juno with an almost existential threat. Another Odyssey would presumably have no more place for Juno than the original one had for Hera. Between the two Homeric poems, only another Iliad would give her an appropriate sphere of action.[54] For this reason as well, Juno wants, or even needs the new poem to be an Iliad.

---

53. Hera's name appears at *Odyssey* 4.513, 8.465 (= 15.112, 15.180), 11.604, 12.72, 20.70—never, I would venture to say, with any narrative consequence. For the *Iliad*, see the index of names in Monro and Allen 1920, or Prendergast 1875/1983, 182–83.

54. This seems the appropriate place to cite Maura Lafferty's superbly epigrammatic observation (*viva voce*) that the point of Juno's speech, which is so visible in its opening words, is to "put the *me* in *mênin*."

Displaced Persons

Some readers may feel that I am not being entirely fair to Juno, and for the sake of the argument, I might concede the point. Although she is an Iliadic character, it may be that she does what she can to cope with the requirements of an ostensibly Odyssean poem—not to adapt to it, however, so much as to infiltrate it. Having practically no Odyssean experience in her previous epic repertoire, Juno draws upon her most relevant Iliadic exploit, which she finds in an episode of deception. This should be a good move. Unlike the *Iliad*, the *Odyssey* celebrates deception. For that reason alone, Juno might reasonably hope that a reprise of "The Deception of Zeus" would turn out better for her in a new, possibly Odyssean environment.

Not only that: a key ingredient in both the old and the new versions of this episode is marriage. Juno, like Hera, is the goddess who presides over marriage.[55] That said, she has a remarkably instrumental view of marriage, not to say a perverse one. This may be in keeping with her history both as the wife of an incorrigible philanderer and as a character in epic poetry. Her bribe at the beginning of the *Aeneid* repeats a similar one in the middle of the *Iliad* and is thus in keeping with Juno's Iliadic character. To that point, it can hardly be said that the *Iliad* devalues marriage. The purpose of the Trojan War was to avenge Menelaus against the adulterous Paris, whose relationship to Helen is set in vivid contrast to the idealized relationship between Hector and Andromache. In general, however, the women of the *Iliad* signify the status of various men in relation to one another. It is the *Odyssey* that celebrates marriage—not, perhaps, in a way that modern readers find unproblematic, but in an unusually positive way within the context of traditional ancient societies. Eventually, the *Iliad* and the *Odyssey* even came to be seen as categorically different poems partly for this reason, the former as a tragedy ending with a funeral, and the latter as a comedy ending with a conjugal reunion and a vindication of marriage as an institution. It is even possible that something like this perspective on the Homeric poems already existed at the time when the *Aeneid* was being written. Aristotle in general regards both the *Iliad* and the *Odyssey* as excellent models for tragic plots. He considers the *Iliad*, however, as exemplifying the best kind of tragedy in an ethical sense, because it focuses on the experience of a noble character who undergoes a reversal of fortune. In contrast, the *Odyssey* employs a double plot in which the ethically better characters move from misery to hard-earned prosperity and the ethically worse characters from

---

55. Juno's authority over marriage is prominent in the *Aeneid*, but always in bizarre or inappropriate ways. I will be returning to this theme from time to time below.

undeserved prosperity to a richly deserved downfall. This kind of plot, he says, is more appropriate to comedy than tragedy.[56] Aristotle himself thus opens the way towards theorizing the *Iliad* and *Odyssey* as tragic and comic poems, respectively. It is also obvious that Odysseus and Penelope's trials and eventual reunion are the prototype of both the standard plot of New Comedy and its later derivative, the novelistic romance, both of them genres that regularly end in marriage.[57] Finally, ancient critical awareness of the centrality of marital reunion to the plot of the *Odyssey* is reflected in a famous philological problem. The influential Homeric scholars Aristophanes of Byzantium and Aristarchus of Samos believed that the *Odyssey* reaches its *telos* or *peras* (end, destination, goal, purpose, fulfillment: see above on *finis*) in book 23 when Odysseus and Penelope repair to their marriage bed.[58] It therefore makes sense that Juno draws upon her only experience of Homeric deception *and* her peculiar authority over marriage to find purchase within what may be an incipient Odyssey.

Returning, then, to the one and only Homeric episode in which Hera uses guile instead of the naked force that usually springs from her impetuous anger, Juno employs a stratagem that fails—once again in keeping with its provenance, an Iliadic world in which main force and not sleight of hand is the most effective and most honored of heroic qualities.[59] It is hard not to infer that

---

56. Aristotle identifies both the *Iliad* and *Odyssey* models for tragedy and *Margites*, which he also ascribes to Homer, for comedy (*Poetics* 1448b–1449a in Halliwell et al. 1995, 38–41); but he later distinguishes the ending of the *Iliad* as more appropriate to tragedy and that of the *Odyssey* to comedy (1452b–2453a in Halliwell et al. 1995, 68–73). An explicit statement that the *Iliad* and *Odyssey* represent the ideal tragedy and comedy, respectively, is not found until the fourth century CE in Aelius Donatus' commentary on Terence (1.5), but Donatus certainly draws upon earlier authorities; see H. A. Kelly 1993, 1–15. Hall 2008 considers the limited suitability of the *Odyssey* as a source of tragic plots. Sommerstein 1996/2010, 241–53 illustrates the greater ease with which Aeschylus was able to convert the *Iliad* into a tragic tetralogy in contrast to the *Odyssey*.

57. The prevalence of marriage as resolving the typical New Comic and ancient romance needs no illustration, nor does the affinity of this plot to that of the *Odyssey*. I return to the tragic or comic character of the *Iliad* and *Odyssey* in chapters 2 and 3.

58. On Aristophanes and Aristarchus see scholia MV and HMQ on *Odyssey* 23.296. The question of exactly what they meant by *peras* and *telos* is much debated; for a summary of the issue, see Heubeck in Heubeck et al. 1992, vol. 3, 342–45.

59. Failed stratagems in the *Iliad* include Agamemnon's test of his troops in book 2, Odysseus' embassy speech in book 9, and Patroclus' return to battle in Achilles' armor in book 16. Even Achilles' withdrawal from battle could be considered, if not a strategic failure, at least a Pyrrhic victory. The "Doloneia" in book 10, which is exceptional in so many ways, is not a stratagem, but is a successful venture carried out by guile. I discuss the implications of this in the section of chapter 3 entitled "The Odyssean *Iliad*, Part 1: 'Embassy' and 'Doloneia.'"

Juno's abidingly Iliadic nature is fundamentally responsible for undermining her plan. Equally striking is the extent to which her very presence seems to draw even characters whom the reader knows mainly from the *Odyssey* into an Iliadic orbit around her or to reveal abiding Iliadic tendencies in them as well. Let us consider three such characters.

Aeolus

In attempting to make the narrative conform to her own purposes, Juno appears to have made a good start. Aeneas, as the reader will soon learn, has reached a point in his personal story similar to that of Odysseus when he is close to his destination but fails to reach it because unruly storm winds drive him away; and Juno causes the same thing to happen in the *Aeneid*. In both cases, the master of the offending winds is Aeolus, who gives his name to a significant episode of the *Odyssey*, but in the world of the *Iliad* is nowhere to be found. Appropriately, when Juno betakes herself to Aeolus, she addresses him in Odyssean terms. Her appeal to him ("for the father of gods and king of men has assigned you to calm the waves and raise them with wind" *Aeneid* 1.65–66) is virtually identical to what Odysseus will tell his Phaeacian hosts about Aeolus ("for the son of Cronus made him warden of the winds, to calm or rouse whichever he pleases," *Odyssey* 10.21–22). The specifically Odyssean nature of the situation is then underlined when Aeolus takes up a spear to set the storm in motion, using the weapon as Poseidon uses his trident to raise the storm in the *Odyssey*. Comparison of the two passages reveals a carefully wrought, six-line correspondence:

> **This said**, inverting his **spear** he struck the hollow
> mountainside; and **winds**, as if in military formation,
> where way is given, **fall** and blow over the lands in **blasts**.
> They have *fallen on the sea*, and from its depths
> together, **both Eurus and Notus and gusty** Africus,
> make it all rush and make **great waves roll** to the shores. (*Aeneid* 1.81–86)

> **So saying** he gathered clouds and stirred up **the sea**,
> taking his trident in hand; he roused all the **blasts**
> of all sorts of **winds**, and with the clouds he hid
> land and sea together; night *fell from the sky*.
> **Both Eurus and Notus** were **falling** together **and gusty** Zephyrus
> and sky-born Boreas, making **a great wave roll**. (*Odyssey* 5.291–96)

In effect, then, Juno enlists one Odyssean character to help her assume the role of another. An innovation is that she takes over the more exalted aspect of

Poseidon's role as the hero's divine antagonist, leaving to Aeolus the more banausic function of rousing the elements, something that Poseidon himself does not shrink from doing in *Odyssey* 5.

With this, Juno appears to have successfully infiltrated a would-be Odyssean narrative and to have gained control of it. Her coup does not succeed, however, because, in reality, her attention to detail is far from perfect. In the first place, the Aeolus of the *Odyssey* is actually the hero's host. After entertaining Odysseus and his crew, he gives his departing guest a bag containing (and so neutralizing) all of the winds except for the one that would carry his ship home to Ithaca. But Odysseus' men, with their destination actually in sight, jealously suspect that their captain is hoarding some treasure for himself instead of sharing it with them. They therefore open the bag and release all the winds, which drive them back to Aeolus' realm (*Odyssey* 10.38–61). In the *Aeneid*, things are quite different. The hero and his crew have been sojourning in Sicily with their Trojan cousin, Acestes; and although they will eventually return to this place, the storm, which they had no part in causing, drives them not there, but to Carthage. Moreover, the Aeolus of the *Aeneid* is no benevolent guest-friend, like his Homeric counterpart, whose good offices are brought to nothing by the folly of his guest's companions. Rather, he is the lackey of the hero's divine antagonist; and again unlike his Homeric counterpart, this Aeolus does not understand his place in the scheme of things.[60] When Odysseus is driven back to Aeolia, his old host refuses him further assistance, *respecting* what he believes is the will of the gods who evidently *hate* the hero (*Odyssey* 10.72–75). When Aeneas is on his way from Sicily, Aeolus whips up the sea, *violating* the province of a more powerful god (Neptune) who (as it will turn out) *favors* the hero. Finally, the character of Aeolus himself is drawn very differently in the two poems. The Homeric Aeolus is king of not only the winds, but of a fairy realm where his six sons and as many daughters are married to one another and live forever (*Odyssey* 10.5–7). In the *Aeneid*, Aeolus seems to live alone in a barren place where he keeps his winds imprisoned in a mountain, having no apparent *raison d'être* other than this.[61] There is certainly no indication that he has a family, and a rather strong indication to the contrary in the form of Juno's offering him marriage to one of her nymphs, who will make him the father of beautiful children (*Aeneid* 1.71–75). This is the

---

60. Of course, he cannot simply refuse Juno, who as "Queen of the Air" (see note 51 above) is his immediate superior, as he emphasizes (1.76–80).

61. Aeolia in the *Aeneid* is evidently the Lipari group in the southeastern Tyrrhenian Sea, an identification first attested by Thucydides, *History of the Peloponnesian War* (3.88) that "vindicates" Homer as a geographer but contributes to the removal of Aeolus' floating island (*Odyssey* 10.3) from the realm of fantasy.

sort of offer that might not tempt a *paterfamilias* like the Homeric Aeolus quite so much as it would a bachelor relegated to a lonely outpost where there is nothing to do but keep his violent charges in check.[62] So, in many ways the Aeolus of the *Aeneid* does not seem like his Odyssean "self," even from the beginning. And with Juno's bribe, his transformation becomes complete: whatever impression the reader may have of Aeolus' Odyssean character is distorted almost beyond recognition as he becomes Juno's henchman, modeled explicitly on Hypnos, who had been Hera's henchman, in a daring but ultimately futile Iliadic gambit.

Neptune

If Juno's intervention effectively converts Aeolus from the Odyssean character of the reader's memory into a quasi-Iliadic one, it is no wonder that she has the same effect on characters who are at home in both Homeric poems. Neptune is one such character: he plays important, but very different roles in both the *Iliad* and the *Odyssey*. In the latter poem, he is the hero's divine antagonist, but in the *Aeneid*, that is the role that Juno wants for herself. I have just discussed how she uses Aeolus to help her take it. Even before Juno approaches Aeolus, though, we are told that she, "while nursing an everlasting wound deep in her bosom, spoke thus to herself" (*Aeneid* 1.36–37); and what follows is her indignant soliloquy. Ursinus compared this passage to one in the *Odyssey* in which Poseidon, before launching his storm at Odysseus, "grew angrier in his heart and, shaking his head," delivered a soliloquy of his own (*Odyssey* 5.284–85).[63] Then, at the end of her speech, Juno complains that in spite of her exalted status among the gods she is unable to accomplish what she most desires—the eradication of the Trojans—and worries that no one will bother worshipping her divinity thereafter (*Aeneid* 1.48–49). This conclusion, as Ursinus also noticed, resembles a complaint that Poseidon once again makes to Zeus in *Odyssey* 13 after watching the Phaeacians deposit Odysseus safe and sound upon the shore of Ithaca. As the Phaeacian ship turns back on its return voyage to its home on the island of Scheria, Poseidon says: "Father Zeus, I shall no longer be honored among the deathless gods, since [these] mortals, the Phaeacians, do not honor me at all, even though they are my descendants" (*Odyssey* 13.128–30).[64] Thus Juno's speech announcing her opposition to

---

62. Lausberg 1983, 204–5.

63. Ursinus 1567, 197. On the relation between Poseidon's speech and Juno's second soliloquy in *Aeneid* 7 see Knauer 1964, 150–52, 231–32, 327, 335 and 1964b, 75–76.

64. Ursinus 1567, 198.

Aeneas is framed by passages that "cite" speeches of Poseidon at the beginning and the end of what ancient critics called the "Phaeacis," the portion of the *Odyssey* (books 5–13) that concerns Poseidon's persecution of Odysseus. This is the very portion of Homer's narrative, in fact, that corresponds to practically the entire "Odyssean *Aeneid*," the first half of the poem as it is traditionally conceived. Juno's motivation, a humiliating perception of *lèse-majesté*, corresponds to that of Odysseus' divine antagonist, as well. As soon as she arrives on the scene, then, Juno begins to inhabit a role that any knowing reader would associate with the Poseidon of the *Odyssey*.

In this respect, Neptune is more directly affected by Juno's meddling than anyone else; and for this reason, the particular course of action that he follows is especially instructive. To understand this, we must be clear about Neptune's specific motivation in quelling Juno's storm. His intervention has far-reaching consequences for Aeneas and for Rome, but in the moment, personal considerations are uppermost in his mind. It is clear that he considers the entire episode an insult to his dignity and a grave trespass. In the manner of a true Roman aristocrat he threatens the menial instruments, the winds themselves, who have actually committed the trespass, and increases their discomfort by ordering them to take a humiliating message to Aeolus, their superior, though he is vastly inferior to Neptune himself (*Aeneid* 1.132–41). Neptune avoids mentioning Juno, his equal and indeed his sister, even though he sees clearly that she is behind the mischief ("nor did Juno's deceit and anger escape her bother," 130), presumably judging it more effective simply to thwart her efforts and assert his own rights.[65] To put the matter simply, in narrative terms Neptune responds to Juno's usurpation by taking back his domain and undoing the trouble she had caused there; and in intertextual terms, when she usurps his Odyssean role as divine antagonist, he responds by reprising the best Iliadic role available to him, that of rescuing Aeneas from certain death, as he does in *Iliad* 20.[66] In this way, Juno is again responsible for creating an Iliadic outcome when she attempts to infiltrate what seems to be an incipiently Odyssean narrative.

To return to the question of motive, although Neptune had rescued Aeneas in the *Iliad*, it is quite clear in *Aeneid* 1 that his main concern is with Juno's trespass, because he acts only incidentally, if at all, with the Trojans' welfare in mind. His speech in this episode (*Aeneid* 1.132–41) is entirely concerned with

---

65. Neptune's alertness to both Juno's guile (*doli*) and her anger (*irae*) might suggest to the reader that she has conflated Odyssean *mētis* and Iliadic *mēnis* narratives. As in "The Deception of Zeus," however, the combination proves to be dangerously unstable.

66. *Iliad* 20.288–340; see Knauer 1964, 149 and especially 343.

Aeolus' transgression and says nothing about Aeneas and his fleet. This point is further illuminated by Neptune's appearance in *Aeneid* 5, a clear pendant to the storm scene in book 1. The relationship between these episodes is established not only by Neptune's calming of the sea in both, but by the fact that Aeneas sets sail from Sicily in both, as well. It is only in the second passage (5.800–15) that Neptune explicitly cites Homeric precedent for helping Aeneas (*Iliad* 20.302–8), thus in the minds of some readers guaranteeing his benign attitude towards the hero throughout the Odyssean *Aeneid*.[67] In book 5, however, Neptune shows more than a little of Poseidon's bloodthirsty, Odyssean nature. Just as in *Aeneid* 1, he remains jealous of his prerogatives as master of the seas. This time, however, his jealousy is directed not only at overreaching sisters and their mischievous underlings, but (in keeping with tradition) also against any mere mortals who dare venture into his domain. In *Odyssey* 13 and *Aeneid* 5, as Odysseus and Aeneas are approaching their respective homelands, Poseidon and Neptune permit their passage, but they do so with reluctance in each case, exacting punishment or compensation from those who convey or guide the heroes to their destinations. In the *Odyssey*, Poseidon turns to stone the Phaeacian ship that had taken Odysseus to Ithaca, putting an end to the Phaeacians' seafaring and to all further contact between them and the rest of the world. In the *Aeneid*, Neptune demands "just" one life in return for the safe passage of the Trojan fleet, and this proves to be the life of Aeneas' helmsman, Palinurus.[68]

The sacrifice of Palinurus is negotiated in one of the most chilling in a series of chilling exchanges between exalted divinities throughout the poem. The episode begins with Venus' effort to secure safe passage for her son, and the goddess wastes no time in getting to the point: "Juno's oppressive anger and her insatiable character force me to beg, Neptune, no matter how abjectly" (*Aeneid* 5.781–82). It is true, even if Venus states her case with the utmost shrewdness, that Juno has put her as well as Neptune into a reactive posture. "You yourself can be my witness as to how suddenly she raised a storm in the waters near Libya, not long ago: she pointlessly confused sea and sky, using Aeolus' storm winds, daring as much as that within your own domain" (789–92). Venus is right to be afraid as Aeneas prepares to embark from the same port as when Juno attacked him just one year before, and all the more so in

---

67. For instance, Williams 1960, 191 on 801–2; see note 71 below.

68. *Aeneid* 5.814–15; *Odyssey* 13.125–87. Surprisingly, this parallel does not seem to have been noticed previously. Knauer 1964, 270, 328, 341–42 instead considers Poseidon's turning of the Phaeacian ship into stone to be Vergil's inspiration for Cybele's transformation of the Trojan ships into nymphs at *Aeneid* 9.77–122, the point (he argues) being that these events mark the end of the heroes' respective voyages.

light of what happened at Carthage during that year.[69] Note that Venus cleverly bases her request not on any apprehension for Aeneas' welfare that she might expect Neptune to share, but rather on Neptune's interest in protecting his own property. This speaks directly and effectively to Neptune's abiding concern, almost as if Venus had overheard his dressing down of Eurus and the other winds in book 1. At any rate, by taking this approach, she opens the door for him to reply with a show of magnanimity. Downplaying his self-interest, Neptune crafts his favorable reply in the language of kinship diplomacy, addressing Venus as "Cytherea"—that is, recalling the circumstances of her birth in his domain, the sea, near the island of Cythera—before going on to claim, rather tendentiously, that it is ever his responsibility to maintain peace in that element (800–802). Only after this (804–11), as if to prove his good will towards Aeneas in particular, does he "remind" Venus of the Iliadic episode (which she had cunningly omitted to mention) in which he saved her son from certain death at the hands of Achilles. In this reminder, Neptune may be hinting to Venus, who was unable to rescue Aeneas earlier, when he had been severely wounded by Diomedes in *Iliad* 5, that she already owes him.[70] Still, it all sounds so friendly that it comes as a shock when Neptune suddenly reverts to form by demanding a victim as payment for his assistance. Neptune's fondness for Venus and her son are evidently not so great that he would forego altogether the grim tribute due to him as ruler of the waves. One has to wonder what Neptune might have done had Venus not acted to ensure his good will.[71]

In fact, as is always the case, behind the elaborate courtesy with which the great gods usually address one another, there is at least one unstated motive,

---

69. Note that "one year before" corresponds to Venus' *nuper*, which I rendered above as "not long ago": a brilliantly incidental illustration of the enormous gap between divine and human perspectives.

70. On Aeneas' Iliadic encounter with Diomedes, see the following section, entitled "Aeneas," in this chapter.

71. In contrast to the critical assumption that Neptune protects the Trojans from storms throughout their voyage, Palinurus infers that Neptune is responsible for the inclement weather that they encounter after leaving Carthage: his words, "what are you up to, father Neptune?" (*quidve, pater Neptune, paras?* 5.14), are an ironic adumbration of the fate that awaits him as sacrificial offering for the good of the fleet. Cairns 1989, 94–95 notes that the Iliadic Poseidon is allied with Hera against the Trojans and that Neptune cooperates in the destruction of Troy at *Aeneid* 2.610–16, so that his taking action against Juno on behalf of the Trojans in books 1 and 5 constitutes a change of sides on his part. Cairns attributes this change to the Trojans' "moral rectitude and the support for their mission of the fates and Jupiter" (Cairns 1989, 95 note 38), but as Austin 1971, 64 on *Aeneid* 1.127 correctly observes, "Neptune's emotional preoccupation is with Iuno and the storm, not with the storm's victims."

and often a thinly veiled threat. In this connection, Neptune's mention of Venus' (and therefore also of Aeneas') kinship with him should be especially unsettling to the reader who recalls the corresponding episode of *Odyssey* 13, in which the Phaeacians successfully convey Odysseus to Ithaca. (This is the second of two episodes that we considered previously as signaling Juno's seizure of Neptune's "rightful" role.) There Poseidon, remonstrating with Zeus, complains that the Phaeacians do not honor him "even though they are his descendants" (*Odyssey* 13.130).[72] For readers of the *Odyssey*, then, Neptune's kinship diplomacy with Venus as good as states both his ability and his willingness to destroy anyone who ventures on his domain, no matter how close to him they may be. Fortunately for Aeneas, Neptune contents himself with a single life, that of Palinurus, rather than insisting on anything more extravagant.[73] Nonetheless, he agrees to guarantee Aeneas' safe passage mainly because Venus focuses his attention on the continuing need to oppose Juno, who has shown no respect for his prerogatives by trespassing into his kingdom and wreaking havoc there.

To put the matter another way, when Venus attempts to secure Neptune's good will by citing an episode from *Aeneid* 1, Neptune assures her of it by citing an episode from *Iliad* 20. He can do this, and perhaps must do this, because Juno's usurpation of Poseidon's Odyssean role as divine antagonist has left Neptune no option but to reprise his other great Homeric role—his Iliadic role—as Aeneas' divine savior. Ironically, this means that twice in the "Odyssean *Aeneid*" an Iliadic Neptune rescues Aeneas, first from certain destruction at sea and then by taking steps to forestall a repetition of that disaster. Such behavior, which would be out of place for Neptune (a.k.a. Poseidon) in a straightforwardly Odyssean narrative, is the direct result of Juno's meddling. Had she not attacked Aeneas in Neptune's element, then Neptune would have no need to get involved; and, to repeat, he gets involved in order to defend his turf, and only incidentally to protect Aeneas. In his second intervention, Neptune's insistence on payment for services rendered, in the form of Palinurus' death, indicates that he is no more unaware of the perquisites that are owed him than is Poseidon, his Odyssean counterpart. It is also relevant that Poseidon does not prevail in the *Odyssey*, just as Hera did not prevail in the Iliadic episode of "The Deception of Zeus," but that unlike Juno Neptune appears

---

72. Poseidon's anger against Odysseus arises from a curse pronounced by Polyphemus, the god's own son (*Odyssey* 10.526–35).

73. A typical reversal of the one-and-many motif: see O'Hara 1990, 7–53; P. R. Hardie 1993, 3–10 and 27–35. The arrangements in book 5 are an Iliadic permutation of Juno's intervention in book 1.

capable of responding flexibly and prudently to different circumstances. Above all, it is evident that protecting his province from continued sisterly encroachment is more important to him than a few human lives, more or less.

Aeneas

The experiences of Aeolus and Neptune illuminate that of Aeneas. When Aeolus, familiar to the reader as an Odyssean character, is drawn into Juno's Iliadic force-field, he is warped almost beyond recognition into an intertextual facsimile of the Iliadic Hypnos. When Neptune, a character who is at home in both Homeric poems, finds Juno trespassing on his domain, he manages to beat her at her own Iliadic game. The position in which Aeneas finds himself bears some relationship to both. Unlike Neptune, however, Aeneas does not enjoy the luxury of choice. His possibilities are limited both because he is not a god and also because, like Aeolus, he appears in only one of the Homeric poems. Unfortunately, it is the wrong one; for if Aeneas is being called to be the hero of an Odyssey, his experience and outlook are those of an Iliadic character who has survived, but can find nothing in his skill set to get him through this challenge. In effect, therefore, his predicament is not unlike that of Juno herself, an Iliadic character who must play an ill-fitting Odyssean role.

Like Juno, Aeneas upon entering the narrative is pulled in two directions. On the one hand, the plot apparently requires him to be a kind of Odysseus. Famously, he even announces himself as such—unwittingly, of course—when, in the midst of Juno's Odyssean storm, he reacts just as Odysseus reacts in similar circumstances, even "quoting" the words that the Homeric Odysseus himself speaks on that occasion:

> **Then Aeneas' limbs go slack** with cold;
> he groans, and lifting his twin palms to the stars,
> such words as these **he speaks** *aloud*: "O, **three and four times blessed** were you who, before your fathers' eyes, beneath the high walls of **Troy**, had the good fortune **to die!**" (*Aeneid* 1.92–96)

> **Then Odysseus' limbs went slack**, and grieving his heart
> in anguish **he spoke** *to his own great-hearted spirit*:
> ...
> "**Three times and four times blessed** were the Danaans **who died** then in broad **Troy**, gladdening Atreus' sons." (*Odyssey* 5.297–98, 306–7)

If the concept of *Leitzitat* means anything at all, this quotation must be telling the reader that Aeneas at this point in his story is directly comparable to Odysseus when he shudders in fear and speaks virtually these same words. What is important, though, is that this comparison does not really answer any questions, but instead raises them; because in spite of the very clear, but superficial similarities between the two heroes, their differences are more impressive. The main points are regularly taught even to first-time students of the poem:

- Odysseus at this point has lost all his companions, whether by his own recklessness or by their legendary foolishness; Aeneas, since leaving Troy (where he lost Creusa, his wife) has lost Anchises, his father, to old age just before the Trojan fleet left Sicily; but otherwise, his fleet is intact.
- Although both heroes long to have died at Troy, Odysseus bitterly regards dying in another man's fight as a bad thing, even if not so bad as dying at sea. For Aeneas, to die defending his own people would have given his life real meaning.
- Odysseus, in short, is defined by his egotism and his heroic isolation, Aeneas by his heroic devotion to and leadership of a community in exile.

These are, then, quite different figures, and it is not hard, for these very reasons, to make a case for Aeneas as the morally superior hero. Surprisingly, though, the burden has often been on his defenders: already in antiquity critics debated whether Aeneas in this very passage lived up to the heroic standard set by Odysseus.[74] Much of the discussion focused on the apparently unassuming phrase "such words as these he speaks aloud" (*talia voce refert* 94), which corresponds to, but revises, the Homeric formula "he spoke to his own great-hearted spirit" (*eipe pros hon megalētora thymon, Odyssey* 5.298). It is easy for the modern reader to treat both phrases as typically epic verbiage, but that would be a mistake.[75] The Greek and Latin phrases have very different meanings, so that some ancient critics took it amiss that Aeneas uttered his complaint aloud (*voce*, literally, "with his voice") while Odysseus spoke to his "great-hearted spirit," which is to say, to himself. They did so because silence in difficult circumstances is "more elevated and more in keeping with heroic character" than giving voice to such

---

74. Servius, *Commentary on Vergil's Aeneid* 1.92, a very full and interesting entry, reports that this passage was criticized for adapting *Odyssey* 5.297–98 improperly. Such comments are generally thought to originate with Vergil's "detractors" (*obtrectatores*) of the early 1st century CE, who were refuted by Asconius Pedianus in about the middle of that century. The most useful treatment of this subject in English remains that of Nettleship's 1881 essays "On Some Early Criticisms of Virgil's Poetry" and "The Ancient Commentators on Virgil" (Conington and Nettleship 1963, vol. 1, xxix–liii, liv–xcix).

75. In fact, while Vergil does use a number of quasi-formulaic phrases (e.g. "when he finished saying these things," *haec ubi dicta dedit*), he employs this particular phrase only twice, the other occurrence being at line 208 of this same book, where Aeneas again "quotes" Odysseus' words at *Odyssey* 10.174–75; see note 152 below.

feelings.[76] They also criticized Aeneas for raising his hands to the sky, finding this gesture "weak" or "soft" (*molle*), and wondering why, if he were going to do so, he did not at least make some appropriate prayer rather than pronouncing a benediction on those who had died at Troy.[77] Such a remark looks as if it were intended to undermine the usual defense of Aeneas, that he is a new type of hero, not an existential egotist but a man of "dutiful responsibility" (*pietas*), someone who knows the right thing to do and does it on all occasions. What good is a man of *pietas* if he can't even pray properly?

It is entirely characteristic of ancient criticism to correlate poetics with ethics, and I agree that this passage is resonant with ethical significance. At the same time, it is equally attentive to poetics in a way that brings out the relationship between poetics and ethics. In evaluating the phrase *talia voce refert* ("thus he speaks aloud"), I have noted that most ancient critics focus on the second word, *voce* ("with his voice," i.e., "aloud"); but Servius also has a brief notice about *refert* ("he speaks"), which he glosses as *profert* (he gives voice to, utters, pronounces).[78] The prefix *re-* "is superfluous" (*abundat*), Servius continues, noting that elsewhere *refert* means *respondet*, "answers"; and in support he cites a different passage of the *Aeneid* as well as common usage.[79] This is all quite correct. One often finds *refert* used as a verb of speaking, almost always in the way that Servius insists is normal. Here, no one has spoken to Aeneas, so that he is not "answering" anyone in any simple sense. But rather than "superfluous," one might say that the prefix is overadequate to the context and so points beyond it.[80] This makes excellent sense, because *refert* is one of those words that critics have learned to regard as an "Alexandrian footnote," an indication of "response" to some intertextual precedent, as if the point of using the word were to stimulate the reader's poetic memory.[81] Here, of course, it points in the first

---

76. Servius, *Commentary on Vergil's Aeneid* 1.92 *frigore*. In the same entry Servius goes on to state that Odysseus kept his thoughts to himself in order to avoid discouraging his men—evidently forgetting that Odysseus is alone at this point. But in doing so, Servius indicates the point of the charge against Aeneas.

77. It is pretty clear that, for some critics, the point was to find fault in any way possible; Servius, *Commentary on Vergil's Aeneid* 1.92 reports that someone complained, absurdly, that it made no sense to raise one's hands "to the stars" (*ad sidera*) during the day.

78. See the *Oxford Latin Dictionary* s.v. profero 4.

79. Servius, *Commentary on Vergil's Aeneid* 1.94.

80. This would, I believe, be a perfectly reasonable way of rendering Servius' *abundat*. It all depends how one evaluates the metaphor that the verb contains. Similarly, *abundans* as a stylistic term can have positive or negative connotations (*Oxford Latin Dictionary* s.v. abundo 4).

81. The term "Alexandrian footnote" was coined by Ross 1975, 78 to designate a phenomenon discussed by Norden 1927/1957, 123–4 on *Aeneid* 6.14 (a note that goes back to the first edition of 1903). Aeneas' memory of Homeric events will figure extensively in chapter 3 below.

instance to the words spoken by the storm-tossed hero of the *Odyssey* as a model for those of Aeneas. At the same time, since one might have thought that Aeneas' response is such an obvious quotation that no such signposting would be called for, we might infer that *refert* points to some further "response," inviting readers to look beyond the obvious; and if we do, we will not be disappointed. Aeneas continues to say that he wishes he had died in battle at Troy:

> **O strongest of the nation of the Danaans,**
> son of Tydeus! That I couldn't have fallen on the plains
> of Ilium and poured out this spirit by your right arm,
> where savage Hector lies beneath the spear of Aeacus' grandson, where great
> Sarpedon [died], where Simois rolls so many shields of men
> and helmets and strong bodies caught in his waves. (*Aeneid* 1.96–101)

That is very similar to what Odysseus also goes on to say:

> How I ought to have died and met my doom
> on that day when most of the Trojans were throwing
> bronze-tipped spears at me around the dead son of Peleus.
> Then I would have had burial, and the Achaeans would have celebrated
> my fame; but now my fate is to be caught by a dismal death. (*Odyssey* 5.308–12)

The point, however, is not just that the *Aeneid* is responding to the *Odyssey*, but that both Aeneas and Odysseus in these passages are responding to the *Iliad*, each in a characteristically metapoetic way. A famous principle of *Odyssey* criticism, "Munro's Law," has to do with the poem's careful avoidance of referring directly to any episode of the *Iliad*.[82] The present passage illustrates that principle: Odysseus wishes he had died in battle; and in the *Iliad*, the battle epic *par excellence*, he almost did.[83] In *Odyssey* 5, however, as the hero contemplates death by drowning, that is not the brush with death that he recalls. Instead, he specifies that he would prefer to have died in the battle over Achilles' body—which is to say, after the events of the *Iliad*, even after the hero of the *Iliad* had himself been consigned to the epic past.[84] In contrast, Aeneas' death wish is explicitly Iliadic, though once again an element of avoidance is

---

82. The most compelling perspective on this principle is that of Nagy 1979, 20–25, who ascribes the classic statement of it to Monro 1901, 395. It is discussed with reference to the *Aeneid* by Dekel 2012, 19–20.

83. Odysseus was wounded by the otherwise obscure Socus, whom he managed to slay before being forced to retreat with the help of Menelaus (*Iliad* 11.401–88).

84. According to Proclus' *Chrestomathia*, the death of Achilles was the concluding event of the *Aethiopis*, a poem of the Epic Cycle that immediately followed the *Iliad* in narrative time: see

involved. As I mentioned in passing above, not once but twice in the *Iliad* does Aeneas come close to death. Both episodes are memorable, but the second was more consequential. In book 20, Achilles nearly ran Aeneas through with his spear before Poseidon rescued the Trojan hero and told him that he would survive the war to rule over his people. This passage was recognized already in antiquity as the charter myth of the Roman Empire.[85] It therefore seems at first that this must be the episode that Aeneas remembers when he apostrophizes the "strongest of the nation of the Danaans" (*Danaum fortissime gentis* 96), before making it clear at the beginning of the following line that he means not Achilles, but Diomedes, whom he apostrophizes as "son of Tydeus" (*Tydide* 97). With that, it becomes clear that he is remembering his first brush with death, in *Iliad* 5, when Diomedes crushed Aeneas' hip with a boulder and was ready to finish him off until Aphrodite came to the rescue. Diomedes, nothing daunted, attacked and wounded the goddess herself, causing her to abandon her son, who was then rescued by Apollo.[86] It is on this occasion, then, and not the later one, that Aeneas says he would prefer to have died.

The difference between the *Aeneid* passage and its Odyssean model illustrates the difference in intertextual dynamics between the two poems. The *Odyssey* may in effect "cite" other poems (or poetic traditions) quite openly, but it circles the *Iliad* warily, alluding to it, if at all, only with the utmost obliqueness, almost as if pretending that it did not exist.[87] The *Aeneid* cites the *Iliad*, just as it cites the *Odyssey*, with great clarity, at times almost pedantically, here going so far as to specify precisely which of two episodes Aeneas wishes had been his death scene. The Homeric procedure produces a strange effect, in that Odysseus, who lived through the entire Trojan War, at no point in the *Odyssey* recalls anything that happened in the fifty or so days covered by the *Iliad*. It is almost as if he were not a major character in that poem—or, in metapoetic terms, as if he had never read it. Aeneas, on the other hand, remembers those fifty days vividly, even if somewhat selectively.[88]

By surviving his encounter with Diomedes, Aeneas lived to come face to face with the hero who really was the strongest of all the Greeks, Achilles himself; but that is not what he remembers. He wishes he had fallen to

---

Davies 1989, 51–59; West 2003, 108–17 and 2013, 129–62. This poem was composed after the *Iliad* and *Odyssey*, so that the *Odyssey* poet is alluding to a traditional epic theme rather than to a fixed text.

85. On the reception of the Homeric passage in this context see Gabba 1976, 85–86; P. M. Smith 1981, 34–43; Gruen 1992, 12–13 and 41; Barchiesi 1994a, 441–42; Casali 2010, 40–41.

86. *Iliad* 5.166–453. On Diomedes in the *Aeneid*, see Knauer 1964, 317–20 and 1964a, 81.

87. See Eisenberger 1973, 107; Lausberg 1983, 206–7.

88. Fifty days is a round number; the exact duration of the *Iliad* is a question that has been debated since antiquity. The most recent consideration of the issue is Beck 2019.

Diomedes, not Achilles, before he could witness the death of Hector, the death of Sarpedon, Achilles' superhuman battle against the very landscape of Troy, and before he could learn that Fate required him to keep on surviving for the sake of his people's future. In psychological terms, then, Aeneas' wish that he had died in *Iliad* 5 is extremely complex.[89] He wishes that he had died instead of ignominiously surviving his encounter with Diomedes, because that would have given him a glorious death in battle at the hands of a great warrior. It would also have spared him a second defeat, albeit at the hands of a still greater one. Even worse, perhaps, than either defeat was the sentence pronounced by Poseidon, that Aeneas must keep on living and struggling to make the best of many defeats, rather than claiming the simple honor of dying like a hero in defense of his country. Not only did Aeneas have to face these traumas in the past, he must repeat them now in the present and again the future.

The rest of Aeneas' speech further betrays his strongly Iliadic obsession. He has not yet heard the Sibyl's prophecy concerning the second Iliad that awaits him in Latium, a prophecy that will speak of wars, of a Tiber bubbling with blood, of Simois and Xanthus, a Greek encampment, another Achilles, and Juno's continuing opposition.[90] Already, however, he sees his present disaster at sea not as anticipating Odysseus' shipwreck (about which he can know nothing, since it has yet to happen), but instead as the fulfillment of Achilles' own near-death encounter with the River Xanthus, one Iliadic book after Aeneas himself escaped death at Achilles' hands.[91] It is no accident that Aeneas recalls seeing the River Simois clogged with "so many shields of men and helmets and strong bodies caught in his waves" when he himself is trapped in a storm at sea, just before he gazes with horror upon "a few swimmers in the vast abyss, arms of men, planks of ships, and Trojan treasure upon the waters."[92] The similarity between these passages suggests that the hero experiences what

---

89. I note in passing that Aeneas is living through an episode that will occur in *Odyssey* 5 while remembering an episode that he lived through in *Iliad* 5. He is in the fifth book of a Homeric poem, but the intertext leaves it to the reader to decide which of them is the more relevant, and how.

90. *Aeneid* 6.84–91, a passage I discuss in the section of chapter 3 entitled "Cumae."

91. *Iliad* 21.136–382. On Aeneas' knowledge of Odysseus' adventures see the section on "Intertextual Chronology" below in this chapter. Since Achilles, like Odysseus in the passage just discussed, is in danger of drowning, an ancient commentator may have noted the verbal similarity of *Odyssey* 5.312 to *Iliad* 21.281 and inferred that the former alluded directly to the latter. In that case, the *Aeneid* passage under discussion might reflect an awareness of his interpretation.

92. *Aeneid* 1.118–19, a passage I discuss below; see Lausberg 1983, 205–6, citing Raabe 1974, 79–83; Conway 1935, 40 on 100 (Simois instead of Scamander); Pöschl 1950/1962, 34–41.

the reader "knows to be" an Odyssean storm as the repetition of a specifically Iliadic trauma.[93]

With this in mind, it is worthwhile to recall the Iliadic episode of the "Battle against the River" in greater detail. In book 21, the River Xanthus (and not Simois, as Aeneas for some reason remembers it) becomes so angry with Achilles for clogging his channel with corpses that he tries to drown the hero, and almost succeeds. As he faces death by drowning, here is how Achilles reacts:

> The son of Peleus groaned, looking into the broad sky:
> "Father Zeus, that none of the gods has undertaken to rescue me,
> pitiable as I am, from the river! After that, I might endure anything.
> None of the other sky-dwellers is responsible
> but my own mother, who deceived me with lies;
> she said that below the wall of the breastplated Trojans
> I would die by Apollo's swift arrows.
> I wish Hector had killed me, who is the best of those raised here:
> then the killer would have been a good man, and would have killed a good one.
> But now it is my fate to die a dismal death hemmed in
> by the great river like a boy who tends pigs,
> whom a torrent washes away as he crosses during a storm." (*Iliad* 21.272–83)

The Vergilian commentator Christian Gottlob Heyne, who also notes the similarity between Aeneas' speech and that of Odysseus, was the first to suggest that Achilles' speech was "another model" (*aliud exemplum*) for the *Aeneid* passage.[94] Knauer includes this correspondence in his lists, but only to state that it was not part of Vergil's plan; nor has any other critic picked up on it.[95] This is extremely puzzling, for Vergilians tend to be, if anything, hyperalert to any possible intertextual gesture, especially where Homer is concerned. Here, moreover, it is easy to see that Aeneas' outburst resembles that of Achilles in several respects, and that these include some of the departures from Odysseus' speech with which ancient critics found fault. For instance, Aeneas, like Achilles, not only speaks aloud but groans, speaks as if in prayer to the gods above, mentions dying at the foot of Troy's defensive walls, and wishes he had been slain by the best hero the enemy had and not by great numbers, as Odysseus

---

93. Pöschl 1950/1962, 36; Austin 1971, 62 on *Aeneid* 1.119. The storm predicts further Iliadic repetitions in books 7–12: see Pöschl 1950/1962, 36 note 3; Lausberg 1983, 206. Here one could borrow and adapt an idea from Dekel 2012 to say that Aeneas views his Odyssean circumstances through an Iliadic lens.

94. Heyne 1830–1841, vol. 2, 83 on *Aeneid* 1.92.

95. Knauer 1964, 364 (for the designation "sicherlich von Vergil nicht bedacht") and 372.

does. Finally, where Achilles in *Iliad* 21 wishes that he had fallen to Hector, Aeneas remembers the exactly opposite thing, that Hector did fall to Achilles, in the very next book of the *Iliad*, as a matter of fact. Such details suggest that Achilles' speech in Homer is a significant point of reference for that of Aeneas, which is also the hero's first appearance in the *Aeneid*.

The remains of ancient scholarship on these passages suggests that they were connected in antiquity as well. We even have indirect evidence that some ancient readers criticized Achilles, much as Servius criticized Aeneas, in a scholium explaining that Achilles' behavior is not in fact cowardly, but heroic:[96]

> DECEIVED ME WITH LIES] like a true hero, he means that he was deceived in his expectation of such a death, as if having put credence in pleasant words. So, it is not death that pains him, but the manner of it. (Scholia abT on *Iliad* 21.276)

This note does not explain precisely what it is that distresses Achilles about the manner of death that he foresees, but it just so happens that there is a bit more information in a comment on the passage in which Odysseus makes his similar complaint. This information refers to Achilles' outburst, as well:

> BY A DISMAL DEATH] the lexicographers define "a dismal death" as one in the moist element, both from this passage and from what is said by Achilles in "The Battle against the River" [*Iliad* 21.281]. It is better to be slain than to be overwhelmed. (Scholia Q on *Odyssey* 5.312)

Eventually, in accordance with a fairly common pattern of transmission, a commentator of the *Aeneid* took over this information, so that it is more fully elaborated in Servius' commentary—which is, after all, a comparatively early source—than it is in the Homeric scholia that survive as marginalia in later medieval manuscripts:[97]

> HE GROANS] not because of death—for there follows "O three and four times blessed" [*Aeneid* 1.94]—but because of the kind of death. For according to Homer it is a grave matter to perish by shipwreck, since the soul is fiery (as

---

96. The note's careful parsing of the reasons behind Achilles' distress suggest that his speech had been criticized by one critic as unheroic, and then defended by another. Eustathius on *Iliad* 16.22, where Achilles learns of Patroclus' death, illustrates such a controversy, citing criticisms of Achilles' grief by Plato and Zoilus, and the rebuttal of Zenodorus; see also scholia A on *Iliad* 18.22–35.

97. The importance of Servius as an early witness to ancient scholarship, in comparison to the marginal scholia found in medieval manuscripts of Homer, is stressed by Fraenkel 1949, 153.

is shown by "they possess a fiery vigor" [*Aeneid* 6.730]) and is considered to be extinguished in the sea, that is, by its opposite element. (Servius, *Commentary on Vergil's Aeneid* 1.93)

One could easily believe that Servius' source conflated material from separate commentaries on the *Iliad* and *Odyssey*, since Servius' note reproduces some of the language found in the *Iliad* scholia and gives a fuller explanation of the elemental theory behind the dismal character of death by drowning that is merely hinted at in the *Odyssey* scholia. On the other hand, Servius does not connect Aeneas' outburst with that of Achilles, and it may just be that his entry depends ultimately on a fuller version of the note on the *Odyssey*. Even that would be interesting, however, because the Greek scholia show that the *Iliad* and *Odyssey* passages were linked in the minds of Homer's ancient critics, who criticized Achilles for an ethical lapse (which Aeneas repeats) while praising Odysseus. There is nothing surprising in that, but it raises the possibility, or I would say the likelihood, that the *Aeneid*, by alluding to both Homeric passages, is in a sense alluding to a commonplace of Homeric criticism that many readers would know.[98] This in turn means that recognizing the similarities between Aeneas' outburst and that of Achilles would hardly have been out of the question—particularly since Aeneas quotes Achilles' "Battle against the River" almost as specifically as he cites his own face-off with Diomedes.[99]

We will notice further traces indicating that Aeneas' poetic memory of Troy includes Achilles' speech. Before that, to conclude this section, we must reckon with a very brief passage in Aeneas' speech that radiates both intertextual and intratextual energy. Again it will be useful to quote the Latin first:

mēne‿Īlĭăcīs | ōccūmbĕrĕ | cāmpis
nōn **pŏ**tŭīsse...
That I couldn't have fallen on the plains of Ilium... (*Aeneid* 1.97–98)

mēne‿īncēptō | dēsīstĕrĕ | uīctam
nēc **pōs**se‿Ītalia Teucrorum auertere regem?

Shall I withdraw in defeat from what I've begun,
unable to keep the king of the Trojans from Italy? (*Aeneid* 1.37–38)

---

98. Mühmelt 1965 believes that similar passages in ancient commentaries reflect the standardized, rote memorization that was typical of grammatical education. My own view is that in certain especially striking cases, it is more likely that one commentator is quoting a specific, written source. In this case, however, I would say that Mühmelt may well be correct.

99. It is worth remembering that the vehicle of a simile from the Iliadic "Battle against the River" contributes a point of agricultural instruction in the *Georgics*: see Farrell 1991, 211, with further references.

Here—as Fowler was first to notice—Aeneas echoes not just this or that passage of Homer, but the first word of the *Iliad* as a whole, responding to, recalling (*refert*), and confirming the presence of the specifically Iliadic exordium that Juno had pronounced upon her own entry into the *Aeneid*.[100]

I noted above that Aeneas, like Juno, is pulled in two directions, one represented by the *Odyssey*, the other by the *Iliad*, and I have been exploring ways in which the narrative seems to require Aeneas to become the hero of a proto-Odyssey, even though he is an Iliadic character obsessed with Iliadic memories. The fact that his first words echo Juno's in echoing the first word of the *Iliad* points to his predicament, and his reaction to the "Odyssean" storm that he is experiencing underlines it. Joy Connolly has built on Fowler's observation about the similarity between Juno's and Aeneas' initial utterances to emphasize how the hero "laments the limits placed on his will using the word *mene*, which he, like her, elides with a word that begins with 'I' (in his case, the dramatically loaded word *Iliacis*), creating a combination that ... may be a punning reference to the first word of the *Iliad*, *menis* or wrath."[101] To this we can add that Aeneas, like Juno, begins his Iliadic utterance in mid-line (see above); that he wishes to have died at a time before the death of Achilles, even before Achilles killed Hector—at a time when Troy's doom had not been sealed, in other words, when victory still seemed possible. But there is more. When we realize that Aeneas, like Juno, not only alludes to the first word of the *Iliad* but cites a number of that poem's most memorable moments (not omitting explicit or implicit reference to both of the most important episodes in which he himself appears), we see that Aeneas, too, can be regarded as harboring the metapoetic ambitions of a would-be, and rather self-interested (not to say, obsessive) narrator.[102] Connolly, again, puts it well: "These passages are more than verbal echoes: they disclose the two desires that Juno and Aeneas share. First, she does not want Rome to be founded; and he does not want Rome to be founded.... Second, Juno wants Aeneas dead, along with the rest of the Trojans; and Aeneas wants to be dead, along with the rest of the Trojans."[103] This is just about right. Aeneas may not want the rest of the Trojans dead, certainly not in the same way that Juno does. Presumably, he would not mind if they had lived on without him, especially if his death had helped them to do so. But mainly, and just as much as Juno, he would prefer his

---

100. Fowler 1997, 260.

101. Connolly 2010, 409.

102. Aeolus speaks before Aeneas, but does not speak or act on his own authority, explicitly renouncing any agency whatsoever. Functionally, he offers the clearest possible contrast to characters like Juno or Aeneas, who want to be in a very different poem.

103. Connolly 2010, 409–10.

personal story to have ended within the confines of the *Iliad*. And it is eerie to realize that, if he could control the narrative of the poem that bears his name, he no less than Juno would prefer that it not be written at all.

The implications of all this are staggering. Upon his first appearance in the poem, the hero presents himself almost as a would-be Homeric narrator. Moreover, he looks shockingly like a Junonian narrator, as well, one who would prefer the entire story in which he is involved to have ended with the destruction of Troy—or, to be more exact, *before* the destruction of Troy, an event that Juno must have been delighted to watch, but that Aeneas wishes he had never lived to see. This makes him in an even more complete sense than Juno a character whose worldview is defined by the *Iliad*—indeed, one who regrets that his own life has extended beyond the confines of that poem. As if to make this point as clear as possible, he wishes that he had died not just in the *Iliad*, but quite early in it: specifically, in book 5, when Diomedes nearly did him in. Finally, it is extremely suggestive that Aeneas' memory of this Iliadic episode occurs in a passage in which he speaks words so similar to those of Odysseus in *Odyssey* 5. That *Leitzitat* or guide citation, as Knauer has remarked, appears to situate the hero at a very precise point in the plot of his personal Odyssey; but the reminiscence exists only in the mind of poet and reader. Aeneas cannot realize that he is speaking the same words as Odysseus, or that he is quoting the Homeric *Odyssey*, not least because, in narrative time, Odysseus has not yet spoken them.[104] Aeneas' initial speech thus opens up quite differing perspectives on (so to speak) his familiarity with the two great Homeric poems. In these terms, the *Iliad* is a work that Aeneas knows quite well, whereas the *Odyssey* is to him not only a closed book but one that has yet to be written. The *Iliad* tells a story through which Aeneas himself has lived and in which he wishes he had died, so that he would not have to endure living through what he cannot comprehend as his own, unfinished Odyssey.

What Is at Stake?

At this point it will be helpful to step back to gain a wider perspective. Our discussion has been concerned chiefly with formal considerations and with the light that they throw upon the motivation of certain characters. The most important of these characters are Juno and Aeneas, both of whom are peculiarly interested participants in this story. Juno's narrative preferences are utilitarian and selfish, those of Aeneas driven by trauma. What would a more disinterested perspective look like? In a larger sense, what would it mean to most

---

104. See the section entitled "Intertextual Chronology" below in this chapter.

of us, who are readers and not actual participants, what difference would it make if the *Aeneid* proved to be an Iliad instead of an Odyssey, or vice versa?

Horace on Iliadic and Odyssean Ethics

The answer to this question goes beyond issues of literary interpretation to those of ethical philosophy. To understand why, let us change focus and turn briefly to Horace, who in one of his verse epistles tells a young friend, Lollius Maximus, about the lessons one can learn from Homer.[105] As we will see, these lessons shed a very interesting light on the interpretive decisions that confront the reader of the *Aeneid*.

The poet of the Trojan War, Horace writes, teaches us what is fine or despicable, what is advantageous or not, better and more completely than do philosophers. The *Iliad*, which tells of the Greeks' clash with barbarians in a long war on account of Paris' illicit love affair, contains the emotional tides of foolish kings and nations. The Trojan hero Antenor advocates eliminating the cause of the conflict by returning Helen; but Paris rejects this good advice, because he will not let Antenor "force him" (as Horace ironically puts it) to rule in safety and live in comfort. The Greek hero Nestor works to quell the strife between Achilles and Agamemnon: the latter is afflicted by lust, both of them by anger. Treachery, guile, crime, lust, and anger cause the blunders committed inside and outside the walls of Troy.

On the other hand, Horace continues, as a useful model of what courage and wisdom can accomplish, Homer gives us Ulysses (the Roman Odysseus), who, after subduing Troy with his foresight, investigated the cities and cultures of many peoples, enduring many hardships over the broad sea as he strove to obtain a homecoming for himself and his companions, refusing to be sunk in a tide of disasters. You know, Horace tells Lollius, about the Sirens' songs and Circe's cups; if in foolish gluttony Ulysses had drunk those down, as his companions did, he'd have ended up base, witless, and enthralled to an immoral mistress, living like a dirty dog or a mud-wallowing pig. We ourselves, Horace concludes, are the rabble: Penelope's suitors, born to eat up the hero's substance, and Alcinous' slacker subjects, who are rather too devoted to their manicures and think it fine to sleep every day till noon, prolonging their nocturnal revelry until the harp falls silent.[106]

---

105. *Epistles* 1.2.1–31; lines 6–16 summarize the *Iliad*, 17–31 the *Odyssey*. On Horace's use of the *Odyssey* and its antecedents see Kaiser 1964; Moles 1985; Eidinow 1990; Perutelli 2006, 43–51. On the programmatic force of *Epistles* 1.2 see Citroni 2001; Cucchiarelli 2019, 209–36.

106. The text of line 31 is uncertain. Here I tentatively follow Mayer 1994, 116–17.

One purpose of this Homeric homily is surely to amuse: there is in such a brief summary of two massive and complex poems some of the same quality that one finds in our contemporary versions of five-minute Shakespeare and other parodies of the classics.[107] But it is Horace's practice, as he says elsewhere, "to tell the truth with a smile," and this is a case in point.[108] In fact, what he says here agrees closely with more serious authorities, and it deserves to be taken seriously, as well.

Let us begin with what Horace does not say. He does not praise Homer for his excellent plot construction, as Aristotle does in *Poetics*. He does not praise him as an exponent of that ineffable quality of "the sublime," as does pseudo-Longinus. He does not praise him for observing generic decorum, as Horace himself does in his *Art of Poetry*. Here Horace focuses not on literary or aesthetic qualities, but on ethical and moral lessons.[109] The *Iliad* shows what happens when men are ruled by their passions and fail to recognize not only what is right, but even what is in their own best interest. The *Odyssey* shows how one man alone, if guided by reason, can prevail while everyone around him acts like a fool. The Homeric poems offer patterns of behavior and moral lessons, few for imitation, many to avoid, all susceptible of abstraction and reapplication to whatever our own situations require. Reading Homer, in short, is for Horace the ultimate model of an ethical education.

Observe that Horace's differentiation between the *Iliad* and the *Odyssey* is extremely stark. Not only do the two poems offer contrasting ethical exempla, he argues, but the *Iliad* is dominated almost entirely by negative ones. Horace criticizes Achilles, the poem's principal hero, along with most of its other characters for indulging their passions in ways ruinous to themselves and their followers. The *Odyssey*, too, abounds in negative exempla; but Ulysses is not

---

107. M. J. Edwards 1992, 85 calls the passage "perhaps the most tendentious sketch of the Iliad ever written."

108. *Satires* 1.1.24. The character of Horace's satiric smile varies: he gives a much more bathetic summary of the *Iliad* at *Satires* 1.7.11–15 and adopts a much more ironic attitude towards Odysseus in *Satires* 2.5. Perutelli 2006, 48–50 rightly contrasts *Epistles* 1.2 with Horace's earlier, more overtly humorous treatments of the *Odyssey*.

109. The concepts on which Horace focuses are *pulchrum*, "beautiful" in an ethical sense, like the Greek *kalon*; *turpe*, "base" or "disgraceful"; and *utile*, "useful." The philosophers he mentions are Chrysippus, an important Stoic writer who quoted poets extensively in his treatises (so that people would refer jokingly to "Chrysippus' *Medea*" with reference to his frequent citations of Euripides' tragedy) and wrote *On the Right Way of Reading Poetry* in two books; and Crantor, an Academic who wrote especially on moral and ethical philosophy and was a great admirer of Homer as well as of Euripides. See Diogenes Laertius, *Lives of Eminent Philosophers* 4.26, 7.180 in Hicks 1925, vol. 1, 402–3 and vol. 2, 288–89.

among them. Quite the opposite: he differs both from the heroes of the *Iliad* and from other characters in the *Odyssey* by mastering his passions so that his intelligence may prevail. All the rest that Horace names—the Sirens, Circe, the hero's crew, the suitors, the Phaeacians—represent either temptations to avoid or examples of what happens to those who cannot resist them.[110] As a result, Ulysses emerges as the chief positive exemplum in Homer, the one man of good sense, the single hero truly worthy of emulation.[111]

Readers familiar with representations of Achilles and Odysseus in canonical poetry may be puzzled by the contrast that Horace draws. That said, the fact that he does contrast them is hardly surprising. The *Iliad* and the *Odyssey* themselves each celebrate the particular qualities of their respective heroes, and have been seen as antithetical in this respect.[112] In Greek the contrast can be represented pointedly in lexical terms. Odysseus' "cunning intelligence" and "circumspection" are denoted by *mêtis*; its near-homonym *mênis* is also its opposite, Achillean anger, which is related to *menos*, a synonym of *biê*, "force." Authors of the "higher" genres tended to prefer Achilles to Odysseus. Pindar, for instance, goes so far as to blame Homer for making Odysseus seem worthy to inherit Achilles' arms, partly to gratify addressees who claimed descent from Ajax, but also because Ajax and Achilles better exemplify the straightforward ethical ideals of Pindar's victory songs.[113] But even in the *Iliad* Achilles embodies unsurpassed courage and capacity for physical force to a troubling

---

110. Works on topics like *The Cyclops*, *Circe*, and *Odysseus*, lost but known from the title catalogues preserved by Diogenes Laertius, are well represented among the moralizing essays written by various followers of Socrates. Murray 2008, 14–15 characterizes the early fourth century BCE as the period "that created a general conception of monarchy that influenced the rest of antiquity."

111. In *Odes* 1.6 Horace adopts a more jaundiced perspective on "shifty Ulysses" (*duplicis . . . Ulixei* 7) as well as Achilles (using the coarse word *stomachum* for Achilles' "anger" in the preceding line); see Ahern 1991. Of course, Horace is deprecating the entire genre of epic poetry as a way of emphasizing the importance of his lyric project.

112. Nagy 1979 represents the two poems as the products of ideologically opposed poetic traditions. See also Edwards 1985, who argues that the *Odyssey* responds to the primacy of Achilles in the *Iliad* by promoting Odysseus as an alternative type of hero. D. Cairns 2015 shows that the Iliadic Odysseus is a constructive foil to the less able Agamemnon and that the character informs later kingship theory. I discuss some less admirable aspects of the Iliadic Odysseus in two sections of chapter 3, "A Leadership Vacuum" ("The Odyssean *Iliad*, Part 1: 'Embassy' and 'Doloneia'") and "The Reader's Sympathies" ("The Odyssean *Iliad*, Part 2: Words and Deeds").

113. See Pindar, *Nemean Odes* 7.17–30, 8.18–34, both poems for victors from Aegina. These are the only odes in which Odysseus is named, both times to disparage him. Pindar mentions Ajax in at least five other odes, Achilles in at least ten, always to praise them.

and even frightening extent.[114] Aeschylus, Sophocles, and Euripides were more ambivalent about Achilles' angry, violent nature, but they generally saw him as the greatest and most irreplaceable of heroes, nevertheless.[115] Conversely, they tended to treat Odysseus, for all the evident appeal of the Homeric archetype, as a highly ambivalent figure in ethical terms, often assigning him the role of "stage villain," as W. B. Stanford memorably put it.[116] Under these conditions, the contrast that Horace draws between the two Homeric poems and their respective heroes would have been more or less unthinkable. At about the end of the 5th century BCE, however, in large part under the influence of Socrates and several of his closest followers, a decisive reorientation of attitudes took place. These intellectuals, even more than the earlier tragedians, were troubled by Achilles' inflexibility and solipsism.[117] At the same time, Odysseus came to be exalted precisely for his extraordinary adaptability and versatility.[118] The significance of this peripeteia can hardly be exaggerated. Silvia Montiglio has documented how quickly the situation changed and with what long-lasting results.[119] In spite of the major differences that existed among rival philosophical schools, throughout the Hellenistic and Roman periods the intelligent, adaptable Odysseus was praised as an ethical paradigm in implicit and sometimes explicit contrast to the obstinate Achilles. The difference between them came to involve not only Odysseus' cunning intelligence (*mêtis*) in contrast to Achilles' capacity for violence, but also the self-control and circumspection of the former in contrast to the latter's uncontrollable anger (*mênis*). Montiglio focuses mainly on the more abundant evidence for this tradition in Greek culture, but even the highly fragmentary remains of archaic Latin literature attest the impact of these attitudes on poets like Livius Andronicus, Gnaeus Naevius,

---

114. In book 11 Nestor effectively equates Achilles' self-absorption and lack of pity for his fellow warriors with his "virtue" (*aretês* 763), complaining to Patroclus that Achilles alone will profit from it. Patroclus himself, addressing Achilles, later calls his rage (*cholos*) "a dreadful virtue" (*ainaretê* 16.31). See King 1987, 13–28.

115. See King 1987, 50–104; Michelakis 2002.

116. Stanford 1954, 102–17.

117. King 1987, 104–9.

118. See Lampert 2002. The philosopher Antisthenes, an associate of Socrates, argued that the first word of the *Odyssey*, *andra* (the accusative form of *anêr*, "man"), referred to *andreia*, etymologically "manliness" but in a larger sense "courage" and then "virtue" more generally. In view of its modifier *polytropon*, "versatile," Antisthenes claimed, Homer was equating "manliness" and "versatility": see Montiglio 2011, 20–37. A similar development later took place with Latin *vir* "man" and *virtus* "courage, manliness," as is reflected in modern derivatives like "virtue": see McDonnell 2006.

119. Montiglio 2011.

Quintus Ennius, Marcus Pacuvius, and Lucius Accius.[120] By the first century BCE, we find Cicero, in clear imitation of how earlier Greek philosophers had interpreted Homer and the tragedians, making ethical arguments with reference to Achilles and Ulysses as they appear in archaic Latin poetry.[121] The evidence is clear that Roman intellectuals were influenced by the philosophical preference for Ulysses as an ethical hero.[122]

When Horace cites the philosophers Crantor (335–275 BCE) and Chrysippus (279–206 BCE), both of Soli, he places himself squarely in this tradition. Of particular relevance is the fact that Horace's perspective on Homer's principal heroes is entirely characteristic of the tradition as a whole.[123] His letter to Lollius Maximus is consistent with a perspective on Achilles and Odysseus in ethical philosophy that had been prevalent for about three centuries. It happens that the poetry book in which it appears was made public about a year before Vergil died, when the *Aeneid* must already have reached a form very much like the one in which we have it today. This is not to say that the attitudes voiced by Horace agree with those explored in the *Aeneid*. Rather, Horace's poem is a precious witness to the horizon of expectations that he and other literary people of the Augustan period will have brought to the ethical evaluation of Iliadic and Odyssean heroism. In these terms, it would not be surprising if the first readers of the *Aeneid* expected to find in it a celebration of qualities such as endurance, self-restraint, perspicacity, and adaptability, and not a celebration of hyperbolic emotion and capacity for extreme violence. And we can be confident, when the poem begins in a way that has signaled to different students of the poem either a specifically Iliadic or Odyssean orientation, that those first readers would have noticed that they were being confronted with an unlikely combination or else an explicit choice, and that they understood the ethical issues at stake.

Horace on Ethical Citizenship

A second aspect of Horace's ethical instruction involves a contrast between the *Iliad* and the *Odyssey* as poems that focus on the public and private spheres, respectively, but the reality is more complex than that. Horace presents the

---

120. On the reception of Achilles and Odysseus in archaic Latin poetry see the section of chapter 2 entitled "Historical Intertexts in Roman Epics" and Farrell 2021a.

121. Perutelli 2006, 17–29; Farrell 2021a.

122. Perutelli 2006, 30–42 regards Catullus' sympathetic portrayal of, and identification with, the sufferings of Odysseus as an important precursor to the Ulysses of the *Aeneid*. I very much agree with what he says about Catullus, but offer a somewhat different perspective regarding the *Aeneid*.

123. On Chrysippus' opinion of Achilles in particular see Cullyer 2008.

Iliad as a tale "of foolish kings and peoples," and it is the kings whom he repeatedly censures for behaving as if they were private individuals, responsible to no one but themselves, when in fact they are answerable for the welfare of their followers. Their shortcomings are immediately magnified into failures of leadership for which both the Greeks and the Trojans suffer. In contrast, the hero of the *Odyssey* is not criticized for losing his entire crew and saving only himself. As Horace tells the story, there is in Ulysses' behavior no tension between public and private responsibilities. The hero's ethical position is exemplary, and any failure rests with his comrades, who are unable, or perhaps just unwilling, to follow his lead. A clear implication of Horace's summary is that in the face of such reckless intransigence, a man of good sense is not obliged to perish while trying to rescue all those around him, but is finally under a higher obligation to save himself, at least.

The ethical tradition on which Horace draws puts a particular emphasis on heroes as paradigms of "kingly" behavior. Thus modern scholars speak of "kingship theory" with reference to the generic title of numerous treatises "on kingship" (*peri basileias*).[124] Again the roots of kingship theory go back to the time of Socrates and his followers, including Plato and Xenophon, all of whom in different ways debated the extent to which Homer's "kings" offered ethical models of engaged citizenship under a democratic or an oligarchic constitution. In the late Classical period, Aristotle dedicated a treatise *On Kingship* to his pupil Alexander the Great. The rise of powerful kingdoms under Alexander's successors and their rivals in the Hellenistic period gave relevance to theoretical and practical reflections on citizenship under a monarchy, not just for the individual who happened to be king, but for anyone who wished to play an active role in such a government. The fact that some Roman poets of the Middle Republic had absorbed these lessons about "kingship" underlines the flexibility of kingship theory and anticipates the intervention of a later Greek philosopher whom Horace does not cite. The single essay on kingship best known to modern readers must be "On the Good King according to Homer" by Philodemus of Gadara. Oswyn Murray has shown in detail how Philodemus adjusts his observations about the political and social dynamics among Homer's "kings" to suit the realities that prevailed among the Roman senatorial elite in the mid-first century BCE.[125] The philosopher does so to make the essay interesting and useful to his friend and patron Lucius Calpurnius Piso, to whom he may have presented it on the occasion of Piso's

---

124. Murray 2008, 14–15.
125. Murray 1965, 176–78.

inauguration as consul in 60 BCE or shortly afterwards when he was proconsul in Macedonia, about a generation before Horace composed his epistle.[126] There is every likelihood that Horace knew Philodemus' essay and that Vergil did, as well. Vergil, in fact, is actually named as dedicatee of another ethical essay by Philodemus, *On Flattery*, along with Plotius Tucca, Lucius Varius Rufus, and Publius Quintilius Varus.[127] All of these men, like Horace, were members of Maecenas' literary sodality.[128] We need not consider Philodemus to be the poets' philosophical guru, but it is obvious that their acquaintance with him was real.[129] Nor does Horace have to cite "On the Good King according to Homer" to imply that Homer's ethical teachings are directly applicable to the contemporary Roman scene.

In fact, it is not at all difficult to read Horace's summary of the Homeric poems as a political allegory with contemporary reference. He presents the *Iliad* as a tale of civic failure. The Greeks and Trojans are both ruled by a plurality of kings—that is, by aristocracies or oligarchies, or even factions. The most powerful leaders on both sides ignore the sound advice of their nominal peers and indulge their passions, bringing disaster upon their respective peoples. In contrast, Horace does not call Ulysses a king, nor are his men mere subjects: they are his "companions" (*socii*), which implies a comparatively unhierarchical form of government.[130] However, Ulysses is his companions' ethical superior: unlike them, he was not so foolish as to drain Circe's potions.[131] We

---

126. Farrell 2020, 236; fuller surveys of possible dates in Murray 1965, 78–180; Braund 1996, 31–34; Asmis 1991, 1 note 1; Fish 2018, 154.

127. The (partial) names are written on a scrap of papyrus found in Herculaneum (*PHerc*. Paris, 2); see Gigante and Capasso 1989.

128. Other poems of Horace besides the one we are considering seem indebted to Philodemus, such as *Satires* 1.5 and 1.10: see Michels 1944; Greenberg 1958; Sider 1997, 19–23; Armstrong et al. 2004.

129. Horsfall 1995, 82; Cairns 2004, 314; Farrell 2014, especially 87–89.

130. Homer habitually speaks of Odysseus' *hetairoi*, "companions," which in Latin would be *comites*. In Horace's time this word had no political meaning, whereas *socii* meant "allies," primarily in a military or diplomatic sense.

131. *stultus* in *Epistles* 1.2.24 may reflect *nêpios*, "fool, foolish," which Homer uses to describe Odysseus' companions very prominently at *Odyssey* 1.8 and frequently thereafter, but Horace has already called the kings and peoples of the *Iliad* as well *stultorum* (8); and at *Epistles* 1. 1.41–42 he writes, "excellence (*virtus*) is the avoidance of vice, and the beginning of wisdom is to lack foolishness (*stultitia*)." In *Epistles* 1.6.61–63 Odysseus' crew are demoted from *socii* to the virtually instrumental *remigium* and are charged with caring more about pleasure (*voluptas*) than about their homeland (*patria*).

ourselves, Horace says, are no better than they or than Penelope's suitors and the pleasure-loving subjects of Alcinous. It would be quite in keeping with Horace's more overtly political poetry to find in this contrast between Iliadic and Odyssean kingship a comment on the failure of the rival camps that dominated Rome's Late Republican and Triumviral governments, and on Augustus' subsequent success in emerging from such confusion in a way that would give his people a chance to save themselves, if they would only continue to follow his lead. Characteristically, Horace worries that contemporary Romans may not be up to the challenge.

The political orientation of Horace's Homeric homily permits us to draw a second inference. His reliance on kingship theory will have suggested to his readers ethical lessons not only for personal edification but also for the common good. Here as well a parallel with the *Aeneid* is easy to draw. Since antiquity it has been taken for granted that "Vergil's intention is to imitate Homer and to praise Augustus on the basis of his ancestors."[132] Horace's epistle shows how a poem informed by mainstream ethical perspectives on Homeric heroism might offer implicit praise to Augustus with reference to Roman politics in the late 1st century BCE. It is not far-fetched to imagine that the first readers of the *Aeneid* would have expected something similar. The question is whether that is what they got.

It is hard to believe that when Horace wrote his epistle he was unaware that Vergil's work was nearing completion. It would be entirely like Horace to issue a "response" to his friend's masterpiece before most people could even read it. How could he, as a fellow poetic craftsman, resist the opportunity to scoop Vergil by combining the *Iliad* and *Odyssey* into a single poetic structure in just twenty-six lines—written, no doubt, in much less time than the eleven years that Vergil had spent on the *Aeneid*? It also seems important that Horace's almost doctrinaire representation of kingship theory does nothing to resolve the differences between Homer's two masterpieces and their principal heroes; rather, he greatly accentuates them. Did Horace imagine Vergil as aiming to combine these incompatible paradigms into one plot and the single figure of Aeneas? Was he "helpfully" reminding a fellow craftsman just how difficult a trick that would be? Or was Horace showing his friend the correct way to handle the Homeric poems—by adopting the dichotomous perspective that his epistle exemplifies? However one may answer these questions, did Horace himself emphasize this dichotomy to such an extent because he knew that Vergil was doing exactly the same thing or that he was taking a very different approach?

132. Servius, *Commentary on Vergil's Aeneid*, preface.

Reflections on Juno's Aeneid *in the Light of Horace's Homer*

Whatever Horace may be hinting about the reception of Homeric ethics in the *Aeneid,* his epistle to Lollius Maximus can help us understand why Juno, or anyone, might expect the *Aeneid* to favor Odyssean values. In terms of ethical heroism, Juno may well share the assumptions of ancient Roman readers that a poem about Aeneas would praise the Trojan hero not as a second Achilles, violent and angry, but as another Odysseus, prudent and circumspect. This general preference sheds additional light on Juno's own Iliadic preferences. Above all, she wants to prevent Aeneas from becoming the singular hero who prevails against all odds, and she wants everyone on all sides to be ruled not by their reason, but by their passions, just as she is ruled by her own. That, in addition to Juno's perceived self-interest, is a large part of what is at stake in the Homeric battle for the ethical identity of the *Aeneid* as an Iliad or an Odyssey and for the heroic identity of Aeneas himself.

The stakes for Juno, then, are high; but for the reader, they are really much higher. According to a long-established consensus among ethical philosophers, Odysseus and not Achilles is the superior model of "kingship." The idea that the *Aeneid* combines both of Homer's masterpieces into a stable, harmonious whole is, in fact, much less plausible than the likelihood that the new poem must be one or the other, *either* an Iliad *or* an Odyssey, and not both. If the *Aeneid* it is to be another Odyssey, then it would make sense to read it, in the light of ancient kingship theory, as praising its hero; if another *Iliad,* then the opposite. Interpreting the *Aeneid* in this way is therefore obviously consequential in a literary sense and also in philosophical terms. Offering the reader a choice between incompatible possibilities is one of the properties that makes the poem such a powerful meditation on the human condition and an enduring touchstone of personal as well as public values. An important corollary both for ancient readers and also for ourselves is that Aeneas is the legendary ancestor of Augustus, and that the reader's estimate of the hero reflects on his descendant. To represent Aeneas as another Odysseus is to imply, as I have suggested Horace implies, that Augustus is like the better of Homer's heroes; and vice versa. Everyone, whether as narrator or reader, will evidently have to choose.

Intertextual Chronology

In spite of the extreme confusion, at all levels, that Juno creates with her storm, with Aeneas' landfall some sense of order seems to have been restored. Just as Odysseus survives a storm and washes up in the coast of Scheria, home of the Phaeacians, so Aeneas lands in Africa, home of the Carthaginians. The hero's experiences at Dido's court will closely track those of Odysseus at the court of

Alcinous. Indeed, as Knauer argues, Aeneas' departure and subsequent adventures, including his arrival first in Latium and then at Pallanteum, and even his battle against the pretender Turnus to vindicate his right to marry Lavinia, can all be read as following the course of Odysseus' return to Ithaca, his vanquishing of the suitors, and his reunion with Penelope. This perspective on the *Aeneid* is freely available to anyone who has read the *Odyssey*. Someone to whom it is not available is Aeneas. The point goes beyond the fact that Aeneas has not read the *Odyssey* or heard the story told; it is rather that most of the *Odyssey*, in narrative time, has not yet happened. Everyone knows this, but very seldom does anyone take account of it.[133] It is not always important to do so, but for our purposes it most definitely is. The reason is very simple: this is another, very clear and unambiguous difference between the two Homeric poems as models of the *Aeneid*.

In the most basic sense, of course, the *Iliad* and *Odyssey* assumed their characteristic forms many centuries before Vergil wrote. In literary–historical terms and from the perspective of readers they are both, in their entirety, anterior to the *Aeneid*, which alludes to them constantly and pervasively. From the perspective of characters within the *Aeneid*, one could say, the same is true of the *Iliad*. From beginning to end, the entire plot of the *Iliad* takes place before the earliest events that belong to the main plot of the *Aeneid*. With the *Odyssey*, things are quite different. Whereas the plot of the *Iliad* ends in the year that Troy fell, the plot of the *Odyssey* begins later in that same year, after the fall of the city; and so does that of the *Aeneid*. This means that the plots of the *Odyssey* and the *Aeneid* are broadly contemporary. It is not always easy to synchronize events in the two poems with great precision, but the few points of obvious synchronism that do exist are very informative.

The first of these synchronic moments is registered at the very end of *Aeneid* 1. After peppering Aeneas with questions about what happened during the Trojan War, Dido asks the hero to tell her about the fall of the city and the entire story of his wanderings since that time.[134] In making her request, Dido observes that seven summers have passed since the city fell (1.755–56).[135] Since

---

133. Barchiesi 1984/2015, Cairns 1989, and Dekel 2012 are notable exceptions, as I discuss in the Introduction above.

134. Knauer 1964, 169–72.

135. The accuracy of this statement is complicated by a famous interpretive crux cited by Servius, *Commentary on Vergil's Aeneid* 5.626 as one of the "unsolvable" problems of the *Aeneid*, which he believes Vergil would have cleared up if he had lived to finish the poem: see Dyson 1996; O'Hara 2007, 93 note 39. The relative dating of Aeneas' wanderings and those of Odysseus is not affected by this problem.

Odysseus begins the analogous tale of his own wanderings (his "Apologoi") with the fall of Troy, we can assume that both he and Aeneas began their adventures at approximately the same time. Now, seven years later, Aeneas has arrived at Carthage and is being royally entertained by Dido, while Odysseus, who arrives in Ithaca ten years after the fall of Troy, is right in the middle of a seven-year period of languishing on the island of Ogygia as Calypso's toy boy.[136] That means—crucially for our purposes—that Odysseus has not built his raft, set sail for Ithaca, been spotted by Poseidon, nearly drowned in a storm, washed up on the Scherian coast, or been hospitably received and entertained by Alcinous. All of that is in store for him, but all of it (*mutatis mutandis*) happens to Aeneas *before* it happens to Odysseus.

A second synchronism is established in book 3 when Aeneas rescues Achaemenides from the Cyclops Polyphemus. The castaway, formerly one of Ulysses' companions, informs the hero that he has been living in fear of being eaten by Polyphemus since the Ithacan's departure some three months previously (3.645–48). In the *Odyssey*, before his encounter with Polyphemus, Odysseus had undergone only two other adventures en route from Troy. The first of these, his disastrous attack on the Ciconians in Thrace, takes place (so to speak) in the real world; the second occurs after a storm struck his ship as he was rounding Cape Malea in the south of Greece and drove him for ten days to the land of the Lotus Eaters. After that, he remains in the separate reality of his "Apologoi" until the Phaeacians deposit him on Ithaca some ten years later. His next adventure after the Lotus Eaters is with Polyphemus, and in the *Aeneid* it was when Ulysses was making his escape from this monster that he left Achaemenides behind, according to Achaemenides himself. When Aeneas rescues Achaemenides, three months have passed, during which time Ulysses has presumably gone on to his other adventures, including those with Aeolus, the Laestrygonians, Circe, his journey to the land of the dead, the Sirens, Scylla, the Cattle of the Sun, and Charybdis, eventually to find himself on Ogygia with Calypso. By that time he will have lost all of his companions. Therefore, only Achaemenides survives to tell of Ulysses' few adventures up to and including that of the Cyclops, but even he can know nothing of the later adventures. Aeneas for his own part has already had a

---

136. Odysseus is away from Ithaca during the ten years of the Trojan War (*Iliad* 2.134–35 etc.) and a subsequent ten years of wandering (*Odyssey* 2.170–76; 17.327; 23.97–103, 166–72). The hero spends seven years of his wanderings with Calypso (*Odyssey* 7.259–66). The bulk of his adventures therefore make up the first three years of his wanderings, while Aeneas' own wanderings take seven years (or more; see the preceding note).

number of quasi-Odyssean adventures of his own. He has stopped at Thrace (where he tried to found a city instead of sacking one), Delos, Crete, the Strophades, Actium, and Buthrotum; and then, after giving wide berth to Scylla and Charybdis, he landed in Sicily and found Achaemenides. All that remains is for him to continue skirting the southern and western coast of Sicily until he arrives at Drepanum, his final port of call, before he tells Dido, "I left this place and a god drove me to your shores" (3.715). Thus Aeneas had almost completed his wanderings at a time when Odysseus was just beginning his own. That, and not any further chronological fine-tuning between the *Aeneid* and the *Odyssey*, is what seems to be the point.[137]

If we give this fact its full weight, we may certainly continue to say that the *Aeneid* "follows" the *Odyssey* in its representation of Aeneas' wanderings, but it is not quite right to say that Aeneas "follows" Odysseus. The fact is that Aeneas *precedes* Odysseus in many respects. Not all: Aeneas has not yet, in the seventh year of his wanderings, visited the underworld, whereas Odysseus must have done so, even if the *Aeneid* takes no notice of this fact, since Odysseus should be languishing on Ogygia with Calypso by the time of Aeneas' descent. Nevertheless, by the time Aeneas returns to the upper world in the seventh or eighth year of his wanderings, Odysseus will still have at least two years to spend with Calypso before she releases him in the tenth year since the fall of Troy. Not until after that will Poseidon's storm strike him, or will he make his way to Scheria, recite his "Apologoi" to Alcinous, and be taken by the Phaeacians to Ithaca, where, with the help of Eumaeus, Telemachus, Penelope, and above all Athena, he will re-establish himself as king. In the meantime, Aeneas will return from the underworld, make his way to Latium, request Lavinia's hand in marriage, forge military alliances among the peoples of Italy, and defeat Turnus in single combat. He will then rule as king of Lavinium for three years, as specified in Jupiter's prophecy to Venus (1.261–66). The reader, therefore, may consider the *Aeneid* a belated imitation of the *Odyssey*, but in the story of the *Aeneid*, Aeneas himself is not a belated imitator of Ulysses. Rather, he undergoes the trial of a heroic journey with virtually no knowledge of Ulysses' experiences, even anticipating those experiences in many respects.

Attention to this chronology makes possible at least three observations.

---

137. It will be noted that fine-tuning is actually impossible. Odysseus completes all of his other adventures within three years before landing on Ogygia, but Aeneas does not rescue Achaemenides until he has been wandering for almost seven years. Does the *Aeneid* create this discrepancy to cast doubt on the veracity of Odysseus' "Apologoi" in comparison to Aeneas' more "realistic" account of his wanderings?

First, this sort of allusive relationship partakes in what Alessandro Barchiesi has called the "future reflexive" mode.[138] From an authorial point of view, this now familiar form of intertextual rivalry allows the belated poem to exploit its privileged chronological perspective to improve upon or outdo its model in some way. Here one could say that the hero of the *Aeneid* anticipates the hero of the *Odyssey* at virtually every point in their adventures. One could even say that in the time that it took Odysseus to reclaim his place on Ithaca, Aeneas not only reached Italy but founded a new city there, provided for Ascanius to succeed him as king, earned divinity, and perhaps even experienced apotheosis. The belated poem not only improves upon its model, but "anticipates" it as well, not in literary–historical time but in that of mythological narrative, since its story is set in large part before that of its model. I am not aware that much has been made of this aspect in the Homeric program of the *Aeneid*, but it seems worthy of notice. However, that is not what interests me most about it in this context.

The second observation, which is much more germane to my argument, involves the ethical inferences that can be drawn from this kind of allusion. Although the Homeric *Odyssey* can serve as a model for the *Aeneid*, within the story Aeneas cannot emulate the hero of that poem, first because he knows virtually nothing of his counterpart's post-war adventures, and second because the Greek hero's homecoming has not even happened yet.[139] We may judge Aeneas harshly, and perhaps we should, but not because he failed to learn from the resourceful Odysseus, since he had no possibility of doing so.

My third observation has to do with what one might call intertextual psychology. In the previous paragraph, I wrote as if Aeneas, had he actually known about all of Ulysses' adventures and followed in his wake, might have profited from his example, like a reader of the *Odyssey*, much as Horace advises Lollius Maximus to do. To imagine Aeneas as a reader of Homer is, if you like, a critical license, not unlike treating Juno as a rival to the narrator of the *Aeneid*. But just as that license amounts to little more than a modest extension of Juno's role as a blocking figure, the same can be said of treating Aeneas as a reader who might learn something from heroic example. He cannot learn from Homer, of course, but he does not have to *read* heroic stories because he has both heard them sung by epic bards and has even lived through some of them himself.

---

138. Barchiesi 1993 actually speaks of two such modes, one in which a text has a dramatic date earlier than that of another text to which it alludes, and a second mode in which the alluding text seems to acknowledge its priority. The *Aeneid* employs both of these modes vis-à-vis the *Odyssey*.

139. See note 136 above.

Not all, however; for in Homeric terms, Aeneas is analogous to a reader who is an expert in the *Iliad* but knows nothing of the *Odyssey*.[140] That is to say, he has lived through and witnessed the events of the one poem, but knows virtually nothing of the other, parts of which have not yet taken place. This difference in the hero's "familiarity with Homer" could be seen as decisive for our understanding of Aeneas' psychology.[141] We have seen already and will see repeatedly that Aeneas experiences the narrative present in terms of the Iliadic past, even when we as readers "know" that the *Odyssey* is the "correct" point of reference. Even when we might think he is "wrong" to do so, Aeneas is predisposed to integrate new experiences according to the world that is familiar to him, the world of the *Iliad*, along with the values that are native to that world, of which Achilles is the definitive, and most frightening, exemplum.

With this insight, we have extended the idea that the *Aeneid* is an intertextual contest from analysis of the plot into ethical considerations and even into the psychology of the hero. How widely does the insight apply? What if the intertext could give us access not only to the hero's memory of specific events, or to the lack of it, but also, at least occasionally, to the hero's *unconscious* mind?

Enigmas of Arrival

To answer this question, let us consider the Homeric identity of Africa as it is elaborated through reference to several Odyssean arrival scenes. Individually, these references seem to place Aeneas in particular Homeric episodes. Together, they create a shifting pattern of possibilities that make Aeneas' Odyssey a much less straightforward thing than one might have supposed. The swirling nature of this arrival scene suggests that neither Aeneas nor the reader can expect either of Homer's epics to serve as a reliable roadmap for the *Aeneid*. There is nothing surprising in this, because, to paraphrase something that I wrote some time ago, the Vergilian intertext is not a skeleton key that unlocks the secret meaning of a poem, but rather a device that discloses vistas of interpretive possibility that would otherwise remain unglimpsed and inaccessible.[142] This particular sequence of allusions ought to confuse anyone who has read the *Odyssey*, because it puts Aeneas, who is arriving in just one place, in the position of Odysseus when he arrives in at least three and probably four

---

140. The notion of Aeneas as "in a sense" a reader of the *Iliad* is, as far as I know, first mooted in an *obiter dictum* of Barchiesi; see Fowler 1991, 33 note 51.

141. Schiesaro 2005 and 2008 pioneered this approach with reference to Dido; Schiesaro 2015 applies it to Aeneas.

142. Farrell 1997, 237.

different places. I take it, as well, that the reader's confusion is meant to reflect a certain cognitive dissonance on the hero's part—which he could never explain in these terms, of course—as he struggles to understand what has happened to him in the wake of Juno's storm.

As Knauer rightly notes, Juno's storm in *Aeneid* 1 is, so to speak, the same storm as that of Poseidon in *Odyssey* 6. Accordingly, Knauer considers Aeneas' subsequent adventures in books 1–7 to be, intertextually, those of the Greek hero in *Odyssey* 7–13. In a general sense, this is unarguably true. Differences there are, and Knauer is far more attentive to them than many critics; but he tends to explain them with reference to necessity, convenience, or some other such factor, rather than to any more dynamic hermeneutic significance they might have. My own view is that the intertextual *Aeneid* always invites interpretation in a way that goes well beyond utilitarian considerations. Let us test that assumption on the poem's treatment of several Homeric arrival scenes.

Intertextual Africa

Phorcys' Harbor on the Island of Ithaca

Immediately after the storm, Aeneas' arrival on the African coast is marked by an apparent *Leitzitat*. The battered Trojan fleet finds shelter in a harbor, and the narrator's description of it is an elaborate specimen of topothesia in which key details come from Homer's description of the harbor of Phorcys on Ithaca.[143] The suggestion seems to be that Aeneas, the wandering hero, has finally arrived at the place where he will accomplish his "homecoming"—not a literal one, as in Odysseus' case, but a definitive arrival and an end of wandering— presumably at the place where the gods intend for him to found his city. This putative *Leitzitat*, like the one that Juno pronounces when she bribes Aeolus to unleash his winds, is therefore misleading; but again like Juno's intervention, it is not merely that. It also makes a great deal of sense in at least two ways. One of these corresponds to the perspective of the reader and the other to that of Aeneas himself.

From the reader's point of view, it is not entirely clear how unexpected it should be to find Aeneas arriving in Africa. In terms of any realistic geography, it should be rather surprising; in terms of epic precedent, perhaps less so. To

---

143. *Aeneid* 1.157–69; see Pöschl 1950/1962, 141–43; Buchheit 1963, 183–85; Knauer 1964, 244 note 2. Knauer himself places little emphasis on this correspondence, presumably because he considers Odysseus' arrival on Scheria as the relevant Homeric prooftext, just as he argues that Aeneas' arrival in Latium corresponds to Odysseus' return to Ithaca (1964, 228–39; 1964a, 76 and 78).

take the latter point first, Macrobius states that Juno's storm in the *Aeneid* imitates one that strikes Aeneas in Gnaeus Naevius' epic, *The Punic War*, which was composed about two hundred years before the *Aeneid*. We cannot be sure, but it is at least possible that Naevius' storm drove Aeneas to Africa and that he met Dido there.[144] If so, then the reader of the *Aeneid* might even expect Juno's storm to drive the hero to Carthage. On the other hand, to be told that the Trojans "turn towards the shores of Africa" just before they take refuge in an intertextual version of Phorcys' harbor on Ithaca ought to be very unexpected. The Trojans obviously did not settle in Africa, and for any reader of the *Aeneid*, the mere suggestion that Africa might be an intertextual Ithaca, a site of "homecoming," should be disorienting indeed.

From Aeneas' point of view, this *Leitzitat* functions rather differently. Surprise at finding himself specifically in Africa does not enter into it. He has no idea where he is. That much is made clear a bit later, once the hero has fed and encouraged his followers before passing a largely sleepless night and rising at the crack of dawn to find out where he might be (1.305–9). At that point the reader will have been told three times that the Trojans have landed in Africa (158, 226, 301) and once that they will be hospitably received at Carthage (298), which makes the gap between the reader's perspective and that of Aeneas very great. Further, while the reader may know that Aeneas visits Carthage in Naevius' poem, Aeneas evidently does not. At the very least, he shows no actual awareness of this.[145]

From a geographical point of view, Africa is almost the last place where Aeneas would expect to find himself. When the storm struck, the Trojans were

---

144. Macrobius, *Saturnalia* 6.2.31 in Kaster 2011, vol. 3, 58–59 states that the entire storm scene and its aftermath derive from Naevius' poem; see Servius, *Commentary on Vergil's Aeneid* 1.198 and also 4.9, where he reports that Dido and her sister Anna were both mentioned in *The Punic War*. In a comment on *Aeneid* 4.682 Servius cites a tradition that Anna and not Dido perished for love of Aeneas, but he does not explicitly connect this tradition to Naevius. See, variously, Buchheit 1963, 32–53; Wigodsky 1972, 29–34; Luck 1983, 267–75; Goldberg 1995, 54–55.

145. The fragmentary condition of *The Punic War* makes it impossible to guess how Aeneas' experiences in that poem might be reflected in the *Aeneid*. One might simply assume that the *Aeneid* "overwrites" *The Punic War* in this respect, and that however much the reader might discern a palimpsestic relationship between the two poems, the hero would not. On the other hand, if (say) the Naevian storm did not drive Aeneas to Africa, Aeneas' disorientation upon arriving there in the *Aeneid* could be considered an intertextual effect. In somewhat this way, when Aeneas later tells Venus that an entire day would not suffice for her to hear the "annals" of his sufferings (1.373), he unwittingly alludes to the version of those adventures contained in the *Annals* of Quintus Ennius (and also perhaps to Ennius' account of the Second Punic War in that same poem; so Giusti 2018, 226).

presumably near the Aeolian Islands, i.e., Aeolus' kingdom, where they would be especially vulnerable to any mischief caused by Aeolus' errant winds. Aeneas, having never sailed in those waters before, can only have known that he was heading east towards Italy, with the broad expanse of Sicily lying south of him all the way. After the storm, he made for the closest patch of dry land he could find. If one asks what land he thought this was, he might have guessed it was Sicily, and that he had been blown back to more or less the same place that he had just left. (For that matter, a reader who remembered Aeolus' role in the *Odyssey* might have expected this too.) Otherwise, the hero might have hoped that, by some great stroke of unaccustomed good fortune, he and his people had washed up on the shores of their promised land, after all: that this place was Italy—that they had arrived "home," at last.

This accessing of the reader's and of Aeneas' expectations is managed with great subtlety. The reader knows that for Aeneas to arrive in an Africa that is also this poem's Ithaca does not make sense. Aeneas does not even know where he is, has never landed on Ithaca, and would never think of Ithaca as a place of homecoming. Nevertheless, by inducing a state of cognitive dissonance in the reader, the narrator communicates the hero's unstated hopes in terms that the reader can comprehend, even if the hero cannot. Aeneas hopes that his wanderings, in spite of everything, are at an end, because that is exactly what, with each new landfall, he always hopes. The reader does not know this yet, because the point is mainly developed in book 3, as Aeneas tries over and over to put an end to his wandering by founding a city wherever he arrives, hoping that every arrival will be his last. In this sense, the reference to Phorcys' harbor is a kind of *Leitzitat*, but one that guides the reader towards an insight not so much about the course that the narrative is about to take, as about the hero's dreams and desires and the immense, ironic gulf between his continuing hope and the reader's certainty that this time, just as every other time right up to now, Aeneas will be disappointed.

More on that in a moment. First, to this reading of the harbor I would like to add one further observation. The signals (mis)informing the reader that the harbor of *Aeneid* 1 is an Ithacan harbor are extremely obvious and have been noted and discussed since antiquity.[146] Africa is not Ithaca, however; and even if that is no reason to scant the importance of this misleading correspondence, neither should it prevent us from seeking other possible points of reference.

---

146. See Macrobius, *Saturnalia* 5.3.8–19 in Kaster 2011, vol. 2, 246–47. The parallel is not mentioned by Servius, who states (*Commentary on Vergil's Aeneid* 1.159) that Vergil bases his description of the harbor on that of Carthago Nova in Spain, an idea now corroborated by Shi and Morgan 2015.

Odysseus puts into several harbors, but there is only one other that shares the particular topographical features of the Phorcys harbor (a pair of steep cliffs jutting out into the sea forming a narrow entrance and a deep recess).[147] That is the harbor of Telepylus, the land of the Laestrygonians, where Odysseus arrives immediately after the adventure with Aeolus that took him within sight of Ithaca, but no closer. So here, Aeneas moves from his own adventure with Aeolus to a harbor that resembles the one on Ithaca *and also* that of Telepylus. For the reader, who knows at least that Africa cannot be Ithaca (whatever Aeneas may be hoping), this could be a signal that the inhabitants of this place are as wild and dangerous as the Laestrygonians.[148] And why should they not be? Just before Aeneas goes exploring, the narrator specifies that Jupiter has sent Mercury to make sure that "the Carthaginians put off their wild nature and the queen above all assumes a peaceful attitude and kindly intention towards the Trojans."[149] For that matter, reference to the harbor of Telepylus as the beginning of a Laestrygonian adventure falls in the "right" position between Aeolus and Aeneas' hunting expedition, as the following chart makes clear:

Odyssey 10	*Aeneid* 1
Aeolus, 1–76	
release of the winds, 47–55	storm, 50–156
Laestrygonians, 80–132	
harbor near Telepylus, 87–94	harbor near Carthage, 157–79
Circe, 133–574	
deer hunt, encouraging speech, 144–76	deer hunt, encouraging speech, 180–222

---

147. G. Williams 1968, 637–44 emphasizes the multiplicity of Homeric and other elements that contribute to the Libyan harbor as a means of activating the reader's imagination. His approach, which I try to extend, is foundational to my own; see also Austin 1971, 71–78 on line 159; Dekel 2012, 81.

148. Some ancient authorities place the Laestrygonians either on Sicily (Hesiod, fragment 98.26 in Most 2018, 186–87; Thucydides, *History of the Peloponnesian War* 6.2.1) or in Campania (Cicero, *Letters to Atticus* 2.13.2; Horace, *Odes* 3.17), two of the more likely places that Aeneas might have made landfall after the storm; for more information, see Heubeck and Hoekstra 1989, 47–48 on *Odyssey* 10.80–132.

149. *Aeneid* 1.302–4. Similarly, Aeneas goes out to discover "who controls [the place] men or beasts, for what he sees is wild" (308), much as Odysseus states that beyond the harbor of Telepylus, "there the works of neither men nor oxen were to be seen" (*Odyssey* 10.98, a correspondence first noted by Germanus 1575, 169 on *Aeneid* 1.307–8).

One could thus say that, in order for Carthage to answer for Scheria, the Carthaginians must be converted, via Mercury's intervention, from savage Laestrygonians into welcoming Phaeacians—a conversion that readily suggests itself, in fact, since Homer's Laestrygonians are a kind of nightmare version of the Phaeacians, in any case.[150] There may even be a verbal token pointing to a relationship among these places in the form of a specific topographical similarity that the harbors of Africa, Telepylus, and Ithaca all share. The African harbor is formed by "enormous cliffs" (*vastae rupes*) with "twin peaks" (*gemini... scopuli*) that rise towards the sky on either side of it. These details evidently correspond to the Homeric "jutting headlands" (*problêtes... aktai*), which are found only in the *Odyssey* and only three times. Two of these figure in the harbors of Telepylus and Ithaca, while the other is applied to the reefs that give Odysseus trouble as he attempts to swim ashore on Scheria.[151]

Deer Hunting on the Island of Aeaea

Only one of the three Homeric coastlines that feature "jutting headlands" is Scheria, which does not have a harbor like Ithaca or Telepylus; and yet some version of Scheria is precisely where Juno's storm, an intertextual doublet of Poseidon's storm in *Odyssey* 5, "ought" to have driven Aeneas. The ensuing narrative does little to confirm that this is the case. As soon as the hero reaches land, he goes hunting for deer and lifts the spirits of his weary followers with venison and an encouraging speech.[152] This is not what Odysseus does when he washes up, alone and unconscious, on the beach at Scheria. Instead, it is what happens in a story he tells Alcinous, much later, about arriving on the island of Aeaea, the home of Circe. Both the verbal and the narrative parallels involved are just as clear as those of the storm episode, and they could just as

---

150. When Odysseus sends three of his men to inquire about the Laestrygonians, they first encounter the king's daughter, who has come out to perform her chores, and she points them the way to her father's house. There they find the queen, who summons the king from assembly, whereupon he seizes one of the men and prepares to eat him (*Odyssey* 10.116). See Thornton 1970, 20; Dougherty 2001, 410–41.

151. *Odyssey* 5.405, 10.89, 13.97–98. A similar phrase, *aktêi epi problêti* ("on a jutting headland") occurs in *Homeric Hymn* 7.3 (to Dionysus). Vergilians have not made much of the correspondences between the Homeric passages, as far as I am aware. The harbor on Aeaea where Odysseus takes shelter is more briefly described (10.140–41) and lacks the specific features that are ascribed to the other places.

152. Repetition of the phrase *talia voce refert* invites comparison with Aeneas' first speech (1.94, discussed above), emphasizing that this time Aeneas keeps his disappointment unspoken and even manages to feign a hopeful expression (*Aeneid* 1.208–9).

easily be taken as *Leitzitate*, as well. Specifically, they seem to indicate that Aeneas is about to make his way to the court not of another Alcinous, but of another Circe; and this inference too would be correct. When Aeneas introduces himself to Dido, she replies that she knows his story; and her speech, as Knauer shows, closely tracks that of Circe after Odysseus reveals his identity to her.[153] Not only that, but the alert reader may realize that Dido's words promise Aeneas much more than they seem to; for when she says, "come then, my young fellows, and enter our homes," she paraphrases Circe, who at a similar point in her speech says to Odysseus, "but come . . . we shall go to my bed."[154] Dido of course will eventually welcome Aeneas into her bed, as well, and her role as an avatar of Circe will continue to develop in other ways, both through her very close resemblance to Circe's niece, Medea, and through her use of magic when she attempts to keep Aeneas from leaving Carthage.[155]

Here we see that, from a certain distance, Knauer is perfectly right. After the storm, the narrative of the *Aeneid* proceeds along lines that, *grosso modo*, resemble the narrative of the *Odyssey*. One might even say that it was necessary after this arrival, or at least that it served the requirements of narrative decorum, for Aeneas to think of providing for the needs of his still substantial fleet, rather than to collapse, naked and exhausted like Odysseus, on the shore. "Moving" the arrival on Aeaea from the hero's own tale of his wanderings to the narrator's account of his arrival in Africa serves this purpose; but it is vastly overadequate to it. In particular, the narrator cannot make this change without suggesting that this Africa is like the Homeric Aeaea, and thus that Dido will be like Circe—as, in certain respects, she is. The two characters are not absolutely and definitively alike, any more than Aeneas is absolutely and definitively like Odysseus: intertextual poetics does not work like that. But the idea that there is a resemblance between Dido and Circe is, or should be, disquieting. In particular, we have seen that Horace, in his summary of the *Iliad* and the *Odyssey* as ethical texts, prominently mentions Circe as a potential snare for the hero, and as an actual snare for his companions, whom she turns into swine. Horace's allegorizing treatment of this episode rests on a rich tradition

---

153. *Aeneid* 1.613–30, *Odyssey* 10.323–35; see Knauer 1964, 178–79; 1964b, 71–72.

154. *Aeneid* 1.627, *Odyssey* 10.333–34.

155. See Preshous 1964–1965; Collard 1975; and especially Schiesaro 2008. Apollonius' Medea already owed much to the Homeric Circe, while Dido too is a version of the Homeric Circe at *Aeneid* 1.631–42 (see *Odyssey* 10.467–68; Knauer 1964, 205 note 2 and 377; Hunter 1993, 175–82; Nelis 2001, 116). Dido is also by implication an Apollonian Circe when Jupiter orders Aeneas' departure from Carthage (*Aeneid* 4.223–37, *Argonautica* 4.757–69; *Aeneid* 4.262–63, *Argonautica* 1.722–68; *Aeneid* 4.279–95, *Argonautica* 4.865–88; Nelis 2001, 155–58); see Weber 1998–1999 and Tsakiropoulou-Summers 2006.

of treating Circe in just this way.[156] Dido is not an enchantress who uses magic literally to turn men into swine, but the narrator, by signaling to the knowledgeable reader that she may be the Circe of the *Aeneid*, introduces Aeneas' Carthaginian sojourn with a foreboding that the reader can hardly ignore, but that the hero is in no position to share. This foreboding will of course play out, though in a very unexpected way.

Disguise and Recognition on the Island of Ithaca

But first, back to Ithaca. The Odyssean sequence of the hero's arrival in Phorcys' harbor followed by a meeting with the goddess who is his divine patron suggests that Aeneas' encounter with Venus, who is in disguise, is modeled on Odysseus' encounter with Athena, also in disguise.[157] This similarity in narrative sequence is supported by verbal quotation, but the real interest of this apparent *Leitzitat* lies elsewhere. Comparison between the *Aeneid* and the *Odyssey* at this point should focus our attention on ethos or characterization and on the crucially important Odyssean themes of disguise and recognition.[158]

In the *Odyssey* passage, these two foci are intimately linked. When Odysseus wakes up to find himself in unfamiliar surroundings, he behaves with a caution that is simultaneously his abiding and defining trait and also a defense mechanism that he learns at enormous cost during his wanderings. His first thought is that he has been ill-used by the Phaeacians, who he thinks have not taken him to Ithaca, but have merely left him somewhere convenient for them, though not for him, where someone else is likely to come along to rob him (*Odyssey* 13.187–216). Accordingly, Athena chooses to present herself in the unthreatening disguise of a young man, whom Odysseus, encouraged, takes the initiative to interrogate. When Athena informs him that he has, in fact, reached Ithaca, Odysseus is overjoyed, but still cautious. He replies by telling Athena an elaborate lie that both is plausible and contains a thinly veiled threat. The hero claims to have fought at Troy and then returned to his home on Crete (that epicenter of Greek falsehood), where he killed a man, Orsilochus—a younger man, fast on his feet, perhaps not unlike his addressee—who tried to rob him of his war booty; and because of this crime, he has had to go into exile and has wandered far. Athena, delighted by this deceptive tale, reveals herself to Odysseus and revels with him in the crafty intelligence that they both share (221–440).[159]

---

156. On the antecedents of Horace's use of Circe, the Sirens, and the luxurious Phaeacians as representing vice see Kaiser 1964.

157. *Aeneid* 1.305–409, *Odyssey* 13.184–440.

158. Murnaghan 1987/2011.

159. On Odysseus' Cretan tales see Haft 1984; Reece 1994; Clayton 53–82.

The *Aeneid* passage has a similar structure, but a very different ethical point. Aeneas heads off from the harbor to discover where he has arrived, taking along Achates with a brace of spears for personal protection. Suddenly Venus appears to him, potentially threatening but also alluring, in the guise of a huntress. Since Aeneas' own hunting skills were on display in the previous episode, his mother's disguise could be meant to establish a rapport between herself and her son, not unlike the rapport between Athena and Odysseus in the corresponding Homeric scene. Nothing is made of that possibility, though. To the contrary, like the *Odyssey*, the *Aeneid* dwells on elements of the goddess' disguise, her physical appearance and attire; but while the effect of Homer's description is to convince the reader that Athena really did look just like a young man, Vergil's description drives home the fact that Venus looks like anything but. Her manners are different from those of Athena, as well. She does not wait for Aeneas to address her, but speaks first.[160] What is more, instead of letting him ask her for information, as Athena does in the Homeric episode, she asks him for some, as if he knew his way around the place. She pretends to have lost one of her sisters, and hopes that Aeneas and Achates might have seen her. Aeneas replies that he has not and goes on to suggest that Venus' disguise is really not that effective. He is convinced that she must be a goddess, or at least a nymph.[161] But on the other hand, her disguise is somewhat effective, because the hero takes his mother for the goddess who is least like herself, the chaste Diana. And he insists, truthfully, that it is he and Achates who are lost, having wandered here from afar without any idea where they might be. Venus, sticking to her unbelievable lie, insists that she is no goddess and that all the local girls just dress that way; but then she changes tack and tells Aeneas a truthful story of murder, robbery, and exile that inverts Odysseus' lie about Orsilochus almost point by point. She then does not, like Athena, drop her disguise, but asks Aeneas who he is; and he, without a trace of guile, gives a frank account of himself, emphasizing his tribulations, but not forgoing a heroic vaunt: "I am Aeneas the true, who carry with me in my fleet my ancestral gods, seized from my enemy, [and am] famed above the heavens."[162] Venus is unimpressed, and tells him that,

---

160. As if to underline the point, Venus hails Aeneas and Achates with a colloquialism: see Austin 1971, 121 on 321 *heus*.

161. *Aeneid* 1.327–29. This is what Odysseus says to Nausicaa when he meets her on Scheria (*Odyssey* 6.149–52). I discuss a similar passage of *Homeric Hymn* 5 to Aphrodite below in this section.

162. *Aeneid* 1.378–79. The passage recalls the opening words of Odysseus' "Apologoi," in which he identifies himself to Alcinous only after being entertained at his court over the previous two days. I return to these passages in the next section of this chapter entitled "Intertextual Dido."

whoever he is, things can't be that bad; and she predicts that he will soon recover those of his companions who got lost in the storm—casting an ironic light upon her opening gambit, when she pretended that she could not find a lost companion of her own (385–401).

It is at this point that Venus reveals herself to Aeneas in a way that exposes the enormous distance between her relationship with her own son and Athena's relationship with Odysseus. Where Athena's revelation introduces a scene of warm appreciation between goddess and hero, Venus, after a brief epiphany, speaks not another word but turns and walks away, leaving her son to call after her in bitter reproach. It is a curious thing: Odysseus and Athena lie to one another, but in a plausible way that somehow emphasizes certain basic truths about the heroic wanderer and the divine *virago* while she, seeing through his deception, delights in it. Venus, conversely, lies to Aeneas in a most implausible way, ignoring the fact that she is anything but a *virgo*; and he sees through her lame deception, intuiting that he is in the presence of a divine being. Nevertheless, though he answers her in the frankest possible way, she maintains her disguise as best she can till she has delivered her message; then, dropping all pretense, she leaves Aeneas feeling alienated, abandoned, and (in effect) pointing out to the reader the enormous differences between this scene of divine epiphany and its Homeric model. "Why do you, too, mock your son cruelly and so often with false appearances? Why can't we join hands and talk face to face?" Aeneas' complaint that this sort of thing happens "so often" (*totiens* 407) may be a rhetorical exaggeration; at least, the text of the *Aeneid* does not present the reader with many similar occurrences. But the detail requires us to entertain the possibility that this is Venus' habitual way of dealing with Aeneas.[163] On the other hand, the phrase "you, too" (*tu quoque*) is a bit harder to account for, since this is the first time that the reader has witnessed an encounter between the hero and anyone else. In fact, the poem will not represent any other occasion in which someone, whether mortal or divine, deceives Aeneas in a similar way.[164] As I noted before, Aeneas has not "read" the *Odyssey* or lived through it; but anyone who has read it might justifiably refer the phrases "so often" and "you, too" to the metapoetic character of a passage in

---

163. According to Servius, *Commentary on Vergil's Aeneid* 1.407 the reader should infer that Venus did this sort of thing all the time; the major epiphany at 2.589 is cited as an exception. Alternatively, Servius connects *totiens* with *crudelis*; see the following note.

164. Servius implicitly takes *tu quoque* closely with *crudelis*, "cruel," in reference to Juno and the other divinities who were enemies of the Trojans—a perfectly reasonable explanation, but one that shows he felt the passage ambiguous enough to require one. The phrase *crudelis tu quoque* quotes *Eclogue* 8.48 and 50, where the question is whether Venus or her son Cupid is the crueler.

which, once again, a goddess is wearing a disguise, and in which this time Venus, though looking like Diana, is in effect playing the role of a different virgin goddess, the Homeric Athena. In doing so, however, far from comforting her heroic protégé, as Athena did, she frustrates and disappoints him. Why, Aeneas seems to say (though without knowing it), must you, too, just like Athena in the *Odyssey*, try (not very successfully, and pointlessly, at that) to work through deception?

So far I have been attempting to understand this encounter within an Odyssean frame of reference; but now it seems necessary to admit how difficult this is. The problem is not so much that *Aeneid* 1 is rife with verbal or structural parallels to the *Iliad*. A glance through Knauer's lists will show that centuries of scholarly investigation have turned up few of these, most of them being confined to Iliadic episodes that appear in Juno's temple precinct in Carthage (450–93), or to the questions Dido asks Aeneas during her banquet (748–56). But this does not mean that other kinds of Iliadic motif are absent. Here our earlier discussion of Aeneas' outburst during the storm is again relevant. As I noted above, Heyne, while acknowledging that Aeneas' speech ("O three and four times blessed") is based on that of Odysseus in similar circumstances, was the first to adduce "another model," Achilles' speech when he is near being drowned by the river Xanthus in *Iliad* 21. Among Achilles' grievances there is the fact that *he had been deceived by his mother*, who promised him a choice between a long but ignoble life and a short, glorious one. By returning to battle, he believed that he had chosen the latter fate, but by drowning, he would have the worst of both worlds, a short life and a disgraceful death. It therefore makes sense that Aeneas, too, when facing death by drowning (and remembering his one of his own near-death experiences in the *Iliad*), spoke much as Achilles had done. Now, when he meets Venus, we have him complaining about maternal deceit, as well. This should remind the reader that both Achilles and Aeneas are the sons of goddesses (as Achates and Dido will soon emphasize, addressing Aeneas as *nate dea*, "goddess-born," 582 and 615) and that Venus has just come from Jupiter, having complained to him on behalf of her son, much as Thetis complains on behalf of Achilles in the first book of the *Iliad*. This is another correspondence first mentioned by Heyne, but otherwise strangely overlooked.[165] Of course it is understandable that Jupiter's

---

165. Heyne 1830–1841, vol. 2, 111 on *Aeneid* 1.229, noting that the exchange between Zeus and Athena in *Odyssey* 1 is comparable, finds the one between Zeus and Thetis in *Iliad* 1 much more so. Note that there is a very similar and unmistakably Iliadic episode involving the Hero Aristaeus and his mother, the nymph Cyrene, at *Georgics* 4.315–86; see Farrell 1991, 104–13; Morgan 1999, 36–39 and 94–96.

meeting with Venus should be interpreted in the light of Zeus's interviews with Athena in *Odyssey* 1 and, especially, 5; but only by focusing on those passages exclusively and ignoring the *Iliad* altogether can one maintain that there is no overall Iliadic structure into which the plot of the *Aeneid* as a whole can be seen to fit.[166] If instead one begins with the observation that the *Iliad* and the *Aeneid*, each in its opening book, features an episode in which a goddess intervenes with the king of gods and men on behalf of her son; that this same goddess, much later in the poem, will intervene with Hephaestus/Vulcan to obtain divine armor for her son just before the hero commits himself to battle; and that each poem moves towards a climax in which the hero avenges a dear friend by slaying his killer in single combat; then the plot trajectory of the *Aeneid* will be seen, *as a whole*, to be no less Iliadic than Odyssean, and in some ways even more straightforwardly so. To return to the immediate passage at hand, Venus learns in her interview with Jupiter that her son will live three years after winning this victory (1.263–66). His remaining lifespan will not be as short as that of Achilles, but neither will it be long. On the other hand, his death will certainly not be glorious. Although the *Aeneid* does not say as much, several passages are best understood according to the tradition that Aeneas was not slain by a god, or even by another hero, but that he died at the river Numicus, perhaps drowning in it.[167] In this sense, in spite of the success that Fate holds in store for the Trojan hero, everything that Achilles fears will happen to him in the "Battle against the River" will eventually come true for Aeneas.

For his own part, Aeneas is candid almost to a fault, proving that he is no Odysseus. Servius' reaction to his speech of self-introduction is instructive.[168] Anxious that readers may find Aeneas arrogant, he notes that the hero speaks according to heroic convention, and cites Odysseus' own words in support of this idea:

> **I am Aeneas** the true, **who** carry with me in my fleet my ancestral gods, seized from my enemy, [and am] **famed above the heavens**.
> (*Aeneid* 1.378–79)

> **I am Odysseus**, son of Laertes, **who** for deceptions am familiar to all men, **and my fame reaches the heavens**.
> (*Odyssey* 9.19–20)

Although Aeneas' words are so close to those of Odysseus, however, similarity once again reveals not just a difference, but a key and a very familiar difference.

---

166. Knauer 1964, 223–26, 327–31; 1964a, 73, 76–78, 80–81; Cairns 1989, 179.
167. O'Hara 1990, 105–11 and 115–16 remains essential reading on this point.
168. Servius, *Commentary on Vergil's Aeneid* 1.378.

Odysseus introduces himself, according to heroic convention, as the son of Laertes. Aeneas dispenses with lineage in favor of his perpetual epithet, *pius*, which I have rendered as "true"; I might have used a word like "constant" or "dutiful." Such qualities are very different from Odysseus' cunning intelligence" (*mêtis*), represented in the Homeric text by "deceptions" (*doloisin*), which makes the difference between the heroes very pointed. For many critics, this could be Exhibit A in a case that Aeneas is an improved version of the Odyssean prototype.[169] Before assenting, let us focus instead on how the differences between the two heroes play out.

The passages in which Odysseus and Aeneas reveal their identities belong to the heroes' arrivals on Scheria and in Africa, respectively. That is, according to Knauer and most other critics, they belong intertextually to "the same" episode; but the two passages are placed very differently in their respective texts. Homer's Odysseus famously does not reveal his identity until he has spent a day with the Phaeacians, feasting and celebrating, listening to heroic and divine tales, and doing his best to conceal who he is until Alcinous, his host, cannot stand the suspense any longer and finally asks his guest's name (*Odyssey* 8.532–86). Aeneas, in the sharpest contrast imaginable, does not wait but reveals himself to the very first person he meets before even reaching Dido's court. That is as if Odysseus had blurted out his identity to Nausicaa when she noticed him lurking in the bushes.[170] Ancient Roman readers may have wondered why Aeneas departs so decisively from the Odyssean prototype, since they will have expected there to be a need for caution in dealing with the dangerous Carthaginians.[171] That may be why Venus puts so much emphasis on injustice and treachery when she introduces her brief history of Dido, not only dwelling on Pygmalion's deceit but also touching upon Dido's own cunning escape from Sidon and her cleverness in securing a place of adequate size for her settlement in Africa.[172] For ancient readers familiar with ethical

---

169. Thus Knauer 1964, 160–61 rightly calls attention to the contrast between *penatis*, "ancestral gods" in the *Aeneid* and *doloisin*, "deceptions" in the *Odyssey*, noting that they occupy exactly the same metrical positions (or *sedes*) in their respective lines.

170. See note 161 above. Note that Odysseus, hearing Nausicaa and her attendants, wonders whether they might be nymphs (*Odyssey* 6.122–24).

171. That "Punic dependability" (*Punica fides*)—which is to say, treachery—is proverbial in Roman culture requires no demonstration. I will just mention the denunciation of Hannibal's "more than Punic treachery" (*perfidia plus quam Punica* 21.4.9) in Livy's *History of Rome* and Valerius Maximus, *Memorable Deeds and Sayings* 7.4, external exemplum 2. For probing analysis of the concept see Giusti 2018, 140–41 and 237; Biggs 2019.

172. *Aeneid* 1.340–68. Venus' account illustrates Dido's resilience: after her brother, Pygmalion, murders her husband, Sychaeus, she adapts quickly, becoming the leader of her people,

criticism of Homer, Venus is portraying the clever Dido not only as a someone who shouldn't be taken lightly, but also as a "good king" who has (so to speak) learned the lessons offered by the Homeric Odysseus, lessons that any leader, according to mainstream ethical philosophy, would do well to study. But if Venus means to warn Aeneas that he should be wary, the hero does not get the message: once arrived at Dido's court wrapped in mist, he bursts forth into the clear air at the appropriate time, just like Odysseus; but unlike Odysseus, he again discloses his name immediately.[173]

In such ways as these, an apparent *Leitzitat* directs the reader not merely to a particular episode or sequence of episodes in Homeric narrative, but into the character and even the psyche of a hero who is very different from his putative Homeric prototype. In fact, the psychological aspect is what the *Aeneid* makes most evident; and, though evident, it continues to astonish readers by disclosing ever deeper layers of significance. If Venus means to advise Aeneas to be cautious and crafty in his dealings with Dido or in general—that is, if she advocates that he adopt, in accordance with most ancient kingship theory, an Odyssean model of ethical heroism—then she is not a very convincing teacher. Her own stratagem of dressing as Diana not only seems ill-advised, but comes close to emphasizing the goddess's essential nature by trying to deny it. Venus ought to have known this, of course, because she had employed the same technique once before with a very specific purpose in mind.

Like Juno in "The Bribing of Aeolus," Venus is reprising one of her own most memorable starring roles—not from the *Iliad* or the *Odyssey*, however, since neither poem is very flattering to her, but from the *Homeric Hymn to Aphrodite*—a sort of off-Broadway role, then, but a significant one, nevertheless. The episode in question is "The Seduction of Anchises" (*Homeric Hymn* 5.45–90) and its outcome is the conception and birth of Aeneas himself.[174] In

---

and shows cunning, both in seizing Sychaeus' treasure without Pygmalion's knowledge and in her clever purchase of Byrsa, which would become the site of the Carthaginian citadel. Venus' allusive treatment of the story is explained by other sources (Servius, *Commentary on Vergil's Aeneid* 1.362–67; Justin, *Epitome of the Philippic History of Pompeius Trogus* 18.5.9 in Yardley and Develin 1994, 157; Livy, *History of Rome* 34.62.11–12): the Libyan natives were willing to let Dido purchase only as much land as could be contained by a bull's hide (*byrsa* in Punic; hence the citadel's name), but Dido cut a hide into strips, tying them together to form a single leather cord, and successfully insisted that be allowed to buy as much land as she could *surround* with the cord, not the tiny amount that she could cover with the intact hide.

173. *Aeneid* 1.595–96, *Odyssey* 7.146–52.

174. Sainte-Beuve 1870, 251–59, commended by Wlosok 1967 note 1 as "stimulating *in spite of* the *questionable* comparison with the meeting between Aphrodite and Anchises in the *Homeric Hymn to Aphrodite*" (my translation and bewildered emphasis); she does cite the hymn

the hymn, Aphrodite names her child Aeneas because of the "terrible pain" (*ainon... achos*) it causes her that she "fell into the bed of a mortal man" (198–99). To accomplish this, Zeus "cast a sweet longing for Anchises into her heart" (45) so that she disguised herself as a maiden and presented herself in a lonely place on Mount Ida, where Anchises usually tended his sheep. It did not take Anchises long to respond to Aphrodite's charms, even though she was disguised. In fact, he more or less saw through the disguise, addressing her as one of the blessed ones, either Artemis or Leto, even Aphrodite herself, Themis, Athena, or one of the Graces or nymphs, and he offered to build her an altar (91–106).[175] She, of course, denied that she was a goddess and told him a very implausible lie about how Hermes brought her to him because the gods wanted them to be married; whereupon Anchises decided they should consummate the relationship immediately (107–67). So, the *Aeneid* episode departs from its model in the *Odyssey* by tracking the plot of the *Hymn*, right up to the point where the goddess and her son pointedly do not "join hands and converse face to face," as Aeneas wishes they could do. The barely sublimated sexuality that is so evident even to readers unfamiliar with the hymn is greatly intensified for those who recall it.

Sublimation is a powerful force in other ways, as well. If it were not, someone might long ago have come to Kenneth Reckford's brilliant realization that the words in which the narrator describes Venus' putting off her costume can be taken in two ways. Everyone had always assumed—or, at least, no one had possessed the courage to say otherwise—that when Venus' gown "dropped down to her feet," she merely released the belt she used to keep it hitched up above her knees, like a huntress.[176] But as Reckford saw, the same words could just as easily mean that her clothing dropped off entirely. This would be in keeping with the fact that Venus is the only Olympian goddess whom ancient artists frequently depicted fully nude; the fact that the text goes on to say that "the true goddess **stood revealed**" (*et vera... patuit dea* 405) is hardly incompatible with this idea. Naturally, the forces of sublimation remain strong, and there are also good reasons for insisting that the Latin actually says not that

---

occasionally for details typical of Aphrodite in literature. Otis 1964, 235 note 1 praises Sainte-Beuve as the only one "to have grasped Virgil's mixture of sensual and maternal elements in this scene." See E. L. Harrison 1972–1973, 12–13; Paschalis 1984; Reckford 1996, 7–8; Oliensis 2009, 62–63; Olson 2011; Gladhill 2012.

175. There is some irony in the fact that Anchises includes Aphrodite's name but Aeneas does not.

176. "her dress flowed all the way down to her feet" (*pedes vestis defluxit ad imos* 404; the narrator describes Venus' appearance at 314–20; see Austin 1971, 120–21 on 320 *nuda genu* ("bare-kneed").

"the true goddess *stood revealed,*" period, but that "she stood revealed *as the true goddess herself,*" not by her iconographic nudity but "by her gait" (*incessu* 405). It is not possible, or even necessary, to decide what happens to Venus' gown, but it clearly was necessary for Reckford to propose the more scandalous interpretation if the latent sexual energy of the passage was to be fully appreciated. On balance, Ellen Oliensis puts it perfectly when she writes: "Though the first interpretation"—that is, the traditional, family-friendly one—"seems the more likely, this does not mean that we ought to discard the other as irrelevant. To the contrary, the oscillation between the two reproduces, in the reader's experience, the fundamental dynamic of the encounter. Behind the matronly image of Venus Genetrix shimmers the naked Aphrodite—and this is just Aeneas' problem."[177]

Like Reckford's realization about Venus' gown, the idea that Aeneas' encounter with his mother alludes to Odysseus' meeting with Athena on Ithaca does not go back (so far as the record shows) to Vergil's earliest readers. The correspondence was first pointed out, yet again, by the perceptive Ursinus, who was aware that Macrobius considered the model to be an earlier meeting with Nausicaa on Scheria in *Odyssey* 6.[178] Both parallels were duly noted by most subsequent commentators, but by the middle of the last century more emphasis, for reasons that are not clear, tended to be placed on the Ithacan encounter.[179] Knauer, taking note of this tendency, stressed the primary importance of the Scherian episode, in keeping with his general insistence that Aeneas' Carthaginian adventure as a whole corresponds to Homer's "Phaeacis."[180] By his method, the Phaeacian elements in book 1 reinforce one another in establishing the predominant character of the narrative at this point, while the other elements play only a secondary role.[181] This is hardly

---

177. Oliensis 2009, 62–63; my treatment of the reader's experience as an index to that of Aeneas himself in book 1 and elsewhere owes much to Oliensis' brilliant discussion of this episode, and more generally to Schiesaro 2005 and 2008.

178. Ithaca: Ursinus 1567, 208–9, mistakenly citing μ' (*Odyssey* 12) instead of ν' (13). Scheria: Macrobius *Saturnalia* 5.2.13 and 5.4.6 in Kaster 2011, vol. 2, 230–33 and 250–51. Cerda 1612/1642, vol. 2, 64–65 states that Aeneas' meeting with Venus draws on Odysseus' encounters with Athena in disguise, first as a young girl on Scheria (*Odyssey* 7.14–36) and then as a youth on Ithaca (*Odyssey* 13.221–329).

179. Pöschl 1950/1962, 25, Büchner 1955, 427; 1449, lines 51–54.

180. Knauer 1964, 248.

181. This point of view has been influential: Austin 1971, 118 on *Aeneid* 1.314, citing Macrobius and Knauer, identifies the meeting on Scheria as Vergil's model (while insisting that "Virgil's scene has nothing secondhand about it"). He does not mention the meeting on Ithaca, although he does quote *Odyssey* 13.232–33 as the source of *Aeneid* 1.331 *quibus in oris* ("on what shores"),

unreasonable, but it goes without saying that this form of interpretation involves privileging a unified perspective that can be fully realized only in retrospect. Such an emphasis on unity was a nearly universal concern among literary critics at the time when Knauer's book appeared, only a year after Adam Parry's paper on the "two voices" of the *Aeneid*, before the "dynamics of reading" had come to the attention of classicists, and before an active interest in the proliferation of meanings and the fundamental indeterminacy of language had entered *Aeneid* criticism. In such a critical climate, it would make sense that knowing or having decided that the "Phaeacis" is Vergil's primary model in *Aeneid* 1 should permit the reader to relegate elements at odds with that conclusion to secondary importance, depriving them of significance and dispensing entirely with any confusion that might arise from competition between Phaeacian and other Odyssean intertexts. From a different point of view, to read the *Aeneid* without attention to these discordant notes and the interpretive possibilities that they raise, the alternate narratives that they potentially represent, is to ignore a powerful and a characteristic element of the poem, not to say an engaging and a beautiful one. It is, in my view, a remarkable aspect of the poem's artistry that the "discordant" Homeric intertexts in book 1 work within the more "dominant" Phaeacian narrative—much like the alternative interpretations of Venus' gown—to enrich the interpretive possibilities available to the reader and to serve as something like an image of the hero's psyche, even though these intertexts cannot exist, in any simple sense, within his consciousness. The point is that they are in the reader's consciousness while he or she experiences this narrative arc along with Aeneas. For that reason it is possible to imagine Africa not only as Scheria, but as Aeaea, Telepylos, and Ithaca, as well, and to project those possibilities into the mind of the hero.[182] Not, of course, in any definite way; to repeat, Scheria, Aeaea, and Ithaca are not part of the hero's consciousness. The intertext can, however, function as a very effective substitute for Aeneas' unconscious mind. His encounter with Venus, a replay of the primal scene in which she seduced his father and conceived the hero himself, seems to have been written almost as

---

without further remark. Williams 1972–1973, vol. 1, 185 on *Aeneid* 1.314 f. observes, "Virgil is following Homer *Od.* 7.19 f., where the disguised Athena meets Odysseus (cf. also *Od.* 13.221 f.)."

182. See note 177 above. By the same token, the suggestion that Aeneas' Ithaca might be found in Africa and that he might have joined forces and peoples with Dido opens up a fleeting glimpse of an alternative destiny for the hero, and of an alternative history for his descendants, one defined not by conflicts of world-historical moment between well-matched competitors, but by peace and cooperation between those who find themselves in similar circumstances. But the poem opens these vistas, it seems, only to emphasize that this is not the way history unfolded, or unfolds.

proof that literature can represent the fears and the desires of the unconscious mind. In this respect, the discordant provenance of Vergil's model for this episode is not only un-Phaeacian and un-Odyssean, but un-Homeric as well, or at least not canonically Homeric; and yet it works brilliantly to emphasize the emotional energy that informs that episode and to make it relevant to Aeneas with reference to a narrative of sexual possibility that must never come to pass.

Intertextual Dido

The barely latent forces that pervade Aeneas' encounter with his mother extend to other aspects of the Trojans' arrival in Carthage. As Macrobius explains, "the description of the storm is a wonderful imitation of Homer ... and Venus took the place of Nausicaa, Alcinous' daughter, while Dido herself is the very image of king Alcinous convening his banquet."[183] The verbal parallels involved are precise, but Macrobius' distribution of roles does little justice to the suggestive redeployment of Homeric material in the *Aeneid*. Ursinus, as was noted above, saw that Aeneas' interview with Venus resembles two Homeric encounters between Odysseus and Athena, the one on Ithaca that we have been considering and also the earlier one on Scheria. Knauer, in keeping with his idea that the "Phaeacis" is the primary model for these books of the *Aeneid*, accords the latter encounter more importance than the former, but does not make much of aspects that differ slightly in each case. Here is the *Odyssey*:

1. Odysseus staggers ashore on Scheria during the night and falls asleep (*Odyssey* 5.436–93).
2. During the night, Athena inspires Nausicaa to go down to the shore with her attendants to prepare her trousseau (6.1–98).
3. While Nausicaa and her attendants play during a break from their chores, the narrator compares Nausicaa to Artemis among her nymphs (99–109).
4. Odysseus wakes up and sees Nausicaa with her attendants (110–48)
5. Odysseus addresses Nausicaa, saying "I implore you, mistress: are you some goddess, or a mortal? If you are some goddess, of those who hold high heaven, I make you out to be most like Artemis, the daughter of great Zeus, in appearance and size and figure" (149–52).
6. Athena pours a cloud of mist around Odysseus so that he might make his way to the city unobserved (7.14–17).
7. In the guise of a little girl, Athena briefs Odysseus about King Alcinous (18–77).

183. *Saturnalia* 5.2.13 in Kaster 2011 vol. 2, 230–33.

And here is the *Aeneid*:

1. Aeneas lands in Africa, goes hunting, and encourages his people (*Aeneid* 1.157–222).
2. Venus complains to Jupiter about Aeneas' troubles, and is reassured about the future (223–96).
4. Aeneas wakes up after a sleepless night, goes exploring with Achates, and meets Venus, who is disguised as a young huntress and hails the two heroes (305–24).
5. Aeneas addresses Venus, saying, "O—how shall I call you, maiden? For your face hardly looks mortal, nor does your voice sound human. O, certainly, a goddess, either Phoebus' sister or one of the family of nymphs" (327–29).
7. Venus briefs Aeneas about Queen Dido (335–68).
6. Venus pours a mist around Aeneas and Achates so that they might make their way at the city unobserved (411–14).
3. When Aeneas arrives there, he sees Dido, whom the narrator describes as looking like Diana among her nymphs (494–504).

The most important difference here is that the simile of Artemis/Diana among her nymphs has moved from third to seventh position. In the process, the point of the simile becomes much more explicit and powerful. In the *Odyssey*, the narrator compares Nausicaa to Artemis. The point is simply to express how much more beautiful Nausicaa is than the others, who are beautiful themselves, and also that she is a virgin. When Odysseus shortly afterwards likens the girl to the same goddess, the reader might draw any number of inferences, but the main point seems still to be that she is, indeed, quite lovely and, of course, still a virgin. In the *Aeneid*, however, when the narrator compares Dido to Diana, the hero has already spoken to Venus, his mother, when she is disguised as Diana and approaches him in a way that strongly recalls her seduction of his father. When Aeneas then gazes upon Dido, it is again the narrator, as in Homer, who compares her to Diana. Unlike the Homeric simile, however, this comparison is not presented "objectively" but is very obviously "focalized" through the hero, informing the reader not only how one *might* react to Dido's beauty, but how Aeneas *did* react to it.[184] And since he has just come from an encounter with another, highly sexualized "Diana," the reader is invited not only to connect the two occurrences but to infer that they are connected in the hero's mind, as well.

---

184. On focalization see Fowler 1990; S. C. Smith 1999.

This ought to be worrying. In the earlier scene, Aeneas saw through his mother's inappropriate disguise, at least to the extent of realizing that she was not mortal, but a goddess. Now he sees Dido, and again (by implication) he thinks of Diana; but the widowed Dido among her male courtiers, unlike Diana among her nymphs, is, like Venus, no virgin, nor is she, like Nausicaa, in any sense an ingenue.[185] As Aeneas has learned from Venus, Dido is a capable, even a powerful and resourceful leader who possesses certain key characteristics of "the good king" as exemplified by Odysseus.[186] She is also someone who has succeeded in doing what Aeneas has been trying and failing to do for years.[187] The scene before him, which presents her as the central figure in a conspicuous display of regal authority, and one in which all of the other players are men, ought to confirm for Aeneas what Venus has said. But when Aeneas looks at her, she seems to him like the virgin huntress, and for that reason not unlike the disguised Venus herself.

It is possible to tidy up this welter of misleading signals. After Dido appears, book 1 proceeds mainly according to the pattern of Odysseus' sojourn among the Phaeacians, and interference from other parts of the *Odyssey* (not to mention the *Iliad*, Naevius' *The Punic War*, or the *Homeric Hymns*) is much less pronounced.[188] Purely as a matter of narrative and intertextual economy, the idea of a principal model that is seamlessly combined with various secondary models works beautifully: Knauer has explained very well that, if the idea is to write a recognizably "Homeric" poem, there is no need to include more than one example of each "typical scene"—a scene of arrival, of banqueting, of arming, or what have you.[189] From the standpoint of poetic design on the most basic level, combining multiple episodes into individual specimens of each

---

185. Clausen 1987/2002, 211–12 emphasizes Dido's youth at the expense of her remarkable accomplishments, which (as he notes) have led most commentators, rightly I believe, to see her as somewhat older than a barely marriageable girl.

186. See note 173 above. Cairns 1989, 39–42 praises Dido as a "good king" (without reference, however, to specifically Odyssean elements) but then (42–46) comments on her rapid deterioration from this status. See chapter 3 below and Keith 2021.

187. Aeneas himself registers his appreciation and envy of Dido's success (*Aeneid* 1.437).

188. Aeneas has already perused the Trojan War scenes on Juno's temple, which is a strong indication that the Carthaginians, though wanderers themselves, share their patron goddess' taste for Iliadic narrative; and when Dido questions Aeneas about his experiences, she focuses mainly on Iliadic characters and events (Priam, Hector, Memnon, the horses of Diomedes—i.e. those of Rhesus—Achilles himself, and the sack of Troy) before asking to hear the story of Aeneas' wanderings (1.753–56). On Aeneas' war record and Dido's possibly loaded questioning of him about it see the excellent observations of Dekel 2012, 83–87.

189. Knauer 1964, 335; 1964b, 65.

type makes perfect sense. There are analogous reasons for combining characters, as well, some of which seem to be motivated by peculiarities of the Homeric narrative. For instance, in Scheria the ruler is a king, but there is also an influential queen; and, according to Athena's advice, Odysseus upon arrival at court is to ignore the former and present himself in supplication to the latter (*Odyssey* 7.48–77). The situation that Aeneas faces is simpler: there is only a queen. Venus makes quite a lot out of this, pointedly telling Aeneas, *dux femina facti* (1.364)—"a woman managed all of this," namely, the escape from Sidon, the voyage to Africa, and the acquisition of land for a new settlement. Dido is not just any queen, but a woman playing a man's role. This circumstance is a basic part of the Dido legend; but in Homeric terms, Dido is both Alcinous and Arete.[190] The combination of these figures, who are king and queen, husband and wife, adds a lot to the characterization of Dido as a woman who has succeeded her own husband as ruler of their people and who honors his memory with a vow of chastity. But Dido is more than that: when she enters with her courtiers she is Diana surrounded by her nymphs, like Homer's Nausicaa. Thus, as Pamela Gordon felicitously puts it, "Dido at moments looks like Nausikaa, stands in for Arete, and speaks like Alcinous."[191] In this sense, she is all three members of the Phaeacian royal family. This would be a satisfying combination of attributes, if Dido could be, simultaneously, a ruler, the conjugal power behind the throne, and a nubile young woman awakening to love.

Unfortunately for Dido and her people, she will not be able to combine these disparate roles. While Dido's husband Sychaeus was still alive, she was presumably a convincing Arete, the ideal royal consort; but his death demanded that she become Alcinous, a ruler in her own right, and one without a supportive partner to back her up. She will not live up to this demand and will instead (through the machinations of several divinities) behave like another Nausicaa, except that she will fatally lack that character's exemplary self-control. So, if we look beyond intertextual logistics, the model of combination does not explain everything. In fact, it does not explain much at all. Dido cannot in the end be Alcinous, Arete, and Nausicaa all at once, except in a very superficial sense. She may borrow certain traits from each of these characters and at different times behave more or less like one or another of them. But in the end, the narrative requires that she fail in each of these roles—as in fact she ultimately does.

190. Knauer 1964, 164–65, 174, 343, 354; 1964b, 66, 68; see too Van Nortwick 2013.
191. Gordon 1998, 198. Ancient critics found fault with the simile in comparison to Homer: see Aulus Gellius, *Attic Nights* 9.9.12–17 in Rolfe 1927, vol. 2, 178–83; Servius, *Commentary on Vergil's Aeneid* 1.497. The inconcinnities that bothered ancient critics are of course the point: they emphasize telling incongruities, rather than the superficial similarities, between the *Odyssey* and the *Aeneid*.

To tell the truth, Dido's intertextual identity is more fragmented still. As we have seen, to the extent that Aeneas' arrival in Africa resembles Odysseus' arrival in Ithaca, Dido is presumably his Penelope.[192] But to the extent that Africa is Aeaea, and that Aeneas spends a year with Dido, she is also his Circe.[193] Both possibilities are fundamentally incompatible with one another and with the Phaeacian hypothesis. Knauer, somewhat surprisingly, "resolves" that problem by compounding it, arguing that, in book 4, Dido becomes "a new Calypso": the goddess, although she ultimately relents, wants to keep Odysseus from returning to Penelope, while Dido, although she knows that Aeneas "has another wife," attempts to keep her guest with her in Carthage.[194] Interestingly, Knauer posits that in this respect the intertext functions dynamically: Dido does not simply add another Homeric role, but rather stops being a happy combination of Alcinous, Arete, and Nausicaa in order to become a much less compliant version of Calypso. From one point of view, this solves the problem of Dido's intertextual identity; but from another, it merely complicates the problem further.

Knauer's approach results in a satisfying conclusion if one starts by assuming that the *Aeneid*, in intertextual as well as narrative terms, tells a single, stable, unified story. This is something that many readers do, however much they feel the story is enriched by elements that do not quite fit into the master narrative. At the same time, Knauer's survey of these elements gives a reader who is differently inclined virtually all the material necessary to interpret the story as one of multiple possibilities, as unstable, disunified, and never finally resolved. Dido in particular is not so much a coherent combination of intertextual precedents as a living embodiment of Juno's storm, itself the symbol of a universe in disorder and of a poem that is disordered as well, one in which rival divinities struggle against one another in pursuit of selfish goals, while rival narrators cannot agree on which of the possible Homeric, or any other directions the story of Aeneas should take.[195]

Unintended Consequences

At the beginning of this chapter, I referred to different ways of reacting to mixed intertextual signals in the *Aeneid* proem as to whether the poem was to be another Iliad or another Odyssey. I further distinguished between two

---

192. See Schmitz 2008.
193. On the motif of the year-long stay see Knauer 1964, 180, 205, 208.
194. Knauer 1964, 211–18, 222, 343, 354; 1964b, 66, 68, 70 ("another wife"), 72, 74.
195. The classic discussion of Juno's storm remains Pöschl 1950/1962, 13–24; further essential discussion in P. R. Hardie 1986, 90–97 and 237–40.

different kinds of reader, one who cannot tolerate uncertainty but must make a choice, and one who gets more out of asking questions while deferring any immediate decisions. It is clear which kind of reader Juno is: she interprets the proem and the Trojans' departure from Sicily as disturbing evidence that she is standing on the threshold of a proto-Odyssean narrative. To prevent this from happening, she tries to infiltrate that narrative to make it another Iliad instead. Ironically, the Odyssean trajectory that Juno acted to prevent would have described, literally, a straight line, the most direct possible route from Sicily to the Italian coast. Instead, her would-be Iliadic misdirection takes Aeneas around in circles, like those of the very whirlpools created by the storm in which his fleet is trapped, and like his grand, tragic detour from Sicily to Carthage and back to Sicily. Had Juno held back—had she simply allowed the Trojans to land in Italy, as they do in book 7, and then intervened not for the second but for the first time—Aeneas would never have visited Carthage (as Odysseus visits Scheria), or narrated his wanderings since the fall of Troy (as Odysseus narrates his "Apologoi") or undertaken a journey to the underworld (like Odysseus' "Nekyia"). In the absence of those elements, the *Aeneid* would look like a much less Odyssean poem than it does. Juno would not only have had her Iliad, but she would have bypassed the entire Odyssean *Aeneid* as it is traditionally conceived. This is to say nothing of the disastrous results for Dido and Carthage, the greatest and most tragic of the unintended consequences that follow Juno's first intervention. Therefore, to focus simply on Juno's narrative designs, the point is as inescapable as it is paradoxical: in terms of her Iliadic ambitions, the goddess' first intervention was not only unnecessary, it was counterproductive as well. Without it, there might never even have been an Odyssean *Aeneid*.

It is easy to think of the epic narrator as Juno's real antagonist, and in some sense as himself a character within the poem. One thinks of narrators as existing on a different plane from other characters, but it is also difficult to say just how much autonomy a narrator has, or how much control he may exert over the course that his narrative takes. Moreover, we are not dealing here with a Pirandello play or a Fellini film. Juno's behavior in the *Aeneid* is really just a logical extension of the roles she had played in earlier epic poetry. We should not be surprised, then, if she invites comparison between herself and the poem's narrator, or even threatens to blur the boundary between their generically defined roles. Any transgressive act on Juno's part makes sense, given this goddess's history of resistance. At the beginning of the *Aeneid*, she once again resists the course that she believes the narrative is taking, and as a result the poem that we read—even though it does not turn out exactly as she had hoped—is, to a remarkable extent, one of her own making.

Going Forward

Before ending this chapter I feel compelled to admit that I have been applying a kind of double standard. In evaluating the opinions of other scholars regarding the intertextual *Aeneid*, I have been advocating a more open perspective than some of them adopt. Knauer, for instance, whose work has been my main point of reference, generally identifies one Homeric passage as the dominant model for a given passage of the *Aeneid* and considers any influence from elsewhere in Homer as secondary. In my readings of specific passages, I have generally advocated more openness to reconsideration of such matters. At the same time, despite making occasional references to other potential sources of influence (such as the *Homeric Hymn to Aphrodite* and Naevius' *The Punic War*), the general thrust of my own inquiry is also closed in that it focuses on just two possibilities: that the *Aeneid* is to be either another Iliad or another Odyssey. Is this an inconsistency on my part? Are there no other possibilities? These are questions that have to be faced; and face them we will in the chapter that follows.

2

Third Ways

None of the Above?

Despite my efforts so far, you may be thinking, reader, that there is something in all of this, but that the binary nature of my discussion is very reductive, as indeed it is. I have to admit that binary choices, even when choice is difficult, or perhaps especially then, are seductive in their apparent simplicity, compelling because they restrict the number of possible outcomes while promising a definitive resolution. Sometimes they actually provide what they promise. In practice, however, few dichotomies encompass all possibilities and many misrepresent the complexity of how things really are. They also have a way of breaking down into pluralities: dialogue becomes polyphony, formal duel pitched battle or mere melee.[1] My privileging of the Homeric binary will surely represent the *Aeneid*—and indeed Homer himself—in terms that some will find too simple and schematic, limiting the universe of possibilities to Iliad or Odyssey, Achilles or Odysseus. Whether in literary, ethical, social, or other terms, this either/or dilemma exists within an array of other possibilities that is much wider and more complex. I acknowledge all of this, and indeed I embrace it; but I have three points to make in response.

First, while the *Aeneid* certainly resists reductive treatments of any kind, it is also full of binary choices.[2] There is no real need to illustrate this claim, but it may be helpful to cite, very briefly, two famous examples of seemingly ineluctable alternatives that resolve themselves in curious ways.

In book 6 the Sibyl of Cumae tells Aeneas that he must find and pluck a Golden Bough that grows in the woods around Lake Avernus, to take as an

---

1. Quint 2018 carefully and persuasively explores how the *Aeneid* generates meaning by positing binary oppositions and then reversing them or breaking them down to suggest multiple interpretive possibilities that it does not express more openly.
2. See Suerbaum 1998.

offering to Proserpina, the price of his admission to the kingdom of the dead.[3] She tells him that when he tries to pluck the bough one of two things will happen. If he is fated to undertake this labor, the bough will come off "willingly" (*volens*). If such is not his fate, no amount of force will suffice to break it off (146–48). In the event, the bough does not come willingly: it comes, but "with hesitation" (*cunctantem* 211). We may compare this passage with the very end of the poem, when Aeneas must choose whether to spare Turnus, who is seriously wounded and begging for his life, or to finish him off. The hero listens to Turnus' plea "with hesitation" (*cunctantem* 12.940), like the bough; then he kills the suppliant.[4] The hesitation of the bough and of the hero seem to suggest that no binary is adequate to encompass the available possibilities, that there is always a "third way." For a moment this way may seem very real, if ill-defined; but it is quickly revealed to be an illusion. It cannot persist. Very quickly it falls over to one side of the binary or the other and vanishes, along with the very idea that there must be some "third way." There is nothing for it but to choose, one or the other, yes or no, life or death.

My second point is that ethical and existential choices go to the very heart of epic poetry and its central function of exploring the nature of heroism. These choices are usually between two opposite, incompatible possibilities. Achilles must choose between a short life with everlasting fame and a long life with posthumous obscurity. Odysseus will obtain long life and everlasting fame, but only by rejecting Calypso's offer of immortality in favor of Penelope and, eventually, death. Such heroic choices become a focal point of philosophical meditations on ethics. Hercules must choose between a life of virtuous exertion and one of easy pleasure.[5] Odysseus again, when he faces rebirth in Plato's "Myth of Er," chooses a quiet life over one of adventure.[6] In view of this tendency in heroic poetry and ethical philosophy—and especially in Homeric poetry and its reception—the *Aeneid* would be a poor excuse for an epic if it did not exemplify the theme of ethical choice in defining its hero. Characteristically, it puts this theme into play at every level of significance as symbolized by characters, narrators, and readers. In this sense, it may be the ultimate epic of choice.

---

3. In the vast literature on the Golden Bough, Brooks 1953 remains fundamental; on the Bough's hesitation see Segal 1965–1966 and 1968.

4. Or, as the hero puts it, Pallas does, further occluding the starkness of the alternatives that he and Turnus, from their very different perspectives, confront; see Putnam 2011, 64; Tarrant 2012, 338. On Aeneas' hesitation see Putnam 1984/1995; Holoka 1999; Ziolkowski 2004, 9–33.

5. Prodicus in Xenophon, *Memorabilia* 2.1.21–33; see Galinsky 1972, 101–3, 162; Sansone 2004.

6. Plato, *Republic* 10, 619b2–620d5; see Montiglio 2011, 47–52.

My final point is that the competing paradigms of Iliadic and Odyssean ethics are extremely powerful. In the Homeric program of the *Aeneid* they vie with one another to determine whether the poem is a tragic meditation on destructive anger or a comic celebration of resourceful intelligence. One of the many wonderful things about the poem is that it remains so long in a state of hesitation between these alternatives, all the while seeming to offer the possibility that there must be some "third way." In this chapter, we will explore some of the narrative paradigms that might have allowed Aeneas to escape from or surpass the Homeric binary to become something else. Each of them for a time appears to offer a chance to circumvent the choice between a predominantly Iliadic or Odyssean *Aeneid* and an Aeneas who must be a second Achilles or a second Odysseus. Ultimately, all of these apparent "third ways" either favor one of the two Homeric possibilities, or else seem to do so while leaving the final choice up to us.

With that, let us turn to the first of these "third ways."

Failure Is Always an Option: The *Aeneid* and the Epic Cycle

The most obvious way of avoiding the Homeric dilemma is a very simple one. Many poets set out to rival Homer and simply failed. In fact, that is certainly the likeliest outcome. At the same time, the product of such attempted rivalry is likelier to be a failed Iliad *or* a failed Odyssey than is to be both. It is obviously impossible to consider all the ways in which a would-be Homeric poet might fail. Fortunately, it is also unnecessary, because the history of Homeric ambition includes a well-known example of what it means to fall short of Homeric success in the poems of the so-called Epic Cycle. If Homer is the genre model of epic poetry, the Epic Cycle is the genre model of epic failure. This particular kind of failure is extremely relevant to our discussion of Homeric alternatives and "third ways."

The Narrator's Ambition

We have seen that it is not quite clear what kind of story the narrator of the *Aeneid* wants to tell. Perhaps the truth is not that his intentions are inscrutable, but that he himself really isn't sure what he wants. Perhaps his problem isn't uncertainty, but diffidence. One does not have to read far before this suspicion is confirmed. The third word of the poem, *cano* ("I sing"), might be taken as an act of self-assertion on the narrator's part, but knowledgeable readers would probably draw a very different conclusion. The reasons are familiar and can be stated briefly.

One reason Homer is so vastly superior to all other poets is that he did not have to remember anything. The Muse did that for him. In line 1 of the *Iliad*, he tells the goddess to do the singing, and he requests access to her memory at key points throughout his narrative. So too in line 1 of the *Odyssey* he asks the Muse to sing to or for him. Homer's earliest epic successors seem to have lacked or to have gradually lost this advantage. The poets of the Epic Cycle, a series of half a dozen archaic Greek epics that that collectively told about everything connected with the Trojan War that the Homeric poems did not, told their stories on their own authority.[7] Critics came to judge them very harshly. For Aristotle, their main flaw was shoddy plot construction.[8] Callimachus deplored their obsession with strictly serial story lines that left nothing out, and he also objected to their excessive length, pretentious style, and unimaginative intertextual engagement with Homer.[9] Horace in his *Art of Poetry* speaks of them disparagingly, for similar reasons.[10] Nevertheless, "I sing" in line 1 of the *Aeneid* has long been seen as a specifically Cyclic gesture. This is very odd. Why would any narrator align himself with the kind of epic that was definitive of the second-rate?

If we take "arms and a man" as signaling an effort to combine the *Iliad* and the *Odyssey*, as so many do, then "I sing" can be seen as adding the whole Epic Cycle to the syllabus of the *Aeneid*. This addition makes sense in terms of what follows. Not long after announcing that he is doing the singing himself, the narrator will mention "The Judgment of Paris," an early episode of *Cypria*, the first poem of the Epic Cycle in narrative order.[11] In book 11, "Diomedes in Italy," an episode from the *Homecomings* of the Greek heroes after the Trojan War, will figure in an important plot development. Allusions to numerous other Cyclic episodes occur throughout the *Aeneid*.[12] Perhaps the narrator aims not merely to combine an Iliad and an Odyssey into a single poem, but to encompass the entire Epic Cycle, as well. Rather than choose between or

---

7. See Austin 1971, 26 on *Aeneid* 1.1 and especially Scafoglio 2006 with further references. On the formation of the Epic Cycle see West 2013, 16–20.

8. *Poetics* 1459a–b in Halliwell et al. 1995, 114–19, where he specifically criticizes *Cypria* and the *Little Iliad*.

9. *Palatine Anthology* 12.43 = Callimachus, *Epigram* 28 in Pfeiffer 1953, 88; essentially identical Greek text in Paton 1918, 300–301 and Mair and Mair 1955, 156–57, no. 30, each with a slightly different English translation. This is the poet's most explicit denunciation of Cyclic poetry; see Pfeiffer 1968, 227–30; Hopkinson 1988, 86; Asper 1997, 56 note 140; Heerink 2015, 9–12; Fantuzzi 2015; Sistakou 2015.

10. See Brink 1971, 212–16 on lines 136–39.

11. On *Cypria* see Davies 1989, 32–50; West 2013, 55–128 and 2015.

12. On the *Aeneid* and the Epic Cycle see Kopff 1981; Gärtner 2015.

be confined by alternative Homeric paradigms, perhaps he means to exceed Homer by producing a "Sum of All Trojan Mythologies." If so, he is playing a dangerous game.

When the narrator alludes to "The Judgment of Paris" from *Cypria* he is far from following Homer's practice of "objective" narration, as the Cyclic poets presumably did. He is summarizing Juno's reasons for hating the Trojans. To do so, he employs a storytelling technique known as "free indirect discourse," putting the reader in touch with Juno's silent nursing of her ancient grudge as if he were quoting her.[13] Soon after that, when Juno spies Aeneas sailing happily towards Italy, she recalls "The Death of Ajax the Locrian," like "Diomedes in Italy" an episode from *Homecomings*.[14] These references, which encompass the limits of virtually the entire Trojan Cycle, suggest the actual scope of Juno's obsession. Recalling that these Cyclic episodes inspire the goddess to act as she (i.e., Hera) had done in *Iliad* 14, I take this all to mean that Juno's Iliad is not the *Iliad* alone, but a "Long Iliad," an expansive and continuing anti-Trojan narrative of which the *Iliad* is always the core.[15] Surrounding that core is a vast array of individual episodes, most of them brief. By acting to destroy Aeneas at the very start of this new poem, Juno shows that she would be happy for the *Aeneid* to take its place as one more brief, episodic addition to this undistinguished and unloved encyclopedia of pre- and post-Homerica.

This inference is supported by the episodes that Juno's Carthaginian worshippers depicted on the temple they built for her, episodes defined collectively as "a seriatim account of the Trojan War" (1.456).[16] The individual episodes are not, in fact, presented in chronological order. A few of them might occur at almost any point in the war (Greeks fleeing Trojans, Trojans chased down by Achilles). Most of them, however, can be located precisely within the *Iliad* itself. These include "The Aristeia of Diomedes" (book 5), "The Supplication of Pallas" by the Trojan women (book 6), the "Doloneia" (book 10), and "The Ransom of Hector"—that is, of his corpse (book 24). Others involve more prequels and sequels from the Epic Cycle. "The Death of Troilus" was narrated in *Cypria*, which ended at the point where the *Iliad* begins.[17] "The Arrival of Memnon and Penthesilea," allies of the Trojans, was narrated in

---

13. See Laird 1999, 96–99 with further references.

14. See Davies 1989, 77–83; West 2013, 245–83, especially 260–62.

15. In keeping with the insights of Feeney 1984; 1991, 130–34 and 145–55.

16. Among many studies of this episode see especially Williams 1960a; Leach 1988, 314–323; Fowler 1991, 32–33; Lowenstam 1993, especially 43–44; Putnam 1998/1998a, 23–54; La Penna 2000; McNelis and Sens 2010; Kirichenko 2013, 66–75; Schiesaro 2015; Squire 2016; Freudenburg 2017, 134–35.

17. See Davies 1989, 47; West 2013, 56–57.

Aethiopis, which began right where the *Iliad* ended.[18] The temple scenes make no obvious distinction between actual Iliadic episodes and those told in Cyclic epics.[19] In another sense, however, it seems important that the number of Iliadic episodes mentioned exceeds that of all others combined. Also important is the fact that the two specifically non-Iliadic episodes mentioned come from the poems that immediately preceded and followed the *Iliad* in the Trojan Cycle. This seems to suggest what the phrase that I translated above as "seriatim" (*ex ordine*) really means: it is very much a reference to the sequence not of individual episodes, but of Cyclic poems, with the *Iliad* occupying the essential, unarguably central position, extending back in time through its Cyclic prequel, *Cypria*, and forward through its sequel, *Aethiopis*.[20] Since the temple is dedicated to Juno, moreover, it must represent a perspective that the Carthaginians believe she approves, one that is decidedly Iliadic, but in a highly inclusive sense.

This being the case, what can we now make of the narrator's assertion that *he* is the singer of "arms and a man," without Musal assistance? Is he asserting his wish to be comprehensive, unlike Homer and like the poets of the Epic Cycle? Does he share Juno's slanted perspective on the Epic Cycle as a "Long Iliad"? His motives and intentions remain not merely inscrutable, uncertain, or diffident, but at points even nonsensical. After launching the poem without invoking any Muse, he invokes her belatedly in line 8 to advise him about the Callimachean theme of the "causes" (*causas*) of Juno's anger against Aeneas, even employing Callimachus' characteristic trope of questioning the Muse.[21] To identify oneself as a Cyclic poet in line 1 and a follower of Callimachus in line 8 is a baffling contradiction in terms, like attempting to sing an Iliad and an Odyssey at once. Perhaps the narrator's ambitions are simply confused or unrealistic. Indeed, if *cano* really is a sign of his self-confidence, he must be delusional. More likely it is an attempt to keep indecision and self-doubt at

---

18. See Davies 1989, 51–55; West 2013, 129–34; 138–49.

19. This is not unusual, especially in ancient visual designs. Carpenter 2015 discusses the greater popularity of Cyclic episodes, relative to Iliadic and Odyssean ones, in archaic Greek art. With time, the concept of Trojan themes becomes, if anything, more expansive still: see Squire 2011, 31–54; 2015; 2016.

20. Aeneas will bring the Carthaginians up to date in book 2 with a narration that overlaps with the Cyclic *Iliupersis*, i.e., *The Sack of Troy* (see Davies 1989, 70–76; West 2013, 223–43, especially 224) and perhaps also with the *Little Iliad* (see Davies 1989, 60–70; West 2013, 163–220, especially 165–69).

21. In books 1 and 2 of his *Aetia* Callimachus represented himself in a dream as questioning the Muses about the origins of various Greek cities, cults, customs, and so on. In general, the Muses' replies made up the individual episodes of the poem. See Harder 2012, vol. 1, 52.

bay. To repeat, for any storyteller, trying and simply failing to match either of Homer's masterpieces, never mind both, is by far the most likely outcome. The Cyclic poets tried to imitate Homer without access to his sources of inspiration, and they failed miserably. Perhaps the narrator realizes this. Shifting suddenly from a Cyclic to a Callimachean mode of presentation looks like a panicky course correction right at the outset. The ensuing narrative seems to confirm it is exactly that.

Juno and Memory

In the *Odyssey*, as I have noted, Hera is barely mentioned. It is therefore not surprising that in our very sparse remains of Livius Andronicus' Latin translation of the *Odyssey*—a foundational work of Latin literature written roughly two hundred years before the *Aeneid* and known to us only from about fifty passages, most of them single lines, quoted by other authors—Juno's name does not appear at all. For that same reason it is all the more surprising that two fragments among the scanty remains of the poem refer to this goddess, each by one of her most important Roman cult titles.

The one that concerns us here is Juno Moneta, whose temple stood prominently on the Capitoline Hill overlooking the Forum since at least the mid-fourth century BCE.[22] The cult title Moneta is related to the verb *moneo*—to bring to the notice of, remind, tell (of).[23] This is the meaning of the name that Livius gives to the mother of his Camena, the goddess he invokes in place of Homer's Muse at the opening of his poem.[24] The Camenae were nymphs who inhabited a spring just outside the walls of Rome near the Porta Capena.[25] They had probably always been associated with song, and by the end of the fourth century BCE their similarity to the Greek Muses may already have been

---

22. According to Livy, *History of Rome* 7.28.4–6 the temple was built by Lucius Furius Camillus in 344 BCE, possibly on a site already consecrated to Juno. For discussion of the evidence from somewhat differing perspectives see Meadows and Williams 2001, 31–32; Littlewood 2006, 57–58, 59–60; A. Hardie 2007, 556–60. Curiously, the 10th-century CE Greek encyclopedia of antiquity known as the *Suda* (s.v. *Monēta*, M 1220 in Adler 1928–1938, vol. 1.3, 408) traces the origin of the cult to the Roman conquest of Tarentum in 272 BCE, which happens also to be the occasion when Livius is thought to have come to Rome as a prisoner of war.

23. *Oxford Latin Dictionary* s.v. moneo 1. This ancient etymology has been doubted (indeed, by *OLD* itself s.v. Moneta 1), but most modern authorities now accept it: see Meadows and Williams 2001, 33–34; A. Hardie 2007, 556.

24. For text and translation, see Warmington 1936, 24–25, fragment 1 (invocation) and 34–35, fragment 30 (parentage).

25. Richardson 1992, 63–64 s.v. Camenae.

recognized in cult.[26] Invoking a Camena was a brilliant, culturally appropriate response to an important feature of the Homeric text. Making Juno Moneta the Camena's mother was also brilliant and culturally appropriate, but it was definitely not motivated by anything in Homer. As Alex Hardie observes, "Livius had no need to supply a Latin name for the Camena's mother, for the *Odyssey* does not name the Muse-mother."[27] Nor is the name of the Camena's mother otherwise known, nor did the Camena have any association with Juno Moneta before Livius gave her one. The Muses' mother is Mnemosyne—literally, "Memory" personified—and she is famous not from Homer, who never mentions her, but from Hesiod and other sources undoubtedly known to Livius.[28] Hardie thus concludes that "Livius' Camena-mother derived from Juno Moneta" of the Roman state cult, but was "a distinctive literary goddess, not identical with Mnemosyne, yet connecting with her as divinised memory, and not identical with Juno either, yet recalling her ancient title and her active advisory role. Livius' creation had affinities with the goddess of the Capitol, as well as with Mnemosyne. Moneta linked central Rome with wider Greece."[29]

The fascinating implications of Hardie's argument go far beyond my immediate purposes. The point on which I want to focus is that Livius had no need to make his Camena the daughter of such a prominent figure in the Roman state cult.[30] By doing so, he inserted an avatar of Juno into his *Odyssey*, not merely as part of the "divine apparatus" of the epic but at the wellspring of poetic inspiration as he represented it. His immediate epic successor, Gnaeus Naevius, seems not to have followed him in this but to have responded in a way that could be seen as either challenging or complementary.[31] Quintus Ennius then brought the Muses to Latin poetry, emulating his aristocratic

---

26. *Camena*, though possibly an Etruscan word (Macrobius, *Commentary on Scipio's Dream* 2.3.4; translation in Stahl 1952, 194), was thought to be etymologically connected to *carmen*, "song" (Varro, *The Latin Language* 7.26 in Kent 1938, 292–93). The Muses danced by the banks of a spring on Mt. Helicon and bathed in the springs Permessus, Hippocrene, or Olmeius (Hesiod, *Theogony* 1–9). On cultic resemblances see A. Hardie 2016, 66–69.

27. A. Hardie 2007, 556 citing Fraenkel 1931, 613 and Mariotti 1986, 23.

28. See West 1966, 174 on Hesiod, *Theogony* 54.

29. A. Hardie 2007, 558–59 citing Palmer 1974, 98–99, Otto 2005, 29–30, and Littlewood 2006, 57–58, 59–60.

30. Livius, as I noted above, does not use the name Juno, but only her cult title Moneta. A. Hardie 2007, 557–58 argues that the epithet "represented an early aspect of the supreme goddess," namely the ability "to remind, advise, or warn," and no goddess called Moneta had any existence apart from Juno at the time when Livius wrote.

31. For text and translation, see Warmington 1936, 46–47, fragment 1; for discussion see A. Hardie 2016, 72–74.

friend Marcus Fulvius Nobilior, who imported the first cult of the Muses to Rome from Ambracia to commemorate his victory over that city in in 189 BCE.[32] After Ennius, the Camena and Juno Moneta did not continue to define the standard genealogy of poetic inspiration at Rome, but they did become part of the literary–historical and intertextual record. The names Muses and Camenae came to be used interchangeably, and Juno acquired Musal associations that might be activated at any time.[33]

If the narrator of the *Aeneid* is aware of Juno as a potential rival, it is not surprising that he is wary of invoking any Muse to help him: her complex relationship with Juno Moneta might involve her in divided loyalties, at best. He is clearly aware of these associations when he speaks of Aeneas' trials as something brought about "on account of savage Juno's **remembering** anger" (*saevae **memorem** Iunonis ob iram* 4). A few lines later, having already declared that he is doing the singing himself, the narrator belatedly enlists the Muse's help in "**reminding**" him about the causes of Juno's anger (*Musa, mihi causas **memora*** 8). In the space of eight lines, both Juno and the narrator's Muse are twice linked to memory, and so to one another. A few lines later Juno is once again "showing remembrance, unforgetting" (*memor* 23), this time specifically of the Trojan War.[34] Just afterwards we learn of all the real or perceived offenses to her godhead that she keeps put away deep in her mind: the judgment of Paris, that slight to her beauty, the sheer hatefulness of those people, the abduction of Ganymede and his theft of her daughter Hebe's place of honor among the gods (26–28). Juno is a goddess who just cannot forget; and the mnemonic link that is forged between herself and the Muse in the opening lines becomes in what follows all the more firmly connected to Juno herself. It is Juno, then, as much as any Muse, who is in this poem the goddess of memory.[35]

It is therefore not surprising, when the narrator belatedly does invoke the Muse, to learn that the tale he begins to tell is all about Juno; no more surprising that she herself is then introduced as the first person, other than the narrator, to speak; no surprise either that her first words take us back to the first word of the *Iliad*. To put it another way, whatever the narrator's intentions may be, virtually every imaginable force is ranged against his telling the story of Aeneas as a story that would displease Juno, as one of successful homecoming, as a comedy of dynastic marriage, because at every turn he is opposed by a

---

32. See Skutsch 1985, 144–45; Coarelli 1997, 459; Rüpke 2011, 88–90.

33. A. Hardie 2007, 552–56 explores the Musal association shared by Hera and Juno in literature and cult.

34. See the *Oxford Latin Dictionary*, s.v. memor, where this passage is cited.

35. On Juno and memory see Seider 2013, 68–75.

goddess who is a kind of Muse and the divinity who presides over the institution of marriage itself. If this were not enough, Juno has another yet another advantage. An important part of the narrator's memory is, precisely, his memory of Homer. The new poem, as an elaborate and all but explicit exercise in intertextual composition, is to be an essay in poetic memory of a very particular kind, a kind unknown to Homer. But it is not unknown to Juno, who has her own memories of Homer, and of Livius, as well. Thus, in a sense, the narrator's daunting challenge is not to beat Homer at his own game, but to beat the goddess of memory at hers.

The Narrator's Anxiety

When the narrator uses free indirect discourse to explain why Juno hates Aeneas, he seems to be entering her mind and showing the reader her innermost thoughts. But what happens when a narrator uses this technique to represent the thoughts of a rebellious character who covets control of the narrative for herself? Might the device allow control to flow dangerously in the wrong direction? In common parlance, would we say that the narrator is channeling the character, or vice versa? In either case, by performing this mind meld with Juno, the narrator seems to give her the opening she needs to seize control, as she immediately does. The spectacularly Iliadic irruption in which she fulminates about her supposed powerlessness allows her to recall a literal fulmination in *Homecomings*, in which Pallas Athena borrows Jupiter's thunderbolt to blast Ajax the Locrian out of the sea and impale him on a jagged rock (*Aeneid* 1.40–45). The situations are not really parallel. Like Juno, Athena favored the Greeks during the war, but she destroyed many of them in *Homecomings* because Ajax had *defiled* her cult image, the Palladium, during the sack of the city; and she borrowed Jupiter's lightning bolt, *with* his permission, to blast the malefactors.[36] Juno on the other hand wants to destroy Aeneas despite the fact that he *rescued* the Palladium from the Greek plunderers and is dutifully carrying it with him to Italy; nor does she borrow, but rather usurps Neptune's prerogative, *without* his permission. Indulging in fuzzy logic, Juno seizes upon trivial or misleading parallels to justify her trespass.

From another perspective, however, Juno's view of the situation makes perfect sense. If *Homecomings* is a kind of sequel to the *Iliad*, so too is the *Odyssey*, which for us is the definitive epic of homecoming; but in that sense it is truly

---

[36]. The details behind Juno's allusive account are given by Servius, *Commentary on Vergil's Aeneid* 1.41 *noxam* and *Oil(e)i*, with partial attribution to the otherwise unknown Annaeus Placidus.

exceptional. It is a tale of homecoming that ends happily when a singular hero is reunited with his faithful wife and works with his son to vanquish those who have been consuming his property. It is not like the Cyclic *Homecomings*, which strung together the stories of multiple heroes, some of which involved adulterous wives, alienated offspring, and either death or further wandering for the heroes themselves. Indeed, the *Odyssey* thematizes its similarity to and its difference from *Homecomings*, not casually but repeatedly and insistently. In book 1 of the *Odyssey* (28–43) Zeus complains that mortals blame the gods for their misfortunes, citing the disastrous homecoming of Agamemnon as an example. This unhappy homecoming will run throughout the poem as a leitmotif, always raising the question of whether Odysseus' homecoming will be similar to or different from it.[37] A second development begins later in book 1 (325–64) when the bard Phemius strikes up his own version of *Homecomings* and Penelope objects that it pains her to hear these tales when Odysseus has still not returned. Here, in contrast to the story of Agamemnon, the theme of homecoming is implicitly represented as one of success. This continues when Telemachus visits Nestor in book 3 and Menelaus in book 4. Both these heroes have obtained their homecomings, Nestor without much difficulty; but he traveled part of the way with Diomedes, who at his home in Argos was met with a welcome almost like Agamemnon's, though he survived and went into exile. Menelaus experienced a mini-Odyssey of his own, eventually reaching home successfully, again in contrast to Agamemnon, his brother. In this way, the *Odyssey* minimizes the significance of happy endings in *Homecomings* and emphasizes the difficulties that the Greek captains faced in their returns. That may be a tendentious interpretation of the Cyclic poem, but it was effective both in establishing the magnitude of the challenge that Odysseus had to overcome and in characterizing the theme of "homecoming" as "*disastrous* homecoming."[38] Thus when the *Aeneid* starts out with the hero nearing the successful completion of a potentially successful "homecoming," Juno immediately intervenes to make it a catastrophic one. That is why her citation of Ajax's fate makes sense: it represents her idea of the entire Epic Cycle as part of a "Long Iliad" while indicating the kind of disastrous and abbreviated homecoming that she wants for Aeneas.

The *Odyssey*, then, is unique in that it bears comparison to the *Iliad* while being, as a continuation of the *Iliad* and as an epic of homecoming, uniquely un-Iliadic and un-Cyclic, exploring an exceptional hero and celebrating his success in overcoming the tragic fate of so many others who fought at Troy. Bearing this in mind, the reader of the *Aeneid* who finds Juno citing the Cyclic

---

37. See for instance *Odyssey* 11.385–464, 13.383–85, and 24.19–97.
38. Danek 2005; 2015, 359–60.

Homecomings as a precedent for what she is about to do should be *en garde*. Even more, the narrator whom Juno has just interrupted should be seriously alarmed. Not only is Juno about to end his poem before it has got underway; as if that were not bad enough, she plans to do so in the most tasteless way possible. In comparison to the measured, dignified tone of the narrator's proem and summary of the back-story, Juno's soliloquy might be considered almost bombastic. Her description of Ajax's fate is certainly that, and the shipwreck episode that she produces is bombastic in the extreme. Philip Hardie has written of how the storm of *Aeneid* 1 represents a hyperbolically elemental disturbance, a revolt against universal order with overtones of Gigantomachic rebellion against the Olympian cosmos.[39] If anything, this disturbance is all the greater because it is Juno, herself an Olympian, who is behind this cosmic rebellion. Such an episode might be counted not as bombastic, but sublime; but the impact of this spectacle upon the reader is scripted in the reactions of both hero and narrator.[40] When the storm hits, the reader experiences it, feels it, along with the hero, whose "limbs suddenly go slack *with cold*" (92). That is not an encouraging reaction. In ancient literary criticism, frigidity is the polar opposite of the sublime.[41] Aeneas is paralyzed "with cold" (*frigore*) as he watches, and we watch with him, waves lifted high, oars snapped, prows spun round, hulls breached and buried in mountainous waves, as men and ships fight for their lives on crests that rise to the stars and in troughs that expose the floor of the sea (92–123). A few individual fates are recounted, and in their midst we find a summarizing couplet, justly famous, and brilliantly symbolic of all that is at stake. The Latin demands close attention:

apparent rari nantes in gurgite vasto,
arma virum, tabulaeque, et Troia gaza per undas.

Here and there, swimmers appear upon the vast deep,
arms of men, planks, and Trojan treasure across the waters.
(*Aeneid* 1.118–19)

The first of these lines has become a textbook illustration of metrical artistry.[42] The narrator remains in control at least to this extent. One can add that the

---

39. P. R. Hardie 1986, 90–97.

40. P. R. Hardie 1986, 241–42 on the misguided disparagement of Vergilian hyperbole by some earlier critics.

41. See Russell's text and translation of "Longinus," *On the Sublime* 4–5 in Halliwell et al. 1995, 170–75 and Russell 1964, 76 on chapter 4.1.

42. In the first half of the line, the first long syllable of each foot receives no stress because the natural accent of each word falls on the syllable (*āppá/rēnt rá/rī nán/tēs*) in what is called

verb *apparent* ("they appear") is, once again, a focalizing gesture that causes the reader to gaze upon this bathetic disaster with the hero's own sense of failure and responsibility. The same impulse can be felt in the following line, which summarizes the dashed hopes of the Trojan survivors: "arms of men, planks, and Trojan treasure across the waters." All that Aeneas has is about to sink to the bottom of the sea. At the same time, it is hard not to infer that Aeneas' perspective overlaps with that of another interested party—namely, the epic narrator himself.[43] In effect, line 119 is a biting parody of the poem's opening line:

arma virum *tabulae***que et Troia gaza** *per undas* 1.119
arma virumque *cano,* **Troiae** *qui primus ab oris* 1.1

As all commentators note, this is the first (but far from last) occurrence of the collocation *arma virum(que)* since the opening of the poem. In it, the meaning of the phrase is distorted as *virum* changes its case (from accusative to genitive) and loses its enclitic conjunction (*-que,* "and"), which gets shunted over to make room for *tabulae*, the "planks" or "boards" into which Aeneas' ships have begun to dissolve. The intrusion of this word into the middle of *arma virum . . . que*, the quasi-titular opening phrase of the poem, graphically represents not just the disintegrating fabric of the ships, but also that of the poem itself.[44] The *Aeneid* is coming apart before our eyes, and in this connection it seems relevant that *tabulae* is also the *mot juste* not only for the planks of a ship but also for another kind of board, one that was covered with wax to make a writing tablet.[45] This is an image of elemental dissolution in another sense.[46] Thus the shipwreck takes on not only cosmic but also metaliterary, self-reflexive significance. It is important that this image involves writing tablets in

---

"heterodyne movement" or "ictus-clash." The jostling of these two patterns against one another represents the struggles of the doomed swimmers. Then suddenly in the second half of the line the two patterns coincide (*gŭ́rgĭtĕ/vā́stō*) in "homodyne movement" as the swimmers give in to the insuperable power of the element that dooms them. See Wilkinson 1963, 120–32.

43. On what follows see Oliensis 2004, 31–32.

44. On *arma virum(que)* as a titular phrase, see Austin 1971, 25–26 on *Aeneid* 1.1–7; Abbot 2012–2013; Mac Góráin 2018.

45. For the commonplace analogy between poetry and seafaring see, e.g., Vergil, *Georgics* 2.39–45; Horace, *Epodes* 10, *Odes* 1.3; Propertius, *Elegies* 3.9.1–4, 3.21, 3.24; Ovid, *Fasti* 1.4, *Tristia* 1.2. On metapoetic *tabulae* in general see Roman 2006; in connection with metapoetic voyaging or shipwreck see Horace, *Odes* 1.5.13 and Ovid, *Ibis* 18 with Heerink 2016, 187–88; Propertius, *Elegies* 2.26.33; Ovid, *Metamorphoses* 11.428–29, *Tristia* 1.2.47, 1.6.8.

46. The *Oxford Latin Dictionary* defines "elementum" as (2) "a letter of the alphabet." Some of the cultural implications of this equivalency are explored by Frampton 2019, 55–84.

particular, since an easily erased wax-covered tablet was the device on which a poet would work out the various drafts of his composition before consigning the finished work to inked papyrus book rolls (*libri* or *libelli*).[47] The image thus expresses the poet's fear of failure, but not in the eyes of some putative reading public. That is the sort of failure that Catullus predicts for Volusius, whose *Annals*—in published form, since they are written on papyrus—will be used to wrap mackerel.[48] Rather, it expresses a writer's anxiety about being able to finish a poem at all or, in a context like this, even to get past the first important episode.[49] This is, then, a multivalent shipwreck that expresses both the hero's sense of failure as he watches his fleet being overwhelmed by wind and water and the narrator's anxiety that he, too, will fail to write either an Odyssey or an Iliad, but will be just another Cyclic poet destined to watch his pretentious epic ambitions founder on the sea of Homeric expectations like so much Trojan foppery.[50]

All of this would be quite acceptable to Juno, of course. She has two shortened lives in view here: a premature end both to the story (arrested by storm) and to the poem (doomed by Cyclic inadequacy). A brief, unimpressive *Aeneid* ending with the hero drowned at sea after little more than a hundred lines would align perfectly with her determination to make every Trojan epic merely another short, unimpressive episode of her ever-expanding Cyclic Iliad. In contrast, the narrator seems to have something more ambitious in mind, an Iliad or an Odyssey, we cannot be sure which; perhaps he is aiming for both, or maybe he would be satisfied with either outcome. In that case, Juno's effort to steer the poem one way instead of the other could be viewed as a complication,

---

47. On these distinctions see Birt 1882, 12–14, 85–87, 95–96 and Kenyon 1932, 89–91.

48. Catullus 36; NB *charta* ("papyrus") 1. The image of writing tablets does, however, find its counterpart in Catullus' alarm when he finds that his girlfriend is cross with him and has stolen the "notebooks" (*codicilli*, which consist of several tablets bound together like a modern book) that contain the unpublished drafts of his work which she has sworn to burn: see poems 36 and 42 with Roman 2006, 353–57.

49. Note as well that the metapoetic *tabulae* in line 119 can be taken as responding to the metapoetic *cano* in line 1, and that here too different stages of poetic production—namely, composition and recitation—come into play. This time, however, the stages chosen represent different kinds of metaphorical significance, the grossly physical tablets standing (paradoxically) for impermanence and corruptibility, in contrast to (putatively) immaterial song, according to a widespread ideological prejudice, suggesting the permanence and stability of a classic utterance; see Farrell 1999, 2007, 2009; Kennerly 2018. On *cano* in this sense see Lowrie 2009, 1–23.

50. For the conceit of Homer as the sea or the ocean, see Callimachus, *Hymn to Apollo* 105–13 with Williams 1978, 85–90 and 98–99; Morgan 1999, 32–39, 63–75.

but just one among many, and hardly as an existential disaster. But literary disaster remains a real possibility, because any narrator is more likely to fail utterly than to succeed in an attempt to rival the greatest poet of all.[51] That is how the poets of the Epic Cycle failed, producing all-but-forgotten works that were proverbial among ancient critics, as well as poets of talent and ambition, as the very embodiment of the second-rate. In reality, it may be the likelihood of such failure, even more than Juno's opposition, that haunts the narrator of the *Aeneid*. For this reason, it seems possible that the opening words of the poem, "Arms and a man *I sing*," betray the anxiety with which the narrator launches his effort. And who can blame him?

Aeneas' "Misfortunes"

Internal narrators are a common feature of epic poetry. That is not the kind of narrator Juno wants to be. Her goal is to replace the principal narrator, or at least to make him tell a story that she could accept. There is some reason to believe that Aeneas would also accept a story that would satisfy Juno. Being a mere mortal, however, he can express his preference, but lacks the capacity to challenge the narrator for control of the plot. On the other hand, he enjoys an opportunity that is not granted to Juno when he is given two entire books of the poem to narrate in whatever way he sees fit. What kind of narrator does he prove to be?

One might expect him to be an Odyssean narrator. By the time Aeneas tells his story, the chaos introduced by Juno's storm seems to have dissipated and he finds himself squarely in (what the reader recognizes as) a version of Alcinous' court where he is entertained with a lavish banquet. When Odysseus is entertained by Alcinous, he will recite his "Apologoi," the tale of his wanderings since the Trojan War. Similarly at Carthage, Dido asks Aeneas to tell the story of what I will call his "Misfortunes."[52] According to Knauer's general plan, the narrative of the "Misfortunes" as a whole corresponds to Odysseus' "Apologoi."[53] In that sense, if a contest is underway to decide whether the

---

51. Quintilian's judgment on Antimachus, that he stands second on the canon of Greek epic poets, but a lot closer to third place than first (*The Orator's Education* 10.1.53 in Russell 2002, vol. 4, 278–79), sums up the challenge faced by Homer's would-be rivals.

52. Both Dido and Aeneas refer to the Trojans' postwar adventures as their *casus* in the plural (1.754, 2.10), with the meaning of "a chance occurrence," often an unfortunate one (see the *Oxford Latin Dictionary* s.v. casus 5). I therefore use "Misfortunes" to designate Aeneas' entire narration in books 2 and 3, referring to book 2 alone as "The Sack of Troy" and to book 3 alone as Aeneas' "Wanderings."

53. Knauer 1964, 169–72, 183–84; 1964a, 68.

Aeneid is an *Odyssey* or an *Iliad*, it would seem that the *Odyssey* leaps strongly into the lead at this point and that Aeneas himself is an Odyssean narrator.[54] But it is not as simple as that.

Knauer himself acknowledges some interesting differences between the banquets of Alcinous and Dido in regard to storytelling. In the *Odyssey*, there is a clean division between the three brief tales sung by the bard Demodocus in book 8 and the hero's lengthy "Apologoi" in books 9–12. There is a further distinction between Demodocus' second song, "The Adultery of Ares and Aphrodite" (*Odyssey* 8.266–369), on the one hand, and a pair of Trojan War stories, "The Quarrel of Achilles and Odysseus" (8.72–82) and "The Trojan Horse" (8.499–520), on the other. In the *Aeneid*, the bard Iopas sings just one song about celestial mechanics and its relationship to the rhythm of the seasons on earth, including the origin of species (*Aeneid* 1.740–47). This is widely recognized as corresponding to Demodocus' second song, which in antiquity was interpreted as an allegory of natural philosophy.[55] By the same token, Demodocus' Trojan War songs—especially his final performance, "The Trojan Horse"—correspond thematically to the first half of Aeneas' "Misfortunes," his rendition of "The Sack of Troy" in book 2. Conversely, Odysseus' "Apologoi" correspond more closely to Aeneas' "Wanderings" in book 3 than to the "Misfortunes" as a whole. In addition, Aeneas' telling of "The Sack of Troy" is much longer than Demodocus' version of "The Trojan Horse," and the reader will recognize that it draws plentifully on more extended treatments of that and related stories.[56] Chief among these, according to Knauer, is the Cyclic poem *The Sack of Troy* attributed to Arctinus.[57] That is to say, there is no question but that the first half of Aeneas' narrative, like Demodocus' third and final song itself, is devoted to a consummately Cyclic theme.

On the other hand, Aeneas' "Wanderings" in book 3 are generally considered to be modeled quite closely on Odysseus' "Apologoi," and from the reader's point of view it is impossible not to draw this inference. Nevertheless, when Aeneas tells his story to Dido, Odysseus has not yet told his tale to

---

54. See Lenta 2012. At the same time, the question of artful and even deceptive narrative comes very much into play: see Powell 2011.

55. Knauer 1964, 168 note 2; 1964a, 82 note 4; P. R. Hardie 1986, 51–66; Nelis 2001, 96–112, 348–51.

56. On the sources of book 2 see Casali 2017, 7–40 and passim.

57. Knauer 1964, 165–73; 1964a, 82 note 4. "The Sack of Troy" was also an episode of the Cyclic *Little Iliad* ascribed to Lesches: see Davies 1989, 60–70; West 2013, 164–68. Other works drew on it, especially the several Greek tragedies and their Roman adaptations that dealt with particular episodes. I return to these points below in this chapter and devote a section of chapter 3 to "The Sack of Troy."

Alcinous. No living person knows anything about Odysseus' adventures except Achaemenides, a former companion abandoned by Ulysses and rescued by Aeneas, who therefore knows only about the first few of the Ithacan's adventures up to and including his encounter with the Cyclops Polyphemus.[58] In terms of narrative chronology, then, Aeneas' "Wanderings" are mainly pre-Odyssean in that they take place with virtually no knowledge of Odysseus' adventures. For this reason, to the extent that they are Odyssean in character, they are better regarded as proto-Odyssean instead of derivatively so. In this sense they resemble a Trojan version of the Cyclic *Homecomings*.[59] Aeneas himself suggests as much at the beginning of book 3 when he says that after the fall of the city, "we are driven by the auguries of the gods to seek various places of exile and uninhabited lands" (3.4–5). Servius correctly identifies two ways of understanding "we" in this sentence, stating:

> Many refer this to [*Aeneid* 1.602, where the Trojan people are described as being] "spread throughout the great globe." For it is agreed that such Trojans as Helenus and Antenor occupied different regions of the globe; but it is better that the poet gives this speech to Aeneas in particular, who was driven by auguries to seek different lands, i.e. lands situated in different regions.[60]

Here Servius draws attention to Antenor as one of the leaders of the Trojan diaspora that followed the war, much as Venus does when she remonstrates with Jupiter in book 1 (242–49). Servius also alludes to the most substantial episode of book 3, the "homecoming" of Helenus and Andromache to Buthrotum (294–505). Aeneas' rendition of the latter story is in effect a version of one found in the Cyclic *Homecomings*, that of Pyrrhus, told from the Trojan instead of the Greek point of view.[61] These facts invite a clear inference. Aeneas' "Wanderings" is really one among many tales of Trojan War veterans and

---

58. I return to Achaemenides in the section of chapter 3 entitled "Wanderings."

59. The parallelism of the *Homecomings* tradition is thematized in the *Odyssey* via the song of Phemius in book 1 (325–27), in the homecoming tales told to Telemachus by Nestor in book 3 (130–98) and Menelaus in book 4 (332–586), and in repeated references to the fate of Agamemnon (e.g. 1.30–43, 11.380–466, 13.383–85, 24.19–97). For a list of explicit references to the subject matter of Cyclic epics in the *Aeneid* see Kopff 1981, 925; on tragic sources see Fenik 1960, 1–31; König 1970, 28–88.

60. Servius, *Commentary on Vergil's Aeneid* 3.4. There are two versions of this note (see Fowler, Casali and Stok 1997/2019, 88), each of which contains details peculiar to it; my translation is a synthesis of both versions. Servius' comment on *Aeneid* 1.602 is a fuller version of this note.

61. On Pyrrhus' homecoming see the section of chapter 3 entitled "Wanderings."

survivors making their ways "home." It parallels the Cyclic *Homecomings*, concluding as that poem does before Odysseus, the last of the Greek heroes, arrives at Ithaca. In this sense, Aeneas' "Wanderings" can be seen as an addition to the Epic Cycle and a precursor to, rather than an imitation of, Odysseus' "Apologoi."

For these reasons, it is reasonable to regard both halves of Aeneas' "Misfortunes" as specimens of Cyclic poetry. At the same time, the reader of the *Aeneid* is free to measure Aeneas' story against the Homeric poems. This is true not only of Aeneas' "Wanderings," but of "The Sack of Troy" as well. Book 2 is the only book of the *Aeneid* that is actually set in Troy and is the first to feature armed conflict. This makes it a kind of Iliad, while book 3, as a tale of post-war seafaring in search of one's home, is a kind of Odyssey.[62] Moreover, unlike Odysseus, Aeneas resembles Homer himself by narrating a tale of warfare in book 2 and one of wandering in book 3. Because he deals with war first and wandering second, he even follows same order as Homer, rather than inverting it, as does the *Aeneid* as a whole. To this extent, Aeneas looks like a narrator who is capable of realizing the kind of poem that the *Aeneid* has traditionally been thought to be: a Homeric poem that combines (post-)Iliadic warfare and (proto-)Odyssean wandering in equal measure within a smaller compass, and one that celebrates a single hero—Aeneas himself—from start to finish. Aeneas' "Misfortunes" is thus a miniature Cyclic facsimile of both Homeric masterpieces. The hero is not a poet, of course, and does not have a poet's ambitions, but one may still ask, what kind of success does Aeneas achieve?

Here I would refer to the critical reception of his two-book performance. In general, book 2 is among the most admired of the poem, while book 3 is frequently counted among the least exciting.[63] Whether one agrees with this division of opinion is beside the point. It is an abundantly documented fact of the poem's reception history, and as such it is interpretable. For immediate purposes, there are several points to make. First, because Aeneas' "Misfortunes" consists of quasi-Iliadic and quasi-Odyssean halves, it is difficult not to regard it as a miniature Aeneid.[64] Second, its reliance on mainly Cyclic

---

62. Hexter 1999, 67.

63. Typical are Allen 1951–1952; Williams 1962, 2–3; Williams 1983. Heyworth and Morwood 2017, ix–x offer a brief, but forthright and refreshing defense of book 3, with which I am very much in sympathy. See also Putnam 1980/1995; Quint 1982, 1989, and 2018, 28–60.

64. Hershkowitz 1991, 70 argues that book 3 in itself "can be read as a mini-epic which structurally reflects the *Aeneid* as a whole." Although she does not make this point, her position is compatible with the idea that "the *Aeneid* as a whole" is an Odyssey. In fact, she does not mention or cite the *Iliad* even once. A similar argument (Galinsky 1968) finds book 5 a microcosm of the *Aeneid* but with a greater balance between Iliadic and Odyssean elements.

material suggests that the Epic Cycle is a relevant point of reference for the Homeric program of the *Aeneid*, as well. More than that, it suggests that an epic fashioned out of Cyclic materials can very easily take the form of a bipartite Iliad plus Odyssey; that is, its affinity with the Epic Cycle per se does not predispose it to be more like one Homeric poem or the other. Third, and perhaps surprisingly, the critical reception of book 2 suggests that a Cyclic Aeneid need not be a second-rate failure. Aeneas' recitation of "The Sack of Troy" is the proverbial ripping good yarn.[65] On the other hand, the reception of his "Wanderings" does not encourage the inference that a combination of Iliad plus Odyssey will be equally effective in both parts. It remains an open question just why this is so. Perhaps readers prefer the narrative unity of book 2 to the episodic nature of book 3. Perhaps Aeneas' Iliadic orientation makes him a better exponent of battle narrative than of wandering. Perhaps the hero simply tired as the night wore on, much as Homer's powers (according to "Longinus") declined with age, so that the *Iliad* is (in his eyes) superior to the *Odyssey* in aesthetic terms.[66] To be clear, I am not in any way suggesting that any of these inferences is dispositive. If it were, then the success of Aeneas' quasi-Iliadic "Sack of Troy" ought to correlate with the relative popularity of the "Odyssean" and "Iliadic" *Aeneid*. In fact, the opposite is the case; books 1–6 have always been more popular with readers than books 7–12, until fairly recently, at least. The particular intertextual characteristics of Aeneas' turn as an epic narrator do not tell us what kind of poem the *Aeneid* as a whole will be; and that is the main point. Specifically, any affinity that the poem may have with the Epic Cycle need have nothing to do with any struggle between Iliadic and Odyssean forces. A strategy of risking or courting Cyclic disaster is in the end no "third way" and no solution to our main problem. The narrator of a Cyclic Aeneid would face more or less the same Iliadic and Odyssean choices and pitfalls as the narrator of the *Aeneid* itself.

65. Aristotle does not mention *The Sack of Troy* as an epic by the Cyclic poet Arctinus, but in disparaging the loosely episodic structure of *Cypria* and the *Little Iliad* as capable of yielding multiple tragic plots, he describes "The Sack of Troy" as one of these, and there were a number of tragedies based on that theme (*Poetics* 1459a–b in Halliwell et al. 1995, 114–19). The well-organized plot of *Aeneid* 2 may well derive from successful tragic treatments and tacitly present itself as a tragedy by adopting tragic economy of plot, in contrast to the much more episodic book 3. On the Epic Cycle and Greek tragedy in general see Sommerstein 2015.

66. See Russell's text and translation of "Longinus," *On the Sublime* 1.11–14 in Halliwell et al. 1985, 192–95. Not quite the same thing, but not incompatible with the "poetics of tiredness" thesis promulgated by Allen (1951–1952); quite incompatible with the idea that the book contains "many features that strike the reader as authorial and dissonant with Aeneas as narrator": so G. Williams 1983, 262.

Cyclic Ethics

Aeneas' recitation of his "Misfortunes" suggests that an aesthetically successful Cyclic narrative is not a contradiction in terms, but neither is it a foregone conclusion. It further suggests that Cyclic narratives tend to focus either on battles or on voyaging, and thus conform to the Homeric binary with which we have been concerned. As such, it is not surprising that they are inhabited by a number of would-be successors to Achilles. These include Odysseus himself, who defeated Achilles' own cousin, Ajax son of Telamon, in a debate to determine who would inherit Achilles' god-forged armor. This contest was an episode of the *Little Iliad*, and it later became a favorite with tragic poets. It is not the only episode of "posthomerica" to confront Achillean and Odyssean values to determine who, if anyone, might succeed the best of the Achaeans. On the other hand, Odysseus is hardly the only figure of the Epic Cycle who contrasts with the type represented by Achilles and his kinsmen, his cousin Ajax and his son Pyrrhus (or Neoptolemus). In Aeneas' own narrative we hear of Palamedes, who for once got the better of Odysseus, and of the duplicitous Sinon, who invoked a personal connection with Palamedes to convince the Trojans that Odysseus conspired with the prophet Calchas against him, to have him named a suitable human sacrifice so as to obtain for the rest of the Greeks a safe journey home from the war. Among the Trojans, as well, post-Homeric traditions tell us that Antenor and Aeneas himself collaborated with the Greeks to secure their escape from Troy, either to avoid being caught up in the city's destruction, or perhaps to help bring it about.[67] We will return to these themes and to Aeneas' recital of his "Misfortunes" in chapter 3. For now, it is sufficient to note that this material, and Aeneas' handling of it, is full of complex ethical issues governed by Iliadic and Odyssean values. Above all, neither Cyclic poetry in general nor Aeneas' own record as a Cyclic character outlines a "third way" by which to escape this ethical dilemma.

A Second Argo: The *Aeneid* and Apollonius

The history of *Aeneid* criticism is informed by an expectation that Aeneas ought to be the perfect hero, uniting Achillean might and Odyssean wisdom in a single paragon of heroic virtue.[68] This expectation is also haunted by the fact that many readers consider Aeneas, purely as a character, something of a

---

67. See Ussani 1947; Galinsky 1969, 40; Horsfall 1986, 14–17; Ahl 1989, 26–25; Scafoglio 2015.

68. "Aeneas, of course, is meant to be the prototype as well as the mythical ancestor of Augustus. In the narrative, he belongs to his own heroic age.... Yet the distinction between any

failure, a hero manqué.[69] On this view, far from combining in full measure the virtues of Homer's incompatible heroic paradigms, Aeneas measures up to neither. As the previous section indicates, this outcome might be explained if Aeneas' nature is simply that of a Cyclic hero, a would-be Achilles or Odysseus who is far from equaling either of them, let alone surpassing both. Indeed, because he strikes many readers as less compelling a character than Achilles or Odysseus, the hero of the *Aeneid* can be seen as one of the poem's weakest elements, and he has been. Critical explanations of why this is actually not the case almost always come off as pious homilies unconcerned with the experience of readers, indifferent to how they *do* react to Aeneas and focused on telling them how they *should* react. Many readers therefore understand that the hero is supposed to surpass both of his Homeric models without actually believing that he does. They can write the essay they need to ace the exam, but they keep their own counsel.

One way around this experiment in false consciousness is to identify what I have been calling a "third way;" and one of these readily presents itself in the person of Jason, hero of the *Argonautica* by Apollonius of Rhodes. Since antiquity it has been a critical commonplace that parts of the *Aeneid* imitate Apollonius' poem very closely indeed. The point most often made is first found in Servius: "Apollonius wrote an *Argonautica* and in its third book represented Medea in love; this book [i.e., *Aeneid* 4] in its entirety is translated from it."[70] In mentioning Medea, Servius accentuates the positive, as he usually does.[71] Medea and Dido are widely regarded as sympathetic and impressive characters. The flip side of this perception is that Apollonius' Jason is regarded as less than admirable in his readiness to profit from the good will and superior abilities of others to further his personal goals. Readers of Apollonius look askance at Jason's exploitation of Medea, the young and inexperienced princess of Colchis. Her infatuation with Jason is very much against her

---

genuinely Homeric hero is quite fundamental. His ethos is utterly different from that of Achilles, Hector or Odysseus" (Otis 1964/1995, 222); see also Williams 1963.

69. "Aeneas has much in common with Jason, a hero forced into a quest not of his choosing, and whose erotic history is tarnished by a lack of constancy and consistency" (P. R. Hardie 2014, 77). More generally, some find him "an unheroic hero" (H.-P. Stahl, 1981) or even a "wimp" (Griffin 1993). Kluth 2010 describes Aeneas as "the first 'almost modern' hero." The idea that Aeneas is an "anti-hero" has become so hackneyed that it is possible to download a 2,000-word essay on the subject—"to battle writer's block and get inspiration for your next assignment"—from a number of online "paper mills," which I refrain from citing.

70. Servius, *Commentary on Vergil's Aeneid* 4, preface.

71. The remainder of his introduction notes the various criticisms that had been leveled at book 4 in the context of the narrative as a whole.

family's interests and, ultimately, her own. Readers of the *Aeneid* who see Dido in similar terms are bound to regard Aeneas as her exploitative Jason. One can ask whether that is all he is, whether he improves upon Jason in any way, and so forth; predictably, there is no consensus on such matters. The tragic consequences of Dido's love for Aeneas play out almost entirely in book 4, so that critical discussion tends to focus largely on that book. Such a focus encourages the idea that Aeneas at his worst may be another Jason, but that this is not his abiding character. The hero's defenders may thus conclude that, even if he is no Achilles or Odysseus, at least he surpasses Apollonius' hero as an ethical paradigm.

A more comprehensive approach to the idea of an Argonautic *Aeneid* shows that there is more to the story. Such an approach is now possible thanks to Damien Nelis, who has argued convincingly that the Apollonian program of the *Aeneid* is as extensive as its Homeric one, and that the two are intricately related.[72] So detailed is this relationship, in fact, that scholars and critics have not yet come fully to terms with Nelis' work, which holds considerable implications for my own argument.[73] To understand why, let me summarize Nelis' general perspective on this fascinating intertextual relationship in the light of its immediate antecedents and then focus on a few important details.

Odyssey *and Argosy*

Few readers consider the *Argonautica* a primarily Iliadic poem. Its similarities to the *Odyssey* are more obviously compelling.[74] Both the *Odyssey* and the *Argonautica* are poems of seafaring, and many of Jason's adventures are squarely based on those of Odysseus. The theme of "homecoming" is prominent in both poems. Indeed, Jason's double voyage, out and back, has been characterized as a double *nostos*—literally, and paradoxically, a double "homecoming," and in effect, a double Odyssey.[75] The motif of doubleness, at least, is readily comprehensible, because the poem's Odyssean program develops in a bipartite structure that is iterative and increasingly explicit in its intertextual

---

72. As I explain in the Introduction above.

73. A provocative exception is Kelly 2014.

74. Knight 1995, 29 states that the *Iliad* contributes significantly to the *Argonautica* in the form of phraseology, extended similes, set-pieces, and typical scenes, but not in respect of the plot, so that "in these broad terms, the poem would be entirely Odyssean." She does admit: "The Argonauts as a group are more like the Greek or Trojan army than Odysseus' fellow sailors, since the party consists of named and characterised men . . . rather than a (mostly) nameless group."

75. For the *nostos* theme in Apollonius, see Fränkel 1968, 65–66; Vian 1973, 92–93; Hutchinson 1988, 97–106; Clare 1993, 114–19; Nelis 1993 and 2001, 24; Knight 1995, 163–69.

design. The concept of a double *nostos*—a metaphorical one away from home and a literal one in the return—is but one aspect of this. Similar repetition with increasing explicitness informs numerous episodes of the poem's first half that are modeled on Homer and that find counterparts in the second half. These counterparts are again modeled on the same Homeric episodes, but with greater clarity and emphasis. Here are two illustrations.

The Argo's passage through the Clashing Rocks (Symplegades) into the Black Sea in book 2 (549–606) reappears as a passage through the very similar Wandering Rocks (Planctae) in book 4 (783–965). Both episodes are modeled on Odysseus' daring passage between Scylla and Charybdis in *Odyssey* 12 (234–59). This modeling is clear enough in the earlier episode, but it is made almost glaringly obvious in the second when the Argonauts *avoid* Scylla and Charybdis by successfully hazarding passage through the Planctae. In making this choice, Jason does the opposite of what Odysseus does in *Odyssey* 12 when Circe informs him that Jason is the only person to have sailed through the Planctae on the "the world-famous Argo" (70). Apollonius, then, gives us Jason choosing his route through the Planctae before the Homeric Odysseus chooses the other route between Scylla and Charybdis, which he does to avoid having to repeat Jason's amazing accomplishment. The laws of intertextual causality are thrown into momentary confusion, as if the intersection of the two narratives created a temporal anomaly. This is a clear example of Apollonius' exploitation of the "future reflexive" mode.[76] My immediate point, however, is that this virtuoso display of intertextual craftsmanship makes the Argo's passage through the Planctae in book 4 even more explicitly Homeric than its passage through the Symplegades in book 1.[77] This is entirely typical of the way in which similar episodes in the two halves of the *Argonautica* are related.

To be fully appreciated, the example just cited requires a bit of erudition and imagination on the reader's part. The next example proves that Apollonius was not above providing extremely broad hints to help readers get the point. In book 1 (609–909), the Argonauts stop on the island of Lemnos and are hospitably received by Queen Hypsipyle, who would have liked Jason to remain with her and be her husband. Careful analysis guarantees that this episode is modeled on the Homeric "Phaeacis" (books 5–13 of the *Odyssey*) in which the hero is hospitably received by King Alcinous, who offers Odysseus

---

76. On the "future reflexive" mode see the section of chapter 1 entitled "Intertextual Chronology." On "Homeric time" in Apollonius see Knight 1995, 27–41.

77. Apollonius' imitation of the *Odyssey* was greatly facilitated by the fact that the "Apologoi" appear to have been modeled on earlier Argonautic material: see West 2005.

his daughter, Nausicaa, in marriage.[78] That said, the correspondences are sufficiently understated that they might not be obvious to all readers. More apparent is the fact that Jason's Colchian adventure in book 3, even if King Aeetes is much less friendly to Jason than Alcinous is to Odysseus, is also modeled on the "Phaeacis."[79] For alert readers, the latter, more explicit imitation should confirm the earlier, less explicit one. Nevertheless, in case more definite assurances should be required, in book 4 (982–1222) the Argonauts actually visit the Phaeacians and are received at the court of Alcinous and Arete themselves! As another token of Apollonius' "future reflexive" approach to the *Odyssey*, Jason and Medea meet the Phaeacian royal couple before their daughter, Nausicaa, whose role in the *Odyssey* is so important, has yet been born. This, in addition to most of the other significant correspondences between the first and second halves of the poem, may also be taken as indicating that Apollonius does not in fact digest Odysseus' story as a whole into the double *nostos* of the Argonauts, but rather focuses on the "Phaeacis," the portion of the *Odyssey* that research has shown to be based on the Argonautic legend, and especially on the "Apologoi," the portion of the "Phaeacis" that comprises Odysseus' narration of his adventures.[80]

I shall return to the pattern of repetition with emphasis. For the moment, this summary lends support to the idea that the plot of the *Argonautica* as a whole can be considered a kind of Odyssey. This point has not been lost on critics. Knauer, as I have noted, was the first to challenge seriously the traditional conception of the *Aeneid* as consisting of a six-book Odyssey followed by a six-book Iliad by stressing the continuing importance of the *Odyssey* for the plot of *Aeneid* 7–8 and, less explicitly, for books 9–12 as well. Knauer also acknowledged the importance of allusion to Apollonius, but left to others further consideration of this aspect and its relation to the poem's Homeric program.[81] This challenge was first accepted by Francis Cairns who, taking his bearings from Knauer, wrote about the *Aeneid* as follows:

> the *Odyssey* retains the structural and thematic importance it had in Books 1–6 well into, and indeed throughout, the 'iliadic' Books 7–12, while iliadic or quasi-iliadic episodes surface also in the 'odyssean' *Aeneid* 1–6. This makes the *Aeneid*, not a bipartite work divided by subject matter

---

78. Clauss 1993, 106–47; Hunter 1993, 47–52; Knight 1995, 32–34, 223; Nelis 2001, 112–20.

79. Along with works cited in the preceding note see Hunter 1989, 26, 29–30; Knight 1995, 32–34 and 224–44.

80. Nelis 2001, 23–25.

81. Knauer 1964, 528, entries on "Apollonios v. Rhodos" and on specific passages of the *Argonautica*.

(i.e. voyages or battles), but a unitary *Odyssey* with significant iliadic episodes. Nothing could be more natural, since both the *Odyssey* and the *Aeneid* are 'Returns,' and the outline structures of both are similar.[82]

This insistence on the "conceptual dominance" of the *Odyssey* in the *Aeneid* has far-reaching consequences, some of which I have already explored in a preliminary way. For the moment I am more concerned with one of Cairns' supporting arguments:

> External confirmation [that the *Aeneid* is essentially an Odyssey] comes in Virgil's ready acceptance of additional influence in his characters, motifs, and emotional tone from Apollonius Rhodius' *Argonautica*, which is in important respects a hyper-odyssean epic, choosing, in accordance with hellenistic taste, to stress and enhance those episodic and folkloristic features which distinguish the *Odyssey* from the *Iliad*.[83]

Cairns' conception, then, is that the *Aeneid* is more Odyssey than Iliad from start to finish. For this reason, he suggests, it easily incorporates elements of Apollonius' epic, because it too is predominantly Odyssean, or even (as Cairns puts it) "hyper-odyssean."

On this interpretation, the *Aeneid* is an Odyssey, but not because of Apollonius: rather, as Cairns sees it, the fact that it is conceived as primarily an Odyssey facilitates "additional" allusion to the *Argonautica*, as well. This is not what I mean when I ask whether Apollonius or the *Argonautica* offers a "third way," a different kind of heroic narrative and ethical universe from those offered by Homer. Damien Nelis, however, takes a different approach and goes much further, employing a method of analysis similar to Knauer's and applying it with comparable ambition, as I have explained.[84] In doing so, he not only makes a convincing case that the Apollonian program of the *Aeneid* is equally extensive and important as is its Homeric program. Crucially, Nelis inverts the direction of causal relations as Cairns, and in fact Knauer, conceives them. That is to say, he argues that allusion to the *Argonautica* in the *Aeneid* is not a casual or secondary matter, but that Apollonius' Homeric program actually guided that of the *Aeneid*. That is almost to say that the *Aeneid* is an Odyssey because it is also—and, in some sense, primarily—an Argosy.[85]

---

82. Cairns 1989, 178.

83. Cairns 1989, 179.

84. Nelis 2001: see above in the section of the introduction entitled "The Dialogic Intertext."

85. To be clear, I do not believe that Nelis himself makes this exact claim, and I do not know whether he would agree with it if stated in these terms. To my mind, however, it is one of several unavoidable, and very exciting inferences that his work makes possible.

Such an idea is much closer to what I mean when I speak of "third ways." Unlike Cairns, Nelis argues that the Argonautic *Aeneid* largely determined the form of the Homeric *Aeneid*. To the extent that Apollonius either succeeded in avoiding the horns of the Homeric dilemma, succumbed to them, or readily accepted the need to make a choice and did make it, this would presumably mean that the Argonautic *Aeneid* necessarily did so, as well. This is a fascinating, radically revisionist approach that forces us to rethink the intertextuality of the *Aeneid* from the ground up.

In my view, the idea that the *Aeneid* is Homeric *because* it is Apollonian—that its Homeric identity *is contingent on* its Apollonian one—is certainly right. This does not mean that the poem is no more than accidentally or opportunistically Homeric. The point is rather that Apollonius was the only poet who managed to craft an epic *chanson de geste* through active intertextual engagement with the Homeric poems to produce an imitative work that stands comparison with the originals. This reason above all would make the *Argonautica* the best possible guide to Homeric intertextuality.

A few questions remain. First, must the *Aeneid*, to the extent that it is an Apollonian Argosy, be a Homeric Odyssey, as well? Second, if yes, in ethical terms should we expect the heroes of both poems to be avatars of Odysseus—flexible, adaptable survivors rather than stubborn devotees of a traditional warrior code? Third, is Jason essentially another Odysseus, or does he represent a significant modification of the general type? Finally, what does this mean for Aeneas?

The Aeneid *as Argosy*

Before we can confront questions of character and ethical identity, let me return to some of Nelis' most insightful observations about poetic architecture. I have already mentioned that the intertextual structure of Apollonius' epic is bipartite and iterative between the poem's first and second halves. This feature does not derive from the structure of either Homeric epic. The *Aeneid* of course is also bipartite in structure; and, even if it were not traditional to see the poem specifically as an Iliad followed by an Odyssey, its bipartite structure would still be obvious. Among the most impressive indications of it are Juno's operatic soliloquies in books 1 and 7, the initial books of the first and second halves of the poem. Each soliloquy is followed by an intervention that enlists lesser entities, celestial or infernal as the case may be, to do Juno's dirty work of opposing Aeneas. The soliloquies themselves and the episodes that follow them form an obviously iterative pair. By virtue of their placement, they characterize the architecture of the *Aeneid* as binary and iterative, as well. What is more, this iteration creates emphasis: if the first soliloquy and its aftermath are hyperbolic in character, the second is even more so. In that second speech, line 312, Juno actually comments on the greater lengths to which she is now willing to go: "if I can't move heaven [as I tried to do in book 1, then right here in book 7] I'll raise hell!"[86] To my knowledge, these familiar features of the *Aeneid* are generally regarded as being among the poem's most brilliantly original and successful elements. I have certainly always thought so. After reading Nelis, however, I am convinced that the symmetrical architecture of the *Aeneid* must derive from Apollonius.[87] Let me explain.

The most obvious and best known indication of structural symmetry between the *Aeneid* and the *Argonautica* is the invocation by each poem's narrator of the Muse Erato as he begins the second half of his epic.[88] It would be extravagant to posit a grand architectural relationship between two massive poems on the basis of this single gesture alone; but Nelis has now made it clear that this correspondence is not isolated at all. Rather, each invocation stands at the center of a poetic structure that is not only bipartite, but iterative in precisely the same way and with reference to the same Homeric—and, in the case of the *Aeneid*, Apollonian—material. These similarities, once pointed out, are so easy to see that it is amazing they escaped notice for so long. The probable explanation of this oversight is a general critical inability to see through the Homeric superstructure of the *Aeneid* to its Apollonian substrate. For instance, Knauer regards the events of *Aeneid* 1–7 as tracking those of *Odyssey* 5–13—i.e., the entire "Phaeacis," together with Odysseus' voyages to and from the island of Scheria. Aeneas' Carthaginian sojourn, as Knauer rightly notes, corresponds to Odysseus' visit to Alcinous' court. On this account, *Aeneid* 4 can only be regarded as an Apollonian intrusion—a splendid one, no doubt, but one that might be considered additional to a fundamentally Odyssean plot. On the other hand, if one considers the architecture of the *Aeneid* as a whole in comparison to that of the *Argonautica*, the idea of book 4 as a mere intrusion becomes untenable. In the *Argonautica*, Jason visits two places, Lemnos in book 1 and Colchis in book 3, where he meets two royal women, a queen and a princess, Hypsipyle and Medea. The first of these wishes him to marry and settle with her, and the second he actually does marry. So too in the *Aeneid*, the hero visits two places,

---

86. *Aeneid* 1.37–49, 7.293–322. On both occasions, Juno takes action through a minor divinity under her control, Aeolus in book 1 and Allecto in book 7, who bring storm and warfare, respectively; see Pöschl 1950/1962, 24–33.

87. Again, I do not mean to foist this position on Nelis. He certainly does regard the structure of both the *Argonautica* and the *Aeneid* as bipartite, iterative, and symmetrical, but I do not know whether he would endorse the idea that those features of the *Aeneid* actually derive from the *Argonautica*.

88. *Aeneid* 7.37, *Argonautica* 3.1; see Nelis 2001, 267–75.

Carthage in book 1 and Latium in book 7, where he meets two royal women, a queen and a princess, Dido and Lavinia. The first of these wishes him to marry and settle with her, and the second he actually will marry (after the *Aeneid* reaches its end). In both poems, the action that fills the first and second halves revolves around these relationships.[89] I would find it difficult to agree that such a fundamental element of any poetic design could be considered secondary or additional instead of primary and fundamental. To repeat, neither of the Homeric poems has this binary, iterative structure. In the *Aeneid*, therefore, it cannot derive from Homer, but thanks to Nelis' research, it is obvious that it can, and in my view certainly does, derive from Apollonius.

That is not all. One must also reckon with the fact that all of these episodes—the Lemnian and the Colchian in the *Argonautica*, and the Carthaginian and Latin in the *Aeneid*—are iterative in another, intertextual sense: both pairs follow the pattern of single Homeric episode. This is Odysseus' encounter with yet another royal woman, the princess Nausicaa, daughter of Alcinous and Arete, king and queen of the Phaeacians. As Nelis makes unarguably clear, the Homeric "Phaeacis" establishes a pattern which Apollonius follows in two symmetrically placed episodes, one on Lemnos and the other in Colchis; and the *Aeneid* follows suit in two symmetrically placed episodes in Carthage and in Latium.[90] Unsurprisingly, the intertextual fabric gains complexity with each iteration. The single episode of the Homeric "Phaeacis" informs both the Lemnian and the Colchian episodes in Apollonius: Lemnos and Colchis are each an intertextual Scheria, Hypsipyle and Medea are each an avatar of Nausicaa, and so forth. Then in the *Aeneid*, both Carthage and Latium are the Homeric Scheria, Dido and Lavinia the Homeric Nausicaa; but they are also in each case both the Apollonian Lemnos and Colchis and the Apollonian Hypsipyle and Medea, as well. That is to say, the *Aeneid* episodes are classic instances of "window reference," or what Nelis calls "two-tier allusion": verbal as well as structural correspondences with the Homeric "Phaeacis" and with Apollonius' Lemnian and Colchian episodes inform Aeneas' reception both at Carthage and in Latium. In the two halves of the *Aeneid*, the Odyssean and Argonautic plots are combined and repeated in such a way that it is clearly wrong to speak of Apollonian "interruptions" or "additions." Instead, as Nelis argues, imitation of Apollonius' imitation of Homer renders the plot of the *Aeneid*, like that of the *Argonautica*, a double *nostos* that is also a symmetrical, binary, and iterative version of Homer's "Phaeacis."

---

89. For detailed analysis see Nelis 2001, 112–85, especially 112–25 and 180–85; 267–326, especially 305–26.

90. Nelis 2001, 112–20 and 312–26.

Full appreciation of this far-reaching Apollonian program, then, entails a radical re-evaluation of the Homeric program, as well. That said, by accepting the main thrust of Nelis' argument, and drawing a few additional inferences from it, I have so far done nothing to weaken the case that the Apollonian program takes the *Aeneid* in a primarily Odyssean direction. There is, however, an additional inference that points to a simple, but momentously important difference between the bipartite structures of the *Argonautica* and the *Aeneid*.

As I noted above, Apollonius tends in the first half of his poem, books 1–2, to imitate passages of the "Phaeacis," and especially of Odysseus' "Apologoi," without calling much attention to the relationship; but in books 3–4 imitations of those same passages become much more explicit. The same is true for Jason's erotic and conjugal relationships. As I noted, Hypsipyle and Lemnos in book 1 are plausible versions of Nausicaa and Scheria, but Medea and Colchis in book 3 are much more vivid avatars of both; and for good measure, the Argo later puts in at Drepane, the actual home of the Phaeacians in Apollonius' epic. In this way, the Homeric character of the *Argonautica* as an iterative and ever more explicit "Phaeacis" is extremely pronounced. The *Aeneid*, however, reverses this pattern. Proof of this consists in the fact that critics including Knauer have long considered Carthage to be the Scheria of the *Aeneid*. Much less well appreciated, indeed hardly ever mentioned, is that fact that Latium, Latinus, and his family correspond to Scheria and the Phaeacians, as well.[91] The reason is clear: imitation of these and other Odyssean elements is much more emphatic in books 1–6 than in 7–12. That is to say, where the Odyssean character of the *Argonautica* becomes more vivid with repetition, that of the *Aeneid* becomes less so. By the same token, while the bipartite structure of Apollonius' *Argonautica* unmistakably informs the *Aeneid* from start to finish in terms of theme, character delineation, and related matters, the Apollonian color of the *Aeneid* 1–6 is much more pronounced than that of books 7–12. I invite anyone who doubts this to answer the following deceptively simple question: Who is the Medea of the *Aeneid*? Nelis shows beyond question that there really are two.[92] Where Dido is a dominant figure who fully inhabits the role, however, Lavinia, though undeniably an intertextual avatar of the Apollonian heroine, does not even come across as a convincing understudy. The inference is inescapable: the *Aeneid* follows Apollonius' Homeric program

---

91. Knauer 1964, 264–65, 327–29, 333, 335, 343; note that Knauer bases this observation solely on Homeric parallels, without reference to Apollonius. This aspect was not mentioned in Knauer 1964a, where Apollonian influence is acknowledged (63, 72), but not discussed in any detail.

92. Nelis 2001, 124–80, 275–82.

extensively and in great detail *but in reverse*, so that Odyssean and Argonautic elements fade with repetition instead of gaining force.

Again, the implications of this are far-reaching. I began by asking whether following the pattern of Apollonius offered the narrator of the *Aeneid* a "third way" around or between the Homeric alternatives of reciting another Odyssey or Iliad. Initially it appeared that an Argonautic *Aeneid* would inevitably become another Odyssey. More detailed attention to the poem's Apollonian program then required me to modify this inference: a truly Apollonian approach would make the *Aeneid* an Odyssey that is more circumscribed than the original, like the *Argonautica* itself, with its plot largely confined to the Homeric "Phaeacis." At the same time, it would become a bipartite, iterative "Phaeacis," as indeed it is; but then it proved necessary to modify this conclusion, as well. Unlike the *Argonautica*, which with repetition becomes more clearly and emphatically a "Phaeacis," the *Aeneid* instead becomes less so.[93] We must therefore ask: In this same process, does it also become less of an Odyssey altogether?

Juno's Argonautic Diversion

At this point let us turn to *Aeneid* 4. According to Nelis, in the first half of the *Aeneid* there is a congruency between the Odyssean and Argonautic intertexts such that this book occupies its expected place in both structures.[94] Nevertheless, there is something to Knauer's position that book 4 appears to leave the Odyssean plot behind and become much more explicitly Argonautic. It is difficult not to see the hand of Juno in this. In book 1 she tried to divert the poem from an apparently Odyssean path onto an Iliadic one. Now she tries to divert it from an apparently Odyssean path onto an Argonautic one. Both moves make sense, because Hera is not an important character in the *Odyssey*, whereas in the *Iliad* and the *Argonautica* she certainly is.[95] In fact, Apollonius' poem is exceptional in this regard. Not only is it, apart from the *Iliad*, the only surviving Greek epic in which Hera plays a major role, it is also the only one in which the goddess acts on the hero's behalf instead of trying to destroy

---

93. Recall the statement by Knauer 1964a, 77 that even if the structure of the *Aeneid* as a whole is congruent with that of the *Odyssey*, books 16–24 of that poem "defied transformation," even in the corresponding part of the *Aeneid*. Similarly, Cairns 1989, 178 admits that Odyssean influence begins to decline in *Aeneid* 9.

94. Nelis 2001, 67–71.

95. As I noted in the section of chapter 1 entitled "In Medias Res." On Hera in the *Argonautica* see Hunter 1993, 96–100.

him.[96] This aspect makes her an unexpected model for Juno. Nevertheless, channeling her Argonautic counterpart could be an effective strategy. Apollonius' Hera is a much more subtle figure than her impetuous Iliadic predecessor. Though motivated by hatred for Pelias, Jason's uncle, she embraces Jason mainly as an instrument of Pelias' eventual destruction.[97] She also hates Heracles, but when he joins the crew of the Argo she manages to control her anger against him for the sake of Jason's success. She even calls attention to this fact when she urges the nymph Thetis, mother of Achilles (who at this point is just a baby) to follow her example and help the Argonauts, even though Peleus, Achilles' father and the mortal husband whom Thetis reviles, is another member of the Argo's crew (*Argonautica* 4.783–832). To persuade Thetis, Hera resorts once again to bribery, once again exploiting her role as goddess of marriage, promising Thetis that Medea, who has only just married Jason, will one day be Achilles' wife in the Elysian Fields (810–16).[98] With this it becomes clear that Medea's marriage to Jason within the poem is a purely instrumental matter that has nothing to do with the welfare of bride or groom beyond the success of Jason's mission, which is itself merely a necessary step towards Pelias' destruction. That, in turn, is a step that will inevitably lead to Jason's ruin as it is depicted in Euripides' *Medea*. This is not Hera's objective, but is an outcome she is willing to accept as collateral damage. Jason himself remains unavenged in the mythic tradition, while Medea is at least rewarded with marriage to Achilles—a fact that tends to characterize the entire Argosy and its aftermath as a parergon that subtends Hera's larger and more important project of bringing destruction upon Troy.

But this is to anticipate. In the *Aeneid*, after the storm in book 1, Juno plays very little role in the plot until book 4.[99] There she re-enters it to conspire with Venus in bringing about yet another wedding, this time between Dido and Aeneas. The meeting between the goddesses is fashioned from Apollonian

---

96. The Iliadic Hera favors the Greeks, of course, but shows no particular favoritism towards Achilles. Her importance in Quintus' *Posthomerica* (3rd century CE?) is comparable and may reflect her role in the Epic Cycle. She is also a prominent opponent of Dionysus, the issue of Zeus' extramarital affair with Semele, in Nonnus' *Dionysiaca* (5th century CE). In general, the hero whom Hera persecutes most relentlessly is Heracles, and in Apollonius the goddess must accommodate herself to the fact that the Argo sets sail with Heracles as a member of its crew: see Hunter 1993, 26. On this and related issues see further below.

97. Hunter 1993, 87–88.

98. Hunter 1993, 98–99 draws attention to similarities between the Apollonian passage and "The Deception of Zeus" in *Iliad* 14.

99. After book 1, Juno appears among the deities who are dismantling Troy (2.612); otherwise she is occasionally named (2.761, 3.347 380, 547) but does not intervene in the plot.

material, as is the uncanny "wedding" itself.[100] Here we see Juno trying to plan for the *longue durée* in the manner of Apollonius' Hera, attempting to forestall the historical destruction of Carthage in the Punic wars by keeping Aeneas from Italy and preventing his descendants from founding Rome. She can almost be seen as acting on behalf of the weary hero, who has been wandering for seven years without reaching his goal and seems ready to settle wherever the storm has brought him. Nevertheless, as often in intertextual reading, it makes a difference how deeply the reader peers into the glass onion. The episode in question is clearly modeled on Hera's far-sighted intervention in the *Argonautica*, but that in turn is modeled on the same short-sighted Iliadic ploy, "The Deception of Zeus," that was the basis of Juno's prior intervention in *Aeneid* 1.[101]

The intertextual development of this episode from the *Iliad* to the *Argonautica* to the *Aeneid* has been carefully studied. It is remarkably subtle, with strong continuities serving to highlight some striking reversals. The Iliadic and Argonautic Hera carries out a stratagem of sexual deception soon after each poem has passed its halfway point. In *Iliad* 14 her purpose is to deceive Zeus. Accordingly, in *Argonautica* 3 Hera schemes with Athena on behalf of the Argonauts "apart from Zeus himself and the other immortal gods" (8–9). This is a clear sign that Hera's guile has Homeric roots, specifically in "The Deception of Zeus" episode of *Iliad* 14.[102] This time, however, Hera's purpose is to deceive Aphrodite, whom she had previously duped in the same Iliadic episode. There she enlisted Hypnos to help her deceive Zeus by putting him to sleep and made Aphrodite her unwitting accomplice by borrowing from her a garment guaranteed to induce sexual longing. The focus of the Apollonian episode (25–110) is entirely on Hera's manipulation of Aphrodite. As Richard Hunter in particular has shown, Aphrodite behaves as if to prove that she had learned something from the Iliadic encounter, but to no avail.[103] She enjoys the fact that Hera has come to ask for a favor, until she learns what it is: Hera wants her to get Eros, Aphrodite's son, to make Medea fall in love with Jason. At this, Aphrodite becomes despondent and confesses that she has no control over her unruly boy. Hera smiles at her, passive-aggressively, and assures her that

---

100. Meeting: *Aeneid* 4.90–128, *Argonautica* 3.25–110; "wedding": *Aeneid* 4.160–72, *Argonautica* 4.1128–69.

101. Lennox 1980, 45–73; Feeney 1991, 77–78; Hunter 1989, 101–2 on *Argonautica* 3.36–110; Knight 1995, 291–97; Nelis 2001, 146–48.

102. See *Iliad* 14.188–89, "summoning Aphrodite / apart from the other gods," and 18.168, "without the knowledge of Zeus and the other gods," with Campbell 1983, 7; Feeney 1981, 65–66.

103. Hunter 1989, 43–47; 101–8, especially 101–2 on lines 36–110; 1993, 96;

she will think of something, then leaves. Subsequently, it is Aphrodite who must use bribery to obtain her child's cooperation (111–66). The episode is full of reminders that Aphrodite is no match for the devious Hera.

In *Aeneid* 4 the power relationship between these goddesses is quite different. Venus has shown already in book 1 that, unlike the Apollonian Aphrodite, she wields complete maternal control over Cupid (the Roman Eros).[104] Juno also understands this: she refers with scorn to the way Venus and her "child" had joined forces to make Dido fall in love. (This, ironically, is exactly what Hera had required of Aphrodite and Eros in the *Argonautica*.) In the same way, although Juno herself had first used "treachery" (*doli* 1.130) to subvert the plot of the inchoate epic, she now accuses Venus of using the same tactics (*dolus* 4.95), effectively admitting that the goddess of love has become a worthy adversary. Still, Juno continues to believe she can win at this game. Meanwhile Venus, having learned from previous encounters with this adversary in Homer and Apollonius, now recognizes that Juno's offer of an alliance based on marriage is being made "with deceptive intent" (*simulata mente* 4.105). She therefore pretends to hesitate on the grounds that she is not quite sure whether Juno's proposition will agree with what Fate requires—or what Jupiter will allow. In fact, she is quite sure that it will not. This demurral comes after Venus has remonstrated with Jupiter about Juno's attempt to destroy the Trojans and has been reassured as to what Fate requires by Jupiter's long-range prophecy of world empire for the sons of Aeneas (1.223–96). Now, having been reassured, Venus strategically feigns uncertainty and tells Juno that she should petition her husband: "You're his wife, it's up to you to probe his mind with prayers; lead the way, and I will follow"[105] Here we may recall that in Apollonius, the relevant negotiations take place "apart from Zeus." By reminding Juno to consult her husband, it is almost as if Venus were looking farther back in literary history, through *Argonautica* 3 to *Iliad* 14, restoring Jupiter to his Homeric position as arbiter of Fate and teasing Juno about how poorly her Iliadic attempt to circumvent the will of Zeus had ended. Juno, however, shows no self-awareness at all. This reversion to Homeric type in one of the most Apollonian episodes of the *Aeneid* is remarkable, to say the least, and all the more remarkable for its insistently Iliadic character.

104. Nelis 2001, 147.

105. *Aeneid* 4.113–14, a version of what Athena says to Hera at *Argonautica* 3.34–35: "If what you say pleases you, then I would follow / but you can face [her] and do the talking"; see Nelis 2001, 147. Venus' reference to marriage recalls Juno's entrance to this episode, where she is called "Jupiter's beloved wife" (91), and emphasizes Juno's role—and her surprising ineptitude—as goddess of marriage.

One can understand why Juno might remember the *Argonautica* as an Iliadic narrative of which, as Hera, she was in complete control; but this perspective quickly becomes untenable. Unlike her successful Argonautic intervention, this one will meet with catastrophic failure, like her efforts in *Iliad* 14 and in *Aeneid* 1. And no wonder: Juno overlooks the fact that Hera had obtained short-term success for Jason at the cost of long-term distress for Medea, and eventually for Jason as well. This time she will obtain near-term disaster for Dido, the Medea of *Aeneid*, but merely discomfort for Aeneas, a Jason figure who will enjoy much greater success in the long run. In the process, Juno will concentrate the entire history of Medea's infatuation with Jason all the way to his abandonment of her into the space of a single year. Such are the unintended consequences of remaining obsessed with Iliadic precedent and continuing to use ploys that have failed repeatedly in the past. Juno betrays her obsession with unmistakable clarity at the end of her speech to Venus: the words she chooses to describe her intention to marry Dido and Aeneas repeat precisely the terms of the bribe that Hera had offered Hypnos in *Iliad* 14 ("I will give you . . . to marry and to be called your wife," 268) and that Juno herself more recently had offered Aeolus in *Aeneid* 1 ("I will join to you in proper marriage and call her yours," 73 and 4.126).[106] Somehow, she has not learned. Although she apparently acts with a more successful Apollonian precedent in mind, Juno remains at heart her frustrated Iliadic self. On the other hand, Venus has learned. This time she recognizes Juno's deceptive intent and it is she who smiles triumphantly in the end (4.128).[107]

The reader will also have noticed that Juno's Iliadic behavior in the Apollonian episode is at odds with the idea that an Argonautic *Aeneid* must necessarily be Odyssean. Of course, this particular episode, as Nelis makes very clear, imitates Apollonius' imitation of Homer, which itself imports the Iliadic episode into a predominantly Odyssean plot sequence.[108] Accordingly, one can say that this case of "window reference" or "two-tier allusion" supports Cairns' contention that the *Aeneid* is "a unitary *Odyssey* with significant iliadic episodes" and further suggests that it derives this characteristic from the *Argonautica*, as well. It is clear, however, that contradictory inferences can be drawn from Nelis' account of the Argonautic *Aeneid* as a whole.

---

106. Knauer 1964, 468 credits Paratore 1947 with first noting the parallel between *Aeneid* 4.126 and *Iliad* 268 on the basis of Ursinus' earlier realization that *Aeneid* 1.73 paraphrases the same Homeric line.

107. See Konstan 1986.

108. Nelis 2001, 146–48.

Iliad *and* Argonautica

I suppose nobody would say that the *Iliad* is unimportant to the *Argonautica*, but there is certainly a tendency to describe its importance as circumscribed. According to Virginia Knight, the *Iliad* contributes to the *Argonautica* mainly in terms of phraseology, extended similes, "set-pieces," and typical scenes, so that "in these broad terms, the poem would be entirely Odyssean."[109] Not everyone is so direct, but Knight's opinion is hardly eccentric. Still, in my view, this way of putting it does not take sufficient account of what Iliadic elements there are. For instance, the specific "set-pieces" that Knight refers to are a pair of episodes in book 1, the "Catalogue of Argonauts" (18–233) and the ecphrasis of Jason's cloak (730–67). Both of these are obviously modeled on famous passages of the *Iliad*, and as such they might be described as "set-pieces" detached from any pattern of Iliadic reference. Certainly the actual plot of *Argonautica* 1 would not be different without a lengthy catalogue or if Jason had gone to meet Hypsipyle in his shirt-sleeves. On the other hand, these ostentatious allusions look like the kind of thing that Knauer might have adduced to identify a large-scale structural correspondence. If one asks what the models of the two Apollonian passages have to do with the plot of the *Iliad*, the question answers itself. The "Catalogue of Ships" (*Iliad* 2.494–759), on which the "Catalogue of Argonauts" is based, establishes the magnitude of the Greek host at the point when they march into battle without Achilles. He, their champion, refrains from battle from that point until he must avenge his friend Patroclus, who dies wearing his armor. The description of his shield, which is the model on which Apollonius' description of Jason's cloak is based, occurs just before Achilles returns to the fray (*Iliad* 18.478–608). The two Iliadic passages thus define a hugely significant narrative arc, during which Achilles sulks in his tent, leaving it to the other warriors to determine how badly they need him, and whether anyone might take his place. With these facts in mind, one might ask, is any of this relevant to Apollonius?

Again the question answers itself. Fortunately, it has also been answered in convincing detail by James Clauss, who reads the first book of the *Argonautica* as an essay on heroism and an effort to determine who is, or might become, "the best of the Argonauts."[110] At issue is not just a sequence of events but the specific themes involved. The most crucial is leadership. Achilles' withdrawal from battle represents a challenge to Agamemnon as a leader, a challenge brought about by Agamemnon's refusal to honor Achilles as a warrior. When the Greek army marches off to battle without the one indispensable hero on

---

109. Knight 1995, 29.
110. Clauss 1993.

whom victory depends, they have very much the worst of it until he returns. Leadership and heroic excellence are contested and uncertain issues throughout the *Argonautica*, but especially in book 1. The main point is Jason's fitness to lead the Argonauts in comparison to Heracles, who is by far the greatest hero to take part in the expedition. Like Achilles, Heracles is the very type of physical strength and courage, while in social terms, he behaves early in book 1 almost as an anti-Achilles, chivalrously deferring to Jason's leadership in a cooperative enterprise.[111] Later in the same book, however, in the Lemnian episode, he voices his doubts. While the rest of the Argonauts enjoy the amorous entertainment of Hypsipyle and the other Lemnian women, Heracles stays behind in the ship and upbraids his shipmates for showing more interest in soft living than in their quest (861–74).[112] Apollonius thus reverses the direction in which the theme of leadership develops in the *Iliad*: Homer's poem begins with a quarrel between Achilles and Agamemnon, who are eventually reconciled, while in the *Argonautica*, initial harmony gives way to dissension, which in the aftermath of the Lemnian episode only gets worse.[113] For these reasons, *Argonautica* 1 demands to be understood as an inverted Iliadic structure that puts into play themes of heroic individuality, leadership, collective enterprise, and the apportionment of honor in ways that remain important throughout the epic.

It would be difficult to find a comparably sustained examination of specifically Iliadic themes in *Argonautica* 2, where Odyssean seafaring and adventure dominate the reader's attention. One could thus say that Iliadic structures and themes give way to Odyssean ones between books 1 and 2. In keeping with the binary structure of the epic, this pattern is repeated with greater vividness across books 3 and 4. To be sure, book 3 as a whole is modeled largely on the Odyssean "Phaeacis," as I have noted, but it also contains the poem's most concentrated treatment of physical prowess. The episode in which Jason meets the challenge of yoking the bronze bulls, sowing the field with dragon's teeth, and contending with the earth-born warriors opens as if it were to be a duel between Aeetes and Jason, describing each of the principals armed or arming himself for combat in a sophisticated double-imitation of an Iliadic-type scene

111. Hunter 1993, 19; Clare 2002, 44–47; Mori 2008, 63–70; Thalmann 2011, 63.

112. An echo of the epic theme of choice specifically inflected by the "choice of Hercules" theme, as discussed above.

113. After a stop at the mouth of the River Cios, the Argonauts depart without Heracles and do not notice his absence until they are well underway (1273–83). A ferocious quarrel ensues in which (among other angry words) Telamon accuses Jason of abandoning Heracles deliberately so as to get the better hero out of his way (1284–95). Tensions regarding leadership and heroic excellence, far from being resolved to the degree that they are resolved in Homer, are greater than ever.

(1225–67).[114] Then in what follows, "Apollonius succeeds in writing quite unlike Homer by imitating Homer with such intensity that he packs a whole *Iliad* into the last scene of the book," i.e., the narration of Jason's actual exploits.[115] Thereafter, however, and again like 2, book 4 becomes less Iliadic and more Odyssean than its predecessor, even relentlessly so. In this sense, just as the Iliadic structure and themes visible in book 1 are superseded by an Odyssean paradigm in book 2, this pattern is repeated even more explicitly in books 3–4. At this point, any likelihood that the poem conforms to a fundamentally Iliadic pattern recedes from view; but to say that the *Argonautica* is basically an Odyssey that incorporates occasional Iliadic episodes, as Cairns has said of the *Aeneid*, clearly undervalues the importance of those Iliadic elements. I would say, in fact, that the idea of a choice as to whether the *Argonautica* is to be an Iliad or an Odyssey is very much present, especially in book 1 and again, if briefly, in book 3. Further, while Odyssean (or, more accurately, Phaeacian) story patterns finally win the day, the idea that the poem might have become an Iliad instead never entirely disappears. For this reason, it seems to me very likely that the example of the *Argonautica* plays an important role in the revisiting of this question in the *Aeneid*.

Of course, if the *Argonautica* is predominantly an Odyssean poem, and if we accept Nelis' explanation of Apollonian influence on the *Aeneid*, it would still follow that the *Aeneid*, too, ought to be predominantly Odyssean. In this case, any notion that Apollonius offered a "third way" must be illusory. Instead, even while the *Argonautica* thematizes a choice between Homeric alternatives, it also drives the choice in an Odyssean direction. It is possible, however—and, I would say, necessary—to draw a different distinction.

Here it is crucial to remember that Nelis' purpose is to reveal the comprehensive importance of Apollonian intertextuality throughout the *Aeneid*. I hope it is clear that I consider his findings convincing. The main area that I would look at somewhat differently is the second half of the *Aeneid*. Nelis shows clearly that the preparations for war in *Aeneid* 7 draw particularly on the events of *Iliad* 2 and on portions of *Argonautica* 3.[116] Up to that point, his analysis of *Aeneid* 1–6 and the very earliest portions of book 7 have relied on one main idea, namely that Apollonius' reworking of the *Odyssey* provided a pattern of Homeric imitation that could be largely adopted *en bloc*. The result is that, time and again, the *Aeneid* alludes to Homer through Apollonius in keeping with the technique known as "window reference" or "two-tier allusion." This accords with Nelis' general view that Apollonius served as a

---

114. See Hunter 1989, 232–33 on lines 1225–45; 236 on lines 1247–48.
115. Hunter 1993, 134.
116. Nelis 2001, 291; 295–96.

valuable guide to the imitation of Homer in accordance with Hellenistic aesthetics. In approaching the second half of the *Aeneid*, however, and especially its martial aspects, Nelis flags a change:

> The imitation [in *Aeneid* 7] of both *Iliad* 2 and Apollonius does not, however, imply two-tier allusion at this point. Apollonius does not seem to have *Iliad* 2 in mind in the early part of *Argonautica* 3. Vergil is here combining unrelated models, paralleling the outbreak of hostilities in *Iliad* 2 with the unleashing of erotic passion in *Argonautica* 3.[117]

To be clear, Nelis defines two-tier allusion as a case "in which a poet imitates both a model and the model's model" and goes on to say that attention to this technique is "an ideal framework for the understanding of Vergil's debt to both Homer and his successors."[118] It is basic to his analysis of the *Aeneid* as an Apollonian and Argonautic poem. After finding two-tier allusion virtually everywhere in *Aeneid* 1–6, however, he does not find it to any great extent in *Aeneid* 7. Instead, he sees a shift to combinatory allusion, the simultaneous imitation of two different passages not previously related in any allusive way.[119] This too is a common enough procedure, so it is unsurprising that Nelis does not make too much of it. The chief inference he draws is that reference to Apollonius remains important even when the Homeric program of the *Aeneid* starts following a different course from that of the *Argonautica*. As Nelis puts it, "despite the strikingly Iliadic nature of the material in question ... Vergil's use of Homer is just as indissociable from his imitation of Apollonius' *Argonautica* in the second half of the *Aeneid* as it was in the first."[120] This is perfectly correct; and it is, as Nelis implies, crucial to a proper appreciation of the Argonautic *Aeneid*, which is his main concern. But it is of equally great importance to an appreciation of the Homeric *Aeneid*.

The proposition we are testing is whether Apollonian influence made the *Aeneid* as a whole more Odyssean than Iliadic; and the methodological shift that Nelis notices in *Aeneid* 7 suggests that this is not the case. Throughout books 1–6—according to tradition, the Odyssean *Aeneid*—references to Homer follow those in the *Argonautica* at virtually every point and acknowledge this by referring to Apollonius as well. Suddenly, however, in book 7—according to tradition, the start of the Iliadic *Aeneid*—the poem stops using the *Argonautica* as a

---

117. Nelis 2001, 291.

118. Nelis 2001, 5.

119. As was discussed above in the section of the Introduction entitled "The Dialogic Intertext."

120. Nelis 2001, 267.

guide to Homer *but continues alluding simultaneously to Homer and Apollonius anyway*. It does so not because there is a ready-made Argonautic Iliad embedded in Apollonius' poem, but in spite of the fact that there is not. Effectively, then, and in contrast to the procedure followed in books 1–6, books 7–12 impose an Iliadic and an Argonautic program upon one another to create an Argonautic Iliad *that did not exist until the Aeneid was written*. This joint program involves Apollonian material and is Apollonian in spirit. It is based on existing trends in Homeric interpretation, trends of which Apollonius was aware and in which he participated. But the program itself was not of Apollonius' design. It departs from Apollonius' Homeric program to reinterpret both Homer and Apollonius in far-reaching ways; and this becomes a principal source of the relentless energy that propels the *Aeneid* towards its powerful conclusion.[121]

A corollary to this observation takes us back to what I said earlier about the inversion or reversal of Apollonius' increasingly explicit Odyssean program in the *Aeneid*. Not only does the poem's iterative Argosy pattern become less explicit, and less explicitly Odyssean, in books 7–12 as compared with 1–6, but as Nelis shows it becomes more explicitly Iliadic, as well. This being the case, the obvious conclusion to draw is that Apollonius' influence, although enormous, did not decide whether the *Aeneid* was to become another Iliad or another Odyssey. Furthermore, bearing in mind my earlier point about the contested Homeric character of the *Argonautica*, I would now suggest that the element of flexibility and indeterminacy found in Apollonius' treatment of the Homeric poems should encourage us to find these same qualities in the Argonautic *Aeneid*. The point is not that the poem's Apollonian program ensured that it would become an *Odyssey*, but that the shimmering quality of Apollonius' Homeric program, even in a poem that most would consider more *Odyssey* than *Iliad*, is an element built into the Apollonian and the Homeric *Aeneid*, as well, to an equal and perhaps even greater degree.

So Many Labors: The *Aeneid* as Heracleid

Aeneas' recital of his "Misfortunes" in books 2 and 3 is the longest stretch of internal narration in the poem. The next longest is Evander's story of "Hercules and Cacus" in book 8.[122] On the basis of it, some critics have regarded

---

121. In this connection I find it significant Kelly 2014 makes such a strong case for Apollonian influence, very much as a complicating factor vis-à-vis the more obvious Achillean and Odyssean paradigms, at the very end of the *Aeneid*.

122. As Casali 2010, 39 observes, "Evander is, after Aeneas, the character who speaks the most in the *Aeneid*." For details, see Highet 1972, 327–39.

Hercules, and not Achilles or Odysseus, as the heroic exemplar that Aeneas is really supposed to embody.[123] Evander is a compelling spokesman for this point of view. He is himself a king, and his name (from the Greek *eu* and *anêr*, "good man") suggests that he is a good one. He even presides over a cult commemorating Hercules' victory over Cacus, whose name (from the Greek *kakos*, "bad man") makes him Evander's moral opposite. Moreover, Evander's kingdom is located on the site of what would become Rome. His house is on the Palatine Hill, where Augustus would one day live. The cult over which he presides is no antiquarian or literary fiction: it existed in Augustus' own day and was celebrated at the "Greatest Altar of Hercules the Unconquered." Like everything in *Aeneid* 8, the representation of Hercules is relevant not only to Aeneas but to his notional descendant. Finally, with regard to ethics, although Achilles and Odysseus were constant points of reference in ancient kingship theory, Heracles too offered a prestigious exemplum for emulation.[124] Evander himself actually makes this explicit. After telling the story of Hercules and Cacus and showing Aeneas around his kingdom, he invites the Trojan hero into his home, a humble hut where he had once received Hercules himself. "Dare to have contempt for wealth," he tells Aeneas, "and imagine, my guest, that you too are worthy of the god"—worthy, that is, to follow the example of Hercules—"and enter graciously into my humble estate" (364–65).

Evander's status as a narrator gives his recommendation of Hercules a certain weight. The principal narrator of the *Aeneid* may not be sure what kind of story he wants to tell, and may chiefly fear that it will not be very good. Aeneas may tell his own story as a Cyclic saga that combines quasi-Iliadic and quasi-Odyssean halves, with partial success; there may even be in his performance a clue as to the way he would like his story to continue, but he appears to have little control over that. Juno evidently does have such control, at least to a degree, and she wants the story to be part of her "Long Iliad." When her attempt to make it so produces what seems to be a proto-Odyssey, she tries to make it an Argosy instead, to ward off disaster for her beloved Carthaginians in the distant future, until her effort brings about a near-term disaster for Dido that she did not anticipate. Evander, like Aeneas, lacks the power to make the story he prefers a reality, but he makes it clear that he wants Aeneas to follow Hercules' example. He is somewhat late to the game: We have seen the *Iliad*, the *Odyssey*, the entire Epic Cycle, and the *Argonautica* are all proposed,

---

123. Important discussions of the episode include Buchheit 1963, 116–33; Putnam 1965, 105–50; Galinsky 1966; Binder 1971; George 1974; Labate 2009; Quint 2018, 114–16, 130–35.

124. See Lenssen 1990; Kuntz 1993; Montiglio 2011, 100–103; Moles 2000, 423 and 432; Stafford 2012, 121–70; Atack 2020, 92–121.

explicitly or implicitly, as models for the plot of the *Aeneid*, all within the first four books; for Evander's intervention we must wait until book 8. That should not worry us: the dynamic model of intertextuality that I am exploring ought to allow uncertainties to appear or be resolved at any point. If choice among the various options proposed thus far proves impossible—and anyway, none of them either determines or obviates the choice between Achilles and Odysseus—then Evander's belated promotion of an emergent Hercules paradigm might offer a very viable "third way." His articulation of this paradigm may even suggest some reinterpretation of Aeneas' experiences in earlier books.

Grappling with Heracles

Evander is Hercules' first explicit advocate, but he is hardly the first character to mention the hero, directly or indirectly. Yet again the epic narrator himself in the opening passages of the poem asks his Muse why the queen of the gods drove Aeneas "to undergo so many labors" (*tot adire labores* 10). There was no need to add, "just as she did to Hercules." In books 3 and 5, Aeneas' voyage to Italy twice intersects with Hercules' wanderings, keeping the theme of "labors" relevant.[125] At other points Aeneas is associated with Hercules in more casual ways.[126] Anything but casual, however, was Hercules' final labor, the harrowing of hell, a feat that Aeneas not only emulates, but cites when he begs the Sibyl to give him access to the underworld.[127] Aeneas' descent may even be modeled on a lost poem about Hercules' catabasis.[128] Finally, by completing

---

125. The first time Hercules is named in the poem is when Aeneas tells Dido about sailing by Tarentum, which was founded by Hercules (3.551). In Sicily, Aeneas presides over a boxing match in the same place where Hercules had defeated Eryx, son of Venus and Aeneas' own half-brother (5.410–16).

126. Aeneas is draped in a lion skin when he hoists Anchises onto his shoulders (2.721–23). Antores, a former companion of Hercules who settled in Pallanteum, dies from a spear meant for Aeneas while fighting on his side in the Italian war (10.779–82).

127. When the Sibyl tells Aeneas that a repetition of the Trojan War awaits Aeneas in Italy (6.83–97), he replies that no unanticipated form of "labors" (103) could possibly intimidate him; then, so that he might confer with Anchises, he asks to descend to the world of the dead as other heroes had done, specifically citing Hercules among them (123). The Sibyl famously says that the descent to Avernus is easy, but the return journey will be the real "labor" (129; compare 135). I return to these passages in the section of chapter 3 entitled "Cumae."

128. Norden 1927/1957, 1–48 argues that an Orphic and a Heraclean catabasis tradition informs *Aeneid* 6. Horsfall 2013, vol. 2, 142–44 lays out the new evidence and arguments in favor of this idea that have accrued since Norden's time. For Heracles, the most important

his canonical twelve labors in service to Eurystheus, Hercules earned the divinity that would be his, following further adventures, after his death. Aeneas, too, faces many trials after returning to the upper world, and is also destined to become a god.[129] One could thus say that there is an episodic "Heracleid" embedded within the *Aeneid*. Evander's intervention may not be a belated effort to steer the narrative in an unprecedented direction, but the long-delayed revelation of the course it was always meant to follow.

Like the concepts of a Cyclic *Aeneid* or an Argonautic *Aeneid*, any notion of the *Aeneid* as a Heracleid concerns not only ethics but aesthetics as well. I mentioned above Aristotle's criticism of the Cyclic poets for combining too many unrelated episodes into a single poem; he makes the same complaint against the authors of a Heracleid or a Theseid on the grounds that the diverse adventures of a single man do not add up to a unified plot.[130] He does not mention the *Odyssey* in the same breath with such poems although it is clear, primarily because of the hero's "Apologoi," that it differs from the *Iliad* in somewhat similar terms. One may infer that after Aristotle a title such as *Aeneid*, no less than *cano* in the poem's opening line, could be seen as provocative, or perhaps a worrying sign.

The Greek tragic poets dealt successfully with Heracles by focusing on individual episodes of his multifarious career. I will consider a few examples in the next section of this chapter.[131] In narrative poetry, Theocritus followed the tragedians' lead, but exemplified contemporary taste by treating the slaying of the Nemean lion in miniature, alongside less ponderously heroic themes involving the hero's infancy and the loss of his beloved Hylas.[132] Focusing on individual stories about Heracles in discrete poems was probably a necessary and decisive step towards what I believe we find in the *Aeneid*, but a further intermediate step was also necessary. With regard to narrative form, the most important forerunners of the Heraclean *Aeneid* are, once again, Apollonius of Rhodes and also Callimachus. Both these poets devised ways of embedding a discontinuous "Heracleid" within longer compositions, one epic (Apollonius' *Argonautica*) and one elegiac (Callimachus' *Aetia*), the former a continuous story not primarily about Heracles and the latter a discontinuous collection of stories in which the hero emerges as one of the most prominent themes.

---

contributions are those of Lloyd-Jones 1967; Graf 1974, 142–47; Clark 1979, 2000, and 2001; Setaioli 1985, 958; Bremmer 2009.

129. Cf. *Aeneid* 1.259–60 and 12.794–95 with Tarrant 2012, 292–93.
130. *Poetics* 1451a in Halliwell et al. 1995, 56–57.
131. Silk 1985.
132. *Idylls* 25 ("Heracles the Lion-slayer"), 13 ("Hylas"), and 24 ("Baby Heracles").

If there is an episodic "Heracleid" embedded in the *Aeneid*, this is even more clearly true of the *Argonautica*, and Denis Feeney has shown that the poems are related by this shared element.[133] As often, the relationship involves inversion. The Apollonian Heracles, as I mentioned in the preceding section, starts out as an important member of the Argo's crew, but ends as a remote, solitary figure pursuing his own adventures. He plays his familiar role as a culture hero and civilizer, but in terms of personal ethics, he devolves from being a paragon of self-control as the poem opens into a violent, vengeful brute of monstrous appetite as it approaches its end.[134] The *Aeneid*, as Feeney shows, reverses this pattern as Hercules' presence, barely hinted at in the narrator's early reference to the "labors" imposed on Aeneas by Juno, becomes steadily more explicit. Along the way, Hercules pursues a career full of *labor*, scorning ease but accepting humble hospitality. After Evander challenges Aeneas to emulate the divinized hero, Hercules himself appears at last in book 10, seated in Olympus next to Jupiter, but grieving for the death of Pallas, Evander's son and Aeneas' protégé.[135]

Apollonius' *Argonautica* therefore offers an important model for the *Aeneid* not only in those elements considered in the preceding section, but also by embedding an episodic and discontinuous "Heracleid" within a single, continuous narrative that is indisputably both epic and specifically Homeric. Callimachus' *Aetia* is a different kind of poem, but an equally important model. Really it is a highly organized collection of elegiac narratives all having to do with "origins" or "causes"—the meaning of its title—that are otherwise ostentatiously discontinuous and varied. That and the fact that the *Aetia* survives only in fragments makes it difficult to discern whatever unifying strands hold it together. After decades of effort by some very talented scholars, however, it can be said that an episodic "Heracleid" embedded within it is one of these strands. Rudoph Pfeiffer noted long ago that in the famously rich prologue to the *Aetia* Callimachus develops the theme of his own advancing age with reference to a choral ode from Euripides' *Heracles*. More recently, Annette Harder has pointed out that the same ode goes on to celebrate Heracles' role as a culture hero, which "is also of interest, because this is what will happen in the

---

133. Feeney 1986.

134. On the Apollonian Heracles in the *Aeneid* see Nelis 2001, 37–38 (3.225–340: the Harpies' attack borrows features of Heracles' battle with the Stymphalian birds), 142 (4.483–86: the Massylian witch who assists Dido with her magical rites, a former priestess of the temple of the Hesperides); 157–58 (4.265–95: Mercury's appearance to remind Aeneas of his duty incorporates elements of Heracles' reproach of Jason's amorous ways on Lemnos).

135. On Hercules' failure to attain perfect self-control, even as a god, see Feeney 1986, 75–76; and 1991, 156.

Aetia too."[136] But Callimachus approaches this theme indirectly. In two consecutive early episodes of *Aetia* 1, Heracles appears as a cattle rustler of voracious appetite; in one of these appearances he is presented "in a rather burlesque way as an indifferent glutton." In later episodes, however, "Heracles' role is positive and he appears as a civilizer of mankind; he puts an end to the robbery of Thiodamas and the Dryopians, kills the villain Busiris, kills the Nemean lion, and plays a noble role at Elis after cleaning the stables of Augeas."[137] That is to say, where the Apollonian Heracles starts out as almost the perfect hero but ends as a more complex, more obviously flawed character, Callimachus takes Heracles in the opposite direction. It seems very likely that these two treatments of the hero are in dialogue with one another, even if the question of priority is impossible to resolve. For my purposes, it is also unnecessary, because the *Aeneid* is clearly in dialogue with both treatments.[138] Apollonius' example takes its place within a comprehensive response to the *Argonautica*, but reversing Heracles' Apollonian trajectory aligns the *Aeneid* with Callimachus' treatment of the hero in the *Aetia*.

One would have expected to find Callimachean influence in *Aeneid* 8, and influence from his *Aetia* in particular. When Aeneas arrives at Pallanteum, Evander and his people are celebrating an exploit that gave rise to a Hercules cult on the site of what would be Rome. The motif of mythic origins points to the major unifying theme of the *Aetia*. In explaining to Aeneas the origin of the cult, Evander follows a typically Callimachean script. The opening episode of *Aetia* 3, "The Victory of Berenice," is an especially relevant intertext.[139] Berenice was the wife of King Ptolemy III Euergetes, who ruled Egypt from 246 to 222 BCE. To celebrate a chariot-racing victory by a team that Berenice sponsored, Callimachus relates the achievement to Heracles' slaying of the Nemean lion and his commemoration of that labor by founding the festival in which the queen's team prevailed. In typical Callimachean fashion, the actual narrative focuses not on great events, but on very small ones—specifically on the figure of Molorcus, a poor farmer who extends hospitality to Heracles on the night before his contest with the lion. Molorcus entertains his guest by telling

---

136. Pfeiffer 1928, 328; Harder 2012, vol. 2, 73. I return to the Euripidean *Heracles* below in the a subsequent section of this chapter, "Heraclean Tragedy in the *Aeneid*."

137. Harder 2012, vol. 2, 213.

138. It seems likely that scholars of the late 1st century BCE regarded Apollonius and Callimachus as contemporaries who lived two centuries previously and perhaps as rivals: see Lefkowitz 2012, 113–25, especially 121–25. If so, perhaps the *Aeneid* exploits this tradition by adapting the two poets' treatments of Heracles, which differ in matters of genre and aesthetics as well as personal and public ethics.

139. For a general assessment of its influence on Latin poetry see Thomas 1983.

him how he invented a mousetrap to keep vermin away from his grain. Thus the labors of Heracles and (humorously) Molorcus in the *Aetia*, and of Hercules in Evander's tale, are united by the theme of *alekikakia*, or "salvific monster-slayings," as E. V. George puts it.[140] Molorcus and Evander both exemplify the "humble hospitality" topos, as well.[141] The etiological element is, if anything, even more important in Evander's story than in Callimachus. The tale of "Hercules and Cacus" involves the origin not of a panhellenic festival in which a certain queen of Egypt happened to be just one in a long line of quadrennial victors, but of a Hercules cult older than the city of Rome itself that celebrates the hero's making the area safe for civilized life. The institutional relevance of this cult to an Augustan audience would have been much more direct than that of any Molorcus cult to Callimachus' readers.[142] Finally, in respect to the victory theme, Evander's story, the cult of Hercules the Unconquered, and the entire *Aeneid* itself reflect upon a regal patron's success not in a sporting contest, but in the Battle of Actium.[143] The difference in seriousness of purpose between Molorcus' story and Evander's is immense. In particular, the paradigmatic relationship between Evander's story about Hercules, the challenges that Aeneas would soon face, and the nature of Augustus' victory—over another Egyptian queen, no less, and one descended from Callimachus' honorand—are vastly more significant than Berenice's culturally prestigious, but otherwise trivial accomplishment. Indeed, Augustus' victory exemplifies *alexikakia* in a way that Berenice's winning the chariot race does not. At the same time, the themes that I have been mentioning are not the only Callimachean elements present in book 8, which is pervaded with motifs borrowed from elsewhere in the *Aetia* or from other poems by Callimachus.[144] The importance of Callimachus and the Callimachean Heracles in *Aeneid* 8 is thus enormous.

140. See George 1974, 112.
141. See O'Rourke 2017.
142. The same is true of the cult of Zeus Hecaleus in *Hecale*: on aetiology in "The Victory of Berenice" and *Hecale* see Harder 2012, vol. 2, 387–88 and 479 on fragment 54i, line 15; Ambühl 2004, 43–44; and 2005, 96–97.
143. The centrality of Actium among the images on Aeneas' shield clearly defines Augustus' victory as the cardinal moment (Thomas 1983a; P. R. Hardie 1986 97–110; Putnam 1998, 119–88), and in many ways as the culmination of Roman history.
144. These include (e.g.) the motif of the speaking Tiber or Nile (*Aeneid* 8.36–65 and Callimachus, fragment 384.27–28 in Pfeiffer 1949, 311–315, another victory poem); the vignette of the Cyclopes at their forge (*Aeneid* 8.424, 452–53 and Callimachus, *Hymn to Artemis* 46–61, 59–61); reference to the Chalybes (*Aeneid* 8.421 and Callimachus, *Aetia* 110.48–50, "The Lock of Berenice"); mention of the Euphrates (*Aeneid* 8.726 and Callimachus, *Hymn to Apollo* 726: see Thomas and Scodel 1984; Clauss 1988; Tueller 2000).

For these reasons, one could very well say that Evander does not just call, belatedly, for the story of Aeneas to become a Callimachean "Heracleid," but reveals that it actually is one. This is remarkable, among other reasons, because to date the Callimachean aspect of the *Aeneid* has been seen chiefly as relating to the poem's exquisite style, to its constant display of recherché learning, and so forth, but not to its plot, structure or, on the whole, its treatment of heroic themes. That is to say, Callimachus is the genre model not for a canonical poetic genre but for a kind of poetry defined by learning, extremely careful composition, and an often indirect approach. It is clear, however, that the structure of the *Aeneid* contains an episodic Heracleid that alludes to the contrasting approaches of both Apollonius and Callimachus. Apollonius involves Heracles directly in the tension between Achillean and Odyssean models of heroism that is constantly present in his poem, and at the end his Heracles is far from resolving this tension. In Callimachus' treatment, Heracles becomes ever more virtuous while comparison to the Homeric paradigms is never an obvious factor. Callimachus thus circumvents the ethical roadblock that Achilles and Odysseus represent, making Heracles look like a very convincing "third way." This raises the obvious question: does the "Heracleid" that is embedded in the *Aeneid* follow a Callimachean trajectory as a way of avoiding a dilemma that Apollonius leaves unresolved?

Difference and Essence

There is no doubt that Heracles surpasses even Achilles in terms of physical strength and capacity for violence. He seldom matches Odysseus in cunning, but he does in sheer endurance and, in some episodes, of self-control.[145] That said, to focus on these two, or any two qualities alone, is misleading. Hercules can appear to combine the otherwise incompatible qualities of Achilles and Odysseus as well as any other hero or villain because he is above all else the most inconsistent of figures, one whose character varies most wildly from one story to another.[146] This is not just a Callimachean or an Alexandrian approach. As Michael Silk has written, "Heracles lies on the margins of the human and the divine; he occupies the no-man's-land that is also no-god's-land; he is a

---

145. For a reference to Hercules' capacity for "reason" (*ratio*) in the *Aeneid* see note 151 below.

146. "The figure of the hero who is always strong, never defeated, and exceptionally potent sexually seems, like many fairy-tale motifs, to be drawn from a wish-fulfilment fantasy. Yet not only does this hero meet a terrible or, at any rate, ambivalent end, he contains his own antithesis. The glorious hero is also a slave, a woman, and a madman." So Burkert 1985, 210.

marginal, transitional or, better, *interstitial* figure."[147] Feeney, citing this passage, goes on to emphasize its relevance for Heracles in literature, going even so far as to call him "the most protean and ambivalent figure in Greek myth."[148] In this respect, what I have just presented as contrasting treatments by Apollonius and Callimachus are really not very different. Both poets, in keeping with a delight in variety (*poikilia*) that was so characteristic of their age, celebrate the hero's complexity and variability. If Heracles is defined by any one thing, it is a tendency to exemplify incompatible qualities, and to do so hyperbolically, but in a way that conforms to particular situations.[149] Given such a bafflingly inconsistent character, it is not difficult to see how someone might cherry-pick among individual traits to build a case that Heracles is both more powerful than Achilles and more enduring than Odysseus, and that this combination of qualities makes him the ideal hero. This is, in fact, the implicit argument of those who believe that Evander offers Hercules as Aeneas' true heroic model. To hold this position is to ignore the essence of Hercules, who combines all opposite and incompatible qualities into a single, though hardly ideal, paradigm of heroic, human, and even divine character and behavior, never dependably at their best or worst, often at their most extreme.

Evander in no way challenges Aeneas to emulate Hercules in the fullest possible sense. To the contrary, Evander's tale shows no interest at all in the majority of qualities associated with Hercules. That would be to no purpose: Aeneas' character exhibits a certain degree of variability, but he could never rival Hercules in that regard. And thank goodness! Admirers of Aeneas do not have to conjure with themes like heroic gluttony, parricide, and other Herculean traits. Evander does not exhort Aeneas to emulate Hercules in any of these senses. When he challenges Aeneas to earn divinity by following Hercules' path, he already has made clear what he thinks that path is in his story about "Hercules and Cacus." In that story, there is one Herculean trait that occludes all others: the hero's propensity for violence on a superhuman scale.

This is hardly a new point. Generations of critics have explored the theme of violence in this story and have formed opinions as to whether Hercules is morally compromised by his embrace of violence or justified in using it by some contingent or categorical imperative.[150] I have my own opinions about that, but they are not important here. What interests me is how Evander's

---

147. Silk 1985, 6, who glosses "interstitial" with reference to anthropological commentary on transitional states in traditional cultures.

148. Feeney 1986, 51; and 1991, 95; Effe 1980.

149. Feeney 1991, 95.

150. See for instance Putnam 1965, 129–36; Galinsky 1966; Heiden 1987; Morgan 1998; Boyle 1999; Newman 2002; Quint 2018, 130–35.

exhortation to Aeneas relates to the Homeric dichotomy that is the basis of my inquiry. In urging Aeneas to become another Hercules, does he offer a "third way" that either combines the essential qualities of both Achilles and Odysseus or else represents an entirely different pattern of heroism? And that question is not hard to answer, at all.

If Achilles is the embodiment of violence and anger and Odysseus that of intelligence and versatility, then Evander represents Hercules as a consummately Achillean hero.[151] When Hercules tears open Cacus' cave, Evander illustrates the result by saying that it was no different than if the earth were caused by some violent force to gape open and unseal the pale kingdom of the underworld (8.241–46).[152] But the mysteriously specific, extremely graphic violence of the simile sums up a series of forceful, violent words used to describe Hercules' own efforts: "This [cave], where it sloped down the hill towards the river, [Hercules'] right arm, *with an effort, struck* head-on, *tore away* and *broke apart* from its foundations, and then suddenly *pounded*; and with that *pounding* all heaven thundered, the river banks drew apart, and the river flowed backwards in terror" (236–40).[153] The cosmic dimensions of Hercules' violence are characteristic of his hyperbolic nature. This violence is also supported by anger. Like "violence" (*vis*), the word "anger" (*ira*) appears just once in Evander's story, but it is ascribed to Hercules directly when he searches the entire Aventine three times for his cattle, "burning with anger" (*fervidus ira* 230), and it appears in other guises, as well. When Hercules hears his stolen cattle lowing, "pain caused by black bile suddenly burst into flames of fury" (*furiis* 219)." Language like this (along with "furious," *furens* 228) certainly emphasizes anger, but in the light of other important episodes in the hero's career one is tempted to give them their full Herculean weight and render them as "madness" and "insane." For these reasons, if the question is where Evander's Hercules falls on a spectrum of Homeric heroism, in this story he is unquestionably closer to the violent, angry Achilles than to the crafty, patient Odysseus.

---

151. In a hymn the people of Pallanteum praise Hercules as "not lacking reason" (*non... rationis egentem* 299) in his battle against the Lernaean Hydra. I take this as alluding to the tradition that he defeated the Hydra thanks to the Athena's guidance (Hesiod, *Theogony* 316).

152. Mention of the underworld here cannot but recall Aeneas' recent (and Herculean) catabasis; on book 6 as a means of access to hellish energies that follow Aeneas to the upper world and drive the action of books 7–12, see P. R. Hardie 1993, 57–87.

153. I note in passing that the river's checking its current in reaction to the hero's deadly violence has more than a little in common with Achilles' stopping the Scamander's flow with the number of corpses he left in its channel in *Iliad* 21. This is one of the primal traumatic episodes that Aeneas' recalls in his first speech (*Aeneid* 1.100–101, a passage I discussed in chapter 1).

Let me revise that last statement. Evander's Hercules is, if anything, even angrier and more violent than the Homeric Achilles, a point to which I will momentarily return. First, I want to note that in Evander's story it is not Hercules but Cacus who exemplifies Odyssean qualities. Cacus, after all, does not attempt to take Hercules' cattle by force (as Hercules himself had taken them from Geryon), but rather by stealth; and he not only uses stealth, but almost escapes the hero's notice altogether.[154] This is no surprise, because Hercules in this tale is not the provident hero that he is in some others. Cacus, we are told, daringly but cleverly stole just eight of the cattle, a number small enough that Hercules did not notice they were missing as he prepared to leave.[155] Presumably he would have noticed if he had prudently counted them himself. It was only the lowing of an unseen heifer that told him something was wrong, and kindled his heroically violent anger.

Evander represents Cacus as hyperbolically violent, as well, and in subhuman rather than heroic terms. For that reason, it is all the more significant that he ascribes to Cacus the consummately Odyssean quality of bold willingness to attempt any form "of villainy or clever deception" (*scelerisve dolive* 206). The significance of this phrase is multiplied if we recall that the ruse with which Cacus fooled Hercules is borrowed from Hermes, the god of thieves, who is celebrated for it in the fourth *Homeric Hymn*. There, when the baby Hermes steals cattle from his brother Apollo by driving them backwards into a cave, Apollo (unlike Hercules) does notice, and protests; but Hermes counters any threat of violence with his own cleverness, placating his brother by offering him the tortoise-shell lyre that he had just invented, so that the two become the best of friends.[156] In other words, the original telling of this tale celebrates a thief's cleverness and defuses any potentially angry violence. Evander instead denigrates a thief's cleverness and celebrates punitive violence. Within Evander's version, Cacus exemplifies Odyssean cleverness to an exaggerated degree, but in a negative sense, and is punished for it, just as Hercules exemplifies Achillean anger and violence to an exaggerated degree but (in Evander's eyes, at least) in a positive sense, and is praised for it.

---

154. It is curious that Cacus is not only wily, like Odysseus himself, but is also monstrous, like some of Odysseus' opponents, most of all the Cyclops: see Glenn 1971; Jacobson 1989; Sansone 1991.

155. Evander accuses Cacus of both "unstable mind" (*mens effera* 205) and "clever deception" (*doli* 206). As Casali 2010, 38 observes, there is an interesting textual issue in this speech: "manuscripts and editors are divided [in line 205] between *furis Caci*, "of the thief Cacus," and *furiis Caci*, "by the madness of Cacus." The latter reading would of course accentuate the idea of Cacus' mental instability.

156. See Farrell 2019a with further references.

This, then, is the hero whom Aeneas is exhorted to emulate. Evander wants Aeneas to be another Hercules, a hyper-Achillean figure unrestrained in his anger. This perspective is corroborated by an aspect of Evander's Homeric identity, as well, though in a way that seems not to have been recognized before now. Intertextually, Evander has long been regarded as an amalgam of several Odyssean characters.[157] There is also a relevant Iliadic model. Aeneas' mission to Pallanteum is frequently called an embassy, though I am not aware that any specific parallel between it and the "Presbeia" or "Embassy" episode of *Iliad* 9 has ever been drawn. That is surprising, because Aeneas while on this embassy is absent from battle, like Achilles in *Iliad* 9, although for different reasons.[158] Aeneas plays the role of a successful ambassador, while Achilles instead receives an unsuccessful embassy. As often, however, such differences enrich the interpretive possibilities. In this case, the most important of these concern Evander.

Among the ambassadors whom Agamemnon dispatches to lure Achilles back into battle is Phoenix, Achilles' aged tutor—and so a figure who conspicuously represents the "instruction of princes" motif. Phoenix tells Achilles a story, "The Wrath of Meleager" (*Iliad* 9.524–99). The story speaks directly to Achilles' immediate situation and indicates a clear course of action: Achilles should act *differently* from Meleager and return to battle the following day. Evander also speaks to Aeneas' immediate situation and indicates a clear course of action: Aeneas should act *like* Hercules when he returns to battle the following day. In this way, Evander's mini-Heracleid is precisely analogous to an episode of mise-en-abyme narration in the *Iliad* that has obvious implications for the poem as a whole.[159] If we read the *Aeneid* as a contest between Iliadic and Odyssean forces, it is clear that Evander's identity as an avatar of Achilles' tutor is implicated in this contest; and if we take seriously his

---

157. I will return to this point in the section of chapter 3 entitled "Pallanteum."

158. Aeneas' visit to Pallanteum fits easily into an Iliadic plot sequence. *Aeneid* 7 closes with a "Catalogue of Italian Forces" modeled unmistakably on the "Catalogue of Ships" in *Iliad* 2, and book 8 concludes with a description of arms made for Aeneas by Vulcan, like those made for Achilles by Hephaestus in *Iliad* 18. Aeneas' leaving his people to defend themselves in his absence (as they do in book 9) while he visits Pallanteum thus corresponds to Achilles' withdrawal (for very different reasons) from the rest of the Greek army. See Knauer 1964, 240–41 on what he sees as a comparable situation between Achilles' withdrawal to his camp and Odysseus' arrival at Eumaeus' homestead. I return to this point in two sections of chapter 3, "Pallanteum" and, especially, "A Leadership Vacuum."

159. It is, of course, analogous in precisely the same way to Menelaus' tale of his own homecoming in book 4 is related to the plot of the *Odyssey*, although this point does not seem to have been made previously, either.

representation of Hercules as a hero of anger and violence, recognizing the implications of his story for the character of Aeneas, then one might well conclude that he, his heroic audience, and the entire episode in which they are involved anticipate an increasingly explicit sequence of Iliadic events.

A Hesiodic Heracles

The Iliadic character of book 8 becomes much more explicit in its final episode, "The Description of Aeneas' Shield" (626–728), which of course is emphatically modeled on that of Achilles' shield in *Iliad* 18 (478–608). So obviously important is this correspondence that little of the voluminous literature on the episode even mentions its relationship to another poem, the Hesiodic *Shield of Heracles*.[160] In the context of my own argument, this model is very important indeed. As in the case of Apollonius and Callimachus, it is less important whether Aeneas' shield alludes through one of these models back to the other than that it clearly alludes to both. The effect of this is to underline the hyper-Achillean character of Hercules as represented in Evander's epyllion. Corroboration of this point comes early in Hesiod's poem, which opens with the phrase *ê hoiê*, "or such as she." This is the refrain that Hesiod uses in his genealogical poem, *Catalogue of Women*, where it appears so often that the poem was also known as the *Ēhoiai*. At the opening of the *Shield*, this phrase represents the poem not only as Hesiodic but as an actual episode of the *Catalogue*. The woman to whom it points is Alcmene, who is said to have followed her husband, Amphitryon, into exile from their home near Argos to Thebes after "he subdued her father with force and killed him out of anger over cattle" (11–12). The reader learns this more than a hundred lines before the actual description of Heracles' shield begins, but its relevance to Evander's Hercules, who kills Cacus out of anger over cattle, is perfectly clear. More generally, critics agree that *The Shield of Heracles* differs from "The Shield of Achilles" in its representation of violence. The Homeric "Shield" depicts a world in which the forces of war and peace each have their place, perhaps even working with one another to maintain a kind of balance in the affairs of humankind. The Hesiodic *Shield* instead focuses exclusively on violence—both the violence of monsters and miscreants, and the violence that Heracles and heroes like him must use to subdue them.[161] Not surprisingly, there is less agreement as to

---

160. See Faber 2000; Heckenlively 2013.

161. Russo 1950/1965, 115 on lines 161–67; Thalmann 1984, 62–64; Toohey 1988; Edwards in Kirk 1985–1993, vol. 5, 139–41 and 200–209, esp. 208; Faber 2000, 55–56; Heckenlively 2013, 660. Martin 2005, surprisingly, does not mention violence as an element of the pulp aesthetic.

whether "The Description of Aeneas' Shield" is more closely allied with Hesiodic violence or with Homeric balance.

One way of deciding that matter could involve a second difference between the Hesiodic and Homeric shields. As Robert Lamberton has pointed out, "the integration of the Hesiodic shield into its context is more easily appreciable and, I would argue, more ingenious" than its Homeric counterpart.[162] Here again it is crucial to remember that the ecphrasis is not Hesiod's entire poem: it is, in effect, a typical scene on steroids, taking up 179 lines of a 480-line composition that depicts Heracles in the act of girding himself for battle against Cycnus, son of Ares, the god of war. The battle follows the ecphrasis, and it is here that Lamberton's point about integration applies. The meaning of Achilles' shield for the *Iliad* as a whole is an enigma that fueled critical discussion throughout antiquity and continues to do so.[163] In contrast, the Hesiodic ecphrasis, with its emphatically violent imagery, insistently and specifically prefigures that battle between Heracles and Cycnus that follows. As Lamberton again puts it: "The shield *is* the battle about to occur, and what it conveys includes the consequences of battle, depicted with extraordinary horror and expanded to cosmic dimensions."[164] In this sense as well, Aeneas' intertextual shield puts into play elements of both its Homeric and its Hesiodic models. On the one hand, like Homer's shield, it is enigmatic, not least to Aeneas, who famously "delights in its appearance without understanding its meaning."[165] Unlike Achilles' shield, however, and like that of Heracles, Aeneas' shield does prefigure the battles that are to come, not only those in the rest of the poem, which it prefigures symbolically, but those that it graphically depicts, which will be fought throughout Roman history down to the time of Actium.

The *Aeneid* does not subsequently dwell on the indestructible nature of the hero's divine weaponry, but instead celebrates its symbolic value. In book 10, when Aeneas' ship approaches the beleaguered Trojan camp, the hero stands high on the stern and raises his blazing shield (10.260–75). Tellingly, this gesture incites not only hope but also anger in the Trojans.[166] Just once is the shield said to protect Aeneas, but the narrator does not advert its divine nature, as

---

162. Lamberton 1988, 143.

163. P. R. Hardie 1985 and 1986, 340–46.

164. Lamberton 1988, 143.

165. *rerumque ignarus imagine gaudet* 8.730. I would just note in passing that this famous phrase, which has attracted so much commentary, must be one of the most pregnant throwaway lines in the *Aeneid*, and possibly even a metapoetic signal pointing to the hidden meaning, i.e., the allegorical nature of the ecphrasis that precedes it and of its Homeric model.

166. *spes addita suscitat iras* ("the hope given to them incites their anger," 263).

Homer and Hesiod both do.[167] As a result, what stands out is the symbolic value of the shield as representing Aeneas' fateful success (and the success of his Roman descendants down to Augustus), as well the irresistible anger with which he and his Trojans overwhelm their opponents. In this respect, the Hesiodic character of Aeneas' shield casts a baleful light on its Iliadic character, as well.

A *Heraclean* Aeneid

The Heraclean character of Aeneas' shield works not just within an isolated episode, but as a part of the discontinuous "Heracleid," modeled on those of Apollonius and Callimachus, that is embedded within the *Aeneid*. We have seen that Hercules becomes ever more vividly and directly present in the *Aeneid*, as he does in the *Aetia*, but that he also becomes angrier, more emotional, and more violent, as in the *Argonautica*. The narrator's early, implicit reference to Herculean labors stresses endurance rather than violence, and Aeneas' glancing reference to the founding of Tarentum (3.551) underlines Hercules' civilizing activities. Subsequent references more directly connected to the narrative emphasize his propensity towards violence. In book 5 memories of Hercules shared by the participants in "The Memorial Games for Anchises" focus on a pair of boxing gloves that the hero Eryx wore when he faced Hercules in the ring, and died doing it. The mere sight of them, stained and spattered with blood and brains, causes everyone else to blanch, and Entellus, a pupil of Eryx, to ask them: "What would you say if you saw the gloves that were Hercules' own weapons (*arma*) and that grim bout on this very shore?" (410–12). Hercules' violence destroyed even the hero who wore the "weapons" before Entellus' audience; the hero's own gloves remain undescribed, perhaps even indescribable. In book 6, when Aeneas appears in arms (*armatus* 388) seeking passage across the Styx, the infernal ferryman Charon tries to send him away, recalling Heracles on his descent to the underworld not as an ethical paragon, but as a kind of burglar of whom he was happy to see the last (384–97). The hyperbolically violent tale of "Hercules and Cacus" we have just discussed. In Hercules' final appearance, when he weeps at the impending death of Pallas, violence is not stressed, but as Feeney correctly points out, his emotion at the death of a favorite mortal shows that he hardly acquired the capacity for detachment and philosophical indifference that one might expect him to possess after actually achieving divinity.[168]

---

167. *Aeneid* 10.324–32. The shield is mentioned twice more, as a kind of talisman, at 10.242–43 and 638–39.

168. Feeney 1986, 75–76; and 1991, 156.

In such ways, the Hercules theme clearly adds a great deal to the *Aeneid*, in narrative, thematic, and ethical terms. In the end, however, it certainly does not offer a way of avoiding a decision as to whether the poem is "really" to be an Iliad or an Odyssey. Like the *Aetia* and the *Argonautica*, the *Aeneid* incorporates a Heracleid within it; unlike the *Aetia*, it does not in the end represent Heraclean heroism as a "third way" (as the *Aetia* arguably does) that stands apart from or subsumes Achillean and Odyssean paradigms. Rather, like the *Argonautica*, it identifies superhuman violence as Hercules' principal trait while making him a touchstone of Aeneas' progress towards an ability and a willingness to achieve his objectives through violence. If Evander's Hercules and the hero who wore the Hesiodic shield into battle tilt the balance within Aeneas' character and behavior between Achilles and Odysseus, he can only do so in favor of the former.

Weddings, Funerals, and Madness: Dramatic Plots in the *Aeneid*

To this point, we have concentrated almost exclusively on the epic models of the *Aeneid*, the only exception being Callimachus' elegiac *Aetia*. It would never be possible to deal comprehensively with the intertextual *Aeneid* between the two covers of any book, or for that book to find readers with the strength to lift it, let alone read it. There is one additional genre of poetry that I cannot exclude, however, and that is tragedy. Ancient critics and theoreticians considered epic and tragedy to be close relatives. Modern critics too regard the affinities of the *Aeneid* to tragedy as intimately bound up in its reinterpretation of the epic genre. The issue has been approached from a variety of perspectives, some focusing on specific textual relationships, some on "the tragic" as a literary mode, some on the social function of tragedy in a ritual sense.[169] My own view is that the *Aeneid* is obviously not a tragedy in any of these senses alone, and yet that all of them have relevance to the question of what kind of story it tells. In keeping with my general approach, however, I will have less to say about overarching theories of the tragic than about tragic plots, both typical and specific. This has the advantage of building on Aristotle's perception of an affinity between epic and tragic plots, his insistence that the most effective tragic plots follow principles best learned from Homer, and also of his

---

169. See, variously, De Witt 1930; Garstang 1950; Fenik 1960; Reckford 1961; Putnam 1965, 151–201; Quinn 1968, 324–49; König 1970; Jenkyns 1985; Pavlock 1985; Elliott 2008; Panoussi 2009; P. R. Hardie 1997/2019; Scafoglio 2007.

articulation of an important difference between the plots of the *Iliad* and the *Odyssey*.

In chapter 1 I broached the subject of how Aristotle opens the way towards theorizing Homer's twin masterpieces as tragic and comic poems, respectively, with an emphasis on how they end. A well-constructed plot, he says, should represent a single action, not a double one, and should involve a change of fortune from better to worse as the result not of wickedness but of some great mistake. What he means by a double action emerges when he turns to the second-best kind of plot, like that of the *Odyssey*, in which the good prosper while the bad come to grief. This sort of ending he considers more appropriate to comedy, like plots in which "those who are deadliest enemies in the plot, such as Orestes and Aegisthus, exit at the end as new friends, and no one dies at anyone's hands."[170] The double plot of the *Odyssey* concerns the contrasting fates of Odysseus, who triumphs, and the suitors, who are punished. The reconciliation of bitter enemies is also satisfied at the very end of the *Odyssey* when Athena carries out Zeus's wish that, "since brilliant Odysseus has taken vengeance on the suitors, they [i.e., their survivors] should swear a solemn oath and let him be king all his days, and we on our part should bring about a forgetfulness of the slaying of their sons and brothers, *and they should love one another as before and let wealth and peace abound*" (*Odyssey* 24.482–86, my emphasis). In spite of these irenic orders, a battle does in fact break out and blood is shed before Athena can put an end to it, but she does do so. A comic ending, then, even if one that flirts with the possibility of a more tragic one in which Odysseus might have raged like Achilles until he had sated his desire for revenge.[171]

I dwell on Aristotle's perception of a certain kinship between tragedy and comedy for two reasons. One is that, if one were to follow him in a very general way and accept that epic and tragedy are closely related, but assume that comedy is simply a different thing, then there would be little point in considering the tragic character of the *Aeneid* from this point of view. Since Aristotle sees the difference between the *Iliad* and the *Odyssey* as analogous to that between tragedy and comedy, however, his perspective has an obvious relevance to my inquiry. A second point consists in the perception that tragedy and comedy are not merely different genres or even opposites, but that they are closely related— not in the way that epic and tragedy are related, but in a way that seems somehow more intimate while also involving a greater and more decisive difference between the two. This at any rate will be the theme of what follows immediately before I turn to consider the relevance of a few specific tragic plots.

---

170. Aristotle, *Poetics* 1453a in Halliwell et al. 1995, 72–73.
171. See the suggestive comments of Dekel 2012, 69–70.

Setting the Scene

There is pretty wide agreement that the theme of tragedy is signaled repeatedly in *Aeneid* 1 not by intertextual reference to specific tragedies, but by the appearance of certain tragic symbols. Central to this argument are three episodes that I have already discussed from a different point of view. They include Aeneas' landing on the coast of Africa, his meeting with Venus, and his arrival at Carthage. I agree that tragedy figures in these passages, but not in a straightforward way. Instead, I see the theme of tragedy as developing across these episodes in ways that involve relations between tragedy and other dramatic genres.

When Aeneas lands in Africa, he puts in to a harbor that resembles one on Ithaca. A difference between them is that there stands behind the shore in the innermost recesses of the African harbor a shimmering forest described as a *scaena* (164). Like the English "scene," this is a loan word from the Greek *skênê*, a technical term of the theater denoting a building that formed a "backdrop" or "stage set" before which the actors played their parts and, in the *orchêstra* before them, the chorus danced and sang. In a natural setting like the African harbor, it is a bold metaphor. Few would deny that it should make the reader watch for further dramatic elements in the ensuing narrative.[172] But what kind of drama does it signify? Tragedy is the usual answer; but this involves reading back into this passage what is not disclosed until later.

Vitruvius in his great treatise *On Architecture* devotes an entire book to public buildings and five of its twelve chapters to theaters. One of these chapters explains that there are three different kinds of *scaena* corresponding to the three major kinds of drama: tragedy, comedy, and satyr drama (5.6.9). Each *scaena* has its own kind of decoration. The one for satyr drama involves trees, grottoes, and other rustic iconography. That is exactly the kind of *scaena* that the narrator of the *Aeneid* describes in the Libyan harbor where Aeneas takes refuge. A reader who notices this might well be puzzled as to what, if anything, it might mean, and could be forgiven for dismissing it. That would be a mistake.

Satyr drama is not tragedy, but it is intimately associated with it. Tragic poets who were commissioned to compete in ancient Athenian dramatic festivals were required to produce three tragedies and one satyr drama. This fourth play was humorous and is assumed to have promoted the release of pent-up tension generated by watching the previous three. Satyr drama shared its humorous element with comedy, but the forms and occasions for performance of these two genres were distinct. One might say that satyr drama is

---

172. See E. L. Harrison 1989, 4–5; Martina 1990; Malaspina 2004; Polleichtner 2013.

tragic in virtue of its institutional association with tragedy but comic in virtue of its humorous ethos.[173]

In regard to the "stage set" at the back of Aeneas' African landing place, a reasonable hypothesis might be that it signals not the beginning of a tragedy but an end to the series of tragedies that have been the hero's fate up to this point. This series includes the storm that he has barely survived at the beginning of book 1 and also the previous "Misfortunes" that he is asked to recount at its end. Indeed, Aeneas' stories in books 2 and 3 are replete with references to specific tragic intertexts, as we shall see.[174] But those tragedies are in the past. Aeneas does not know where he has arrived, but the reader recognizes this African harbor as an intertextual doublet of the Phorcys harbor on Ithaca. In my previous discussion of it, I suggested that this poetic memory could represent Aeneas' hope that he has arrived at his place of "homecoming" at last. It makes sense that the metaphorical "stage set" that is added to this intertextually Ithacan harbor is not a tragic stage set, but one that announces the end of tragedies in favor of something very different that promises a resolution of tragic tension. Perhaps the hero can now look forward to less trying times. In fact, after providing his followers with venison to feast upon, he ends a speech of encouragement by advising them to do just that: "Be tough, and keep safe for better days to come" (1.207).

We next turn again to Aeneas' meeting with Venus. Like the metaphorical stage set in the harbor, Venus herself has been taken as a symbol of tragedy, even as a character who is about to deliver the prologue of a tragedy (338–68), because she wears a certain kind of boot—the *cothurnus* (337), another loan word from the Greek—that was worn by tragic actors and is familiar in classical rhetoric as a symbol of tragedy.[175] She, however, explains her outfit quite differently: all of it, including her *cothurni*, is characteristic of the girls who live in the area because they are hunters (336–37), not tragic actors; and indeed, *cothurni* were also worn by ancient hunters and were also familiar in classical rhetoric as a symbol of hunting. Venus' *cothurni* are thus ambiguous. In fact, Venus herself, as we have already seen, is extremely ambiguous throughout this episode, in every way. Much of her ambiguity involves her costume— which, *qua* costume, itself associates her with theatricality. Her boots,

---

173. It is an open question whether satyr drama was ever performed at Rome, but it was certainly familiar to students of literary history and theory: see Horace, *The Art of Poetry* 220–50 with Brink 1971, 273–77; Wiseman 1994, 68–85. On the relationship between comedy and satyr drama see Shaw 2014.

174. I return to this topic in two sections of chapter 3, "The Sack of Troy" and "Wanderings."

175. E. L. Harrison 1989, 5–8; P. R. Hardie 1997/2019, 336.

however, while theatrical and specifically tragic, are also hunting boots. By the same token, she is the sexiest of all gods and goddesses; but hunting in classical poetry is frequently figured as antithetical to *eros*. Euripides' tragedy *Hippolytus* is actually built upon this antithesis.[176] Dressed as a huntress, Venus looks like the chaste Diana. Finally, as we have seen, when Venus drops her disguise, it is not clear whether her clothing remains on her body or falls off altogether.[177] In this explosion of polyvalent symbols and messages, it would be no more than wishful thinking to imagine Venus' footwear as the one unambiguous element, especially at the cost of ignoring her explanation of it.

In view of all this, when some interpret Venus' account of Dido's history as a tragic prologue, I can agree, but only to a point. Certainly it begins tragically with the murder of Dido's husband, Sychaeus. From that point onward, however, it becomes a story of Dido's resourcefulness and success. The good prosper and the bad suffer. It is clearly meant to encourage Aeneas: Venus tells him how fortunate he is to have washed up on Dido's shores, implying that he will receive a warm welcome there. Although comforting her son *in propria persona* is evidently not on her agenda, Venus has already begun to work behind the scenes (as it were) on his behalf, and she will continue to do so. Like the sylvan stage set from which Aeneas has just come, Venus and her *cothurni* are polyvalent in a generic as well as a narrative sense, linked to tragedy, certainly, but to tragedy survived and to the promise of relief in the immediate future.[178]

Finally we come to Aeneas' arrival in Carthage, where last we find a signal that is decisively tragic and nothing but. As the hero gazes with envy on the rising

---

176. Fenik 1960, 151–77 sees Venus' intervention in book 1 as being modeled on both the surviving and the lost versions of Euripides' *Hippolytus*. His focus is on Dido as an intertextual Phaedra, i.e. a woman callously manipulated by a goddess; but in view of her chastity Dido is also an avatar of Hippolytus himself. Her fate is a good example of what can happen in the *Aeneid* where utterly incompatible characters are "combined" into a single figure. As for Venus, it is clear enough how she wants the *Aeneid* to turn out. There is no need to consider her a would-be narrator in this passage, but she proves to be an effective director or stage manager for the remainder of book 1, to the extent that she can happily acquiesce to Juno's Apollonian intervention in book 4, as was discussed above.

177. Reckford 1995; Oliensis 2009; see my discussion in chapter 1, "Disguise and Recognition on the Island of Ithaca."

178. I cannot resist raising the possibility of additional satyr play relevance. As I discussed in chapter 1 (see the preceding note), Aeneas' encounter with Venus closely resembles "The Seduction of Anchises" in the *Homeric Hymn to Aphrodite*. Later in that poem, Aphrodite tells Anchises that she does not plan to raise their child herself but will give him to be raised by tree-nymphs who mate with Silenoi (i.e. satyrs) and Hermes (256–63), who is the father of Pan and is very much at home among satyrs himself. I will refrain from unpacking the implications of this intertext, but I invite the reader to consider them at leisure.

city, one of the amazing things he sees is the building of theaters, like those that were going up in Rome during the twenties BCE, when the *Aeneid* itself was taking shape. Aeneas watches the workers "lay deep foundations for theaters, cut huge columns from cliff faces, suitable adornments for the *scaenae* that are to come" (1.427–29). The word *scaenae* of course takes the reader back to Aeneas' landing in a harbor "decorated" as if for a satyr drama; but here in Carthage, as Vitruvius once again makes clear, they are building a different sort of stage set. "Tragic *scaenae* consist of columns and pediments and statues and all the other royal appurtenances," he writes (5.6.8). The huge columns thus declare the kind of *scaena* for which they are destined. Even so, I want to suggest that these "suitable adornments for the *scaenae* that are to come" are not merely or simply tragic. Famously, the reader's perspective on this Carthaginian construction site is focalized through the character of Aeneas, whose eyes move from the dredging of a harbor for the city's port to the building of the theaters (427–28); and while the laying of foundations for these massive structures will have taken place before Aeneas' eyes, the next, crucial detail, the quarrying of the columns (428–29), cannot be taking place within the city. The columns that Aeneas sees, destined for the theaters whose foundations are just being laid, have been carved out of cliffs (*rupibus* 429), a word previously found in the description of the harbor where Aeneas landed (*rupes* 162; *rupe* 310), where it denotes a part of the same landscape that was described as the stage set of a satyr drama. It is as if Aeneas imagined these columns as having been quarried out of those cliffs. On this level of significance, whatever else Aeneas' landing in the sylvan harbor may have meant to him, the idea that will be uppermost in his mind now is the swift progression that he has witnessed from that rustic place to the rising cityscape before him. The reader will share this perspective, but is also in a position to understand, as Aeneas is not, that the "stage" he found in the harbor where he left his fleet is set for a drama that has ties to both tragedy and comedy, but the stage being set before him in the city is unambiguously tragic.

The Tragedies of Dido and Aeneas

When I typed the phrase "unambiguously tragic" just now, I winced. Is anything in the *Aeneid* unambiguous? The tragic stage that the hero watches being built is for the drama that dominates book 4, "The Tragedy of Dido and Aeneas." This episode has been called tragic more often than probably any other in the *Aeneid*, and it has been studied so often from this point of view that there is no need to labor the point here.[179] I have just two observations to make.

---

179. Heinze 1915/1993, 251–58 and 370–73; De Witt 1907; Sikes 1923, 190; Fenik 1960, 216–30; Wlosok 1976/1999; Moles 1984 and 1987; E. L. Harrison 1989; P. R. Hardie 1997/2019, 336–37; Panoussi 2009, 36–38, 133–38, 92–100, 182–98; Giusti 2018, 88–147.

First, the trajectory that leads from satyr drama to tragedy in book 1 correctly predicts Dido's role as a tragic heroine in book 4; there is no question about that. At the same time, the theme of tragedy as the opposite of comedy, and of satyr drama as its own kind of "third way"—not between Iliadic and Odyssean epic but between tragedy and comedy—does not entirely disappear. One sees this above all in one of the most heart-breakingly beautiful passages ever written, the very end of book 4, when Dido, lying on her pyre and struggling to die, is unable to end her life (693–705). Juno, in what may be her solitary act of kindness in the poem, dispatches Iris to release Dido from her pain. As Iris cuts a lock of Dido's hair, she says, "I, as I was bidden, take this sacred offering to Dis and release you from this body." The narrator continues: "So she spoke and with her right hand cut a lock of hair, and at once all the warmth slipped from her body and life withdrew into the winds." Since antiquity, this passage has been seen as alluding to a speech made by Thanatos—Death—near the beginning of Euripides' *Alcestis*: "The woman is going down to the house of Hades. I go to her to take the first sacrificial cutting of her hair. For when this sword has consecrated the hair of someone's head, they are the sacred property of the gods below."[180] This is not the only reference to *Alcestis* in book 4, but it is by far the most powerful.[181] The quite appropriately grim tone of Euripides' Thanatos been converted into something deeply sympathetic. In addition to this overwhelming pathos, moreover, the reminiscence extends the poem's meditation on the relationship between tragedy and comedy in way that is both highly sophisticated and quite moving. My explanation moves from the pedantic to the sublime.

An ancient report on the dramatic competition at the City Dionysia of 438 BCE tells us that Euripides took second place that year with the plays *Cretan Women*, *Alcmaeon*, *Telephus*, and *Alcestis*. The titles, given in that order, put *Alcestis* fourth, following three tragedies, in the place normally reserved for the satyr drama. As if to justify this, the report notes that "the play has a somewhat comic conclusion" and goes on to call it "rather satyric because its ending is in accordance with delight and pleasure in contrast to the essence of tragedy."[182] No one could say that about the end of *Aeneid* 4.[183] The contrast is striking, but not surprising: generating intertextual dialogue by comparing the

---

180. Euripides, *Alcestis* 73–76; see Servius, *Commentary on Vergil's Aeneid* 3.46, 4.694 (where he mistakenly attributes the speech to Mercury, not Death), and 4.703; Macrobius, *Saturnalia* 5.19.1–5 in Kaster 2011, vol. 2, 432–35.

181. See Fenik 1960, 32–43; König 1970, 204–32.

182. For the Greek text see Diggle 1984, 34.

183. Or could they? James O'Hara reminds me of a remark that Servius makes at the beginning of his commentary on book 4 to explain its relationship to *Argonautica* 3: "Almost the whole book is concerned with love, although it has pathos at the end, where Aeneas' departure

beginnings, middles, and ends of related poems is a hallmark of Roman poetry, as we have noticed more than once in this study. Thus in *Alcestis*, when Thanatos speaks these words at the beginning of a tragedy that ends as if it were a comedy, the effect is very much in accordance with the function of satyr drama in an Athenian tragic competition. Even in the *Aeneid*, when the narrator utters them at the end of book 4, some of that function is fulfilled in the release of tension that allows Dido's struggling soul to escape her body, and in the reader's vicarious experience of this release. Thus a trajectory that began in book 1 with fleeting references to stage sets suited first to satyr drama and then to tragedies is pathetically and beautifully concluded. Rather than hope that a tragic prologue might find its counterweight in a comic resolution focusing on marriage, a potentially comic story is instead retold in a way that "restores" to it a tragic ethos focusing on death.

And yet this is not really the end of the story. With Dido's release from life, she comes into her own as an Alcestis figure according to her own character and the demands of Fate—that is, the demands of the epic plot, from which release is impossible. In contrast to the tragedy of book 4 as it is generally understood, the fact that death separates Dido from Aeneas is not the end of it. To say the least, it is far from obvious that Dido, like Alcestis, dies in place of her "husband," Aeneas (although that too might be a possibility to explore). The problem is that Sychaeus, her real husband, has already died, so that there is no question of dying in his place. Still, just as in Euripides, the loving wife is united with her husband in the end, but with a crucial difference. In keeping with the "restoration" of a tragic ethos and a tragic ending to her story, Dido–Alcestis is reunited with Sychaeus–Admetus not in life, but in death. Sadly, in book 6 when Aeneas sees Dido in "The Fields of Mourning," the hero seems to betray a wish that he, and not Sychaeus, could play Admetus to Dido's Alcestis. At the end of Euripides' play, when the real Admetus is reunited with his wife, he is overjoyed, but puzzled by one thing: Alcestis does not speak to him. Heracles, who has braved the underworld to bring Alcestis back to life, explains that she will remain in the power of Thanatos for three days before she can speak (1143–46). Similarly, in "The Fields of Mourning" Dido does not speak to Aeneas (6.469–71), but for a different reason: not because she is in the power of Death, because Aeneas converses freely with everyone else he meets on his underworld journey. The point is that Dido simply refuses to speak to Aeneas, just as Ajax refuses to answer Odysseus in the Homeric "Nekyia" (*Odyssey* 11.563–64).[184]

---

produces pain; as a whole of course it deals with plots and deception, *for the style is almost comic*; and no wonder, where one is dealing with love." (My emphasis.)

184. Servius, *Commentary on Vergil's Aeneid* 6.468.

With reference to Homer's *dramatis personae*, Aeneas of course "is" Odysseus at this point. With reference to Euripides, however, he must be the hero who defies death to reunite his Alcestis with her Admetus. His "restoration" of Dido and Sychaeus to a ghostly imitation of their former married state reinforces the idea of weddings as the most satisfying and emblematic of comic endings. In an infinitely sad inversion of Heracles' feat, however, Aeneas does not reunite Dido with her husband in life but finds that he has sent her to be with him in death. Dido's story is thus imagined as a more tragic *Alcestis* in which Aeneas plays the role of an anti-Heracles.

A separate point, which concerns a larger pattern of tragic intertextuality, is that plays specifically involving the Trojan legend are most relevant to the plot of books 2 and 3. They tell us nothing that would decide whether the *Aeneid* is to be a more Iliadic or more Odyssean poem.[185] Paradoxically, it is when these Trojan plays are left behind that the issue becomes more urgent. The transition involves a shift to intertextual material involving other myths and other themes. Above all, the theme that becomes most prominent from book 4 onwards is that of madness.

The tragic madness of book 4 is clearly signaled and well understood. Within the book, Dido, the intertextual avatar of the Argonautic Medea, inherits Apollonius' exquisite exploration of his character's divided, tormented psyche. The reader of his *Argonautica* recognizes these traits as a "future reflexive" allusion to Medea's post-Argonautic career in Euripidean tragedy. The extensive Apollonian program that informs the *Aeneid*, as Nelis has shown, provides many opportunities for this and related themes to develop.[186] Then, still in book 4, when the reader learns of Dido's nightmares about Pentheus and Orestes driven mad by Furies—in another passage marked by the fatal word "stage" (*scaenis* 471)—it is very clear what this means.[187] As the plot advances beyond book 4, these very specific references to Bacchic and Furial frenzy extend their influence, as well.[188] Ultimately the motif of god-driven madness threatens to pervade the entire poem. In fact, it would not be too much to say that madness becomes the theme under which the tragic intertext of the *Aeneid* finds its unity. This process is abetted by the growing prominence

---

185. See Fenik 1960, 1–33 and König 1970, 28–88 on allusions to Euripides' *Andromache*, *Hecuba*, and *Trojan Women*.

186. Nelis 2001, 160–66.

187. On Euripides' *Bacchae* in book 4 see E. L. Harrison 1972–1973, 15 and 23 note 34; Paschalis 1997, 153; Weber 2002; Panoussi 2009, 133–38. On the *Oresteia* see P. R. Hardie 1991; on Orestes and the Furies see Rebeggiani 2016.

188. See Krummen 2001 and 2004; Weber 2002; Bocciolini Palagi 2007; Mac Góráin 2013.

of a particular figure and a particular play. Both of them, once again, go by the name of Heracles.

Heraclean Tragedy in the Aeneid

Alcestis is not the only Hercalean intertext that informs book 4 (and beyond). Euripides' ambivalent tragedy in which Heracles defeats Death works in counterpoint with Sophocles' *Women of Trachis*, in which Heracles himself dies. The contrasting models create a productive dialogue between Heracles' comic and tragic aspects.

In *Women of Trachis*, not only Heracles but his estranged wife, Deianeira, comes to a tragic end. It was yet again the sharp-eyed Ursinus who noticed the similarity between Deianeira's suicide and that of Dido.[189] This similarity identifies Aeneas as the Heracles who causes the heroine's death, not as a pseudo-Heracles who should have saved his Alcestis from death instead of sending her there. At the same time, although critics have not made much of this connection, *Women of Trachis* ends not with Deianeira's death, but with that of Heracles himself. It is he who in this tragedy cannot find release from the suffering caused by Deianeira's misguided attempt to win back his affections, and he who requires assistance to release his agonized body from the fetters of mortal suffering. Thus there is more than a little Heraclean heroism in Dido's end. As I have noted more than once, however, it is Aeneas who will be compared to Hercules more and more frequently as the poem proceeds. In this respect the theme of god-driven madness as well bears a particular relevance to the Trojan hero.

With Aeneas' descent to and, especially, his return to from the underworld, a different tragic script assumes a much larger relevance to the plot of the *Aeneid*. Earlier in this chapter I noted that Callimachus' *Aetia* prologue contains reference to a passage of Euripides' *Heracles* that celebrates the hero as a civilizing force. As that play begins, Heracles is completing the last of his twelve labors, his journey to the underworld—not to fetch Alcestis, but to steal Cerberus, the three-headed beast that guards the gates of death. It is this attempt of which Charon complains to Aeneas when he presents himself to be ferried across the Styx (*Aeneid* 6.384–97). During the play, after Heracles returns to the upper world, Hera's messenger, Iris, and Lyssa, personified Madness, appear on stage to reveal Hera's plan to drive the hero insane, which will cause

---

189. Ursinus 1568, 300 on *Aeneid* 4.445–65 comparing Sophocles, *Women of Trachis* 912–31. Cerda 1612/1642, vol. 2, 477 on *Aeneid* 4.445–62 compares Euripides, *Alcestis* 175–84. Heinze 1915/1993, 116–17 note 42, Fenik 1960, 32–43, and König 1970, 204–25 consider both intertexts relevant to Dido's end.

him to murder his wife and children (822–74). Similarly, in book 7 of the *Aeneid*, the hero has endured his catabasis and has just returned to the upper world. Shortly afterwards, Juno and Allecto appear to reveal and carry out Juno's plan to unleash infernal madness and thus delay, if not prevent, the Trojans from settling in Italy (7.286–340). It has long been acknowledged that the conception of Allecto at this point owes a lot to Euripides' depiction of Lyssa–Madness, but the more extensive congruency that hinges on this resemblance has not received much emphasis. Perhaps this is explained by the fact that Aeneas, whom Evander in book 8 explicitly challenges to emulate Hercules himself, does not actually murder Ascanius, his only remaining family member. Perhaps it is because Allecto visits her Furial madness directly on Amata, Turnus, and the Latin peoples, not on Aeneas (7.341–571). At the same time, as is all too well known, madness (*furor*) does visit Aeneas more than once in the final books of the poem, causing him to visit indiscriminate slaughter on all those who come in his way.[190] It is clear as well that Seneca read the *Aeneid* exactly this way. In *Hercules Furens* ("Hercules Insane"), a tragedy closely based on Euripides' *Heracles*, Seneca "glosses" quotations and paraphrases of the Greek play with allusions to previous borrowings that he found in the *Aeneid*—an exemplary instance of "window reference" or "two-tier allusion" with clear implications for how one expert reader interpreted the epic's tragic intertext.[191]

A few inferences seem inescapable. Above all, the tragic intertext of the *Aeneid* is extensive. I have not come close to accounting for all of it here. It is also heterogeneous in a way that does not encourage the identification of any single tragedy as more important than any other. On the other hand, and increasingly as the epic proceeds, most of the tragic intertexts, in spite of their diversity, tend to converge on the theme of madness in a way that concerns not just Aeneas but also many of the other most important characters in the poem. The point is that Aeneas is not exempt, and this fact leaves the reader with a familiar decision to make about what madness does to him and how much it matters.

It also seems clear that the theme of tragedy develops in such a way as to insist that tragedy is not merely a thing in itself, but is always to be understood as existing in tension with comedy. A plot is tragic or comic, one or the other, because it is one and not the other. References to ambivalent genres like satyr drama and "tragicomedies" like *Alcestis* are managed in such a way that persisting in such an in-between state seems, in the *Aeneid*, to be an extremely

---

190. Germanus 1575, 380 and Heyne 1830–1841, vol. 3, 46 draw a connection between Allecto and the Euripidean Lyssa in this passage; see also Otis 1964, 323–24; Panoussi 2009, 126.

191. Putnam 1992/1995; Morelli 2007.

remote possibility, one that can perhaps be imagined for only a moment before some decision has to be made. In the epic's dramatic intertext, that decision is always in favor of tragedy.

With respect to Homer, it appears on the one hand that dramatic intertexts more than any other offer a "third way" of sorts. As a drama, the *Aeneid* is sometimes a Medea, an Alcestis, even a Bacchae. In all cases, it seems to be a fully tragic version of these stories, even more tragic in some cases than the originals. In terms of the Aristotelian categories with which I began this section, it is left up to the reader to decide whether the point is that a good man makes a terrible mistake or the good prosper while the bad suffer. If that is so, then any decision one might make as to the Homeric identity of the *Aeneid* would seem to have a clear dramatic counterpart in tragedy or comedy.

Historical Intertexts in Roman Epics

One final step remains in this survey of potential "third ways," a step not only beyond the genre of epic poetry but, in part, beyond poetry altogether. Among the many prose genres that contribute to the incredibly rich intertext of the *Aeneid* are philosophy (which we have been considering as a major influence), oratory (which has been studied fairly intensively since antiquity), technical disciplines such as geography, augury, architecture (as we saw in the previous section), and many others. The one I have not mentioned that is most germane to this study is history, especially when considered not in the abstract but as a literary genre. The point is not just what happened but how historians wrote about it. For that reason it seems useful to speak of history and historiography as the relevant genre. It takes various forms, including verse. In what follows, I will briefly consider a few important moments in prose historiography before coming back to poetry in the form of early Roman epic as a historiographical intertext.

History and Historiography

As I was saying earlier in this chapter, Greek culture treated mythical events as causal, explanatory, or otherwise relevant to historical realities.[192] For poets like Apollonius and Callimachus, the adventures of the Argonauts, the labors of Heracles, and other myths were foundational for the world in which they lived, both in general and with specific relevance to the contemporary political dispensation. In this, they take their bearings from Hesiod rather than Homer,

---

192. See Moles 1993.

who was interested in the Trojan War more as the end of the mythical period than as the beginning of history. That did not stop anyone from citing Homer as providing historical justification for contemporary political arguments, or from finding in him a prediction that Troy would one day be reborn as Rome.[193] No wonder, then, that history is a central theme in the *Aeneid* or that mythical narrative is mediated by the poem's engagement with historiography.[194] In book 2, the image of Sinon skulking among reeds and that of Priam as a headless corpse lying on the shore were recognized in antiquity as alluding to historical accounts of the Roman generals Gaius Marius and Gnaeus Pompeius Magnus, respectively.[195] In book 7, when the epic narrator invokes divine assistance to begin the second half of the poem, he asks the Muse for details concerning "the kings, the conditions and the state of affairs in ancient Latium when the foreign army first drove its fleet to the shores of Ausonia," declaring his intention to "recall the very beginning of the conflict" and to tell of "fearsome warfare, battle formations, kings driven to death by their emotions, all Etruria and all Hesperia mobilized for war" (37–45). This invocation owes a lot to the language of prose historiography, and it is a sign of things to come. For instance, Andreola Rossi has pointed out that when battle narrative begins in earnest the poem seems to accelerate in its impetuous rush past the end of heroic time and into the historical era.[196] This becomes especially evident as specific events in Aeneas' Italian war are presented as prefigurations of actual Roman battles, of tactics, fortifications, weaponry, and other military elements that anachronistically anticipate those of much later times.[197] In terms of more specific historical comparisons, these anachronisms encourage the realization that Aeneas' legendary war against Turnus at various points resembles particular episodes during the Samnite, Punic, Social, and Civil Wars.

Great historical events, and not merely vignettes, lurk behind mythic narratives in the early books, as well. In this regard the role of Carthage has always been obvious. In particular, the curse that Dido pronounces on her funeral pyre, that an avenger might rise from her bones to ensure perpetual enmity

---

193. Cf. the infamous story of Plutarch (*Life of Solon* 10) that Solon attempted to interpolate into the Homeric "Catalogue of Ships" lines that would bolster an Athenian claim to sovereignty over Salamis.

194. See Woodman 1989.

195. Servius, *Commentary on Vergil's Aeneid* 2.135 and 557; see Moles 1983; Delvigo 2013.

196. Rossi 2003.

197. See P. R. Hardie 1994, 255–8, index entries "Hannibal" and "Roman reference"; Marincola 2010; Goldschmidt 2013, especially 101–48; Giusti 2018, especially 199–278, on Carthage in the *Aeneid* as standing for the Punic Wars as an anticipation of and replacement for the Roman and Italian Social and Civil Wars; Biggs 2020.

between her people and that of Aeneas (4.625–29), looks forward unmistakably to Hannibal and the Punic Wars. Nora Goldschmidt, Elena Giusti, Thomas Biggs, and others have explored the more general relevance of Carthaginian history in the *Aeneid* and its early Roman forerunners.[198] If one looks beyond Carthage to Africa and Egypt as a whole, it has long been known that the love affair of Dido and Aeneas invites comparison with the historical encounters involving Sophonisba and Scipio, Cleopatra and Julius Caesar, Mark Antony, and the future Augustus.[199] Finally, commenting on Anchises' "Parade of Heroes" in book 6 and on the ecphrasis of Aeneas' shield in book 8, Servius states that those who read these passages carefully will discover that they give an account of Roman history in its entirety from the time of Aeneas' wanderings down to the poet's own age.[200] In view of all this, the question must be asked: does history itself offer any guidance as to the Homeric question of what kind of poem and what kind of hero this epic and this hero are to be?

Homer and Historiography

It is clear that ancient prose historiography displays an awareness of, and places a certain emphasis on, the most basic Homeric antinomy between Achilles and Odysseus. Let us consider a passage in which Livy exploits a familiar stereotype that presents Romans as paragons of straightforward military valor while various enemies, be they Greeks, Gauls, or Parthians, rely instead on duplicitous strategies. Here the Carthaginians are involved, and it is they whom the Romans most insistently branded with this stereotype. The scene is a naval encounter off Lilybaeum in 218 BCE at the onset of the Second Punic War. According to Livy, the Romans, remembering their success in these waters during the previous war, were "confident in their numbers and their **valor**" (*virtute* 21.49.13).[201] When they tried to engage, however, the Carthaginians adopted evasive maneuvers, "preferring to wage war by **artifice** instead of **force**" (*arte non vi rem gerere* 21.50.2). To be sure, Livy is recording the particular tactics followed by a specific pair of commanders in a single encounter; but it is not hard to believe that he uses this episode to characterize two entire

---

198. See Elliot 2013 for a soberingly skeptical perspective on these approaches insofar as they involve the reconstruction of fragmentary literature on the basis of presumptive imitations by Vergil and other authors.

199. Giusti 2018, 239–46 on Sophoni(s)ba.

200. Servius, *Commentary on Vergil's Aeneid* 6.752 and 8.625.

201. In 241 BCE, Gaius Lutatius Catulus won a decisive victory over Hanno in the Battle of the Aegates Islands, which caused the Carthaginian senate to sue for peace rather than prolong the war any further. For references see Broughton 1951, vol. 1, 218.

peoples on the eve of the decisive conflict between them. The Romans are programmatically associated with straightforward military might, their enemies with craft and strategy; and this is no surprise. One might have expected Roman readers and writers always to have such a preference. On the other hand, we have seen that in ethical philosophy this was not the case. Is historiography then different in this regard?

In isolation, the passage seems to recommend bluff *virtus* and to deplore cunning strategy as a way of passing judgment on two entire peoples. From a wider perspective, it may ironically forecast very different encounters later in the war when Hannibal, the master tactician, would inflict heavy losses on Roman armies led by brave but thoroughly outclassed commanders. If so, Livy may also be hinting that the straightforwardness that had allowed the Romans to prevail in the last war would not be sufficient in the next. Not overwhelming force but the singular insight of "one man" would eventually save the state thanks to a controversial strategy that earned Quintus Fabius Maximus the derisive, but later glorious name Cunctator, "The Delayer." So successful was his strategy of not engaging that Fabius eventually maneuvered Hannibal into a disadvantageous position that enabled the Romans to recapture Tarentum, a city that Hannibal had previously taken in a daring nocturnal raid.[202] This turn of events reportedly caused Hannibal himself to comment: "The Romans seem to have found another Hannibal, for we have lost Tarentum in the same way that we took it."[203] In fact, Fabius' evasive strategy was not unlike that of the Carthaginians at Lilybaeum, whereas the aggressive approach favored by the Romans on that occasion would later prove disastrous in battles at the Ticinus, the Trebia, Lake Trasimenus, Geronium, Cannae, and elsewhere, when unimaginative leaders repeatedly came to grief. Late in the war, the aging Fabius came to fear that the youthful Scipio would fare no better; but he would prove the greatest strategist of all.[204] Scipio's invasion of Africa forced Hannibal's departure from Italy to defend his country, where Scipio won a decisive victory. Thus (I might venture to say) the Carthaginian's homecoming turned out to be no Odyssean *nostos*, but an admission of defeat no less than Achilles' threatened return to Phthia would have been.

Livy does not develop this theme in explicitly Homeric terms; one would hardly expect this. But David Levene has commented on Livy's rivalry not just with the Greek historian Polybius but also with Homer to tell the story of a

---

202. Livy, *History of Rome* 27.12.15–16; Plutarch, *Life of Fabius* 21–23; Polybius, *Histories* 1.10.

203. Plutarch, *Life of Fabius* 23.

204. And another double of Hannibal: see Rossi 2004.

war that Livy calls "the most memorable war of them all" (21.1.1). [205] The simple distinction that Livy makes between "force" (*vis*) and "cunning" (*ars*) in book 21 is in fact a close approximation of Homeric *biê* and *mêtis*, the signature traits of Achilles and Odysseus and symbols of the values that inform the ethical universes of the *Iliad* and the *Odyssey*, respectively. Perhaps Livy expected his readers to prefer Achillean might as compatible with Roman character and to associate Odyssean craft with their shifty enemies. Possibly he hoped that some readers would see through the simple distinction he seemed to have drawn. In either case, Livy was preparing them for a major strand of thematic development across the following ten books of his history. By invoking an exemplary contrast between "force" and "cunning" to begin a narrative in which the Romans must learn to rely less on the former and more on the latter, Livy challenges readers to respond flexibly to stereotypical ideas and to take the long view themselves. This is just one of many examples that could be cited to show that the Roman tradition of rhetorical exemplarity shares important terms of reference with Homeric themes. Moreover, it is consistent with a pronounced tendency in historiography to present Odyssean intelligence in a favorable light.[206]

A pat response to the question of whether the ideal Roman historical epic would be an Iliad or an Odyssey might nevertheless favor the former, especially if the poem's major theme happened to be war. Our brief discussion of Livy suggests that it may be more complicated than that, and we shall see that inferences drawn from early Roman epics both mythical and historical are correspondingly complex, as well. Two of these poems, Gnaeus Naevius' *The Punic War* and Quintus Ennius' *Annals* are undeniably historical and also undeniably Homeric. What may be surprising is that even Livius Andronicus' translation of Homer's *Odyssey* can profitably be considered from a historical perspective, and it is with it that we begin.

Myth and History in Livius' Odyssey

Although one could say that Roman historiography begins with Poseidon's revelation about Aeneas' future in *Iliad* 20, Livius decided to translate the *Odyssey* instead. Can the poet's historical consciousness have driven this decision? It has recently been argued that Livius' poem celebrates in a quasi-

---

205. Levene 2010, 88–99 and 107–11; see also Marincola 2007; Flatt 2017; Giusti 2018, 152–67.

206. See Strasburger 1972, 40–41; Hartog 2001; Montiglio 2005, 118–46; Marincola 2007; Biggs 2018; Gerolemou 2018. My thanks to Cynthia Damon for discussion of Livy's narrative strategy.

allegorical way Rome's success in the First Punic War (264–241 BCE), a naval conflict that took place in the same waters as Odysseus' wanderings supposedly did.[207] This idea is supported by the fact that in 240 BCE Livius wrote dramatic scripts to celebrate the end of this same war the previous year. Years later, during the second war with Carthage (218–202 BCE), he composed a hymn for ritual use at a moment of crisis.[208] That hymn, as it happens, was written to propitiate Juno, and it is on Livius' treatment of this goddess that I wish to concentrate here.

In the first section of this chapter we saw that in Livius' *Odyssey*, in which Juno herself presumably plays no more of a role than does Hera in the Homeric original, the goddess gains unexpected prominence via her cult title Moneta as a Roman equivalent of Mnemosyne and mother of the Camenae, the first Roman "Muses." Juno's association, via Moneta, with Mnemosyne scrambles the traditional genealogy of the Greek pantheon and creates difficult working conditions for the narrator of the *Aeneid*. Here I turn to a second passage in which Livius names Juno by one of her cult titles, calling her, "venerable child, daughter of Saturn, **queen**" (*sancta puer Saturni filia* **regina**).[209] This is probably an expansion of the much simpler phrase "**mistress** Hera" (***potnia** Hērē*) in the original.[210] Expansive grandiloquence is in keeping with Livian poetics when it comes to names, but this conversion of a perfectly ordinary noun-epithet phrase into an impressive tricolon that fills an entire line is extraordinary. It is especially so if one considers that Livius' chosen form, coincidentally known as the Saturnian verse, is shorter than Homer's dactylic hexameter. This leaves word space in his version of the *Odyssey* very much at a premium. Giving his additions their full weight, we see immediately that the word "venerable" (*sancta*) corresponds to nothing in the Greek. It is also out of keeping with the straightforward style of Homeric narrative and more reminiscent of a prayer or hymn. As such, it establishes a solemn tone that continues in the word or words that it modifies, "child ... daughter" (*puer ... filia*). Literal rendering of these near synonyms produces an effect that in English seems merely awkward, but in Latin is recognizably archaic and impressive.[211] The doublet also emphasizes the theme of parentage, a traditional feature of this verse form. Saturnians had long been used in the funeral inscriptions of

207. Leigh 2010; Biggs 2020.

208. The ancient evidence is reasonably consistent except for that of Accius, which Cicero considered mistaken (*Brutus* 71–73). See Goldberg 1995, 28–30; Suerbaum 2002, 94–96.

209. Text and translation in Warmington 1936, 30–31 (fragment 16).

210. *Odyssey* 4.513, the corresponding Homeric passage, according to most editors; *contra* Goldberg 1995, 65–66. See the citation in the following note.

211. Mariotti 1952/1986, 33.

Roman aristocrats who were mightily concerned to advertise their distinguished ancestry. Thus Juno here is "daughter of Saturn" in the same way that Lucius is son of Gnaeus in an inscription on the tombs of the Scipios.[212] Other divinities and heroes get similar treatment in Livius' *Odyssey*.[213] The effect is to inscribe the ideology of the Roman ruling elite onto the divine and heroic genealogy of the Greeks, a notable "familiarizing" or "domesticating" gesture, in the language of translation theory.[214]

The epithet "Saturnian" is special in another way. Although most of the elder Olympians are children of Saturn, in the *Aeneid* only Juno is regularly called "Saturnian." Apart from her, only her brothers Jupiter and Neptune are ever called by that name, and then only to express their similarity to her, or else to their father in ways that she exemplifies even more than they. These are frightening, even bloodthirsty qualities; but conversely, the same epithet can evoke powerful ideas about peace and justice in the remote Italian past.[215] In Greek myth, Cronus, after Zeus deposed him, was confined to Tartarus with the rest of the Titans; but the Romans said that Saturn hid (*latuit*) in Latium where he ruled in Golden Age conditions.[216] He long remained an important Roman divinity: the Temple of Saturn in the Forum was dedicated in the late 6th or early 5th century BCE, possibly before that of Jupiter Optimus Maximus; it was rebuilt and enlarged a number of times, most recently in the 4th century CE, about a thousand years after it was first built. Its "birthday," the date of its dedication, was celebrated along with the Saturnalia, one of the most important and popular festivals in the Roman religious calendar, on December 17. Unfortunately, we cannot say whether Livius himself knew the myth of Saturn's Golden Age kingdom in ancient Latium. In all other respects, though, the poet's reference to Juno as the child of Saturn lends an aura of antiquity and prestige as compared with Homer's almost unadorned mention of Hera.

Why did Livius think this necessary, when Juno herself occupied a central position in the Roman state cult? In the presumptive Homeric original, as Agamemnon tries to sail around the notoriously treacherous Cape Malea (the same place from which a storm blew Odysseus for ten days to the land of the Lotus Eaters), Hera rescues him from a storm (*Odyssey* 4.513). No doubt she performs this uncharacteristically good deed because Agamemnon is king of Argos, the Greek town that she loved above all others. By stressing her cultic

---

212. See Courtney 1995, 40–44 and 216–29; Goldberg 1995, 63–66.
213. Mariotti 1952/1986, 33.
214. To use the familiar, if blunt distinction popularized by Venuti 1995.
215. See Johnston 1980, 62–89; Wallace-Hadrill 1982; Perkell 2002.
216. *Aeneid* 8.319–27 with O'Hara 1996, 207–8.

identity in general along with her place in the divine genealogy of Rome, then, Livius emphasizes an act of cultural translation (the so-called *interpretatio Romana*) in the religious sphere that parallels his own intervention as a translator of canonical literature.

The climax of this performance comes in the final word of this remarkable line. The Latin word for "queen," *regina*, is more or less equivalent to *potnia*, "mistress," in the Greek. More to the point is that Juno Regina had been a specific cult title in the Roman state religion since at least (according to legend) 396 BCE. How it became one greatly corroborates what I have written so far. This cult, like that of Juno Moneta, was founded by the great (and possibly legendary) Marcus Furius Camillus, who conquered the Etruscan city of Veii after performing a rite of *evocatio*, petitioning the goddess to abandon her patronage of his enemy and come to Rome (Livy, *History of Rome* 5.21–22). It seems unlikely that Livius in our passage selected this cult title, out of many possibilities, at random. Even more than in the case of Moneta, reference to the goddess' transfer of her allegiances from an enemy people to the Romans is remarkably apt.

The only pity is that we do not know when Livius wrote these lines. In 207 BCE, some thirty-three years after he staged his first translations from the Greek at the Roman Festival of 240 BCE, he composed a hymn to be sung by a chorus of twenty-seven girls as they processed through the city. While the chorus was practicing, the temple of Juno Regina was struck by lightning. In consequence, it was decided that the goddess required special propitiation, which she received in the form of a golden bowl dedicated in that temple and of a procession by that chorus of twenty-seven girls, now if not before singing explicitly in her honor. The ceremony had originally been planned in response to a series of alarming portents that followed a number of serious military defeats dealt by Hannibal, who for years had been running roughshod over the Italian peninsula during the Second Punic War. To make matters worse, Hannibal's brother Hasdrubal was reported to be crossing the Alps into Italy, as well. Livy (27.37.7–14) explains the decision to propitiate Juno in this particular way by the fact that many of the portents had to do with matters related to her role as goddess of marriage and childbirth. He does not say, but it is difficult not to believe, that it also had to do with the fact that Juno, like the Greek Hera, was identified with the Punic goddess Tanit, one of the chief patron deities of the Carthaginians.[217] In any case, the ceremony that featured Livius' hymn was soon followed by a major victory. It was in fact Livius' own

---

217. The impact of this identification on Latin epic is explored by Feeney 1991, 116–17, 127, 131, 149.

patron, Marcus Livius Salinator, who stopped Hasdrubal's advance at the Battle of the Metaurus, in which the invading general fell. These events probably mark the occasion when later poets remembered that Juno not only abandoned Carthage, much as she had abandoned Veii almost two centuries previously, but also put away the pathological grudge that she had nursed against the Trojans and their Roman successors since time immemorial, as the epic narrator describes so hauntingly in the opening lines of the *Aeneid*.[218]

To repeat, we do not know when Livius wrote his *Odyssey*. It seems likely that he did so sometime between the two fixed dates that we have, 240 and 207 BCE, which suggest that he had enjoyed a long career and a long life by the time he composed his hymn to Juno Regina. His epic may be even earlier than the dramas produced in 240. The fact is, however, that what we know of Livius' poetic career is that it was associated at the beginning and the end with service to the state. Whenever he introduced Juno Regina into his *Odyssey*, it is not at all surprising that he chose to do so in a context that invites reflection upon the goddess' history of abandoning her former protégées, be they Argives, Veientes, or Carthaginians, in favor of the Romans, and one that stresses her abidingly Roman character.

This way of looking at Livius' *Odyssey* reveals the shadow of a warlike Iliadic ethos lurking in its references to Juno, in Homeric terms an almost exclusively Iliadic goddess to whom Livius grants unexpected prominence both as a Musal figure and as a symbol of Roman conquest. If we could be sure that Livius' poem was written and read with reference to the First Punic War, the notion that it alluded in some way to the Homeric *Iliad* as well as the *Odyssey* would be that much easier to assert. One might then infer that Rome's first epic poet established a pattern of treating Odyssean wandering, his overt subject, as prior in some sense to implied Iliadic warfare, reversing the relationship between Homer's epics. We cannot with confidence ascribe this reversal to Livius himself, but the pattern emerges more clearly from consideration of Livius as Naevius' precursor, and also from critical engagement with Naevius himself.

Myth and History in Naevius' The Punic War

If Livius' *Odyssey* implicitly celebrates Roman success in the First Punic War (and, as I have suggested, in earlier conflicts as well), Naevius' epic, *The Punic War*, addresses that subject directly. Scevola Mariotti, writing before Livius began to be discussed in terms of contemporary Roman militarism, suggested that Naevius' poem might be considered an Iliadic and historical response to

---

218. See Feeney 1984; some qualifications tentatively proposed by Farrell 2020a, 74–76.

Livius' mythological *Odyssey*, but then went on to admit that there might be more to it than that. Since the first half of Naevius' poem was (as seems probable) almost entirely taken up with mythical origins from Aeneas' escape from Troy to Romulus' foundation of Rome, and the second half entirely devoted to contemporary battle narrative, Mariotti notes that the structure of Naevius' poem could be seen as beginning with Odyssean wandering and "homecoming" followed by Iliadic warfare. This would anticipate the structure of the *Aeneid* as it has traditionally been understood.[219] Here I return to a subject broached previously in chapter 1, the possibility that the plot of the *Aeneid* follows that of *The Punic War* in some detail. Macrobius writes: "In Book 1 of the *Aeneid* a storm is described [81–123], and Venus complains to Jupiter about the dangers her son faces [227–53], and Jupiter comforts her by telling her that her posterity will flourish [254–96]. All of this is taken from Book 1 of Naevius' *The Punic War*. There too Venus complains to Jupiter while the Trojans are beset by a storm, and after her complaint Jupiter comforts her by speaking of her posterity's great expectations."[220] Of course there are limits to how far we can press such a notice: recall Servius' statement that *Aeneid* 4 was translated "in its entirety" from *Argonautica* 3.[221] We cannot assume that Naevius anticipated the *Aeneid* in any detail that Macrobius does not specify—for instance, by making his storm the work of Juno, the cause of Aeneas' arrival in Carthage, and the prelude to an affair with Dido—nor can we assume that other fragments of *The Punic War* that look as though they might fit into the same narrative sequence actually do belong there. All of that said, if Naevius did inflict a storm at sea upon the Trojans early in his epic, and did follow that episode with an interview between Venus and Jupiter, then it is hard to ignore Macrobius' testimony that the *Aeneid* opens on a markedly Naevian note. Knowledgeable readers would obviously factor any such similarity between *The Punic War* and the *Aeneid* into their interpretation of the later poem.

It is also true that the main theme of *The Punic War* was the beginning of an epochal clash between Rome and Carthage, and this is a major historical theme of the *Aeneid*, as well. Whether or not Naevius' storm drove Aeneas to Carthage, when the storm of *Aeneid* 1 does so it alludes to Naevius' connection

---

219. Mariotti 1955/2001, 19–21; Buchheit 1963, 23–53; Wigodsky 1972, 22; Horsfall 1973–1974, 9–13. Servius, *Commentary on Vergil's Aeneid* 1.170 cites Naevius' *The Punic War* for the information that Aeneas had one ship built for him by Mercury (text and translation in Warmington 1936, 50–51). The phrasing leaves it unclear whether Aeneas had only one ship, and it was made by Mercury, or had only one such ship in addition to others. In either case, the motif of a ship built by a god recalls the building of the Argo by Athena; see Biggs 2019a.

220. Macrobius, *Saturnalia* 6.2.31 in Kaster 2011, vol. 3, 58–59.

221. See note 70 above.

between Aeneas' heroic adventures and the First Punic War. As a result, the theme of Rome and Carthage remains marked as a Naevian one throughout the *Aeneid*, and not only in those passages that allude directly to Naevius' epic.

A major problem is that reconstructions of Naevius' highly fragmentary poem tend to rely heavily on passages of the *Aeneid* that seem to be imitating it. It is easy to assume that verbal allusion to Naevius betokens a more extensive narrative congruency. This is the same principle on which Knauer bases his concept of *Leitzitate*. As we have seen, however, it is never a straightforward matter to determine which of Knauer's allusions to Homer really work this way. The same is probably true of allusions to Naevius, as well.[222]

Still, the main point is that *The Punic War* does seem to have anticipated the *Aeneid* in consisting of approximately equal Odyssean and Iliadic halves, in that order. The remains of it do not permit us even to guess at exactly what that means. Does the architecture of *The Punic War* respond to Livius' *Odyssey* primarily as yet another, new and improved Odyssey, based this time on the wanderings of the proto-Roman Aeneas instead of the Greek Ulysses? Does it self-importantly trump Livius' effort by presenting itself as an Iliadic *maius opus*? Does it succeed in combining both Homeric poems? Are all of these ideas in play, or some of them, or others, or none? Such questions might be answerable if we had *The Punic War* entire; more likely they would remain highly debatable. Since the Naevian Aeneas seems to have experienced Odyssean wanderings in the largely mythological first half of *The Punic War*, but not to have figured directly in the (perhaps) Iliadic warfare of the historical second half, he remains a fascinating but elusive point of reference, but one that for this inquiry perhaps raises more questions than can be answered.

Knauer, while admitting that Naevius may have anticipated the bipartite architectural approach to large-scale Homeric relationships for which the *Aeneid* is celebrated, dismisses any idea of such a thing in Ennius' *Annals*.[223] But Ennius too told of Aeneas' journey from Troy to Italy and Romulus' founding of Rome. The entire sequence seems to have been contained in the poem's first book out of an original fifteen.[224] Those proportions hardly describe a balanced structural and thematic division between myth and history, voyaging and warfare. Nevertheless, Virginia Fabrizi has shown that the *Annals* stresses themes like diplomacy and wisdom as the foundations of Roman success, and these qualities are especially evident in the earlier books.[225] In book 1, someone

---

222. See Spielberg 2020 on the tendency of passages that Ennius presents as direct quotations of historical speeches to be "transferred" by later writers to other historical contexts.

223. Knauer 1964, 239 note 1, 344; 1964a, 82.

224. I stress "seems," admonished by the arguments of Elliott 2012.

225. Fabrizi 2012.

observes that settling differences by force is to act like stolid swine.[226] In (probably) book 6, someone else says that the Aeacidae, the descendants of Achilles down to King Pyrrhus of Epirus, are themselves stolid, being powerful in war, but not in wisdom.[227] In book 9, Philip V of Macedon, another of the Aeacidae, is said to be devouring Greece like a ravenous Cyclops.[228] Such passages express a preference for strategy over force while aligning Rome's enemies with Iliadic heroes or Odyssean monsters. It is hard to imagine the *Annals* as an Odyssey in terms of plot, but it is evident that passages like these associate the Romans with Odyssean prudence, and their opponents with opposite qualities, whether specifically Iliadic or anti-Odyssean.

Curiously, however, Ennius seems to have ended the *Annals* rather differently, and in doing so he gave the entire poem a bellicose reputation. After completing the *Annals* in fifteen books, the poet embarked on an extension of (eventually) three more. In book 16, to justify this decision, he speaks of his subject up to that point as "the ancient wars of men."[229] Scholars have accordingly designated the theme of books 16–18 as "more recent wars" (*bella recentiora*), and the surviving fragments of these books bear out this designation. Ennius may be deliberately misrepresenting the prominence of battle narrative in the original *Annals*, or at least focusing on just one aspect of the poem, perhaps one that became more prominent in the course of the narrative.[230] Book 6 opened with the rhetorical question: "Who can unroll the vast boundaries of the war?"[231] The question has metaliterary import for the subject of this particular book, the Pyrrhic War of 280–275 BCE; but could it have a more general significance? Books 7, 8, and 9 seem to have been almost entirely concerned with the First and Second Punic Wars. Book 10 opens by invoking the

---

226. Ennius, *Annals* fragment 1.47 (line 96) in Goldberg and Manuwald 2018, 156–57. For what follows see Farrell 2021a.

227. Ennius, *Annals* fragment 6.14 (lines 197–98) in Goldberg and Manuwald 2018, 210–11. The passage is not attested for this book, but Cicero, who quotes the passage (*On Divination* 2.116), associates it with King Pyrrhus, who was certainly a major character in book 6 of the *Annals*.

228. Ennius, *Annals* fragment 9.15 (lines 319–20) in Goldberg and Manuwald 2018, 266–67.

229. Ennius, *Annals* fragment 16.3 (line 403) in Goldberg and Manuwald 2018, 320–21.

230. Ennius may well be tendentiously characterizing his earlier work in a way that serves the purpose of a new project. Horace introduces book 4 of his *Odes* by complaining to Venus that he has grown too old for love poetry, as if love poetry were all that *Odes* 1–3 contained. This facilitates a re-imagination of Venus in the context of imperial court panegyric as divine ancestress of Augustus and his family (*Odes* 4.15.31–32) instead of as the "savage mother of Desires" (4.1.4). Perhaps Ennius, in similar fashion, re-imagines *Annals* 1–15 as predominantly martial in character in order to facilitate a transition to martial themes in books 16–18.

231. Ennius, *Annals* fragment 6.1 (line 164) in Goldberg and Manuwald 2018, 198–99.

Muse to help narrate the Second Macedonian War. The fragments of books 11–15 as well have mainly to do with war. One could thus take the opening of book 6 as announcing a decisive turning point in the poem as a whole, and with it in Ennius' conception of Roman history. Books 1–5 tell how a band of Trojan refugees, following the destruction of their city by the Greeks, went into exile to find a new home far away in Italy, where they established themselves—not simply through warfare, but especially because they enjoyed the gods' favor, cherished sound institutions, and practiced prudent leadership—to become a leading city.[232] Indeed, the remains of these books suggest that war was hardly their most important theme.[233] Thus, as the narrator girds himself for the Pyrrhic War, he must ask whether he has it in him to narrate the first in what would be a continuous series of conflicts waged by these same Romans on a world stage against so many Hellenistic super-states, including several lineal descendants of the very Greek heroes who sacked Troy, Aeneas' homeland.[234] In this case, a statement at the beginning of book 16 that it was time to turn from old wars to new would not look very tendentious, at all. In addition to this thematic turn, a few passages securely placed in book 15—the last book in the poem's original edition—take their bearings directly from Iliadic, and in one case specifically Aeacid, values. As it happens, both passages involve not only the *Iliad*, but the *Aeneid* as well.

Macrobius, our source for the passages, tells us that in one case, the heroics of Pandarus and Bitias, a pair of gigantic brothers fighting to defend the Trojan encampment in *Aeneid* 9, is based on a passage from *Annals* 15. In the Ennian passage, which Macrobius paraphrases, a pair of Istrian soldiers open the gate of their camp to attack and wreak havoc among the Roman troops that are besieging them.[235] Elsewhere, Macrobius treats the same passage from *Aeneid* 9 as a direct imitation of Homer; although he does not say that Ennius must

---

232. Fabrizi 2012 makes a convincing case that Ennius was especially concerned to represent the Romans as ethically and morally suited to be the rulers of a world empire on the basis of their trustworthiness, respect for diplomacy, and piety rather than on sheer military might. The material she discusses extends to book 15 of the *Annals*, but her analysis of the early books is particularly important.

233. Fragments assigned to *Annals* 1–5 take up 163 lines in Goldberg and Manuwald 2018, 118–97. By my count, 22 of these lines (14, 71, 92, 94, 104, 120–126, 130–32, 142–43, 151, 159–62), or 13 percent, have to do with general warfare or individual combat.

234. Fragments assigned to *Annals* 6–18 take up 278 lines in Goldberg and Manuwald 2018, 98–345. By my count 184 of these lines, or 66 percent, have to do with general warfare or individual combat.

235. Macrobius, *Saturnalia* 6.2.32 in Kaster 2011, vol. 3, 58–59; Ennius, *Annals* 15 testimonium 1 in Goldberg and Manuwald 2018, 310–13.

have been imitating Homer as well, it is obvious that he was and that the episode in *Aeneid* 9 is Homeric as well as Ennian.[236] Pandarus and Bitias thus correspond both to the Istrian soldiers of the *Annals* and, through them, to the Homeric Polypoetes and Leonteus, who in *Iliad* 12 (127–94) successfully defend an open gate in the wall surrounding the Greek ships. So far, so good; but then a third passage, noted still elsewhere by Macrobius (who does not connect it with this previous one), also comes into play. Later in *Aeneid* 9, when Turnus has broken into the Trojan camp but then must fight his way out, Macrobius tells us that this passage too is modeled on one of Ennius, also from *Annals* 15, concerning the bravery of a Roman military tribune in the Istrian war, and that Ennius had modeled this passage on Ajax's defense of the Greek ships in *Iliad* 16.[237] This Homeric passage comes from an entirely different book from that of the defense of the gate in *Iliad* 12. What they have in common is that they celebrate three Greek heroes, Polypoetes and Leonteus in the first passage, Ajax in the second, who are especially conspicuous for their sheer size and strength, as they display great physical courage in defending their camp. Ennius imitates both passages in *Annals* 15, though we cannot be sure that he connected them as closely they are connected in *Aeneid* 9, or indeed at all. What we can say is that he (so to speak) distributes these paradigms of physical courage between the Romans and their Istrian opponents. The *Aeneid* follows suit, basing the Trojan defenders, Pandarus and Bitias, on the Greeks Polypoetes and Leonteus, and the Italian attacker, Turnus, on Ajax. Without further context, it is difficult to interpret the Ennian passages as anything but another instance of the "worthy foe" motif: both the Romans and their Istrian opponents are likened to Homeric warriors, Greeks in both cases.[238] It also seems significant that Ennius' characters are hardly aristocratic warriors: they are a pair of particularly imposing Istrians and a Roman military tribune.[239] We have nothing like this in any earlier book of the *Annals*, nor is there a comparable instance of closely imitated Iliadic battle narrative among the unplaced fragments of the poem. The general impression, then, is that Ennius in the later books of the *Annals* employed hyperbolically Iliadic comparisons to lend impressiveness to his account of contemporary conflicts, which in and of themselves

---

236. Macrobius, *Saturnalia* 5.11.26–29 in Kaster 2011, vol. 2, 334–37, comparing *Aeneid* 9.675–82 with *Iliad* 12.131–36.

237. Macrobius, *Saturnalia* 6.3.2–4 in Kaster 2011, vol. 3, 60–65, comparing *Aeneid* 9.806–14 with *Iliad* 16.102–11 and *Annals* fragment 15.3 (lines 391–98) in Goldberg and Manuwald 2018, 314–17. Servius, *Commentary on Vergil's Aeneid* 9.808 notes that "the entire passage is Homer's" (*totus locus Homeri est*).

238. Another appearance of the "worthy foe" motif: see note 227 above.

239. On the question of whether Ennius named the tribune, see Skutsch 1985, 557–59.

lacked either the legendary importance of events like the Latin and Samnite wars or the proven historical significance of the conflicts with Pyrrhus and the Carthaginians.

The *Aeneid* does not seem to be following Ennius in this. Above all, it is clear that Trojans and Italians of the *Aeneid* are waging intertextual war over their Homeric identities.[240] This is most apparent in Turnus' view of the situation: he regards the Trojans as merely Trojans and himself as a descendant of Argos, and thus the heir of those who vanquished Troy. It does not seem likely that a similar dynamic informed Ennius' account of the Istrian War. Further, whereas Ennius' comparison of Istrians and Romans to Homeric Greeks emphasizes the valor of both sides, the entire episode of *Aeneid* 9 verges on bathos. The hyperbolic size of Pandarus and Bitias is almost grotesque, while both they and Turnus, at the moment when they are compared to Iliadic warriors, have committed grave blunders, as is not the case in Homer. In *Iliad* 12, the gates of the Greek encampment have been opened to allow soldiers retreating before the Trojan onslaught to reach safety, and Polypoetes and Leonteus are fighting heroically outside the open gate to defend it. In *Aeneid* 9, Pandarus and Bitias open the gates of the Trojan encampment, against the express orders of Aeneas, because they and their comrades are spoiling for a fight. Almost immediately their plan backfires when Turnus enters the gate and slays Bitias, among others. His success does not last, though: eventually, Pandarus thinks to close the gate behind Turnus, who then barely escapes with his life. The passage in which he does so is modeled on one in *Iliad* 16 in which Ajax stands in the open gate, not to fight his way out of the Greek encampment, but to keep Hector from entering—exactly what Turnus, who will die as the Hector of the *Aeneid*, has just done. Thus the Iliadic originals in all cases behave nobly, and it seems likely that Ennius' Istrians and his Roman tribune do so, as well; but in the *Aeneid*, warriors on both sides blunder their way into hyperbolic comparisons with their models.

From the evidence that we have, then, a pattern emerges. Macrobius observes that the *Aeneid* imitates both the *Iliad* and the *Odyssey*, but of necessity does so in the opposite order to Homer's, because Aeneas' Odyssean journey to Italy preceded his Iliadic war there.[241] At the most literal level, it is certainly true that Naevius' rendition of Aeneas' journey in his foundation saga preceded the bulk of his battle narrative of the First Punic War. At an intertextual level, his poem may be a mythical Odyssey followed by a historical Iliad. If so,

---

240. I discuss this topic in greater detail in the sections of chapter 3 entitled "A Leadership Vacuum" and "More Contested Identities."

241. See chapter 1 note 5.

Aeneas in part 1 would be an exemplary Trojan and proto-Roman Odysseus. In part 2 there was no single dominant figure, so that if anything it seems possible that a plethora of commanders may have presented both positive and negative examples of leadership. Ennius as well began, literally, with Aeneas, and especially in the early books of the *Annals* seems to have expressed a preference for Odyssean leadership, as this was understood by contemporary kingship theory. He associated such qualities with the Romans while painting their opponents in opposite colors as would-be avatars of Achilles or as a metaphorical Cyclops. Nevertheless, as the poem progressed, it appears to have embraced martial themes more and more and eventually to have celebrated Roman military expansion, as well as resistance to it, in specifically and even hyperbolically Iliadic terms. Finally, if a pattern of following Odyssean with Iliadic themes describes the practice of both Naevius and Ennius, it could be that both of them are adopting a pattern used by earlier historical poets, particularly in the genre of "foundation epic."[242] This would make sense, in that the history of many cities—and especially of colonies—incorporates the theme of arrival as an origin motif, and then may well involve the new city in a period of military struggle as the colonizers work to establish themselves among their new neighbors. If this is so, then historical epic, far from offering a "third way" around the Homeric impasse, may actually have encouraged the pattern that critics have traditionally found in the *Aeneid*, in which a poem that begins as an Odyssey ends instead as an Iliad. Whether and how these earlier poets may have negotiated the relationship of this narrative pattern to the general tendencies of ethical philosophy are questions that we cannot answer. The evidence that we have seen regarding Naevius and, especially, Ennius suggests that in these poets, at least, significant account was taken of this tradition, even if we cannot explain their response to it in every detail.

If nothing else, a pair of general tendencies may be relevant. I noted previously that writers of history sometimes present themselves as followers of Odysseus, and many of them show a certain fondness for generals who are tactical and strategic geniuses rather than proponents of blunt force. At the same time, few of them could resist describing their own subject, whatever it may be, in terms that invite comparison to the greatest war of all time, or that even suggest that it far surpasses the Trojan War. As writers, it seems, many of them found it hard to resist the lure and the challenge of writing "something greater than the *Iliad*."[243]

---

242. Foundation (or *ktisis*) epic is a fairly well-attested genre of Hellenistic Greek poetry, but only scraps of it have survived. For its possible influence on early Latin epic see Goldberg 1995, 52–54.

243. See chapter 1 note 14 above.

Some Conclusions

Ancient critics regarded Homer as the greatest of all poets, and Roman critics saw the *Aeneid* as rivalling Homer in almost every respect. We may include comprehensiveness under this heading, in the following way: just as Homer was thought to be the source of all poetic genres, so the *Aeneid* can be seen as subsuming them all along with Homer's masterpieces.[244] This perspective has been influential on modern critics, as well, who find it difficult to imagine that there was any limit to the erudition that the *Aeneid* contains, including masterly control over previous Greek and Latin literature, not to mention entirely separate areas of knowledge.

As the reader is aware, I am following a different approach. Without wishing to deny the *Aeneid* its traditional status as the kind of poem that I have just described, I am considering its diversity not as somehow fitting into a coherent whole, but as presenting different possibilities, often simultaneously, but in varying combinations as the narrative proceeds, and often serially as one model gains ascendency over the others, if only for a time. My working assumption is that the poem derives much of its impetus from a contest between interested parties as to whether it will be another Iliad or another Odyssey; but the poem clearly aligns itself with a multiplicity of models, and not just a duality. In this chapter, I have considered whether any of its more notable models might represent a way around the Homeric dilemma that I defined in chapter 1, and I have to conclude that they do not. All of these "third ways," as I have called them, are very much in play, some of them virtually from the beginning to the end of the poem, some of them to a more limited, but still highly significant extent. All of them add immeasurably to the mythological, narratological, intertextual, and ethical texture of the *Aeneid*. None of them, however, offers a either an aesthetic or an ethical model for heroic poetry that is free of what Homer defined as the essential, inescapable alternatives represented by Achilles and Odysseus. All of them acknowledge, address, and deploy Iliadic anger and violence alongside Odyssean patience and strategy in distinctive ways, but never in a way that is free of Homeric influence, often in a way that avoids making choices in favor of one or the other alternative. The *Aeneid*, a poem that is more thoroughly pervaded by reference to Homer, specific and pointed as well as general, than any other that has ever been written, consistently, and even relentlessly relates the poetry of the Epic Cycle, of Apollonius, of Callimachus, of the tragedians, of Livius, Naevius, Ennius, and no doubt many others, to the polar coordinates defined by the *Iliad* and the

---

244. As I discussed above in the "Coming Attractions" section of the Introduction.

Odyssey. Within Vergil's epic, different actors and would-be narrators emerge from time to time in order to urge that the poem either choose between the Homeric alternatives or else follow some "third way;" but all of these eventually reduce to one or the other kind of Homeric heroism, and the choice of whether the *Aeneid* will ultimately be an Iliad or an Odyssey remains very much in play, very much in doubt.

The chronological trajectory of this chapter, from the poetry of the Epic Cycle to that of Naevius and Ennius, has followed a more complex trajectory of subject matter. It begins with Homer's stories of the Trojan War, the liminal event dividing the mythical from the historical period, then continues with sophisticated "future reflexive" prequels to the *Iliad* and *Odyssey*, and then to tragic sequels and analogues, before finally moving on to historical sequels to Homer that represent Roman history as a comparable theme. The *Aeneid*, above all, reflects upon the relevance of its Homeric or post-Homeric tale to Roman history, ancient and modern, and this question of relevance is central to any ethical judgment that the reader may make. In the next chapter we will come at the question of ethics from a different angle by considering Aeneas' own evaluation of events in the poem in the light of his past experience. Among the insights that this process will yield, the most important is this: Aeneas' personal desire is not to do what his fate and the gods require him to do, but to become a proper Homeric hero, and the *Aeneid* is the story of how he succeeds in doing so.

3

Reading Aeneas

A New Kind of Hero?

Aeneas' personal desire is not to do what his fate and the gods require him to do, but to become a proper Homeric hero, and the *Aeneid* is the story of how he does so. This statement, if true, is full of implications, possibly decisive ones, for the interpretation of the poem as a whole. Above all, it is at odds with the idea that Aeneas represents a new pattern of heroism.[1] Many other inferences flow from this, and many questions, too. Which Homeric hero does Aeneas become? How fully does he inhabit this role? When does he begin to do so, and when does he complete his transformation? Finally, does this transformation satisfy his desire? There may be no way to answer this last question, but I believe that it is important to ask.

All of these issues pertain to what Servius describes as the double purpose of the *Aeneid*.[2] The first part of it, he says, is "to imitate Homer." Whatever other purposes there may be, I do not see how anyone could say that Servius is wrong about this. What about the second part, though: "to praise Augustus on the basis of his ancestors"? If it emerged that Aeneas wanted to become another Achilles—the greatest warrior who fought at Troy, but one regarded by philosophically minded critics as an example to avoid, especially for leaders—would that support the idea that the poem praises Augustus on the basis of his ancestors? Or would it suggest that it has some purpose different from or beyond what Servius believes?

---

1. In fact, a number of new patterns have proposed: see, for example, Heinze 1915/1993, 223–27; Pöschl 1950/1962, 34–60; Knauer 1964, 345–69 and 1964b, 81; Otis 1964, 222–24; Camps 1969, 21–30; Putnam 1972/1995; Galinsky 1981, 1007–9; Wlosok 1982 and 1985; Clausen 2002, 59–61; Clauss 2002; Reed 2007, 173–202; Schmidt 1983.

2. Servius, *Commentary on Vergil's Aeneid*, preface.

Aeneas, a Heroic Reader

An asymmetrical perspective on the Homeric poems agrees with Aeneas' behavior and with the decisions that he makes. This is especially true where the polar Homeric values of force and intelligence are concerned, along with their attendant values—violence, anger, and passion on the one hand, strategy, restraint, and subtlety on the other. Moreover, Aeneas is not only the protagonist of this drama. As I observed in chapter 1, he is also in a position not unlike our own. In facing the Homeric challenges of warfare and wandering, he must draw on his own experience, his "reading of Homer." Similarly, we ourselves must read Aeneas against the Homeric paradigms of Achilles and Odysseus. It is impossible not to have some sympathy for Aeneas, not only because he has to act while we get to judge him; we also have the advantage of him in having read both the *Iliad* and the *Odyssey*. What is more, we are familiar with the reception of both poems in later epic and tragic poetry, in history, and in philosophy. In every way, our understanding of Homer as an authority on ethical heroism is much more extensive than his. On the other hand, since we have this greater knowledge, our responsibility to understand and apply the lessons of this tradition is itself, in some sense, that much greater as well.

As we track Aeneas' experiences in the light of his "reading of Homer," some of what we find will seem familiar, but some familiar ideas will appear in an unfamiliar light. For the sake of simplicity and clarity, we will proceed in linear fashion, to the extent that this is possible, dividing the poem not into Odyssean and Iliadic halves, but into thirds, an approach that a number of critics have found useful.[3] For our purposes, this division corresponds to important stages in Aeneas' ethical development. The first third of the poem (books 1–4) establishes the theme of ethical heroism in light of the very different qualities that Achilles and Odysseus represent. Throughout these four books, although Aeneas does not lack altogether the qualities of a "good king," he is hardly a paragon of ethical heroism at virtually any point. The second third of the poem (books 5–8) is informed by the theme of heroic education. Thanks to Aeneas' experiences in these books, he emerges from them much better prepared for the challenges that await him than he was for those in the past. The final third (books 9–12) is dominated by battle narrative, and it is in this theater that Aeneas' ethical heroism is most fully on display. To repeat, many of the issues under discussion will be familiar, but many will appear in a new light. The chapter will conclude with some retrospective remarks and a few summary observations about readership, both that of Aeneas and our own.

---

3. Cf. Mackail 1930, 298; Camps 1954, 52–53 and 1959; Duckworth 1957; Pöschl 1950/1962, 172. More recently Giusti 2018, 206 invokes this scheme to emphasize the unitary character of books 1–4.

Books 1–4, Good Kings and Bad

It is the Homeric "Phaeacis" and especially Odysseus' own "Apologoi," the account of his adventures that he gives to Alcinous, that recommended the hero to ethical philosophers as a paradigmatic "good king."[4] From the time that Aeneas arrives in Carthage in book 1 until he leaves in book 4, he finds himself in a precisely analogous situation.[5] That in itself, however, does not make Aeneas too a good king, and it is easy to see why. The point is not just that he is in an analogous situation, but what he does in it; and Aeneas is no Odysseus. That is hardly surprising, since the *Aeneid* contains no indication that he wants to be one. In part, that is because his "reading" of Odysseus is different from ours. He knows Odysseus as the duplicitous figure who helped defeat the Trojans by trickery instead of martial valor. He knows next to nothing about Odysseus' exemplary post-war adventures. He has not "read" the *Odyssey*, as we have, because, for him, much of it has not yet happened, and most of what has happened remains unknown. Odysseus' most exemplary accomplishments are therefore not yet available to Aeneas, or to anyone, for emulation. The world Aeneas knows is that of the *Iliad* and its Cyclic prequels and sequels, including the post-war *Homecomings* of the combatants *except* for Odysseus. Finally, having experienced only this half of the Homeric universe, Aeneas not only detests Odysseus, but he is to a similar degree in awe of Achilles beyond all others. Again, this preference is readily explained by Aeneas' "reading." His memory is dominated by the Trojan War itself, but during the seven years since the fall of the city, his experiences in the war are of almost no use to him, either practically or psychologically. There are as yet no more wars for him to wage. He must endure a long sea voyage to obtain a "homecoming" for himself and his followers. The situation clearly calls for an Odysseus, not an Achilles, and Aeneas flounders because his experience gives him no access to the Odyssean resources that he needs. In psychological terms, he remains obsessed with his lost city and with the kind of hero that he believes destroyed it. He can barely even admit the obvious, which is that Troy did not fall to Achillean force but to Odyssean trickery, and he certainly cannot reconcile himself to that reality.

As a result of this mismatch between Aeneas' experience and the challenges before him, he is in no way comparable to either Achilles or Odysseus, and

---

4. See for example Kaiser 1964, 100; Rutherford 1986; Gerolemou 2018. Some ancient critics, however, criticized Odysseus for his nostalgia (see Kindstrand 1973, 137; Montiglio 2011, 85–87), a point that could be significant for Aeneas' persistent longing for Troy.

5. Knauer 1964, 148–222 and 1964b, 67.

this causes him worlds of trouble. The intertext constantly invites the reader to evaluate him against one or the other of these Homeric paradigms. Sadly, as he makes his way from Troy to Carthage, he almost never measures up to either standard; and the very fact that he is in a situation that calls for the kind of hero that he most despises remains beyond his ken.

Since we are trying to understand how Aeneas experiences his adventures within the poem, let us begin with the hero's "Misfortunes" in books 2 and 3. In chronological terms, these books contain the earliest events narrated in the *Aeneid*, and since they are narrated by Aeneas himself, they offer numerous insights into the hero's reflections on his ethical ideals.

"The Sack of Troy"

We have seen that in book 1 Achilles looms large in Aeneas' memory of Troy and in Dido's, as well. He continues to loom large in book 2 even though the events of that book all take place after Achilles' death.[6] Conversely, Ulysses is not named in book 1, but in book 2 he is named before Achilles and more often as well.[7] Nevertheless, in Aeneas' rendition of "The Sack of Troy," he comes off as a much less imposing figure than Achilles and certainly as a less worthy foe. Even in death Achilles remains the greatest of the Greek heroes, striking awe into Aeneas' heart. In contrast, Aeneas does not represent Ulysses as the heroic protagonist of the *Odyssey*—a story that lies almost entirely in the future as Aeneas looks back on "The Sack of Troy"—or even as the formidable supporting character that he might know from his experience, his "reading," of the *Iliad*. Instead, Ulysses is the ruthlessly deceitful rogue of the Epic Cycle and, especially, of the tragic stage. This only makes sense in the light of Aeneas' experience and of Ulysses' experience, as well. The Ithacan has yet to face the superhuman trials that would define him as an ethical hero. His career to date has been largely that of the devious, manipulative scoundrel once familiar from Epic Cycle and now better known from treatments of individual episodes in Athenian tragedy. No wonder Aeneas represents Ulysses as no better than a "stage villain."[8] Further, unlike the reader, Aeneas has no access to a philosophical perspective on ethical heroism. He thus regards Achilles as terrifying, but nevertheless as the consummate hero, obviously worthy of

---

6. In fact, book 2 is just behind book 1 in terms of the frequency with which Achilles (Aeacides, Pelides) is named, six and seven times, respectively: see the index of proper names in Mynors 1969, 423–52. On memories of Achilles in book 2 see S. C. Smith 1999, 242–43.

7. Achilles is named six times in the book, Ulysses (or Ithacus) eleven.

8. Chapter 1 note 116.

emulation even if all his would-be surrogates, rivals, and successors—Patroclus, Hector, Ajax, Pyrrhus, Aeneas himself—fall woefully short of his unattainable standard.

Perhaps the very fact that Achilles is now dead also enters into it. Aeneas may envy Achilles the simplicity of the role he had to play: after defeating his enemy's champion he died as the greatest hero of them all. He chose, and obtained, a short, glorious life instead of a long one without honor.[9] It is a choice that Aeneas would happily have made, whether in defending his city successfully or dying in the attempt. In addition, Aeneas obviously credits Achilles more than anyone with the fall of Troy. That seems strange until he describes the actions of those who actually brought the city down at last, as we shall presently see. Safely dead, like Hector and so many others, Achilles already belongs to a heroic age that is receding into the past. He can still be feared and admired but, unlike his unworthy successors, he is beyond blame and beyond replacement.

Aeneas first mentions Achilles when he tells how the Trojans, believing the war over, spill out of the city and onto the plain where the Greek army had made their camp: "here was the Dolopian contingent, and here savage Achilles pitched his tent" (2.29). Achilles' singularity, his heroic isolation, and the implication that he alone was worth any number of others, is emphasized in a phrase that balances him against an entire contingent. What is more, the contingent named represents the theme of succession: as Servius notes, the Dolopians are led by Pyrrhus, Achilles' son, just as the Myrmidons were led by Achilles himself.[10] Thus Aeneas begins his tale by implicitly sounding the theme of succeeding Achilles.

It is extremely interesting that Achilles' greatness in the eyes of Aeneas consists not only in his unparalleled excellence, but also in the limits set upon it. Of particular importance is the fact that Achilles does not live to participate in "The Sack of Troy." This allows Aeneas to remember him as the most frightening, most dangerous of the Greek champions and to feel nothing but awe at his memory rather than hatred or contempt. He speaks of even Achilles'

---

9. It is true that fate intervened to complicate Achilles' position when Patroclus died, but this complication does not enter into Aeneas' memory of Troy or of Achilles in particular. It is hardly surprising that the death of Pallas, Aeneas' personal Patroclus, inspires some of the hero's most Achillean behavior: see S. J. Harrison 1991, 201 on *Aeneid* 10.510–605; Quinn 1968, 223–27; Renger 1985, 52–69; Anderson 1993, 168–69 on 595–98; Mazzocchini 2000, 67–96; Heil 2001, 194–203.

10. Servius, *Commentary on Vergil's Aeneid* 2.7; Servius is commenting on Aeneas' earlier remark, "in telling of such things, who among the Myrmidons or Dolopians or what soldier of hard Ulysses could keep from weeping?" (*Aeneid* 2.6–8).

inability to bring down the walls of Troy in order to stress his indignation at the city's fall: "By such deceit and the artistry of treacherous Sinon was a story believed, and we were taken by trickery and forced tears, we whom neither [Diomedes] son of Tydeus, nor Thessalian Achilles, nor ten years, nor a thousand ships could overcome" (2.195–98). Sinon's weapons are deceit, lies, and cunning, which are consummately Odyssean weapons, and Aeneas makes him the proximate cause of Troy's downfall and the definitive example of Greek treachery. He does this with explicitly didactic intent: "listen now to what Greek treachery is, and from a single crime **learn about** [*disce*] them all" (65–66). The effect is almost to deny Ulysses his role as the mastermind of the entire plot. Sinon contributes to this impression by representing himself, a companion of Palamedes, as a victim of Ulysses, that "deviser of wickedness" (164).[11] His account of how the Trojan horse came to be repeatedly denigrates Ulysses' character.[12] Aeneas later tells how, on the night after the Trojans brought the horse into their city, it was Sinon who released the soldiers hidden within it (259). Among them is Ulysses, distinguished from the others by an epithet, "abominable" (*dirus* 261), but not as the author of the ruse, an honor that is reserved for Epeos (264).[13] Aeneas, both in his own words and in those he attributes to Sinon and other characters, like Laocoon, singles Ulysses out for his cruelty and duplicity in a way that suggests moral deficiency rather than efficacy.[14] Ulysses is mentioned often indeed, but always for denunciation in explicitly ethical terms, and not for material contributions to the Greek victory.

With his self-defeating devotion to Achillean arms and his utter lack of Odyssean insight and self-restraint, Aeneas is singularly ill-prepared to face the challenges that await him during his city's final night. In this respect, his account of Hector's appearance to him in a dream is especially revealing.[15] Hector is significantly clad in Achilles' mortal armor, which he stripped from Patroclus' dead body after defeating him in *Iliad* 16, and he is deformed by

---

11. See Ganiban 2009; Casali 2017, 128–30 on *Aeneid* 2.81–100.

12. Three times Sinon contemptuously calls Ulysses "the Ithacan" (*Ithacus* 104, 122, 128), refusing even to use his proper name. Achaemenides does the same thing just once (3.629).

13. The phrase *dirus Ulixes* occurs again at 2.762 and then not before Statius, *Achilleid* 1.94; see also Apuleius, *Metamorphoses* 2.14 (*tam diram, immo vero Ulixeam peregrinationem*, "such a baleful, or rather Odyssean journey").

14. Laocoon's rhetorical question, *sic notus Ulixes?* ("is *that* what you know about Ulysses?" 2.44) forcefully sums up the Trojans' experience of Odysseus.

15. On Aeneas' dream of Hector see Steiner 1952, 29–37; Kühn 1971, 41–43; Raabe 1974, 84–86; Kragelund 1976; Kyriakou 1999; Smith 1999, 243–34; Walde 2001, 267–75; Scafoglio 2002; Dufallo 2007, 100–105; Elliott 2008.

Achilles' abuse of his own corpse in *Iliad* 22 and 24.[16] The image is worth a brief digression.

To slay an opponent in single combat and strip the armor from his lifeless body is the act of a great warrior. To wear or even covet Achilles' armor, however, is to invite disaster. Aeneas' description of Hector's shade—"How different he was from the Hector who came back wearing the spoils of Achilles" (274–75)—would make better sense if Hector had slain Achilles, stripped him of his armor, and come back to the city wearing it. He did not come back at all, however, and he took these "spoils"—*exuvias* (275), a word that in this context properly means armor stripped from a vanquished enemy[17]—from Patroclus, Achilles' surrogate. The reader also understands that by challenging Hector, Patroclus trespassed beyond the limit that Achilles set for him, lest Patroclus win glory that Achilles insisted belonged to him alone (*Iliad* 16.80–100). Patroclus effectively brought doom upon himself just by wearing Achilles' armor; and Hector, by stripping it from Patroclus' corpse, similarly sealed his own fate. In the *Iliad*, Achilles' divine armor replaces what Patroclus had lost; the Epic Cycle and a number of tragic scripts trace the history of that divine armor after Achilles' death.[18] Telamonian Ajax, as Achilles' own cousin and the warrior most like him, expected to inherit the weapons, but after a contest of words, "The Judgment of the Arms," the Greek leaders awarded them to Odysseus instead. Unable to accept this, Ajax ultimately committed suicide. Odysseus prudently decided never to wear the arms himself and saved them instead for Pyrrhus, Achilles' son and heir, who will appear wearing them in this very book of the *Aeneid*; but that is to anticipate. The important point now is that the image of Hector, dead and disfigured, wearing Achilles' mortal armor, vividly expresses the futility both of Patroclus' offering himself as Achilles' surrogate and of Hector's dressing himself up as if he were another Achilles. It is a potent emblem of a problem that drove Greek intellectuals to embrace Odysseus as an ethical model instead of the irreplaceable Achilles. Hector's appearance should tell Aeneas that, however much he may admire Hector or even Achilles himself, however much he may aspire to be a that kind of hero, it will never be possible. Achilles was unique, and his time is gone.

---

16. In the *Iliad* (24.14–21) Apollo prevents Achilles' mistreatment from damaging Hector's corpse; see Fuqua 1982, 235–37.

17. See the *Oxford Latin Dictionary*, s.v. exuviae.

18. "The Judgment of the Arms" is an episode of the Cyclic *Aethiopis* and *Little Iliad* (Davies 1989, 57–58, 61–63; West 2013, 132–34, 158–62, 166–67, 174–78) and the subject of tragedies by Aeschylus and perhaps other Greek playwrights as well as by the Romans Pacuvius and Accius; see Schierl 2006, 131–33.

In case Aeneas does not understand this, Hector tells him explicitly that if Troy could have been defended by force, he himself would already have done that (291–92). Aeneas must therefore be a different kind of hero, the very opposite of Achilles. Hector tells him that he must undergo what the reader cannot help but recognize as an Odyssean journey. "Take these [gods] as the companions [*comites*] of your destiny and seek for them the great walls that you will build when at last you have finished wandering the entire sea" (*pererrato... denique ponto* 294–95). To be sure—and this is an elementary point in *Aeneid* criticism—there is a sacral dimension to Hector's injunction that is entirely unlike anything in Homer. The proem of the *Odyssey* speaks of the hero as simply "trying to save his own life and achieve the homecoming of his companions" (*hetairoi* 5), with no mention of opposition to, support from, or service to the gods.[19] In contrast, Aeneas is "battered on land and sea by the force of those above on account of savage Juno's unforgetting anger ... until he could found a city *and bring his gods to Latium*" (1.3–6; my emphasis). Nevertheless, Aeneas' quotation of Hector echoes the narrator's words in the proem of the *Aeneid*, emphasizing the theme of Odyssean wandering in contrast to Iliadic warfare, effectively ordering Aeneas not to continue fighting the war that defined Hector's own life and now threatens to consume that of Aeneas, as well. Instead, Hector urges Aeneas to forget about saving Troy by force of arms and to accept a specifically Odyssean or proto-Odyssean future that he is unfortunately ill-equipped to comprehend.

Although Hector's message is clear to the reader, Aeneas forgets it entirely when he wakes up and sees his city in flames.[20] "Out of my mind," he tells his audience, "I take up arms, but there is no adequate plan in those arms" (314). Instead of forsaking Iliadic arms in favor of Odyssean voyaging, as Hector had urged, he takes up Iliadic arms and neglects Odyssean intelligence and strategy. Of the rudimentary strategy that does occur to him—to assemble a band of men and rush to the citadel—he says that "madness and anger [*furor iraque* 316] hurry my thinking, and it seems a beautiful thing to die under arms" (315–17). That is to say, Aeneas is motivated not just by passion instead of prudence, but by the most Achillean form of passion, anger, and its near-cousin, madness, as well as by impetuosity instead of Odyssean restraint.

---

19. The divine enters into it only with mention of the Cattle of the Sun, which the hero's companions were foolish enough to eat (*Odyssey* 1.7–9). Critics have long considered the prominence of this episode in the poem's opening lines as something of a puzzle: see Fenik 1974, 212 ff.; S. West in Heubeck et al. 1988–1992, vol. 1, 71–72 on lines 7–9.

20. On Aeneas' initial reaction to the sight of the city in flames see Anderson 1968, 1–7, 16; D. A. West 1969, 429–30; Johnson 1976, 75–78; H.-P. Stahl, 1981, 165–74; Chew 2002.

Under the influence of these passions, Aeneas shows no leadership or even individual initiative. Instead, he allows circumstances and questionable counsel to lead him astray.[21] When a band of Greeks led by Androgeos mistake Aeneas and his band for their own comrades, the Trojans exploit their advantage and quickly dispatch them (370–85). Unfortunately, this success causes the Trojan Coroebus to suggest they put on their victims' armor, the better to infiltrate the Greek forces. To carry his point, Coroebus poses a loaded rhetorical question: "Who asks about courage or trickery in the case of an enemy?" (390).[22] This is as if to say, what is the difference between Achilles and Odysseus? The Trojans soon find out. Abandoning Achillean force in favor of Odyssean disguise, they have some success until their countrymen mistake them for Greeks and attack them (391–430). Here again we encounter the motif of wearing another's armor, which in the *Iliad* proves fatal to Patroclus and Hector, just as coveting it would later prove fatal to Ajax, and would no doubt have undone Odysseus, if he had lacked to foresight never to wear it and save it for Pyrrhus instead. Aeneas, however, under Coroebus' influence, lacks such foresight, and is lucky to escape with his life.[23]

There is no need to catalogue every instance of Aeneas' futility in Troy's final hour. My point is to define that futility in terms of his unrealized Achillean aspirations and lack of Odyssean adaptability. That said, there is another dimension to his obsession with Achilles that reveals itself with particular force in the presence of Achilles' lineal successor, his son Pyrrhus.

When Pyrrhus emerges from the wooden horse among the other Greek leaders, he is assimilated to his father by being called called "Pelides," the patronymic common to both of them, "son (or) grandson of Peleus."[24] In that same passage, he is presented as something new by the use of his second name, Neoptolemus, which means "new battle." Finally, after Aeneas makes his way to Priam's palace, he witnesses a terrifying episode of which Pyrrhus, emphatically represented as an avatar of Achilles, is the baleful star. Aeneas first catches sight of Pyrrhus' arrival at the entrance to Priam's palace. It is one of the most

---

21. On the Androgeos episode see D. A. West 1969, 433–44; Briggs 1980, 61–68; H.-P. Stahl, 1981, 165–74; Lyne 1987, 210–12; Rauk 1991; Schmit-Neuerburg 1999, 232–34; Abbot 2000.

22. See Farron 1993, 4–7; Horsfall 2008, 303–6 on 370–401. On Coroebus in the Aeneas legend see Casali 2017, 25–27.

23. Hornsby 1966. I return to this episode immediately below.

24. *Pelidesque Neoptolemus* 263. The patronymic is seldom if ever used of Neoptolemus (only here according to Casali 2017, 190); Ovid even uses it in contrasting Neoptolemus with Pelides, i.e. Achilles (*Heroides* 8.82–83).

famous passages of the poem.[25] It also marks the second time that Aeneas is confronted with the unexpected sight of someone wearing Achilles' armor. In contrast to Hector, the pretender who had appeared in a dream wearing Achilles' mortal armor, the very image of a lesser warrior who dared to challenge the greatest and came to grief, Pyrrhus now bursts onto the scene, refulgent in Achilles' divine armor, revealing himself as Achilles' true successor and almost as his father reborn. This idea of renewal animates the centerpiece of Aeneas' reaction to Pyrrhus, which is a celebrated passage repeated from the *Georgics* describing a rustic pest, a snake that has shed its old skin, its new scales gleaming brilliantly against the sun (3.437–39). In that *Georgics* passage, exchanging old skin for new represents the motif of death and rebirth, which is perhaps the most important theme that the *Georgics* shares with the *Aeneid*. Aeneas makes this image the vehicle of a magnificent simile of which Pyrrhus is the tenor (2.471–75).[26] Needless to say, redeployment of the image in epic narrative exemplifies in itself the motifs of renewal and terrifying threat that the image conveys. It is as if both father and son, merely by stripping off their mortal arms in favor of divine weaponry, revealed and realized the true nature they shared. To drive home the point that Pyrrhus is virtually Achilles reborn, Aeneas notes that he is attended by Automedon, Achilles' former armor-bearer (*armiger* 477), as he batters down the door and "presses ahead with the violence that is his patrimony" (*instat vi patria* 491). These words convey Aeneas' own impression of the young hero as both the inheritor and the very embodiment of his father's defining trait.

The apparitions of Hector, the failed Achilles, and Pyrrhus, the new Achilles, affect Aeneas in diametrically opposite ways. Where Aeneas woke from his dream of Hector and ignored his friend's Odyssean advice, driven by madness and Iliadic anger to take up arms, the sight of Pyrrhus seems to put him into a trance. Paralyzed, he merely watches as Pyrrhus chases down Polites, one of Priam's few remaining sons, and slaughters him before the eyes of his parents and sisters, who have taken refuge by clinging to an altar. Not even then does Aeneas remember to be a man at arms and rush to defend the pitiable old king (453–558).

What follows illustrates a point that I made earlier, that Achilles' greatness in Aeneas' eyes seems to be defined by certain limits. Up until Pyrrhus slays

---

25. On the Pyrrhus episode see Knox 1950; West 1969, 430–33; Raabe 1974, 124–25; Kenney 1979; Moles 1983; Lyne 1987, 53–55; Bowie 1990; Conte 1999, 20–21; Smith 1999, 244–50; Morgan 2000; Berno 2004; Delvigo 2013, 32–38; Quint 2018, 36–51.

26. See Briggs 1980, 61–68.

Polites he has done nothing—other than concealing himself in the wooden horse with the other Greek ambushers (264)—that Achilles himself had not done. In view of how differently Achilles and Odysseus are treated in myth and literature, it is hard to believe that Achilles would have agreed to take part in such a scheme, and as I noted before he was fortunate in not having to choose.[27] Pyrrhus' participation in the stratagem agrees with other episodes in which Odysseus guided or manipulated the young man to act against his native instincts.[28] Aeneas does not emphasize or even acknowledge any special relationship between Pyrrhus and Ulysses, but he does make Pyrrhus every bit as violent as Achilles and even crueler, as if he were an Achilles who had not been humanized by his encounter with the aged, pitiable Priam, father of the enemy whom he had slain in hateful vengeance. Excoriating Pyrrhus in this passage, Priam himself gives voice to this idea, praising Achilles as a chivalrous warrior for allowing him to ransom Hector's body, as he famously does in the last book of the *Iliad* and in a number of tragedies based on that episode, and denying that the vicious Pyrrhus could possibly be Achilles' son (533–46). In response, Pyrrhus drags the old king from the altar and slaughters him as well, but not before bidding him tell Achilles in the underworld what a disgrace Pyrrhus is to his ancestors (547–53). Aeneas as he develops this damning portrayal of Pyrrhus' character can have no knowledge of Odysseus' adventures among the dead; but the reader, who knows the *Odyssey*, will understand this as a very pointed contradiction of what Odysseus tells the shade of Achilles about his son. When Achilles asks Odysseus about Pyrrhus, his heart is gladdened by Odysseus' report that he excelled in counsel as well as in battle (*Odyssey* 11.492–540). That is conventional praise for any hero.[29] In this context, however, it is almost as if Odysseus were praising the young man for possessing both Achillean might and Odyssean prudence in equal measure. As I have noted, the subsequent tradition is more various and in many ways more subtle, sometimes representing Pyrrhus as a match for his father in simplicity, but not in ruthlessness. Aeneas' account of Pyrrhus is very different. There is no gap between Priam's contempt for Pyrrhus and the bitterness of

---

27. Achilles' only participation in a subterfuge was supervised by Thetis, his mother, who disguised him as a girl among the daughters of King Lycomedes of Scyros. Odysseus found him there and identified him by distributing presents, including arms, which attracted Achilles' interest alone. See Dilke 1954, 10–12; Rosati 1994, 5–61; Heslin 2005.

28. This is an especially prominent theme in Sophocles' *Philoctetes* (see Nussbaum 1976; Blundell 1987 and 1988; Roisman 1997; Fulkerson 2006). The treatment of Ulysses in *Philocteta* by the early Roman tragedian Lucius Accius seems to have been rather different (Latin fragments and translation in Warmington 1935–1940, vol. 2, 504–19).

29. A. T. Edwards 1985, 52–68.

the narrator who tells Dido of the young hero's monstrous impiety. If Aeneas were capable of explaining his ideals in terms of kingship theory, it seems very unlikely that he would describe Pyrrhus as Odysseus does, in terms that are so favorable to Odysseus himself.[30] Rather, the Trojan hero appears to regard the combination of Achillean force governed by Odyssean cynicism as the worst thing imaginable, a nightmarish parody of the ethical heroism to which he himself aspires.

"Wanderings"

Aeneas' recitation of "The Sack of Troy" is the last story of the Trojan War per se. When he turns to his "Wanderings" in book 3, his purview expands to include stories about the returns or exiles of the Greeks and Trojans after the war.[31] For the reader of the *Aeneid*, the general structure and several of the episodes derive from sources representing various "third ways" that we surveyed in chapter 2. For instance:

- As a narrative of multiple post-Iliadic, pre-Odyssean tales of wandering and city-foundation, the entire book bears comparison to the Cyclic *Homecomings* and analogous tales of colonization in Italy and Sicily. To avoid confusion, I will continue to call this the book of Aeneas' proto-Odyssean "Wanderings," but the hero's multiple attempts to establish a new home would justify naming it after his quasi-Cyclic "homecomings," plural and all. Aeneas' frequent failures to found a city where he and his followers can remain, and thus obtain their "homecoming," only underlines the similarity of his narration to the unsuccessful *nostoi* told of in the Cyclic poem.
- Aeneas' focus is mainly on the experiences of Trojan captives and refugees, but the stories of a few Greek victors also come into play, and several of these recall tragic models. For instance, Aeneas' first adventure after embarking on his voyage incorporates the story of Polydorus, known to readers primarily from Euripides' *Hecuba*; and his visit to Buthrotum, which we will consider below, reminds the reader of the same playwright's *Trojan Women* and *Andromache*, not to mention other scripts.[32]

---

30. Dekel 2012, 61–66.

31. On book 3 in general see Heinze 1915/1993, 68–94; Knauer 1964, 181–99, 382–85; Knauer 1964a, 69–70; Putnam 1980/1995; Quint 1982; 1991; 1993, 50–96; Hexter 1999; Dekel 2012, 96–109.

32. Several early Roman tragedies dealt with these themes, including Ennius' *Andromache*, *Astyanax*, and *Hecuba*, Pacuvius' *Hecuba* and *Iliona*, and Accius' *Hecuba*. Fenik 1960, 15–19,

- A major episode of book 3 comes directly out of Apollonius' *Argonautica*.[33] When Aeneas lands on one of the Strophades Islands and the Trojans try to make a meal, the Harpies, a trio of monstrous birds, swoop down and befoul the wanderers' food with their droppings. This is exactly what the Harpies had done to the hero Phineus when he was living in Thynias on the south coast of the Black Sea. To explain the Harpies' presence in the Strophades, not far from Crete, Aeneas tells the story of how two of the Argonauts rescued Phineus by chasing the Harpies away.
- Aeneas' adventures in northwest Greece underline the fact that the southern Adriatic coasts of Italy and Epirus were an important contact zone between eastern and western Mediterranean peoples. On the eastern side, Epirus was the home of King Pyrrhus, the Romans' first military opponent from the larger Hellenistic world in 280–275 BCE. As was noted above, the story of this war seems to have taken up an entire book of Ennius' *Annals*. I also noted that Ennius celebrated a Roman victory in this same region over Ambracia in 179 BCE, both in the *Annals* and in a historical drama. The Ambracian Gulf was also the site of the Battle of Actium in 31 BCE, an event that the *Aeneid* represents as the foundation of Augustus' regime.
- Soon after Aeneas leaves Buthrotum and catches sight of Italy for the first time, he passes the Greek town of Tarentum, founded (as he notes) by Hercules (3.551). This anticipates Hercules' presence in books 5 and 8 and marks the Greek hero as a forerunner of Aeneas in colonizing Italy. As such, it is a miniature episode of the embedded "Heracleid" that I discussed in chapter 2.

Aeneas' wanderings, then, are much more diverse, both geographically and intertextually, than his very focused experience of Troy's final night.

At the same time, if one pulls back to regard the narrative of book 3 as a whole, these diverse episodes get absorbed into a dominant impression of Iliadic and Odyssean contrasts as Aeneas continues to dwell on the Trojan past and to give evidence of his fascination with Achilles' emulators and successors as well as his antipathy towards Odysseus. Very early in the book, for instance,

---

24–26; König 1970, 244–49. On the Thracian episode in general see H.-P. Stahl, 1998a, 43–44; Gibson 1999; Casali 2005; Dufallo 2007, 106–9. On the Buthrotum episode see Knauer 1964, 199–206; Bright 1981; P. R. Hardie 1986, 261–63; and 1993, 15–17; Bettini 1997; H.-P. Stahl, 1998a, 44–46; S. C. Smith 1999, 250–52; Nelis 2001, 38–44.

33. Recognition of this relationship goes back at least to Servius, *Commentary on Vergil's Aeneid* 3.209; see Nelis 2001, 32–38. On other aspects of the episode see Harrison 1986; H.-P. Stahl, 1998a; Labate 2009.

Aeneas prays for Apollo to pity the Trojans, whom he calls "those left by the Greeks and harsh Achilles" (87), a phrase previously used by the epic narrator early in book 1 (30). This repetition increases one's impression that Aeneas and the narrator are speaking the same language and playing analogous roles. It may further suggest that they share a certain perspective on the Trojan War as Achilles' personal accomplishment, even though the city ultimately fell to trickery and not main force. In contrast, when Aeneas sails past Ithaca, he expresses no awe or respect, nor even envy at the thought that Odysseus may already have reached his home (as of course he has not). Instead, the Trojans bitterly curse the land that nourished this "savage" enemy (3.273). These attitudes are wholly consistent with those expressed in book 2. In structural terms, as well, although book 3 less unitary and more episodic than book 2, David Quint has shown that it conspicuously mirrors the preceding book's treatment of Sinon and Pyrrhus in chiastic order via the episodes of Helenus at Buthrotum and of Achaemenides on Sicily.[34]

As he recalls passing Ithaca and cursing Ulysses, Aeneas pronounces a lovely mini-catalogue of other islands in the vicinity that the reader will recognize as a quotation of the *Odyssey*: "now in mid-flood there appear wooded Zacynthus, Dulichium, Same, and Neritos, steep and rocky."[35] It is disorienting to realize that Aeneas utters these words to Dido *before* Odysseus speaks them at a pivotal moment in the *Odyssey*, when he reveals his identity to Alcinous.[36] This perception of a wrinkle in intertextual time encourages an inference that Aeneas is entering an area of temporal convergence. That impression soon becomes more vivid when the hero puts in at Actium and celebrates a festival of Jupiter with "Trojan Games" (280). The celebration clearly prefigures that of the Actian Games held in 30 BCE (and quadrennially thereafter) at Nicopolis, the "City of Victory" that Augustus founded near the site of the decisive battle to commemorate his defeat of Antony and Cleopatra.[37] To commemorate his own celebration, Aeneas performs another symbolic act, reversing a blunder that he committed in book 2 when he wore armor captured from the Greeks. This time he dedicates to Jupiter a bronze shield that had

---

34. See Quint 2018, 36–60.

35. See O'Hara 1990a.

36. "I am Odysseus, son of Laertes, who for deceptions am familiar to all men, and my fame reaches the heavens. I live on sunny Ithaca; there is a mountain on it, Neritos of rustling leaves, easily spotted; and around it lie many islands close to each other, Doulichion and Same and wooded Zacynthus" (*Odyssey* 9.19–24). The first part of Odysseus' speech echoes that of Aeneas when he introduces himself to Venus at 1.378–80, as I discussed in the section of chapter 1 entitled "Disguise and Recognition on the Island of Ithaca."

37. See Horsfall 2006, 223–24 on *Aeneid* 3.280 and H.-P. Stahl, 1998a; Miller 2009, 54–96.

once belonged to the Argive hero Abas and gives it the inscription "Aeneas [took] these arms [*arma*] from the victorious Greeks" (288). As John Miller explains, this act "points allusively to the mythical past as well as the Augustan future."[38] Abas, according to Servius, was the inventor of the Greek shield; the mythographer Hyginus states that his shield was in fact a dedication made to Hera in her temple at Argos by the hero Danaus, Abas' grandfather. Abas later carried the shield into battle before rededicating it to Hera. At this point the reader's imagination must come into play, and the 19th-century commentator Albert Forbiger suggested that a descendant of Abas carried the shield to Troy.[39] It is a matter of pure guesswork when Aeneas might have taken it, but in the *Aeneid* his best opportunity was when he took part in Coroebus' ill-fated ruse during "The Sack of Troy." Whenever Aeneas acquired it, here we find him dedicating it instead of wearing it, perhaps having learned from his earlier misadventure, and in any case expressing thanks that he has got past the homeland of Ulysses and thus clear of the Greek world, as well. It is for the reader to understand that Aeneas does all this in a place where his descendant, Augustus, would commemorate his victory over the entire east.[40] It is also relevant that Aeneas dedicates these *arma*, once sacred to Argive Juno, to Jupiter instead. One recalls the narrator's statement in book 1 that Carthage is where Juno keeps her *arma* (1.16). Ultimately Aeneas is wise to throw in his lot with Jupiter, but Helenus does well in the following episode to emphasize that the hero must do all he can to propitiate Juno as well (3.433–40).

It is at Buthrotum, soon after he makes this dedication, that Aeneas finds a group of Trojan refugees living in a pathetic mock-up of their fallen city (291–505).[41] The community is led by the prophet Helenus, a son of Priam now married to Andromache, widow of his brother Hector. Aeneas' description of their settlement conveys both the enormous difference in grandeur between Priam's city and this Potemkin village, but also the depth of Aeneas' own envy for these friends who have already found a home to call their Troy.[42] There

---

38. Miller 1993, 445; see also Rebeggiani 2013.

39. Forbiger 1872–75 vol. 2, 353 on *Aeneid* 3.286.

40. Servius, *Commentary on Vergil's Aeneid* 3.287 also notes that Aeneas made this dedication in Samothrace. The information must derive from much earlier Greek sources. By "relocating" the dedication to Actium, Aeneas "authenticates" this specifically Augustan version; see Miller 1993, 447.

41. *See* Bright 1981; P. R. Hardie 1993, 15–17; Bettini 1997. Horsfall 2006, 235–36 interprets the Trojan settlement at Buthrotum in a more positive way.

42. Aeneas' words as he takes his leave of Helenus and Andromache (492–505) express his envy of their good fortune in finding a new home, while he must continue searching for "the ever-receding lands of Ausonia" (496).

Aeneas learns from Andromache that Pyrrhus, after fathering a child on her, gave her to Helenus in a marriage of enslaved captives and went off to marry Hermione, daughter of Menelaus and Helen. From the Euripidean tragedy to which Andromache gives her name we know that Menelaus offered Pyrrhus his only daughter in marriage, having learned (from Helenus, in fact) that Troy would not fall unless Achilles' son joined the Greek forces.[43] This story is not incompatible with others involving Pyrrhus' indispensability to the success of the Greeks, although unlike them it credits Odysseus with no role at all. It also involves the familiar motif of marriage used as a bribe, not to mention treachery. The reader of Euripides knows that Menelaus' offering Hermione to Pyrrhus meant breaking a prior arrangement with his nephew Orestes. At this, the disappointed bridegroom, "on fire with great desire for his stolen bride," as Andromache puts it in Aeneas' account, "and driven by the Furies of his crimes, took [Pyrrhus] unawares and slaughtered him at his ancestral altars" (3.330–32). This is a history that repeats itself more than once.[44] Just as Menelaus' quarrel with Paris over Helen brought their peoples to war, so rivalry over Helen's daughter brought the sons of Achilles and Agamemnon into conflict. This time Pyrrhus finds himself not in the avenging role of his father and the sons of Atreus, but in that of the interloper Paris. Moreover, as Stefano Rebeggiani has argued, the situation prefigures Turnus' attempt to vindicate his claim to Lavinia against Aeneas. Rebeggiani also makes the case that Aeneas as Lavinia's rightful suitor will take the role of Orestes away from Turnus.[45] In much the same way he will disabuse Turnus of any pretensions he may have to be another Agamemnon, Menelaus, or Achilles. Rebeggiani further argues that identification of Aeneas with Orestes becomes a persistent point of reference as the poem develops. This is barely visible in Andromache's report to Aeneas, and only to a reader who is already intimately familiar with the plot and the intertextual dynamics of *Aeneid* 7–12.[46] In any case, Aeneas will no

---

43. Ursinus 1568, 265; Fenik 1960, 20–31; König 1970, 67–79.

44. I note in passing that a part of Pyrrhus' kingdom passed into Helenus' hands, so that the defeated Trojans come to rule in place of his Greek conqueror. This theme of reversal may well have informed the grand structure of Ennius' *Annals* (Fabrizi 2012) and, more specifically, Ennius' representation of the Romans' war against King Pyrrhus, the descendant and namesake of Achilles' son. In the *Aeneid*, the same motif informs the "conversion" of the defeated Aeneas into a proto-Roman victor over the "Argive" hero Turnus: see Quint 2018, 188–90.

45. Rebeggini 2016.

46. The crucial points are a pair of details that disagree with the dominant tradition regarding Pyrrhus' death. First, that event is regularly set at Delphi (Euripides, *Andromache* 998–1000, 1085–1172; compare "Apollodorus," *Library of Greek Mythology*, epitome 6.14 in Hard 1997, 160). This does not agree with Andromache's statement that Pyrrhus died "before his ancestral altars"

doubt have felt that poetic justice was done when Pyrrhus' slaughter of Priam "at an altar" (*ad aras* 2.663) was repaid in kind (*ad aras* 3.332).[47] Moreover, since Venus has told Aeneas that Dido's own brother murdered her husband "before an altar" (*ante aras* 1.349), Aeneas might well have expected Dido to take special notice of this detail as he told this story to her.[48]

Here Aeneas' description of Orestes as "driven by the Furies of his crimes" (3.331) comes into play. One might consider this phrase a kind of "perpetual epithet," since the episode of Orestes' madness, brought on by the Furies in retribution for the murder of his mother, is such a crucial element of his story. On its face, however, the phrase means that Orestes murdered Pyrrhus *while the Furies were driving him mad*. This is a problem: in most versions of the myth, Orestes is cured of his madness before his quarrel with Pyrrhus occurs. All commentators note this discrepancy and offer various attempts to explain it, none of which has won general approval. This brings me to the main point of Rebeggiani's paper, which is that the figure of Orestes, precisely as an avenger of his father, had a place in Augustus' management of his own public image. Having begun his career by committing violence against Roman citizens in pursuit of what was in essence a personal vendetta originating in the murder of Julius Caesar, the future Princeps compared himself to Achilles and Orestes precisely as avengers—the former of Patroclus and the latter of Agamemnon.[49] The effect of such a comparison would be to remove some of the young Caesar's most brutal acts from the realm of civil disturbance in the here and now to a mythic plane, thus endowing them with both epic and tragic dimensions, while making the implicit point that the acts themselves, however gruesome, not only punished wrongdoing but brought about conditions of peace. This general approach agrees with Philip Hardie's position that the tragic element of the *Aeneid* functions as institutional tragedy is supposed to have functioned in the 5th century BCE in Athens, as a means of creating communal solidarity by displaying the resolution of violent personal and social forces within the ritual setting of mythical re-enactment.[50] In Rebeggiani's argument, Orestes is of particular importance because he is so closely identified with the theme of madness: assimilation of the Princeps to such a figure

---

(*Aeneid* 3.332), presumably in Epirus. There are of course excellent reasons for "moving" the event to Epirus or some other ancestral place, and especially to ancestral *altars*, since Pyrrhus slaughters Polites and Priam at an altar in the Trojan royal palace (*Aeneid* 2.512–32, 547–53, 663).

47. Conington and Nettleship 1858–1898, vol. 2, 207 on *Aeneid* 3.332 comment on this similarity; see also Barchiesi 1984/2015, 143 note 47; Horsfall 2006, 262–63; Quint 2018, 55–56.

48. See Heyworth and Morwood 2017, 172 on *Aeneid* 3.330–32.

49. Rebeggiani 2016, 58–61.

50. P. R. Hardie 1997/2019.

thus invites the interpretation that Caesar's heir performed his most heinous acts of vengeance "not as a blood-thirsty tyrant, but as a tragic hero under the influence of *furor*." At the same time, Rebeggiani acknowledges that an apologetic strategy of this kind "is certainly problematic," admitting that Augustus' opponents could easily turn it against him.[51] Both points are obviously correct, and I would suggest that both deserve some weight in relation to the intertextual *Aeneid*.

Aeneas' visit to Buthrotum presents Pyrrhus not as the terrifying, irresistibly violent figure that he was in book 2 but as deserving the insult that Priam hurled at him, that he is merely a degenerate Achilles. His treatment of Andromache is as callous as his treatment of the old king; this time he does not get away with it. Above all, he no longer sits as king on his ancestral throne, which at the moment is not occupied by an heir of his blood: the Trojan Helenus, his former slave, now rules in his place. The vanquished have triumphed over their conqueror. This situation will not last: Molossus, Pyrrhus' bastard son by Andromache, will presumably inherit, and King Pyrrhus of Epirus—Molossus' descendant according to the heroic self-fashioning of dynastic genealogy—will one day present himself as the champion of those Greek cities in Italy that were coming under the hegemony of Rome.[52] His efforts on their behalf would give his name to the "Pyrrhic victory," but would not prevent Rome from becoming a world imperial state. Aeneas as he tells the story of his visit with Helenus and Andromache has not yet heard what Fate has in store for his people centuries hence.[53] He can, however, and does envy his friends their good fortune, and no doubt takes satisfaction in the reversals suffered by Achilles' unworthy heir. Ultimately, he learns, Pyrrhus is just one more would-be Achilles who comes to a bad end.[54]

Aeneas crosses the Adriatic to Italy and, following Helenus' advice, he skirts the southern coast until he can land on Sicily. There he encounters Achaemenides, a companion of Ulysses whom the Ithacan hero had inadvertently

51. Rebeggiani 2016, 72–73.

52. As is implied by Euripides' *Andromache* (1243–52), the Aeacid line of Peleus, Achilles, and Neoptolemus is to live on in Andromache's child Molossus, whose descendants will rule over the Molossians. Plutarch, however (*Life of Pyrrhus* 1), states that a line of legitimate Molossian kings, the Pyrrhidae, were descended from the mythical Pyrrhus and Lanassa, daughter of Cleodaeus, and he implies that the historical Pyrrhus was of this line.

53. On the mythical Pyrrhus and his historical namesake see Quint 2018, 54–60.

54. Remarkably, Helenus gives Aeneas the arms of Neoptolemus as a parting gift (3.463–69). Are these meant to be Achilles' divine arms, which the prudent Odysseus refrained from wearing, keeping them for Neoptolemus instead? Is one to infer that Aeneas wore them, or that Venus provided her son with his own divine armor to forestall this very possibility?

abandoned in his narrow escape from the Cyclops Polyphemus (570–691).[55] The Greek castaway has every reason to resent Ulysses for abandoning him while escaping from the very jaws of the Cyclops, but many readers hear grudging admiration in the words with which (in Aeneas' report) he describes the blinding of Polyphemus. Yes, Achaemenides says, the monster devoured two of our crewmates—but he didn't get away with it! Ulysses wouldn't allow that, or lose his head in such a crisis. This is the one passage in the *Aeneid* that I have found in which anyone says anything about Ulysses that might, almost convincingly, be construed as praise; but that is not how I understand it. In summarizing Achaemenides' speech, I just rendered the Latin phrase *oblitus sui* (629) as meaning that Ulysses would never "lose his head," i.e., fail to maintain his exemplary self-control; more literally, it means "(be) forgetful of himself."[56] To "forget oneself" can certainly mean "to lose one's head," but in the most literal sense possible—especially in the mouth of someone whom Ulysses actually did forget—it may be a bitter comment on Ulysses' me-first attitude. As things turned out, Achaemenides could not know how fortunate he actually was. Had he remained with Ulysses, he would eventually have perished along with all of his crewmates, save their captain. This is the weak point in Horace's epistolary summary of the *Odyssey* as the story of one man who saves himself despite the foolishness of those around him; for the poem is also the story of a man who does not save anybody but himself. It is for this reason above all that I cannot agree with the idea that, when Achaemenides introduces himself as "a companion of unhappy Ulysses," the reader is to understand him, and still less Aeneas, as expressing any pity for Ulysses' sufferings.[57] The Latin word that I here render as "unhappy" is *infelix*, which at its root does not refer so much to someone's mood, or even to what he has suffered from forces external to himself, but to the capacity of a person or thing to produce positive results. Someone who is *felix* is someone who prospers and creates prosperity; *infelix* means the opposite.[58] Thus I would argue that Aeneas or Achaemenides or both of them see Ulysses as a man who creates trouble for all concerned, and who survives thanks only to his remarkable knack for deflecting pain and death away from himself onto others.

In addition to insight regarding Aeneas' attitude towards Odyssean ethics, this episode raises questions, once again, about Aeneas' role as an Odyssean

---

55. See Knauer 1964, 192–96; Galinsky 1968, 161–63; E. L. Harrison 1986; P. R. Hardie 1986, 264–67; Traill 1993; Gibson 1999; Erdmann 2000, 103–4; Hutchinson 2007; Biggs 2019b.

56. See the *Oxford Latin Dictionary* s.v. obliuiscor 4b and 5b (where this passage is cited).

57. See, most recently, Heyworth and Morwood 2017, 242 and 260 on *Aeneid* 3.613–15 and 687–91.

58. See the *Oxford Latin Dictionary* s.vv. felix and infelix.

narrator. In his account of finding Achaemenides, is he being perfectly straightforward and candid, or does he artfully tailor his story to a specific narratological situation? Here above all we must ask, is it even truthful?[59] If Aeneas can refer to himself and his fellow refugees as "the leavings of the Greeks and ungentle Achilles," Achaemenides is more literally someone left behind by Ulysses. And yet this is the first episode in which, in order to believe Aeneas, the reader must in effect disbelieve Homer; for it offers the first direct contradiction, or apparent contradiction, between the *Aeneid* and the *Odyssey*. The point is not that Odysseus' story is wrong, but that it is incomplete, perhaps in a self-serving way. Odysseus never tells Alcinous that he had a crewmate named Achaemenides whom he accidentally left while escaping from the Cyclops; but why would he? Here we run into the tradition of Odysseus not only as an unreliable narrator but as an outright liar. At the same time, we have to ask whether Aeneas' tale about Achaemenides is an artful or unreliable narrative, or even a lie.

Like the question of what Aeneas was doing when he saw himself depicted in Juno's temple among the leaders of the Greeks, the question of how far one can trust the entire recitation of his "Misfortunes" in books 2–3 becomes most urgent in the Achaemenides episode. It is no good to wave it away by saying, the story must be true, mustn't it? What else would Achaemenides or anyone be doing there in the land of the Cyclops, at risk of being devoured by the brutish Polyphemus? If Aeneas were making it up, wouldn't he be taking a terrible risk? What if Dido asked to see this remarkable fellow? And so on. That all makes sense, as far as it goes, but it doesn't even begin to get at the issues raised by Aeneas' narration.

The first point, which many have noted, is that the tale of Achaemenides, a Greek castaway rescued by Trojans, is like that of Sinon, a Greek scapegoat rescued by Trojans.[60] Sinon turned out to be a bogus scapegoat who brought about the destruction of Troy. In trusting Achaemenides, does Aeneas show good judgment and situational flexibility?[61] Or has he simply forgotten what he told Dido about Sinon: "listen now to what Greek treachery is, and from a single crime learn about them all" (*Aeneid* 2.65–66). Does the Trojans' readiness to believe Achaemenides' story—which on its face is far more incredible than Sinon's—betray a simple failure to learn from experience?

The reader who does not entertain such questions is missing an opportunity to explore the narrative richness of the *Aeneid* and, in my opinion, to

---

59. See Ahl 1989, 26–31.
60. In the eyes of many critics, the episode proves that Aeneas has not lost his humanity even towards the Greeks: see Heinze 1915/1993, 84–84; Putnam 1980/1995, 63–64.
61. See, e.g., Heyworth and Morwood 2017, 234 on *Aeneid* 3.588–691.

appreciate the categorical difference between Aeneas and Odysseus. This difference finds expression not only in Aeneas' contempt for Ulysses, but also in how frequently he acts in the most un-Odyssean ways imaginable. He does so for good and bad reasons and with good and bad outcomes. Disguising himself as a Greek in an effort to save Troy was a very bad idea, and it quickly backfired. Rescuing Achaemenides was a humanitarian act that was soon repaid when Aeneas' new follower was able to retrace Ulysses' route along the Sicilian coast.[62] The main point, though, is that Aeneas both detests Ulysses and consistently acts very differently from Ulysses, as well. He does so when he knows what Ulysses did or would have done (as in the case of Achaemenides) and when he does not (as when he lands in Thrace and tries to found a city where Odysseus either did or would sack one).[63] In view of just how extremely unlike Ulysses Aeneas makes himself seem, one would have to conclude either that he is vastly *more* duplicitous than even the master of deception himself, or else that he is generally telling the truth and unwittingly confessing a degree of naïveté that is almost culpable in a person with kingly responsibilities. In my view, the latter possibility is by far the more likely.

In short, it is difficult to believe that Aeneas is the clever manipulator of truth and falsehood that Odysseus is. In terms of his immediate audience, it is impossible to regard his story as conveying any single message, particularly a self-serving one.[64] By the same token, when it comes to Achilles, Aeneas' perspective is also extremely clear. As he narrates his own experiences in books 2 and 3, it is true that he has little opportunity to recall explicitly his experiences in the *Iliad*, and only one to recall the *Odyssey* itself. He does, however, have ample opportunity to express his opinions about Achilles and Ulysses and about the heroic values that they, and characters more or less like them (Pyrrhus, Sinon) represent. What emerges is that Aeneas continues to regard Achilles a uniquely gifted hero, unsurpassed as a soldier, virtually responsible by himself for the fall of Troy, and fortunate in having given his life

---

62. Nelis 2001, 52–57 notes that the Argonauts assist or rescue several people in trouble who return the favor with useful advice. Papanghelis 1999, 284 observes that when Achaemenides helps the Trojans by "retracing" his previous wanderings in this area, the word used is *relegens* (690; see the *Oxford Latin Dictionary* s.v. relego 3). Achaemenides' retracing is thus like a rereading of the *Odyssey*. Similarly, Gasti 2010, 16 comments that the narrator's use of *renarrabat* (717) acknowledges the intertextual basis of Aeneas' narrative "based on a reworking of Ulysses' adventures."

63. Knauer, 1964, 184 and 1964b, 69; Horsfall 2006, 56 on *Aeneid* 3.17.

64. See, variously, Gasti 2006 and 2010; Bowie 2008. Bednarowski 2015 strikes an excellent balance in evaluating the theme of deception in books 2 and 3 with respect to its importance for Dido and Aeneas' relationship. See also Spence 1999.

in return for everlasting fame. It does not hurt that when Troy fell Achilles was enjoying his heroic afterlife and thus, unlike his son, was unable to participate in the taking of the city by base trickery, not martial valor. Ulysses above all is associated with such reprehensible tactics, but in the *Aeneid* he receives no credit for ending the Trojan War. That credit goes to Epeos, who built the Trojan horse, and to Sinon, who sold the ruse to the Trojans. Pyrrhus, Achilles' successor, plays a vicious role in the fall of city and, in Aeneas' eyes, disgraces himself as unworthy of his father. In book 3, it is not surprising that Pyrrhus soon comes to grief in Buthrotum; nor is it surprising that Aeneas voices his disgust with Ulysses at every opportunity.

Aeneas and Dido

After the Trojans arrive in Africa, the most explicit evidence cited to show that Aeneas is a good king in book 1 is the ambassador Ilioneus' statement when he explains to Dido who he and his people are and how they happen to find themselves in her territory.[65] As he tells her, "our king was Aeneas, than whom there was no other more just, or greater either in his sense of duty [*pietate*] or in waging war [*bello et ... armis*]" (1.544–45). But what would anyone expect him to say? The first point he is making is that this rag-tag band of castaways have up to this point actually been under the leadership of a real king. That makes them somebody, and it means that, if Aeneas does appear, Dido will have to deal with him as a peer, however needy he may be. In addition to that basic point, Servius comments perceptively on Ilioneus' characterization of Aeneas, noting first that the speaker is at pains to excuse his leader's absence from the scene. The grammarian maintains that the tense of the verb Ilioneus uses to say that Aeneas "was" their king (the imperfect *erat* instead of the perfect *fuit*) avoids any implication that Aeneas has in any way forsaken his people once and for all.[66] Servius then praises the speech for making two points that ought to strike Dido in the description of a foreign king: that he is dutiful, because he wants Dido to show the same sense of responsibility towards himself and his fellow refugees, and that he is a great warrior, so that she will fear him and his followers.[67] To be clear, my contention is hardly that Ilioneus

---

65. Cairns 1989, 29–30; Keith 2021.

66. Servius, *Commentary on Vergil's Aeneid* 1.544: "He does well to use the imperfect verb *erat*, lest he seem to have lost hope, [as would be the case] if he had used *fuit*," since the perfect tense would imply that Aeneas' days as king of the Trojans were over.

67. Servius, *Commentary on Vergil's Aeneid* 1.545: "He does well to praise two qualities in Aeneas, his sense of duty [*pietas*], which he is trying to elicit in Dido, and his courage [*virtus*], which he wants her to fear."

misrepresents Aeneas. It is that he himself is represented as a skillful speaker shaping his utterance to achieve specific goals. Quite apart from that, one can hardly allow what any character says about any other in a very particular situation simply to determine one's own summary judgment.

That said, if we do give full weight to what Ilioneus says, we are bound to observe that the two qualities he specifies when he says that Aeneas excels "in his sense of duty" (*pietate*) and "in waging war" (*bello et... armis*) make a significant pair. Since the first words of the poem, "arms" has been marked as the first of the epic's two great themes, and one with clear Iliadic connotations. The other theme, denoted in the proem as "man" (*vir*), poses the question, just like the first word of the *Odyssey* (*andra*), what kind of man? This is a question that Homer answers almost immediately with the epithet *polytropon*, "of many turns." Since the time of Antisthenes, Odysseus' heroic excellence was seen to consist in this quality." in a way that established him as an ethical paradigm superior to the inflexible Achilles.[68] The narrator of the *Aeneid* leaves open for the moment what kind of man Aeneas is. As I argued in chapter 1, this is not accidental. Rather, it is the central question that the poem was written to pose. Only after the *Aeneid* proem is complete and the narrator turns, belatedly, to invoke his Muse does he grant his hero, again belatedly, his perpetual epithet, *pius*, "dutiful," or at least gesture towards it when he asks the Muse why Juno drove "a man so distinguished for his sense of duty" (*insignem pietate virum* 1.10) to undergo so many trials. It is up to the reader to triangulate what the narrator says about his hero in these two passages with Ilioneus' praise of his king to infer that the Trojan ambassador represents Aeneas according to a quasi-Homeric binary as man of "arms," like Achilles, but not "of many turns," like Odysseus; rather he is a man of "responsibility"—which is as if to say, almost precisely *unlike* Odysseus. In the language of Homeric kingship theory, this is remarkably strange. Aeneas is said in effect to be like Achilles, a highly problematic ethical exemplar, and quite unlike Odysseus, the preferred kingly paradigm. What does that make him?

In other respects, there is little in book 1 to suggest that Aeneas is a paradigmatically good king. In particular, all of the intertextual signals that invite comparison between Aeneas and Odysseus illustrate the ways in which the Trojan hero departs from the Ithacan's standard precisely where the signature Odyssean traits of cleverness, strategy, deception, and disguise are concerned. We have seen as much in our discussion in chapter 1 of Aeneas' frankness in his meeting with the disguised Venus, which is so different from Odysseus' wary encounter with the disguised Athena. What emerges with painful clarity is that

---

68. Montiglio 2011, 20–37; Moles 2017.

the latter pair are united by their expertise in duplicity and caution, while Venus and her son are quite inept and divided by these same practices.[69]

The fact is that, if there is an ideal Homeric king in book 1, it is Dido. Some critics have recognized the applicability of kingship theory to an evaluation of the Queen of Carthage, spelling out the implications of her dispensation of justice, the industry of her people, even her extreme physical beauty as attributes of the ruler.[70] None of this should be in doubt. The notion remains strong, however, that Dido's primary function in the plot of the Odyssean *Aeneid* is to tempt the hero to abandon his mission. Intertextual signals that she might be in Homeric terms a Nausicaa, a Circe, or a Calypso align with ethical philosophy to identify her with some of the temptations that Odysseus had to overcome in order to achieve his homecoming. Even the inference that she might be Aeneas' Penelope is a problem in these terms, because the reader knows that the hero cannot make Carthage his home. That is one side of the story. The other is that Dido is argued to be not just a potential temptress but also a foil for Aeneas precisely in terms of kingly excellence. Francis Cairns, for instance, stresses that by book 4 "Dido deteriorates into a bad monarch while Aeneas emerges at its end as an improved good king."[71] There is no doubt, of course, that Dido in the end fails both herself and her people. The question is how to understand this failure in the light of Homer and of the philosophical reception of the Homeric "Phaeacis."

We have seen that Venus in book 1 paints Dido as a "good king" in explicitly Odyssean colors. Her personal history proves not only her resilience but even more her capacity for cunning intelligence, both in her stealthy escape from Sidon and in the clever bargain she struck with the Libyan natives from whom she purchased land for her new city (1.357–68). As leader of a community in exile and in founding a new home for her people, she is far ahead of Aeneas. Indeed, Dido at first seems a match not only for Odysseus but for Penelope, as well, not as the woman whom Aeneas is fated to marry, but as the devoted wife who overcomes enormous difficulties to maintain her husband's estate, whether in his absence or after his death. In this respect, Dido even surpasses Penelope by using her husband's wealth to found a new city of her own, thus becoming a "king" in her own right, and by resisting the advances of many

---

69. Later, in book 4, Dido accuses Aeneas of trying to disguise his departure—"Did you think you could you could conceal [*dissimulare*] so great a crime, you betrayer [*perfide*]?" (305–6). The narrator too has characterized Aeneas' attempt to leave without telling Dido as an act of deception (*dolos* 296). Both passages, like the Coroebus episode in book 2, go to show that when Aeneas tries to use guile, he is not very good at it.

70. Cairns 1989, 39–42; Gordon 1998; Keith 2021.

71. Cairns 1989, 38.

suitors. Only with Aeneas' arrival and under overwhelming divine influence does Dido's devotion to duty and to the memory of her murdered husband begin to fade.

The Homeric intertext supports this perspective on Dido through its refractions of her "Phaeacian" identity. I discussed in chapter 1 the ways in which she corresponds not only to the marriageable Nausicaa, but to Arete, the ideal royal consort, as well as to the ruler Alcinous. It is true that ethical philosophers did not altogether approve of the Phaeacians' luxury-loving ways, and to this extent their king's reputation was somewhat equivocal. Horace in *Epistles* 1.2 treats the Phaeacians as luxurious hedonists, and when he disapprovingly refers to them as "Alcinous' slacker subjects" (*nebulones Alcinoi* 28) he may be blaming the king for his people's behavior. But then, he may not: he mentions the Phaeacians in parallel with Penelope's suitors, and he presumably does not hold Penelope responsible for their dissolution. Moreover, he equates both groups with "us" (*nos* 27); and if, as I have suggested, Horace's summary of Homer in his epistle to Lollius Maximus is a thinly veiled allegory of recent Roman history, he seems not to be holding a good ruler responsible for his people's fecklessness. In any case, with regard to Dido as a version of the Homeric Alcinous, it is worth remembering, with Pamela Gordon and Alison Keith, that Philodemus in his treatise "On the Good King according to Homer" praises Alcinous quite unambiguously as the ruler of an orderly, peaceable kingdom where pleasures were enjoyed in moderation and laws like those of hospitality were observed.[72] Such complexity in the ancient ethical commentary on Alcinous is very much to the point in the reader's assessment of Dido and her people.

Additional complexity arises from the fact that, despite the powerful and powerfully disorienting presence of the *Odyssey* in *Aeneid* 1, Carthage is in many ways a more Iliadic than a Phaeacian place. The Phaeacians are good seamen, but above all they are luxurious. As Alcinous himself tells Odysseus, "ever dear to us is the banquet, the lyre, dances, changes of clothing, warm baths, and [the pleasures of] bed" (8.248–49). The first thing said about Carthage in the *Aeneid* is that it is "rich in resources," which may hint at luxury, "and most fierce in zeal for war," which certainly does not (1.14). As was previously noted, it is in Carthage that Juno kept her arms (*arma* 16) and her chariot. (This is the second occurrence of the thematic word *arma*, the first word of the poem.) Soon afterwards, to prevent the Carthaginians from harming the Trojan castaways, Jupiter dispatches Mercury to visit them, "and the Carthaginians put aside their fierce nature [*ferocia corda*] as the god desired" (1.302–3). Even so, the Trojan

---

72. Gordon 1998, 195–97; Keith 2021.

ambassador Ilioneus must remonstrate with Dido about his reception: "What kind of people is this? What country is so uncivilized as to allow such behavior? We are being denied permission to land! They are starting a war [*bella cient*] and forbidding us to set foot on the beach" (1.539–41). In the light of all this, one could say that Jupiter—in response to Juno's meddling—mitigates the Carthaginians' Iliadic instincts by converting the them into quasi-Odyssean Phaeacians, but that his effort is only partly successful.

It soon becomes clear that Dido herself shares an Iliadic orientation. As the builder of Carthage, she must be responsible for the Temple of Juno in which Aeneas finds depicted the story of the Trojan War, including Cyclic episodes that establish the beginning and end of the narrative arc that it covers. Moreover, the episodes mentioned suggest that Dido, like Aeneas, is obsessed not only with Troy but with Achilles in particular, for they describe a virtual Achilleid from start to finish.

In these episodes Achilles is named four times, first as the enemy of both Priam and the Atridae (1.458); next, as the equal of the entire Trojan or Greek force (468); then as the slayer of Troilus (475; his name makes him an obvious representative of his entire people); and finally as he desecrates and sells Hector's corpse (484; the loss of Troy's greatest champion stands, as in the *Iliad* itself, for the eventual loss of the war). In these four passages, Achilles' name is always emphatically in verse-final position, and it appears at fairly regular intervals. The paragraph continues for nine more lines, long enough to have fitted in one more occurrence near the end, where instead two more of his victims are named. The first, Memnon, is mentioned in the fifth line from the end (489); the last four lines (490–93) are devoted to Penthesilea. Both characters, the African hero and the Amazonian queen, prepare the reader for the appearance of Dido, the African queen, in the very next sentence. No interpreter has failed to connect Dido with Penthesilea in particular. Of course, if we follow the logic of this comparison, we realize that Dido is to Penthesilea as Aeneas is to Achilles, each hero causing the death of a woman whom he loved.[73]

In these ways Dido is firmly associated with Troy and with Achilles. At the end of the book, as well, she is fascinated by Aeneas' Trojan War stories and especially with Achilles himself. At the banquet she gives in the Trojans' honor, she questions Aeneas obsessively about the heroes who took part in the war, including Priam, Hector, Memnon, and Diomedes before Achilles is

---

73. Davies 1989, 51–52; West 2013, 130–43. In addition to appearing implicitly as the lover/slayer of Penthesilea, Achilles is also the slayer of a younger man (Troilus) and of his people's champion (Hector), both of which figures are conflated into that of Turnus, Aeneas' final victim (although the slaying of Lausus is relevant here, as well).

named in the climactic position (749–52). Thus Dido, who is effectively the Alcinous of the Odyssean *Aeneid*, before listening to the hero tell about his wanderings, wants to hear about the war itself, and about Achilles above all.

But this is to anticipate. The absence of Achilles' name at the end of his catalogue of victims, where the symmetry of the paragraph might have led us to expect it, is both an elegant sophistication, a sign that the reader should be alert to Achilles' presence even where he is not named, and a means of posing and answering an important question. We have seen that if Dido can be regarded as representing the entire Phaeacian royal family, she is an unstable amalgam who ultimately fails in all three of her assigned roles. This implicit comparison of her to Penthesilea predicts this failure. Like Penthesilea, Dido is a heroic figure, a queen not just in the sense of royal spouse but one who is the equal of any king, and a beautiful, marriageable woman, as well. Like Penthesilea, she meets her match, and this proves the end of her. Though seeming to combine successfully the Odyssean roles of king, royal consort, and nubile daughter, she meets Aeneas and, under pressure brought by his mother, she comes apart; but as a worshipper of Juno, sharing to some extent Juno's Iliadic obsession, she is drawn further into the "Long Iliad" of which Juno wants the *Aeneid* to be just one more component. As yet another of the unintended consequences that Juno must endure, she effectively casts Dido as Penthesilea to Aeneas' Achilles. By the same token, if anyone means Aeneas to be some sort of Odysseus, he too fails. The real Odysseus does not cause the death of any woman or goddess who loved him, as Aeneas causes Dido's death, which represents the symbolic destruction of her city in the time of the mythic narrative and forecasts the literal destruction of Carthage many centuries later at the hands of Aeneas' descendants.[74] In these ways, the idea that Carthage "is" the Odyssean Scheria is distorted to the point that it ultimately seems a failed comparison that need not, and perhaps should not, govern one's perspective on the entire *Aeneid*. Instead, in some simpler and deeper sense, Aeneas causes the death of a woman who loves him and whom he apparently loves as well, and he is in large part responsible for destroying the city that she, like Penthesilea, playing a man's role, has chosen to defend. Carthage is, in this respect, not so much Scheria as it is Troy, a comparison already strongly suggested the opening lines of the narrative.[75] In the tragedy of Dido and Aeneas, the hero

---

74. This theme has recently been explored in detail by Giusti 2018.

75. On the surprise involved in the immediate progression from "there was an ancient city" to "Tyrian colonists occupied it" in *Aeneid* 1.12 see Barchiesi 1994/1999, 341. On the wordplay between "ancient city" at the beginning of line 12 and "Carthage" (which means "New City" in Punic) at the beginning of line 13, see Maltby 1991, 111 s.v. Carthago; O'Hara 1996/2017, 115.

is clearly fated to play Achilles to Dido's Penthesilea; and he is quite the equal of Achilles in at least this respect.

In other ways, even if Aeneas' experiences throughout book 1 seem to be modeled on those of Odysseus, he certainly does not understand this. Instead, his perspective draws exclusively on what he learned in the Trojan War, often during the fifty or so days that comprise the plot of the *Iliad* itself. Further, like Aeneas, Juno and Dido as well are almost obsessed with what happened at Troy and, to a surprising extent, with Achilles' role in the war. Achilles and Odysseus are never directly compared in book 1. Indeed, it is almost exclusively Achilles' martial heroism that is repeatedly associated with the fall of Troy, while Odysseus' role in the war is never even mentioned. Aeneas, as well, when he finds himself in situations that the reader "knows" to be Odyssean, never acts like Odysseus. In particular, he is consistently open and straightforward, almost to the point of naïveté, even in situations that, to judge by their Homeric analogues, call for Odysseus' characteristic cunning and restraint. To this extent, the "Odyssean *Aeneid*" could almost be said to lack an Odysseus.

Almost, but not quite. I noted in passing above that Dido is introduced by Venus as a consummate example of the "good king" according to the paradigm of Odysseus. In the face of hardship, Dido is enduring, resilient, resourceful, prudent, and clever to the point of duplicity when the situation demands it. It is she if anyone who exemplifies the ideal ruler—at least in book 1. In the course of that book, however, something happens to her. Ironically, it is Venus, who paints such an impressive and appreciative portrait of Dido's qualities as a leader, who also acts to distort her behavior. After Venus sends Cupid to make Dido fall in love with Aeneas, the good queen stops acting like Odysseus and starts behaving more like the women of the "Apologoi," whom ethical philosophers regarded as so many allegories of the snares that threaten a man of poor judgment. Aeneas of course succumbs, and from that point on they both behave like the passion-driven Iliadic rulers of Horace's *Epistle* to Lollius Maximus. A key difference, of course, is that they are not at war with one another, but in love. In this case, Paris is living in Helen's city. At the same time, when Aeneas turns to building up and beautifying Carthage, he might as well be sacking and destroying it.[76] In Horace's terms, both he and Dido have become bad Iliadic kings, and to the extent that Dido began as a far more

---

76. At 4.215–18 Iarbas, a disappointed suitor of Dido, in a prayer to Jupiter refers to Aeneas as "that Paris" and contemptuously describes his outlandish Trojan costume. When Jupiter in reply sends Mercury to goad Aeneas into action, he finds Aeneas wearing luxurious Punic attire and directing the construction and renovation of buildings and upbraids him for laying "the foundations of towering Carthage" (260–67). It is his evident investment in Dido's project that will prove so devastating to her when he suddenly leaves in response to Mercury's command.

convincing example of good Odyssean kingship, it is Aeneas who has led her astray, distorted her character, and pulled her into his own gravity well of Iliadic futility. We saw that it was easy for Juno to do this with Aeolus, Neptune, and Aeneas himself, because they were each to varying degrees susceptible to Juno's Iliadic designs; and the same is true of Dido. The scenes on Juno's temple and the questions Dido asks Aeneas during the banquet suggest as much. Still, if one can speculate on what Horace made of *Aeneid* 1–4, the poet of the *Epistles* might easily have recognized in it a tragedy of ethical philosophy, the downfall of a "good king" who had been an exemplar of resourceful Odyssean kingship but was herself seduced into passionate self-indulgence by an Iliadic refugee.

Books 5–8, Aeneas' Heroic Education

If the first four books of the *Aeneid* take the measure of the hero and find him lacking, the middle four books represent his education. Books 5 and 6, though dissimilar in many other respects, are very similar in emphasizing this theme.[77] Offering much more than a transition from the disastrous love affair with Dido to the bitter war with Turnus, they show Aeneas evaluating his past, assessing his immediate circumstances, and girding himself for the future. They also put him in contact with various teachers who school him in ethical heroism even as he begins to inhabit his role as king more successfully than before. His progress is not easy or straightforward, but it is progress. The question is, towards what end? What kind of hero does he become?

To summarize this middle section, "The Memorial Games for Anchises" in book 5 are an opportunity for Aeneas to practice leadership in a ritual context. This should be easy, and yet it almost ends in disaster. When Juno intervenes via Isis to make the Trojan women set fire to their fleet and destroy several ships, Aeneas is badly shaken and unsure what to do. He cannot even process the excellent advice given him by a wise counselor until Anchises himself appears in a dream, repeats the same advice, and issues the additional command that Aeneas come to visit him in the underworld for further instruction. In book 6, Aeneas receives an oracular lesson about his future from the Cumaean Sibyl who then guides him through the underworld to Anchises. Along the way Aeneas revisits episodes of his own life since the fall of Troy while the

---

[77]. A simple lexical illustration may be helpful. In books 5 and 6 the verb *doceo*, "to teach," occurs ten times as against eight times in the rest of the poem. Forms of *disco*, "to learn," occur six times in these books as against five other times in the rest of the poem. See below in this section on *magister* in book 5.

Sibyl dispenses commentary of an overwhelmingly ethical and moral nature. Upon reaching Elysium the hero is reunited with his father, who gives him a lesson in metaphysics and eschatology before teaching him about the Roman future that that awaits their descendants. All of this, too, is described in explicitly ethical and moral terms.

Book 7 stands in contrast to the previous two. At the end of book 6, after Anchises finishes teaching Aeneas about their remarkable descendants, he tells the hero what he will need to know in the near term to establish himself in Latium. The narrator simply informs the reader about this in a very few lines: "After Anchises finished taking his son through the individual details [of their descendants' glorious future] and igniting his soul with desire for the renown that would come, he then told what wars the hero would next have to wage, taught him about the peoples of Laurentum and Latinus' city, and how he might avoid or endure each challenge" (6.888–92). That is all. No details are given, and the summary is presented "objectively," with no hint of focalization through Aeneas.[78] By the same token, when the reader in book 7 begins to learn about the things that this brief passage summarizes, Aeneas is not a major presence, either as an actor or as a focalizer. In fact, he spends most of the book supervising the construction of the Trojan's camp, which is perhaps intended to be their city, although it will soon become a military fort under siege by Turnus. In book 8, during this siege, Aeneas goes to seek an alliance with Evander, the king of Pallanteum, an Arcadian settlement on the site of what will be Rome. This book, in contrast to book 7, is focalized almost entirely through Aeneas and is devoted in very large part to his education. By prophecy, recitation of heroic deeds, and ritual observance, the river god Tiber, King Evander, and the people of Pallanteum all play their parts in the education of Aeneas.[79]

These central books thus expose Aeneas to a rich assortment of lessons that are pertinent to a kingly education and exquisitely calibrated to his own needs. The question is, how well does he learn them? This, in one form or another, is one of the central questions of *Aeneid* criticism. By framing the issue in terms of heroic education, I am putting it into a different context from most previous critics and am giving it a particular emphasis. Above all, it is important how the lessons offered to Aeneas, and those that he actually learns, comport with

---

78. Horsfall 2013, 2.608 on *Aeneid* 6.886–901 comments on a number of issues in this passage that have not received much critical attention to argue that they were never fully revised. In the dreamy atmosphere of Aeneas' return to the upper world, perhaps a certain vagueness is appropriate; see Michels 1981, who remarks (141–42 note 2) that Aeneas never seems to recall any of the detailed instruction he receives about the challenges he is about to face.

79. Van Nortwick 1992, 148–152 considers Aeneas' visit to Pallanteum under the rubric of "the hero's education."

ancient evaluations of Homeric heroism in ethical philosophy. In what follows I will focus on what I regard as particularly illustrative episodes in each of these books while adverting occasionally to the presence of Iliadic and Odyssean ethics in them.

Sicily

If the motif of contest is woven into the intertextual fabric of the *Aeneid*, then "The Memorial Games for Anchises" in book 5 should illustrate its significance. Georgia Nugent, in a valuable and justly admired paper, has commented on the intertextual rivalry that surfaces in a simile during the boat race episode:

> Chariots released from the starting gate in a contest of two-horse teams have not sped over the ground and do not rush as fast, nor have charioteers let their teams run so free as they shake their rippling reins and lean into the strokes of their whips.[80]

The simile thus stages a contest between boats and chariots. This is effective, if hyperbolic, since no ship could move as fast as a two-horse team off the mark. The real point of the simile is that these boats, as Nugent points out, are faster than the Homeric chariots in "The Funeral Games of Patroclus" on which they are modeled.[81] The simile's explosive metapoetic force greatly expands the reader's capacity for reflection on its significance. The *tertium comparationis*, the "third term of comparison," is contest itself. The imitative poem is in competition with its model, and it implicitly comments on this fact. Within the "Games," as well, there is competition between Iliadic and Odyssean values, and between the *Iliad* and the *Odyssey* as well.

To that last point, the critical record is one of competition between *Iliad* and *Odyssey* for intertextual primacy. For Servius, as I discussed above, the "Games" are Iliadic games.[82] Richard Heinze builds his masterly analysis of them on this assumption. At the same time, he acknowledges, with many others, that Iliadic games are "out of place" in the "Odyssean *Aeneid*." Knauer argues that the episode was "transferred" from the end of the *Aeneid*, where (he says) it would have been inappropriate, to a location approximating that

---

80. *Aeneid* 5.144–47; see Nugent 1992, 257–58.

81. Servius, *Commentary on Vergil's Aeneid* 5.1 is explicit about this point, noting that "everything the poet mentions here is on display around the tomb of Patroclus [in *Iliad* 23], except there is a chariot race there and a boat race here." On what follows see the section entitled "The Systematic Intertext" in the introduction above.

82. Heinze 1915/1993, 121–41.

of the Phaeacian games in *Odyssey* 8.[83] Cairns takes this argument farther, arguing that the Odyssean games are actually the more important model.[84] Other scholars have taken a more eclectic approach, emphasizing that the episode draws widely on sources that include not just epic poetry but Roman history as well.[85] It would thus be very easy to show that the "Games" are animated by shifting intertextual perspectives, much like Aeneas' landing in Africa in book 1. The themes of sport and warfare, however, instantiate the motifs of contest and decisive outcome, even as they entertain numerous ways of avoiding simple decisions. They do not celebrate either Iliadic or Odyssean ethics exclusively, but neither do they offer a "third way" that is convincingly distinct from the two Homeric paradigms.

With respect to Aeneas himself, it seems important that, like Achilles but unlike Odysseus, he presides over these games but does not take part as a contestant; that he holds them in honor of a person dear to him whom he has lost; and above all that he does so in a way that restores him to his proper position of leadership in his community. For Achilles all of this was necessary because he had put his personal quarrel with Agamemnon ahead of his public obligation to his peers. It is necessary for Aeneas because, since the death of his father, he has (thanks to Juno) totally lost his way to Italy and landed in Africa instead, lost (for the first time) an entire ship from his fleet, (in effect) lost his head and his vaunted sense of responsibility by falling in love with Dido, and (finally) lost an entire year to the building of her city instead of his. The need for him to reorient himself towards the needs of his people and his mission is obvious. If one accepts the relevance of such Iliadic considerations, then some obvious inferences suggest themselves. After succumbing to a period of Odyssean turbulence and confusion, Aeneas goes back to Sicily, the place he left before his year among the "Phaeacians" in Carthage, and binges there on Iliadic and Achillean contests. What could be more characteristic of him than that?[86] Not that it is entirely his choice. Although it is welcome, Aeneas is driven back to Sicily by bad weather—nothing like the storm that

83. Knauer 1964, 156; 1964a, 65, 72 note 2, 73–74.

84. Cairns 1989, 215–48.

85. Nelis 2001, 8–21 gives an excellent account of the boxing match (5.362) as an episode that draws on a multitude of poetic sources. Critics have for some time emphasized the "Games" as alluding to historical events associated with the Roman presence in Sicily, especially the First and Second Punic Wars: see Traill 2001; Leigh 2007 and 2010; Goldschmidt 2013, 115–27; Giusti 2018, 276–77.

86. In playing his Achillean role, Aeneas can also draw on the experience of other heroic games, such as the funeral games of Hector, in which the Trojan Dares defeated the Bebrycian giant Butes (*Aeneid* 5.368–74).

drove him from Sicily to Carthage, but bad weather nonetheless. It is hard to say who is responsible for this. Palinurus ominously wonders what Neptune has in store for him, but he will not find out until the end of this book. There, when Aeneas sets sail for Italy, Venus is nervous that Juno—who is still, after all, "Queen of the Air"—may attack Aeneas once again. Therefore, as I discussed in chapter 1, she bargains away Palinurus' life to obtain Aeneas' safe passage. At the beginning of the book, when Palinurus expresses severe doubts about trying to reach Italy in such weather, and Aeneas decides to make for the shores of Mount Eryx nearby, favorable winds immediately start to blow from the west (5.32–33). These westerly winds, or Zephyrs, are associated with Venus. Is she using what influence she has in Juno's element to steer the plot not just away from danger, but away from further Odyssean disasters and into a specifically Iliadic direction? Perhaps one advantage that comes from dividing the poem into thirds is that book 5 looks less like an Iliadic interruption of an Odyssean plot, and more like a turning point away from what may have been unintended Odyssean entanglements and towards an inevitably Iliadic future.

One could look at it another way, as well. In chapter 1, I noted that Venus' audience with Jupiter in book 1 can be seen as the beginning of a narrative arc that reaches its climax when she delivers arms to Aeneas in book 8. Such an arc would parallel the one defined by Thetis' audience with Zeus in *Iliad* 1 and her delivery of Achilles' arms in book 18. Both of these arcs serve as the long, complex prelude to the vendetta that dominates the final books of the poem. At the same time, just as Aeneas' embassy to Pallanteum in book 8 parallels Achilles's absence from battle, his dallying in Carthage also represents a kind of absence or dereliction of duty. With his return to Sicily, he resumes doing what he is meant to do. An episode of Iliadic games at just this point could be a sign that the Iliadic program of the *Aeneid*, no less than the Odyssean one, conforms to a bipartite, Apollonian model. As we have seen, the *Aeneid* inverts the Odyssean program of the *Argonautica*: instead of a somewhat faintly adumbrated "Phaeacis" in the poem's first half, followed by an ever more explicit one in the second, as in Apollonius, we find that the Carthaginians are quite convincing Phaeacians while the Latins are a relatively attenuated version of them. However, if one thinks of Aeneas' Carthaginian sojourn in Iliadic terms, as I have just suggested, then his return to duty, marked by the celebration of Iliadic games, in the first half of the poem anticipates his actual return to battle in book 9, after which the plot follows a relentlessly Iliadic trajectory. This is very much in keeping with Nelis' observation that the later books of the *Aeneid* imitate the *Iliad* as well as the *Argonautica* even when Apollonius does not take the *Iliad* as his model. Perhaps the Iliadic program of Apollonius' poem should be revisited from this point of view, and the Apollonian program of the *Aeneid*, as well.

However this may be, in both the *Iliad* and the *Aeneid* the "Games" episodes involve "likenesses of battle," as is said of one of the events in Sicily which is actually conducted "under arms."[87] Nevertheless, "transferring" the episode from the end of the *Iliad* to the middle of the *Aeneid* creates a significant difference. When Achilles celebrates Patroclus' games, his real battles, at least for the moment, are behind him. In contrast, all of Aeneas' most important battles—his personal Iliad—lie ahead. The games of *Iliad* 23 are a respite from the furious battle that has been raging for days. The games of *Aeneid* 5, which follow a period of luxuriating in Carthage, symbolically and even practically prepare Aeneas' followers for battles to come while preparing Aeneas himself to meet his responsibilities as their king.[88]

Training is a form of education, and I noted above that references to teaching and learning are prominent in this book and the next.[89] It is also true that the word *magister*, from which we derive the English "master," occurs three times as often in book 5 as in any other.[90] As in English, the word has several meanings. The first officer of a naval vessel is its *magister*. A teacher or coach is also a *magister*. So is a supervisor. Thus *magistri* figure in the boat race, the boxing match, and the "Troy Game" that concludes the competition, in the immediate aftermath of the "Games," and then at the very end of the book. Let us quickly go through these in order.

It is a bad sign in the boat race when Gyas, as captain of the Chimaera, becomes exasperated with Menoetes, his ship's *magister*, and throws him overboard, taking over the post himself (5.159–82). Result: the Chimaera comes in last except for the Centaur, which breaks its oars against a rock that serves as turning post in the race (183–209; 266–85). That boat's captain was Sergestus, ancestor of that consummately bad Roman "king," the seditious Lucius Sergius Catilina, whose defeat was the glory of Cicero's consulship (and, later, the ex-consul's undoing).[91] It is not difficult to work out a general truth applicable to sailing and to all forms of government that a master may know what needs to be done, but ultimately someone else is in charge. If that person is ruled by

87. *pugnaeque cient simulacra **sub armis*** 5.585.
88. Putnam 1965, 64–104; Feldherr 1995 and 2002.
89. It seems worth noting that in the Iliadic chariot race, Nestor famously and rather obtrusively gives his son Antilochus some last-minute advice about charioteering (*Iliad* 23.301–50). Richardson in Kirk et al. 1985–1993, 6.209 describes it as "a sermon on the uses of *mêtis* (practical intelligence)." His speech belongs to the "instruction of princes" genre (see note 128 below) and as such establishes the Iliadic "Games" episode as a kind of school. In Aeneas' "Games" the theme is more widely distributed, as I explain.
90. Six occurrences in this book, no more than two in any other, none in six of the books.
91. See Fratantunono and Smith 2015, 224 on *Aeneid* 5.121.

his own daring, overconfidence, fear of losing, or anything other than his "master's" knowledge and expertise, he may come to a bad end. Gyas' ship moreover is a trireme—a "modern" ship that did not exist in the age of heroes—which the narrator describes as "the size of a city" (*urbis opus* 119). This introduces an explicitly civic association and a contemporary political resonance to this leader's disdain for experts.[92]

The meaning of *magister* as "teacher" comes explicitly into play in the boxing match when the Sicilian Entellus boasts of having been a pupil of the hero Eryx, who dared enter the ring against Hercules. That was long ago, however, and Entellus is now old. His friend Acestes has to shame him into competing. "Where now, I ask you, is the god, Eryx, the teacher [*magister*] of whom you boast, but to no purpose [if you refuse to fight]?" (391–92). Early in the bout it looks as though Entellus ought to have resisted Acestes' goading. Though still massively powerful, he is nearly worn out by the superior technique of Dares, his younger opponent. It is thus a clear confrontation of force against strategy, and when Dares causes Entellus to swing, miss, and collapse, it looks very much as if strategy will prevail. Entellus, however, "returns to the battle all the keener and he rouses his force with his anger [*ira*]; then shame and self-conscious courage [*virtus*] ignite his strength."[93] Powered by these emotions, the older fighter pummels the younger one nearly to death. After Aeneas stops the bout, Entellus sacrifices his prize, a fully-grown steer, with single blow of his fist to the animal's skull—a sign of the fate that Dares narrowly avoided. The lessons Entellus learned from his boxing master evidently had less to do with technique than with main force.[94]

The festival concludes with the spectacle of the "Troy Game," an equestrian display in which opposing "forces" mimic cavalry warfare under the watchful eyes of "supervisors" (*magistris* 562; cf. 669); the title blends their military and pedagogical roles.[95] This is the event that I mentioned above as being called "likenesses of battle under arms." The passage is represented as the origin story

---

92. Feldherr 1995, 253.

93. 454–55; with *vim suscitat ira* ("he rouses his force with anger," 454) compare *se suscitat ira* ("he rouses himself with anger," 12.108), of Aeneas preparing for single combat with Turnus.

94. Many pertinent observations to this point in Feldherr 2002.

95. According to Roman antiquarians, the emergency office of dictator was originally known as "Master of the People" (*magister populi*), and a dictator's junior colleague was always known as "Master of Horse" (*magister equitum*). The dictatorship was revived as a permanent office in the 1st century BCE by Lucius Cornelius Sulla and then by Julius Caesar, so that these associations will have been fresh in the mind of readers in the time of Augustus. See Lintott 1999, 109–13.

of a "custom" (*morem* 596) that was "revived" under Augustus to promote the "moral" education of Roman youth, very much in the "instruction of princes" tradition. The concluding lines embed the theme of education in a brief allusion to the Trojan, Alban, and Roman "king list" as it might appear in an ancient chronicle: the custom is the same one that Ascanius "taught" (*docuit* 598) to the Latin peoples after he founded Alba Longa, that the Albans later "taught" (*docuere* 600) to their sons, and which the Romans now continue as an ancestral tradition.

For the contestants, then, "The Memorial Games for Anchises" are clearly marked as an exercise in the moral education of citizen soldiers. For the presider, the lessons it imparts are less explicit. In comparison to Gyas, the captain who impetuously hurls his prudent master into the sea and takes his place, Aeneas fares well. When the god Sleep descends from heaven at the end of the book to cast Palinurus into the sea, the hero somehow senses that his ship has lost its own master (*magistro* 867). He then rises and takes poor Palinurus' place. Not in any practical sense, because even if Aeneas were a better helmsman than Gyas, Palinurus took the tiller with him when he went overboard. Aeneas' replacing his ship's master thus belongs very much to the realm of the symbolic, and the symbolism is very much in his favor.

In adjudicating the "Games" themselves, Aeneas' role is ceremonial, but also practical, and he generally plays it well. That said, it is worth asking whether he does the right thing in adjudicating the footrace (286–361). Only in this event do Odyssean traits of a suspect kind come into play, as dirty tricks are unexpectedly rewarded. The Iliadic intertext is informative. In Achilles' "Games," Ajax the Locrian is leading in the footrace when Athena, responding to a prayer made by Odysseus, no less, causes him to slip and fall, allowing Odysseus to sprint past him and take first place.[96] In Aeneas' "Games," when the Trojan Nisus leads but suddenly slips and falls, without divine intervention, he deliberately takes down the next runner, the Sicilian Salius. This allows Nisus' friend Euryalus to win and promotes Helymus and Diores to second and third place, respectively. Protests ensue, but Aeneas, amused, settles them by lavishing prizes on everyone.[97] It is an irenic outcome, and for first-time readers of the *Aeneid* a comic one; but experienced readers know that Nisus and Euryalus will

---

96. In the boat race, Cloanthus prays for victory (5.232–48) and, like the Iliadic Odysseus, wins, but without causing misfortune to any competitor.

97. When Nisus protests that he should receive a prize, in spite of the fact that he had the bad luck to fall *and then* cheated by tripping Salius so that Euryalus might win, Aeneas smiles at him (*risit* 358), his only smile in the poem. In the *Iliad*, Achilles too smiles just once, when he awards a prize to a disappointed loser in the chariot race (23.555–56). The parallel was first noted by Clarke 1729–1732, vol. 2, 317 on *Iliad* 23.555. On Aeneas' smile see Uden 2014.

return in an episode that unfolds in a similar way, but ends tragically. As we shall see, on that occasion too an emphasis on prizes and the questionable judgment of the Trojan high command will be at issue. In retrospect the precedent that Aeneas sets in the "Games" does not look well advised.

However well Aeneas manages the "Games," he falters badly when faced with a real crisis. This becomes clear immediately when Juno ruins the end of the "Games" by sending Iris to make the Trojan women set fire to their ships (604–778). This sudden fit of madness deals Aeneas a heavy psychological blow. Whatever confidence he had gained by presiding successfully over the "Games" is virtually shattered. He has no idea what to do. As I noted above, he cannot even recognize the good advice given him by the Trojan elder Nautes until Anchises himself appears in a dream to repeat it, adding that Aeneas should descend into the very underworld for a reunion with his father. Both episodes are highly symbolic; both very explicitly involve kingly instruction in the form of specific advice to a king by an advisor. The nub of it is that in the wake of the "Games" Aeneas must make decisions about which of his people can face the challenges ahead, culling all those who shrink from or are otherwise not ready for them. It is significant that this advice comes first from Nautes, who is introduced as a pupil of Pallas Athena distinguished for his abundant skill (*arte* 705) and a character whose name means "sailor." Seafaring is of course the heroic adventure that Aeneas never wanted to face, but Nautes' advice focuses specifically on readiness for war.[98] Aeneas should advance to Italy with only those of his followers whose martial valor will be equal to the challenges ahead. It is a clear sign that Aeneas is not yet ready to lead that he cannot recognize the wisdom of Nautes' advice until he hears it repeated by the ghost of his father. This episode is followed by the death of Palinurus, whose place as *magister* Aeneas assumes, as was discussed above. The "epitaph" that he pronounces, pitying Palinurus for trusting too much in in a calm sky and sea (870–71), shows the reader how little Aeneas understands of the situation. It is Venus' influence with Neptune and her willingness to use Palinurus' life as a bargaining chip that ensure Aeneas' success, more than any insight or experience that he has gained up to this point.

Cumae

Even before Aeneas arrives in Cumae his descent to the underworld is framed as an educational experience. When Anchises' shade commands his son to visit him in Elysium, he promises: "You will learn [*disces* 5.737] about your

---

98. On Nautes see Fratantuono and Smith 2015, 630–31.

entire progeny and the walls that are being granted you." When they meet, Anchises amplifies these words, promising "I shall teach [*docebo* 6.759] you your destiny." Between and after those two moments, the theme of education appears repeatedly.[99] What is it that Aeneas learns?

Much of Aeneas' education comes in the form of prophecy. Before he descends to Avernus, the Sibyl—speaking on behalf of Apollo, the god who inspires her prophecy—addresses him in no uncertain terms as one who has "at last escaped the dangers of the sea" (83). She then famously predicts that he will find in Italy not only "wars, terrible wars, and the River Tiber bubbling with blood," but specifically Iliadic wars: "nor will you be without a Simois, a Xanthus [that is, the two major rivers in the Troad], a Greek encampment, another Achilles, born in Latium, himself a goddess' son, and neither will Juno ever be far away.... The cause of such great trouble for the Trojans will again be an alien wife, again a foreign marriage" (86–94). Remarkably, Aeneas answers this frightening prediction with a confidence so out of keeping with anything he has previously said that it seems preposterous: "Maiden, absolutely no new or unexpected form of challenge is rising before me. I have anticipated them all and have gone over them beforehand in my mind" (103–5). Commentators never fail to remark upon these words, generally focusing on elements of Stoic terminology and exaggerating the extent to which Aeneas can be considered a Stoic or suggesting how he might have become one.[100] The philosophical register is obviously an important element of this poem's

---

99. Aeneas asks the Sibyl of Cumae to "teach" him the way to the underworld (*doceas* 109). En route she is his "learned companion" (*docta comes* 292). The infernal judge Minos "learns" (*discit* 433) about the misdeeds (of each soul before assigning it a place in the underworld. The Trojan dead are eager "to learn" (*discere* 488) why Aeneas has come. When Aeneas and the Sibyl reach a crossroads, she will not let him visit Tartarus to the left, but she can describe it because the goddess Hecate "taught" (*docuit* 565) her about it. Still, there are so many punishments there that Aeneas must not ask "to be taught" (*doceri* 614) about each one. She does mention the mythical sinner Phlegyas, who undergoes eternal torture and proclaims in a great voice: "Be advised, learn [*discite* 620] justice and not to scorn the gods!" The travelers then follow the right-hand path to Elysium, where Anchises takes them to a mound from which he might "learn" (*discere* 755) the faces of the souls awaiting rebirth. It is then that Anchises tells Aeneas that he will "teach" (*docebo* 759) him his destiny. Finally, after this, the narrator informs us that Anchises "teaches" Aeneas (*docet* 891) what he must know to establish himself in Italy.

100. Austin 1977, 74 (on line 105): "This is Stoic language.... Aeneas has come a long way from his earlier fears and bewilderment ... he can take the Sibyl's gloomy prediction without flinching, and is prepared for the ordeal of going to the Underworld if the Sibyl will be his guide." Horsfall 2013, 132 (on lines 102–23): "Aen[eas] assures the Sibyl that he will not be unnerved; he is already prepared for everything; not in the sense that he knows it all, but because he is mentally, as a good Stoic, prepared."

exceptionally rich stylistic lexicon. My own argument concerning heroic virtue depends upon this fact. Philosophical confessionalism, however, is beside the point.[101] Even a character's actual agreement with or awareness of whatever philosophical import his words might suggest to us may be irrelevant. Rather, the difference between the character's intended meaning and their specifically philosophical significance may be the point. So it is here, because whatever philosophies may be in play, Aeneas is actually saying something very simple. The Sibyl has just addressed Aeneas as someone who has completed his proto-Odyssean wanderings and predicted that he will have to fight another Trojan War in Italy. His reply to this prediction is that he finds nothing new or unexpected in that: he has gone over it all in his mind. That should not be surprising. The Sibyl has told him that he must live through another Iliad, and he replies, yes, fine, that's all I ever think about; the thing is, I want to go to the underworld, can you help me there? From our perspective, it is as if Aeneas were acknowledging that his heroic wandering is now behind him and declaring that he is perfectly ready to face heroic warfare once again. And why not? He never knew what to expect from heroic wandering because he had never "read the *Odyssey*" (most of which has not yet even happened) and never before lived through anything like that himself. He has, on the other hand, "read the *Iliad*," because he has lived through the entire Trojan War, and the fifty days covered in Homer's epic, in which he is actually a character, are seared into his memory. What he tells the Sibyl is not that he has got philosophy but just that another Trojan War cannot confront with him with any challenge that he has not faced before and replayed obsessively in his mind ever since the city fell. He is more than ready for his Iliadic do-over. That way, either his previous experience will make him successful or, in spite of it, he will die like a hero, as he wishes he had done in the first place.[102]

To put it another way, Aeneas has not changed. The starkly dichotomous view of the world with which he has made his way from Troy to Cumae still has him in its grip. Not surprisingly, throughout his underworld adventure

---

101. See Farrell 2014.

102. See Seider 2013, 33. Anderson 1957, 19 correctly observes that upon hearing the Sibyl's description of the war to come, "Aeneas might well leap to the conclusion that the whole pattern would repeat itself, that the Trojan settlement would eventually be assaulted, captured, and destroyed by the combined forces of the enemy." He goes on to note that her reference to unexpected salvation coming from a Greek city "shatters the apparent parallelism" and saves Aeneas from despair, but this may be going too far. The parallelism, as this classic paper so clearly shows, remains extremely close, the crucial difference of course being that the Trojans will exchange their Homeric identity with the Italian resistance for that of Homer's Greek invaders, as I discuss below in the section of this chapter entitled "Books 9–12, Becoming Achilles."

Aeneas remains true to himself, the very image of a man at arms. In the vestibule of the underworld, when he finds a motley collection of insubstantial shapes, he takes fright and would have tried to rout them with his sword, had the Sibyl not explained how pointless that would be (6.268–94). When he presents himself before Charon to seek passage across the Styx, the infernal boatman demands to know what he means by trying to enter "under arms" (*armatus* 388), recalling Hercules, Theseus, and Pirithous as unruly brawlers who forced their way into the realm of the dead. These are some of the very predecessors whom Aeneas cited to persuade the Sibyl to honor his request for her guidance (119–23). Similarly, when Aeneas reaches the shades of those who died at Troy, the Greeks all try to shout in fear and flee him like the dangerous warrior that he is, even though he can no longer harm them (489–93). In spite of the fact that his underworld journey aligns with that of Odysseus point by point, Aeneas remains primarily a soldier, not a voyager, and a man of force, not a strategist. Finally, it is significant that the hero, despite the progress that he has made over the first half of the poem, remains in the grip of his heroic death wish. When the Anchises informs him about the process of purification and rebirth that the dead undergo, he cannot believe that anyone would willingly submit to enduring another life: "What lust, so baleful, for the light do these poor creatures have?" (721). The reader is not told who these dead were in their previous lives, but those whom Anchises shows to Aeneas are mainly the military heroes of Roman history (756–887). A soldier who dies valiantly in service to his country is precisely who Aeneas wants to be, so it is entirely understandable that he would expect the dead to prefer to remain dead rather than go through it all again. To face second Iliad while still alive is something that he has gone over in his mind, as he tells the Sibyl; but having to be reborn in order to do it is quite another matter. In this sense, Aeneas' values are very much those of the Iliadic Achilles, and not of the Odyssean version, who would rather be enslaved to a poor man among the living than to be honored as king among the dead (*Odyssey* 11.487–91).

What is equally significant is that the Sibyl—or Apollo through her—encourages Aeneas to think that way! Her message about the ease with which one can descend to Avernus and the difficulty of the ascent (6.124–29) might actually speak to Aeneas' death wish. If he could not return, he would at least die in an effort to do something truly heroic. Returning to endure a second Trojan War, however, does not bother him. Having suffered through seven years of Odyssean wandering, another Iliad will be a different challenge, but at least a familiar one. Learning this, Aeneas may not be elated, but he may well feel grimly determined, and somewhat encouraged that he will again be in familiar territory, at last.

The Sibyl's utterance is inspired, and it ought to be reliable. That is, her own power to shape the narrative does not seem to extend beyond book 6, but

Apollo, speaking through her, seems to be a very traditional narrator, declaring that the "Odyssean *Aeneid*" has reached its end and that the "Iliadic *Aeneid*" is about to begin. Nevertheless, questions remain. In the first place, prophecy is always a slippery medium of instruction. In the *Aeneid*, moreover, as James O'Hara above all has shown, oracles and other forms of prophecy are often encouraging in the moment, but become misleading the more one learns about their meaning.[103] Apollo may just be telling Aeneas what he thinks he must to steel the hero for trials to come. In any case, oracles are oracular. Why should the reader expect clarity from this one?

There may be a reason, or a partial one. Even if there definitely will be a second Trojan War, the Sibyl is vague about who the new Achilles is going to be—and by the same token, who will be the victorious Greeks this time around and who the vanquished Trojans. By oracular implication, the Trojans are to remain themselves and their Italian opponents will be the new Greeks. This is Juno's perspective, as well, and there is every reason to believe that Aeneas shares it. Seeing the world in Iliadic terms, it haunts him that he did not measure up to Achilles and that he did not even attempt to face Pyrrhus, Achilles' lineal successor. What another Trojan War can give him is a chance to atone for those past failures by prevailing or else dying in the attempt. How could he ever believe that he himself might actually become the new Achilles? Still less would he ever dream that he might surpass an Achillean Turnus by representing the opposite type of hero, in accordance with the highest ideals of kingship theory, as a flexible, resourceful Odysseus; nor does the Sibyl say anything that so much as hints at such a future.

As if to confirm that Aeneas remains impervious to Odyssean influence, even in this unmistakably Odyssean book, even as he endures what the reader cannot help but recognize as an Odyssean trial, the hero's utterly anti-Odyssean nature continues to assert itself. In the first part of his underworld journey, his experience—what I have been calling his "reading"—becomes a major theme as he encounters the shades who represent his life since the fall of Troy. This period of Odyssean wandering, of comrades and lovers lost, remains painful. Among the souls he sees waiting to be judged by Minos are those condemned to death by a false accusation (430). In the Fields of Mourning he meets Dido who in life accused him of perfidy, and he now sees it confirmed that he himself was the cause of her death (450–76). Farther on he meets his old comrade Deiphobus and learns that on Troy's final night Helen betrayed him to Menelaus, hoping to curry favor with her victorious husband, and to Ulysses himself, that "counselor of crimes, the spawn of

---

103. See O'Hara 1990.

Aeolus."[104] Eventually he gets past this area of the underworld and approaches the walls of Tartarus. When the Sibyl informs Aeneas about the terrors within, he learns that punishments for crimes of treachery—deceit (*dolos* 567), theft (*furto* 569), deception (*fraus* 609), breaking oaths (*fallere dextras* 613)—are especially prominent there. As if to state the entire meaning of everything that Aeneas has learned on this journey so far, the Sibyl quotes a particular prisoner of Tartarus, the great mythological sinner Phlegyas, who, as he undergoes eternal torture, proclaims in a great voice: "Be warned, learn justice [*discite iustitiam* 620] and not to scorn the gods!" (620).

The Sibyl delivers this account of Tartarus at a crossroads (540–43). In the ethical and eschatological texts from which the topography of this underworld derives, a crossroads symbolizes a binary choice that is absolutely decisive.[105] Here Aeneas has no opportunity to choose because the Sibyl will not allow it. He cannot enter Tartarus, on the left, even to visit. He is bound for Elysium, to the right. This crossroads will take the hero away from a place that is absolutely bad to one that is absolutely good. It will also take him away from his own past to a vision of the distant future that his own quite limited future will bring into existence. Everything about this crossroads should therefore focus the reader's attention on the great choice with which this book is concerned. What kind of hero must Aeneas be if all this is to happen?

Although Aeneas at the crossroads cannot choose his route, the theme of choice pervades his journey. The Golden Bough, as I discussed at the beginning of chapter 2, must choose whether he will be allowed to make the journey at all. Along the way he sees two of the three mythological judges traditionally said to hold sway over the dead, the aforementioned Minos (432) and his brother Rhadamanthus (566). The third, Aeacus, is nowhere to be found.[106] That is interesting for many reasons, not least because Aeacus is the grandfather of Achilles. It is Anchises, I suggest, who takes Aeacus' place. There a couple of reasons for this.

First, although Anchises is not a Greek mythological judge, Eric Kondratieff has shown very convincingly that he is represented as a Roman censor. A censor is not a judge in any narrow sense, but he exercised much broader

---

104. *hortator scelerum Aeolides* 529. The reference is not to Aeolus, king of the winds, but to the father of the Sisyphus, a great liar and thief, whose bastard son Odysseus' detractors alleged him to be: so Servius, *Commentary on Vergil's Aeneid* 6.529; see Austin 1977, 177.

105. See Horsfall 2013, 384–85 on *Aeneid* 6.540–43.

106. Minos, who presides over an area between the Fields of Mourning and Tartarus, appears at 6.432 as a *quaesitor*, which is the title of the presiding judge in a Roman court; see Horsfall 2013, 326 on *Aeneid* 6.432. Rhadamanthus presides over the "most harsh realms" (*durissima regna* 566) of Tartarus itself, but has no title.

powers of judgment over Roman society more generally. As Kondratieff writes, "censors could wield tremendous influence in shaping Roman society, especially through their *regimen morum* (supervision of morals)."[107] This is very much the narrator's point when he says that Anchises "was reviewing [*recensebat* 682] the entire number of his descendants, his dear grandsons, and the fates and fortunes of those men, their character [*mores* 683] and their strength." There is, in my view, no question but that Anchises is represented as, in effect, conducting Rome's first census. The idea that in doing so he "replaces" Aeacus as the third infernal judge can be no more than a suggestion, but it is one that makes sense. First of all, identification of Anchises with Aeacus, the ancestor of Achilles, would prefigure that of Aeneas with Achilles himself.

Second, the glorious vision of Roman history that Anchises offers Aeneas is entirely militaristic from start to finish. This should be surprising, but in the context of the *Aeneid* it is not. However much philosophers, poets, and historians had come to favor an affirmative interpretation of Odyssean ethics as a guide for good citizenship and political leadership, the *Aeneid* almost obstinately refuses to recognize that fact and continues to depict Ulysses as a despicable villain. Aeneas is unquestionably the most determined spokesman for that point of view. It would be a true peripeteia if Anchises at this extraordinary moment of revelation were to tell his son: Be like Ulysses! Be flexible! Use your *mêtis*, not your *mênis*! Needless to say, he says no such thing. Instead, he glories in the militaristic inevitability of his descendants' transformation from stateless, wandering refugees into citizens of a world empire.

For these reasons, Anchises' treatment of Lucius Junius Brutus is particularly instructive. Here is what he says:

> Do you want to see the Tarquin kings and the proud soul
> of Brutus the avenger, and the rods of command that he took from them?
> He will be the first to receive the absolute authority and savage axes of a consul;
> and despite being their father, when his sons start a rebellion
> he will summon them to punishment on behalf of lovely freedom—
> a man of ill fortune [*infelix*], however posterity shall treat his accomplishments:
> love of country will prevail and immeasurable desire for approval.
> (*Aeneid* 6.817–23)

---

107. Kondratieff 2012, 125; Freudenburg 2017, 132.

Having used restraint in this translation, I must follow it with a few comments. First, as is very well known, Anchises' introduction of Brutus along with the Tarquin kings, whom he overthrew, is rather curious. These figures represent a major inflection point in Roman history, between the Regal Period and the Republic, and they stand on opposite sides of it. All of them find their place in the "Parade of Heroes." It is Brutus who as first consul receives not only the emblems and instruments of regal authority, the bundle of rods and axes used to beat or behead the unruly; he also receives the epithet of Rome's last king, Tarquinius Superbus, "Tarquin the Proud." Brutus is also called "the avenger" (*ultoris*) for his role deposing the regime after a member of the royal family, Sextus Tarquinius, raped the virtuous noblewoman Lucretia Collatini and left her to commit suicide after reporting the atrocity. "Avenger" is not a common epithet for this Brutus; still less common is it for his descendant, Decimus Junius Brutus, who led an uprising against Julius Caesar, a descendant of Anchises and Aeneas, when it appeared that Caesar intended to establish a new form of monarchy in Rome. It was Caesar's adoptive son, who has already appeared in the "Parade of Heroes" (791–807) and who began his career by punishing his father's assassins, including Brutus, to whom the epithet "avenger" better applies. In the heat of battle against these assassins at Philippi in 42 BCE, the young Caesar even vowed to build a temple to Mars the Avenger (*Mars Ultor*), as he eventually did, decades later, by which time he preferred to associate the temple with a very different, more public and less personal, act of vengeance.[108] Like the first Brutus, however, the second is also a champion of "lovely freedom." The word *libertas*, in fact, was used as a slogan by Caesar's assassins before it was taken up by Caesar's heir in his struggle for supremacy.[109] This is just to say that "freedom" and "avenger" are extremely loaded words in any Augustan context, and particularly in situations that involve anyone named Brutus.

Anchises' treatment of Brutus is remarkable not only for what it says about him, but also for what it does not. The first Brutus was not remembered primarily as a military figure. Indeed, he is one of the few Roman leaders who is remembered primarily for his cunning intelligence. His very name reflects this. According to the *Oxford Latin Dictionary* (s.v. brutus 1 and 2) it means "heavy,

---

108. See Ovid, *Fasti* 5.569–96; Suetonius, *Augustus* 29.2. Weinstock 1971, 131–32 argues that the vow at Philippi is not historical, but it escapes me why Ovid would have invented such a story half a century after the supposed fact, and why Suetonius would have believed the story if Ovid was his only available source. In any case, the first two feats mentioned in Augustus' own account of his *Accomplishments* (the *Res Gestae*) are (1) liberating the republic from the oppression of a "faction" (headed by Brutus and Cassius) and (2) avenging the murder of his father.

109. Wirszubski 1950, 100–106; Gosling 1986; Brunt 1988; Arena 2012, 42–43; G. Kennedy 2014.

inert, brute," and so "devoid of intelligence or feeling, irrational, insensitive, brutish." Brutus' name means the opposite of "intelligent" because he carefully concealed his intelligence so as to avoid being identified as an opponent of the oppressive Tarquins. His exquisite timing in deceptively deploying that intelligence to solve a riddle posed by the Delphic oracle enabled Brutus to take down the regime. These qualities are the ones for which Brutus was most famous, but Anchises does not even hint at them. Instead, he focuses on Brutus' decision to execute his own sons for plotting a return to monarchical government; and he declares that, no matter what posterity will say about him—and it is his shrewd policy of low-key resistance to the Tarquin regime, his clever interpretation of the riddling oracle, and his sudden, decisive self-revelation as the very man to lead the overthrow of the tyrants, that posterity did principally remember—Brutus is not to be counted among the fortunate. The specific word Anchises uses here is significant, as well. He calls Brutus *infelix*, which is what Achaemenides, and then Aeneas imitating Achaemenides, calls Ulysses in book 3; and the reader will recall that I took issue with those who regard either instance as an expression of sympathy. Rather, I see it as a comment on Ulysses' character as one that creates trouble for himself and especially for those around him. As applied to Brutus's execution of his own sons, the word comes about as close as possible to its etymological and primary meaning of "yielding nothing useful, unproductive."[110] You do not have to agree with me, however, to see that Anchises' use of *infelix* here is a further connection between Brutus and Ulysses. Whether this word bespeaks pity for Ulysses before and for Brutus now or instead condemns them, Anchises pointedly ignores those positive Odyssean qualities that enabled Brutus to overthrow the tyrants and establish a republic. Instead he focuses on the brutal measures that he used against his own sons "on behalf of lovely freedom"— freedom (*libertas*) being the slogan under which the second Brutus would rally Caesar's assassins.

By characterizing Brutus as a man of force, Anchises assimilates him to the majority of those who appear in the "Parade of Heroes," who were renowned for their military achievements. All of this comports with his injunction "to establish a tradition of peace, to spare the humble and overcome the proud" (*paci imponere morem, / parcere subiectis et debellare superbos* 852–53). Here too my translation is treading carefully, for to "impose" anything on peace is to regard peace itself as an unruly thing, which is the opposite of how peace is usually conceived. Nicholas Horsfall well brings out the strangeness of the

---

110. *Oxford Latin Dictionary* s.v. infelix 1.

expression, both in his rendering of it ("to set the force of habit upon peace") and in his commentary.[111] The rest of it can be stated more clearly just by emphasizing the basic meaning of the words: "to spare the humble" is really "to spare your subjects, those whom you have subjected," i.e., "cast down," while "overcome the proud" is really "war down the proud." The only difference between these two groups is that the former accept their subject condition while the latter as yet do not. Anchises advocates a policy of continuous warfare until all of the "proud" have become "subjects." It is no wonder that he has no time for Brutus' ingenuity, and even if he regrets Brutus' severity, he must consider it needful.

Latium

Book 7 begins with two minor events that may say something about Aeneas' frame of mind. Neither is very encouraging. The first event is the death of Aeneas' nurse, Caieta. She gives her name to the place where she dies (7.1–4), as do the trumpeter Misenus (6.232–35) and the helmsman Palinurus (6.376–83). After them, she is the third follower or companion to perish, like Elpenor in the *Odyssey* (11.51–80), while the hero himself returns from the underworld alive. In the *Aeneid*, multiplying Homeric characters is rarer than combining them. When Aeneas is struck by the storm in book 1, he has already lost only Creusa and Anchises, although the reader does not learn this until the ends of books 2 and 3. By the time Odysseus faces a similar storm he will already have lost all of his companions. In Aeneas' version of that storm, however, he loses a ship and its entire crew.[112] He then causes Dido's suicide at the end of book 4 and leaves a large number of followers behind on Sicily before losing Palinurus at the end of book 5 and Misenus in book 6. Now in book 7, the death of a third Elpenor figure signals ominously how many more Aeneas is about to lose. It is a question that may well be troubling the hero's mind.

The second event occurs en route to Latium, Aeneas' "Ithaca" according to Knauer.[113] We have seen that Africa is already represented as a potential Ithaca, but also as Aeaea, the home of Circe in the *Odyssey*; and here Aeneas passes Monte Circeo, now a peninsula but once an island identified by Hellenistic

---

111. Horsfall 2013, vol. 1, 59 and vol. 2, 585 on *Aeneid* 6.852.

112. *Aeneid* 1.113, 584–85. Aeneas sees Orontes, the captain of the lost ship, in the underworld at 6.334. See O'Hara 1990, 7–24, 110–11.

113. Knauer 1964, 239–53 and 1964a, 76, building on Heyne 1830–1841, vol. 3, 22–23, who finds a parallel between the prayers the heroes make upon arrival to the local nymphs at *Aeneid* 7.133–40 and *Odyssey* 13.356–60.

geographers with this Homeric place.[114] The Trojan fleet glides along by moonlight, coming close enough that the "angry groaning" of lions, chafing at their chains, as well as boars, bears, and wolves can be heard. All of them are men whom Circe has transformed with her drugs. If Dido was a kind of Circe, here (in good Apollonian fashion) is the real thing. The reader eventually learns that Aeneas' future father-in-law is a descendant of Picus, a consort of Circe whom the goddess bizarrely turned into a woodpecker. Eduard Fraenkel and Kenneth Reckford have both focused on the Trojans' non-encounter with Circe as a symbol of what Reckford calls "latent tragedy in *Aeneid 7*."[115] Neither scholar explicitly invokes ancient allegories that regarded Circe as a trap for the ethical hero to avoid or overcome, but their readings are perfectly compatible with this tradition. As readers we may ask whether Circe's appearance here is a warning of what Aeneas must avoid, a representation of his fears, a prediction of what will happen in these last six books, or perhaps all of the above.

Caieta's death and the bestial growling of Circe's pets create an atmosphere of gloom and foreboding, and the intertext may once again give access to the hero's thoughts and emotions; but that is a matter of conjecture. Before we can even begin to ponder it, the Trojans arrive at the mouth of the Tiber and the narrator invokes the Muse Erato, to whom we shall presently return. After the invocation, he tells the reader about the ancestry of King Latinus, which includes Circe's Picus, about Latinus' lack of male offspring and the many local suitors of his daughter, Lavinia, all vying to be his heir, and the preeminence among them of Turnus, whom the girl's mother, Amata, especially favors. The reader also learns about omens advising Latinus not to marry Lavinia to any Latin suitor, and others portending greatness for Lavinia herself but war for her people. Latinus seeks further advice from the oracle of his father, Faunus, who confirms the necessity of seeking a foreign bridegroom. The king tells no one, but a rumor is going around when the Trojans arrive (45–106). The narrator introduces this account by saying, "I shall lay out who were the kings, what were the conditions and the state of affairs in ancient Latium when the foreign army first drove its fleet to the shores of Ausonia," also promising to "recall the very beginning of the conflict" (37–40). Very similarly, after the "Parade of Heroes" in book 6, Anchises tells Aeneas "the wars he would next have to wage, the peoples of Laurentum and Latinus' city, and how he might

---

114. On the Apollonian background of this brief Circe episode see Nelis 2001, 259–62. On repetitions with increasing emphasis and clarity of Odyssean episodes in the *Argonautica* see the section of chapter 2 entitled "The *Aeneid* as Argosy."

115. Fraenkel 1945; Reckford 1961; see also Thomas 1986/1999; Hunter 1993, 175–82; Kyriakidis 1998, 75–117; Keith 2000, 48–49.

avoid or endure each challenge" (6.890–92). The obvious similarity between these summaries suggests that the narrator's exposition in book 7 spells out the details of Anchises' teaching in book 6. Or does it? If so, then all of it? Part of it? The details that the narrator shares with the reader would be useful for Aeneas to know. The question is, does he actually know them? Famously, Aeneas never once mentions learning any such details, and major events in Latium take him quite by surprise. Some critics are therefore convinced that Aeneas remembers nothing of his underworld excursion; others suspect that it happened only in a dream.[116] For the present argument, it is sufficient to infer that Aeneas' education is not a simple matter. As became very clear in book 2, people try to tell him things with the utmost clarity and force, but he either misunderstands, forgets, or becomes distracted and must be told repeatedly. This is especially true when he is told to do something that does not comport with his Iliadic worldview. We have seen both the Sibyl and Anchises give Aeneas lessons that appear to agree with and reinforce that worldview, but those lessons are short on specifics and are in part confusing. The one thing we can be sure is that Aeneas should expect to fight another Trojan War in Latium. Does he truly understand that much, at least?

At first glance, the narrator's invocation of Erato seems to promise not an Iliad but the second half of an Argonautica. As Nelis has shown, we do get that, although, as I have argued, it comes in an attenuated and surprisingly Iliadic form. Erato's name speaks of erotic love, and the narrator picks up this theme when he continues, "I shall sing frightening wars, I shall sing pitched battles and kings driven to death by their passions [*animis*]," before he ends with the ringing phrase, "a greater series of events rises before me; greater is the task I set in motion" (7.37–45). This statement is almost universally regarded as evidence that the narrator is shifting from an Odyssean to an Iliadic program. Whether doing so has been his intention from the beginning of the poem or Juno's intervention in book 1 causes him to improvise, as I have suggested, remains an open question. In contrast to the invocation of book 1, however, this time the narrator's intentions seem clear. Characterizing his Iliadic program as a tale of kingly passions told under the auspices of the Muse whose name virtually means "sex" agrees closely with Horace's representation of the *Iliad* as a story that "contains the passions of foolish kings and peoples." The question again is, does Aeneas know that this is the kind of Iliad that awaits him?

Immediately after the narrator spells out the situation regarding Latinus' succession, the reader is granted clear access to Aeneas' mind in a way that

---

116. Michels 1981, 143 note 8, cites half a dozen scholars, beginning with Eduard Norden, who suggested or argued that Aeneas' "Catabasis" could be a dream. See also Gotoff 1985.

establishes one point while raising a number of additional questions. In book 3 (223–28) the hero tells Dido how the Harpy Celaeno predicted that the Trojans would not accomplish their "homecoming" until starvation forced them to consume their very tables. Here in book 7 (107–47), after landing near the mouth of the Tiber, they must eke out their dwindling supplies by foraging. Using slabs of bread (really as plates, but never mind) to hold their simple meal, they finish by devouring those, as well, and Ascanius makes a joke: "Hey, we're eating our tables!" Aeneas recognizes this as the prophecy's fulfillment and is cheered. He is also confused, because now he remembers not Celaeno but Anchises as the source of the prophecy. This represents the reader's most direct access to Aeneas' consciousness in book 7, and it is significant that he is encouraged. It may or may not be significant that his memory is bad.

After this episode, which is at once decisive and enigmatic, the rest of book 7 denies the reader access to Aeneas' mind, with just two minor exceptions. On the day that follows the omen of the tables, Aeneas sends ambassadors to state his case to King Latinus and request Lavinia's hand in marriage (148–55). Having done so, "he outlines [a foundation for] walls by [making] a shallow trench and builds the place up, and surrounds his first home on the coast with a parapet atop a rampart, in the manner of a military camp" (157–59). In the remaining 658 lines of this book, Aeneas will of course be mentioned, but he will be actually seen again only once, by Juno, busying himself with this same work: "Up in the sky, all the way from Pachynus in Sicily she caught sight of a joyful Aeneas and his Trojan fleet. She sees that buildings are going up, that they have confidence in this land, that they have left seafaring behind them. She stood transfixed by a piercing pain" (288–91). That is all. Aeneas then evidently spends almost the entire book doing what he does when he arrives almost anywhere: building a settlement. He envisions this settlement as a kind of fort, and Juno's reaction when she sees him proves that he will need one. That he seems "joyful" is therefore a bit odd. Perhaps that is just how he seems to Juno. Perhaps the word (*laetus*), which in Roman augury has the technical meaning of acting in accordance with the will of the gods, means that here Aeneas is, for the first time in the poem, exactly where he is supposed to be.[117] The "Omen of the Tables" has just confirmed this. On the other hand, the Trojans on their way from Sicily to Italy the first time were "joyous" (*laeti*) when Juno noticed them and almost finished them with a storm (1.35). Therefore, the word is in effect a reminder that Aeneas is not acting in accordance with the will of *all* the gods. Maybe he is simply happy because he is doing something he knows how to do, possibly even something that Anchises told

---

117. On the augural significance of *laetus* see Linderski 1993/1995, 615–16.

him to do upon arriving in Latium: First of all, build yourself a fort! Sooner or later, you will be fighting another war! One might hope that Anchises' instruction would be both more detailed and more extensive than that, but possibly not. Helenus in book 3 (433–40) warns that Aeneas should propitiate Juno at every opportunity, but he does not make it clear that she would try to destroy him with a storm because both the Fates and Juno herself prevent him from saying too much (380). By the same token, the Sibyl in book 6 warns that in the second Iliad Juno would still be against the Trojans; but even if Apollo inspires her, is she forbidden to say that Allecto, a denizen of the hellish regions that she and Aeneas are about to visit, would also be involved? Does she even know? Does Anchises?

In response to this glimpse of a joyful Aeneas, Juno delivers her second great soliloquy (7.293–322), which further explains the narrator's invocation of Erato to tell of "kings driven to death by their passions" (42). This passionate war is being fomented by the passionate Juno, who has wanted the *Aeneid* to be a passion-driven Iliad from the beginning. Her improvised attempt in book 4 to divert it into an Argonautic channel has had surprisingly long-term results: the narrator's first Musal invocation in book 7, of Erato, proves as much.[118] Indeed, the erotic character of Juno's interventions—her bribing of Aeolus in book 1, her ghastly faux-wedding in book 4, and now her interference with Turnus and Amata in book 7—runs like a red thread through the poem's incredibly dense intertext. At the same time, the energy of Juno's Argonautic intervention eventually becomes another tributary of the swollen river that is her Iliadic obsession. This is perhaps surprising to readers who regard any Argonautic plot as an essentially Odyssean story, even a "future reflexive" Odyssey, something that Apollonius' poem (with the qualifications discussed above) actually is. As book 7 unfolds, however, it becomes obvious that the erotic element signaled by the Erato invocation conforms to Horace's jaundiced reading of Homer's greater opus.

Juno's second soliloquy certainly moves the poem decisively in this direction, but it differs from her first effort in an important way. In book 1 she has her minions attack Aeneas directly to make him just another unlucky Cyclic hero whose demise belongs in *Homecomings*, and not a forerunner of the exceptionally successful hero of the *Odyssey*. That effort not only fails, but actually puts Aeneas into an Odyssean situation that persists, according to some critics, into book 7 and beyond. In book 4 she has to alter her tactics: she cannot coerce or bribe Venus as she does Aeolus, so she tries to reach an understanding with her instead. Since Venus, acting through Cupid, has made

---

118. *Aeneid* 7.37, *Argonautica* 3.1.

Dido infatuated with Aeneas, Juno—to use Odyssean reference points—attempts to offer Dido to Aeneas much as the *Odyssey* presents its hero with Circe, Calypso, and Nausicaa as potential brides who would prevent him from returning to Penelope. In doing so, however, as I pointed out in the previous chapter, Juno acts on Dido as the Apollonian Hera acts on Medea—not for Medea's benefit, but for Jason's. It is hardly surprising that this strategy does not turn out well for Dido or for Juno. Now, in book 7, Juno reverts to her earlier approach in an even simpler form that once again derives from her troublemaking literary past. As we saw in the last chapter, when the title character of Euripides' *Heracles* returns from the underworld, Hera sends her agents, Iris and Lyssa, "Madness," to drive him insane and make him murder his wife and children. Now that the title character of the *Aeneid* has returned from the underworld, too, she has no need to bribe anyone this time, either. She merely summons Allecto and orders this hellion to do her worst; not to Aeneas, however, but to Amata and Turnus. This is to repeat the mistake she made in conspiring with Venus against Dido. Juno ought to have followed the Hercalean script more closely. If she had allowed Aeneas to marry Lavinia, then driven him insane, and forced him to murder Lavinia and Ascanius, Turnus would no doubt have been disappointed in his personal hopes, but Juno would have erased the glorious future that Anchises showed Aeneas in the Elysium. That is presumably why she could not do it, of course; but that does not stop her the first time ("Oh, right; I'm forbidden by the Fates!" 1.39). Why does it stop her now?

This is a question that has an answer. Juno is not an inscrutable character. On the contrary, she is an open book, and that book, as I continue to maintain, is the *Iliad*. Whatever tactics she adopts at any given moment, her goal remains the same. The *Aeneid* must turn out to be a sorry Iliadic sequel, an episode in the seemingly endless Iliad that tells of the utter eradication of Troy. As the poem opens, she thinks she can accomplish this within the confines of the Epic Cycle. When that doesn't work, and the poem starts shaping up to be a proto-Odyssey, she tries to capitalize on her influence within a similar story, the *Argonautica*, in which her control is virtually total, free even from constraints imposed by Zeus. Again, it does not work. Finally, when it appears that she is going to get not just a minor extension of the *Iliad*, but a full-scale remake, she acts in a way that seems entirely logical—to her. But to be fair, it might seem logical to anyone who had listened to the Cumaean Sibyl's oracular description of this remake. Even Aeneas, forecasting his future in the light of his own Iliadic experience after listening to the Sibyl's warning could not possibly imagine that the Achilles awaiting him in Latium is none other than himself. As for Juno, Aeneas must be the last person she would expect to play this role, and certainly the last that she would want. Therefore, taking nothing for granted, she dispatches her minions to breathe Achillean anger, and a bit of madness for good measure, into her own hero to ensure that he is equal to his task. If she resorts to the same measures that she uses against Heracles, that is simply in keeping with the fuzzy logic that determined her immediate tactics involving Aeolus and Dido before. She is no more a flexible Odyssean goddess, like Athena, than Venus is, and no more than Aeneas by his nature is an Odyssean hero. Her strategy remains the same. She means both to enforce Aeneas' Trojan identity and to destroy him along with the last remnants of his kind. If an entirely new Iliad is required to get the job done, so be it; and if that new Iliad requires a champion powered not only by Achillean *mênis*, but by Heraclean *lyssa*, as well, that is what she means to supply.

To make the second half of the poem the Iliad that she requires and so far has not managed to achieve, Juno works to make of Turnus an Achilles even worse than Horace and his sources could have imagined. What is more, as I noted in the previous chapter, she sends Allecto, as the Euripidean Hera sends Lyssa against Heracles, to drive Turnus mad. It is still not obvious whether Juno fully understands what she is doing. It is Aeneas, not Turnus, who like Heracles has just returned from the underworld. It should be he, if anyone, who is thus susceptible to infernal forces. The situation is obviously unsettled, as it usually is when Juno intervenes. Intertextual identities are anything but stable, and as they shift the forces that Juno had brought to bear on one character will eventually infect others.

A second invocation in book 7 (641–46) omits the erotic element to focus squarely on martial matters. Here the narrator comes close to the tone of the actual *Iliad*. His model is an invocation that precedes the "Catalogue of Ships" in *Iliad* 2 (484–93), just as this one precedes a "Catalogue of Italian Forces."[119] As in the Homeric passage, the narrator asks for practical information: "Who were the kings roused to war, what armies followed whom and filled the battlefields, with what men [*viris*] was the nurturing land of Italy even then aflower, with what arms [*armis*] was it ablaze?" (641–46). Again, the detailed information that follows should correspond to what Anchises taught Aeneas about the immediate future that lay before him in Italy after teaching him about the more distant future that awaited their Roman descendants. By the same token, as a character who has "read" the *Iliad*, Aeneas might be expected to recognize this marshaling of forces for what it is, the onset of the war that he has been taught to expect. The strange thing is that Aeneas is nowhere to be found.

---

119. Servius, *Commentary on Vergil's Aeneid* 7.641; Knauer 1964, 233: "Die Musenanruf... ist als 'wörtliches Zitat' sofort erkennbar und diene daher als Leitzitat" ("The invocation of the Muse... as a 'word-for-word citation' is immediately recognizable and thus serves as a guide citation").

In this regard, it is noteworthy that Francis Cairns regards Latinus as fundamentally a good king and in many ways not unlike Aeneas.[120] Not entirely, of course: Latinus is bathetically ineffectual, while Aeneas at his worst shows far more determination in the face of adversity. One would like to see that contrast here. When Amata and Turnus, under Juno's influence, work against Latinus' acceptance of Aeneas' claim to Lavinia, the king simply throws up his hands and declares: "Alas! I am being broken by fate and carried away by a storm!" (594).[121] It would be a good moment for Aeneas to act. But where is he? Has he been working on his fort or city all this time, as he worked on Dido's city in book 4? After the ceremonial laying out of the foundations, is his presence really required? Is he aware of what is happening elsewhere? Can he do nothing to stop it? In his absence, the situation quickly unravels to the point where battalions of troops from many Italian cities present themselves to drive the Trojans out of Italy. If the reader had access to Aeneas' thoughts, would we see that his experience of the first Trojan War, his "reading" of the *Iliad*, had prepared him for this moment? Would the hero share the reader's "understanding" that the "Catalogue of Italian Forces" casts his opponents as the Homeric Greeks of this second war? Would he be buoyed by this "understanding," or depressed? Above all, would he be right about this, and would being right give him some advantage that throughout his Odyssean wanderings he has entirely lacked?

Pallanteum

The short answer to these questions does not arrive until the beginning of book 8, which opens with a paragraph that continues to focus on Italian preparations for war. Then there is a sudden shift: "That is what was happening throughout Latium. The Trojan hero, seeing it all, floats on a great ocean-swell of cares and lets his attention go this way and that, quickly, turning his mind in different directions, everywhere, in a hurry" (8.18–21). That is not the image of a well-prepared or decisive leader.[122] Nor is it encouraging to realize that

---

120. Cairns 1989, 62–66.

121. "I am being carried away" is my rendering of *ferimur* 594. Horsfall 2000, 387 on this passage comments, "the verb is a favourite with V[irgil] . . . to express violent and uncontrolled or involuntary motion." I would add that this form and the singular *fero* regularly associated with leaders confessing or admitting their lack of control over events or themselves (Aeneas, 2.337, 655, 725; 3.11, 16, 78; Dido, 4.376; Latinus, 7.594; Turnus, 10.442, 670; Juno (!) 10.631; a telling progression of speakers? See also 4.110, Venus, dissembling; 5.628, Iris/Beroe, dissembling/rabble-rousing). On Latinus as a "weak king" see Cowan 2015.

122. The description of Aeneas' confused mental state here is almost the inverse of the one he claims when he tells the Sibyl: "No new or unexpected form of challenge is rising before me.

this portrait of indecision is modeled on a passage of Apollonius in which the subject is Medea. This is confirmed by the extraordinary simile that follows.[123] In the *Argonautica*, light reflected from water in a cauldron, glancing about a room, suggests the agitated mental and emotional state of a young girl grappling for the first time with the sensation of falling in love. In the *Aeneid* it represents the confusion of a king who is not at all in love, though he is supposed to be getting married, and whose people are under the threat of imminent war. This can only be the second Trojan War that the Sibyl says is waiting for Aeneas in Latium and for which he tells her, in no uncertain terms, that he is ready. Now, after being instructed by Anchises "how he might avoid or endure each challenge" (6.892), he really should be ready. The previous book ends with a "Catalogue of Italian Forces," which even first-time readers might recognize as alluding, almost ostentatiously, to the "Catalogue of Ships" that concludes *Iliad* 2. Aeneas, as a "reader" of the *Iliad*, might thus be expected to observe this mustering of Italian troops with grim resolve as confirmation that the second Iliad that he expects is finally under way. That is not his reaction. Although he uses Stoic language to assure the Sibyl that he is well prepared for this moment, now the narrator tells the reader something different. Night falls, and Aeneas tries to get some sleep, but is "disturbed in his mind by the bitter war" that is brewing. The Latin for "disturbed" is *turbatus* (29), a word frequently used to convey the mental and emotional state associated with the Greek word *tarachos*, "disturbance (or) agitation," which Epicurean and Stoic philosophers used to describe a state of mind opposite to their shared ideal of calm indifference, *ataraxia*, "lack of disturbance."[124] If Aeneas is disturbed instead of composed as he faces the war for which he said he was ready, then as a philosopher he is not very far advanced, and as a leader he also has a long way to go.

It is in book 8 that Aeneas will complete his journey—or, at least, he will go as far as he can. His embassy to Pallanteum is the final phase of his education. After the opening paragraph on Italian preparations for war, practically the entire book is focalized through him. As in book 5 and especially book 6, from the moment that he manages to fall asleep Aeneas receives a series of "lessons" from gods and mortals via prophecy, storytelling, advice, and ritual. Finally, he receives an omen, which he interprets correctly in terms of both its immediate and long-term significance. Over the course of these episodes,

---

I have anticipated them all and have gone over them beforehand in my mind" (6.103–5), discussed in the preceding section of this chapter.

123. As recognized by Servius, *Commentary on Vergil's Aeneid* 8.19; see Nelis 2001, 331: "The Apollonian model . . . is explicitly, almost blatantly, signalled."

124. On *ataraxia* in Hellenistic and Roman philosophy more generally see Warren 2002.

Aeneas begins, as we have just seen, in a state of troubled uncertainty and evident paralysis as the Iliad that he said he had thoroughly foreseen actually starts to unfold. As the various teachers just mentioned administer repeated doses of advice, he begins to settle down and regain his confidence. At the end of the book he can be seen to have overcome his initial butterflies and actually to be eager for war and confident of victory. How does this happen?

During Aeneas' night of troubled sleep, a dream vision of the river god Tiber reassures the hero by telling him that he is in the right place should not be frightened by the impending war (8.26–67). This is a further sign, by the way, that Aeneas is in fact unsure of himself and frightened by the prospect of an impending second Iliad. In his effort to calm Aeneas, Tiber is even a bit misleading: he claims that "all the passion and anger of the gods have given way" (40–41), when this is manifestly not so.[125] In fact, before he finishes speaking Tiber will command Aeneas upon waking at dawn to "offer prayers to Juno with due ceremony and with solemn vows overcome her threatening anger [*iram* 60]." Aeneas, however, clearly needs even more encouragement, and Tiber means to provide it. The river god goes on to promise an omen that will confirm the long-range success of what he is telling Aeneas to do. Then he shifts back to the present: "Now, pay attention: I shall teach you [*docebo* 50] how to get on with the business at hand [and emerge] victorious."

In what follows, Tiber informs Aeneas about the Arcadian settlement of Pallanteum in the hills up river, instructs him to form an alliance with its king, Evander, who is ever at war with Latinus, and then offers to take Aeneas there himself. It is a baffling passage, because it appears to be the first time that Aeneas has ever heard of Pallanteum. Did Anchises—who, we will soon learn, has actually met Evander when they were both young—not put alliance with the Arcadians on Aeneas' to-do list? Did Aeneas in his confusion forget about that? Whatever the truth may be, the effect of such a passage is to increase the reader's sense that Aeneas has not in fact prepared himself sufficiently for this war, although he continues, as always, to receive timely support.

Hope is strengthened when Aeneas awakens and, following Tiber's instructions, accepts the promised omen of a white sow with thirty piglets, makes his way by night upriver, and arrives at noon the following day at Pallanteum on the future site of Rome (66–101). From the reader's perspective, Aeneas' visit with Evander corresponds not only to Odysseus' sojourn with Eumaeus in *Odyssey* 14–16 but also to Telemachus' visits with Nestor and Menelaus in *Odyssey* 3 and 4.[126]

---

125. *tumor omnis et irae / concessere deum*. On this typically "optimistic" prophecy, see O'Hara 1990, 31–35, 116–18.

126. Knauer 1964, 249–59; Knauer 1964b, 65, 76–77.

A strong indication of this comes when Evander, looking upon Aeneas, recognizes in him Anchises, who visited Arcadia when he and Evander were young men (126–74). This is what happens when Nestor beholds Telemachus and recognizes him as the son of Odysseus.[127] It is odd to think of Aeneas as the callow Telemachus at this point in his career, but we have seen that there are many ways in which his behavior seems, frankly, immature. The practical information that he has gathered since the fall of Troy has brought him, with the greatest difficulty, to this point; but as we have seen, it is still unclear whether he really has all the information that he needs and whether having it is sufficient if he lacks the confidence to use it. Telemachus too is in need of both information and confidence when the goddess Athena appears to him in the guise of Mentes, an aged guest-friend of his father, to suggest that the young man go to Pylos and Sparta in search of useful information from Nestor and Menelaus, the first and last of the Greek leaders to obtain successful homecomings (*Odyssey* 1.280–305). Both Athena/Mentes' interview with Telemachus and the young man's visits with Nestor and Menelaus derive from a deeply archaic genre of poetry devoted to the instruction of princes.[128] In this genre, instruction on any subject at all conveys something more than mere information. It performs a rite of passage by which the old instructor initiates his young pupil in the ways of "manhood" (*andreia* or *virtus*). The intertext suggests that Aeneas at Pallanteum is in a very important sense more Telemachus than Odysseus, needing more than just information but the maturity to use it, as well.

The stories Telemachus hears on his travels are not precisely like the one that Evander tells to Aeneas. Nestor and Menelaus give Telemachus some reason to hope that Odysseus is still alive and may yet return. In Hercules' defeat of Cacus, Evander offers Aeneas a specific heroic example to follow himself. In this respect, as I argued in the preceding chapter, it resembles an Iliadic episode of princely instruction, "The Wrath of Meleager," which Phoenix offers to Achilles as an example to avoid. Readers are free to evaluate these paradigms as they please; but of all the ways that Aeneas might react to Evander's princely instruction, deciding to adopt, all of a sudden, the crafty ways of Odysseus and Cacus, and not the forceful ethos of Achilles and Hercules, does not seem to be even a remote possibility.

It is only as Aeneas is leaving Pallanteum that his perspective changes decisively. There is a practical side to this. The reader has just read a lengthy description of the troops that Evander and his Etruscan allies have mustered to

---

127. *Aeneid* 8.152–56, *Odyssey* 3.123–25; see Eichhoff 1825, vol. 2, 77–78; this and other parallels discussed by Knauer 1964, 250; more generally, 249–62; 1964a, 76–77.

128. On this genre in Greek and Roman antiquity see Martin 1984; Kurke 1990; Fish 1999; Nieto Hernandez 2010; Farrell 2018; Klooster and Van den Berg 2018.

join forces with Aeneas' Trojans (470–519). Leaving Pallanteum with these soldiers behind him, he is that much readier for war than he was previously. Still, we learn, he and his faithful Achates keep their eyes cast down upon the ground thinking troublesome thoughts in their gloomy hearts, and would have kept doing so if not for an omen suddenly sent by Venus (520–23). Strangely, it is this omen that seems to open Aeneas' eyes at last and to complete his heroic education.[129] Recognizing it as the fulfillment of a promise, Aeneas' mood turns exultant as he foresees with almost clairvoyant acuity the course of the war that is about to unfold. The Latin demands to be quoted in full:

> Heu, *quantae* miseris caedes Laurentibus instant!
> *quas* poenas mihi, Turne, dabis! *quam multa* **sub und***as*
> **scuta virum galeasque et fortia corpora volv***es*,
> **Thybri** pater!
>
> Ah, how many disasters loom over the poor Laurentian people!
> *What* penalties you will pay me, Turnus! **Beneath your waters,** *how many* **shields of men and helmets and brave bodies** *will you* **roll,**
> father **Tiber!** (*Aeneid* 8.537–40)

and then compared with Aeneas' words on a very different occasion in book 1:

> mene Iliacis occumbere campis
> non potuisse, tuaque animam hanc effundere dextra,
> saevus *ubi* Aeacidae telo iacet Hector, *ubi* ingens
> Sarpedon, *ubi* tot **Simois** correpta **sub und***is*
> **scuta virum galeasque et fortia corpora volv***it*?
>
> That I couldn't have fallen on the plains
> of Ilium and poured out this spirit by your right arm,
> where savage Hector lies beneath the spear of Aeacus' grandson,
> where great
> Sarpedon [died], *where* **Simois rolls so many shields of men and helmets and strong bodies caught in his waves**?
> (*Aeneid* 1.97–101)

---

129. According to Knauer, Venus' gift corresponds to that given by Helen to Telemachus as he departs from Sparta in *Odyssey* 14, which is followed by a sign from Zeus that Helen interprets as indicating that Odysseus will soon return (1964, 255–59); also of course to that given by Thetis to Achilles in *Iliad* 18 (1964, 259–62). The sign given by Venus before the gift-giving could thus be seen as marking the conclusion of Aeneas' education just as Zeus's sign concludes the "Telemachia." The fact that Helen gives Telemachus a peplos while the goddesses Thetis and Venus both give their sons arms forged by Hephaestus/Vulcan, not to mention the elaborate ecphrases of heroes' shields that follow the gift-giving, seems worth noting.

As I have noted, Aeneas in the second passage recalls a specific episode of *Iliad* 20, in which Achilles slays so many Trojan opponents that their bodies clog the channels of the river Scamander, preventing its waters from flowing down to the sea.[130] In the first passage, Aeneas seems to remember the Sibyl's warning about horrible wars, the Tiber foaming with blood, a Simois, a Xanthus, a Greek encampment, and another Achilles, born in Latium, himself the son of a goddess (6.86–94). It is as if, upon seeing the divine armor, he finally understands something that has eluded him from the beginning. And why would he not? Aeneas knows what Achillean armor is, having faced an Achilles who was clad in it.[131] When he receives similar armor of his own, he has no idea, as the narrator makes clear at the very end of book 8 (729–31), what the images wrought upon it mean, but he now seems to understand perfectly that the new Achilles is not to be Turnus, after all, but rather himself, and to recognize what this means for the coming Iliadic war.

Books 9–12, Becoming Achilles

In the final four books of the poem, the reader finally has the opportunity to observe Aeneas in a situation comparable to one he has lived through before. He has brooded over that previous experience ever since and has been repeatedly warned, advised, and educated in preparation for this second chance. While brooding he has had his moments, but in general he has been a very indifferent leader. As he advances towards his second Iliad, however, he shows more convincing signs that he understands his situation and is ready for it. In these final books, the reader learns more about the kind of leader the Trojans need, about the kind of leader Aeneas is, and about the hero's perspective on his situation.

A Leadership Vacuum

Book 9 is the only book of the poem in which Aeneas does not appear at all. If ever the notion of an "absent presence" were applicable, though, it is applicable here. Obeying Tiber's instructions to leave his settlement and seek an alliance with Evander will pay off when he returns in book 10, but intervening events prove how risky a gambit this is. In the hero's absence, the wisdom of his strategy comes under question through scrutiny not of his own actions, but of the capacity of his Trojans to act as "good kings" by simply following his orders.

---

130. See the section of chapter 1 entitled "Aeneas."
131. On Aeneas and Achilles' mortal armor see note 54 above on Helenus' gift.

THE ODYSSEAN *ILIAD*, PART 1: "EMBASSY" AND "DOLONEIA"

Speaking of "absent presences," book 9 as a whole corresponds to the central books of the *Iliad* when Achilles is absent from battle.[132] Throughout the book, Turnus attacks the Trojan settlement, and the defenders are hard pressed to keep him at bay. The book's own central episode involves Nisus and Euryalus, characters familiar from the footrace of book 5, who volunteer for a dangerous mission to bring Aeneas back to base. In this respect, their mission resembles the Iliadic "Embassy" to Achilles in *Iliad* 9.[133] Unfortunately, along the way they raid an enemy camp where they are themselves captured and killed. This is a replay of the successful "Doloneia" of *Iliad* 10, but with a disastrous outcome.[134] It does put the Trojans of the *Aeneid* in the position of the Homeric Greeks that they must become, but it also suggests that they are much worse off without Aeneas than the Greeks were without Achilles. In his father's absence, Ascanius is nominally in charge of the settlement and is supported by a team of senior advisors. Aeneas has told them not to venture outside the camp or engage with the Italians under any circumstances (40–46). These are sound, simple orders, but the Trojan leadership proves incapable of carrying them out.

Aeneas' absence is differently motivated from that of Achilles. One could even say that the hero's order not to engage is aligned with Odyssean restraint and proper timing rather than Achillean anger and intransigence. That said, a very different aspect of the Odyssean ethos is impossible to overlook in this "Embassy-cum-Doloneia." In *Iliad* 9, Odysseus' silver-tongued effort to lure Achilles back to battle earns him the famous, blood-curdling response in which Achilles states the definitive difference between them:

> "Son of Laertes, descendant of Zeus, Odysseus of many wiles,
> I must declare accurately what I have to say
> as I mean it and as it will come to pass,
> so that you all may not sit there jabbering at me on this side and that;
> for hateful to me as the gates of hell is that man
> who keeps one thing hidden in his heart but says another." (*Iliad* 9.308–13)

Elsewhere in the *Iliad* Odysseus is praised as the most persuasive speaker among the Greeks and is shown to be brilliant in choosing just the right way

---

132. Anderson 1957, 25; Knauer 1964, 266–80 specifies *Iliad* 8–16, with additions from 18 and 22, as the most relevant Iliadic intertexts.

133. Knauer 1964, 266–69. On this episode see especially Fowler 2000.

134. The resemblance is noted by Ovid, *Ibis* 625–30, Servius, *Commentary on Vergil's Aeneid* 9.1, and Macrobius, *Saturnalia* 5.2.15 in Kaster 2011, vol. 2, 232–33; see Casali 2004, 321 note 8.

to persuade different sorts of men.[135] The embassy speech to which Achilles makes this response is his longest set-piece in the poem. It is also a total flop. In contrast, when Nisus presents his idea to the Trojan leaders, he has no difficulty persuading them. In fact, they have been asking themselves who might be able to take word to Aeneas about their precarious position. In a situation that calls for the determination of an Achilles, they behave very differently.

As a matter of fact, they behave like the Greek leaders of *Iliad* 10. After the failure of the "Embassy," Agamemnon and the others give in to a desperate urge to do anything that might inflict some damage on the enemy and raise their own spirits. Their solution is to send Diomedes and Odysseus on a dangerous mission behind enemy lines to capture the horses of Rhesus. This speaks to a prophecy that if those horses should ever taste the grass of the Trojan plain, Troy would never fall. The mission succeeds, but some ancient critics objected so strenuously to the entire episode as a celebration of shifty, duplicitous action under cover of night rather than open combat in the clear light of day that they did not consider it genuinely Homeric.[136] However, the tactics involved are entirely characteristic of those that would finally prevail in the war, and they are characteristic of Odysseus, as well. In Aeneas' Achillean absence, then, the Trojan leadership tries to summon him back to camp by employing the most suspect of Odyssean tactics, and their effort fails utterly.

There is an explicitly philosophical subtext running through this episode. When Nisus tells Euryalus about his plan, he poses a question that has fascinating implications for the poem and for the epic tradition as a whole: "Do the gods apply this burning sensation to our minds, Euryalus, or does one's own desire become each man's god?" (184–85). Having read this theological stumper, the reader is entitled to construe Nisus' follow-up statement in philosophical terms, as well. "For a long time now my mind has been astir to do battle or for some great exploit, nor is it satisfied with peaceful rest" (186–87). Nisus' mental agitation and restlessness bespeak an unhealthy psychological state. Even worse, the Trojan high command are also in spiritual turmoil:

> All other creatures throughout the world were releasing
> their cares and their hearts to sleep, forgetful of their troubles;
> the first leaders of the Trojans, choicest of their youth,

---

135. On Odysseus as a "good king" in the *Iliad* see D. Cairns 2015.

136. See scholia T on *Iliad* 10.1: "It is said that this book was prepared separately by Homer and that it was not part of the *Iliad*, but was introduced into the poem by Pisistratus" (trans. Casali 2004, 322; my interpretation of this episode is greatly indebted to Casali's penetrating analysis). For a general discussion of scholarly opinions on the relationship of the "Doloneia" to the *Iliad*, see Hainsworth in Kirk et al. 1985–1993, vol. 3, 151–55.

were taking counsel about the highest matters of state.
What were they to do? or, Who might take a message to Aeneas, right now? (*Aeneid* 9.224–28)

Taking one's responsibilities seriously is obviously not bad in itself, but inability to let go of one's cares while everyone else can is always a sign of emotional disturbance.[137] It does not help that the narrator calls this war council the "first leaders" of their people and the "choicest" of their youth. That is exactly how Lucretius describes Agamemnon and the other leaders of the Greek expedition against Troy, "the choicest leaders of the Greeks, the first of [their] men."[138] Lucretius' grandiloquence is ironic, because he is condemning these leaders for sacrificing Agamemnon's daughter to the goddess Diana at Aulis to obtain favorable winds for the fleet to sail to Troy. He is condemning an act of religious superstition, the very thing that he wrote his poem to combat. The meaning of the Lucretian intertext in the *Aeneid* is extremely complex, but there can be no doubt that the Trojan leaders here share with Lucretius' Greeks an unphilosophical perspective that leads them to make poor decisions.

The Trojan leaders have just been called their people's "choicest *youth*," but the first to respond to Nisus' proposal is the aged Aletes, who speaks emotionally and promises the adventurers handsome rewards. Ascanius, taking this cue, lists the prizes he will lavish on them. These correspond closely to the ones that the Iliadic Odysseus, speaking on Agamemnon's behalf, offers Achilles in his "Embassy" speech.[139] The correspondence strengthens the "Embassy-cum-Doloneia" character of the episode while underlining a difference between Nisus' and Euryalus' ready acceptance and Achilles' flat rejection of such rewards.[140] The prizes that Ascanius offers also resemble the ones Aeneas used to appease the disgruntled participants in the footrace of book 5, when Nisus cheated so that Euryalus might win.[141] The two episodes reflect upon each other in unflattering ways when it emerges that Nisus and Euryalus might

---

137. See Farrell 1997, 234–36; Casali 2004, 340–43.

138. Compare *ductores Teucrum primi, delecta iuventus* (*Aeneid* 9.226) with *ductores Danaum delecti, prima virorum* (Lucretius, *On the Nature of Things* 1.86).

139. Sabbadini 1908, 151; cf. Knauer 1964a, 269, P. R. Hardie 1994, 122 on *Aeneid* 9.263–74. In case there were any doubt about this, both lists begin at line 263 of their respective books. The prizes, which include tripods, talents of gold, enslaved women, and even territory, go far beyond the black sheep that Nestor promises each man who volunteers for what becomes the "Doloneia" (*Iliad* 10.211–17). On the theme of greed in this episode see Casali 2004, 227–35.

140. In *Iliad* 19.56–275, Achilles and Agamemnon return to the question of the gifts "as a weapon in their ongoing *agon* over honor and status" (Donlan 1989, 6).

141. Aeneas' policy on prizes resembles but is not identical to that of Achilles; see the trenchant analysis of Uden 2014, 72–80, 89.

have carried out their mission unscathed had they not tarried to loot the Rutulian camp. Instead, Euryalus is noticed by enemy troops when moonlight glints off the plundered helmet he wears (367–77). When he is captured, Nisus does not go on to summon Aeneas, but goes back to save or avenge his friend and ends up dying on Euryalus' lifeless body (384–445). Prizes, then, are what the Trojan leaders offer Nisus and Euryalus, and prizes are the material cause of their doom.[142] As in the development of the "stage set" motif in book 1 and that of Dido as Alcestis in books 4 and 6, this grim echo of Nisus' "self-sacrifice" in the footrace exemplifies a general tendency of the *Aeneid* to move from comedy to tragedy, both intertextually and in terms of plot. The upshot of Nisus and Euryalus' failed "Embassy-cum-Doloneia" is merely to enrage their enemies and demoralize their friends when the heads of the unhappy pair are displayed on pikes in front of the Trojan camp (459–502). The further result will be a day of fierce and confused combat and a very narrow escape for the Trojans, whose camp is nearly taken, instead of another day of tedious self-isolation before Aeneas does in fact appear with reinforcements.

FIGHTING TO BE GREEK

By mustering in book 7 as Homer's Greeks had done in the "Catalogue of Ships," the Italian forces begin the second Trojan War predicted by the Sibyl, and they do so on terms favorable to themselves. In book 9 Turnus continues in this vein, especially as a commentator. He repeatedly draws parallels between himself and Agamemnon, the generalissimo, Menelaus, the wronged husband, and Achilles, the greatest warrior.[143] It does not bother him that the *Iliad* begins with a bitter quarrel between Achilles and Agamemnon. He seems to think that he is all of these heroes in one. His actions, though, often tell a different story.

Book 9 begins with Iris, Juno's agent, advising Turnus that Aeneas' absence gives him a chance to make quick work of the Trojans (1–24). In the *Iliad* Iris is sent twice by Zeus and once by Hera to incite either Greeks or Trojans to

---

142. In this respect, Nisus and Euryalus resemble the Homeric Dolon more than Diomedes and Odysseus: see Casali 2004, 324–33.

143. Turnus compares himself to Agamemnon and Menelaus at 9.138–39; like the former he is the supreme commander of his troops and like the latter he sees himself as a wronged husband, even though there has been no wedding. His words, moreover—"the pain [caused by the theft of one's wife] does not affect the sons of Atreus alone"—echo those of Achilles in his indignation at Agamemnon's taking Briseis from him ("Are the sons of Atreus the only members of the human race who love their wives?" *Iliad* 9.340–41). Turnus later declares himself another Achilles (*Aeneid* 9.741–42).

battle, and any or all of those occasions could be relevant here.[144] Collectively they raise the question of just what Turnus' Homeric identity is. After he approaches the Trojan settlement and finds no convenient place to attack it, he tries to lure the Trojans out into open battle by setting fire to their ships (47–76). That is exactly what Hector comes close to doing in *Iliad* 13 and what he actually does in book 16.[145] After the ships are saved by being miraculously transformed into nymphs by the Great Mother of the Gods, Turnus tries to reassure his troops by insisting that effective loss of these ships puts the Trojans in an untenable predicament (123–33). On this occasion, he does in fact speak in the voice of Achilles just before he sends Patroclus out to do battle in his place.[146] Achilles' point, however, is that the *Greeks* are in the kind of untenable position that Turnus says the *Trojans* are now in. Thus Turnus ironically suggests (to a reader who is attuned to such things) that the Trojans are looking like Greeks in this new Trojan War.

An intertextual contest between the Trojans and the Italians to determine who really are the Homeric Greeks in this poem continues throughout book 9. The day of battle that begins in lamentation for Nisus and Euryalus corresponds to the longest day of battle in the *Iliad*, which follows the night of the "Embassy" and the "Doloneia" (books 9–10) and extends over books 11–18 before night falls again. Over this long arc of Homeric narrative, the momentum shifts back and forth between both sides until Achilles receives his divine armor and prepares to rejoin his comrades. The long day of battle in *Aeneid* 9 ends earlier, so to speak, than Homer's does: the book closes at a point comparable to Hector's breaching of the Greek defensive wall in *Iliad* 16, just before Achilles lets Patroclus enter the battle wearing his armor. As in the *Iliad*, momentum shifts back and forth between attackers and defenders. Even more shifting are the intertextual identities of the combatants. The environment is rife with generically Homeric elements and easily recognized "set-pieces" that invite a more pointed response. Very strikingly, Turnus continues to comment on these events in light of Iliadic antecedents.

Among the major signs of shifting momentum and intertextual identity, two episodes stand out. In one of them, Numanus Remulus, Turnus' brother-in-law, takes a stand at the head of the Italian battle formation to hurl insults at the Trojans. His speech, a textbook example of ethnic stereotyping, represents the Trojans as the same battle-shirking, wife-stealing, luxury-loving sissies

---

144. These parallels are well and succinctly discussed by P. R. Hardie 1994, 65–66 on *Aeneid* 9.1–24.

145. Knauer 1964, 27–72.

146. With *Aeneid* 9.131 compare *Iliad* 16.67–70; see P. R. Hardie 1994, 99 on *Aeneid* 9.131.

they have always been.[147] This obviously aligns with Juno's and Turnus' assumption that the Trojans are and always will be Trojans, not only ethnically but intertextually as well. Like Iarbas in book 4, Numanus does not call them Trojans, but Phrygians (*Phryges* 599), associating them with another people of Asia Minor who are proverbial for their "soft" way of life. He thinks they are no match for the "hard race" (*durum genus* 603) of the Italians. Numanus then doubles down on his earlier point: no, these are "not men of Phrygia, at all, but women of Phrygia" (617). This taunt repeats one that two quite different Iliadic characters, Thersites and Menelaus, hurl at their fellow Greeks—the former merely to abuse them, the latter to rally them.[148] Numanus' xenophobic appropriation of this trope thus complicates the intertextual and ethnic relations involved. Further complications ensue when Numanus scoffs: "Here there are no sons of Atreus or that fabricator of speechifying, Ulysses" (602). He means to imply that the Italians are a more formidable enemy than the Greeks were, but Turnus has already compared himself to both of Atreus' sons. Numanus also seems to share Aeneas' contempt for Ulysses, even though he himself is immediately exposed as a mere fabricator of speechifying when an arrow shot by Ascanius punctuates his obnoxious bloviating. It is ironic that Ascanius before shooting prays to Jupiter for success. This recalls the vow to Apollo that the Trojan Pandarus makes in the *Iliad* before he treacherously breaks a truce by shooting Menelaus when he is about to defeat Paris in single combat.[149] Any similarity between Ascanius and Pandarus could be seen as proving Numanus' point. It also suggests that Ascanius shares half of an intertextual identity with a nameless bowman—whether a member of the Rutulian resistance or a god acting in support of them—who shoots Aeneas the first time he attempts to settle his quarrel with Turnus by single combat (12.311–23).[150]

147. See Horsfall 1971.
148. "Women of Achaea, no longer men" (*Iliad* 2.235, 7.96, the former parallel cited by Macrobius, *Saturnalia* 5.9.13 in Kaster 2011, vol. 2, 306–7, the latter by a late supplement to Servius; see Knauer 1964, 451).
149. *Iliad* 4.116–21; noted by Clarke 1754, 111; P. R. Hardie 1994, 200–201 on 625–29. Knauer 1964, 444 lists Nisus' prayer before casting his spear (9.404–9) as a more relevant parallel.
150. The narrator makes it clear that no one claimed credit for shooting Aeneas. Knauer 1964, 292 note 1 states that Pandarus' shot is imitated again when the Italian augur Tolumnius, urged by Juturna, hurls a spear, thus breaking a truce that has just been concluded so that Aeneas and Turnus might settle it by themselves, and causing a general melee (12.257–310). At that point, when Aeneas attempts to restore order, he is hit by the mysterious arrow (311–23; see Servius, *Commentary on Vergil's Aeneid* 12.176, 266). In any case, after Ascanius fells his man, Apollo appears to him in the guise of the Trojan Butes in order to congratulate but also restrain him from further exploits; see Miller 2009, 150–60. Remarkably, Apollo's intervention is based on one at

The Trojans' elation at Ascanius' deed incites them to flout Aeneas' orders entirely. The tumultuous action is bookended by a pair of extraordinary "window references" to Homer via Ennius, which we have briefly considered before. In the first, a pair of enormous brothers named Pandarus, no less, and Bitias, have been given special orders to defend a particular gate. In the second, Turnus has made his way into the Trojan settlement and must back slowly out of it under a shower of missiles. In Homeric terms, Pandarus and Bitias "are" the Greek soldiers Leonteus and Polypoetes while Turnus is the Greek hero Ajax son of Telamon. Similarly, as we have also seen, in Ennius' *Annals* there is a gate being defended by a pair of Istrian soldiers acting like Leonteus and Polypoetes as well as a Roman military tribune who plays the part of Ajax; the principals in Ennius are fighting on opposite sides, presumably in the siege of Ambracia in 189 BCE. We do not have enough Ennian context to make firm judgments, but there is no indication that ethnic difference is the most important theme in his treatment. As I suggested previously, Ennius' purpose is evidently to magnify the significance of a recent and, frankly, not very important war by comparing the valor of combatants on both sides to that of Iliadic Greeks. The Trojan–Italian War of the *Aeneid* is the mythical forerunner of several more recent wars, including the Italian or Social War of 91–88 BCE and the subsequent civil wars that issued in the Augustan regime. Both the mythical prototype and its historical successors involve an underlying ethic unity between the enemy combatants, if only as an achieved state rather than a given. All of that said, the battle for the Trojan settlement in *Aeneid* 9 is the last episode in a book that repeatedly thematizes ethnic difference, and it directly follows Numanus Remulus' jeremiad, which is devoted to that subject. Finally, it does not merely treat both sides as Homeric Greeks, but rather treats Greek intertextual identity as itself something worth fighting for.

Neither side manages to earn that distinction. As I noted above, when Ascanius slays Numanus Remulus, the Trojans no longer refrain from engaging. Pandarus and Bitias, again as noted above, have been given just one job: to defend just one gate, keeping it closed against enemy attack. Instead, they open it and take the fight to the Italians. This is the exact opposite of their specific orders and of Aeneas' general order, as well. It is also precisely opposite to

---

Iliad 17.319–34 in which he appears in mortal guise for the opposite purpose of urging none other than Aeneas on to battle (P. R. Hardie 1994, 207 on 644–60; Dingel 1997, 241 on 646–51; earlier commentators cited by Knauer 1964, 477 note the motif of divine impersonation of a mortal but do not make much of this particular parallel). See also Schmit-Neuerburg 1999, 296–300 and 318–25.

what happens in the comparable Homeric episode.[151] In the *Iliad* (12.127–94), Leonteus and Polypoetes are guarding a gate in the Greek defensive wall that is being kept open to receive any Greek warriors forced to retreat under Trojan attack, and their defense is successful, whereas Pandarus and Bitias' breakout will fail. The commotion that Pandarus and Bitias create attracts the attention of Turnus, whose arrival causes a momentary disruption of Homeric identities and then a kind of intertextual jump-cut. In the *Iliad* (12.191–92), the first Trojan attacker felled by Leonteus is named Antiphates. This is also the name of the first Trojan defender felled by Turnus (696), who now starts to mow down opponents as the Greek defender Leonteus had done in Homer.[152] Ultimately Turnus fells Bitias himself, causing Pandarus to close the gates in panic, shutting out many his fellow Trojans—exactly what Leonteus and Polypoetes did not do to their fellow Greeks—but shutting Turnus inside!

This is where the intertextual action leaps forward from Leonteus and Polypoetes' defense of the Greek camp to Hector's breach of its wall later in the same book (*Iliad* 12.457–66).[153] Upon entering the Trojan settlement, Turnus, like Hector upon breaching the wall, reaches the height of his success. The unusual radiance of his eyes, the resonance of his body armor, the blood-red crest of his helmet, the thunderbolts crackling off his shield, recall not only Hector at this point, but also Achilles, especially in his pursuit of Hector.[154] Turnus virtually says as much: When Pandarus taunts him for letting himself be trapped inside the settlement, Turnus smiles in response and replies with an eerie calm.[155] "You go first, if there's any courage in your heart—start the battle! You can tell Priam that here as well you found an Achilles" (741–42). These words obviously recall those spoken to Priam by Pyrrhus in book 2, making Turnus' penetration of the camp and his brilliant appearance into a repetition of Pyrrhus' penetration of Priam's palace and his refulgent appearance

---

151. Ennius' Istrian soldiers were also represented as "charging out of the gate of the camp and wreaking havoc the besieging enemy" according to Macrobius, *Saturnalia* 6.2.30 in Kaster 2011, vol. 3, 58–59.

152. By the same token, "Leonteus' next three victims form a group of three names in one line, *Odyssey* 12.193; similarly, T[urnus]'s next three victims are contained in 702" according to P. R. Hardie 1994, 219 on *Aeneid* 9.696.

153. Eichhoff 1825, vol. 3, 181–82; Knauer 1964, 275, 464; P. R. Hardie 1994, 213 on *Aeneid* 9.672–755.

154. *Aeneid* 9.731–33. P. R. Hardie 1994, 228–34 offers the most convenient documentation and most penetrating discussion of these points.

155. *sedato pectore*, "with no emotion," 740. This is in marked contrast to Turnus' usual mental and emotional state after Allecto attacks him; see P. R. Hardie 1994, 83 and Dingel 1997, 59 on *Aeneid* 9.57 *turbidus*.

when he cold-bloodedly gives Priam a message to take to Achilles in the underworld.[156] Pyrrhus, however loathsome, looked invincible to Aeneas on that terrible occasion, as if he truly were Achilles reborn as an even more ruthless killer. That must be how Turnus thinks of himself at this moment, perhaps even more so when the enormous Pandarus' spear cast—like that of the aged Priam—falls harmlessly without reaching him. Turnus answers with a cast of his own that gruesomely splits his enemy's head cleanly in two—as the Homeric Achilles himself does to the Trojan Iphition (*Iliad* 20.386–87). However, it will take less time for Turnus than it did for Pyrrhus to realize what it means to try taking Achilles' place.

Turnus inflicts a lot of damage before the Trojans come to their senses. At last, though, they realize that numbers are on their side. The gate is barred shut. Turnus cannot get out, and no one can get in to help him. The end of the day's battle plays out, fittingly, in a final contest over Greek intertextual identity. Mnestheus, the victorious captain in the boat race in book 5 (and thus a kind of anti-Nisus in these paired books), points out to the Trojans that they have nowhere to go, but do have the advantage of numbers, if they would only use it. His speech (781–87) corresponds to one made by Telamonian Ajax in *Iliad* 15 (733–41), which rouses the defenders of the Greek camp before Hector's advance.[157] Mnestheus thus recaptures for the Trojans their Greek intertextual mojo, if only momentarily. Turnus realizes that the advantage has shifted and begins to withdraw warily to the back of the camp, which is open to the Tiber. At first he is compared to a lion surrounded by hunters in a simile that Homer uses to describe Ajax's retreat before Hector.[158] As he goes, moving backwards step by step under a hail of missiles, Turnus repeats what Ajax had done on a second occasion under Hector's assault.[159] Turnus thus (so to speak) wrests the role of Ajax from Mnestheus and with it regains a measure of the Greekness that someone will need to prevail in this second Iliad. He also assumes the identity of a intertextual Roman in the form of Ennius' military tribune.[160] Even more remarkably, when he reaches the riverbank and leaps in, arms and all, he "anticipates" the feat of the legendary Roman hero Horatius Cocles,

---

156. *Aeneid* 2.547–53.

157. The similarity is noted by Macrobius, *Saturnalia* 5.9.14–15 in Kaster 2011, vol. 2, 306–7.

158. With *Aeneid* 9.791–96 compare *Iliad* 11.548–55 (Conington and Nettleship 1875, vol. 3, 220–21 on 789) and 17.657–64 (Menelaus withdrawing from the battle over Patroclus' body, Knauer 1964, 461–62).

159. With *Aeneid* 9.806–14 compare *Iliad* 16.102–11 (noted by Macrobius, *Saturnalia* 6.3.2–4 in Kaster 2011, vol. 3, 60–65).

160. Ennius, *Annals* fragment 15.3, lines 391–98 in Goldberg and Manuwald 2018, 314–17; on the tribune's identity see Skutsch 1985, 557–59.

who single-handedly defended an important bridge across the Tiber from an Etruscan incursion until his fellow soldiers could get across; then, while his comrades from the security of the right bank destroyed the bridge, Horatius prayed to the river god, leapt in arms and all, and swam to safety.[161]

Turnus thus ends this intertextual melee not as the Achilles that he wishes to be, but as Ajax, one of Achilles' would-be successors, and not his most successful one. On the other hand, Ennius had sanctioned and aligned this identity with Roman victory in his treatment of the "Siege of Ambracia." Beyond that, Turnus' prefiguration of the heroic Horatius at the bridge confers on him a measure of exemplary Romanness that is, for once, difficult to map according to Homeric or any other literary or cultural coordinates.

More Contested Identities

When Aeneas returns to battle in book 10, he wears the divine armor given him by his mother, just like Achilles in *Iliad* 19. With his arrival, Turnus' claim to be the new Achilles begins to look very weak. For the Sibyl's prediction to be correct, we must assume that Aeneas has undergone or is undergoing a kind of rebirth, perhaps symbolized or in some sense even caused by his new armor. Whatever is happening to him seems more powerful than Pyrrhus' "rebirth," resplendent as a serpent in Priam's palace, or Turnus' imitation of a fulminating Achilles in the Trojan settlement. If Achilles' return to battle in divine armor represents his "rebirth" as the hero of the *Iliad*, Aeneas' own return seems to mark his "rebirth" as the Achillean hero of the *Aeneid*. Even so, he does not yet fully understand, any more than Turnus does, all that it means to take Achilles' place.

Before Aeneas returns, in the "Council of the Gods" that opens book 10, Venus and Juno say many bitter things to each other, but one exchange is especially striking. Speaking first, Venus states that she is ready to bargain away Aeneas' life and promised destiny if only Ascanius might survive in some place that is dear to her. "By all means," she rants, "let Aeneas be tossed about on unknown waters" (10.48). Different critics understand this differently. Some say that Venus is exaggerating the hazards of Aeneas' voyage up the Tiber. Juno in her mocking reply shows that she takes Venus this way, or at least pretends to.[162] Other critics

---

161. Turnus has not yet relinquished his claim to Achillean status, however: Van Nortwick 1980, 304 finds his leap into the river (9.815–16) reminiscent of Achilles' two leaps into the Scamander (*Iliad* 21.18 and 233), a comparison not found in Knauer 1964.

162. "Did I urge him to leave camp and entrust his life to the winds?" (68–69). Juno may of course be speaking disingenuously to belittle Venus' concerns.

notice that Venus' words echo the poem's opening lines when the narrator notes that Aeneas was "much tossed about on land and on the deep": note in particular the metrically identical phrases *iactetur in undis*, "let him be tossed about on the water" (10.48) and *iactatus et alto*, "and tossed about on the deep" (1.3). She may therefore be imagining that if Italy is closed to Aeneas, he is really facing not a second Iliad but yet another Odyssey. In an eerily similar way, this critical uncertainty echoes Aeneas' own confusion upon entering the poem. In that first appearance, we recall, on the point of drowning in an Odyssean storm at sea, the hero recalls his comrades slain by Achilles and their corpses clogging the flow of an Iliadic river. Now we are made to ask whether Venus is referring hyperbolically to Aeneas' voyage up the Tiber—soon, as per the Sibyl, to be filled with Iliadic blood—in preparation for an imminent Trojan War Redux for which the hero thinks he is ready, or to future wanderings on Odyssean seas that he can never comprehend, this time perhaps to be drowned in another Junonian storm. Even at his late hour, the possibility of an Odyssean *Aeneid* is being debated, and in the poem's only "Council of the Gods," no less.

This council ends indecisively, with Jupiter declaring that "on this day" (*hodie* 107) he will allow the Trojan invaders and the Italian resistance to fight it out, showing no favoritism himself. One might still ask whether he is not putting his thumb on the scale. This is the day when Aeneas will return to battle, and Jupiter says precisely what Zeus says will happen in *Iliad* 20 when Achilles returns to battle "on this day" (*sêmeron* 127).[163] True, there are signals that Aeneas, despite his divine weaponry, is not yet Achilles' equal. As he sails down the Tiber, the Etruscan reinforcements that accompany him are described in a brief catalogue (163–214) that is a pendent to the "Catalogue of Italian Forces" in book 7, just as a less impressive Trojan catalogue follows the great catalogue of Greek forces at the end of *Iliad* 2. On the other hand, as

---

163. This seems like the right place for a word about Jupiter as a narrator, specifically with regard to the *Aeneid* as an Iliad, an Odyssey, both, or neither. Knauer 1964, 302 notes that the narrator, or poet (*Dichter*) as he calls him, comments that Turnus, by stripping Pallas of his armor, seals his own death, just as the Iliadic Zeus narrator comments that death is approaching Hector as he strips Patroclus of Achilles' armor (*Aeneid* 10.501–5, *Iliad* 16.799–800; compare 852–53, 17.198–208). This is also a key passage for Barchiesi 1984/2015, 25–32, whose discussion redefines the *Iliad*, differently from Knauer, not only as the original text but as the entire history of its interpretation. In spite of this difference, however, it appears to me that they agree in finding that this and similar episodes, including Jupiter's consolation of Hercules, cast the father of gods and king of men in a role much more in keeping with that of the Iliadic Zeus than of his Odyssean counterpart. I do not believe that Barchiesi would go so far as Knauer does to identify Jupiter with the narrator or poet, however, and neither would I. See Feeney 1991, 129–87; Hejduk 2009 and 2020, 72–78.

Stephen Harrison writes, "perhaps the most interesting Homeric parallel is that with the short catalogue of Myrmidons in *Il.* 16.168–97, which is closely similar in function in describing reinforcements to the ultimately victorious side which enter the battle late and at a crucial point."[164] That is certainly a more encouraging point of reference. Still, the Myrmidon catalogue of *Iliad* 16 does not accompany Achilles' return to battle. Those Myrmidons accompany Patroclus, who leads them in Achilles' place. By the same token, these Etruscans accompany Pallas. They are his father's allies and are glad for a chance to fight against their enemy Mezentius, who is allied with Latinus, an enemy of Evander. One could thus say that the Iliadic intertext is somewhat disturbed. In the *Iliad*, Patroclus precedes Achilles into battle, and it is his death that causes him to return. Instead, Aeneas and Pallas join the battle together.

There are nevertheless clear signs that Aeneas is readier for this fight than he has been for anything else in the poem thus far. When we find him going over in his mind the different courses that the coming war might take (10.159–60), this seems to be a more concrete version of his reassurance to the Sibyl that he is ready for the second Iliad to come. It is also encouraging that he takes time to field questions from Pallas, identifying constellations for the young man, commenting on their movement through the night sky, and telling him about his own adventures to this point (160–62). This is an exemplary scene of princely instruction, specifically on the eve of battle, with Aeneas at last in the position of teacher rather than pupil.[165] The hero will appear explicitly in the role of teacher one further and final time, with Ascanius as his student (12.432–40). Before going to what he thinks will be a decisive duel with Turnus, Aeneas tells his son, "Learn from me, boy, manhood [*virtutem* 435] and real labor, luck from others. Now my right hand will make you safe and lead you into great prizes [*praemia* 437]. You, soon, when you have come fully of age, be sure to remember, and as you ponder in your soul the ethical standards of your people [*exempla turoum* 439], let your father Aeneas and your uncle Hector inspire you."[166] At that crucial moment, Aeneas will offer himself to his son as an example of *virtus* that Ascanius may emulate when he becomes

---

164. Harrison 1991, 107 citing Knauer 1964, 297.

165. Harrison 1991, 105–6 on *Aeneid* 10.160–61 and 161–62 is excellent on these points, although I agree with Putnam 1985 that there is an erotic element in the passage. The combination of astronomical lore with questions about Aeneas' own adventures recalls the astronomical song of Iopas—allegorized by many critics as referring to the experiences of Dido and Aeneas in the past as well as the future—followed by Dido's eager questioning of Aeneas about the fall of Troy and the wanderings that brought him to Carthage.

166. See Kühn 1957, 37–39; Laird 1999, 192–94; Schmit-Neuerburg 1999, 155–61, 296–300; Bettini 2005/2006. Note Aeneas' emphasis on "prizes" (*praemia*) in light of both the "Footrace"

a ruler in his own right. It seems the culmination of an argument that has been developing from the beginning of the poem. At the same time, it has struck some critics as odd when Aeneas looks as far into the future as it is possible for him to do, that he continues looking backwards to the example of Hector, Troy's failed champion. If Troy could have been defended by force, Hector told Aeneas, he himself would already have done that. Nevertheless, Aeneas still proposes Hector as a source of inspiration equal to himself. Stranger still is a quotation in this scene of leave-taking that Aeneas cannot have intended but the reader cannot avoid noticing and interpreting as a comment on Aeneas' state of mind. It involves a "window reference" to Sophocles' *Ajax* via the Latin version of Lucius Accius. In both plays, Ajax is bidding farewell to his young son Eurysaces just before going to commit suicide.[167] The reminiscence implicitly compares Aeneas to another would-be successor of Achilles, one who coveted Achilles' arms as a sign of succession but lost them to Odysseus, a totally different hero and, in Ajax's eyes and in Aeneas' as well, a vastly inferior, utterly unworthy one. That is in fact the ultimate reason why Ajax ended his own life. What does this comparison tell us? That Aeneas does not expect to survive his duel with Turnus? That he does not want to? That he still harbors the death wish that was so prominent a part of his psychology from his first appearance in the poem and in the stories he tells about events from the past? Such an inference is hardly consistent with the idea that Aeneas' physical strength is about to make Ascanius safe and lead him into great prizes. It agrees, however, with the symbolic pairing of himself with Hector, the paradigmatic honorable soldier who dies in defense of his country, as Aeneas has so often said he wishes he had done. Perhaps the point is that even Achilles by attaining the summit of glory hastened his own death; although Aeneas' knowledge of the future, in spite of Anchises' teachings, in spite of the imagery on his shield, seems to be very limited, it would be like him to feel premonitions of death—perhaps especially if he feels himself to be even more an Achilles than Ajax or Hector. In any case, as Aeneas sails down the Tiber on his way to battle, he does not seem comparable to Ajax. Only later, when he goes to meet his rival, might a reader recall that Turnus too, as he withdrew from the Trojan camp the day before Aeneas' return, did so as an intertextual Ajax. More than any other hero, Ajax longed to be recognized as Achilles' successor. More than any other, except perhaps Achilles himself, he loathed Odysseus. In

---

and the "Nisus and Euryalus" episodes of books 5 and 9, and see Tarrant 2012, 204 on the unusual phrasing of *inter praemia ducet* at *Aeneid* 12.437.

167. See Sophocles, *Ajax* 550–51; Accius, *The Award of the Arms* fragment 123 in Warmington 1936, 2.366–67; Wigodsky 1972, 95–97; Lyne 1987, 8–10, 191–93; Panoussi 2002 and 2007, 177–217.

their similarity to Ajax, both Turnus and Aeneas are vying to become the next Achilles, and there is no Odysseus to challenge them.

Whatever Aeneas may believe after pondering the Sibyl's prophecy and receiving his god-wrought arms, after all that he has experienced he still cannot possibly foresee the course of the war in any detail. No more can the reader. Even though Aeneas appears to be on track to become the Achilles of this new Iliad, that does not mean that he is surrounded by a fixed cast of supporting characters. To come back to Pallas, it does not make things simpler that in his brief hour on the field of battle, he is the intertextual double not of Patroclus but of Sarpedon.[168] In one of the poem's most sublime moments, as Pallas' astonishingly powerful death scene draws near, Jupiter explicitly cites one of the most sublime moments of the *Iliad*, "The Death of Sarpedon," as a precedent for what is unfolding before the reader's eyes.[169] For a moment Pallas becomes almost as closely identified with Sarpedon as it is possible to be. Only when Turnus strips Pallas' baldric from his lifeless body does he become Patroclus. In telling of this act, the narrator mimics the Homeric narrator's account of Hector stripping Achilles' mortal armor from the body of Patroclus, commenting that the day would soon come when Turnus, like Hector, would give much to buy back the life of Pallas or Patroclus. As Pallas becomes Patroclus, so does Turnus' destiny not as the new Achilles, but as another Hector, begin to look inevitable.

Returning to battle in his divine armor, Aeneas is convincing as a potential Achilles, but he is not yet a complete one. Only when he fails to protect Pallas as he had sworn to do does his sense of shame and responsibility issue in the convincingly Achillean anger that he feels then for the first time, but not the last. Under the influence of that anger he mows down rows of enemies, very much in the manner of Achilles after the death of Patroclus, hunting down Turnus as Achilles had hunted Hector (10.510–605).[170] Aeneas does not find Turnus because Turnus finds himself playing an Achillean role at the same time, though hardly the one he would prefer. In the *Iliad*, the Trojan Agenor offers battle with Achilles, but Apollo wraps Agenor in mist, whisks him away, assumes Agenor's form, and runs, distracting Achilles so that the Trojans might withdraw to the safety of the city (21.537–22.24).[171] In the *Aeneid* it is

---

168. Indispensable here is Quint 2018, 150–79.

169. *Aeneid* 10.464–73, *Iliad* 16.431–61; see Barchiesi 1984/2015, 6–15; Farrell 1997, 236–37.

170. See, variously, Farron 1977; 1985; 1986; Putnam 1981/1995, 134–35; Renger 1985, 52–69; P. R. Hardie 1986, 154–56; Glei 1991, 218–20; Putnam 2011, 28–48.

171. Similarly at *Iliad* 20.419–54 Apollo wraps a mist around Hector and spirits him away to save him from Achilles, but no chase ensues.

Juno who fashions a phantom Aeneas for Turnus to chase (10.633–88).[172] The motives of god and goddess are very different: Apollo means to save Agenor from Achilles, while Juno means her phantom Aeneas to save Turnus from the real one. Turnus' humiliation when he learns the truth is warranted, especially if it is beginning to dawn on him that his cause is almost lost.[173] From the reader's perspective the motif of deception exposes Turnus' delusional confidence in his exalted intertextual identity. He is merely a false Achilles chasing a false Aeneas playing the role of a false Agenor.

While Turnus is being saved and humiliated, a plethora of greater and lesser avatars of Iliadic heroes briefly appear, briefly succeed, and are soon killed.[174] This welter of Homeric reminiscences can be seen as merely the intertextual equivalent of the fog of war. At the same time, patterns emerge, and the treatment of certain major figures is instructive. Mezentius, as Harrison writes, no sooner comes to the fore than "he is at once characterized by a series of recognizable Homeric warrior-similes . . . and this together with implicit comparisons with Hector and Achilles . . . establish him as a mighty hero of the traditional Homeric type and a fit opponent for Aeneas."[175] Specifically, with Turnus indisposed, the Etruscan tyrant assumes Turnus' intertextual ambition along with his military role.[176] At the height of his "Aristeia" (689–761), Mezentius slays a warrior who flees before him in an altogether emblematic way:[177]

> He did not deign to fell Orodes as he fled,
> nor deal an unseen wound by spear-cast;
> he ran to cut him off and confronted him man to man,
> face to face, being better not in subterfuge but in strength and arms.[178]
>   (*Aeneid* 10.732–35)

---

172. In the "Council of the Gods" Juno cites a similar Iliadic episode in which Aphrodite tries to rescue Aeneas from Diomedes, who wounds her and drives her away, leaving Apollo to envelop Aeneas in mist and take him to safety (10.81–82). She remembers it all as Venus' own doing, and can be regarded as imitating Venus here.

173. As it dawned on Juno in an exchange with Jupiter just before she resorted to this subterfuge (10.606–32)

174. Schweizer 1967, 55–63; Thome 1979, 48–89, 349–50; González Vázquez 1979–1980; Gotoff 1984; Reed 2006.

175. Harrison 1991, 236 on *Aeneid* 10.689–768.

176. For what follows see Knauer 1964, 307–8 note 3 (cited by Harrison, preceding note).

177. Again see Quint 2018, 67–68.

178. Orodes is the name of the Parthian king who destroyed the army of Marcus Licinius Crassus at the Battle of Carrhae in 53 BCE (Cassius Dio, *Roman History* 40.12.1). Mezentius' victory over this king's namesake is thus a bit of "future-reflexive" payback: Augustus' negotiated

Harrison rightly calls this "an expression of the heroic ethic."[179] More precisely, it is an Iliadic ethic, one that in deprecating "subterfuge" (*furto* 735) explicitly rejects an Odyssean alternative. Achilles is the paramount exemplar of Iliadic heroism, but in this case, the narrator's words echo those of Hector just before his duel with Telamonian Ajax:

> "But I do not wish to strike you, being what you are,
> by spying on you in secret, but openly, if I might hit you."[180]
>   (*Iliad* 7.243–44)

Mezentius brings down Orodes with a spear cast and "pressing with foot and spear upon the man he had cast down," he says,

> "Here lies tall Orodes, men, no contemptible part of this war."
> [Mezentius'] comrades follow him singing a joyous victory song;
> but Orodes said as he died, "Whoever you are, victor,
> you will not long rejoice while I am unavenged; the same fate
> awaits you, too, and soon the same ploughlands will hold you."
>   (*Aeneid* 10.737–41)

Here is another intertextual jump-cut, this time from what Hector says to Ajax before an inconclusive duel in *Iliad* 7 to what the dying Patroclus says to Hector in book 16:

> "No, you yourself will not live long, but already
> death and powerful fate are standing nearby." (*Iliad* 16.852–53)

Mezentius answers, smiling at Orodes with a bit of anger:

> "Die now. As for me, that's up to the father of gods
> and king of men." (*Aeneid* 10.743–44)

This is yet another jump-cut to *Iliad* 22, where Achilles says to the mortally wounded Hector:

> "Die. Then will I accept death, whenever
> Zeus and the other immortals wish to make it so."
>   (*Iliad* 22.365–66)

---

recovery of the Roman battle standards lost by Crassus was a major ideological success achieved in 20 BCE, the year before Vergil's death (Gruen 1996, 159).

179. Harrison 1991, 248 on *Aeneid* 10.734–35.

180. See Conington and Nettleship 1858–1898/1963, vol. 3, 291–92 and Harrison 1991, 248 on *Aeneid* 10.734–35.

Finally, as if to draw together these last two Iliadic moments, the narrator informs us that Mezentius,

> saying this, pulled the spear from his corpse. (*Aeneid* 10.744)

Just so at the death of Patroclus, Hector,

> saying this, the bronze-tipped spear from the wound
> he drew. (*Iliad* 16.862–63)

and just so after killing Hector, Achilles

> spoke and drew the bronze-tipped spear from his corpse.
> (*Iliad* 22.367)

Far from being a pastiche composed of randomly chosen typical motifs and epic diction, "The Death of Orodes" is a compelling micro-Iliad boiled down to its chivalrous, tragic, terrible essence. In a blindingly fast sequence, Mezentius is first Hector facing off against Ajax in what ends as a draw, then Hector felling Patroclus, then Achilles avenging Patroclus, and finally the dying Hector predicting Achilles' death and Achilles declaring his readiness for it. Thus does Mazentius, a powerful warrior, loathsome tyrant, and impious "contemnor of gods" enter a single encounter equivalent to a pair of Achilles' evenly matched, would-be successors, Ajax for the Greeks and Hector for the Trojans, then become Hector's equal in victory over Patroclus, and then grow into Achilles himself in victory over Hector—before being reminded that all heroes are equally mortal and that all will have the same end.

Orodes is a much less memorable character than Mezentius, but he attains a fleeting moment of great significance as an intertextual Patroclus, the victim of Mezentius *qua* Hector. That is easy to overlook because Lausus, a much more prominent character, becomes the next, more pathetic Patroclus. This is only to be expected: the narrator virtually declares that Lausus is Pallas' doppelgänger when he observes that the two were fated not to meet on the battlefield, but both would fall to a greater warrior (10.433–38). In Lausus' case, the greater warrior is Aeneas, who in a fit of Achillean *ira* avenges his own Patroclus by making Lausus another.[181] The narrator confirms this with the words,

> then in sorrow his life through the air
> withdrew towards the shades of the dead and left his body.
> (*Aeneid* 10.819–20)

---

181. "And now the Trojan leader's fierce anger was swelling higher" (*saevae iamque altius irae Dardanio surgunt ductori* 10.813–14; with *Dardanio ... ductori* compare *ductores Teucrum* (9.226; see note 138).

This renders the first half of the Homeric couplet that marks Patroclus' death:

> Flying out of his body, his soul went to Hades
> bemoaning its fate, leaving manhood and youth. (*Iliad* 16.856–57)

In the *Iliad*, that same couplet also describes the death of Hector (22.362–63). In the *Aeneid*, only the second line is repeated. It first marks the death of Camilla, the woman warrior who joins Turnus' resistance.[182] Then, in the very last line of the poem, the same line that marks the death of Camilla is bestowed on Turnus himself. Of both warriors, the narrator says, "and with a groan their life fled in protest to the shades below" (11.831, 12.952).[183] In one way the meaning of this repetition seems simple and direct; especially when considered retrospectively. When it first occurs, however, it greatly complicates the unfolding of this strange new Iliad. In the actual *Iliad*, the exact repetition just cited marks a causal relationship: both Patroclus and Hector die wearing the mortal arms of Achilles; Hector slays Patroclus, puts on the same armor, and suffers exactly the same fate when Achilles slays him in revenge. In the *Aeneid*, Turnus does not slay Camilla, nor do they wear the same arms; to avenge Pallas, Aeneas slays Turnus, not Camilla. Even more strangely, the person who does slay Camilla is himself a kind of Patroclus and even a kind of anti-Achilles, as well. When Arruns prays to Apollo of Soracte that he might bring down the virago, foreswearing any interest in trophies and promising, "I will return to my ancestral cities without renown" (*patrias remeabo inglorius urbes* 11.793), Apollo grants only half of his prayer.[184] This is what Zeus of Dodona does after Achilles prays that Patroclus might drive the Trojans back from the Greek ships and then return to camp (*Iliad* 16.220–52). Patroclus does drive the Trojans away and Arruns does make his kill, but neither of them returns alive. The shared motif of the half-answered prayer suggests that Arruns is both a kind of Patroclus and a kind of Achilles, because he makes Achilles' prayer for Patroclus into a prayer for himself.[185]

---

182. An "Amazonian" ally aligns Turnus with the Trojans of the Cyclic *Aethiopis*: see Knauer 1964, 308–10.

183. See Harrison 1991, 266 on *Aeneid* 10.819–20.

184. It is in his willingness to return home without glory that Arruns resembles Achilles before the latter relents and returns to battle. It is especially strange that he prays for this as well as for success in bringing down a great warrior. On this strange figure see Rosenmeyer 1960; Kepple 1976; Miller 1994; Fratantuono 2006.

185. Indeed, Achilles' concern is not just that Patroclus return, but that he do so after driving the Trojans back from the ships and relieving the pressure on the Greeks, not taking the battle to the city walls and so leaving the Trojans to wonder what Achilles himself might do to them. Achilles' concern is with himself as well as Patroclus.

Confused intertextual identities are bound to occur in any poem that follows the plot of another so extensively, but not exactly. Possibly divisions or multiplications of Iliadic characters such as I have been tracing are simply emergent phenomena or unintended consequences, like those that follow Juno's initial intervention in book 1. On the other hand, K. W. Gransden has made an observation about a crucial difference between the *Iliad* and the *Aeneid* that strikes me as apposite in this connection:

> In the *Iliad*, after nearly ten years of war, an attempt to end the war by single combat between Paris and Menelaus is aborted by divine intervention. The only heroes who "must" die in order to produce the narrative of the wrath of Achilles, are Patroclus and Hector. No other important heroes die in the poem. In the *Aeneid*, Aeneas must get rid of all his rivals as surely, and with as firm a basis in historical necessity, as Octavian had to.[186]

That is to look outside the literary intertext to the historical one, as it seems occasionally necessary to do. My contention is that neither the historical intertext nor any other "third way" can transcend the Homeric terms on which the narrative of the *Aeneid* unfolds, but that any one of these "third ways" may intensify the Homeric character of any given word, idea, episode, theme, or structure, up to and including that of the poem as a whole. In what follows I will consider a few additional historical referents that work with the literary intertext to encourage intuitions like the one I have just quoted.

The Reader's Sympathies

In book 11, before Camilla is drawn into the ever-expanding number of Patroclus avatars who must be killed off, Pallas' intertextual identity is fixed by the preparations for his funeral (29–99). In structural terms this episode corresponds closely to that of Patroclus' funeral in the *Iliad*, where it is also found near the beginning of the poem's penultimate book (23.108–225). Of all episodes in the Iliadic *Aeneid* that recall or reflect on the poem's earlier, Odyssean half, it may be the most powerful. As I have noted, the Homeric "Funeral Games of Patroclus" is an important model of "The Memorial Games for Anchises" in book 5, which performs a similar, socially reintegrative function. Aeneas' presidency of those games is successful and might have been even more so if Juno had not intervened to make the Trojan women burn the ships. This intervention is another aspect of a tendency for the plot of the *Aeneid* to move from comedy to tragedy. Here the same thing happens at a distance. It is hard

---

186. Gransden 1984, 171.

to miss the fact that in book 11, the cheerful, restorative, comic element of the "Games" lies far in the past, and only the grimly tragic business of burial—not only of Pallas, but of the many Trojan and Italian dead—remains.

Here I invoke the concept of tragedy in what might be considered a loose, almost vernacular way, in contrast with the usage of important scholarship that stresses the work performed by ancient tragedy as a civic institution. I explained above why I believe Aristotelian definitions of tragedy and comedy are worth remembering. A further point of reference is what Emily Wilson has named "tragic overliving." The concept is extremely relevant, as she has shown, to Aeneas, whose death wish looks like a form of "survivor guilt."[187] The Augustan period is not one that is especially well known for this malady, which is much more closely associated with several later regimes.[188] Still, it is impossible to believe that the civil wars and proscriptions from the early forties to the late thirties BCE failed to take this form of psychological toll.[189] Frankly, it would not be absurd to say that the *Aeneid* is, in the end, entirely about this. If it is, then its tragic character would indeed play some role in processing the trauma of the recent past. That said, no form of grieving is ever a simple or straightforward process. I cannot imagine how any institutional or artistic experience can be expected fully to contain the energy of such grief and dependably channel it only into social cohesion, or trusted not to exacerbate the very tensions that it was meant to resolve.

In the *Iliad*, even after taking his revenge on Hector, burying his friend, and presiding over the more celebratory ritual of the "Games," Achilles is hardly reconciled to his loss. He continues to abuse Hector's dead body, or try to (since the gods will not allow it to suffer further). Only Priam's determination to humble himself by asking Achilles in person to let him ransom his son's corpse allows the father and his people to impose some measure of closure on their bitter experiences. It is all too true that the *Aeneid* does not end that way. Not only does Pallas' funeral happen before Aeneas takes his revenge, but his body is sent to Pallanteum for burial; Aeneas takes part in the preparations for this ceremony, but he does not witness it. In this and other ways, Pallas' burial itself, unlike Patroclus' or Hector's, is virtually bereft of closural significance. Instead of performing the work to which the *Iliad* devotes its last two books in their entirety, it becomes the occasion for reflecting on those forces that

---

187. "The *Aeneid* is, before *Paradise Lost*, the epic most concerned with the sense of overliving" (Wilson 2004, 13).

188. On survivor guilt in imperial authors see Beutel 2000; Zarifopol-Illias 2000; Freudenburg 2001, 215–34; Baraz 2012.

189. A. Powell 1998 makes many of the essential points.

resist social integration and closure. Let us consider the episode from that point of view.

In the heat of battle during book 10, Aeneas takes eight men captive, intending them to be sacrificed on Pallas' funeral pyre. It is one of his most explicitly Achillean moments.[190] It also pertains to the poem's contemporary frame of reference. Richard Heinze connected this ghastly parallel with a report by Suetonius that the young Caesar—that is, the future Augustus—once sacrificed three hundred captives to his father, the deified Julius, during the civil wars.[191] The report may be false: as Stephen Harrison writes, "even if it were true an allusion to it in a poem which otherwise lauds the *princeps* seems fundamentally unlikely."[192] I agree with this; and yet, even if the story is untrue, it does not seem like the kind of story that would have been invented long after the fact, when Augustus had become Augustus not merely in name, a process that took decades. A spurious accusation pertaining to the Triumviral period would not have been invented long after the supposed event, nor would its memory have died out when the *Aeneid* was taking shape. Even if it is false, *risking the perception of* an allusion to this story in a poem which otherwise lauds the *princeps* seems fundamentally unwise.

Or does it? Augustan panegyric and even Augustan self-praise is a remarkably complex business. In considering tragedy as a "third way," I briefly discussed Stefano Rebeggiani's analysis of the paired themes of revenge and madness, which turns on Augustus' own discursive identification with Achilles and Orestes as mythical avengers. The logic is that Achilles stands for the use of overwhelming force motivated by overwhelming anger to avenge a friend, Orestes for overcoming madness associated with vengeful killing within a family. If that is how it is meant to work—yes, there was bloodshed, but there was also anger, and a kind of madness; but that has passed, and anyway, that's heroic behavior—it seems a high-risk strategy, not unlike that of associating Aeneas with human sacrifice. In any case, is it really possible for anything that the ancestral hero does not to reflect on Augustus?

When Achilles sacrifices Trojan victims on Patroclus' pyre, he is not concerned to be reconciled with his enemy. That makes his unexpected reconciliation with Priam at the end of the poem all the more powerful. Before that, his main motive is to atone for the death of his friend and to rejoin the Greek

---

190. *Aeneid* 10.517–20, 11.81–82, *Iliad* 21.26–33, 23.175–83; see Putnam 2011, 21–30.

191. Suetonius, *Augustus* 15; Appian, *Civil War* 1.541–42; Cassius Dio, *Roman History* 48.14.4; Heinze 1915/1993, 187–88, note 44; cf. Kraggerud 1987; Farron 1985, 21–33; Horsfall 2003, 96–98 on *Aeneid* 11.82.

192. Harrison 1991, 203 on *Aeneid* 10.517–20.

social collective. Aeneas' position is entirely different. Like Achilles, he has failed his young friend and the young friend's father, having promised Evander he would look after his son.[193] The hero may be trying to make amends to an important ally who, even if he is a "good man," is Latinus' enemy and so may regard sacrificing Latin victims as just. The point of this war, though, is that Aeneas must marry Latinus' daughter and live out his life among Latin neighbors. By incorporating this act of barbarism into Pallas' funeral while dispensing with the comic and restorative sequel of the "Games," the *Aeneid* does everything possible to deprive this Iliadic episode of any socially integrative function that it might have had and to emphasize Aeneas' terribly heroic isolation.

THE ODYSSEAN *ILIAD*, PART 2: WORDS AND DEEDS

The Renaissance commentator Cerda, as I noted previously, after embracing Servius' position that the *Aeneid* consists of a six-book Odyssey followed by a six-book Iliad, softened his stance by observing that there are episodes of Iliadic warfare in the first half of the poem and also of Odyssean "diplomacy" in the second.[194] One such episode comes into play after the preparations for Pallas' funeral. As the boy's cortege leaves for Pallanteum, Aeneas is approached by a delegation of Latin ambassadors, who are called *oratores* (100). This means "orators," of course, but also "ambassadors," a usage that Nicholas Horsfall calls "a distinctive Ennian archaism," which it is.[195] Elsewhere in the *Aeneid*, "ambassadors" are simply *legati*, the regular, somewhat prosaic word.[196] In addition to its dignified tone, however, the word *oratores* performs thematic work in accessing the proverbial contrast between words and deeds, which is extremely relevant here, as we shall see.

The ambassadors request an armistice so that they might bury their fallen comrades. Aeneas replies magnanimously: "You ask me to grant peace to those who are dead and taken from us by the fortunes of war? I would willingly make this concession to the living" (11.110–11). Saying nothing about Lavinia, Aeneas

---

193. As Achilles also failed Menoetius, Patroclus' father (Eichhoff 1825, 3.264–65 comparing *Aeneid* 11.45–46 with *Iliad* 18.328–33).

194. See chapter 1, note 26.

195. Horsfall 2003, 105 on *Aeneid* 11.100, with reference to the hundred "envoys" (*oratores*) mentioned at *Aeneid* 7.153 and to Ennius, *Annals* fragment **6.17 (line 202) in Goldberg and Manuwald 2018, vol. 1, 212–13: *orator sine pace redit regique refert rem* ("the honest envoy returns without a peace and refers the matter to the king"). For discussion of the assignment of this passage to *Annals* 6 see Skutsch 1985, 364–65.

196. See *Aeneid* 8.143, 11.227, 239, 296.

blames Turnus for causing the war and offers to settle the matter with him in single combat. The ambassadors look at each other in momentary surprise, and then one of them speaks to this point.

The name of this *orator* is Drances, "an older man who always opposes young Turnus with hateful accusations" (122–23).[197] He immediately lives up to this introduction when he addresses Aeneas. "Great in fame," he calls the hero, "greater in arms, man of Troy, in what terms shall I praise you to heaven, admiring first your justice or your works of war?" (124–26). This is more than diplomatic grandiloquence. Because Drances is introduced as the enemy of Turnus, and has been given an opening, he flatters Aeneas in the most shameless way, because he is much more interested in the prospect of a duel than a truce. He confirms this when he treacherously promises to reconcile Aeneas to King Latinus—or, more literally, to "join" them (*iungemus* 129), a word that hints at a marriage alliance—and presumably let Turnus fend for himself.[198]

Several Iliadic passages illuminate this exchange, but there is one from the Epic Cycle that I do not believe has been discussed. We have encountered it in the depiction on Juno's temple of Aeneas "among the foremost of the Greeks" (1.488). The reader will recall that this intertext alludes to the tradition that Aeneas treacherously negotiated with the Greeks for safe passage out of Troy. I have explained why I do not believe that allusion to this tradition undermines Aeneas' own account of his actions during "The Sack of Troy." At this point, however, we are not looking at pictures on a temple in a hostile city, nor are we listening to the potentially self-serving account of an unreliable narrator. This time, Aeneas is, in fact, negotiating with the enemy for his own self-interest; or, if you prefer, Drances is negotiating with the foremost of his enemy for personal and political advantage. It is a big departure from anything that has yet happened in the poem.

This episode should be fresh in the reader's memory not long afterwards when Latinus holds a war council to consider his position (225–444).[199] His counselors are divided on how to proceed. Among them is Drances, now described as "relentless in his opposition" (*idem infensus* 336). It is not a question of "loyal opposition," and some may feel that my rendering of *infensus* is much too bland. The word connotes active hostility and dangerous threat; but Drances pursues his aims deviously, so much so that he seems almost entirely

---

197. On Drances see Burke 1978; McDermott 1980; Scholz 1999; Horsfall 2002; Fröhlich 2011.

198. Compare Juno's statements, "I will join (her to you/him) in proper marriage," *conubio iungam stabili* 1.73, 4.126, discussed above in chapter 1, "In Medias Res" and chapter 2, "Juno's Argonautic Diversion."

199. See La Penna 1971/1999, 173–78; P. R. Hardie 1998; Rieks 1989, 41–43; Horsfall 1995, 186–91; Suerbaum 1998, 365–67; Fantham 1999; Pagán 2010.

out of place in heroic poetry.[200] Like someone more at home in contemporary parliamentary debate, he speaks in favor of peace, but that is far from his main concern. Like Aeneas before, Latinus now gives him an opening by proposing, among other things, generous concessions of Rutulian territory in return for ending the war. Drances seconds these measures, which would affect Turnus and his people, but he proposes one other: Turnus must also relinquish any claim to Lavinia in favor of Aeneas. This is good advice, of course. Here, however, the way in which the proposal comes about colors the reader's perception of it. Latinus, a sensible if also an ineffectual king, sees that a costly war is in no one's interest. What he fails to see, or lacks the courage to acknowledge, is that Lavinia's marriage is the crux of the matter. It is left for another to raise this point. Drances can be counted on to do so, but he makes a great show of faux-diffidence:

> "O good king, you are asking for advice about a point that no one
>   finds unclear
> and that does not require a word from me. All admit that they know
> what outcome our fortune is bringing us, but they don't say it clearly.
> Let him put an end to his bluster and give me freedom to speak—
> I will say it indeed, though he threaten me with weaponry and death—
> that man under whose ill-starred leadership and untrustworthy
>   character
> we see that so many of our brightest champions have fallen,
> and the entire city has sunk down in grief." (*Aeneid* 11.343–50)

Drances' opponent is Turnus, of course, and this *orator* makes a great show of casting him as an opponent of free speech in the public interest—as, in this instance, he certainly is—and of casting himself as its champion. But the situation is rich and complex. Drances must be right: everyone is wondering whether anything but a marriage alliance would satisfy Aeneas. Latinus himself has regarded Aeneas as the suitor foretold by fate, all along.[201] Because he is a weak character and a weak king, he is afraid to speak directly to the issue in Turnus' presence. Drances, in contrast, welcomes the opportunity, because he has made it his business in life to oppose Turnus.

We learn in this episode that Drances is a man of words, not deeds, the son of an aristocratic mother and an obscure father. His intertextual ancestry is

---

200. "Perhaps because his character is so completely un-epic, Virgil allows himself for once a detailed thumbnail sketch more in the style of a prose historian": Quinn 1968, 240–41; see also Horsfall 2002.

201. See *Aeneid* 7.52–106, 249–58.

also of interest.[202] He has been likened especially to Thersites in the war council of *Iliad* 2; Drances' hatred of Turnus finds a point of contact in Thersites' constant abuse of Achilles and Odysseus (*Iliad* 2.220–21). Further, as Thersites has made it his business to challenge the Greek leaders in general (2.214–15), Drances is "adept at fomenting civic unrest" (*seditione potens* 11.340). Again like Thersites, who correctly points out that Agamemnon is wrong to dishonor Achilles, Drances makes a proposal that is not only perfectly reasonable but actually essential, namely, that Turnus renounce any claim to Lavinia. By the same token, in *Iliad* 7 the Trojans hold a war council in which Antenor advocates the return of Helen to the Greeks, a proposal that Paris immediately rejects.[203] In *Aeneid* 11, when Drances makes his proposal, Turnus does not speak directly to the issue of Lavinia, but he does offer to meet Aeneas in single combat, if the Trojans demand this and it is Latinus' pleasure (434–37). Thus Turnus sways Latinus and the entire council away from Drances' sound, if malevolent proposal, much as in *Iliad* 18 Hector rejects Poulydamas' sound and benevolent recommendation against making the Trojan defenders spend the night outside the city walls; after coming so close to taking the Greek encampment earlier that day, Hector would have none of Poulydamas' good advice, and the council followed him (254–313). For both Hector and Turnus these failures to heed sound advice would prove fatal.

Much like "The Aristeia of Mezentius" in the previous book, then, the war council recapitulates the development of a crucial Iliadic motif. In the former case it was the defining Iliadic motif of hand-to-hand combat as the ultimate arbiter of *andreia* or *virtus*; here it is rather the efficacy of words versus arms in settling differences. In the *Iliad*, Thersites is all talk, and is not only made to be quiet but is beaten for his insolence; then a sensible proposal by the counselor Antenor is vetoed by Paris, a very inferior warrior who was barely rescued from certain death when he faced Menelaus in a duel that would have settled the matter of Helen; and finally Poulydamas is defined precisely as Hector's opposite number in the fields of counsel and arms: "He was companion to Hector, and they were born on the same night; but the one prevailed in words, the other with the spear" (*Iliad* 18.251–52). The sequence of Iliadic counselors that contribute to the complex figure of Drances begins with a man as different as possible from the heroes that he reviles and ends with one who is as much like one of those heroes as he can possibly be. From another point of view,

---

202. The "Homeric antecedents" of his speech are "unexpectedly complex" (Horsfall 2003, 221 on 343–75). Gransden 1984, 176–77 gives a particularly clear and concise account of Drances' Iliadic counterparts.

203. *Iliad* 7.345–64; the episode is recalled by Horace as damning evidence of Paris' kingly incompetence in *Epistles* 1.2.9–11.

although the ugly Thersites is the absolute opposite of Achilles, the paradigmatic man of action, not words, he is not altogether unlike Odysseus. In "The Review from the Walls of Troy" in *Iliad* 3, Odysseus strikes the Trojans as not much to look at, but as a wonder when he begins to speak. In book 2, after Odysseus uses his remarkable powers of persuasion to put down a mutiny, Thersites rises to say his piece against Agamemnon. In response, Odysseus does not waste many words before resorting to blows—symbolically using a speaker's staff as his weapon (265–69). Much as the Iliadic sequence of counselors ends with Poulydamas as Hector's doppelgänger, so it begins with Thersites as that of Odysseus. These relationships bring out more sharply the similarities as well as the differences between Drances and Turnus, as is especially true when Drances keeps expressing concern that by speaking his mind he is actually endangering his life. It is as if he were baiting Turnus to resort to blows, as Odysseus does. When Turnus responds instead with a surprisingly effective speech of his own (376–444), the spirit of the Iliadic Odysseus seems to animate the entire exchange, even though Turnus not only cites his own achievements in the previous day's battle but, as is his wont, persistently describes the conflict in Iliadic terms.

FIGURES OF DISSENT

The case of Drances is just one indication that opposition or dissent in the *Aeneid* is a slippery matter. As a character he is defined by his opposition to Turnus. He speaks, however, not in open opposition but in support of Aeneas and his mission. He embodies the hateful dictum, "the enemy of my enemy is my friend." It is the reader's privilege and the interpreter's burden to know that Drances' support for Aeneas—and, by extension, for everything that Aeneas' mission represents, down to and including the Augustan regime itself—is motivated by base reasons of personal animus on the part of an unappealing character invented for this special role. To make matters worse, before advancing his proposal in the war council Drances wraps himself in the mantle of free speech (*libertatem fandi* 346), even courageous speech in the face of personal danger ("I will say it indeed, though he threaten me with weaponry and death!" 348). Perhaps for this and other reasons, some scholars have suggested that Drances alludes to the historical Cicero, whom others believe is being snubbed when Anchises states that different nations will surpass the Romans in the orator's art.[204] I would not myself recommend reading these passages in

---

204. For this interpretation and a refutation of it see Horsfall 2003, 116 on *Aeneid* 11.122–32, with further references.

such *ad hominem* terms, but I do find in both Drances and Anchises a certain skepticism if not actual hostility to forms of *libertas* that were characteristic of the Republic and that arguably contributed to its chaotic demise. As I mentioned previously in discussing the first and the second Brutus, the word *libertas* was a watchword of Julius Caesar's assassins, the first group upon whom Caesar's heir felt compelled to take revenge. Perhaps all the more if Drances anticipates the last champions of the Republic, he is no defender of real *libertas*; rather, he is merely a *delator*, an imperial-era "informer" *avant la lettre*.[205] He combines elements of several Homeric dissenters, including Thersites, a Greek and a bad man who insincerely took the part of the greatest of the Achaeans and was punished for it, and Poulydamas, a Trojan and a good man whose sound advice would have saved his people's greatest champion, but was ignored. In the figure of Drances all the complexity of opposition as it appears in the *Aeneid* is summed up; easy judgment—indeed, any convincing judgment about the absolute value of opposition to or agreement with the master narrative seems impossible.

This complex case points to a surprisingly simple truth. In the *Aeneid*, those who adopt a stance of opposition, regardless of their personal worth, very often get what they want—not all of them, and not always immediately, but many and eventually. From the largest perspective, that is the story of the Trojans and their Roman descendants. By refusing to accept annihilation at the hands of the Greeks, they come to rule over all of the Greeks, centuries later, en route to obtaining a world empire.[206] On a vastly smaller scale, Drances fails to convince the Italian leaders to abandon Turnus and welcome Aeneas; but in the end he sees Aeneas plunge his sword deep into Turnus' chest. He gets what he wants, perhaps even foreseeing this as the likeliest outcome of his proposal. For this reason we would do well to keep our eye trained on the ultimate resolution of opposition and protest in all their forms.

Simpler and less sinister forms of opposition reinforce this initial impression. In the "Games" of book 5 opposition and protest have no effect on the course of the narrative. Not only in the foot race but in all of the events awards are lavished on winners and losers alike (340–61). More consequential is the disaffection of the Trojan women who burn the ships to avoid journeying any farther (604–99). Aeneas rewards them as well by founding a new city, Segesta, and making their Trojan cousin Acestes their king (767–71). Much later in the First Punic War the people of Segesta would appeal to the Romans for

---

205. See Rutledge 1999.

206. On the winners and losers as defining a structural principle in the *Aeneid* and a constitutive theme of epic poetry in general Quint 1993 remains fundamental.

protection against Carthage on the basis of this shared ancestry.[207] Palinurus too fits into a general pattern of protest rewarded, even if the implications of his case are not so far-reaching. Not once but twice he protests the requirements of Fate. When Sleep tries persuasion to make him relinquish his post, the helmsman replies indignantly, so that the god must use force to make him accept what Fate requires. Aeneas later finds Palinurus in the underworld, still seeking to get around his fate by gaining transport across the River Styx instead of wandering aimlessly for a thousand years (6.337–71). The Sibyl puts an end to this dream, but tells Palinurus to take comfort because the place where he died will be called after him (as indeed it is). There is an enormous gap between the momentary pleasure that Palinurus takes in this news (N.B. *parumper* 382, "for a little while") and the fact that Capo di Palinuro still "glories in his name."[208] Still, he will have his reward, however meager.

What is the reader to make of such events? Insincere orators successfully oppose the leaders of their people by cozying up to invaders. Cheaters complain about their bad luck and thus obtain prizes. Disaffected refugees mutiny and are rewarded with their own city. Are these instances of "real" opposition or merely of Fate working in mysterious ways? Do the principal actors know, or care, whether they are working with Fate or against it? Should they? If we focus on episodes such as these, we may well conclude that opposing Fate is the primary means by which "what must be" is finally realized.

It is not always so easy, though. There are counter-examples, and famous ones. I have already mentioned Amata, whose funeral will coincide with her daughter's marriage.[209] Among mortals, it is perhaps she who is most openly and actively opposed to what Fate requires, and with her no accommodation is possible: she is driven first mad and then to suicide. Although to many her treatment seems unjust, my impression is that most readers feel little actual pity for her. In itself, her death confirms, logically as well as emotionally, that there are limits to how far the *Aeneid* can go in appeasing those who oppose what its narrative requires. On the other hand there is Dido, who also opposes Aeneas' mission in a way that clearly cannot be accommodated and, like

---

207. Diodorus of Sicily, *Library of History* 23.5.1 in Walton 1966, 88–89; Zonaras, *Epitome of History* 8.5.

208. In *gaudet cognomine terra* (383) I take *cognomine* as a substantive and *terra* as nominative, the subject of *gaudet*: for details see Farrell 2008a.

209. On Amata see Heinze 1915/1993, 150–52; Otis 1964, 324–25; Buchheit 1963, 102–8; La Penna 1967; Schweizer 1967, 22–34; Zarker 1969; Burke 1976; Voisin 1979; Lyne 1987, 13–27; Brazouski 1991, 129–36; Cardinali 1995; Fantham 1998; Keith 2000, 75–76; Carney 1988; Bocciolini Palagi 2001 and 2006; Boëls-Janssen 2007; Panoussi 2007, 124–33; Mac Góráin 2013, 134–37 and 143–44.

Amata, is driven first mad and then to suicide. Her treatment too seems unjust, and the reader's pity for her is profound.

Even more complex is a character like Laocoon, another opponent of Fate, who with a passionate address tries to prevent the wooden horse from entering Troy (2.40–56, 199–249). His protest must be ineffectual, but what he says is perfectly true: the horse is a trap, and it ultimately becomes, after long years of war and apparent deliverance, the instrument of Greek victory. He is a Cassandra figure, as her brief appearance at the end of the episode quietly reminds us (246–47). He is not merely disbelieved, however, but is dramatically destroyed, along with his two innocent sons for good measure, even while he is sacrificing to Neptune.[210]

Laocoon's tale is told by Aeneas with pity and remorse, not to say self-reproach. That is, Aeneas makes clear own his sympathy with Laocoon, even though Laocoon must be counted as an opponent of Aeneas' mission. This is not surprising, since Aeneas is the character who registers the most affecting opposition to his own mission, especially in resentful comments on his fate and the fates of others whom he envies. His dissatisfaction with the order of things appears in many guises. It appears in his epitaph for Rhipeus, "the single most just man among the Trojans and most observant of the right, although the gods thought otherwise" (*dis aliter visum* 2.428). It appears in his insistent wish to have died at Troy (as when he first enters the poem, blessing those who fell there, 1.94–95), or else to live in a pathetic facsimile of Troy like Buthrotum (3.493–94), or, best of all, to be living in an unfallen Troy (as he says when he abandons Dido, 4.340–44). It appears in his unwitting quotation of Ajax before he enters his final battle (12.435–36). Aeneas' disaffection is a defining element of his character. To be sure, he grows from the almost suicidal, dysfunctional leader of book 1 into a more decisive and capable one by book 12. But I cannot agree with those who find him ever accepting his fate with wholehearted approval. Whether he actually learned anything from "The Parade of Heroes," whatever he may have recognized in the omen announcing the arrival of his divine armor, whether he was duty-bound to rouse himself to anger for the final battle or the anger that welled up in him spontaneously represents his moral downfall—no matter how each of us settles these issues for herself or himself, one thing, I think, is clear. Aeneas' personal desire is not to do any of the things that Fate and the gods require him to do. He grows by experience, only in that he becomes better able to do what he must, which means suppressing his desire; but that desire remains the same: to become a proper Homeric

---

210. On Laocoon see Kleinknecht 1944; Paratore 1979; Zintzen 1979; Lynch 1980; Pietsch 1980; Tracy 1987; Erler 1992 and 2009; Rüpke 1993; Petter 1994; Bruno 2011; Pigón 2011.

hero; and the *Aeneid*, as I have been arguing, is the story of how he reaches this goal. Who, in the end, is he?

Resolutions and Rewards

The most famous example of protest rewarded, and rewarded lavishly, brings our attention back to Juno.[211] Late in book 12, Jupiter, although introduced as "king of all-powerful Olympus," addresses Juno as his spouse (*coniunx* 793). He thus speaks to their relationship as husband and wife, but also to her particular remit over marriage, framing his speech as one concerned with conjugal harmony, but with world-historical issues very much in play.

On the divine plane, it is important in so many ways that these two most exalted of divinities be reconciled and for marital discord to be finally dispelled. Juno's first act in the *Aeneid* is to reprise Hera's role in "The Deception of Zeus," abusing her power as tutelary goddess of marriage to get Aeolus to trespass on a more powerful god's element.[212] In book 4 she returns to the same episode.[213] Throughout the poem she is at odds with her husband, and she repeatedly abuses her authority over marriage to alter the plot. The unintended consequences, which immediately affect the intertextual identity of the poem, continue to reverberate down to the era of the Punic Wars. In books 7–12, her intervention via Allecto to preserve Turnus' engagement to Lavinia effectively destroys the marriage of Lavinia's mother even before Amata takes her own life. Here at last, weary of his wife's relentless opposition, Jupiter delivers a tactful but firm and unmistakable message. The battle is over. There is no point in deferring what is inevitable. Juno's recent stratagems have become an embarrassment unworthy of a great divinity. "The end is at hand," he says. "You have been able to pursue the Trojans by land and sea, to incite unspeakable war, to disgrace a house and mix the wedding hymn with lamentation." With those words Jupiter returns to the theme of marriage as he approaches the end of this speech, and does so in such a way as to make it clear that Juno has effectively turned what might have been a comedy into a tragedy: there will be a wedding, but also a funeral. Jupiter is thinking of Amata's suicide, which not only marks the end of her life and her marriage but also ensures that her

---

211. See Buchheit 1963, 133–50; Schweizer 1967, 5–14; Suerbaum 1967, 184–190; Kühn 1971, 162–67; Johnson 1976, 123–27; Mack 1978, 83–84; Feeney 1984 and 1991, 146–52; Lyne 1987, 79–81; Gottlieb 1998; Hershkowitz 1998; Dyson 2001, 211–27; Hejduk 2009 and 2020, 80–83.

212. See the section in chapter 1 entitled "In Medias Res."

213. See the section in chapter 2 entitled "Juno's Argonautic Diversion."

daughter's wedding will be full of grief. There will of course be many other funerals, too.[214]

In view of how important the motif of conjugal reunion is at the end of the *Odyssey*, it is hardly tendentious to read Jupiter's message to Juno in Odyssean terms.[215] The *Aeneid* might have ended as a comic affirmation of marriage.[216] Instead, thanks to the goddess of marriage herself, it risks ending as a tragedy instead. Enough damage has been done. Jupiter's final sentence is one of the most direct and unequivocal utterances that anyone makes in the poem: "I forbid you to try anything further" (12.803–6).

Amazingly, Juno's reply is almost like the response of one who didn't hear Jupiter at all. It is remarkable for its sheer gall, and also for Juno's response to Jupiter's playing the marriage card. She begins by admitting that she has acted unbecomingly, but then immediately shifts some of the blame to Turnus' sister, Juturna, for her excessive zeal on her brother's behalf. Naming Juturna is rhetorically effective as a reminder of how much Juno herself has had to put up with, Jupiter's innumerable peccadilloes being a defining characteristic of their bizarre marriage. She also makes the more specific point, which is no less forceful for being left implicit, that if Jupiter had not raped Juturna and then "rewarded" her with immortality, Turnus' sister would never have had the power to cause so much trouble.[217] Juno follows up with an oath by the River Styx and a general show of submissiveness, then makes an important concession specifically regarding marriage: the Trojans and Italians will "make a peace on the basis of propitious marriage rites."[218] The main point of reference is to

---

214. *luctu miscere hymenaeos* (*Aeneid* 12.805), with reference to Amata's suicide (593–611) in advance of her daughter's inevitable marriage to Aeneas; but the phrase would almost equally well describe the ghastly pseudo-marriage between Dido and Aeneas that Juno engineers in book 4 (160–72).

215. Hejduk (2009) 304–7.

216. As D. A. West 1998 argues it actually does.

217. The narrator informs the reader about Jupiter and Juturna just before Juno archly addresses the nymph as her favorite among all of Jupiter's illicit sexual partners—the ones from Latium, that is (12.138–45). She does this when she informs Juturna that her brother is doomed, but that she must do whatever she can to save Turnus, if possible (146–60). Juturna's lament for Turnus and her own lost mortality follows the omen that Jupiter sends directly after his reconciliation with Juno (843–86).

218. Knauer 1964, 322–27 argues that the agreement between Jupiter and Juno is based on one between Zeus and Athena to prevent warfare between Odysseus and the suitors' families. In each poem Zeus or Jupiter calls for "oaths" between the two sides (*horkia* 483, *foedera* 822) and issues a similarly phrased injunction, "**let there be peace** aplenty" (*eirênê halis estô* 486) and "**peace on the basis of propitious marriages; so be it**" (*conubiis pacem felicibus: esto* 821). Conversely, as

the marriage of Aeneas and Lavinia, but Juno has in mind the plethora of marriages destined to take place between Trojan settlers and Italian brides. Nevertheless, she insists that somehow the issue of these propitious unions be not Trojan but entirely Latin, Alban, and eventually Roman. That is to say, she asks Jupiter to accomplish what she has been unable to achieve on her own throughout the entire poem: if not the eradication, then at least the erasure of Troy as a nation, a people, and a name: "Do not bid the native Latins change their ancient name, or become Trojans, or be called Teucrians, or change their speech or dress. . . . Troy has fallen, and let it be fallen, name and all" (823–28).

As Ralph Johnson made chillingly clear so long ago, the cheerfulness with which Jupiter accepts these terms is astonishing, as is the new way in which he now addresses Juno. He smiles at her and says, "you are the very *sister of Jupiter* (*germana Iovis* 830) and a second child of Saturn, who churn such floods of anger in your breast. But come, put down that fury, needlessly conceived: I grant your wish and, vanquished and glad, surrender myself to you. The people of Ausonia will keep their ancestral speech and culture, their name be as it is; sharing bloodlines only, the Teucrians will subside (*subsident Teucri* 836)."[219] Having begun this negotiation as a husband issuing a direct order to his wife, Jupiter ends by meeting Juno's astounding demands and addressing her as his sibling. As a restoration of marital harmony, then, their exchange is not very convincing, especially when Juno, after obtaining what she wants, immediately quits the scene, leaving her husband, or brother, behind (841–42). Whatever hierarchies of power govern their relationship in the pantheon or in their marriage, as a child of Saturn Juno is Jupiter's equal, and in one way his superior: she, not he, is most like their father in temperament.[220] Familiar, no doubt, from long experience with what he is up against, Jupiter cuts his losses and makes a generously irenic concession to a protesting loser.[221]

No one can say that Juno gets everything she wants. Although she has an enormous effect on the plot of the *Aeneid*, she never gains full control of the narrative. The question is whether her bid for control was real and effective or

---

Knauer notes, Homer follows up this agreement with one in which Athena prevents Odysseus from making war on the suitors' families, and there is no such follow-up in the *Aeneid*.

219. On Jupiter's "optimistic prophecy" that seems to promise the cultural obliteration of Troy in spite of the continuities between Troy and Rome that pervade the *Aeneid* see O'Hara 1990, 141–44; Reed 2010, 68–69; more generally, Toll 1991 and 1997.

220. Lyne 1989, 173–77.

221. The similarity between Aeneas' smile in book 5 and Jupiter's smile here was first noted by Kraggerud 1968, 226–29. Theodorakopoulos 2004 stresses Aeneas' similarity as he presides over the games to Jupiter as he placates Juno in book 12, and also to Augustus' performative adjudication of athletic contests. Further exploration of these relationships by Uden 2014.

merely an illusion. From the very first lines she is preceded by her reputation as a character who refuses simply to accept what Fate or any narrator gives her. Whether her suspicion of this poem's narrator is justified we will never know. Is the story as it turns out exactly the one that he meant to tell all along, or did Juno force him to tell a different one, making the *Aeneid*, in a very significant sense, her poem? It is glaringly true that the results of her interventions are not so much futile as contrary to her interests in their outcome. Evidently fearing that the poem will become an Odyssey *avant la lettre*, she is not very effective in preventing it from doing so. She may even cause it to become one for most of its first six books. Eminently qualified interpreters believe that the *Aeneid* is an Odyssey from start to finish. On the other hand, even they agree that after Juno intervenes again in book 7, and even more clearly by book 9, an unmistakably Iliadic plot starts to assert itself in the final books.[222] Does Juno bring this about? In some sense, yes. All of her interventions are at least instrumental in giving the poem the shape that it has, in both narrative and intertextual terms. However, if the question is whether this second Iliad is the one that she wanted and expected, then the answer is obviously no. Her hero is about to die. She has abandoned the resistance, at least for the time being. The *Aeneid* can move quickly towards its fated end.

In spite of this tactical retreat, and whatever else may be true, Juno is a figure who represents dissent. She opposes Aeneas, opposes Jupiter, opposes Fate. If we read her not just as a character, but as a poetological figure as well, then she even opposes the epic narrator. Discussions of the *Aeneid* over the past generation and more have been troubled by the issue of dissent. Is the poem an expression of such dissent? Is it even possible for a poem written under Augustus to adopt such a stance? For an *epic* poem? The debate over that issue has favored one side or the other at different times in a way that suggests it will ever really be settled. It is hardly the only such issue in *Aeneid* criticism. What I would like to do is point out a parallel between the world *of* the poem and the world *in* the poem.

First the inner world. Does the *Aeneid* represent a discursive empire of monologic character ruled by a single narrator whom no mere character can hope to challenge, or one in which the narrator's voice is just one voice, whether or not the principal one, in a dialogic universe, one in which narrative authority is diffused and occluded, in which power can never be reliably traced to any ultimate "source"? The fact that the plot tends in the general direction that it must and in the way that Jupiter early in the poem says it will by clearing the way for Rome's eventual foundation, suggests one answer. The fact that Jupiter

---

222. Knauer 1964, 322–27 and 1964b, 77; Cairns 1989, 78.

must negotiate with Juno before the poem can actually end, and that her opposition will continue for centuries, suggests a different one.

It is easy to transfer the conditions under which the narrator of such a poem works to the world outside the poem. I recommend that we do so as a way of coming to grips with this poem, the ultimate meaning of which continues to prove so elusive. I have purposely described the poem's narrator and his world in terms applicable to the political and social realities of the external world in which the poem took shape. In that world, too, authority was ostensibly diffused and power did not wish to be traced to its ultimate "source." This world too presented itself not as a discursive universe of monologic character, but one in which every voice, even that of the principal player, was just one voice within a dialogic drama. Neither the world inside the poem nor the one outside it is one that permits easy decisions between "pro" and "con," whether we mean pro-*Iliad* or pro-*Odyssey*, pro-Aeneas or pro-Juno, pro-Rome or pro-Italy, or whatever other terms we use. In this way, the poem is a faithful image of a world in which such choices were not possible, however pressing the need to choose may have seemed. A remaining question is whether one individual voice can choose a position that does not aim to silence any others, even if it remains permanently in dialogue, or even in opposition with them.[223]

How to Read the *Aeneid*

There are limits to the agency, and even the perceptiveness that we can grant to any literary character. Juno's interventions at least seem to alter the course of the poem, but it is not clear whether she really escapes the narrator's control. In Aeneas' case we cannot say even this. For much of the poem, he does not understand the sort of plot in which he is caught up and where it is taking him. He may sometimes recognize that he is in an Iliadic situation. He may think he knows what that means. He may even come to understand that another Trojan War not only gives him a second opportunity to fight and die honorably, but actually requires him to emerge victorious as a new Achilles. However accurate his understanding, though, does he have any choice in the matter?

As a last comment on the perceived need to choose, let us return, very briefly, to the motif of Aeneas as a reader—not of Homer, this time, but of the several visual texts that he encounters throughout the poem.[224] The main

---

223. My thanks to one of the press's anonymous readers making this point.
224. For further detail on what follows here see Farrell 2012. In addition to the studies of specific passages cited below, the following studies of ecphrasis in the *Aeneid* in general should be noted: Putnam 1995; Barchiesi 1997/2019; Bartsch 1998.

passages are four, and they are extremely famous. In book 1, Aeneas sees representations of the Trojan War on the Temple of Juno at Carthage (450–93), a passage I have mentioned several times. In book 6, he finds scenes of Daedalus' career depicted on the doors of the Temple of Apollo at Cumae (14–41).[225] In book 8, of course, he receives his divine armor, which includes a shield on which are embossed or engraved scenes from the history of Rome culminating in the Battle of Actium (608–731). Finally, at the end of the poem, he sees the baldric of Pallas (12.940–52) with the myth of the fifty daughters of Danaus who murdered their bridegrooms on their wedding night (as described at 10.495–506). Aeneas' reaction to these works of art, I suggest, has a lot to tell us about him as a reader and as a hero.

The four passages outline a clear trajectory in which Aeneas goes from being one kind of reader to becoming another. There is also an element of consistency in that Aeneas' reaction to what he sees is always emotional. In the first passage, seeing episodes of the Trojan War relieves the hero's fears, gives him confidence and hope, and causes him to weep. In the second, his reaction is more muted, but he is so absorbed by the scenes on Daedalus' doors that he seems to forget why he had come to Cumae in the first place. It is only the Sibyl's arrival that calls him back to his purpose. In the third instance, the shield, Aeneas rejoices and perhaps even intuits that it is he who will become a new Achilles in Latium. The fourth instance, the baldric, calls forth the terrible anger that prevents Aeneas from sparing Turnus and makes him plunge his sword deep in his enemy's chest. Aeneas, then, is an emotional reader, even heroically so, and his reactions develop in a particular way, starting out as relatively calm (a lessening of fear in Carthage, quiet reflection in Cumae), and ending in greater excitement, whether of joy (the shield) or anger (the baldric).

The second aspect of Aeneas' readerly development has to do with the depth of his experience. Here, too, there is a clear progression. I just mentioned his extreme absorption in the scenes at Cumae. He is no less fascinated by the earlier images at Carthage. On both these occasions, Aeneas goes over the scenes in detail, "reading" very closely, as it were. His reading of the shield is a bit harder to assess. The lengthy ecphrasis of the scenes that the shield contains would seem to indicate the length of time that Aeneas' gaze lingered on this dazzling gift. As the narrator tells us, however, though he was delighted at the appearance of the shield, he had no idea what those images meant. This remains true even if he did understand that the gift of divine weapons marked

---

225. See Norden 1927/1957, 120–23; Pöschl 1950/1962, 149–50; Klingner 1967, 495–96; Fitzgerald 1984; Kinsey Putnam 1987; Spence 1988, 38–42; Fowler 1990 and 1991; Boyd 1995, 89–90; P. A. Miller 1995; Erdmann 1998; Staley 2002; Kofler 2003, 56–57, 134–36.

him as a new Achilles: that role is confined to the plot of the poem, not to the Roman and Augustan future that the *Aeneid* "predicts." That future remains beyond the hero's ken. At any rate, Aeneas' reading of the shield seems to have involved less of the absorption that he experienced in viewing Juno's temple and Daedalus' doors, and to have become more reactive and superficial than those earlier readings were. Finally, when Aeneas sees the belt of Pallas, he wastes no time lingering on the scene. In fact, to eliminate any possibility of this, the narrator informs the reader what scene is depicted on the belt not in the final episode, when Aeneas notices it and then instantly kills Turnus, but much earlier, when Turnus dispatches the young Pallas and takes the baldric as a prize. The placement of the ecphrasis in the earlier scene betokens the victor's fatal fascination with his trophy. The absence of any description in the final passage signals Aeneas' absolute lack of interest in the baldric as a work of art—as a text—and proves that he cares for it only as a univocal sign of Pallas' death at Turnus' hands.[226]

Aeneas' absorption in these images thus decreases steadily, at the same time as the emotions that arise from seeing them become more violent. From a few remarks that I have already made, it is clear that Aeneas' literal comprehension of the images he sees decreases as well. At Carthage, Aeneas is able to identify individual figures, such as Priam, himself, and presumably others mentioned by the narrator. At Cumae, it is not clear how much he understands of the story that is being told. In book 8, of course, it is stated clearly that Aeneas has no idea what he is looking at. The scenes on the shield mean nothing to him, though they cause him to rejoice; precisely why is left famously unsaid. In book 12, as well, Aeneas effectively does not even see the representation of the Danaids, but merely reacts to the belt itself as a reminder that Turnus killed Pallas. In other words, in one scene after another, Aeneas' basic comprehension of what he is seeing—what he is reading—diminishes steadily. One begins to wonder what kind of a reader our hero really is. Only at Carthage and possibly at Cumae can Aeneas know enough about what he is seeing to interpret it on any higher or deeper level.[227]

If we ask how skillful Aeneas is at such interpretation, what we find may be disappointing. Does he grasp the relevance of Daedalus' wanderings to his

---

226. In enormous contrast to the significance that critics rightly find in the imagery: see Conte 1970/1986, 185–95; Spence 1991; Van Nortwick 1992, 158–60; Putnam 1994/1998, 189–207; O'Higgins, 1995; Keith 2000, 77–78; Fulkerson 2008.

227. It is ironic that Aeneas is a better reader of ecphrases in books 1 and 6, books in which I have suggested that he resembles someone who has not read the *Odyssey* at all, but an even a poorer reader of ecphrases in 8 and especially 12, where his "reading" of the *Iliad* might presumably be of use to him.

own? Of the labyrinth to the underworld journey in store for him? Maybe yes, maybe no; but whatever this imagery means to him, he does not say. At Carthage he says a lot: he tells Achates that the scenes on Juno's temple prove that Trojan fame has reached even to Libya, and that this fame will be their salvation. His prediction is correct, more or less, because the gods have seen to it that the Trojans receive a warm welcome from Queen Dido; but many have noted the irony in the conclusion that Aeneas draws.[228] Scenes celebrating the destruction of Troy on the temple of the goddess who was the Trojans' chief opponent during the Trojan War and who is the principal divinity of the city where Aeneas now finds himself should not suggest that the Carthaginians will be happy to see him. Aeneas' belief that they do mean this seems less like virtuoso interpretation and more like wishful thinking.

If we use these episodes to assess Aeneas as a reader, we find that about half the time he lacks the basic information to understand what he is reading, and that even when he does have this information his interpretation is likely to be misguided. His attention span diminishes over time in parallel with his basic understanding, and in the process he becomes more agitated, whether by extreme pleasure or extreme anger. This is all beginning to sound a bit worrying, as it should. Together with lessened understanding and greater excitability comes, predictably enough, a greater tendency to act, and act precipitously. Lost in reflection at Carthage and at Cumae, Aeneas has to be jolted out of his absorption in the images that he reads. At Caere, where he receives his shield after leaving Evander and Pallanteum, he seems to realize immediately, even before seeing the gift, that he is being called to perform deeds worthy of Achilles. At the end, on the final battlefield, the sight of Pallas' belt instantly triggers the anger that brings about Turnus' death.

It is worth noting, by the way, that Aeneas' development as a reader parallels his growing tendency to share in one of Juno's defining traits, her irresistible anger.[229] I have emphasized that he also shares her obsession with the *Iliad* as the defining episode of a never-ending war against Troy. When Juno "reads" the beginning of the *Aeneid* as the beginning of another Odyssey, it is not obvious that she is correct, and by her attempt to destroy Aeneas she risks making the poem the very thing that she wants to avoid. Juno starts the poem as a reactive reader, heedless of possible but unintended consequences, and she ends

---

228. See Horsfall 1973–1974, especially 7–8; Leach 1988, 311; Fowler 1991, 23; Barchiesi 1994/1999, 339–31; Putnam 1998/1998a, 24 with note 4.

229. Williams 1972–1973, vol. 2, 503 on *Aeneid* 12.877f.: "the behaviour of Aeneas, as he kills his enemy in a fit of fury (*furiis accensus et ira terribilis*, 946–7), goes counter to all his efforts in the poem to overcome the evil effects of *furor* in himself and in others." See Putnam 1965, 200; 1990/1995; 2011, 12–15, 113; Quinn 1968, 272–76; Johnson 1976, 133;

it the same way. The motif of enemies who come to resemble one another, whether in literature or in life, is depressingly familiar.[230] The fact that Aeneas' reading habits come increasingly to resemble those of Juno is not a development that I think we should view as positive.

There are those who disagree. If the *Aeneid* is the story of how Aeneas becomes a less reflective, but more decisive reader, perhaps he is a model of how we, too, should read the poem. I have to admit that this idea has some appeal even for me. So often and in so many ways, Vergil's poetry presents readers with a dichotomous perspective on the world. Even when one feels a certain sympathy for both sides, it is difficult not to feel the urge to choose between them. At least, it is difficult for me. That is why, as I approach the end of the poem, I tend to see it the way that Aeneas predicts it will be when he recognizes that his divine armor is about to arrive. The poem will end as an Iliad, through and through. How could it not? From that point on, almost everything that Aeneas does follows an Iliadic script; and while Turnus struggles to uphold his claim to be the new Achilles, of course he ultimately fails. When it comes to the end, after the final, quasi-Odyssean note of quasi-comic, not quite conjugal reunion has been sounded among the Olympians, down on the battlefield the Iliadic parallels could not be any clearer. When he plunges his sword into Turnus' chest in vengeful anger, Aeneas *is* Achilles, and Turnus *is* Hector.[231] By the same token, the *Aeneid* ends not as an Odyssean comedy, but as an Iliadic tragedy, not because of its perfectly constructed plot, but because a good man, Aeneas, a man of consummate responsibility, he has finally given in to his emotions. Instead of concluding the battle to establish himself in Italy by accepting his opponent's surrender, as Jupiter accepts Juno's surrender (and she accepts his), and as Odysseus obeys Athena's command to lay down his arms, Aeneas indulges his Achillean anger; and the narrator gives him no opportunity, as Homer gives Achilles himself, to reconcile with his victim's survivors. Critics are divided as to whether Aeneas ignores the counsel of his own father "to spare the submissive and to war down the proud" (6.853).[232] Nevertheless, it is clear that Turnus' pride has been broken; he could not be more submissive at the end. No matter: Aeneas' embodiment of,

---

230. For Turnus as Aeneas' "second self" in comparison to other paradigms see Van Nortwick 1992, 151–161.

231. Anderson 1957; Knauer 1964, 314–16, 320–22, 343; 1964a, 74, 78–81.

232. The point was first made, I believe, by Putnam 1972/1995 and it has remained fundamental to his perspective on the poem. This perspective has also met with committed opposition: see for instance Wlosok 1976/1999 and 1982; Galinsky 1988; Renger 1985, 72–103; Cairns 1989, 78–84; Erler 1992. For some of the weaknesses in their critique, see Thomas 1991; Fowler 1997, 30–34; Dowling 2006, 97–105.

or possession by, the spirit of Achilles is complete. His performance is convincing, and his ambition to fulfill the destiny to which he aspires, to be a Homeric warrior, is tragically fulfilled. By this act, he establishes violence as the founding principle of Roman rule. By choosing this alternative, according to what generations of ancient philosophers maintained, Aeneas makes himself an avatar of Homer's chief example of a bad king.[233]

That is how I would read the end of the poem, if I allowed myself to do so. I am certain that the urge to read it that way will never leave me. At the same time, about half a century, and counting, of engagement with this beautiful and often baffling poem have led me to understand that, by reading it in this way, I would be no better a reader than Aeneas. The perceived need to choose, I repeat, is powerful; but so is the need to reflect. Aeneas over the course of his story becomes steadily less reflective, and more reactive. That is part of his tragedy. His story tempts readers, as well, to become less reflective, and more reactive. It is almost impossible not to conclude that Aeneas must act, and that we must choose. If we can resist that urge and remain reflective, however, the rewards may be greater. If we think back over the journey that we ourselves make over the course of these twelve books; if we bear in mind the multitude of possibilities and uncertainties that confront us at every turn; if we consider the remarkable range of literary and ethical speculation that we find on every page of this inspiring creation; and if we feel, even in the most sobering and repellent moments to which it subjects us, the sheer pleasure that it offers us as a means of evaluating, appreciating, and celebrating our own humanity; after all this, it may be that we will succumb to the urge to choose, to decide, and have done with it, but I think that outcome becomes much less likely. For my part, when I reflect on the *Aeneid* in this way, I respond differently to my own instinctive reaction to the end of the poem. Above all, when I consider the hero's proclivity to superficial reading, I find it impossible to believe that such a poem, which seems to me to support and encourage interpretive approaches of almost infinite subtlety, could have been written in order to encourage such reading—to make us like Aeneas. In the final analysis, I submit, that is not the sort of reader that Vergil calls on us to be.

---

233. In this context the observations of Smolenaars 1993 are pertinent.

APPENDIX

mene in- and *mênin*

WILLIAM LEVITAN'S IDEA that Juno's first words in the *Aeneid* echo the first word of the *Iliad* has been endorsed in print by a number of scholars and seems to be taken for granted by some, but it has proven impossible for others to believe.[1] I personally have encountered both enthusiastic acceptance of and strong resistance to the idea when I have referred to it in lectures related to the argument presented in chapter 1 of this book. It therefore seemed necessary to address the objections that I have heard raised; but for most of the time that I was writing, no one, so far as I know, had expressed his or her reservations in print. Now, however, Gian Biagio Conte has performed the service of publishing his doubts.[2] I can only say that I am grateful for the opportunity to respond.

Conte's objections are very similar to those that I heard from him some years ago, and that I have heard from others from time to time.[3] They are mainly linguistic in nature, the general idea being that the way Latin and Greek were pronounced in Vergil's day would not have encouraged anyone hearing Juno's *mene in-* to think of Homer's *mênin*. What are the specific points at issue?

The first point that I want to mention is not one of those that Conte makes, but it is similar to them, and others have raised it, so that it seems worth discussing here. The concern is that the *ē* of *mēnĕ* in Latin would not have sounded like the eta in *mênin*, because iotacism would have changed the sound represented by the latter from *ē* to *ī*.[4] In fact, as W. S. Allen points out in *Vox Graeca*, the

---

1. Levitan 1993; see (for instance) O'Hara 1996, 115; Fowler 1997, 259; Connolly 2010, 409.

2. Conte 2017, 55.

3. I had the opportunity to discuss the matter with Professor Conte on a visit to the Scuola Normale Superiore di Pisa in 2002. I remain grateful for his hospitality and his spirited engagement on that occasion.

4. I was first alerted to this possibility by Peter Smith when I referred to Levitan's paper in a lecture at the University of North Carolina at Chapel Hill in 2002. Professor Smith himself established within a few minutes that iotacism is not a factor, for the same reasons that I give here.

sound of eta did not undergo this change until after the *Aeneid* was written.[5] To understand that eta did sound like Latin ē, and not like ī, Allen's account of the difference between eta (η) and the epsilon-iota diphthong (ει) is instructive. That they represented different sounds is proved, he writes, by the fact that they develop differently in later times. "This situation is reflected in the transcription of Greek words in Latin, where η is represented by ē until a late date, whereas ει is represented by ī (e.g. *sēpia* = σηπία, *pīrāta* = πειρατής, and *Aristīdēs* = Ἀριστείδης)."[6] This obviously means that, in Vergil's time, *me* in *mene* must have sounded like μη in μῆνιν, and not like ει or ι, which would be represented in Latin as ī.

Conte's own objections begin with the second syllable of *mene* and with the fact that it is elided with the preposition *in*; or rather with the fact that it is not elided, but undergoes synaloepha, which is to say that the final *e* of *mene* does not simply disappear, but is blended with the *i* of *incepto*. Conte does not cite any evidence for this, but his point is familiar. It was established by Soubiran, and it is accepted by other experts in meter and prosody.[7] On the other hand, the general truth does not take very close account of the particular situation that we find here. What Conte argues is that Vergil's audience would have heard in the final syllable of *men(e) in-* two vowels, ĕ and ĭ, that were blended, almost as a diphthong, but kept somehow distinct; and indeed, that is how experts believe synaloepha generally worked. That said, it is important to note that the pronouns *me* ("me") and *te* ("you") with enclitic *–ne* (to indicate a question) are often written in manuscripts as *men* and *ten*, before vowels as well as consonants, which suggests that the final ĕ might be entirely suppressed in all environments. That being the case, I do not see how one can insist that the final vowel of the enclitic always made a distinct contribution to the blended sound that it is supposed to have produced with whatever vowel followed it.

Even if one could be sure that it was fully pronounced, though, we are dealing in this case with two vowels, ĕ and ĭ, that were very close in sound and often confused.[8] Educated speakers will have had no difficulty distinguishing them, of course, but neither will they have found it difficult to minimize the difference between them, if they had any reason to do so. We see this in the case of Vergil's own name, which not only came to be spelled Virgilius as well as (the correct)

---

5. Allen 1987, 69–75.

6. Allen 1987, 70.

7. Soubiran 1966, 55–91; cf. Gratwick 1993, 251–53, Morgan 2010, 5–6.

8. For examples, see Allen 1978, 49. Curiously, confusion of ĕ with ī and of ē with ĭ seems to be more common than of ĕ with ĭ or ē with ī, but Allen also notes "the frequent use of Greek ε to render Latin short *i*."

Vergilius, but also seems to have been felt by his friends, and even by the poet himself, to sound sufficiently like *virgo* as to inspire the nickname Parthenias—an apt enough name for anyone who preferred living in Naples (i.e. Parthenope) to anywhere else, but all the more apt if the nickname puns on that person's proper name.[9] So, even if we grant that maintaining a differentiation in vowel quality and distinctness in pronunciation between ĕ and ĭ might have been possible in *menĕ ĭn-*, it should not have been at all difficult to treat the junction between the words so as to mimic very closely the sound of *mênin*.

Conte raises another point regarding the second syllable of *mênin*: it is short by nature and scans as short in line 1 of the *Iliad*, while the second syllable of Juno's speech scans as long by position (*mēn(e) īncepto*). That is certainly true. I might add that Homer's first syllable, μῆ-, takes a circumflex accent. Latin has no such accent, so that the Greek syllable must have sounded different from that point of view. The question is, once again, would such things have mattered to Vergil's audience, and would they have prevented anyone from hearing *mene in-* as *mênin*? As it happens, we have clear indications that the circumflex would not have mattered a bit.[10] The lengthening of *-nĭn* to *-n(e) īn-* presents no problem, either. Here we must remember that to speak of a "long" syllable in terms of prosody, though convenient, is really a misnomer. Strictly speaking, the syllable in question is "closed" or "heavy." It takes longer to pronounce than an "open" or "light" syllable, but whatever vowel it may contain, in this instance a short ĭ, does not appreciably change its quality. The heavy syllable, to be sure, will have contributed a certain emphasis to the pronunciation of *mēn(e) īn-*, but this will have been welcome, since the point was not to make line 37 of the *Aeneid* sound exactly like line 1 of the *Iliad*—if that had been the point, then *mēn(e) in-* would presumably have stood at the beginning of the line, instead of in the middle—but to call attention to Juno's first utterance, and to make the similarity of these syllables to *mênin* that much more striking.

Conte's final objection has to do with Vergil's (or Juno's) use of the word *incepto*, "beginning," presumably instead of *coeptis*, "undertakings (or) the project that I've begun," to mean "a story or theme," since the former word "never appears in Virgil with this sense; the sense is possible only in the prosaic usage of Latin."[11] If we can take the *Oxford Latin Dictionary* as an authority, we find that it contains a lemma "inceptum, -ī, n." and gives as definition 1b of

---

9. Vergil himself appears to play on the similarity of his name to *virgo* and of *parthenos* to Parthenope at *Georgics* 4.563–64. Confusion between *e* and *i* must therefore have been a factor long before iotacism eradicated the distinction and made possible the connection between Virgilius the magician and his *virga*, or "wand."

10. See below on *cura* and κῶρα (*côra*).

11. Conte 2017, 55.

this word, "the theme or subject of a book or sim.," citing two passages of Sallust and one of Tacitus. It is a pity that it did not cite Lucretius as well, who writes *quo magis **inceptum** pergam pertexere dictis* ("all the more do I hasten to weave my theme in words," *On the Nature of Things* 6.42). The Lucretian commentator H. A. J. Monro compares this to an earlier passage, *ut repetam **coeptum** pertexere dictis* ("to resume weaving my theme in words," 1.418).[12] The comparison might have helped Conte see that Juno's *incepto* can bear the required sense, since Vergil does, famously, write *da facilem cursum atque audacibus adnue **coeptis*** ("grant me an easy course and show favor to the project that I've begun," *Georgics* 1.40), and does so in the opening prayer of a poem. He also uses other forms of the verb *incipere* in reference to starting a poem, more than a few times (***incipe***, "begin" in the imperative, *Eclogue* 3.58; 5.10, 12; 8.21 etc.; 9.32; ***incipit***, "he [Silenus] begins [to sing]," *Eclogue* 6.26; *hinc canere **incipiam***, "from this point I shall begin to sing," *Georgics* 1.5). I would add what Aeneas says as he begins to recite "The Sack of Troy" (*quamquam animus meminisse horret luctuque refugit, / **incipiam***, "although my spirit shrinks from remembering and recoils in grief, / I shall begin, *Aeneid* 2. 12–13), but perhaps that is too close to what I am trying to prove, so I leave it to one side. Even without it, though, I think there is enough evidence here to show that forms of *incipere*, including the substantival use of the participle, could be construed not just as referring to the start of something (which is, in fact, the reference that most concerns me), but that the word is actually used quite frequently, not just in poetry, but in Vergil's poetry, to mean the beginning and the theme of a literary performance, in particular.

Since Conte's objections are quite precise, I have so far replied in kind. I would be remiss, however, if I did not add that Roman poets are not always very precise in this domain. In various passages where Vergil reproduces a Greek word sonically, but not lexically, he does not allow such things as a difference in aspiration or vowel quality to get in the way: thus we find *Orcus*, god of the underworld (*Georgics* 1.277), and Ὅρκος (*Horkos*), personified Oath (Hesiod, *Works and Days* 802); *tua cura, Lycoris*, "the one **you care** for, Lycoris" (*Eclogue* 10.22), and τυ κῶρα (*tu kôra*), "**your girl**(friend)" (Theocritus, *Idyll* 1.82; compare Propertius, *Elegies* 1.1.36, and note the irrelevance of the circumflex accent); <u>aurea mala decem</u> misi, cras altera mittam, "I sent **ten golden apples; tomorrow** I'll send ten more" (*Eclogue* 3.71) and δέκα μᾶλα φέρω... καὶ **αὔριον** ἄλλά τοι οἰσῶ (***deka mâla** pherô... kai **aurion** alla toi oisô*), "I'm bringing you **ten apples** ... / and **tomorrow** I'll bring you another ten" (*Idyll* 1.10–11; note the "equivalency" of Latin ĕ and Greek short ι, as well as the

---

12. H.A.J. Monro 1886, vol. 2, 353 on line 42.

irrelevancy of the different endings of *aurea* and αὔριον); *ut... ut... ut*, "as... as... as" (*Georgics* 4.261–63) and οὔτε... οὔτε... οὔτε (*oute...*), "neither... neither... neither" (Homer, *Iliad* 14.394–98; each passage is a simile featuring three points of comparison).

More generally, Roman linguists like Marcus Terentius Varro did not allow such things as different vowel quantities to stand in the way of their perceiving a good etymology (examples are numerous and well known), nor did diviners with the aid of hindsight refrain from interpreting the braying of a street vendor, who had been hawking figs (*cauneas!*) at the time of Marcus Licinius Crassus' departure for his ill-fated expedition against the Parthians in 55 BCE, as a warning to Crassus not to go (*cau(e) n(e) eas!*).[13] And, speaking of Cicero, his notorious letter to Paetus on double entendres (*Letters to his Friends* 9.22) shows that these were clearly perceptible, perhaps especially between Latin and Greek. According to Cicero, two perfectly innocent words, such as Latin *bini*, "two apiece," and the name of Socrates' lyre instructor, Κόννος (*Konnos*), might be confused, respectively, with Greek βινεῖ (*binei*) and Latin *cunnus*, despite differences of accent between the first pair and of vowel quality between the second. These are quite striking examples, since *binei* and *cunnus* are primary sexual obscenities. The most recent edition of Liddell and Scott's *A Greek–English Lexicon* s.v. βινέω translates the verb into Latin instead of English as "*inire, coire*," noting that it is used "of illicit intercourse." The *Oxford Latin Dictionary* s.v. cunnus renders the word, perhaps less prudishly, but only slightly, not in Greek but via a Latin loan word as "the female pudenda." The meanings of these words have nothing in common with *bini* and *Konnos*, whereas readers have found that the meanings of *mene* and *mênin* actually are related;[14] nor do Cicero's examples sound any more alike than do Juno's outburst and the first words of the *Iliad*.

Conte's concerns about what we should count as perceptible by a Roman audience, therefore, are misplaced. Of course, we should be grateful to him for stating these concerns; but we must conclude that an ancient Roman audience would have been prepared to perceive the kind of wordplay represented by *mene in-* and *mênin* and that, if they were familiar with Vergil's earlier poetry, they ought to have been prepared to perceive it in anything he wrote, above all.

---

13. Examples from Varro are too numerous even to begin mentioning. On differences of vowel quantity in etymological wordplay, see O'Hara 1996, 61–62 with notes 316 and 317. On Crassus and *cauneas*, see Cicero, *On Divination* 2.84 in Falconer 1923, 464–67.

14. See, for instance, chapter 1 note 54.

WORKS CITED

Abbot, James C. 2000. "The *Aeneid* and the Concept of *dolus bonus*." *Vergilius* 46, 59–82.
———. 2012–2013. "*Arma virumque*." *The Classical Journal* 108, 37–63.
Abrahamson, Ernst. 1960. *The Adventures of Odysseus: Literary Studies*. St. Louis: Washington University Press.
Adler, Ada. 1928–1938. *Suidae Lexicon*. Stuttgart: B. G. Teubner.
Ahern, C. F., Jr. 1991. "Horace's Rewriting of Homer in *Carmen* 1.6." *Classical Philology* 86, 301–14.
Ahl, Frederick. 1989. "Homer, Vergil, and Complex Narrative Structures in Latin Epic: An Essay." *Illinois Classical Studies* 14, 1–31.
Allen, A. W. 1951–1952. "The Dullest Book of the *Aeneid*." *The Classical Journal* 47, 119–23.
Allen, W. S. 1978. *Vox Latina*. 2nd ed. Cambridge: Cambridge University Press.
———. 1987. *Vox Graeca*. 3rd ed. Cambridge: Cambridge University Press.
Ambühl, A. 2004. "Entertaining Theseus and Heracles: The *Hecale* and the *Victoria Berenices* as a Diptych." In *Callimachus II*, ed. M. A. Harder, R. F. Regtuit, and G. C. Wakker. Hellenistica Groningana 7. Leuven: Peeters, 23–48.
———. 2005. *Kinder und junge Helden*. Hellenistica Groningana 9. Leuven: Peeters.
Anderson, W. S. 1957. "Vergil's Second *Iliad*." *TAPA* (*Transactions of the American Philological Association*) 88, 17–30.
———. 1968. "*Pastor Aeneas*: On Pastoral Themes in the *Aeneid*." *TAPA* (*Transactions of the American Philological Association*) 99, 1–17.
———. 1993. "The Suppliant's Voice and Gesture in Vergil and Ovid's *Metamorphoses*." *Illinois Classical Studies* 18, 165–77.
Arena, Valentina. 2012. *Libertas and the Practice of Politics in the Late Roman Republic*. Cambridge: Cambridge University Press.
Armstrong, David et al., ed. 2004. *Philodemus, Vergil and the Augustans*. Austin: University of Texas Press.
Asmis, Elizabeth. 1991. "Philodemus' Poetic Theory and *On the Good King according to Homer*." *Classical Antiquity* 10, 1–45.
Asper, Marcus. 1997. *Onomata allotria: Zur Genese, Struktur und Funktion poetologischer Metaphern bei Kallimachos*. Stuttgart: Steiner.
Atack, Carol. 2020. *The Discourse of Kingship in Classical Greece*. London: Routledge.
Austin, R. G. 1971. *P. Vergili Maronis Aeneidos liber primus*. With a commentary. Oxford: Oxford University Press.

Austin, R. G. 1977. *P. Vergili Maronis Aeneidos liber sextus*. With a commentary. Oxford: Oxford University Press.

Babbit, F. C. 1928. *Plutarch, Moralia, with an English translation*. Vol. 2. Cambridge, MA: Harvard University Press.

Baraz, Yelena. 2012. "Pliny's Epistolary Dreams and the Ghost of Domitian." *TAPA* (*Transactions of the American Philological Association*) 142, 105–32.

Barchiesi, Alessandro. 1978/2015. "Il lamento di Giuturna." *Materiali e discussioni per l'analisi dei testi classici* 1, 99–121 / "Appendix: The Lament of Juturna" in Barchiesi 1984/2015, 95–114.

———. 1984/2015. *La traccia del modello: Effetti omerici nella narazione virgiliana*. Pisa: Giardini / *Homeric Effects in Vergil's Narrative*. Trans. Ilaria Marchesi and Matt Fox. Princeton: Princeton University Press.

———. 1993. "*Future Reflexive*: Two Modes of Allusion and Ovid's *Heroides*." *Harvard Studies in Classical Philology* 95, 333–65.

———. 1994. "Alcune difficoltà nella carriera di un poeta giambico: Giambo ed elegia nell'Epodo XI." In *Bimilenario de Horace*, ed. R. Cortés Tovar and J. C. Fernandez Corte. Salamanca: Ediciones Universidad de Salamanca, 127–38.

———. 1994a. "Immovable Delos: *Aeneid* 3.73–98 and the Hymns of Callimachus." *The Classical Quarterly* 44, 438–43.

———. 1994/1999. Rappresentazioni del delore e dell' interpretazione nell'Eneide." *Antike und Abendland* 40, 109–24 / "Representations of Suffering and Interpretation in the *Aeneid*." In P. R. Hardie 1999, vol. 3, 324–44.

———. 1997/2019. "Virgilian Narrative: Ecphrasis." In Martindale and Mac Góráin, 413–24.

———. 2005. *Ovidio: Metamorfosi*. Vol. 1: libri I–II. Saggio introduttivo di Charles Segal. Traduzione di Ludivica Koch. Milan: Mondadori.

Bassett, Samuel E. 1920. "ΥΣΤΕΡΟΝ ΠΡΟΤΕΡΟΝ ΟΜΕΡΙΚΩΣ (Cicero, Att. 1, 16, 1)." *Harvard Studies in Classical Philology* 31, 39–62.

Beck, William. 2019. "The Narrative of the *Iliad*: Time, Space, and Story." Diss. University of Pennsylvania.

Bednarowski, K. Paul. 2015. "Dido and the Motif of Deception in *Aeneid* 2 and 3." *TAPA* (*Transactions of the American Philological Association*) 145, 135–72.

Bell, Andrew J. E. 1999. "The Popular Poetics and Politics of the *Aeneid*." *TAPA* (*Transactions of the American Philological Association*) 129, 263–79.

Berno, Francesca Romana. 2004. "Un *truncus*, molti re: Priamo, Agamemnone, Pompeo (Virgilio, Seneca, Lucano)." *Maia* 56, 45–77.

Bettini, Maurizio. 1997. "Ghosts of Exile: Doubles and Nostalgia in Vergil's *parva Troia* (*Aeneid* 3.294 ff.)." *Classical Antiquity* 16, 8–33.

———. 2005/2006. "Un'identità 'troppo compiuta': Troiani, Latini, Romani e Iulii nell'*Eneide*." *Materiali e discussioni per l'analisi dei testi classici* 55, 77–102 / "Forging identities: Trojans and Latins, Romans and Julians in the *Aeneid*." In *Herrschaft ohne Integration? Rom und Italien in republikanischer Zeit*, ed. Martin Jehne and Rene Pfeilschifter. Studien zur alten Geschichte 4. Frankfurt am Main: Verlag Alte Geschichte, 269–91.

Biggs, Thomas. 2017. "*Primus Romanorum*: Origin Stories, Fictions of Primacy, and the First Punic War." *Classical Philology* 112, 3, 350–67.

———. 2018. "Odysseus, Rome, and the First Punic War in Polybius' *Histories*." In *Polybius and his Legacy*, ed. N. Miltsios et al., Trends in Classics, Suppl. vol. 60. Berlin: De Gruyter: 381–99.

———. 2019. "Roman and Carthaginian Journeys: Punic *Pietas* in Naevius' *Bellum Punicum* and Plautus' *Poenulus*." In *The Epic Journey in Greek and Roman Literature*, ed. T. Biggs and J. Blum. Yale Classical Studies 39. Cambridge: Cambridge University Press, 170–93.

———. 2019a. "Did Mercury Build the Ship of Aeneas?" In *Tracking Hermes, Pursuing Mercury*, ed. John F. Miller and Jenny Strauss Clay. Oxford: Oxford University Press, 209–24.

———. 2019b. "Vergil's Achaemenides and the Idea of Early Latin Epic." *Latomus* 78, 301–13.

———. 2020. *The Poetics of the First Punic War*. Ann Arbor: University of Michigan Press.

———. 2020a. "Generic Innovation and the Mediation of History in Naevius' *Bellum Punicum* and Ennius' *Annales*." In Damon and Farrell, 91–106.

Binder, Gerhard. 1971. *Aeneas und Augustus. Interpretationen zum 8. Buch der Aeneis*. Beiträge zur Klassischen Philologie 38. Meisenheim am Glan: Hain.

Birt, Theodor. 1882. *Das antike Buchwesen in seinem Verhältniss zur Literatur*. Berlin: Wilhelm Hertz.

Bloch, A. 1970. "*Arma virumque* als heroisches Leitmotiv." *Museum Helveticum* 27, 206–11.

Bloom, Harold. 1973. *The Anxiety of Influence: A Theory of Poetry*. New York: Oxford University Press.

———. 1987. *Ruin the Sacred Truths: Poetry and Belief from the Bible to the Present*. Cambridge, MA: Harvard University Press.

Blundell, M. W. 1987. "The Moral Character of Odysseus in *Philoctetes*." *Greek, Roman, and Byzantine Studies* 28, 307–29.

———. 1988. "The *phusis* of Neoptolemus in Sophocles' *Philoctetes*." *Greece & Rome* 35, 137–48.

Bocciolini Palagi, Laura. 2001. "Amata e l'iniziazione dionisiaca." *Maia* 53, 565–81.

———. 2006. "Le alluziazioni di Amata (Nota a Verg. *Aen*. VII 376 *ingentibus excita monstris*)." In *Concentus ex dissonis: Scritti in onore di Aldo Setaioli*, ed. Carlo Santini, Loriano Zurli, and Luca Cardinali. Università degli Studi di Perugia, Quaderni del Dipartimento di Filologia e Tradizione Greca e Latina 4. Napoli: Edizioni Scientifiche Italiane, 113–22.

———. 2007. *La trottola di Dioniso: Motivi dionisiaci nel VII libro dell'Eneide*. Testi e manuali per l'insegnamento universitario del latino n.s. 97. Bologna: Pàtron.

Boëls-Janssen, Nicole. 2007. "Rôles et paroles de femmes dans l'*Énéide*." In *L'intertexte virgilien et sa réception: écriture, récriture et réflexivité chez Virgile et Rutilius Namatianus*, ed. Christina Filoche. Dijon: Université de Bourgogne, 19–43.

Bowie, Angus M. 1990. "The Death of Priam: Allegory and History in the *Aeneid*." *The Classical Quarterly* 40, 470–81.

———. 2008. "Aeneas narrator." *Proceedings of the Virgil Society* 26, 41–51.

Boyd, Barbara Weiden. 1995. "*Non enarrabile textum*: Ecphrastic Trespass and Narrative Ambiguity in the *Aeneid*." *Vergilius* 41, 71–90.

Boyle, A. J. 1999. "*Aeneid* 8: Images of Rome." In Perkell 1999, 148–61.

Braund, D. 1996. *Ruling Roman Britain: Kings, Queens, Governors and Emperors from Julius Caesar to Agricola*. London: Routledge.

Brazouski, Antoinette. 1991. "Amata and Her Maternal Right." *Helios* 18, 129–36.

Bremmer, J. N. 2009. "The Golden Bough: Orphic, Eleusinian, and Hellenistic-Jewish Sources of Virgil's Underworld in *Aeneid* VI." *Kernos* 22, 183–208.

Briggs, W. W., Jr. 1980. *Narrative and Simile from the Georgics in the Aeneid. Mnemosyne* Suppl. 58. Leiden: Brill.

Bright, David F. 1981. "Aeneas' Other Nekyia." *Vergilius* 27, 40–47.

Brink, C. O. 1971. *Horace on Poetry*. Vol. 2: The "Ars Poetica." Cambridge: Cambridge University Press.

Broughton, T. Robert S. 1951. *The Magistrates of the Roman Republic*. 2 vols. New York.

Bruno, Nicoletta. 2011. "Il riscatto di una vittima: L'episodio di Laocoonte (Verg. Aen. 2,40–56; 199–233)." *Euphrosyne* 39, 31–66.

Brunt, P. A. 1988. "*Libertas* in the Republic." In *The Fall of the Roman Republic and Related Essays*. Oxford, 281–350.

Buchheit, Vinzenz. 1963. *Vergil über die Sendung Roms: Untersuchungen zum Bellum Poenicum und zur Aeneis. Gymnasium* Beiheft 3. Heidelberg: Carl Winter Verlag.

———. 1967. Review of Knauer 1964. *Gymnasium* 74, 470–73.

———. 1970. Review of Knauer 1964. *Göttingische Gelehrte Anzeigen* 222, 79–94.

Büchner, Karl. 1955. *P. Vergilius Maro, der Dichter der Römer*. Stuttgart. Alfred Druckenmüller. = s.v. P. Vergilius Maro." In *Paulys Realencyclopädie der classischen Altertumswissenschaft*, Suppl. VIIIA, 1, 1021–1264 and VIIIA, 2, 1265–1486.

Burke, Paul F., Jr. 1976. "Virgil's Amata." *Vergilius* 22, 24–29.

———. 1978. "*Drances infensus*: A Study in Vergilian Character Portrayal." *TAPA (Transactions of the American Philological Association)* 108, 15–20.

Burkert, Walter. 1985. *Greek Religion: Archaic and Classical*. Cambridge, MA: Harvard University Press.

Cairns Douglas. 2015. "The First Odysseus: *Iliad*, *Odyssey*, and the Ideology of Kingship." *Gaia: revue interdisciplinaire sur la Grèce Archaïque* 18, 51–66.

Cairns, Francis. 1989. *Virgil's Augustan Epic*. Cambridge: Cambridge University Press.

———. 2004. "Varius and Vergil: Two Pupils of Philodemus in Propertius 2.34?" In Armstrong et al., 299–321.

Calvino, Italo. 1981/1986. "Italiani, vi esorto ai classici." *L'Espresso*, June 28, 58–68 / "Why Read the Classics?" In *The Uses of Literature: Essays*. Trans. Patrick Creagh. New York: Harcourt Brace Jovanovich, 125–34.

Campbell, Malcolm. 1983. *Studies in the Third Book of Apollonius Rhodius' Argonautica*. Hildesheim: Olms.

Camps, W. A. 1954. "A Note on the Structure of the *Aeneid*." *The Classical Quarterly* 4, 214–15.

———. 1959. "A Second Note on the Structure of the *Aeneid*," *The Classical Quarterly* 9, 53–56.

———. 1969. *An Introduction to Virgil's Aeneid*. Oxford: Oxford University Press.

Cardinali, Luca. 1995. "Tradizione annalistica e versione virgiliana della figura di Amata." *Prometheus* 21, 256–70.

Carney, Elizabeth D. 1988. "*Reginae* in the *Aeneid*." *Athenaeum* 66, 427–45.

Carpenter, Thomas H. 2015. "The Trojan War in Early Greek Art." In Fantuzzi and Tsagalis, 178–95.

Casali, Sergio and Fabio Stok. 2019. "Post-classical Commentary." In Martindale and Mac Góráin, 95–108.

Casali, Sergio. 2004. "Nisus and Euryalus: Exploiting the Contradictions in Virgil's *Doloneia*." *Harvard Studies in Classical Philology* 102, 319–54.

———. 2005. "La vite dietro il mirto: Lycurgus, Polydorus e la violazione delle piante in Eneide 3." *Studi Italiani di Filologia Classica* 3, 233–50.

———. 2006. "The Making of the Shield: Inspiration and Repression in the *Aeneid*." *Greece & Rome* 53, 185–204.

———. 2010. "The Development of the Aeneas Legend." In Farrell and Putnam 2010, 37–51.

———. 2017. *Virgilio, Eneide 2: Introduzione, traduzione, e commento*. Pisa: Edizioni della Normale.

Cerda, Juan Luis de la. 1612/1642. *P. Vergili Maronis Aeneidos libri*. 2 vols. Cologne: Johann Kinckius.

Chew, Kathryn Sue. 2002. "*Inscius pastor:* Ignorance and Aeneas' Identity in the *Aeneid*." *Latomus* 61, 616–27.

Citroni, Mario. 2001. "Orazio lettore di Omero: sulla valenza programmatica dell' epistola I 2." In *Posthomerica* 3, ed. Franco Montanari and Stefano Pittaluga Genova: D.AR.FI.CL.ET. Francesco Della Corte, 23–49.

Clare, Ray J. 2002. *The Path of the Argo: Language, Imagery, and Narrative in the Argonautica of Apollonius Rhodius*. Cambridge: Cambridge University Press.

Clark, Raymond J. 1979. *Catabasis: Vergil and the Wisdom-Tradition*. Amsterdam: Grüner.

———. 2000. "P.Oxy. 2078, Vat. Gr. 2228, and Vergil's Charon." *The Classical Quarterly* 50, 192–96.

———. 2001. "How Vergil Expanded the Underworld in *Aeneid* 6." *Proceedings of the Cambridge Philological Society* 47, 103–16.

Clarke, M. L. 1965. Review of Knauer 1964. *Gnomon* 37, 687–90.

Clarke, Samuel. 1729–1732. *Homeri Ilias, Graece et Latine: annotationes in usum serenissimi principis Gulielmi Augusti, ducis de Cumberland*. 2 vols. 2nd ed. London: John and Paul Knapton.

Clausen, Wendell. 1987/2002. *Virgil's Aeneid and the Tradition of Hellenistic Poetry*. Berkeley: University of California Press / *Virgil's Aeneid: Decorum, Allusion, and Ideology*. Beiträge zur Altertumskunde 162. Munich and Leipzig: K. G. Saur.

Clauss, James J. 1988. "Vergil and the Euphrates Revisited." *American Journal of Philology* 109, 309–20.

———. 1993. *The Best of the Argonauts: The Redefinition of the Epic Hero in Book One of Apollonius' Argonautica*. Berkeley: University of California Press.

———. 1995. "A Delicate Foot on the Well-Worn Threshold: Paradoxical Imagery in Catullus 68b." *American Journal of Philology* 116, 237–53.

———. 2002. "Vergil's Aeneas: The Best of the Romans." In *Approaches to Teaching Vergil*, ed. W. S. Anderson and L. N. Quartarone. New York: Modern Language Association, 87–98.

Clayton, Barbara L. 2004. *A Penelopean Poetics: Reweaving the Feminine in Homer's Odyssey*. Lanham: Lexington Books.

Coarelli, F. 1997. *Il Campo Marzio dalle origini alla fine della republica*. Rome: Quasar.

Collard, C. 1975. "Medea and Dido." *Prometheus* 1, 131–51.

Conington, John. 1863. *P. Vergili Maronis Opera: The Works of Virgil with a Commentary*. Vol. 2, Containing the first six books of the Aeneid. London: Whitaker & Co.; George Bell.

Conington, John and Henry Nettleship. 1883. *P. Vergili Maronis Opera: The Works of Virgil with a Commentary*. Vol. 3, Containing the last six books of the Aeneid. 3rd ed., revised. London: Whitaker & Co.; George Bell and Sons.

Conington, John and Henry Nettleship. 1884. *P. Vergili Maronis Opera: The Works of Virgil with a Commentary*. Vol. 2, Containing the first six books of the Aeneid. 4th ed., revised with corrected orthography and additional notes. London: Whitaker & Co.; George Bell and Sons.

———. 1898. *P. Vergili Maronis Opera: The Works of Virgil with a Commentary*. Vol. 1, Eclogues and Georgics. 5th ed, revised F. Haverfield. London: George Bell and Sons.

———. 1883–1898/1963. *P. Vergili Maronis Opera: The Works of Virgil with a Commentary*. Rpt. of the editions of 1883–1898. 3 vols. Hildesheim: Olms.

Connolly, Joy. 2010. "Figuring the Founder: Vergil and the Challenge of Autocracy." In Farrell and Putnam 2010, 404–17.

Conte, Gian Biagio. 1970/1986. "Il balteo di Pallante." *Rivista di Filologia e di Istruzione Classica* 98, 292–300 / *The Rhetoric of Imitation: Genre and Poetic Memory in Virgil and other Latin Poets*. Trans. from the Italian. Ed. Charles Segal. Ithaca: Cornell University Press, 185–95.

———. 1999. "The Virgilian Paradox: An Epic of Drama and Sentiment." *Proceedings of the Cambridge Philological Society* 45, 17–42.

———. 2017. *Stealing the Club from Hercules: On Imitation in Latin Poetry*. Berlin and Boston: De Gruyter.

Conway, R. S. 1929/1931. "Vergil as a Student of Homer." *The Martin Classical Lectures*, ed. Louis E. Lord. Vol. 1. Cambridge, MA: Harvard University Press, 151–81.

———. ed. 1935. *P. Vergili Maronis Aeneidos liber primus*. Cambridge: Cambridge University Press.

Courtney, Edward. 2003. *The Fragmentary Latin Poets*. Oxford: Oxford University Press.

Cowan, Robert. 2015. "On the Weak King according to Vergil: Aeolus, Latinus, and Political Allegoresis in the *Aeneid*. *Vergilius*, 61, 97–124.

Crosby, H. Lamar. 1946. *Dio Chrysostom: Discourses 37–60*. With an English translation. Cambridge, MA: Harvard University Press.

Cucchiarelli, Andrea. 2019. *Orazio, Epistole 1: Introduzione, traduzione, e commento*. Pisa: Edizioni della Normale.

Cullyer, Helen. "Chrysippus on Achilles: The Evidence of Galen, 'De Placitis Hippocratis et Platonis' 4.6–7." *The Classical Quarterly* 58, 537–46.

Damon, Cynthia and Joseph Farrell, eds. 2020. *Ennius' Annals: Poetry and History*. Cambridge: Cambridge University Press.

Danek, G. 2005. "Nostos und Nostoi." *Aevum Antiquum* 5, 45–54.

———. 2015. "Nostoi." In Fantuzzi and Tsagalis, 355–79.

Davies, Malcolm. 1989. *The Greek Epic Cycle*. London: Bloomsbury Academic.

de Jong, Irene J. F. 2018. "The Birth of the Princes' Mirror in the Homeric Epics." In Klooster and Van den Berg, 20–37.

de Jonge, Casper C. 2018. "Eumaeus, Evander, and Augustus: Dionysius and Virgil on Noble Simplicity." In Klooster and Van den Berg, 157–81.

De Witt, Norman W. 1907. "The Dido Episode as Tragedy." *The Classical Journal* 2, 283–88.

———. 1930. "Vergil and the Tragic Drama." *The Classical Journal* 26, 19–27.

Dekel, Edan. 2012. *Virgil's Homeric Lens*. London and New York: Routledge.

Delvigo, Marialuisa. 2013. "*Per transitum tangit historiam*: Intersecting Developments of Roman Identity in Vergil." In Farrell and Nelis, 19–39.

Dickey, Eleanor. 2007. *Ancient Greek Scholarship: A Guide to Finding, Reading, and Understanding Scholia, Commentaries, Lexica, and Grammatical Treatises, from their Beginnings to the Byzantine Period*. New York: Oxford University Press.

Diggle, J. 1984. *Euripidis Fabulae: vol. 1: Cyclops; Alcestis; Medea; Heraclidae; Hippolytus; Andromacha; Hecuba*. Oxford: Oxford University Press.

Dilke, O.A.W. 1954. *Statius, Achilleid*. With an introduction, critical apparatus, and notes. Cambridge: Cambridge University Press.

Dingel, J. 1997. *Kommentar zum 9. Buch der Aeneis Vergils*. Heidelberg: Carl Winter.

Donlan, Walter. 1989. "The Unequal Exchange between Glaucus and Diomedes in Light of the Homeric Gift-Economy." *Phoenix* 43, 1–15.

Dorandi, Tiziano. 1982. *Philodemo, Il buon re secondo Omero: edizione, traduzione e commento*. Napoli: Bibliopolis.

Dougherty, Carol. 1993. *The Poetics of Colonization: From City to Text in Archaic Greece*. Oxford: Oxford University Press.

Dowling, Melissa Barden. 2006. *Clemency and Cruelty in the Roman World*. Ann Arbor: University of Michigan Press.

Duckworth, G. 1957. "The Aeneid as a Trilogy." *TAPA (Transactions of the American Philological Association)* 88, 1–10.

Dufallo, Basil. 2007. *The Ghosts of the Past: Latin Literature, the Dead, and Rome's Transition to a Principate*. Columbus: The Ohio State University Press.

Dyson, Julia T. 1996. "*Septima aestas*: The Puzzle of *Aen*. 1.755–6 and 5.626." *The Classical World* 90, 41–43.

———. 2001. *King of the Wood: The Sacrificial Victor in Virgil's Aeneid*. Oklahoma Series in Classical Culture 27. Norman: Oklahoma University Press.

Edwards, Anthony T. 1985. *Achilles in the Odyssey: Ideologies of Heroism in the Homeric Epic*. Beiträge zur klassischen Philologie, 171. Königstein im Taunus: Verlag Anton Hain.

Edwards, Mark J. 1992. "Horace, Homer and Rome: *Epistles* I, 2." *Mnemosyne* 45, 83–88.

Effe, Bernd. 1980. "Held und Literatur: Der Funktionswandel des Heracles-Mythos in der griechischen Literatur." *Poetica* 12, 145–66.

Eichhoff, Frédéric Gustave. 1825. *Études grecques sur Virgile*. 3 vols. Paris: A. Delalain.

Eidinow, J.S.C. 1990. "A note on Horace, Epistles 1.2.26 and 2.2.75." *The Classical Quarterly* 40, 566–68.

Eisenberger, Herbert. 1973. *Studien zur Odyssee*. Wiesbaden: Franz Steiner Verlag.

Eliot, T. S. 1945. *What Is a Classic? An address delivered before the Virgil Society on the 16th of October, 1944*. London: Faber.

Elliott, Jackie. 2008. "Ennian Epic and Ennian Tragedy in the Language of the *Aeneid*: Aeneas' Generic Wandering and the Construction of the Latin Literary Past." *Harvard Studies in Classical Philology* 104, 241–72.

———. 2013. *Ennius and the Architecture of the* Annales. Cambridge: Cambridge University Press.

Ellis, R. 1889. *A Commentary on Catullus*. Oxford: Oxford University Press.

Elsner, J. 1991. "Cult and Sculpture: Sacrifice in the *Ara Pacis Augustae*." *The Journal of Roman Studies* 81, 50–61.

———. 1995. *Art and the Roman Viewer: The Transformation of Art from the Pagan World to Christianity*. Cambridge: Cambridge University Press.

———. 2007. *Roman Eyes: Visuality and Subjectivity in Art and Text*. Princeton: Princeton University Press.

Empson, William. 1935. *Some Versions of Pastoral*. London: Chatto & Windus.

Erdmann, Martina. 1998. "Die Bilder am Apollotempel von Cumae und ihre Bedeutung im Kontext der *Aeneis*." *Gymnasium* 105, 481–506.

———. 2000. *Überredende Reden in Vergils Aeneis*. Studien zur klassischen Philologie 120. Frankfurt am Main: Peter Lang.

Erler, Michael. 1992. "Der Zorn des Helden: Philodems 'De Ira' und Vergils Konzept des Zorns in der 'Aeneis.'" *Grazer Beiträge* 18, 103–26.

———. 2009. "Laokoon als Zeichen: Göttliche Einwirkung und menschliche Disposition in Vergils *Aeneis* und bei Homer." In *Laokoon in Literatur und Kunst: Schriften des Symposions "Laokoon in Literatur und Kunst" vom 30.11.2006, Universität Bonn*, ed. Dorothea Gall and Anja Wolkenhauer. Beiträge zur Altertumskunde 254. Berlin and New York: De Gruyter, 14–31.

Faber, Riemer A. 2000. "Vergil's Shield of Aeneas (*Aeneid* 8.617–731) and the Shield of Heracles." *Mnemosyne* 53, 48–57.

Fabrizi, Virginia. 2012. *Mores veteresque novosque: Rappresentazioni del passato e del presente di Roma negli Annales di Ennio*. Pisa: ETS.

Falconer, William Armistead. 1923. *Cicero: On Old Age, On Friendship, On Divination. With an English Translation*. Cambridge, MA: Harvard University Press.

Fantham, Elaine. 1998. "Allecto's First Victim: A Study of Vergil's Amata (*Aeneid* 7.341–405 and 12.1–80)." In H.-P. Stahl, 1998, 135–154.

———. 1999. "Fighting Words: Turnus at Bay in the Latin Council (*Aeneid* 11.234–446)." *American Journal of Philology* 120, 259–80.

Fantuzzi, Marco. 2015. "The Aesthetics of Sequentiality and its Discontents." In Fantuzzi and Tsagalis, 405–29.

Fantuzzi, Marco and Christos Tsagalis, eds. 2015. *The Greek Epic Cycle and its Ancient Reception*. Cambridge: Cambridge University Press.

Farrell, Joseph. 1991. *Vergil's Georgics and the Traditions of Ancient Epic: The Art of Allusion in Literary History*. New York and Oxford: Oxford University Press.

———. 1997. "The Virgilian Intertext." In Martindale 1997, 222–38.

———. 2004. "Ovid's Vergilian Career." In *Re-presenting Virgil: Special Issue in Honor of Michael C. J. Putnam*, ed. G. W. Most and S. Spence. *Materiali e discussioni per l'analisi dei testi classici* 52, 41–55.

———. 2005. "Intention and Intertext." *Phoenix* 59, 98–111.

———. 2008. "Servius and the Homeric Scholia." In *Servio: stratificazioni esegetiche e modelli culturali / Servius: Exegetical Stratifications and Cultural Models*, ed. Sergio Casali and Fabio Stok. Collection Latomus 317. Brussels: Éditions Latomus, 112–31.

———. 2008a. "La ricompensa di Palinuro." *Studi Italiani di Filologia Classica* 4, 5–18.

———. 2012. "Art, Aesthetics, and the Hero in Vergil's *Aeneid*." In *Aesthetic Value in Classical Antiquity*, ed. Ineke Sluiter and Ralph M. Rosen. *Mnemosyne* Suppl. 350. Leiden and Boston, 285–313.

———. 2014. "Philosophy in Vergil." In *The Philosophizing Muse: The Influence of Greek Philosophy on Roman Poetry*, ed. Myrto Garani and David Konstan. Cambridge: Cambridge Scholarly Publishing, 61–90.

———. 2016. "Ancient Commentaries on Theocritus' *Idylls* and Vergil's *Eclogues*." In *Classical Commentaries: Explorations in a Scholarly Genre*, ed. Christina S. Kraus and Christopher Stray. Oxford: Oxford University Press, 397–418.

———. 2018. "The Genre of Princely Instruction in Classical Antiqiuty." In *I volti del Principe*, ed. Fabio Finotti. Padova: Marsilio, 19–46.

———. 2019. "Virgil's Intertextual Personae." In Martindale and Mac Góráin, 299–325.

———. 2019a. "Hermes in Love: The Erotic Career of a Mercurial Character." In *Tracking Hermes, Pursuing Mercury*, ed. John F. Miller and Jenny Strauss Clay. Oxford: Oxford University Press, 121–40.

———. 2020. "Was Memmius a Good King?" In *Approaches to Lucretius: Traditions and Innovations in Reading the De Rerum Natura*, ed. Donncha O'Rourke. Cambridge: Cambridge University Press, 219–40.

———. 2020a. "The Gods in Ennius." In Damon and Farrell, 63–88.

———. 2021. "Latin." In *How Literatures Begin: A Global History*, ed. Joel Lande and Denis Feeney. Princeton: Princeton University Press.

———. 2021a. "Kingship Theory in Archaic Latin Poetry." In *Latin Poetry and Its Reception: Essays for Susanna Braund*, ed. C. W. Marshall. New York and London: Routledge.

Farrell, Joseph and Michael C. J. Putnam, eds. 2010. *A Companion to Vergil's Aeneid and its Tradition*. Chichester: Wiley-Blackwell.

Farrell, Joseph and Damien P. Nelis, eds. 2013. *Augustan Poetry and the Roman Republic*. Oxford: Oxford University Press.

Farron, Steven G. 1977. "The *furor* and *violentia* of Aeneas." *Acta Classica* 20, 204–8.

———. 1985. "Aeneas' Human Sacrifice." *Acta Classica* 28, 21–33.

———. 1986. "Aeneas' Revenge for Pallas as a Criticism of Aeneas." *Acta Classica* 29, 69–83.

———. 1993. *Vergil's Aeneid: A Poem of Grief and Love*. Mnemosyne Suppl. 122. Leiden: Brill.

Feeney, D. C. 1984. "The Reconciliations of Juno." *The Classical Quarterly* 34, 179–94.

———. 1986. "Following after Hercules, in Apollonius and Virgil." *Proceedings of the Virgil Society* 18, 47–83.

———. 1991. *The Gods in Epic: Poets and Critics of the Classical Tradition*. Oxford: Oxford University Press.

———. 1999. "Epic Violence, Epic Order: Killings, Catalogues, and the Role of the Reader in Aeneid 10." In Perkell 1999, 178–94.

Feldherr, Andrew. 1995. "Ships of State: *Aeneid* 5 and Augustan Circus Spectacle." *Classical Antiquity* 14, 245–65.

———. 2002. "Stepping out of the Ring: Repetition and Sacrifice in the Boxing Match in *Aeneid* 5." In *Clio and the Poets: Augustan Poetry and the Traditions of Ancient Historiography*, ed. D. S. Levene and D. P. Nelis. Mnemosyne Suppl. 224. Leiden: Brill, 61–79.

Fenik, Bernard C. 1960. "The Influence of Euripides on Vergil's *Aeneid*. Diss. Princeton University.

Ferris, Jennifer L. 2009. "Catullus Poem 71: Another Foot Pun." *The Classical Journal* 104, 376–84.

Fish, Jeffrey. 1999. "Philodemus on the Education of the Good Prince: PHerc. 1507, col. 23." In *Satura: Collectanea philologica Italo Gallo ab amicis discipulisque dicata*, ed. Giancarlo Abbamonte, Andrea Rescigno, Angelo Rossi, and Ruggero Rossi. Naples: Arte Tipografica. 71–77.

———. 2002. "Philodemus' *On the Good King According to Homer*: Columns 21–31." *Cronache Ercolanesi* 32, 187–232.

Fish, Jeffrey. 2018. "Some Critical Themes in Philodemus' *On the Good King According to Homer.*" In Klooster and Van den Berg, 141–56.

Fish, Stanley E. 1976/1980. "Interpreting the *Variorum.*" In *Is there a Text in this Class: The Authority of Interpretive Communities.* Cambridge, MA: Harvard University Press.

Fitzgerald, William. 1984. "Aeneas, Daedalus, and the Labyrinth." *Arethusa* 17, 51–65.

Flatt, T. 2017. "Anēr Poluplanēs: Geography and the Odyssean Tradition in Polybius." *The Classical World* 110, 451–73.

Forbiger, Albertus. 1872–1875. *P. Vergili Maronis Opera.* 3 vols. 4th ed. Leipzig: Hinrichs.

Fowler, Don P. 1986. "Homer and Philodemus." Review of Dorandi 1982. *The Classical Review* 36, 81–85.

———. 1990. "Deviant Focalisation in Virgil's *Aeneid.*" *Proceedings of the Cambridge Philological Society* 36, 42–63.

———. 1991. "Narrate and Describe: The Problem of Ekphrasis." *The Journal of Roman Studies* 81, 25–35.

———. 1991a. "Subject review: Roman literature." *Greece & Rome* 38, 85–97.

———. 1997. "Virgilian Narrative: Story-telling." In Martindale 1997, 259–70.

———. 1997a. "Epicurean Anger." In *The Passions in Roman Thought and Literature*, ed. Susanna Morton Braund and Christopher Gill. Cambridge: Cambridge University Press, 16–35.

———. 2000. "Epic in the Middle of the Wood: *Mise en Abyme* in the Nisus and Euryalus Episode." In *Intratextuality: Greek and Roman Relations*, ed. Alison Sharrock and Helen Morales. Oxford: Oxford University Press, 89–113.

Fowler, Don P., Sergio Casali, and Fabio Stok. 1997/2019. "The Virgil Commentary of Servius." In Martindale 1997, 73–78 / revised Sergio Casali and Fabio Stok. In Martindale and Mac Góráin, 88–94.

Fraenkel, Eduard. 1931. "Livius Andronicus." In *Paulys Realencyclopädie der classischen Altertumswissenschaft*, Suppl. 5, 598–607.

———. 1945. "Some Aspects of the Structure of *Aeneid* 7." *The Journal of Roman Studies* 35, 1–14.

———. 1949. Review of *Servianorum in Vergilii Carmina Commentariorum Editionis Harvardianae Volumen II, Quod in Aeneidos Libros I et II Explanationes Continet* by E. K. Rand, J. J. Savage, H. T. Smith, G. B. Waldrop, J. P. Elder, B. M. Peebles, A. F. Stocker. Part 2. *The Journal of Roman Studies* 39, 145–54.

Frampton, Stephanie Ann. 2019. *Empire of Letters: Writing in Roman Literature and Thought, from Lucretius to Ovid.* Oxford: Oxford University Press.

Fränkel, Hermann. 1968. *Noten zu den Argonautika des Apollonios.* Munich: C. H. Beck.

Fratantuono, Lee. 2006. "*Tros Italusque*: Arruns in the *Aeneid.*" In *Studies in Latin Literature and History* 13, ed. Carl Deroux. Collection Latomus 301. Brussels: Éditions Latomus, 284–90.

Fratantuono, Lee and R. Alden Smith. 2015. *Virgil, Aeneid 5: Text, Translation and Commentary.* Mnemosyne Suppl. 386. Leiden: Brill.

Freudenburg, Kirk. 2001. *Satires of Rome: Threatening Poses from Lucilius to Juvenal.* Cambridge: Cambridge University Press.

———. 2017. "Seeing Marcellus in *Aeneid* 6." *The Journal of Roman Studies* 107, 116–39.

———. 2019. "Epic Anger, and the State of the (Roman) Soul in Virgil's First Simile." In *Augustan Poetry: New Trends and Revaluations*, ed. Paulo Martins, Alexandre Hasegawa and João Angelo Oliva Neto. São Paolo: Editora Humanitas, 287–311.

Fröhlich, Uwe. 2011. "*Nulla salus bello*: Vergils Drances." In *Noctes Sinenses: Festschrift für Fritz-Heiner Mutschler zum 65. Geburtstag*, ed. Andreas Heil, Matthias Korn and Jochen Sauer. Kalliope 11. Heidelberg: Winter, 15–20.

Fuchs, H. 1947. "Rückschau und Ausblick im Arbeitsreich der lateinschen Philologie." *Museum Helveticum* 4, 147–98.

Fulkerson, Laurel. 2006. "Neoptolemus Grows Up? 'Moral development' and the Interpretation of Sophocles' *Philoctetes*." *The Classical Journal* 52, 49–61.

———. 2008. "Patterns of Death in the *Aeneid*." *Scripta Classica Israelica* 27, 17–33.

Fuqua, Charles. 1982. "Hector, Sychaeus, and Deiphobus: Three Mutilated Figures in *Aeneid* 1–6." *Classical Philology* 77, 235–40.

Gabba, Emilio. 1976. "Sulla valorizzazione politica della leggenda delle origini troiane di Roma fra III e II secolo a. C." *Contributi dell'Istituto di Storia antica dell'Università del Sacro Cuore* 4, 84–101.

Galinsky, G. Karl. 1966. "The Hercules-Cacus Episode in *Aeneid* VIII." *American Journal of Philology* 87, 18–51.

———. 1968. "*Aeneid* V and the *Aeneid*." *American Journal of Philology* 89, 157–85.

———. 1969. *Aeneas, Sicily, and Rome*. Princeton: Princeton University Press.

———. 1972. *The Herakles Theme: The Adaptations of the Hero in Literature from Homer to the Twentieth Century*. Oxford: Blackwell.

———. 1981. "Vergil's *Romanitas* and His Adaptation of Greek Heroes." *Aufstieg und Niedergang der römischen Welt* 2.31.2, 985–1010.

———. 1988. "The Anger of Aeneas." *American Journal of Philology* 109, 321–48.

———. 1996. *Augustan Culture: An Interpretive Introduction*. Princeton: Princeton University Press.

———. 2006. "Vergil's Uses of *libertas*: Texts and Contexts." *Vergilius* 52, 3–19.

Ganiban, R. 2009. "The *Dolus* and Glory of Ulysses in *Aeneid* 2." *Materiali e discussioni per l'analisi dei testi classici* 61, 57–70.

Garstang, J. B. 1950. "The Tragedy of Turnus." *Phoenix* 9, 47–58.

Gärtner, U. 2015. "Virgil and the Epic Cycle." In Fantuzzi and Tsagalis, 543–64.

Gasti, Helen. 2006. "Narratological Aspects of Virgil's *Aeneid* 2.1–13." *Acta Classica* 49, 113–20.

———. 2010. "Narrative Self-consciousness in Virgil's *Aeneid* 3." *Dictynna* 7, https://journals.openedition.org/dictynna/348.

George, E. V. 1974. *Aeneid VIII and the Aitia of Callimachus*. Mnemosyne Suppl. 27. Leiden: Brill.

Germanus, Valens Guellius. 1575. *P. Vergilius Maro et in eum commentationes et paralipomena*. Antwerp: Christophe Plaintin.

Gerolemou, Maria. 2018. "Educating Kings through Travel: The Wanderings of Odysseus as a Mental Model in Polybius' *Histories*." In Klooster and Van den Berg, 124–40.

Gibson, C. A. 1999. "Punitive Blinding in *Aeneid* 3." *The Classical World* 92, 359–66.

Gigante, Marcello. 2001/2004. "Virgilio all'ombra del Vesuvio." *Cronache Ercolanesi* 31, 5–26 / "Vergil in the Shadow of Vesuvius." In Armstrong et al. 2004, 85–99.

Gigante, Marcello and Mario Capasso. 1989. "Il ritorno di Virgilio a Ercolano." *Studi Italiani di Filologia Classica* 7, 3–6.

Giusti, Elena. 2016. "Did Somebody Say Augustan Totalitarianism? Duncan Kennedy's 'Reflections,' Hannah Arendt's *Origins*, and the Continental Divide over Virgil's *Aeneid*." *Dictynna* 13, https://journals.openedition.org/dictynna/1263.

Giusti, Elena. 2018. *Carthage in Virgil's Aeneid: Staging the Enemy under Augustus*. Cambridge: Cambridge University Press.

Gladhill, C. W. 2012. "Sons, Mothers, and Sex: *Aeneid* 1.314–20 and the *Hymn to Aphrodite* Reconsidered." *Vergilius* 58, 159–68.

Glei, Reinhold. 1991. *Der Vater der Dinge: Interpretationen zur poetischen, literarischen und kulturellen Dimension des Krieges bei Vergil*. Bochumer Altertumswissenschaftliches Colloquium 7. Trier: Wissenschaftlicher Verlag Trier.

Glenn, Justin. 1971. "Mezentius and Polyphemus." *American Journal of Philology* 92, 129–55.

Goldberg, Sander M. 1995. *Epic in Republican Rome*. New York and Oxford: Oxford University Press.

Goldberg, Sander M., and Gesine Manuwald, ed. and trans. 2018. *Fragmentary Republican Latin*. Vol. 1. *Ennius: Testimonia, Epic Fragments*. Cambridge, MA: Harvard University Press.

Goldschmidt, Nora. 2013. *Shaggy Crowns: Ennius' Annales and Virgil's Aeneid*. Oxford: Oxford University Press.

González Vázquez, José 1979–1980. "Mezencio: Su caracterización a través de las imagenes, *Aen*. X, 689–772." *Cuadernos de Filología de la Complutense* 16, 127–38.

Gordon, P. 1998. "Phaeacian Dido: Lost Pleasures of an Epicurean Intertext." *Classical Antiquity* 17, 188–211.

Gosling, Anne. 1986. "Octavian, Brutus and Apollo: A Note." *American Journal of Philology* 107, 586–89.

Gotoff, Harold C. 1984. "The Transformation of Mezentius." *TAPA (Transactions of the American Philological Association)* 114, 191–218.

———. 1985. "The Difficulty of the Ascent from Avernus." *Classical Philology* 80, 35–40.

Gottlieb, Gunther. 1998. "Religion in the Politics of Augustus: *Aeneid* 1.278–91; 8.714–23; 12.791–842." In H.-P. Stahl, 1998, 21–36.

Graf, Fritz. 1974. *Eleusis und die orphische Dichtung: Athens in vorhellenistischer Zeit*. Religionsgeschichtliche Versuche und Vorarbeiten 33. Berlin: De Gruyter.

Gransden, K. W. 1984. *Virgil's Iliad: An Essay on Epic Narrative*. Cambridge: Cambridge University Press.

Gratwick, A. S. 1993. *Plautus: Menaechmi*. Cambridge: Cambridge University Press.

Greenberg, N. A. 1958. "Metathesis as an Instrument in the Criticism of Poetry." *TAPA (Transactions of the American Philological Association)* 89, 262–70.

Griffin, Alan. 1983. "Pius Aeneas or Aeneas the Wimp?" *Akroterion* 38, 81–85.

Gruen, Erich S. 1992. *Culture and National Identity in Republican Rome*. Ithaca: Cornell University Press.

———. 1996. "The Expansion of the Empire under Augustus." In *The Cambridge Ancient History*. 2nd ed. Vol. 10: The Augustan Empire, 43 B.C.–A.D. 69, ed. Alan K. Bowman, Edward Champlin and Andrew Lintott. Cambridge: Cambridge University Press, 147–97.

Gutting, Edward. 2006. "Marriage in the *Aeneid*: Venus, Vulcan, and Dido." *Classical Philology* 101, 263–79.

Habinek, Thomas. 1998. *The Politics of Latin Literature: Writing, Identity, and Empire in Ancient Rome*. Princeton: Princeton University Press.

Haecker, Theodor. 1931/1934. *Vergil, Vater des Abendlandes*. Munich: Kösel / *Virgil, Father of the West*. Trans. A. W. Wheen. New York: Sheed & Ward.

Haft, A. 1984. "Odysseus, Idomeneus and Meriones: The Cretan Lies of *Odyssey* 13–19." *The Classical Journal* 79, 289–306.

Hall, Edith. 2008. "Can the *Odyssey* Ever be Tragic? Historical Perspectives on the Theatrical Realization of Greek Epic." In *Performance, Iconography, Reception: Studies in Honour of Oliver Taplin*, ed. M. Revermann and P. Wilson, 499–523.

Halliwell, Stephen et al. 1995. *Aristotle: Poetics*. Ed. and trans. Stephen Halliwell. *Longinus: On the Sublime*, Trans. W. H. Fyfe. Rev. Donald Russell. *Demetrius: On Style*. Ed. and trans. Doreen C. Innes. Based on W. Rhys Roberts. Cambridge, MA: Harvard University Press.

Hard, Robin. 1997. *Apollodorus: The Library of Greek Mythology*. Translated with an introduction and notes. Oxford: Oxford University Press.

Harder, Annette. 2012. *Callimachus: Aetia*. 2 vols. Oxford: Oxford University Press.

Hardie, Alex. 2007. "Juno, Hercules, and the Muses at Rome." *American Journal of Philology* 128, 551–92.

———. 2016. "The Camenae in Cult, History, and Song." *Classical Antiquity* 35, 45–48.

Hardie, Colin. 1967. "Homer in the *Aeneid*." Review of Knauer 1964. *The Classical Review* 17, 158–61.

Hardie, P. R. 1985. "*Imago mundi*: Cosmological and Ideological Aspects of the Shield of Achilles." *The Journal of Hellenic Studies* 105, 11–31.

———. 1986. *Virgil's Aeneid: Cosmos and Imperium*. Oxford: Oxford University Press.

———. 1991. "The *Aeneid* and the *Oresteia*." *Proceedings of the Virgil Society* 20, 29–45.

———. 1993. *The Epic Successors of Virgil: A Study in the Dynamics of a Tradition*. Cambridge: Cambridge University Press.

———. 1994. *Virgil: Aeneid, Book IX*. Cambridge: Cambridge University Press.

———. 1997/2019. "Virgil and Tragedy." In Martindale and Mac Góráin, 326–42.

———. 1998. *Virgil. Greece & Rome*. New Surveys in the Classics 28. Oxford: Oxford University Press.

———. 1998a: "Fame and Defamation in the *Aeneid*: The Council of Latins. *Aeneid*, 11.225–467." In H.-P. Stahl, 1998, 243–70.

———. ed. 1999. *Virgil: Critical Assessments of Classical Authors*. 4 vols. London and New York: Routledge.

———. ed. 2009. *Paradox and the Marvellous in Augustan Literature and Culture*. Oxford: Oxford University Press.

———. 2014. *The Last Trojan Hero: A Cultural History of Virgil's Aeneid*. London: I. B. Tauris.

———. ed. 2016. *Augustan Poetry and the Irrational*. Oxford: Oxford University Press.

Harrison, E. L. 1972–1973. "Why Did Venus Wear Boots? Some Reflections on *Aeneid* 1.314f." *Proceedings of the Virgil Society* 12, 10–25.

———. 1986. "Foundation Prodigies in the *Aeneid*." *Papers of the Liverpool Latin Seminar* 5, 131–64.

———. 1989. "The Tragedy of Dido." *Echos du monde classique* 33, 1–21.

Harrison, S. J. 1991. *Vergil: Aeneid 10*. With introduction, translation, and commentary. Oxford: Oxford University Press.

———. 2007. *Generic Enrichment in Vergil and Horace*. Oxford: Oxford University Press.

———. 2007a. "Henry Nettleship and the Beginning of Modern Latin Studies at Oxford." In *Oxford Classics: Teaching and Learning, 1800–2000*, ed. Christopher A. Stray. London: Bristol Classical Press, 107–116.

Hartog, F. 2001. *Memories of Odysseus: Frontier Tales from Ancient Greece.* Chicago: University of Chicago Press.

Havelock, E. A. 1967. *The Lyric Genius of Catullus.* New York.

Hawkins, Tom. 2016. "The Underwood of Satire: Reading the *Epodes* through Ovid's *Ibis*," in *Horace's Epodes: Contexts, Intertexts, and Reception,* ed. Philippa Bather and Claire Stocks. Oxford: Oxford University Press, 175–98.

Heckenlively, T. S. 2013. "*Clipeus hesiodicus: Aeneid* 8 and the *Shield of Heracles.*" *Mnemosyne* 66, 649–65.

Heerink, Mark. 2015. *Echoing Hylas: A Study in Hellenistic and Roman Metapoetics.* Madison: University of Wisconsin Press.

Heiden, Bruce. 1987. "*Laudes Herculeae*: Suppressed Savagery in the Hymn to Hercules, Verg. A. 8.285–305." *American Journal of Philology* 108, 661–71.

Heil, Swantje. 2001. *Spannungen und Ambivalenzen in Vergils Aeneis: Zum Verhältnis von menschlichem Leid und der Erfüllung des fatum.* Hamburg: Verlag Dr Kovač.

Heinze, Richard. 1915/1993. *Vergils epische Technik.* 3rd ed. Leipzig: B. G. Teubner / *Virgil's Epic Technique.* Tr. Hazel Harvey, David Harvey, Fred Robinson. Berkeley: University of California Press.

Hejduk, Julia D. 2009. "Jupiter's *Aeneid: fama* and *imperium.*" *Classical Antiquity* 28, 279–327.

———. 2017. Introduction: Reading Civil War." *The Classical World* 111, 1–5.

———. 2020. *The God of Rome: Jupiter in Augustan Poetry.* New York and Oxford: Oxford University Press.

Henderson, John. 1998. "Exemplo suo mores reget." Review of Galinsky 1996. *Hermathena* 164, 101–16.

Henkel, John. 2014. "Metrical Feet on the Road of Poetry: Foot Puns and Literary Polemic in Tibullus." *The Classical World* 107, 451–75.

Hershkowitz, Debra. 1991. "The *Aeneid* in *Aeneid* 3." *Vergilius* 37, 69–76.

———. 1998. *The Madness of Epic: Reading Insanity from Homer to Statius.* Oxford: Oxford University Press.

Heslin, Peter. 2005. *The Transvestite Achilles: Gender and Genre in Statius' Achilleid.* Cambridge: Cambridge University Press.

Heubeck, Alfred et al. 1988–92. *A Commentary on Homer's Odyssey.* 3 vols. Oxford: Oxford University Press.

Hexter, Ralph. 1999. "Imitating Troy: A Reading of *Aeneid* 3." In Perkell 1999, 64–79.

———. 2010. "On First Looking into Vergil's Homer." In Farrell and Putnam 2010, 26–36.

Heyne, Christian Gottlob. 1830–1841. *P. Vergilii Maronis Opera varietate lectionis et perpetua adnotatione illustrata.* 4th ed. G. P. E. Wagner. 5 vols. Leipzig and London.

Heyworth, S. J. 2001. "Catullan Iambics, Catullan Iambi." In *Iambic Ideas,* ed. A. Carvazere, A. Aloni, A. Barchiesi. Lanham: Rowman and Littlefield, 117–40.

Heyworth, S. J. and J.H.W. Morwood. 2017. *A Commentary on Vergil, Aeneid 3.* Oxford: Oxford University Press.

Hicks, R. D. 1925. *Diogenes Laertius: Lives of the Eminent Philosophers.* With an English translation. Vol. 1. Cambridge, MA: Harvard University Press.

Hinds, S. 1985. "Booking the Return Trip: Ovid and *Tristia* 1." *Proceedings of the Cambridge Philological Society* 31, 13–32.

———. 1987. *The Metamorphosis of Persephone: Ovid and the Self-conscious Muse*. Cambridge: Cambridge University Press.

———. 1998. *Allusion and Intertext: Dynamics of Appropriation in Roman Poetry*. Cambridge: Cambridge University Press.

Holoka, James P. 1999. "Heroes cunctantes—Hesitant Heroes: Aeneas and Some Others." In *Euphrosyne: Studies in Ancient Epic and Its Legacy in Honor of Dimitris N. Maronitis*, ed. John N. Kazazis and Antonios Rengakos. Stuttgart: Franz Steiner, 143–53.

Hölscher, T. 1987/2004. *Römische Bildsprache als semantisches System*. Heidelberg: Carl Winter / *The Language of Images in Roman Art*. Trans. A. Snodgrass and A. Künzl-Snodgrass. Cambridge: Cambridge University Press.

Hopkinson, Neil. 1988. *A Hellenistic Anthology*. Cambridge: Cambridge University Press.

Hornsby, R. A. 1966. "The Armor of the Slain." *Philological Quarterly* 45, 347–59.

Horsfall, N. M. 1971. "Numanus Remulus: Ethnography and Propaganda in *Aeneid* 9.598ff." *Latomus* 30, 1108–16.

———. 1973–1974. "Dido in the Light of History." *Proceedings of the Virgil Society* 13, 1–13.

———. 1986. "The Aeneas-legend and the *Aeneid*." *Vergilius* 32, 8–17.

———. 1995. *A Companion to the Study of Virgil*. Mnemosyne Suppl. 151. Leiden: Brill.

———. 2000. *Vergil, Aeneid 7: A Commentary*. Mnemosyne Suppl. 198. Leiden: Brill.

———. 2002. "Sallustian Politician and Vergilian Villain." *Scripta Classica Israelica* 21, 79–81.

———. 2003. *Vergil, Aeneid 11: A Commentary*. Mnemosyne Suppl. 244. Leiden: Brill.

———. 2006. *Virgil, Aeneid 3: A Commentary*. Mnemosyne Suppl. 273 Leiden: Brill.

———. 2008. *Virgil, Aeneid 2: A Commentary*. Mnemosyne Suppl. 299. Leiden: Brill.

———. 2013. *Vergil, Aeneid 6: A Commentary*. 2 vols. Berlin and Boston: De Gruyter.

Hunter, Richard L. 1989. *Apollonius: Argonautica, Book III*. Cambridge: Cambridge University Press.

———. 1993. *The Argonautica of Apollonius: Literary Studies*. Cambridge: Cambridge University Press.

Hutchinson, G. O. 2007. "The Monster and the Monologue: Polyphemus from Homer to Ovid." In *Hesperos: Studies in Ancient Greek Poetry Presented to M. L. West on his Seventieth Birthday*, ed. P. J. Finglass, C. Collard, N. J. Richardson. Oxford: Oxford University Press, 22–39.

Jacobson, Howard. 1979. "Cacus and the Cyclops." *Mnemosyne* 42, 101–2.

Jenkyns, Richard. 1985. "Pathos, Tragedy and Hope in the *Aeneid*." *The Journal of Roman Studies* 75, 60–77.

Johnson, W. R. 1976. *Darkness Visible: A Study of Vergil's Aeneid*. Berkeley and Los Angeles: University of California Press.

Johnston, P. A. 1980. *Vergil's Agricultural Golden Age: A Study of the Georgics*. Mnemosyne suppl. 60. Leiden: Brill.

Kaiser, E. 1964. "Odyssee-Szenen als Topoi." *Museum Helveticum* 21, 109–36, 197–224.

Kaster, R. A. 2011. *Macrobius: Saturnalia*. 3 vols. Cambridge, MA: Harvard University Press.

Katz, Joshua T. 2018. "Μῆνιν ἄειδε, θεά and the Form of the Homeric Word for 'Goddess.'" In *Language and Meter*, ed. Olav Hackstein and Dieter Gunkel. Brill's Studies in Indo-European Languages and Linguistics 18. Leiden: Brill. 54–76.

Keith, Alison. 2000. *Engendering Rome: Women in Latin Epic*. Cambridge: Cambridge University Press.

Keith, Alison. 2021. "The Good King according to Vergil in the *Aeneid*." In *Latin Poetry and Its Reception: Essays for Susanna Braund*, ed. C. W. Marshall. New York and London: Routledge.

Kelly, Adrian. 2014. "Apollonius and the End of the *Aeneid*." *The Classical Quarterly* 64, 642–48.

Kelly, Henry Ansgar. 1993. *Ideas and Forms of Tragedy from Aristotle to the Middle Ages*. Cambridge: Cambridge University Press.

Kennedy, Duncan F. 1992. "'Augustan' and 'anti-Augustan': Reflections on Terms of Reference." In *Roman Poetry and Propaganda in the Age of Augustus*, ed. Anton Powell, London: Bristol Classical Press, 26–58.

———. 1995. "Tradition and Appropriation: T. S. Eliot and Virgil's *Aeneid*." *Hermathena* 158, 73–92.

———. 1997/2019. "Modern Receptions and their Interpretive Implications: The Case of T. S. Eliot." In Martindale and Mac Góráin 2019.

Kennedy, Geoff. 2014. "Cicero, Roman Republicanism and the Contested Meaning of *Libertas*." *Political Studies* 62, 488–501.

Kennerly, Michele. 2018. *Editorial Bodies: Perfection and Rejection in Ancient Rhetoric and Poetics*. Columbia: University of South Carolina Press.

Kenney, E. J. 1979. "*Iudicium transferendi*: Virgil, *Aeneid* 2.469–505 and Its Antecedents." In *Creative Imitation and Latin Literature*, ed. David West and Tony Woodman. Cambridge: Cambridge University Press, 103–20.

Kenyon, F. G. 1932. *Books and Readers in Ancient Greece and Rome*. Oxford: Oxford University Press.

Kent, Roland G. 1938. *Varro: On the Latin Language*. With an English translation. 2 vols. Cambridge, MA: Harvard University Press.

Kepple, Laurence R. 1976. "Arruns and the Death of Aeneas." *American Journal of Philology* 97, 344–60.

Kindstrand, J. F. 1973. *Homer in der Zweiten Sophistik: Studien zu der Homerlektüre und dem Homerbild bei Dion von Prusa, Maximos von Tyros und Ailios Aristeide*. Uppsala: Acta Universitatis Upsaliensis.

King, Catherine Callen. 1991. *Achilles: Paradigms of the War Hero from Homer to the Middle Ages*. Berkeley: University of California Press.

Kirk, G. S. et al. 1985–1993. *The Iliad: A Commentary*. 6 vols. Cambridge: Cambridge University Press.

Kleinknecht, Hermann. 1944. "Laokoon." *Hermes* 79, 66–111.

Klingner, Friedrich. 1967. *Virgil: Bucolica, Georgica, Aeneis*. Zürich: Artemis Verlag.

Klooster, Jacqueline and Baukje Van den Berg, eds. 2018. *Homer and the Good Ruler in Antiquity and Beyond*. Mnemosyne Suppl. 413. Leiden: Brill.

Kluth, Andreas. 2010. "The First 'Almost Modern' Hero: Aeneas." http://andreaskluth.org/tag/aeneas. Accessed July 27, 2010.

Knauer, Georg Nicolaus 1964. *Die Aeneis und Homer: Studien zur poetischer Technik Vergils mit Listen der Homerzitate in der Aeneis*. Hypomnemata: Untersuchungen zur Antike und ihren Nachleben 7. Göttingen: Vandenhoeck & Ruprecht.

Knauer, Georg Nicolaus 1964a. "Vergil's *Aeneid* and Homer." *Greek, Roman, and Byzantine Studies* 5, 61–84.

Knight, Virginia. 1995. *The Renewal of Epic: Responses to Homer in the Argonautica of Apollonius.* Mnemosyne Suppl. 152. Leiden: Brill.

Knox, B.M.W. 1950. "The Serpent and the Flame: The Imagery of the Second Book of the *Aeneid*." *American Journal of Philology* 71, 379–400.

Kofler, Wolfgang. 2003. *Aeneas und Vergil: Untersuchung zur poetologischen Dimension der Aeneis.* Heidelberg: Carl Winter.

Kondratieff, Eric. 2012. "*Anchises censorius*: Vergil, Augustus, and the Census of 28 BCE." *Illinois Classical Studies* 37, 121–40.

König, Annemarie. 1970. "Die *Aeneis* und die griechische Tragödie: Studien zur *imitatio*-Technik Vergils. Diss. Berlin, Freie Universität.

Konstan, David. 1986. "Venus's Enigmatic Smile." *Vergilius* 32, 18–25.

Kragelund, Patrick. 1976. *Dream and Prediction in the Aeneid: A Semiotic Interpretation of the Dreams of Aeneas and Turnus.* Opuscula Graecolatina. Suppl. Musei Tusculani 7. Copenhagen: Museum Tusculanum.

Kraggerud, Egil. 1968. *Aeneisstudien. Symbolae Osloenses* Suppl. 22. Oslo: Universiteitsforlaget.

———. 1987. "Perusia and the *Aeneid*." *Symbolae Osloenses* 62, 77–87.

Kroll, W. 1959. *C. Valerius Catullus.* Stuttgart: Teubner.

Krummen, Eveline. 2001. "*Totam incensa per urbem bacchatur* . . . Liebe und bacchantischer Wahnsinn: Zur Bild- und Tragödientradition in Vergils Didoerzählung." *Ianus: Informationen zum altsprachlichen Unterricht* 22, 7–16.

———. 2004. "Dido als Mänade und tragische Heroine: Dionysische Thematik und Tragödientradition in Vergils Didoerzählung." *Poetica* 36, 25–69.

Kühn, Werner. 1957. "Rüstungsszenen bei Homer und Vergil." *Gymnasium* 64, 28–59.

Kuntz, Mary. 1993. "The Prodikean 'Choice of Herakles': A Reshaping of Myth." *The Classical Journal* 89, 163–181.

Kurke, Leslie. 1990. "Pindar's Sixth Pythian and the Tradition of Advice Poetry." *TAPA (Transactions of the American Philological Association)* 120, 18–107.

Kyriakidis, Stratis. 1998. *Narrative Structure in the Aeneid: The Frame of Book 6.* Le Rane 23. Bari: Levanti Editori.

Kyriakou, Poulheria. 1999. "Aeneas' Dream of Hector." *Hermes* 127, 317–27.

La Penna, Antonio. 1967. "Amata e Didone." *Maia* 19, 309–18.

———. 1971. "Spunti sociologici per l'interpretazione dell'*Eneide*." In *Vergiliana: Recherches sur Virgile*, ed. Henri Bardon and Raoul Verdière. Roma Aeterna 3. Leiden: Brill, 283–93

———. 1999. "Sociological Approaches to the Interpretation of the *Aeneid*." In P. R. Hardie 1999 vol. 3, 173–82.

———. 2000. "L'ordine delle raffigurationi delle guerra troiana nel tempio di Cartigigne (*Aen.* 1.469–493)." *Maia* 52, 1–8.

Labate, Mario. 2009. "In Search of the Lost Hercules: Strategies of the Fantastic in the *Aeneid*." In P. R. Hardie 2009, 126–44.

Laird, Andrew. 1999. *Powers of Expression, Expressions of Power: Speech Presentation and Latin Literature.* Oxford: Oxford University Press.

Lamberton, Robert. 1988. *Hesiod.* New Haven: Yale University Press.

Lampert, L. 2002. "Socrates' Defense of Polytropic Odysseus: Lying and Wrong-doing in Plato's *Lesser Hippias*." *The Review of Politics* 64, 231–60.

Lausberg, Marion. 1983. "Iliadisches im ersten Buch der *Aeneis*." *Gymnasium* 90, 203–39.

Leach, Eleanor Winsor. 1988. *The Rhetoric of Space: Literary and Artistic Representations of Landscape in Republican and Augustan Rome*. Princeton: Princeton University Press.

Lefkowitz, Mary P. 2012. *The Lives of the Greek Poets*. 2nd ed. Baltimore: Johns Hopkins University Press.

Leigh, Matthew. 2007. "Troia, Sicilia, Roma: Virgilio, il pugilato e il problema d'Erice." In *Eroi, eroismi, eroizzazioni: dalla Grecia antica a Padova e Venezia: Atti del convegno internazionale, Padova, 18–19 settembre 2006*, ed. Alessandra Coppola. Padova: Sargon, 27–35.

———. 2010. "Boxing and Sacrifice: Apollonius, Vergil, and Valerius." *Harvard Studies in Classical Philology* 105, 117–55.

Lenssen, José G.A.M. 1990. "*Hercules exempli gratia*: de Hercules-Cacus-episode in Vergilius *Aeneis* 8.185–305." *Lampas* 23, 50–73.

Lenta, Giovanni. 2012. "L'eroe epico si racconta: Odisseo, Enea e la narrazione di sé." In *Figure e autori dell'epica: Atti del convegno, Sala Ghislieri, Mondovì (CN) 8–11 aprile 2011*, ed. S. Casarino and A. Raschieri. Rome: Aracne Editrice, 93–110.

Levene, D. S. 2010. *Livy on the Hannibalic War*. Oxford: Oxford University Press.

Levitan, William. 1993. "Give up the Beginning? Juno's Mindful Wrath (*Aeneid* 1.37)." *Liverpool Classical Monthly* 18, 14–15.

Linderski, J. 1993/1995. "Roman Religion in Livy." In *Livius: Aspekte seines Werkes*, ed. W Schuller. Xenia: Konstanzer Althistorische Vorträge und Forschungen 31. Konstanz: Universitätsverlag Konstanz, 53–70 / *Roman Questions*. Stuttgart: Franz Steiner Verlag, 608–25.

Lintott, A. W. 1999. *The Constitution of the Roman Republic*. Oxford: Oxford University Press.

Littlewood, R. Joy. 2006. *A Commentary on Ovid's Fasti, Book 6*. Oxford: Oxford University Press.

Lloyd-Jones, Hugh. 1967. "Heracles at Eleusis. P. Oxy. 2622 and P. S. I. 1391." *Maia* 19, 206–29.

Lovatt, Helen. 2005. *Statius and Epic Games: Sport, Politics and Poetics in the Thebaid*. Cambridge: Cambridge University Press.

Lowrie, Michèle. 2009. *Writing, Performance, and Authority in Augustan Rome*. Oxford: Oxford University Press.

Luck, Georg. 1983. "Naevius and Virgil." *Illinois Classical Studies* 8, 267–75.

Lynch, John P. 1980. "Laocoön and Sinon: Virgil *Aeneid* 2.40–198." *Greece & Rome* 27, 170–79.

Lyne, R.O.A.M. 1987. *Further Voices in Vergil's Aeneid*. Oxford: Oxford University Press.

Mac Góráin, F. 2013. "Virgil's Bacchus and the Roman Republic." In Farrell and Nelis, 2013, 124–45.

Mac Góráin, Fiachra. 2018. "Untitled/*Arma Virumque*." *Classical Philology* 113, 423–48.

Mack, Sara. 1978. *Patterns of Time in Vergil*. Hamden: Archon Books.

Mackail, J. W. 1930. *The Aeneid*. Edited with introduction and commentary. Oxford: Oxford University Press.

Mair, A. W. and Mair, G. R. *Callimachus: Hymns and Epigrams*. Trans. A. W. Mair. *Aratus*. Trans. G. R. Mair. Cambridge, MA: Harvard University Press.

Malaspina, E. 2004/2008. "I fondali teatrali nella letteratura latina (Riflessioni sulla *scaena* di *Aen*. I 159–169). *Aevum Antiquum* 4, 95–123 / *La riflessione sul teatro nella cultura romana: Atti del congresso internazionale 10–12 maggio 2006, Milano, Università cattolica del Sacro Cuore*, ed. Giuseppe Aricò and Massimo Rivoltella. Milan: Vita e Pensiero, 95–123.

Maltby, Robert. 1991. *A Lexicon of Ancient Etymologies*. ARCA Classical and Medieval Texts, Papers and Monographs 25. Leeds: Francis Cairns.

Marincola, John. 2007. "Odysseus and the Historians." *Syllecta Classica* 18, 1–79.

———. 2010. "Eros and Empire: Virgil and the Historians on Civil War." In *Ancient Historiography and Its Contexts: Studies in Honour of A. J. Woodman*, ed. Christina S. Kraus, John Marincola and Christopher Pelling. Oxford: Oxford University Press, 183–204.

Mariotti, Scevola. 1952/1986. *Livio Andronico e la traduzione artistica: Saggio critico ed edizione dei frammenti dell'Odyssea*. 2nd ed. Milano: Urbino.

———. 1955/2001. *Il Bellum Poenicum e l'arte di Nevio: Saggio con edizione dei frammenti del Bellum Poenicum*. 3rd ed. Bologna: Pàtron.

Martin Richard P. 1984. "Hesiod, Odysseus and the Instruction of Princes." *TAPA (Transactions of the American Philological Association)* 114, 29–48.

———. 2005. "Pulp Epic: the 'Catalogue' and the 'Shield.'" In *The Hesiodic Catalogue of Women: Constructions and Reconstructions*, ed. Richard L. Hunter. Cambridge: Cambridge University Press, 153–75.

Martina, A. 1990. "Teatro Romano." *Enciclopedia virgiliana* 5, 59–63.

Martindale, Charles, ed. 1997. *The Cambridge Companion to Virgil*. Cambridge: Cambridge University Press.

Martindale, Charles. 2017/2019. "Introduction: 'The Classic of all Europe.'" In Martindale and Mac Góráin, 1–20.

Martindale, Charles and Fiachra Mac Góráin, eds. 2019. *The Cambridge Companion to Virgil*. 2nd ed. Cambridge: Cambridge University Press.

Mayer, Roland. 1994. *Horace: Epistles, Book 1*. Cambridge: Cambridge University Press.

Mazzocchini, Paolo. 2000. *Forme e significati della narrazione bellica nell'epos virgiliano: I cataloghi degli uccisi e le morti minori nell'Eneide*. Fasano: Schena editore.

McDermott, William C. 1980. "Drances/Cicero." *Vergilius* 26, 34–38.

McDonnell, Myles. 2006. *Roman Manliness: Virtus and the Roman Republic*. Cambridge: Cambridge University Press.

McGill, S. 2006. "*Menin Virumque*": Translating Homer with Virgil in *Epigrammata Bobiensia* 46, 47 and 64." *The Classical Journal* 101, 425–431.

McNelis, Charles Anthony and Alexander Sens. 2010. "*Quasi indignum heroo carmine*: Lycophron, *Alexandra* 258–313 and Dido's Temple of Juno (Verg. *Aen*. 1.456–93)." *Studi Italiani di Filologia Classica* 8, 247–55.

Meadows A., and J. Williams, 2001. "Moneta and the Monuments: Coinage and Politics in Republican Rome." *The Journal of Roman Studies* 91, 27–49.

Michelakis, Pantelis. 2002. *Achilles in Greek Tragedy*. Cambridge: Cambridge University Press.

Michels, A. K. 1944. "*Parrhesia* and the Satire of Horace." *Classical Philology* 29, 173–79.

———. 1981. "The *Insomnium* of Aeneas." *The Classical Quarterly* 31, 140–46.

Miller, John F. 1993. "The Shield of Argive Abas at *Aeneid* 3.286." *The Classical Quarterly* 43, 445–50.

———. 1994. "Arruns, Ascanius, and the Virgilian Apollo." *Colby Quarterly* 30, 171–232.

———. 2009. *Apollo, Augustus, and the Poets*. Cambridge: Cambridge University Press.

Miller, Paul Allan. 1995. "The Minotaur Within: Fire, the Labyrinth, and Strategies of Containment in *Aeneid* 5 and 6." *Classical Philology* 90, 225–40.

Moles, J. L. 1983. "Virgil, Pompey, and the Histories of Asinius Pollio." *The Classical World* 76, 287–8.

———. 1984. "Aristotle and Dido's *hamartia*", *Greece & Rome* 31, 48–54.

———. 1985. "Cynicism in Epistles I." *Papers of the Liverpool Latin Seminar* 5, 33–60.

———. 1987. "The Tragedy and Guilt of Dido." In *Homo Viator: Classical Essays for John Bramble*, ed. Michael Whitby, Philip Hardie, and Mary Whitby. Bristol: Bristol Classical Press, 153–61.

———. 1993. "Truth and Untruth in Herodotus and Thucydides." In *Lies and Fiction in the Ancient World*, ed. C. Gill and T. P. Wiseman. Exeter: University of Exeter Press, 88–121.

———. 2000. "The Cynics." In *The Cambridge History of Greek and Roman Political Thought*, ed. C. Rowe and M. Schofield. Cambridge: Cambridge University Press, 415–34.

———. 2017. "*Romane, memento*: Antisthenes, Dio and Virgil on the Education of the Strong." In *Word and Context in Latin Poetry: Studies in Memory of David West*, ed. A. J. Woodman and J. Wisse. Cambridge: Cambridge Philological Society, 105–30.

Monro, David B. 1901. *Homer's Odyssey*. Vol. 2. *Books XIII–XXIV*. Edited with English notes and appendices. Oxford: Oxford University Press.

Monro, David B. and Allen, Thomas W. 1912–1920. *Homeri Opera*. 5 vols. 3rd ed. Oxford: Oxford University Press.

Monro, H.A.J. 1886. *T. Lucreti Cari De Rerum Natura libri sex*. With notes and translation. 4th ed. 2 vols. Cambridge: Deighton Bell and Co.

Montiglio, Silvia. 2005. *Wandering in Ancient Greek Culture*. Chicago: University of Chicago Press.

———. 2011. *From Villain to Hero: Odysseus in Ancient Thought*. Ann Arbor: University of Michigan Press.

Morelli, Alfredo M. 2007. "Il monologo di Giunone nell'*Hercules furens* e l'*Eneide* di Virgilio: allusività e confronto di paradigmi letterari in Seneca tragico." *CentoPagine* 1, 30–39.

Morgan, Llewelyn. 1998. "Assimilation and Civil War: Hercules and Cacus: *Aeneid* 8." In H.-P. Stahl, 1998, 175–98.

———. 1999. *Patterns of Redemption in Virgil's Georgics*. Cambridge: Cambridge University Press.

———. 2000. "The Autopsy of C. Asinius Pollio." *The Journal of Roman Studies* 90, 51–69.

———. 2001. "Metre Matters: Some Higher-level Metrical Play in Latin Poetry." *Proceedings of the Cambridge Philological Society* 46, 99–120.

———. 2010. *Musa pedestris: Metre and Meaning in Roman Verse*. Oxford: Oxford University Press.

Mori, Anatole. 2008. *The Politics of Apollonius Rhodius' Argonautica*. Cambridge: Cambridge University Press.

Most, Glenn W. 2018. *Hesiod: The Shield, Catalogue of Women, Other Fragments*. Edited and translated. Cambridge, MA: Harvard University Press.

Mühmelt, Martin. 1965. *Griechische Grammatik in der Vergilerklärung*. Zetemata 37. Munich: C. H. Beck.

Murnaghan, Sheila. 1987/2011. *Disguise and Recognition in the Odyssey*. Princeton: Princeton University Press / 2nd ed. Lanham: Lexington Books.

Murray, Oswyn. 1965. "Philodemus on the Good King according to Homer." *The Journal of Roman Studies* 55, 161–82.

———. 1984. "Rileggendo il *Buon Re secondo Omero*." *Cronache Ercolanesi* 14, 157–60.

———. 2008. "Philosophy and Monarchy in the Hellenistic World." In *Jewish Perspectives on Hellenistic Rulers*, ed. T. Rajak, S. Pearce, J. Aitken and J. Dines. Berkeley: University of California Press, 13–28.

Murrin, Michael. 1980. *The Allegorical Epic: Essays in its Rise and Decline*. Chicago: University of Chicago Press.

Mynors, R.A.B. 1969. *P. Vergili Maronis Opera*. Oxford: Oxford University Press.

Nagy, Gregory. 1979. *The Best of the Achaeans: Concepts of the Hero in Archaic Greek Poetry*. Baltimore: Johns Hopkins University Press.

Naumann H. 1981. "Suetonius' Life of Virgil: The Present State of the Question." *Harvard Studies in Classical Philology* 85, 185–87.

Nelis, Damien P. 1993. "Apollonios est un poète sans faille dans les *Argonautiques*—; mais prefereriez vous etre Homère ou Apollonios? (Longin, Du Sublime, 33.4)." *Revue des Études Latines* 71, 14–16.

———. 2001. *Vergil's Aeneid and the Argonautica of Apollonius Rhodius*. ARCA Classical and Medieval Texts, Papers and Monographs 39. Leeds: Francis Cairns.

Newman, John Kevin. 2002. "Hercules in the *Aeneid*: The Dementia of Power." In *Hommages à Carl Deroux. I: Poésie*, ed. Pol Defosse. Collection Latomus 266. Brussels: Éditions Latomus, 398–411.

Nieto Hernandez, Pura. 2015. "Pindar's Other Sources: Catalogue and Advice Poetry." *Gaia* 18, 197–210.

Norden, Eduard. 1915. *Ennius und Vergilius*. Leipzig: Teubner.

———. 1927/1957. *Vergilius, Aeneis Buch VI*. 4th ed. Darmstadt: Wissenschaftliche Buchgesellschaft.

Nugent, S. Georgia. 1992. "Vergil's 'Voice of the Women' in *Aeneid* V." *Arethusa* 25, 255–92.

Nussbaum, M. 1976. "Consequences and Character in Sophocles' *Philoctetes*." *Philosophy and Literature* 1, 26–53.

O'Hara, James J. 1990. *Death and the Optimistic Prophecy in Vergil's Aeneid*. Princeton: Princeton University Press.

———. 1990a. "Homer, Hesiod, Apollonius, and *Neritos ardua* at *Aeneid* 3.271." *Vergilius* 36, 31–34.

———. 1996/2017. *True Names: Vergil and the Alexandrian Tradition of Etymological Wordplay*. New and expanded edition. Ann Arbor: University of Michigan Press.

———. 2004. "The *Aeneid* and Apollonius." Review of Nelis 2001. *The Classical Review* 54, 374–76.

———. 2007. *Inconsistency in Roman Epic: Studies in Catullus, Lucretius, Vergil, Ovid and Lucan*. Cambridge: Cambridge University Press.

O'Higgins, Dolores. 1995. "The Emperor's New Clothes: Unseen Images on Pallas' Baldric." *Hermathena* 158, 61–72.

O'Rourke, Donncha. 2017. "Hospitality Narratives in Virgil and Callimachus: The Ideology of Reception." *The Cambridge Classical Journal* 63, 118–42.

Oliensis, Ellen. 2004. "Sibylline Syllables: The Intratextual *Aeneid*." *Proceedings of the Cambridge Philological Society* 50, 29–45.

———. 2009. *Freud's Rome: Psychoanalysis and Latin Poetry*. Cambridge: Cambridge University Press.

Olson, S. Douglas. 2011. "Immortal Encounters: *Aeneid* 1 and the *Homeric Hymn to Aphrodite*." *Vergilius* 57, 55–61.

Otis, Brooks. 1964/1995. *Virgil: A Study in Civilized Poetry*. Oxford. Oxford University Press / Rpt. Foreword by Ward W. Briggs, Jr. Norman: University of Oklahoma Press.

———. 1976. "Virgilian Narrative in the Light of Its Precursors and Successors." *Studies in Philology* 73, 1–28.

Otto, W. F. 2005. *Le Muse e l'origine divina della parola e del canto*. Trans. Susanna Mati. Rome: Fazi Editore.

Pagán, Victoria Emma. 2010. "Forestalling Violence in Sallust and Vergil." *Mouseion* 10, 23–44.

Palmer, R.E.A. 1974. *Roman Religion and Roman Empire: Five Essays*. Philadelphia: University of Pennsylvania Press.

Pandey, Nandini B. 2018. *The Poetics of Power in Augustan Rome: Latin Poetic Responses to Early Imperial Iconography*. Cambridge: Cambridge University Press.

Panoussi, Vassiliki. 2002. "Vergil's Ajax: Allusion, Tragedy, and Heroic Identity in the *Aeneid*." *Classical Antiquity* 21, 95–134.

———. 2007. "Threat and Hope: Women's Rituals and Civil War in Roman Epic." In *Finding Persephone: Women's Rituals in the Ancient Mediterranean*, ed. Maryline Parca and Angeliki Tzanetou. Bloomington: Indiana University Press, 114–34.

———. 2009. *Greek Tragedy in Vergil's Aeneid: Ritual, Empire, and Intertext*. Cambridge: Cambridge University Press.

Papanghelis, Theodore D. 1999. "*Relegens errata litora*: Virgil's Reflexive 'Odyssey.'" In *Euphrosyne: Studies in Ancient Epic and Its Legacy in Honor of Dimitris N. Maronitis*, ed. J. N. Kazazis and A. Rengakos. Stuttgart: Franz Steiner Verlag, 275–90.

Paratore, Ettore. 1947. *Virgilio: Eneide, libro quarto*. Rome: Gismondi.

———. 1979. "Sull'episodio di Laocoonte in Virgilio." In *Studi di poesia latina in onore di Antonio Traglia*. Storia e letteratura, Raccolta di studi e testi 141 and 142. Roma: Edizioni di storia e letteratura, 405–30.

Parry, Adam. 1963. "The Two Voices of Virgil's *Aeneid*." *Arion* 2, 66–80.

Paschalis, Michael. 1984. "The Affair Between Venus and Anchises and the Birth of Aeneas in the *Aeneid*." *Dodone* 13, 25–40.

———. 1997. *Virgil's Aeneid: Semantic Relations and Proper Names*. Oxford: Oxford University Press.

Paton, W. R. 1918. *The Greek Anthology*. Vol. 4: Books 10–12. Cambridge, MA: Harvard University Press.

Pavlock, Barbara. 1985. "Epic and Tragedy in Vergil's Nisus and Euryalus Episode." *TAPA (Transactions of the American Philological Association)* 115, 207–24.

Peirano, Irene. 2013. "*Ille Ego Qui Quondam*: on Authorial (an)Onymity." In *The Author's Voice in Classical and Late Antiquity*, ed. Anna Marmodoro and Jonathan Hill. Oxford: Oxford University Press, 251–85.

Perkell, Christine. 1997. "The Lament of Juturna: Pathos and Interpretation in the *Aeneid*." *TAPA (Transactions of the American Philological Association)* 127, 257–86.

———. ed. 1999. *Reading Vergil's Aeneid: An Interpretive Guide*. Norman: University of Oklahoma Press.

———. 2002. "The Golden Age and Its Contradictions in the Poetry of Vergil." *Vergilius* 48, 3–39.

Perutelli, Alessandro. 2006. *Ulisse nella cultura romana*. Firenze: Le Monnier.
Petter, Gerald J. 1994. "Laocoon's Fate According to Virgil." In *Studies in Latin Literature and Roman History* 7, ed. Carl Deroux. Collection Latomus 227. Bruxelles: Éditions Latomus, 327–37.
Pfeiffer, Rudolf. 1928. "Ein neues Altersgedicht des Kallimachos." *Hermes* 63, 302–41.
———. 1949. *Callimachus*. Vol. 1: Fragmenta. Oxford: Oxford University Press.
———. 1953. *Callimachus*. Vol. 2: Hymni et epigrammata. Oxford: Oxford University Press.
———. 1968. *History of Classical Scholarship from the Beginnings to the End of the Hellenistic Age*. Oxford: Oxford University Press.
Pietsch, Wolfgang. 1980. "Laokoon: Bemerkungen zur Episode in der Äneis, zur Wirkungsgeschichte und zur unterrichtlichen Behandlung eines antiken Mythologems." *Anregung* 26, 158–75.
Pigón, Jakub. 2011. "A Priest, Two Snakes, and a Bull: The Laocoon Episode in the *Aeneid* once Again." In *Birthday Beasts' Book: Where Human Roads Cross Animal Trails. Cultural Studies in Honour of Jerzy Axer*, ed. Katarzyna Marciniak. Warsaw: Interdiscipinary Research Institute "Artes Liberales," 321–34.
Polleichtner, Wolfgang. 2013. "*scaenis decora apta futuris*: Das Theater und die *Aeneis*. In *Innovation aus Tradition: Literaturwissenschaftliche Perspektiven der Vergilforschung*, ed. Manuel Baumbach and Wolfgang Polleichtner. Bochumer Altertumswissenschaftliches Colloquium, Band 93. Trier: Wissenschaftlicher Verlag Trier, 139–65.
Pöschl, Viktor. 1950/1962. *Die Dichtkunst Vergils: Bild und Symbol in der Äneis*. Innsbruck: Rohrer Verlag. / *The Art of Vergil: Image and Symbol in the Aeneid*. Trans. Gerda Seligson. Ann Arbor: University of Michgan Press.
———. 1969. "Forschungsbericht: Virgil." 3. Fortsetzung. 2. Teil. *Anzeiger für die Altertumswissenschaft* 22, 1–38.
Powell, Anton. 1998. "The Peopling of the Underworld: *Aeneid* 6.608–27." In Stahl, H.-P. 1998, 85–100.
Powell, J.G.F. 2011. "Aeneas the Spin-Doctor: Rhetorical Self-Presentation in *Aeneid* 2." *Proceedings of the Virgil Society* 27, 184–202.
Prendergast, Guy Lushington. 1875/1983. *A Complete Concordance to the Iliad of Homer*. London: Longman, Green & Co. / Rpt. 1983. Hildesheim: Olms.
Preshous, J. D. M. 1964–1965 "Apollonius Rhodius and Virgil." *Proceedings of the Virgil Society* 4, 1–17.
Putnam, Michael C. J. 1965. *The Art of the Aeneid: Four Studies in Imaginative Unity and Design*. Cambridge, MA: Harvard University Press.
———. 1972/1995. "The Virgilian Achievement." *Arethusa* 5, 53–70 / chapter 1 in Putnam 1995, 9–26.
———. 1980/1995. "The Third Book of the *Aeneid*: From Homer to Rome." *Ramus* 9, 1–21 / chapter 3 in Putnam 1995, 50–72.
———. 1981/1995. "*Pius* Aeneas and the Metamorphosis of Lausus." *Arethusa* 14, 139–56 / chapter 7 in Putnam 1995, 134–51.
———. 1984/1995. "The Hesitation of Aeneas." In *Atti del Convegno nazionale 1984*. Vol. 2, 233–52 / chapter 8 in Putnam 1995, 152–71.
———. 1985/1995. "Possessiveness, Sexuality and Heroism in the *Aeneid*." *Vergilius* 31, 1–21 / chapter 2 in Putnam 1995, 27–49.

Putnam, Michael C. J. 1987/1998. "Daedalus, Virgil, and the End of Art." *American Journal of Philology* 108, 173–98 / chapter 3, "Daedalus' Sculptures," in Putnam 1998, 75–96.

———. 1990/1995. "Anger, Blindness and Insight in Virgil's *Aeneid*." In *The Poetics of Therapy: Hellenistic Ethics in Its Rhetorical and Literary Context*, ed. Martha C. Nussbaum. *Apeiron* 23, 7–40 / chapter 9 in Putnam 1995, 172–200.

———. 1992/1995. "Virgil's Tragic Future: Senecan Drama and the *Aeneid*." In *La storia, la letteratura e l'arte a Roma da Tiberio a Domiziano: Atti del Convegno* 63–5058, 231–91 / chapter 11 in Putnam 1995, 246–85.

———. 1994/1998. "Virgil's Danaid Ekphrasis." *Illinois Classical Studies* 19, 171–89 / chapter 6, "The Baldric of Pallas," in Putnam 1998, 189–207.

———. 1995. *Virgil's Aeneid: Interpretation and Influence*. Chapel Hill: University of North Carolina Press.

———. 1998. *Virgil's Epic Designs: Ekphrasis in the Aeneid*. New Haven: Yale University Press.

———. 1998/1998a. "Dido's Murals and Virgilian Ekphrasis." *Harvard Studies in Classical Philology* 98, 243–75 / chapter 1, "Dido's Murals," in Putnam 1998, 23–54.

———. 2011. *The Humanness of Heroes: Studies in the Conclusion of Virgil's Aeneid*. Amsterdam: Amsterdam University Press.

Quinn, Kennneth. 1968. *Virgil's Aeneid: A Critical Description*. London: Routledge.

———. 1973. *Catullus: The Poems*. London: Macmillan.

Quint, David. 1982. "Painful Memories: *Aeneid* III and the Problem of the Past." *The Classical Journal* 78, 30–38.

———. 1989. "Repetition and Ideology in the *Aeneid*." *Materiali e discussioni per l'analisi dei testi classici* 24, 9–54.

———. 1993. *Epic and Empire: Politics and Generic Form from Virgil to Milton*. Princeton: Princeton University Press.

———. 2018. *Virgil's Double Cross: Design and Meaning in the Aeneid*. Princeton: Princeton University Press.

Raabe, Hermann. 1974. *Plurima mortis imago: Vergleichende Interpretationen zur Bildersprache Vergils*. Zetemata 59. Munich: C. H. Beck.

Race, William H. 2008. *Apollonius Rhodius: Argonautica*. Edited and translated. Cambridge, MA: Harvard University Press.

Rauk, John. 1991. "Androgeos in Book Two of the *Aeneid*." *TAPA (Transactions of the American Philological Association)* 121, 287–95.

Rawson, Elizabeth. 1985. *Intellectual Life in the Late Roman Republic*. London: Duckworth.

Rebeggiani, Stefano. 2013. "*De Danais Victoribus*: Virgil's Shield of Abas and the Conquest of Greece." *Studi Italiani di Filologia Classica* 11, 82–106.

———. 2016. "Orestes, Aeneas, and Augustus: Madness and Tragedy in Virgil's *Aeneid*." In P. R. Hardie 2016.

Reckford, Kenneth J. 1961. "Latent Tragedy in *Aeneid* VII, 1–285." *American Journal of Philology* 82, 252–69.

———. 1995. "Recognizing Venus (I): Aeneas Meets His Mother." *Arion* 3, 1–42.

Reece, S. 1994. "The Cretan *Odyssey:* A Lie Truer Than Truth." *The American Journal of Philology* 115, 157–73.

Reed, J. D. 2006. "Virgil's Corythus and Roman Identity." *Studi Italiani di Filologia Classica* 4, 183–97.

———. 2007. *Virgil's Gaze: Nation and Poetry in the Aeneid*. Princeton: Princeton University Press.
———. 2010. "Vergil's Roman." In Farrell and Putnam 2010, 66–79.
———. 2017. "*Solvuntur Frigore*." *The Classical World* 111, 103–6.
Renger, Cornelia. 1985. *Aeneas und Turnus: Analyse einer Feindschaft*. Frankfurt am Main: Peter Lang.
Richardson, L., Jr. 1992. *A New Topographical Dictionary of Ancient Rome*. Baltimore: Johns Hopkins University Press.
Richardson, Nicholas. 1975. "Homeric Professors in the Age of the Sophists." *Proceedings of the Cambridge Philological Society* 201, 65–81.
———. 1992. "Aristotle's Reading of Homer." In *Homer's Ancient Readers: The Hermeneutics of Greek Epic's Earliest Exegetes*, ed. Robert Lamberton and John J. Keaney. Princeton: Princeton University Press, 30–40.
Rieks, Rudolf. 1989. *Affekte und Strukturen: Pathos als ein Form- und Wirkprinzip von Vergils Aeneis*. Zetemata 86. Munich: C. H. Beck.
Rogerson, Anne. 2013. "Conington's 'Roman Homer.'" In *Oxford Classics: Teaching and Learning, 1800–2000*, ed. Christopher Stray. London: Bristol Classical Press, 94–106.
Roisman, H. M. 1997. "The Appropriation of a Son: Sophocles' *Philoctetes*." *Greek, Roman, and Byzantine Studies* 38, 127–71.
Rolfe, John C. 1927. *Aulus Gellius: Attic Nights*. With an English translation. 3 vols. Cambridge, MA: Harvard University Press.
Roman, Luke. 2006. "A History of Lost Tablets." *Classical Antiquity* 25, 351–88.
Rosati, Gianpiero. 1994. *Stazio, Achilleide: Introduzione, traduzione e note*. Milan: Rizzoli.
Rosenmeyer, Thomas G. 1960. "Virgil and Heroism: *Aeneid* XI." *The Classical Journal* 55, 159–64.
Ross, David O., Jr. 1975. *Backgrounds to Augustan Poetry: Gallus, Elegy, and Rome*. Cambridge: Cambridge University Press.
———. 1987. *Virgil's Elements: Physics and Poetry in the Georgics*. Princeton: Princeton University Press.
Rossi, Andreola. 2003. *Contexts of War: Manipulation of Genre in Virgilian Battle Narrative*. Ann Arbor: University of Michigan Press.
———. 2004. "Parallel Lives: Hannibal and Scipio in Livy's Third Decade." *TAPA (Transactions of the American Philological Association)* 134, 359–81.
Rüpke, Jörg. 1993. "Vergils Laokoon." *Eranos* 91, 126–8.
———. 2011. *The Roman Calendar from Numa to Constantine: Time, History, and the Fasti*. Trans. D.M.B. Richardson. Chichester: Wiley-Blackwell.
Russell, D. A. 1964. *"Longinus": On the Sublime*. Edited with introduction and commentary. Oxford: Oxford University Press.
———. 2002. *Quintilian: The Orator's Education*. Edited and translated. 5 vols. Cambridge, MA: Harvard University Press.
Russell, D. A. and David Konstan. 2005. *Heraclitus: Homeric Problems*. Edited and translated. Writings from the Greco-Roman World 14. Atlanta: Society for Biblical Literature.
Russo, Carlo-Ferdinando. 1950/1965. *Hesiodi Scutum: Introduzione, testo critico, e commento con traduzione*. Biblioteca di Studi Superiori 9. 2nd ed. revised and augmented. Florence: La Nuova Italia.
Rutherford, R. B. 1986. "The Philosophy of the *Odyssey*." *The Journal of Hellenic Studies* 106, 145–62.

Rutledge, S. H. 1999. "*Delatores* and the Tradition of Violence in Roman Oratory." *American Journal of Philology* 120, 555–73.

———. 2012. *Ancient Rome as a Museum: Power, Identity, and the Culture of Collecting.* Oxford: Oxford University Press.

Sabbadini, Remigio. 1908. *P. Vergili Maronis Aeneis commentata.* Vol. 3, books 7–9. 2nd ed. Turin: Loescher.

Sainte-Beuve, A. 1870, *Études sur Virgile.* 2nd ed. Paris: M. Lévy frères.

Sansone, David. 1991. "Cacus and the Cyclops: An Addendum." *Mnemosyne* 44, 171.

Scafoglio, Giampiero. 2002. "L'apparizione onirica di Ettore nel libro II dell'Eneide: Intertestualità e mediazione filosofica." *Philologus* 146, 299–308.

———. 2006. "Two Fragments of the Epic Cycle." *Greek, Roman, and Byzantine Studies* 46, 5–11.

———. 2007. "Elementi tragici nell'episodio virgiliano di Sinone." *Antike & Abendland* 53, 76–99.

———. 2013. "The Betrayal of Aeneas." *Greek, Roman, and Byzantine Studies* 53, 1–14.

Schierl, Petra. 2006. *Die Tragödien des Pacuvius: Ein Kommentar zu den Fragmenten mit Einleitung, Text und Übersetzung.* Berlin and New York: De Gruyter.

Schiesaro, Alessandro. 2005. "Under the Sign of Saturn: Dido's *Kulturkampf.*" In *La représentation du temps dans la poésie augustéenne / Zur Poetik der Zeit in augusteischer Dichtung,* ed. Jürgen Paul Schwindt. Heidelberg: Carl Winter, 85–110.

———. 2008. "Furthest Voices in Virgil's Dido." *Studi Italiani di Filologia Classica* 6, 60–109, 194–245.

———. 2015. "Emotions and Memory in Virgil's *Aeneid.*" In *Emotions between Greece and Rome,* ed. D. Cairns and L. Fulkerson. *Bulletin of the Institute for Classical Studies* Suppl. 125. London: Institute of Classical Studies, School of Advanced Study, University of London, 163–76.

Schlunk, Robin R. 1974. *The Homeric Scholia and the Aeneid: A Study of the Influence of Ancient Homeric Literary Criticism on Vergil.* Ann Arbor: University of Michigan Press.

Schmidt, Ernst Günther. 1983. "Achilleus, Odysseus, Aeneas: Zur Typologie des vergilischen Helden." *Listy Filologické/Folia Philologica* 106, 24–28.

Schmit-Neuerburg, Tilman. 1999. *Vergils Aeneis und die antike Homerexegese, Untersuchungen zum Einfluss ethischer und kritischer Homerrezeption auf imitatio und aemulatio Vergils.* Berlin and New York: De Gruyter.

Schmitz, Christine. 2008. "Ist Penelope ein Modell für Vergils Dido? Möglichkeiten und Grenzen einer intertextuellen Lektüre." In *Vergil und das antike Epos: Festschrift Hans Jürgen Tschiedel,* ed. Volker Michael Strocka, Raban von Haehling, Stefan Freund, and Meinolf Vielberg. Altertumswissenschaftliches Kolloquium, 20. Stuttgart: Franz Steiner, 85–103.

Scholz, Udo W. 1999. "Drances." *Hermes* 127, 455–66.

Schweizer, Hans Jörg. 1967. *Vergil und Italien: Interpretationen zu den italischen Gestalten der Aeneis.* Aarau: Sauerländer.

Seider, A. M. 2013. *Memory in Vergil's Aeneid: Creating the Past.* Cambridge: Cambridge University Press.

Setaioli, Aldo. 1985. "Inferi (loci)." *Enciclopedia Virgiliana* 2, 953–63.

———. 1995. "Ulisse nell'*Eneide.*" In *Presenze classiche nelle letterature occidentali: Il mito dall'età antica all'età moderna e contemporanea: Convegno Internazionale di Didattica, Perugia, 7–10 novembre 1990, Atti,* ed. M. Rossi Cittadini. Citta di Castello: GESP, 167–86.

Shaw, Carl. 2014. *Satyric Play: The Evolution of Greek Comedy and Satyr Drama*. Oxford: Oxford University Press.

Shi, Veronica S.-R. and Morgan, Llewelyn. 2015. "A Tale of Two Carthages: History and Allusive Topography in Virgil's Libyan Harbor (*Aen.* 1.159–69)." *TAPA* (*Transactions of the American Philological Association*) 145, 107–33.

Shorey, Paul. 1927/1931. "Sophocles." *The Martin Classical Lectures*, ed. Louis E. Lord. Vol. 1. Cambridge, MA: Harvard University Press, 57–95.

Sider, David. 1997. *The Epigrams of Philodemus: Introduction, Text, and Commentary*. New York and Oxford: Oxford University Press.

Sikes, E. E. 1923. *Roman Poetry*. London: Methuen.

Silk, Michael. 1985. "Heracles and Greek Tragedy." *Greece & Rome* 32, 1–22.

Sistakou, E. 2015. "The Hellenistic Reception of the Epic Cycle." In Fantuzzi and Tsagalis, 487–95.

Skutsch, Otto. 1985. *The Annals of Quintus Ennius*. Oxford: Oxford University Press.

Smith, P. M. 1981. "*Aineiadai* as Patrons of *Iliad* XX and the Homeric *Hymn to Aphrodite*." *Harvard Studies in Classical Philology* 85, 17–58.

Smith, Stephen C. 1999. "Remembering the Enemy: Narrative, Focalization, and Vergil's Portrait of Achilles." *TAPA* (*Transactions of the American Philological Association*) 129, 225–62.

Smolenaars, J.L.L. 1993. "De dood van Pallas en van Turnus in Vergilius' *Aeneis* (X en XII): de sturende invloed van het Homerische model." *Lampas* 26, 332–55.

Sommerstein, A. H. 1996/2010. *Aeschylean Tragedy*. Bari: Levante / 2nd ed. London: Bristol Classical Press.

———. 2015. "Tragedy and the Epic Cycle." In Fantuzzi and Tsagalis, 461–86.

Soubiran, Jean. 1966. *L'Élision dans la poésie latine*. Paris: Klincksieck.

Spence, Sarah. 1988. *Rhetorics of Reason and Desire: Vergil, Augustine, and the Troubadours*. Ithaca: Cornell University Press.

———. 1991. "Cinching the Text: The Danaids and the End of the *Aeneid*." *Vergilius* 37, 11–19.

———. 1999. "*Varium et Mutabile*: Voices of Authority in *Aeneid* 4." In Perkell 1999, 81–95.

Spielberg, Lydia. 2020. "Ennius' *Annals* as Source and Model for Historical Speech." In Damon and Farrell, 147–66.

Squire, M. J. 2015. "Running Rings round Troy: Recycling the 'Epic Circle' in Hellenistic and Roman Art." In Fantuzzi and Tsagalis.

———. 2016. "*Iliacas ex ordine pugnas*: Ordering Time and Space in Virgilian Ecphrasis." *Lampas* 49, 223–51.

Stafford, Emma J. 2012. *Herakles*. London: Routledge.

Stahl, H.-P. 1981. "Aeneas: An 'Unheroic Hero'?" *Arethusa* 14, 157–77.

———. 1998a. "Political Stop-overs on a Mythological Travel Route: From Battling Harpies to the Battle of Actium: *Aeneid* 3.268–93." In H.-P. Stahl, 1998, 37–84.

———. ed. 1998. *Vergil's Aeneid: Augustan Epic and Political Context*. London: Duckworth.

Stahl, William Harris. 1952. *Macrobius: Commentary on the Dream of Scipio*. Translated with an introduction and notes. New York: Columbia University Press.

Staley, Gregory A. 2002. "Vergil's Daedalus." *Classical Outlook* 79, 137–43.

Stanford, W. B. 1964. *The Ulysses Theme: A Study in the Adaptability of a Traditional Hero*. 2nd ed. Oxford: Oxford University Press.

Steiner, Hans Rudolf. 1952. *Der Traum in der Aeneis*. Noctes Romanae 5. Bern: Haupt.

Stok, Fabio. 2010. "The Life of Vergil before Donatus." In Farrell and Putnam 2010, 107–20.
Strasburger, H. J. 1972. "Homer und die Geschichtsschreibung." *Sitzungsberichter der Heidelberger Akademie der Wissenschaften.* Heidelberg: Carl Winter.
Suerbaum, Werner. 1967. "Aeneas zwischen Troja und Rom: Zur Funktion der Genealogie und der Ethnographie in Vergils Aeneis." *Poetica* 1, 176–204.
———. 1998. "*Si fata paterentur*: Gedanken an alternatives Handeln in Vergils *Aeneis*." In *Candide Iudex: Beiträge zur augusteischen Dichtung. Festschrift für Walter Wimmel zum 75. Geburtstag*, ed. Anna Elissa Radke. Stuttgart: Franz Steiner Verlag, 353–74.
———. 2002. "L. Livius Andronicus," in *Handbuch der lateinischen Literatur der Antike*, ed. Reinhart Herzog and Peter Lebrecht Schmidt. Vol. 1: *Die archaische Literatur von den Anfängen bis Sullas Tod*, ed. Werner Suerbaum. Munich: C. H. Beck, 93–104.
Syme, Ronald. 1939. *The Roman Revolution*. Oxford: Oxford University Press.
Tarrant, Richard, ed. 2012. *Vergil: Aeneid, Book XII*. Cambridge: Cambridge University Press.
Tatum, James. 2013. "Mrs. Vergil's Horrid Wars." *Arion* 21.1, 3–46.
Thalmann, William G. 1984. *Conventions of Form and Thought in Early Greek Epic Poetry*. Baltimore: Johns Hopkins University Press.
———. 2011. *Apollonius of Rhodes and the Spaces of Hellenism*. New York and Oxford: Oxford University Press.
Theodorakopoulos, E. 2004. "The Name of the Game: The *Troia*, and History and Spectacle in *Aeneid* 5." *Proceedings of the Virgil Society* 25, 63–72.
Thomas, Richard F. 1983. "Callimachus, the *Victoria Berenices*, and Roman Poetry." *The Classical Quarterly* 33, 92–113.
———. 1983a. "Virgil's Ecphrastic Centerpieces." *Harvard Studies in Classical Philology* 87, 175–184.
———. 1986. "Virgil's *Georgics* and the Art of Reference." *Harvard Studies in Classical Philology* 90, 171–98.
———. 1986/1999. "From *recusatio* to Commitment: The Evolution of the Vergilian Program." *Papers of the Liverpool Latin Seminar* 6, 61–73 / *Reading Virgil and His Texts: Studies in Intertextuality*. Ann Arbor: University of Michigan Press, 101–113.
———. 1991. "*Furor* and *Furiae* in Virgil." *American Journal of Philology* 112, 261.
———. 2001. *Virgil and the Augustan Reception*. Cambridge: Cambridge University Press.
Thomas, Richard F. and Ruth Scodel. 1984. "Virgil and the Euphrates." *American Journal of Philology* 105, 339.
Thome, Gabriele. 1979. *Gestalt und Funktion des Mezentius bei Vergil, mit einem Ausblick auf die Schlußszene der Aeneis*. Europäische Hochschulschriften 15. Reihe: Klassische Philologie und Literatur 14. Frankfurt am Main: Peter Lang.
Thornton, Agathe. 1970. *People and Themes in Homer's Odyssey*. London: Methuen.
Toll, Katharine. 1991. "The *Aeneid* as an Epic of National Identity: *Italiam laeto socii clamore salutant*." *Helios* 18, 3–14.
———. 1997. "Making Roman-ness and the *Aeneid*." *Classical Antiquity* 16, 34–56.
Toohey, Peter. 1988. "An [Hesiodic] *danse macabre*: The *Shield of Heracles*." *Illinois Classical Studies* 13, 19–35.
Tracy, S. V. 1987. "Laocoon's Guilt." *American Journal of Philology* 108, 451–54.

Traill, D. A. 1993. "Between Scylla and Charybdis at *Aeneid* 3.684–86: A Smoother Passage." *American Journal of Philology* 114, 407–12.

———. 2001. "Boxers and Generals at Mount Eryx." *American Journal of Philology* 122, 405–13.

Traina, Alfonso. 1990. "Le troppe voci Virgilio." *Rivista di Filologia e di Istruzione Classica* 118, 490–99.

Tsakiropoulou-Summers, Tatiana. 2006. "Dido as Circe and the Attempted Metamorphosis of Aeneas." In *Studies in Latin Literature and Roman History* 13, ed. Carl Deroux. Collection Latomus, 301. Bruxelles: Éditions Latomus, 236–83.

Tueller, Michael A. 2000. "Well-Read Heroes: Quoting the *Aetia* in *Aeneid* 8." *Harvard Studies in Classical Philology* 100, 361–80.

Uden, James. 2014. "The Smile of Aeneas." *TAPA (Transactions of the American Philological Association)* 2014, 71–96.

Ursinus, Fulvius. 1568. *Virgilius collatione scriptorum graecorum illustratus*. Antwerp: Christophe Plantin.

Ussani, V. 1947 "Enea traditore." *Studi Italiani di Filologia Classica* 22, 108–23.

van der Valk, M. 1971–1987. *Eustathii Archiepiscopi Thessalonicensis commentarii ad Homeri Iliadem pertinentes*. 4 vols. Leiden: Brill.

Van Nortwick, Thomas. 1980. "Aeneas, Turnus, and Achilles." *TAPA (Transactions of the American Philological Association)* 110, 303–14.

———. 1992. *Somewhere I Have Never Travelled: The Second Self and the Hero's Journey in Ancient Epic*. New York and Oxford: Oxford University Press.

———. 2013. "Woman Warrior? Aeneas' Encounters with the Feminine." In *Roman Literature, Gender, and Reception: Domina Illustris*, ed. Donald Lateiner, Barbara K. Gold, and Judith Perkins. London and New York: Routledge, 136–52.

Venuti, Lawrence. 1995. *The Translator's Invisibility: A History of Translation*. London: Routledge.

Verrall, A. W. 1913. *Collected Studies*. Cambridge: Cambridge University Press.

Vian, F. 1973. "Notes critiques au chant 2 des *Argonautiques* d' Apollonios de Rhodes." *Revue des Études Anciennes* 75, 82–102.

Vian, F., ed. and Delage, E., trans. 1974–1996. *Apollonios de Rhodes: Argonautiques*. 3 vols. 2nd ed. Paris: Les Belles Lettres.

Voisin, J. L. 1979. "Le suicide d'Amata." *Revue des Études Latines*, 254–66.

von Albrecht, Michael. 1966. Review of Putnam 1965. *Gnomon* 38, 564–68.

———. 1999. *Roman Epic: An Interpretative Introduction*. Mnemosyne Suppl. 189. Leiden: Brill.

Walde, Christine. 2001. *Die Traumdarstellungen in der griechisch-römischen Dichtung*. Munich and Leipzig: Saur.

Wallace-Hadrill, Andrew. 1982. "The Golden Age and Sin in Augustan Ideology." *Past & Present* 95, 19–36.

Walton, Francis B. 1957. *Diodorus of Sicily: Library of History*. With an English translation. Vol. 11, books 21–33. Cambridge, MA: Harvard University Press.

Warmington, E. H. 1935–40. *Remains of Old Latin*. With an English translation. 4 vols. Cambridge, MA: Harvard University Press.

Warren, James. 2002. *Epicurus and Democritean Ethics: An Archaeology of Ataraxia*. Cambridge: Cambridge University Press.

Weber, Clifford. 1987. "Metrical *Imitatio* in the Proem to the *Aeneid*." *Harvard Studies in Classical Philology* 91, 261–71.

———. 1998–1999. "Dido and Circe 'Dorées": Two Golden Women in *Aeneid* 1.698 and 7.190." *The Classical Journal* 94, 317–27.

———. 2002. "The Dionysus in Aeneas." *Classical Philology* 97, 322–43.

Weidner, Andreas. 1869. *Commentar zu Vergils Buch I und II*. Leipzig: Teubner.

West, D. A. 1969. "Multiple-correspondence Similes in the *Aeneid*." *The Journal of Roman Studies* 59, 40–9.

———. 1998. "The End and the Meaning: *Aeneid* 12.791–842." In H.-P. Stahl, 1998, 303–18.

West, M. L. 1966. *Hesiod: Theogony*. Edited with prolegomena and commentary. Oxford: Oxford University Press.

———. 2003. *Greek Epic Fragments from the Seventh to the Fifth Centuries BC*. Cambridge, MA: Harvard University Press

———. 2005. "*Odyssey* and *Argonautica*." *The Classical Quarterly* 55, 39–64.

———. 2013. *The Epic Cycle: A Commentary on the Lost Troy Epics*. Oxford: Oxford University Press.

———. 2015. "The Formation of the Epic Cycle." In Fantuzzi and Tsagalis, 96–107.

Whitman, Cedric. 1958. *Homer and the Heroic Tradition*. Cambridge, MA: Harvard Universtiy Press.

Wigodsky, Michael. 1972. *Vergil and Early Latin Poetry*. Hermes Einzelschriften, 24. Wiesbaden: F. Steiner.

Wilkinson, L. P. 1963. *Golden Latin Artistry*. Cambridge: Cambridge University Press.

Willcock, Malcolm M. 1988. "Homer's Chariot Race and Virgil's Boat Race." *Proceedings of the Virgil Society* 19, 1–13.

Williams, Frederick. 1978. *Callimachus, Hymn to Apollo: A Commentary*. Oxford: Oxford University Press.

Williams, Gordon. 1968. *Tradition and Originality in Roman Poetry*. Oxford: Oxford University Press.

———. 1983. *Technique and Ideas in the Aeneid*. New Haven: Yale University Press.

Williams, R. D. 1960. *P. Vergili Maronis Aeneidos liber quintus*. Edited with a commentary. Oxford: Oxford University Press.

———. 1960a. "The Pictures on Dido's Temple (*Aeneid* 1.450–93)." *The Classical Quarterly* 10, 145–51.

———. 1962. *P. Vergili Maronis Aeneidos liber tertius*. Edited with a commentary. Oxford: Oxford University Press.

———. 1963. "Virgil and the *Odyssey*." *Phoenix* 17, 266–74.

———. 1967. Review of Knauer 1964. *Classical Philology* 53, 225–27.

———. 1972–1973. *The Aeneid of Virgil*. Edited with introduction and notes. 2 vols. London: Macmillan.

Wilson, Emily R. 2004. *Mocked with Death: Tragic Overliving from Sophocles to Milton*. Baltimore and London: Johns Hopkins University Press.

Wirszubski, C. 1950. *Libertas as a Political Idea at Rome during the Late Republic and Early Principate*. Cambridge: Cambridge University Press.

Wiseman, T. P. 1994. *Historiography and Imagination: Eight Essays on Roman Culture.* Exeter: University of Exeter Press.

Wlosok, Antonie. 1967. *Die Göttin Venus in Vergils Aeneis.* Heidelberg: Carl Winter.

———. 1973. "Vergil in der neueren Forschung." *Gymnasium* 80, 129–51.

———. 1976/1999. "Vergils Didotragödie: Ein Beitrag zum Problem des Tragischen in der Aeneis." In *Studien zum antiken Epos,* ed. Herwig Görgemanns and E. A. Schmidt. Beiträge zur klassischen Philologie 72. Meisenheim am Glan: Hain, 228–50 / "The Dido Tragedy in Virgil: A Contribution to the Question of the Tragic in the *Aeneid.*" In P. R. Hardie 1999, vol. 4, 158–81.

———. 1982. "Der Held als Ärgernis: Vergils Aeneas." *Würzburger Jahrbücher für die Altertumswissenschaft* 8, 9–21.

———. 1985. "Zur Funktion des Helden (Aeneas) in Vergils Aeneis." *Klio* 67, 216–23.

———. 2001. "Viktor Pöschl." *Gnomon* 73, 369–78.

Woodman, A. J. 1989. "Vergil the Historian." In *Studies in Latin Literature and its Tradition in Honour of C. O. Brink,* ed. J. Diggle, J. B. Hall, and H. D. Jocelyn. *Proceedings of the Cambridge Philological Society* Suppl. 15, 132–45.

Yardley, J. C. and R. Develin. 1994. *Justin: Epitome of the Philippic History of Pompeius Trogus.* Atlanta: Scholars Press.

Zanker, Paul. 1987/1988. *Augustus und die Macht der Bilder.* Munich: C. H. Beck / *The Power of Images in the Age of Augustus.* Trans. Alan Shapiro. Jerome Lectures, 16th series. Ann Arbor: University of Michigan Press.

Zarker, John W. 1969. "Amata: Vergil's Other Tragic Queen." *Vergilius* 15, 2–24.

———. 1972. "The Hercules Theme in the *Aeneid.*" *Vergilius* 18, 34–48.

Zintzen, Clemens. 1979. *Die Laokoonepisode bei Vergil.* Akademie der Wissenschaften und der Literatur. Abhandlungen der Geistes und Sozialwissenschaftlichen Klasse, 1979, 10. Wiesbaden: Franz Steiner Verlag.

Ziolkowski, Jan M. and Michael C. J. Putnam. 2008. *The Virgilian Tradition: The First Fifteen Hundred Years.* New Haven and London: Yale University Press.

Ziolkowski, Theodore. 1993. *Virgil and the Moderns.* Princeton: Princeton University Press.

———. 2004. *Hesitant Heroes: Private Inhibition, Cultural Crisis.* Ithaca: Cornell University Press.

Zissos, Andrew. 2008. *Valerius Flaccus' Argonautica, Book 1: A Commentary.* Oxford: Oxford University Press.

INDEX OF PASSAGES CITED

Accius, *The Award of the Arms*, fragment
    123 in Warmington 1936, 2.366–67,
    266
Aelius Donatus, *Commentary on Terence* 1.5, 58
"Apollodorus," *Library of Greek Mythology*,
    epitome 6.14, 211
Apollonius of Rhodes, *Argonautica*
    Books 1–2, 142, 149, 150
    Book 1, 140, 142, 148–50
        1.18–233, 148
        1.609–909, 136, 141, 149
        1.722–68, 96
        1.730–67, 148
        1.861–74, 149
        1.1273–95, 149
    Book 2, 149–50
        2.549–606, 136
    Books 3–4, 142, 149, 150
    Book 3, 9, 37, 134, 140–42, 146,
        149–51, 173
        3.1, 140, 245
        3.8–9, 145
        3.25–110, 145
        3.34–35, 146
        3.36–110, 145
        3.111–66, 146
        3.1225–1407, 149–50
    Book 4, 150
        4.757–69, 96
        4.783–965, 136
        4.783–832, 144
        4.810–16, 144
        4.865–88, 96
        4.982–1222, 137
        4.1128–69, 145

Appian, *Civil War* 1.541–42, 274
Apuleius, *Metamorphoses* 2.14, 201
Aristotle, *Poetics* 1448b–1449a, 58
    1451a, 155
    452b–2453a, 58
    1453a, 168
    1459a–b, 117, 132

Callimachus
    Aetia, 38
        Books 1–2, 119
        Book 1, 157
            prologue (fragment 1.32–40 in
            Harder 2012), 156, 176
        Book 3, 157
            "The Victory of Berenice"
            (fragment 54i, line 15 in
            Harder 2012), 158
        Book 4
            "The Lock of Berenice"
            (fragment 110.48–50 in
            Harder 2012), 158
    Hymn to Apollo 105–13, 127
        726, 158
    Hymn to Artemis 46–61, 158
    The Victory of Sosibius (fragment
        384.27–28 in Pfeiffer 1949), 158
Cassius Dio, *Roman History*
    40.12.1, 268
    48.14.4, 274
Catullus, poems 36 and 42, 127
Cicero
    Brutus 71–73, 183
    Letters to Atticus 1.16.1, 41
        2.13.2, 94

Cicero (*continued*)
    Letters to His Friends 9.22, 297
    On Divination 2.84, 297
        2.116, 189

Dio Chrysostom, *Discourse* 52, "On Homer", 9
Diodorus of Sicily, *Library of History* 23.5.1, 281
Diogenes Laertius, *Lives of Eminent Philosophers* 4.26, 7.180, 78

Ennius, Quintus, *Annals* (in Goldberg and Manuwald 2018)
    Books 1–15, 188, 189, 190
    Books 1–5, 190
    Book 1, 188
        fragment 1.47 (line 96), 189
    Books 6–18, 190
    Book 6, 189, 190
        fragment 6.1 (line 164), 189
        fragment 6.14 (lines 197–98), 189
        fragment **6.17 (line 202), 275
    Books 7–9, 189
    Book 9, 189
        fragment 9.15 (lines 319–20), 189
    Book 10, 189
    Books 11–15, 190
    Book 15, 190, 191
        fragment 15.3 (lines 391–98), 191, 262
        testimonium 1, 190
    Books 16–18, 189
    Book 16, 190
        fragment 16.3 (line 403), 189
Epic Cycle (*see* the general index)
    Aethiopis, 34
    Cypria, 34
    Homecomings (*Nostoi*), 34, 55
    Little Iliad, 34
    The Sack of Troy (*Iliupersis*), 34
    Telegony, 55
Euripides
    Alcestis 175–84, 176
        73–76, 173
        1143–46, 174
    Andromache 998–1000, 211
        1085–1172, 211
        1243–52, 213
    Heracles 822–74, 177
Eustathius, *Commentary on the Iliad* 16.22, 73

Gellius, Aulus, *Attic Nights* 9.9.12–17, 110

Heraclitus, *Homeric Problems* 39, 53
Hesiod
    Catalogue of Women, fragment 98.26 in Most 2018, 186–87, 94
    The Shield of Heracles, 38
        161–67, 164
    Theogony 1–9, 121
        54, 121
        316, 161
    Works and Days 802, 296
Homer
    Iliad, 1, 5, 7, 8, 9, 10, 11, 13, 15, 16, 17, 18, 21, 22, 23, 24, 25, 26, 28, 30, 33, 34, 35, 36, 37, 40, 42, 43, 44, 48, 50, 55, 56, 57
    Books 1–18, 228
    Book 1, 10, 11, 48, 100
        1.1, 47, 50, 51, 117, 122, 293
        1.1–7, 45, 46
    Book 2, 12, 58, 150, 151, 163
        2.134–35, 87
        2.214–15, 278
        2.220–21, 278
        2.235, 259
        2.243–69, 279
        2.484–93, 247
        2.494–759, 148, 163, 179, 247, 249
        2.760, 12
    Books 3–19, 12
        3.121–244, 279
    Book 4
        4.116–21, 259
    Book 5, 64, 70, 71, 76, 118
        5.166–454, 70

Book 7
   7.96, 259
   7.243–44, 269
   7.345–64, 278
Books 8–16, 254
Books 9–18, 258
Books 9–10, 258
Book 9, 58, 79, 163, 254–58
   9.308–13, 254
   9.340–41, 257
   9.356–63, 48
   9.434–605, 163
   9.524–99, 163
Book 10, 10, 58, 79, 118, 254–58
   10.214–17, 256
Book 11
   11.401–88, 69
   11.548–55, 262
   11.763, 80
Books 11–18, 258
Book 12, 192
   12.127–94, 191, 261
   12.131–36, 191
   12.191–92, 261
   12.459–66, 261
Book 14, 145, 146, 147
   14.135–52, 54
   14.153–353, 53, 54, 56, 62, 65, 145, 283
   14.187–88, 145
   14.263–70, 52, 53
   14.268, 147
   14.354–401, 54
   14.394–98, 297
Book 15, 54
   15.34–46, 54
   15.733–41, 262
Books 16–22, 15
Book 16, 58, 192
   16.22, 73
   16.31, 80
   16.80–100, 202
   16.102–11, 191, 262
   16.168–97, 12, 265
   16.220–52, 271

   16.419–507, 267
   16.431–61, 267
   16.799–800, 264
   16.852–53, 264, 269
   16.856–57, 271
   16.862–63, 270
Book 17
   17.201–8, 264
   17.319–34, 260
   17.657–64, 262
Book 18, 12, 163, 254
   18.168, 145
   18.251–52, 278
   18.254–313, 278
   18.328–33, 275
   18.478–608, 148, 163–64
Book 19, 263
   19.56–275, 256
Book 20, 12, 65
   20.127, 264
   20.300–8, 63
   20.386–87, 262
   20.419–54, 267
Book 21, 100, 161
   21.18, 263
   21.26–33, 274
   21.136–382, 71–74, 101, 161, 253
   21.233, 263
   21.272–83, 72
   21.281, 71, 73
   21.537–22.24, 267
Book 22, 12, 202, 254
   22.363–64, 271
   22.365–66, 269
   22.367, 270
Book 23, 9, 13, 23, 226, 229, 231, 272
   23.108–225, 272
   23.175–83, 274
   23.287–650, 229
   23.301–50, 229
   23.555–56, 231
Book 24, 118, 202
   24.14–21, 202
Odyssey
   Books 1–4, 10, 252

Homer (*continued*)
   Book 1, 101
      1.1–5, 44, 45
      1.1, 10, 45, 51, 117
      1.4, 46
      1.5, 203
      1.7–9, 203
      1.8, 83
      1.20, 46
      1.28–43, 124
      1.30–43, 130
      1.280–305, 251
      1.325–27, 130
      1.325–64, 124
   Book 2
      2.170–72, 87
   Books 3–4, 250
   Book 3, 124
      3.123–25, 251
      3.130–98, 130
   Book 4, 124, 163
      4.332–586, 130
      4.351–586, 163
      4.513, 56, 183
   Books 5–12, 11
   Books 5–13, 49, 62, 136, 140
   Book 5, 11, 60, 62, 69, 71, 76, 101, 106–107, 136–37, 140–43, 149, 198
      5.43–261, 87
      5.282–85, 50
      5.284–85, 61
      5.291–96, 59
      5.297–98, 66–67
      5.306–7, 66
      5.308–12, 69
      5.312, 71
      5.405, 95
      5.436–93, 107
   Book 6, 91
      6.1–152, 107
      6.122–24, 102
      6.149–52, 98, 107
   Books 7–13, 91
   Book 7
      7.14–17, 107
      7.14–36, 105
      7.19–20, 106
      7.48–77, 110
      7.146–52, 103
      7.259–63, 87
   Book 8, 14, 129
      8.72–82, 129
      8.248–49, 220
      8.266–369, 129
      8.465, 56
      8.470–522, 129
      8.499–520, 129
      8.532–86, 102
   Books 9–12, 11, 14, 87–88, 98, 112, 128–29, 131, 136–37, 142, 155, 198, 223
   Book 9
      9.19–24, 209
      9.19–20, 101
      9.39–61, 87
      9.82–104, 87
      9.105–566, 130
   Book 10
      10.1–76, 59, 87, 93–94
      10.3, 60
      10.5–7, 60
      10.21–22, 59
      10.38–61, 60
      10.47–55, 94
      10.72–75, 60
      10.80–132, 87, 94
      10.87–94, 94
      10.89, 95
      10.98, 94
      10.116, 95
      10.133–574, 87, 94
      10.140–41, 95
      10.144–76, 94
      10.174–75, 67
      10.323–35, 96
      10.333–34, 96
      10.467–68, 96
      10.526–35, 65
   Book 11, 11, 14, 87, 112, 174
      11.51–80, 241

11.385–464, 124, 130
11.487–91, 235
11.492–540, 206
11.563–64, 174
11.604, 56
Book 12
   12.70, 136
   12.72, 56
   12.153–200, 87
   12.193, 261
   12.234–59, 136
   12.260–402, 87, 203
Books 13–24, 12
Books 13–15, 12
Book 13, 12, 61, 63, 65, 105
   13.97–98, 95
   13.125–87, 63
   13.128–30, 61
   13.130, 65
   13.184–440, 97
   13.187–216, 97
   13.221–22, 106
   13.221–329, 105
   13.221–440, 97
   13.232–33, 105
   13.356–60, 241
   13.383–85, 124, 130
Books 14–16, 250
Book 15
   15.112, 56
   15.180, 56
Books 16–24, 10, 11
Book 17
   17.327, 87
Book 20
   20.70, 56
Book 24
   24.19–97, 124, 130
   24.481–86, 168
   24.483, 284
   24.486, 284
Homeric Hymn 5 (to Aphrodite)
   45–90, 103
   45, 104
   91–106, 104

107–67, 104
198–99, 104
256–63, 171
Homeric Hymn 7 (to Dionysus), 95
Horace
   Art of Poetry 136–39, 117
      220–50, 170
   Epistles 1.1.42, 83
      1.2.1–31, 77
      1.2.8, 83
      1.2.9–11, 278
      1.2.24, 83
      1.2.27–28, 220
      1.6.61–63, 83
   Epodes 10, 126
   Odes
      Books 1–3, 189
      1.3, , 44, 126
      1.5.13, 126
      1.6, , 79
      3.17, 94
      Book 4, 189
      4.1.4, 189
      4.15.31–32, 189
   Satires 1.1.24, 78
      1.5, 83
      1.7.11–15, 78
      1.10, 83
      2.5, 78

Justin, *Epitome of the Philippic History of Pompeius Trogus* 18.5.9, 103

Livius Andronicus, *Odyssey* (in Warmington 1936)
   fragment 1, 120
   fragment 16, 183
   fragment 30, 120
Livy, *History of Rome*, 5.21–22, 185
   7.28.4–6, 120
   21.1.1, 182
   21.4.9, 102
   27.12.15–16, 181
   21.49.13, 180
   21.50.2, 180

Livy (continued)
    27.37.7–14, 185
    34.62.11–12, 103
"Longinus," *On the Sublime* 1.11–14, 132
    4–5, 125
Lucretius, *On the Nature of Things* 1.86, 256
    1.418, 296
    6.42, 296

Macrobius
    Commentary on Scipio's Dream 2.3.4, 121
    Saturnalia 5.2.6, 42
    5.2.7, 46
    5.2.13, 105, 107
    5.2.15, 254
    5.3.8–19, 93
    5.4.3, 52
    5.4.6, 105
    5.9.13, 259
    5.9.14–15, 262
    5.11.26–29, 191
    5.19.1–5, 173
    6.2.30, 261
    6.2.31, 92, 187
    6.2.32, 190
    6.3.2–4, 191, 262

Naevius, Gnaeus, *The Punic War*
    Book 1 187
    fragment 1 (in Warmington 1936), 121

Ovid
    Fasti 1.4, 126
    5.569–96, 239
    Heroides 8.82–83, 204
    Ibis 18, , 126
    625–30, 254
    Metamorphoses 1.2, 50
    11.428–29, 126
    Tristia 1.2.47, 126
    1.6.8, 126

Palatine Anthology 12.43, 117
Philodemus of Gadara
    On Flattery, 83
    On the Good King according to Homer, 6
Pindar, *Nemean Odes* 7.17–30
    8.18–34, 79
Plato, *Republic* 3, 390b–c, 53
    10, 619b2–620d5, 115
Plutarch
    Advice to Bride and Groom 38, 53
    Life of Pyrrhus 1, 213
    Life of Solon 10, 179
    Life of Fabius 21–23, 181
"Plutarch," *On the Life and Poetry of Homer*, 2.4
Polybius, *Histories* 1.10, 181
Proclus, *Chrestomathia*, 69
Propertius, *Elegies* 1.1.36, 296
    2.34.66, 44
    2.26.33, 126
    3.9.1–4, 126
    3.21, 126
    3.24, 126

Quintilian, *The Orator's Education* 10.1.53, 128

Scholia A on *Iliad* 1.1, 43
Scholia A on *Iliad* 18.22–35, 73
Scholia abT on *Iliad* 21.276, 73
Scholia bT on *Iliad* 14.176, 53
Scholia MV and HMQ on *Odyssey* 23.296, 58
Scholia Q on *Odyssey* 5.312, 73
Scholia T on *Iliad* 10.1, 255
Servius, *Commentary on Vergil's Aeneid*
    preface (*vita Servii*), 9, 13, 42, 84, 196
    1.1, 9, 41–42
    1.41, 123
    1.92, 67, 68
    1.93, 74
    1.94, 68
    1.170, 187

INDEX OF PASSAGES CITED   337

    1.198, 92
    1.159, 93
    1.264, 41
    1.362–67, 103
    1.378, 101
    1.407, 99
    1.497, 3, 110
    1.544, 217
    1.545, 217
    1.602, 130
    2.7, 200
    2.135, 179
    2.557, 179
    3.4, 130
    3.46, 173
    3.209, 208
    3.287, 210
    4, preface, 134, 173
    4.9, 92
    4.682, 92
    4.694, 173
    4.703, 173
    5.1, 226
    5.626, 86
    6.529, 237
    6.468, 174
    6.752, 180
    7.641, 247
    8.19, 249
    8.625, 180
    9.1, 254
    9.808, 191
    12.176, 259
    12.266, 259
Sophocles
    Ajax 550–51, 266
    Women of Trachis 912–31, 176
Statius, *Achilleid* 1.94, 201
Suda, s.v. Monêta (M 1220 in Adler XXXX), 120
Suetonius
    Augustus 15, 274
    29.2, 239
    Life of Vergil, 42

Theocritus, *Idylls*
    1.10–11, 82, 296
    13, 155
    24, 155; 25, 155
Thucydides, *History of the Peloponnesian War*
    3.88, 60
    6.2.1, 94

Valerius Flaccus, *Argonautica* 1.1, 50
Valerius Maximus, *Memorable Deeds and Sayings* 7.4, external exemplum 2, 102
Varro, *The Latin Language* 7.26, 121
Vergil, *Aeneid*
    Books 1–8, 228
    Books 1–7, 47, 91, 140, 245
    Books 1–6, 2, 10, 13–15, 41, 47, 53, 62–63, 65, 112, 116, 132, 137, 142, 150, 151, 152, 219, 222–223, 226, 236, 272, 286
    Books 1–4, 154, 197, 198, 224
    Books 1 and 4, 141
    Book 1, 50, 54, 63, 64, 65, 91, 93, 125, 139, 141, 144, 145, 147, 170, 173, 199, 220, 223, 227
    1.1a–d ("preproemium"), 42, 45
    1.1, 41–42, 45, 116, 117, 119, 126, 127, 155
    1.1–7, 44–46, 126
    1.2–3, 46
    1.3–6, 203
    1.3, 45, 264
    1.4, 46, 55, 122
    1.8, 10, 47, 119, 122
    1.10, 154, 218
    1.11, 55
    1.12–33, 46, 48
    1.12–28, 56
    1.12, 222
    1.14, 210, 220
    1.16, 220
    1.23, 122
    1.25–26, 55
    1.26–28, 122

Vergil (*continued*)
    1.30, 209
    1.35, 244
    1.36–37, 61
    1.36, 56
    1.37–49, 140
    1.37–38, 49, 74
    1.37, 55
    1.39, 246
    1.40–45, 123
    1.48–49, 61
    1.50–156, 94, 170
    1.57, 55
    1.64–76, 52–53
    1.65–66, 59
    1.71–75, 60
    1.73, 147, 276
    1.76–80, 60
    1.81–123, 187
    1.81–86, 59
    1.92–123, 125
    1.92–96, 66
    1.92, 72, 125
    1.94, 67, 73, 95
    1.94–95, 282
    1.96–101, 69
    1.96, 70
    1.97–101, 252
    1.97–98, 74
    1.97, 70
    1.100–1, 161
    1.113, 241
    1.118–19, 71, 125
    1.119, 126
    1.127, 64
    1.130, 62, 146
    1.132–41, 62
    1.157–222, 108
    1.157–69, 91
    1.157–79, 94, 169–70
    1.162, 172
    1.164, 169
    1.180–222, 94
    1.207, 170
    1.208, 67

    1.208–9, 95
    1.223–96, 108, 146
    1.223, 50
    1.227–53, 187
    1.229, 100
    1.242–49, 130
    1.254–96, 187
    1.259–60, 155
    1.261–66, 88
    1.263–66, 101
    1.302–3, 220
    1.302–4, 94
    1.305–24, 108
    1.305–409, 97
    1.307–8, 94, 169–70
    1.308, 94
    1.310, 172
    1.314–20, 104
    1.320, 104
    1.321, 98
    1.327–29, 98, 108
    1.331, 105
    1.335–68, 108
    1.336–37, 170
    1.337, 170
    1.338–68, 170
    1.340–68, 102
    1.349, 212
    1.357–68, 219
    1.36–37, 61
    1.364, 110
    1.373, 92
    1.378–79, 98, 101
    1.378–80, 209
    1.385–401, 99
    1.404, 104
    1.405, 104–105
    1.407, 99
    1.411–14, 108
    1.418–39, 169, 171
    1.427–28, 172
    1.428–29, 172
    1.429, 172
    1.437, 109
    1.450–93, 100, 288

INDEX OF PASSAGES CITED 339

1.456, 118
1.458, 221
1.468, 221
1.475, 221
1.484, 221
1.488, 276
1.490–93, 221
1.494–504, 108
1.539–41, 221
1.544–45, 217
1.582, 100
1.584–85, 241
1.595–96, 103
1.602, 130
1.613–30, 96
1.613–15, 214
1.615, 100
1.627, 96
1.631–42, 96
1.740–47, 129
1.748–56, 100
1.749–52, 222
1.750–55, 109
1.754, 128
1.755–56, 86
Books 2–3, 11, 14, 128–33, 170, 175, 199, 215, 216
Book 2, 47, 128, 129, 131, 132, 199, 209, 213, 243
  2.6–8, 200
  2.10, 128
  2.12–13, 296
  2.29, 200
  2.40–56, 282
  2.44, 201
  2.65–66, 201
  2.81–100, 201
  2.104, 201
  2.122, 201
  2.128, 201
  2.164, 201
  2.195–98, 201
  2.199–249, 282
  2.246–47, 282
  2.259, 201
  2.261, 201
  2.263, 204
  2.264, 201, 206
  2.274–75, 202
  2.275, 202
  2.291–92, 203
  2.294–95, 203
  2.314, 203
  2.315–17, 203
  2.316, 203
  2.337, 248
  2.370–401, 204
  2.370–85, 204
  2.390, 204
  2.391–430, 204
  2.428, 282
  2.453–558, 206
  2.471–75, 205
  2.477, 205
  2.491, 205
  2.512–32, 212
  2.533–46, 206
  2.547–53, 206, 212, 262
  2.589, 99
  2.610–16, 64
  2.612, 144
  2.655, 248
  2.663, 212
  2.721–23, 154
  2.725, 248
  2.761, 144
  2.762, 201
Book 3, 22, 128–32, 154, 170, 207
  3.4–5, 130
  3.11, 216
  3.17, 216
  3.78, 248
  3.87, 209
  3.223–28, 244
  3.225–340, 156
  3.273, 209
  3.280, 209
  3.286, 210
  3.288, 210
  3.291–505, 210

340 INDEX OF PASSAGES CITED

Vergil (*continued*)
 3.294–505, 130
 3.330–32, 211
 3.330–32, 212
 3.331, 212
 3.332, 212
 3.332, 212
 3.332, 212
 3.347, 144
 3.380, 144, 245
 3.433–40, 210, 245
 3.437, 144
 3.463–69, 213
 3.492–505, 210
 3.493–94, 282
 3.496, 210
 3.547, 144
 3.551, 154, 166, 208
 3.570–691, 214
 3.588–691, 215
 3.613–15, 214
 3.629, 201, 214
 3.645–48, 87
 3.687–91, 214
 3.690, 216
 3.715, 88
 3.717, 216
 Book 4, 9, 37, 134, 135, 140, 143, 146, 171, 172, 173, 175, 176, 187, 219
 4.90–128, 145
 4.91, 146
 4.95, 146
 4.105, 146
 4.110, 248
 4.113–14, 146
 4.126, 147, 276
 4.128, 147
 4.160–72, 145, 284
 4.215–18, 223
 4.223–37, 96
 4.260–67, 223
 4.262–63, 96
 4.265–95, 156
 4.279–95, 96
 4.296, 219
 4.305–6, 219
 4.340–44, 282
 4.376, 248
 4.445–65, 176
 4.445–62, 176
 4.471, 175
 4.484–86, 156
 4.625–29, 180
 4.693–705, 173
 Books 5–8, 197, 224
 Books 5–6, 249, 224
 Book 5, 9, 13, 14, 63, 131, 154, 166, 228, 224, 229
 5.14, 64
 5.32–33, 228
 5.104–603, 13, 14, 166, 226, 229, 231, 232, 272, 273
 5.119, 230
 5.121, 229
 5.144–47, 226
 5.159–82, 229
 5.183–209, 229
 5.232–48, 231
 5.263, 256
 5.266–85, 229
 5.286–361, 231
 5.315–61, 254, 256, 266
 5.340–61, 280
 5.358, 231
 5.362–484, 227, 230
 5.368–74, 227
 5.410–16, 154
 5.410–12, 166
 5.454–55, 230
 5.545–603, 229
 5.562, 230
 5.585, 229
 5.596, 231
 5.598, 231
 5.600, 231
 5.604–778, 232
 5.604–99, 280
 5.628, 248

INDEX OF PASSAGES CITED   341

5.669, 230
5.705, 232
5.737, 232
5.767–71, 280
5.781–82, 63
5.789–92, 63
5.800–15, 63
5.800–802, 64
5.804–11, 64
5.814–15, 63
5.867, 231
5.870–71, 232
Book 6, 11, 14, 161
   6.14–41, 288
   6.83–97, 154
   6.83, 233
   6.84–91, 71
   6.86–94, 233, 253
   6.102–23, 233
   6.103–5, 233, 249
   6.103, 154
   6.109, 233
   6.119–23, 235
   6.123, 154
   6.124–29, 235
   6.129, 154
   6.135, 154
   6.146–48, 115
   6.211, 115
   6.232–35, 241
   6.264–901, 176, 177, 243
   6.292, 233
   6.336–71, 281
   6.376–83, 241
   6.382–83, 281
   6.384–97, 166, 176
   6.388, 166, 235
   6.425–76, 174, 236–37
   6.430–76, 236
   6.430, 236
   6.432, 237
   6.433, 233
   6.450–76, 236
   6.469–71, 174

   6.488, 233
   6.489–93, 235
   6.529, 237
   6.540–43, 237
   6.565, 233
   6.566, 237
   6.567, 237
   6.569, 237
   6.609, 237
   6.613, 237
   6.614, 233
   6.620, 233, 237
   6.682–83, 238
   6.721, 235
   6.730, 74
   6.753–892, 80, 239–40, 242, 282
   6.755, 233
   6.756–887, 235
   6.759, 233
   6.791–807, 239
   6.817–23, 238
   6.852–53, 240
   6.852, 241
   6.853, 291
   6.886–901, 225
   6.888–92, 225
   6.890–92, 243
   6.891, 233
   6.892, 249
Books 7–12, 9, 10, 12, 13, 21, 41, 47,
   132, 137, 142, 151–52, 161, 211, 228,
   236, 243, 247, 272, 283, 286
Books 7–8, 137
Book 7, 11, 12, 54, 139, 141, 150, 151,
   163, 225, 241, 242, 245
   7.1–147, 141
   7.1–4, 241
   7.37–45, 179, 243
   7.37–40, 242
   7.37, 140, 245
   7.42, 245
   7.45–106, 242
   7.52–106, 277
   7.107–47, 244

Vergil (*continued*)
    7.133–40, 241
    7.148–56, 244
    7.153, 275
    7.157–59, 244
    7.249–58, 277
    7.286–340, 177
    7.286–92, 50
    7.293–322, 245
    7.312, 140
    7.341–571, 177
    7.594, 248
    7.641–817, 163, 247, 248, 249, 264
    7.641–46, 247
    Book 8, 11, 12, 152, 153, 154, 157, 163, 225
    8.18–21, 248
    8.26–67, 250
    8.29, 249
    8.36–65, 158
    8.40–41, 250
    8.50, 250
    8.60, 250
    8.66–101, 250
    8.126–74, 251
    8.143, 275
    8.152–56, 251
    8.184–279, 152, 160, 162, 164
    8.205, 162
    8.206, 162
    8.219, 161
    8.228, 161
    8.230, 161
    8.236–40, 161
    8.241–46, 161
    8.299, 161
    8.319–27, 184
    8.364–65, 153
    8.421, 158
    8.424, 158
    8.452–53, 158
    8.470–519, 252
    8.520–23, 252
    8.537–40, 252
    8.608–731, 288
    8.626–728, 163–65, 180
    8.726, 158
    8.729–31, 253
    8.730, 165
    Books 9–12, 12, 137, 179, 197, 253
    Book 9, 143, 163, 190, 191, 192, 228, 253, 254, 257
    9.1–24, 257
    9.40–46, 254
    9.47–76, 258
    9.57, 261
    9.77–122, 63
    9.123–33, 258
    9.131, 258
    9.138–39, 257
    9.176–502, 254, 256, 266
    9.184–85, 255
    9.186–87, 255
    9.224–28, 255–56
    9.226, 256, 270
    9.263–74, 256
    9.367–77, 257
    9.384–445, 257
    9.404–9, 259
    9.459–502, 257
    9.599, 259
    9.602, 259
    9.603, 259
    9.617, 259
    9.625–29, 259
    9.672–755, 261
    9.675–82, 191
    9.696, 261
    9.702, 261
    9.731–33, 261
    9.740, 261
    9.741–42, 257, 261
    9.781–87, 262
    9.789, 262
    9.791–96, 262
    9.806–14, 191, 262
    9.815–16, 263
    Book 10, 12, 15, 156, 263
    10.1–117, 263–64

INDEX OF PASSAGES CITED 343

10.48, 263–64
10.68–69, 263
10.82, 268
10.107, 264
10.159–60, 265
10.160–61, 265
10.161–62, 265
10.163–214, 12, 264
10.242–43, 166
10.260–75, 165
10.263, 165
10.324–32, 166
10.433–38, 270
10.442, 248
10.464–73, 267
10.495–506, 288
10.501–5, 264
10.510–605, 200, 267
10.517–20, 274
10.595–98, 200
10.606–32, 268
10.631, 248
10.633–88, 268
10.638–39, 166
10.670, 248
10.689–768, 268, 278
10.689–761, 268
10.732–46, 270
10.732–35, 268
10.734–35, 269
10.735, 269
10.737–41, 269
10.743–44, 269
10.744, 270
10.779–82, 154
10.813–14, 270
10.819–20, 270–71

Book 11
11.29–99, 272
11.45–46, 275
11.81–82, 274
11.100, 275
11.110–11, 275
11.122–32, 279

11.122–23, 276
11.124–26, 276
11.129, 276
11.225–444, 276, 278
11.227, 275
11.239, 275
11.296, 275
11.336, 276
11.340, 278
11.343–50, 277
11.346, 279
11.348, 279
11.376–444, 279
11.434–37, 278
11.793, 271
11.831, 271

Book 12, 12, 15
12.108, 230
12.138–45, 284
12.146–60, 284
12.257–310, 259
12.311–23, 259
12.432–40, 265
12.435, 265
12.435–36, 282
12.437, 265–66
12.439, 265
12.593–611, 284
12.793, 50, 283
12.794–95, 155
12.803–6, 284
12.805, 284
12.821, 284
12.822, 284
12.823–28, 285
12.830, 285
12.836, 285
12.841–42, 285
12.843–86, 284
12.877–78, 290
12.940, 115
12.940–52, 288
12.946–47, 290
12.952, 271

Vergil (*continued*)
    Eclogues, 27
        3.58, 296
        3.71, 296
        5.10, 296
        6.3, 51
        6.7, 51
        6.26, 296
        8.21, 25, 28a, 31, 36, 42, 46, 51, 57, 296
        8.48, 99
        8.50, 99
        9.32, 296
        10.22, 296
    Georgics, 27
        1.5, 50, 296
        1.40, 50, 296
        1.277, 296
        2.39–45, 126
        3.437–39, 205
        4.261–63, 297
        4.315–86, 100
        4.563–64, 295

Vitruvius, *On Architecture*
    5.6.8, 172
    5.6.9, 169

Xenophon, *Memorabilia* 2.1.21–33, 115

Zonaras, *Epitome of History* 8.5, 281

GENERAL INDEX

Abas, 210
Accius, Lucius, 81,183; *The Award of the Arms*, 202, 266; *Hecuba*, 207; *Philocteta*, 206
Acestes, 60, 230, 280
Achaemenides, 87–88, 130, 201, 209, 213–16, 240
Achaeans, 69, 133, 280
Achates, 98, 100, 108, 252, 290
Achilles, 11, 22, 39, 48, 51, 55, 58, 70, 72–74, 100–101, 109, 114, 118, 144, 149, 154, 159, 160, 162, 165, 168, 181, 201–2, 204–6, 211, 216, 229, 252, 256–57, 267, 273, 275, 291, 292; absence from battle, 12, 58, 148, 163, 254, 228, 254; arms of, 12, 58, 79, 133, 163, 201–2, 205–6, 213, 228, 253, 258, 263–64, 267, 271; battle with Aeneas, 64, 70–71; battle with the River Scamander/Xanthus, 71–72, 100, 161, 253, 263–64; choice of, 115; criticized/defended in ancient scholarship, 73, 78; death of, 35, 69, 75, 199–200, 217, 266, 269; deceived by Apollo, 267; grandson of Aeacus, 69, 213, 237–38; grandson of Aeacides, 199; greatest of Greek warriors, 70, 199–200, 205–6, 216, 257, 269; in kingship theory, 5–6, 7, 28, 35, 38, 77–81, 85, 90, 153, 218; in the *Odyssey*, 40, 206; kills Hector, 15, 73, 75, 200–202, 258, 269–72; kills Penthesilea, 221; marriage to Medea, 144; makes human sacrifice, 274; opposed by Thersites, 278–79; Pelides, 199, 204; princely instruction of, 163–64, 251; quarrel with Agamemnon, 11, 77, 148–49, 227, 257, 274, 278; quarrel with Odysseus, 129; reconciliation with Priam, 206, 213, 261, 273, 291; responsible for the fall of Troy, 35, 199–200, 209, 215, 223; returns to battle, 51, 148, 263–65; shield of, 164–65; smiles, 231; unlike Odysseus, 5–7, 35, 37, 79–81, 85, 159, 161, 180, 182, 194, 197, 204, 254, 266
Achilles, successors, 39, 133–35, 200, 202, 204, 205, 208, 213, 257; Aeneas, 28, 35, 37, 39, 51, 71, 85, 100–101, 133, 116, 167, 196, 198, 203, 218, 221, 223, 227, 229, 233, 235, 236, 237–38, 246, 253, 263, 264, 266–67, 275, 287, 288–89, 290, 291–92; Ajax son of Telamon, 79, 133, 202, 204, 263, 266–67, 269, 270; Arruns, 271; Augustus, 212, 274; Hector, 202, 205, 269, 270; Mezentius, 268, 270; Odysseus, 79, 133, 202; Pyrrhus, King of Epirus, 189, 193, 211; Pyrrhus/Neoptolemus, 133, 199, 202, 204–5, 213, 217, 236, 261–62; Turnus, 71, 211, 233, 247, 253, 257–58, 261–63, 267
Actium, 88, 209, 210; battle of (31 BCE), 158, 165, 208, 288
Admetus, 174
adventure, 49, 55, 87, 94, 105, 115, 149, 190, 207, 232, 252
Aeaea, 95, 96, 106, 111
Aeacidae, 189–90, 213, 252
Aeacus, 69, 237–38, 252
Aeetes, 137, 149
Aegates Islands, battle of (241 BCE), 180

GENERAL INDEX

Aeneas, 2, 3, 7, 11–12, 14–15, 18, 20, 22, 30, 34–35, 37–42, 48–50, 52, 55–56, 59–60, 62–76, 84–116, 118–19, 122–26, 128–35, 139–41, 144–46, 154–58, 160–61, 163–67, 169–74, 176–77, 179–80, 182, 187–88, 190, 192, 195, 196–225, 227–57, 259–69, 271–73, 275–85, 287–92, 296; absence from battle, 253–57; arrival in Carthage, 198; betrayer of Troy, 276; conception and birth, 103, 106; criticism of, 68, 72; death wish, 70, 71, 75, 235, 266, 273, 282; education, 247; experience, 39, 288; frankness, 218; hero, 224, 288; humanity, 215; ignorance of the *Odyssey*, 76, 86, 90, 99, 130, 206; Iliadic orientation, 71, 76, 90, 223, 243, 290; king, 219, 229; labors, 156; memory of Troy, 198–200; name, 104; narrator, 128–33, 152–53, 199–217, 207, 276; opposed by Juno, 286; personal desires, 196, 282; resentment of fate, 282; reader, 40, 196–292, 197–98, 234, 236, 247–48, 287; return to battle, 263–65; teacher, 265; unheroic hero, anti-hero, vel sim., 134; wanderings, 222, 290

Aeneas, intertextual identities, 187–88, 192–93, 253; Achilles, 22, 37, 39, 85, 135, 163, 167, 196, 198, 201, 223, 227, 228, 231, 236, 238, 246, 251, 253, 255, 263, 266–67, 270, 274–75, 287–90; Ajax son of Telamon, 266, 282; Augustus, 180, 274; Cyclic hero, 133–34; Heracles/Hercules, 37, 153, 160, 174–76, 247; Jason, 37, 134, 135, 147; Julius Caesar, 180; Mark Antony, 180; Odysseus, 21, 35, 37, 38–39, 66, 68, 85, 89, 96, 102, 135, 167, 175, 198, 214, 223, 235–36, 245, 247, 250; Paris, 223; Scipio Africanus, 180; Telemachus, 250–51; Trojan, 247

Aeolia(n Islands), 60, 93

Aeolus, king of the winds, 52–5, 59–63, 66, 75, 91, 93–94, 103, 140, 147, 224, 237, 245, 247, 283

Aeolus, son of Sisyphus, 237

Aeschylus, 8, 80, 202; *Oresteia*, 175

Aethiopis, 34, 69, 119, 202, 271

Africa, 35, 85, 90–96, 102, 106, 108, 110–11, 169, 180–81, 217, 227, 241

Agamemnon, 11, 58, 77, 79, 124, 130, 148–49, 163, 184, 211–12, 227, 255–57, 278–79

Agenor, 267

Ajax son of Telamon, 37, 79, 118, 133, 174, 191–92, 200, 202, 204, 262, 266–67, 269–70

Ajax the Locrian, 118, 123–25, 231

Alba Longa, 231

Alcestis, 173, 174, 175, 176, 178, 257

Alcinous, 35, 77, 84, 86–88, 95–96, 98, 102, 107, 110–11, 128–30, 136–37, 140–41, 198, 209, 215, 220

Alcmene, 164

Alexander the Great, 82

Allecto, 54, 140, 177, 245–47, 261, 283

allegory, 2, 55, 83, 96, 165, 183, 223, 242, 265

Amata, 177, 242, 245–46, 248, 281–84

Amazons, 221, 271

ambassadors, 163, 244, 275–76

ambition, 37, 38–39, 75, 112, 119, 127, 131

Ambracia, 122, 208; siege of (189 BCE), 260, 263

Amphitryon, 164

Anchises, 13, 35, 67, 103–4, 154, 171, 180, 224–25, 232–33, 235, 237–49, 251, 279–80; and Evander, 250; as Aeacus, 237–38; as Aeneas' teacher, 266; confused with Celaeno, 244; seduction of, 103, 106, 108

Androgeos, 204

Andromache, 57, 130, 207, 210, 211, 213

Anna, 92

Antenor, 77, 130, 133, 278

Antilochus, 229

Antiphates, 261

Antisthenes, 80, 218

Antony, Mark (Marcus Antonius, 83–30 BCE), 37, 209

Antores, 154

Aphrodite, 70, 98, 103, 104, 105, 113, 129, 145–46, 268

Apollo, 2, 46, 70, 72, 127, 158, 162, 202, 209, 233, 235–36, 245, 259, 267–68, 271, 288; Phoebus, 108

Apollonius of Rhodes, *Argonautica*, 3, 8, 9, 22, 23, 24, 25, 26, 38, 50, 96, 133, 134, 135, 136, 137, 138, 139, 140, 141, 145, 147, 150, 155, 156, 157, 166, 167, 171, 173, 178, 187, 194, 208, 228, 242, 245, 246, 249; plot, 143; structure, 47, 135, 139–40, 142

Apollonius of Rhodes, *Argonautica*, intertextual aspects: Heraclean, 156, 166–67; Iliadic, 135, 145, 147–48, 150, 228; Odyssean, 135, 137–38, 147–48, 150, 152, 245

Arctinus, 129, 132

Ares, 165

Arete, Queen of Scheria, 110–11, 137, 141, 220

Argo, 3, 133, 136, 142, 144, 156, 187

Argos, 124, 164, 184, 192, 210

Aristarchus of Samos, 58

Aristophanes of Byzantium, 58

Aristotle, 7, 57, 58, 78, 82, 117, 132, 155, 167–68, 273

arms (*arma*), 12, 18, 41–48, 50–51, 58, 71, 79, 101, 117, 119, 125–26, 133, 148, 163, 166, 201–6, 209–10, 213, 218, 220, 228–30, 235, 247, 252–53, 258, 262–64, 266–68, 271, 276, 278, 282, 291

arrival scenes, 90, 91

Arruns, 271

Artemis, 104, 107, 108, 158

Ascanius, 89, 177, 231, 244, 246, 254, 256, 259, 260, 263, 265, 266

Asconius Pedianus, 67

Athena, 88, 97, 98, 99, 100, 101, 104, 105, 106, 107, 110, 123, 145, 146, 161, 168, 187, 218, 231, 232, 247, 251, 284, 285, 291

Athenian theater festivals, 169; City Dionysia of 438 BCE, 173; satyr drama in, 174

Augeas, 157

augury, 178, 244

Augustus, Augustan, 20, 28, 30, 42, 84–85, 133, 153, 158, 166, 180, 189, 196, 208–10, 212–13, 230–31, 239, 268, 274, 285–86; *Accomplishments* (*Res Gestae*), 239; Augustan period, 158; Augustan regime, 260, 289; Augustan Rome, 2, 29–30, 81, 210, 239, 273–74, 279, 283; Caesar, 212–13, 239, 274, 280; Octavian, 272

authority, 57–58, 75, 109, 197, 238–39, 287; lexical, 295; narrative, 117, 286

Automedon, 205

Aventine Hill, 161

Avernus, 114, 154, 233, 235

Berenice II, Queen of Egypt (267–221 BCE), 157–58

Bitias. *See* Pandarus and Bitias

bombast, 125

boxing, 154, 166, 227, 229

bribery, 52–54, 57, 61, 144, 146–47, 211, 245–46

Briseis, 257

Brutus: Decimus Junius Brutus (81–43 BCE), 239; Lucius Junius Brutus (d. 509 BCE), 238, 239

Buthrotum, 88, 130, 207–10, 213, 217, 282

Cacus, 152–53, 161–62, 164, 166, 251

Caere, 290

Caesar, Julius (100–44 BCE), 37, 180, 212–13, 230, 239–40, 280. *See also* Augustus, Augustan

Caieta, 241–42

Calchas, 133

Callimachus, 23, 38, 117, 119, 120, 127, 153–59, 166–67, 176, 178, 194

Calypso, 14, 34, 87–88, 111, 115, 219

Camenae, 120, 122, 183

Camilla, 272

Camillus, 120, 185

Cannae, battle of (216 BCE), 181

Carrhae, battle of (53 BCE), 81, 268

Carthage, 11, 14, 35, 48–49, 60, 64, 85, 87, 92, 94, 95–97, 100, 102–3, 105, 107, 109, 111–12, 118–19, 128, 140–42, 153, 171–72, 179–81, 183, 185–86, 187–88, 192, 199, 210, 219, 220–23, 228, 229, 265, 281, 288–90

Cassandra, 282

catabasis, 14, 154, 161, 177, 243

Catiline (Lucius Sergius Catilina, 108–62 BCE), 229

Catullus, 81, 127

causes (*origines, aetia*), 33, 54, 55, 59, 104, 119, 122, 126, 166, 222
Celaeno, 244
Cerberus, 176
Charon, 166, 176, 235
Charybdis. *See* Scylla and Charybdis
cheaters, 281
choice, 4, 23, 34, 36–37, 39, 42, 53, 66, 81, 85, 100, 112, 114–16, 136, 139–50, 154, 195, 200, 237, 287, 292
Chryseis, 48
Chrysippus, 78, 81
Cicero (Marcus Tullius Cicero, 106–43 BCE), 41, 81, 94, 183, 189, 229, 279, 297
Circe, 77, 79, 83, 94–97, 111, 136, 219, 241–42
Civil Wars, 48–31 BCE, 179
Cleopatra VII Philopator (69–30 BCE), 180, 209
Cloanthus, 231
Colchis, 134, 137, 140, 142
Cold War, 1947–1991 CE, 31
comedy, comic, 25, 57–58, 122, 168–74, 178, 257, 273, 291; comic endings, 174–75; comic mode, 116, 291; in the *Aeneid*, 272; relation to satyr drama, 169–70, 172; relation to tragedy, 168, 173
consequences, unintended, 147, 283, 290
contamination. *See* intertextuality: combination
contradiction, 19, 119, 133, 206, 215
Coroebus, 204, 210, 219
cothurnus, 170, 171
Crantor, 78, 81
Crassus (Marcus Licinius Crassus, 115–53 BCE), 268, 297
Crete, 88, 97, 208
Creusa, 67, 241
Cronus, 59, 184
crossroads, 233, 237
Cumae, 71, 114, 154, 232–33, 234, 288–90
Cupid, 99, 146, 223, 245
Cyclops, 79, 87, 130, 158, 162, 214–15
Cycnus, 165
Cypria, 34, 117–19, 132
Cythera, Cytherea, 64

Daedalus, 288–89
Danaans, 66, 69, 70
Danaids, 288–89
Dares, 227, 230
death, 8, 9, 19, 42, 45, 62, 64–67, 69–75, 88, 100–101, 110, 115, 124, 155–56, 166, 173–76, 179, 192, 202–3, 205, 211, 214, 219, 221–22, 227, 230, 232, 235–36, 241, 243, 245, 269–72, 277–79, 281; by drowning, 69, 71–74, 87, 100–101, 127, 264; death wish, 266, 273; dismal, 69, 72–73; glorious, 71; heroic, 234–35; honorable, 71, 287; in tragedy, 174; of Achilles, 199, 270; of Camilla, 271; of Hector, 264, 271; of Orodes, 270; of Pallas, 200; of Patroclus, 265, 267, 271, 274; of Sarpedon, 267 ;of Turnus, 264, 271, 286, 290
Death. *See* Thanatos
decision, 34, 40, 47, 167, 177–78, 182
defeat, 49–50, 71, 74, 88, 181, 198, 209, 229, 251, 259
Deianeira, 176
Deiphobus, 236
Demodocus, 129
Diana, 98, 100, 103, 108–10, 171, 256
dichotomy, 114, 291
Dido, 14, 35, 39, 85–88, 90, 92, 96–98, 100, 102–3, 106–12, 128–29, 134–35, 141–42, 144, 146–47, 153–54, 156, 171–76, 199, 207, 209, 212, 215–17, 219–21, 223–24, 227, 236, 244, 246, 247–48, 265, 282, 284, 290; character, 174; death, 176, 222, 241; Iliadic orientation, 221, 222; in light of kingship theory, 219; in Naevius' *The Punic War*, 187
Dido, intertextual identities: Alcestis, 174, 257; Alcinous, 220, 222; Arete, 222; Calypso, 246; Circe, 242, 246; Cleopatra, 180; Helen, 223; Heracles, 176; Hippolytus, 171; Medea, 175, 246; Nausicaa, 246; Penthesilea, 221–23; Phaedra, 171; Sophonisba, 180
dilemma, 39, 114, 116, 133, 139, 159, 194
Diomedes, 64, 70–71, 74, 76, 109, 117–18, 124, 221, 255, 257, 268; Tydides (son of Tydeus), 69, 70, 201

GENERAL INDEX 349

Dionysus, 95, 144
Dis, 173
dissent, 4, 5, 279–80, 286
diversion, 54, 143
divine antagonist, 2, 3, 5, 34–35, 60–62, 65
divine apparatus, 53, 121
Dolopians, 200
doppelgänger, 270, 279
double entendres, 297
Drances, 276–80
dreams, 21, 119, 201, 205, 224, 232, 236, 243, 250
Drepane, 142
dynamics of reading, 186

Eastern Bloc, 32
ecphrasis, 148, 165, 287–89
education, instruction, 46, 74, 78, 81, 163, 197, 201, 224–25, 229–33, 236, 243, 245, 249–52, 265; teacher (*magister*), 31, 224, 229–30, 232
Egypt, 157–58, 180
elegy, 36, 155, 156, 167
Elpenor, 241
Elysium, Elysian Fields, 144, 225, 232–33, 237, 246
emotion(s), 4, 14, 26, 34–35, 39, 43–44, 46, 47, 53, 55, 58, 61–65, 72, 77, 79–81, 85, 107, 116, 119, 122, 138, 144, 149, 161–66, 179, 197, 203, 205, 230, 242, 244–46, 249–50, 255–56, 261, 269, 270, 274, 281, 285, 288–91; anger, wrath (*ira, mênis*), 10, 14, 34–35, 39, 43–44, 46–47, 49–51, 53, 55, 58, 62, 63, 65, 72, 74–75, 77, 79–80, 85, 116, 119, 122, 144, 149, 161–66, 194, 197, 203, 205, 230, 238, 242, 246–47 250, 252, 254, 267, 269–70, 272, 274, 282, 285, 288, 290, 291, 293–97; confidence, 119, 186, 232–33, 244, 250–51, 268; passion(s), 78–79, 83, 85, 151, 197, 203–4, 223, 243, 245, 250
Ennius (Quintus Ennius), 81, 92, 121–22, 182, 188–95, 207–8, 211, 260–63, 275
Entellus, 166, 230
Epeos, 201, 217
epic, 2, 3, 5, 10–11, 14–16, 18–19, 21, 26, 29, 34, 36–39, 44–46, 50–52, 56–57, 67, 69, 79, 89, 91, 92, 112, 115–17, 121, 123–24, 126–28, 131–32, 138–40, 143, 146, 149, 154–56, 167–68, 173, 178–80, 182, 185–88, 193, 195, 197, 205, 209, 212, 227, 255, 270, 273, 277, 280, 286
Epic Cycle, 34, 38, 55, 69, 116–20, 124–25, 127–34, 144, 153, 155, 194, 195, 198–99, 202, 207, 221, 245, 246, 271, 276
Epicureanism, 6, 249
epiphany, 99
Epirus, 208, 212
Erato, 140, 243, 245. *See* Muse(s)
eros, Eros, 145, 146, 171
Eryx, 154, 166, 228, 230
ethical qualities: courage (*virtus, andreia*), 251; adaptability, flexibility, versatility, 66, 80, 81, 161, 182, 204; anger, wrath (*ira, mênis*), 10, 34, 35, 39, 43–44, 46–47, 53, 55, 58, 62, 63, 65, 72, 75, 77, 79–80, 85, 116, 119, 122, 144, 149, 161–66, 194, 197, 203, 205, 230, 238, 242, 246, 247 250, 254, 267, 269–70, 272, 274, 282, 285, 288, 290; artifice, skill (*ars*), 180, 232; candor, frankness, 101, 215; caution, 12, 97, 102, 103, 219; circumspection, 15, 79, 80, 85; cleverness, 64, 102, 103, 162, 216, 218, 219, 223, 240; consistency, 134, 288; courage, valor (*virtus, andreia, aretê*), 77, 79–80, 83, 133, 149, 180–81, 191–92, 198, 204, 217, 230, 232, 234, 260–61, 277–79; craftiness, deceit, deception, disguise, feigning, guile, sleight of hand, trickery (*dolus, dolos*), 48, 54, 57, 58, 61–62, 72, 73, 77, 97–103, 129, 145, 146, 147, 162, 174, 198–99, 201, 204, 209, 216–18, 219, 237, 268; cruelty, 205; determination, 255; deviousness, 79, 146, 182, 199, 255, 276; diplomacy, 188, 190, 275, 276; disguise, 54, 97, 98, 99, 100, 104, 105, 106, 108, 109, 171, 204, 206, 209, 218, 219; duplicity, 39, 133, 180, 198, 201, 216, 219, 223, 255; endurance, 55, 77, 81, 85, 159, 160, 166, 223, 235; falsehood, lies, 97, 98, 99, 215–16; force, violence (*vis, biê*), 8, 14, 19, 25, 36, 38, 39, 44, 52, 58, 61, 77, 79, 80, 81, 85, 89, 115, 156, 159–62, 164, 165, 166,

ethical qualities (*continued*)
167, 180, 181, 182, 189, 193, 194, 197, 198, 203, 204, 205, 206, 207, 209, 212, 213, 221, 230, 235, 240, 241, 248, 266, 274, 281, 286, 289, 292; foresight, prudence, 66, 77, 85, 162, 189, 190, 202, 203, 204, 206, 213, 223, 231; harshness, 209; inflexibility, 80, 218; insight, 40, 90, 93, 181, 201, 232; intelligence (*sapientia, mētis*), 38, 39, 62, 79, 80, 102, 103, 116, 159, 161, 181, 182, 197, 201, 203, 219, 223, 229, 238, 239, 240; intransigence, inflexibility, obstinacy, stubbornness, 5, 14, 80, 82, 139; lying, 98, 99, 215; might, 206; moderation, 17, 18, 220; obstinacy, 80; patience, 194; perspicacity, 81; pitilessness, 80; resilience, 102, 219, 223; resourcefulness, 55, 89, 109, 116, 171, 223–24, 236; restraint, self-control, self-restraint, 80–81, 110, 156, 159, 197, 201, 203, 214, 223, 239; self-absorption, 80; solipsism, 80; stealth, 162; straightforwardness, 79; stratagem, strategy, 20, 54, 58, 103, 132, 144–45, 180–81, 189, 193–94, 197, 203, 206, 213, 218, 230, 246, 247, 253; strength, 149, 159; stubbornness, 14, 139; subtlety, 93, 197; thievery, 162, 237; treachery, 77, 102, 146, 201, 211, 215, 237; trustworthiness, 190; wiliness, 14, 162

ethics, 4–7, 15, 17, 28–30, 33, 35–36, 38–39, 57, 68, 74, 77–85, 89–90, 96, 98, 102–3, 114–16, 133, 135, 138–39, 153, 155, 157, 159, 166–67, 181–82, 193–95, 197, 199, 201, 202, 218, 220, 225–27, 237, 265, 292; ethical heroism, 6–7, 39, 85, 103, 207, 242; ethical philosophy, 5–6, 35, 77–78, 81, 85, 103, 115, 181, 193, 198, 219, 220, 223–24, 226; Iliadic or Achillean v. Odyssean ethics, 39, 48, 57, 85, 90, 133, 159, 161–63, 182, 190, 197, 204, 216, 226

Etruscan(s), 12, 121, 185, 252, 263–64, 268
etymology, 80, 120–21, 184, 239–40, 243, 297;
  Aeneas, 103–4; Cacus, 153; Erato, 243;
  Evander, 153; Latium, 184; Moneta, 120
Eumaeus, 88, 163, 250
Euripides, 38, 78, 80, 144, 171, 173, 211, 213;
  Alcestis, 173, 174, 176–77; *Andromache*, 175;
  Bacchae, 175; *Hecuba*, 175, 207; *Heracles*, 176, 246; *Hippolytus*, 171; *Trojan Women*, 175
Euryalus. *See* Nisus and Euryalus
Eurystheus, 155
Evander, 38, 154, 155–62, 167, 177, 225, 252–53, 265, 290; enemy of Latinus, 250, 275; good king, 153; name, 153; narrator, 152–53
Evander, intertextual identities: Eumaeus, 250; Menelaus, 250; Nestor, 250, 251; Phoenix, 163, 251
exempla, 182; negative, 30, 78, 193; positive, 7, 39, 79, 82, 110, 193, 198, 214, 263, 265

Fabius (Quintus Fabius Maximus, 280–203 BCE), 37; "The Delayer" (*Cunctator*), 181
failure, 19, 23, 32, 38, 54–55, 58–59, 78, 82–84, 89, 109–10, 116, 120, 126–28, 132, 134, 147, 156, 163, 205, 207, 214–15, 219, 222, 233, 236, 245, 255, 257, 261, 266–67, 273, 275, 277–78, 280, 291
fate, Fate(s), 20, 34, 44, 50, 52, 64, 69, 71, 72, 100–101, 115, 124–25, 130, 146, 170–71, 174, 195–96, 200, 202, 213, 230, 245–46, 248, 269, 271, 277, 281, 282, 286
focalization, 108, 126, 172, 225, 249
forgetfulness, 168
formalism, literary, 4, 5, 25, 27, 41, 76, 114
foundation(s) 154, 157, 166, 207, 216
freedom, freeom of speech (*libertas*), 239, 240, 277, 279, 280
free indirect discourse, 118, 123
frenzy, 175
frigidity, 125
Fulvius Nobilior (Marcus Fulvius Nobilior, consul 189 BCE), 122
funeral(s), 56–57, 167, 179, 183, 272–75, 281, 283–84
Furies, 175, 211–12
fury, 161, 285, 290
futility, 61, 202, 204, 224, 286

Ganymede, 122
genre, 5, 6, 15–16, 29, 36–38, 58, 78–79, 82, 112, 157, 167–69, 171, 177–78, 193–94, 229, 251, 286

geography, 43, 91, 92, 178
Geronium, battle of (217 BCE), 181
Geryon, 162
gluttony, 77, 160
god(s), 2, 3, 5, 10, 12, 14, 19, 34–35, 44–47, 52–57, 59–66, 70, 72, 88–91, 97–105, 107–9, 111–12, 117–18, 120–24, 130, 133, 140, 143–46, 153–56, 159–60, 162, 165–66, 171, 173, 175, 179, 187, 220, 222, 225, 230, 231, 233, 237, 242, 244, 247, 249–53, 255, 256, 258–59, 263, 267–70, 272–73, 282–83, 288, 290–91, 296; apotheosis, divinization, 89, 156. *See also* nymphs
Golden Age, 184
Golden Bough, 114, 115, 237
Graces, 53, 104
Great Mother, 258
Greeks, 12, 53–54, 70, 77, 82–83, 118, 123, 133, 144, 180, 184, 186, 190–92, 204, 207, 209–11, 215, 235–36, 254, 256–59, 261, 270–71, 276, 280
guide citation. See *Leitzitat*
Gyas, 229, 230, 231

Hades, 173
Hannibal, 102, 179–81, 185
Hanno, 180
Harpies, 156, 208
Harvard School, 29
Hasdrubal, 186
Hebe, 122
Hector, 12, 15, 57, 69–70, 72–73, 75, 109, 118, 134, 192, 200–206, 210, 221, 227, 252, 258, 261–62, 264–73, 278–79
Helen, 57, 77, 211, 236, 252, 278
Helenus, 130, 20913, 245, 253
Hephaestus, 101, 163, 252
Hera, 2, 3, 52–58, 61, 64–65, 118, 120, 122, 143–47, 176, 183–85, 210, 246–47, 257
Heracleid, 155–56, 208
Heracles, 37–38, 44, 53, 144, 149, 154–60, 164–66, 175–78, 247; appetite, 157; baby Heracles, 155; comic aspects, 176; compared to Achilles and Odysseus, 160; death of, 176; in Callimachus' *Aetia*, 155, 157, 159–60, 176; in Greek tragedy, 155–56, 174, 176, 247; in kingship theory, 153; in the *Argonautica*, 144, 155–56, 159–60; labors, 155–58, 176, 178; persecuted by Hera, 144
Hercules, 38, 115, 149, 153–67, 177, 208, 230, 235, 251; catabasis, 154; civilizing activities of, 166; consoled by Jupiter, 264; cult of Hercules the Unconquered, 158; propensity for violence, 160; wanderings of, 154
Hermes, 104, 162, 171
hero, 2, 3, 5, 11–12, 14, 28, 34–39, 44–46, 50, 56, 60–61, 63, 67–73, 75–79, 81–82, 85–87, 89–93, 95–99, 101, 103, 106, 108, 115, 124–27, 129, 131–36, 140, 143, 144–45, 148–49, 153–55, 157, 159–67, 170–72, 174, 180, 198–200, 202–3, 205–11, 213, 216, 218–19, 221–22, 224–25, 230–31, 235–37, 241–42, 246–47, 250, 265, 268; "almost modern" hero, 134; anti-hero, 134; culture hero, 156, 158; Cyclic, 134; hero manqué, 134; Homeric, 195–96, 283; Homeric Odyssean, 66; unheroic hero, 134; wimp, 134
heroism, 30, 38, 81, 84, 115, 148, 159, 161, 167, 176, 195, 196, 197, 199, 223, 226, 269
Hesiod, 38, 94, 121, 161, 164–66, 178, 296
hesitation, 115–16, 146
historiography, 36–38, 178–82, 193
historians, 193
history, 2–3, 8, 17–19, 30, 32, 36–38, 43, 48, 55, 57, 89, 94, 102–3, 106, 120, 134, 145, 158, 165, 178–80, 182, 185–88, 190, 192–93, 195, 197, 208, 213, 220, 227, 235, 238–39, 268, 272, 274, 281, 289
homecoming, 34, 44, 55–56, 77, 89, 91–93, 122–24, 130, 135, 163, 170, 181, 187, 198, 203, 207, 219, 244
Homecomings (*Nostoi*), 34, 55, 117–18, 123–25, 130–31, 198, 207, 245
Homer, *Iliad* and *Odyssey*, 1, 3, 6–10, 12, 15–19, 21–28, 30, 33, 35–44, 54, 56, 58, 60, 62, 72–75, 77–85, 89–91, 95, 98, 102, 103, 105–8, 110, 113–14, 116–21, 123, 127–28, 131–34, 136, 138, 141, 149–51, 165–68, 178–84, 186, 188,

Homer (*continued*)
190–92, 194–95, 203, 215, 218–20, 234, 245, 255, 257–58, 260–62, 285, 287, 291–93, 295, 297; ancient scholarship, 43–44, 53, 58, 73–74, 94, 255; source of all genres, 36–37, 194
Homeric Hymn to Aphrodite, 171
honor, 61, 65, 122, 148–49, 185, 200–201, 221, 256
Horace, 44, 76–85, 89, 94, 96, 97, 117, 126, 170, 189, 214, 220, 223–24, 243, 245, 247, 278
Horatius Cocles, 262–63
horizon of expectations, 7, 17, 30, 81
Horkos (Oath), 296
hospitality, 156, 157, 220, 293
Hydra, Lernaean, 161
Hylas, 155
hymn, 103–4, 161, 183, 185–86
hyperbole, 81, 125, 140, 160–62, 166, 191–93, 226, 264
Hypnos (Sleep), 52–54, 61, 66, 145, 147
Hypsipyle, 136, 140–42, 148, 149

Iarbas, 223, 259
ideology, 19, 79, 127, 269
Ilioneus, 217–18, 221
imperialism, 20, 33
impiety, 207
incompatibility, 24, 26, 84–85, 104, 111, 115, 132, 134, 159–60, 171
individuality, 149
informer (*delator*), 280
insanity, 161, 246. *See also* madness
instruction. *See* education
intention(s), 5, 11, 24–25, 34, 84, 94, 116, 122, 147, 179, 243
intertextual chronology, 71, 76; identity, 111, 258, 260, 262, 268, 272, 283; intrusion, 140; inversion, 156; jump-cut, 261; set-pieces, 148
intertextuality, 9–10, 12, 17, 21–24, 27, 35–37, 48, 62, 66, 68, 72, 74, 89–90, 92, 95–96, 106, 109–11, 113, 117, 122–23, 132, 135–36, 139, 141–42, 145145, 150, 157, 165, 167, 169–71, 175–78, 192, 194, 199, 209, 211, 213, 216, 218, 220, 226–27, 231, 242, 245, 251, 256, 258–59, 261–63, 265–70, 276, 277, 286; Alexandrian footnote, 68; characters, division and multiplication of, 272; combination (*contaminatio*), 2, 10–11, 20–21, 25, 35, 37, 62, 75, 81, 84, 109–11, 117, 132, 134, 155, 159–60, 171, 188, 194, 207, 222, 265; conflation or multiple reference, 25; congruency, 143; dialogic, 21, 151, 157, 173, 176; dynamic, 70, 91, 111, 154; dynamics, 70, 85; extended similes, 148; future reflexive mode, 89, 136, 137, 175, 195, 245, 268; historical, 178, 272, 274, 279; imitation, 9, 10, 12, 25–26, 38–39, 42, 44–45, 78–79, 81, 88, 107, 131, 136–37, 141–42, 147, 149–51, 175, 190; interruption, 141; intertextual diversion, 143; metrical, 45, 46, 102; multiplication of Homeric characters, 241; numerical, 71; paraphrase, 147; reversal, 156–57; rivalry (*aemulatio*), 38, 128, 116; sonic, 296; systematic, 9, 13, 15, 26, 27; "window reference" (two-tier allusion), 22–23, 141, 147–51, 177, 260, 266
intertextuality, allusion, 10, 17, 22–25, 89, 137–38, 188, 231; combinatory, 25, 51, 151; two-tier. *See also* intertextuality: "window reference"
intertextuality, model, 7–9, 11, 14–16, 18, 21–23, 26–27, 29, 44, 50, 53, 61, 69, 70, 72, 77–78, 85, 89, 97, 99–100, 103–7, 110, 113, 129, 136–37, 144–45, 148–49, 151, 154, 156, 160, 163–66, 171, 191–92, 194, 202, 227, 247, 249, 272; example model (*modello esemplare*), 15–16, 37; genre model (*modello genere*), 15, 37, 116, 159; primary or principal model, 109, 138; secondary model, 109, 113, 138
intratextuality, 74
Iopas, 129, 265
iotacism, 293
Iphition, 262
Iris, 173, 176, 232, 246, 248, 257
Isis, 224
Istria, Istrian(s) 190–91, 260

GENERAL INDEX 353

Istrian War (189 BCE), 192
Italians, as Iliadic Greeks, 236, 248, 257
Italy, 11, 34, 42, 44, 48–50, 52, 74, 88–89, 93, 112, 117–18, 123, 145, 154, 177, 181, 185, 188, 190, 192, 207–8, 213, 227–28, 232, 233–44, 247–48, 264, 287, 291
Ithaca, 11–12, 34, 49, 54, 60–61, 63, 65, 86–89, 91–95, 97, 105–7, 111, 131, 169–71, 209, 241
Ithacus. *See* Odysseus

Jason, 37–38, 134–37, 139–40, 142, 144–45, 147, 149–50, 156, 246
Juno, 1–4, 33–35, 37, 44, 46, 48–76, 85, 89, 91–92, 95, 99–100, 103, 109, 111–12, 118–28, 139–40, 143–47, 153, 156, 171, 173, 183–86, 187, 203, 210, 215, 218, 220–24, 227, 232, 233, 236, 243, 244–48, 250, 257, 259, 263, 268, 272, 276, 283–87, 291–96; anger of, 250, 290; dissenter, 286; goddess of marriage, 144, 146, 185, 283–84; Iliadic orientation, 59, 147, 186, 245, 246, 290; intertextual identities, 183, 245–46; Juno Moneta, 120, 121, 122, 183, 185; Juno Regina, 183, 185, 186; Jupiter's opponent/sister/spouse, 57, 146, 283, 285; Musal associations, 186, 122, 123; Queen of the Air, 55, 60, 228; reader, 290, 291; Saturnian, child of Saturn, 183–84, 285; Tanit, 2, 185; temple at Carthage, 288–90. *See also* Hera
Juno, soliloquies, 49, 50, 139; first, 139; second, 140, 245
Jupiter, 2, 19, 50, 54, 64, 88, 94, 96, 100–101, 108, 123, 130, 146, 156, 187, 209–10, 220–21, 223, 228, 259, 264, 267–68, 283–86, 291; as Iliadic Zeus, 264; as narrator, 264; as Odyssean Zeus, 284; consolation of Hercules, 264; opposed by Juno, 286; son of Saturn, 184
Juturna, 19, 259, 284

king(s), 6, 28, 30, 35, 49, 52, 55, 59–60, 74, 80, 82–83, 88–89, 95, 101, 107, 110, 136–37, 141, 153, 157, 168, 184, 189, 205–6, 208, 211, 213, 217–20, 222, 224–25, 229, 232, 235, 237, 239, 242, 244, 248–50, 264, 268–69, 275–77, 280, 283; king list, 231; kingship theory, 5–7, 9, 15, 22, 28, 35, 39, 79, 82, 84–85, 103, 109, 153, 193, 197–98, 207, 217–19, 223–24, 236, 248, 255, 277, 292
kinship diplomacy, 64
Konnos, 297

labor, labors (*labor, labores*), 27, 115, 154–58, 166, 172, 265
Laertes, 101, 102, 209, 254
Laestrygonians, 94, 95
Lake Trasimenus, battle of (217 BCE), 181
Laocoon, 201, 282
Latins, as Homeric Phaeacians, 228
Latinus, 142, 225, 242–44, 248, 265, 276, 278; good king, 248; ineffectual king, 277; enemy of Evander, 250, 275
Latium, 11, 71, 86, 88, 91, 141–42, 179, 203, 225, 233, 241–49, 253, 284, 288; as Odyssean Ithaca, 241; etymology, 184
Laurentian, 252
Laurentum, 225, 242
Lausus, 270
Lavinia, 86, 88, 141–42, 211, 242, 244, 246, 248, 275, 277–78, 283, 285
Lavinium, 88
leadership, 5, 22, 67, 79, 82–83, 102–3, 109, 130, 148–49, 163, 181, 190, 192–93, 196, 202, 204, 215, 217, 219, 223–24, 227, 230, 238–39, 248–49, 251, 270, 277–78, 281–82
leadership vacuum, 253–63
Leitzitat ("guide citation"), 53–54, 66, 76, 91–93, 96–97, 103, 188, 247
Lemnos, 136, 140, 142, 156
Leonteus and Polypoetes, 191–92, 260–61
Lesches, 129
Leto, 104
Lilybaeum, 180, 181
Little Iliad, 34, 117, 119, 129, 132–33, 202
Livius Andronicus, 80, 120, 182–83, 186, 194
Livius Salinator (Marcus Livius Salinator, 254–204 BCE), 186
Livy, 181–82
Lollius Maximus, 77, 81, 85, 89, 220, 223

"Long Iliad." *See* Vergil, *Aeneid*, intertextual identity
Lotus Eaters, 184
love, 33, 77, 92, 110, 134–35, 145–46, 168, 173–74, 180, 189, 223–24, 227, 238, 243, 249, 257
lust, 77
Lutatius Catulus (Gaius Lutatius Catulus, 291–220 BCE), 180
luxury, 66, 220, 258
Lycomedes, 206
Lycoris, 296
Lyssa. *See* madness

madness, 161–62, 167, 175, 203, 205, 212, 232, 246–47, 274; and tragedy, 175; as unifying theme, 175; Furial, 177; god-driven, 175, 176; infernal, 177; Madness (personified), 176–77
magister. *See* education, instruction
Malea, Cape, 87, 184
Marius, Gaius (157–86 BCE), 179
marriage, 53, 57–58, 60, 86, 88, 104, 109, 122–23, 137, 140–41, 144, 146–47, 167, 174–75, 210–11, 219–20, 222, 233, 242, 244, 246, 249, 275–77, 281, 283–85; of Lavinia, 284; wedding(s), 144–45, 245, 257, 283, 288
Medea, 78, 96, 134, 137, 140–42, 144–45, 147, 175, 178, 249
Memnon, 109, 118, 221
memory, remembering, etc., 32, 40, 61, 68, 70–71, 74, 76, 84, 90, 100, 110, 117, 120–23, 146, 170, 180, 200, 220, 234, 244, 273–74, 276, 289, 296. *See also* Mnemosyne
Menelaus, 57, 69, 124, 130, 211, 236, 251, 257, 259, 262, 272, 278
mênis. *See* emotion(s): anger, wrath
Menoetes, 229
Mercury, 94–95, 156, 173, 187, 220, 223
metapoetics, 4, 50, 69–70, 75, 99, 126–27, 165, 226
Metaurus River, battle of (207 BCE), 186
mêtis. *See* ethical qualities: intelligence
Mezentius, 265, 268–70
Minos, 233, 236, 237
mise-en-abyme, 163

Misenus, 241
Mnemosyne, 121, 183
Mnestheus, 262
Molorcus, 157, 158
Molossus, 213
monologue, 19, 286, 287
Monte Circeo, 241
Mount Ida, 104
Munro's Law, 69
Muse(s), 44, 117, 119–23, 140, 154, 183, 190, 218, 243, 247; Erato, 242; invocation of, 10, 120, 140, 179, 242–43, 245, 247
Myrmidons, 12, 200, 265
myth, 36, 48, 55, 70, 89, 133, 160, 178–79, 182, 184, 186–88, 194–95, 192, 206, 210, 212–13, 233, 237, 260, 274, 288

Naevius, Gnaeus, *The Punic War*, 80, 92, 109, 113, 121, 182, 186–88, 192–95
Naples (Parthenope), 295
narrative(s), 4, 5, 11, 18, 19–20, 26, 34–36, 38–39, 42, 48, 52–56, 59, 66, 75, 90, 93, 95, 97, 103, 105–7, 109–12, 116–18, 120, 123, 128–30, 134, 138, 147–48, 155, 157, 166–67, 169, 171, 182–83, 188, 193, 194, 205, 207–8, 215–16, 222, 235, 258, 281, 285; authority, 286; continuous/discontinuous, 156; Cyclic, 133; Iliadic, 62; master, 280; Odyssean, 60, 62, 65, 96, 112, 150; rivalry, 89; time, 69, 76, 86
narrative, battle, 132; in Ennius' *Annals*, 189, 191; in Naevius' *The Punic War*, 187, 192; in the *Aeneid*, 51, 132, 179, 197; in the *Iliad*, 51, 191
narrator(s), 5, 85, 112, 128, 190; *Aeneid*, 5, 11, 33–35, 38, 41, 48, 55, 56, 89, 91, 93, 94, 96–97, 104, 107–8, 116–20, 123–28, 143, 154, 156, 165–66, 169, 173–74, 179, 183, 186, 203, 209, 210, 216, 218, 219, 225, 230, 233, 238, 242–43, 245, 249, 253, 256, 259, 269, 284, 286, 287, 288, 289, 291; Argonautic, 140, 243; Cyclic, 132; Iliadic, 247, 264, 267, 270; Odyssean, 108, 128–29, 215, 264; relation to Jupiter, 264; unreliable, 276; would-be, 195

narrator(s), internal, 128; Aeneas, 75–76, 128–32, 206–7; Apollo, 236; Evander, 153
narrator(s), rival, 111, 115, 122, 128, 195; Juno, 51–52, 89, 112; Venus, 171
Nausicaa, 98, 102, 105, 107–11, 137, 141, 142, 219–20
Nautes, 232
Neoptolemus. *See* Pyrrhus/Neoptolemus
Neptune, 3, 52, 54, 60–66, 123, 184, 224, 228, 232, 282
Nestor, 77, 80, 124, 130, 229, 251, 256
New Comedy, 58
New Criticism, 29
New Left, 30
Nicopolis, 209
Nile, 158
Nisus and Euryalus, 231, 254–59, 262, 266
Nonnus, *Dionysiaca*, 144
nostalgia, 198
novelistic romance, 58
Numanus Remulus, 258–60
Numicus River, 101
nymphs, 52, 60, 63, 98, 102, 104, 107–10, 120, 144, 171, 241, 258, 284

Octavian. *See* Augustus, Augustan: Octavian
Odysseus, 3, 5–7, 10–12, 14, 28, 34–35, 38, 40, 48–49, 54–55, 58–63, 65–73, 76–81, 83, 85–91, 94–12, 114–16, 124, 128–31, 133–37, 139–41, 153–54, 159, 161–63, 168, 174, 180, 182, 184, 193–94, 197–98, 201–2, 204, 206–9, 211, 213, 215–16, 218–20, 222–23, 227, 231, 237, 241, 250–52, 254–57, 267, 278, 284–85, 291; Achilles' successor, 266; arrivals of, 35, 102; craftiness of, 251; ethically superior to Achilles, 218; in the *Iliad*, 79, 279; narrator, 137; praise of, 74; "stage villain," 80; wanderings, 183
Odyssey: comedy, 291; limited as a source of tragic plots, 58
Ogygia, 87, 88
Olympus, 156, 283
opposition, 2, 18, 52, 61, 71, 128, 203, 276, 279–83, 287, 290. *See also* protest

orator(s), oratory, 178, 276–77, 279, 281; as ambassadors, 275–76
Orcus, 296
Orestes, 168, 175, 211–12, 274
Orodes, 268–70
Orsilochus, 97, 98
overadequacy, 3, 14, 68, 96

Pacuvius, Marcus, 81, 202, 207
Paetus (Lucius Papirius Paetus), 297
Palamedes, 133, 201
Palatine Hill, 117, 153
Palinurus, 63–65, 228, 231–32, 241, 281
Palladium, 123
Pallanteum, 11, 86, 154, 157, 161, 163, 225, 228, 248–52, 273, 275, 290
Pallas, son of Evander, 18, 115, 118, 123, 156, 166, 232, 264–65, 267, 270–71, 273, 275, 289; baldric, 288–90; death, 200, 289; funeral, 275
Pallas, son of Evander, intertextual identity, 272; as Iliadic Sarpedon, 267; Patroclus, 200, 265, 267, 274
Pan, 171
Pandarus, Trojan archer, 259
Pandarus and Bitias, 190–92, 260–62
panegyric, 189, 274
papyrus, 83, 127
Paris, 57, 77, 83, 117–18, 122, 211, 223, 259, 272, 278
parricide, 160
Parthian(s), 268
passion(s). *See* emotion(s)
Patroclus, 10, 13, 15, 58, 73, 80, 148, 200–202, 204, 212, 226, 258, 262, 264–65, 267, 269, 270–75
patron, patronage, 158; divine patron, 3, 97, 109, 185; literary patronage, 6, 29, 82, 185–86
Peleus, 69, 72, 144, 204, 213
Pelias, 144
Pelides. *See* Achilles; Pyrrhus/Neoptolemus
Penelope, 11, 12, 58, 77, 84, 86, 88, 111, 115, 124, 219, 220, 246
Penthesilea, 118, 221

Pentheus, 175
Phaeacians, 11, 14, 49, 59, 61, 63, 65, 79, 85, 87–88, 95, 97, 102, 105–7, 109–11, 137, 141–42, 150, 220–22, 227
Phaedra, 171
Phemius, 124, 130
Philip V, King of Macedon (238–179 BCE), 189
Philippi, battle of (42 BCE), 239
Philodemus of Gadara, 6, 82–83, 220
philosophy, 6–7, 19, 30, 36, 77–78, 80–83, 85, 115, 129, 166, 197, 199, 219, 233–34, 238, 249, 255–56, 292; as a literary genre, 178; Stoicism, 78
Phineus, 208
Phlegyas, 233, 237
Phoenix, 163
Phorcys, 91–94, 97, 170
Phthia, 48, 181
pietas, pius, 39, 68, 102, 217–18
Pindar, 79
planks, tablets (*tabulae*), 126–27
Plato, 53, 73, 82, 115; Myth of Er, 115
plot(s), 4, 5, 11, 21, 34–36, 38, 41, 49–52, 66, 76, 78, 84, 90, 101, 104, 117, 128, 135, 137, 143–44, 148, 154–55, 159, 163, 211, 272, 291; *Aeneid*, 86, 257, 272, 283, 285–87, 289; Argonautic, 141; comic, 168, 177; double, 57; dramatic, 167; epic, 167, 174; Iliadic, 86, 186; Odyssean, 86, 140–41, 147, 186, 189, 228; tragic, 57, 58, 132, 167–78
ploys, 54, 145, 147
Polites, 205, 206, 212
politics, 6, 8, 20, 29–33, 82–84, 178–79, 230, 238, 287
Polybius, 181
Polydorus, 207
Polyphemus, 65, 87, 130, 214, 215
Polypoetes. *See* Leonteus and Polypoetes
Pompeius/Pompey (Gnaeus Pompeius Magnus, 106–48 BCE), 179
Poseidon, 3, 46, 50, 54, 59–65, 70–71, 87–88, 91, 95, 182
Poulydamas, 278–80

Priam, 109, 179, 204–6, 210, 212–13, 221, 261–63, 273–74, 289
prizes, rewards, 27, 231–32, 256–57, 265–66, 280–83, 292
Prodicus, 115
propaganda, 29
prophecy, 54, 71, 88, 146, 225, 233, 244, 249–50, 255, 267, 285; optimistic, 236
prosaic usage, 295
Proserpina, 115
prosody, 295
prosperity, 168, 171, 178
protest, 51, 162, 231, 271, 280–85
psychology, 71, 89, 90, 103, 106, 175, 198, 232, 255, 266, 273; trauma, 72, 76, 273
Ptolemy III Euergetes, King of Egypt (284–222 BCE), 157
pulp aesthetic, 164
Punic: attire, 223; dependability (*Punica fides*), 102; language, 103, 222
Punic Wars (264–164 BCE), 145, 179–80, 189, 227, 283; as epic theme 92, 182–83, 186–88; First Punic War (264–241 BCE), 92, 183, 186–88, 192, 227, 280–81; Second Punic War (218–201 BCE), 39, 92, 180–83, 185, 188–89, 227
Pygmalion, brother of Dido, 102–3
Pyrrhic victory, 58, 213
Pyrrhic War (280–275 BCE), 189, 190, 192
Pyrrhus, King of Epirus (319–272 BCE), 189, 192, 208, 213
Pyrrhus/Neoptolemus, 37, 130, 133, 200, 202, 204–7, 209, 211–13, 216, 217, 236, 261–62, 263; Pelides, 199, 204

quarrel, 11, 149, 211, 212, 227, 257, 259
queen (*regina, potnia*), 35, 55, 60, 94–95, 108, 110, 136, 140–41, 154, 157–58, 183, 185, 219, 221–22, 223, 228, 290
Quintus of Smyrna, *Posthomerica*, 144

race, 32, 33
rebellion, 125, 238

reception, literary 7, 9, 13, 15–18, 29–30, 33–34, 37, 44, 70, 81, 85, 115, 131–32, 197, 219, 221
reconciliation, 168, 274, 284
resistance, 112, 193, 234, 240, 259, 264, 271, 286, 293
revenge, vengeance, 15, 57, 101, 144, 148, 168, 179–80, 206, 212–13, 238–39, 257, 269–71, 273–74, 280, 291
rewards. *See* prizes, rewards
Rhadamanthus, 237
Rhesus, 109, 255
Rhipeus, 282
Roman(s), 2, 6, 17, 20, 25, 29, 37–39, 44, 49–50, 54, 62, 70, 77, 80–85, 102, 120–21, 126–27, 146, 158, 165–66, 174, 178–86, 188, 190–95, 206–8, 211–12, 220, 225, 227, 229, 230–31, 235, 237–39, 244, 247, 249, 251, 262–63, 268–69, 274, 280, 285; as Iliadic Greeks, 260; as orators, 279; contrasted with duplicitous enemies, 180; descendants of the Trojans, 186; military valor of, 180; Odyssean affinities of, 189, 193
Rome, 6, 12, 20, 29–30, 62, 75, 84, 102–3, 120–22, 153, 158, 170, 183, 185–89, 213, 225, 238–39, 285–87; and Pallanteum, 157, 250; foundation of, 145; Roman Empire, 70; Roman rule, 292; theaters in, 172; Troy reborn, 179
Rutulian, 257, 259, 277

sacrifice of human victims, 274–75
sailing, 34, 48, 52, 118, 154, 229
Samnite Wars (343–290 BCE), 179, 192
Sarpedon, 69, 71, 252, 267
Saturn, 183–84, 285
Saturnian verse, 183
satyr drama, 169, 170–74, 177
satyrs, 171
Scamander (Xanthus), 71–72, 100, 161, 233, 253, 263
Scheria, 11, 14, 34–35, 61, 85, 87–88, 91, 95, 98, 102, 105–7, 110, 112, 140–42, 222
Scipios, 184; Publius Cornelius Scipio Africanus (235–183 BCE), 37, 121, 180–81

Scylla and Charybdis, 87–88, 136
seafaring, 26, 48, 51, 63, 131, 135, 149, 232, 244; and poetry, 126
Second Macedonian War (200–197 BCE), 190
Second World War (1939–1945 CE), 31
Segesta, 280
Semele, 144
Seneca, 177
Sergestus, 229
sex, 53, 105, 107, 145, 149, 159, 243, 284, 297
shipwreck, 71, 73, 125–27
Sibyl of Cumae, 71, 114, 154, 224–25, 233–37, 243, 245–46, 248–49, 253, 257, 263–65, 267, 281, 288
Sicily, 34, 48, 60, 63, 67, 88, 93, 94, 112, 154, 207, 209, 213, 226–29, 241, 244, 281
Sidon, 102, 110, 219
Silenoi, 171
simile, 3, 74, 108, 110, 161, 205, 226, 249, 262, 297
Simois, River, 69, 71–72, 233, 252–53
Sinon, 133, 179, 201, 209, 215–17
Sirens, 77, 79, 97
Sleep, 52–53, 231, 281
Social War (91–87 BCE), 179
Socrates, 79, 80, 82, 297
Socus, 69
Sophocles, 38, 80, 176, 206, 266
stage set (*scaena, skênê*), 169, 170–72, 174–75, 257
Stoicism, 233, 249
storm, 3, 35, 52, 54, 59–64, 66, 69, 71–72, 75, 85, 87–88, 91–96, 99–100, 107, 111–12, 125, 127–28, 140, 144–45, 184, 187, 227, 241, 244–45, 248, 264
story, 4, 5, 11–12, 14, 16, 27–28, 34, 38–39, 42, 48, 51–52, 54, 56, 59, 66, 76, 82, 86, 88–89, 95–96, 98, 103, 109, 111, 116–17, 122, 124–25, 127–29, 131, 137, 150, 153, 158–61, 164, 167, 179, 196, 207–8, 211–15, 219, 239, 243, 257, 295; continuous v. discontinuous, 155
strength, 149, 159, 191, 230, 238, 266, 268
Strophades Islands, 88, 208

structure, 11, 13, 21, 37, 47, 98, 135–36, 139–43, 159, 187–88, 207, 211, 228, 272; bipartite, 132; episodic, 132, 159; Iliadic, 54, 101, 141, 149–50; inverted, 41, 149; iterative, 135, 139–43; Odyssean, 11–12, 49, 53, 138, 141, 143, 149–50; symmetrical, 140–41; tripartite, 197

Styx, 166, 176, 235, 281, 284

sublimity, 43, 78, 125, 132, 173, 267

success, 1, 11, 17–18, 34–35, 54–56, 58, 84, 101, 109, 116, 122, 124, 131–33, 140, 144, 147, 153, 158, 163, 166, 171, 180–81, 183, 186, 188, 192, 195, 204, 211, 221, 232, 234, 245, 250–51, 254, 259, 261, 263, 269, 271, 272

suffering, 55, 82, 171, 178

suicide, 176, 202, 239, 241, 266, 281, 282–84

suitors, 11, 12, 77, 79, 84, 86, 168, 220, 242, 284, 285

Sulla (Lucius Cornelius Sulla Felix, 138–78 BCE), 230

survival, 71; survivor guilt, 273

Sychaeus, 102–3, 110, 171, 174–75

synaloepha, 294

tabulae. *See* planks, tablets

Tanit, 2, 185

Tarentum, 120, 154, 156, 181, 208

Tarquin kings, 238–40

Tartarus, 184, 233, 237

Telamon (Argonaut), 149

Telegony, 55

Telemachus, 88, 124, 130, 251–52

Telepylus, 94

Thanatos (Death), 173

theater(s), 169–72

Thebes, 38, 164

Themis, 104

Theocritus, 155, 296

Thersites, 259, 278–80

Theseus, *Theseid*, 44, 155, 235

Thetis, 100, 144, 206, 228, 252

third ways, 37–39, 114–95, 115, 116, 132, 133, 150, 154, 159, 161, 167, 173, 193, 227, 272, 274

Tiber, 71, 158, 225, 233, 242, 244, 250, 252, 253, 262–64, 266

Ticinus River, battle of (218 BCE), 181

time, 7, 87–89, 118, 136, 195, 199; heroic, 179, 200; narrative chronology, 130; synchronism, 86, 87

Titans, 184

title, 1, 4–5, 13, 34, 42, 44, 53, 79, 82, 120–21, 126, 156, 183, 230, 237, 246

Tolumnius, 259

tragedy, 6, 19, 21, 36–38, 57–58, 78, 132, 167–71, 173, 176–78, 197, 222; and comedy, 168, 173, 177; and satyr drama, 169, 172; as a theme, 169, 177; civic institution, 212, 273; Greek, 38, 129, 132, 155, 167–78, 194, 199, 202, 206, 207, 211; kinds, 57; ritual, 167; Roman, 129, 202, 206; social function, 167; symbols of tragedy, 170, 171; third way, 274; Trojan subjects, 175

tragedy, themes: madness, 175; overliving, 273

tragic: costumes, 170; ending, 174, 176; essence, 173; mode, 19, 21, 30, 37, 58, 112, 116, 124, 130, 133, 135, 167–78, 195, 199, 207, 212–13, 232, 242, 257, 270, 273, 291–92; plots (*see* plot(s): tragic); prologue, 171, 174; symbols, 169

tragic hero or heroine, 173; Aeneas, 292; Dido, 224

transgression, 2, 5, 51–53, 63, 112

Trebia, battle of (218 BCE), 181

trespass, 52, 54, 62, 65–66, 123, 202, 283

Triumviral period, 274

Troilus, 118, 221

Trojan(s), 2, 12, 34, 48–49, 53–54, 56–57, 60–64, 67, 69–72, 74–75, 77, 82–83, 85–87, 91–92, 94, 99, 101, 107, 109, 112, 117–19, 122, 125–30, 133, 135, 146, 153, 165–66, 177, 187, 190–93, 195, 198, 200–201, 204, 207–18, 220–21, 223–24, 227, 231–36, 242, 244–45, 247–48, 252–66, 267, 270–71, 273–74, 278–80, 282–85, 290; hated by Juno, 186; Trojan horse, 201, 204, 206, 217; Trojan women, 272, 280

Trojan(s), intertextual identities, 259; Iliadic Greeks, 254–56, 258, 262; Phrygians, 259
Trojan War, 2, 57, 70, 77, 86–87, 109, 117–18, 122, 128–30, 133, 154, 193, 195, 198, 200, 203, 207, 209, 217, 221–23, 235, 248, 287–88, 290; division between mythical and historical periods, 179
Troy, 14, 34–35, 40, 42, 44–45, 48–49, 51, 55–56, 64, 66–69, 71–72, 74–77, 87–88, 97, 112, 124, 129, 131–33, 144, 187–88, 190, 192, 196, 199, 201, 203–4, 208, 210–11, 215–17, 221, 222–36, 246, 251, 256, 266, 276, 282, 285, 290; Ilium, 52–53, 69, 74, 252; reborn as Rome, 179; sack (fall, destruction) of, 34, 86, 109, 119, 123, 128, 131–32, 170, 198–200, 207, 210, 223–24, 265, 276, 290
Troy Game, 230
Turnus, 12, 17, 19, 30, 48, 86, 88, 115, 177, 179, 191, 211, 221, 224–25, 230, 242, 245–48, 252, 254, 257, 277–80, 283–84, 288; Argive ancestry, 192; death of, 271, 286, 289–90; kills Pallas, 289
Turnus, intertextual identity, 258–68; Achilles, 236, 247, 253, 257–58, 261, 262–63, 267–68, 291; Agamemnon, 257; Ajax son of Telamon, 260, 262–63, 266; Hector, 192, 258, 261, 267, 291; Leonteus, 261; Menelaus, 257; Odysseus, 279; Pyrrhus/Neoptolemus, 261; Roman, 262–63
two-tier allusion. *See* intertextuality: "window reference"
typical scenes, 109, 165
Tyrrhenian Sea, 60

Ulysses, 42, 77–83, 87–89, 188, 199–201, 206, 209, 210, 213–17, 236, 238, 240, 259; Ithacus, 199, 201; "stage villain," 80, 199
underworld, 11, 14, 88, 112, 154, 161, 166, 176, 206, 224, 232–37, 241, 243, 246, 247, 262, 281, 290, 296
unity, 13, 26, 106, 132, 138, 147, 155–57, 175, 197, 209, 260
univocality, 289

unrest, civic, 278
usurpation, 51, 52, 62, 65, 123

variability, 160
variety (*poikilia*), 160
Veii, Veientes, 185, 186
vengeance. *See* revenge, vengeance
Venus, 1, 35–36, 50, 63–65, 88, 92, 97–110, 130, 144, 146–47, 154, 171, 187, 189, 209, 212–13, 218–19, 223, 228, 232, 245–46, 248, 252, 263–64, 268; Cytherea, 64; disguise, 104–5
Venus, intertextual identities, 228, 247; Iliadic Thetis, 228; Odyssean Athena, 247
Vergil, *Aeneid*: ancient scholarship on, 3, 9, 13, 41–43, 55, 67–68, 73–74, 84, 86, 92–93, 99, 101, 103, 110, 123, 130, 134, 173–74, 179–80, 187, 191, 196, 200, 208, 210, 217, 226, 237, 247, 249, 254, 259, 275; "bible," 31, 33; encomium of Augustus, 196; incorporates all genres, 37, 194; plot, 176, 187, 283, 285, 286, 287; purpose of, 196; title, 155
Vergil, *Aeneid*, intertextual identity: Argonautic, 133–53, 155–56, 228, 242–43; comic, 173, 283–84; Cyclic, 116–33, 246; episode of "Long Iliad," 34, 118–19, 124, 153, 222; Heraclean, 152–67, 176–78; historical, 178–95; Homeric, 2–29, 33, 41, 141–42, 151, 178, 187, 192, 196, 272; Iliadic, 7, 8, 13, 26, 28, 35, 38–39, 44–45, 47–48, 51, 54, 56, 58, 77, 85, 101, 111–13, 117, 143–51, 159–67, 199–207, 226–32, 253–91; Odyssean, 7, 8, 13, 26, 28, 35, 38–39, 44–45, 47–48, 51, 58, 66, 75, 77, 85, 89, 96, 111, 113, 117, 119, 127, 129, 131, 137–39, 143, 147, 150, 152, 167, 175, 193–95, 228, 234–35, 243, 246, 264, 290–91; tragic, 167–78, 283–84
Vietnam war, 30
Vitruvius, 169, 172
voice, 18–21, 23–25, 53, 67–68, 106, 108, 206, 217, 233, 237, 258, 286–87
Volusius, 127

voyaging, 13, 34, 42, 44, 49, 61, 63–64, 110, 126, 133, 135, 138, 140, 154, 188, 203, 218, 227, 235, 263–64, 283,
Vulcan, 101, 163, 252

wandering, 10, 41, 48, 86–88, 91, 93, 96–97, 112, 124, 128, 131–32, 145, 183, 186–87, 197, 203, 207–8, 216, 234–35, 238, 281; Odyssean theme, 188, 203, 234, 236, 248, 264; of Aeneas, 265, 290; of Daedalus, 289
war, warfare, 11, 12, 18, 31–32, 40–42, 44, 46–48, 50–51, 70–71, 77, 97, 109, 118, 120, 123, 130–31, 140, 150, 154, 164–65, 179–80, 182–83, 186–87, 189–93, 197–98, 207–8, 211, 217–18, 220–21, 223–25, 227, 230, 232–34, 241–43, 245, 247–50, 252–53, 255–56, 260, 265, 268–69, 272, 274–77, 282–85, 290–91
wedding(s). *See* marriage
Western civilization, 31, 32, 33

window reference. *See* intertextuality
winds, 52, 55, 59–60, 62–64, 91, 93–94, 228, 237, 256, 263
words, 4, 8, 10, 29, 31–32, 41, 43, 45–46, 49, 54, 56, 64, 66–69, 73, 75–76, 96, 98, 101, 104, 122, 128, 147, 149, 161–62, 174, 183, 201–3, 205, 209–10, 214, 218, 233–34, 239, 241, 252, 257, 261, 264, 269–70, 275, 283, 289, 294–96; opposed to deeds, 277–79

Xanthus River. *See* Scamander
Xenophon, 82, 115

Zeus, 104, 144, 158, 168, 184, 254, 269, 284; in the *Argonautica*, 3, 145–46, 246; in the *Iliad*, 53–54, 56, 57, 62, 65, 72, 100, 144–46, 228, 254, 257, 264, 269, 271, 283; in the *Odyssey*, 61–62, 65, 100–101, 107, 124, 168, 252, 264, 284

A NOTE ON THE TYPE

This book has been composed in Arno, an Old-style serif typeface in the classic Venetian tradition, designed by Robert Slimbach at Adobe.